Soviet Economic Structure and Performance

Soviet Economic Structure and Performance

SECOND EDITION

Paul R. Gregory
University of Houston

Robert C. Stuart
Rutgers University

Sponsoring Editor: *John Greenman*
Project Editors: *Robert Ginsberg/Matthew Collins*
Designer: *Frances Torbert Tilley*
Senior Production Manager: *Willie Lane*
Compositor: *American Book–Stratford Press, Inc.*
Printer and Binder: *The Maple Press Company*
Art Studio: *Vantage Art Inc.*

SOVIET ECONOMIC STRUCTURE AND PERFORMANCE, *Second Edition*

Library of Congress Cataloging in Publication Data
Gregory, Paul R
  Soviet economic structure and performance.
  Includes bibliographies and index
  1. Russia—Economic conditions—1918–
2. Russia—Economic policy—1917–   I. Stuart,
Robert C., 1938–   joint author. II. Title.
HC335.G723   1981   330.947′0853   80-24511
ISBN 0-06-042508-3

For Annemarie, Andrei, and Paul Mischa;
Beverly, Andrea, and Craig Robert

Contents

Preface

Since the appearance of the first edition of this book, new material has become available that adds substantially to our knowledge of the Soviet economy. The study of Soviet economics continues to be drawn into the mainstream of contemporary economic analysis, with increasingly sophisticated studies of Soviet production technology, industrial structure, consumption and saving behaviors, and the impact of imported technology on the Soviet economy. Major studies of Soviet income distribution and inflation have been undertaken. These works shed new light on the reasons for the declining rate of Soviet growth, on the measurement of Soviet inflation, and on the prospects for reliance on imported technology. An entirely new source of information has become available: that supplied by recent emigrants from the Soviet Union, many of whom bring with them special insights concerning the operation of the economy. Moreover, public access to analyses of the United States intelligence community has been increased, so that now independent evaluations of Soviet military power and the impact of the military sector on the economy are possible. Government studies of Soviet economic performance are published with greater frequency and supply the foundation for more up-to-date evaluation of that performance.

Subsequent events have not required us to amend major assessments of the Soviet economy since the appearance of the first edition in 1974. Soviet output and productivity growth continue to falter, so much so that our evaluation of long-term Soviet performance must be lowered. The USSR has now experienced two decades of slow growth. Economic reform continues to remain "dead," with little prospect of its revival. Solutions to the problem of lagging technological innovation have yet to be found. The most substantive amendments are the growing recognition of the importance of informal market mechanisms (the "second economy") and the Soviet's increasing trade with the West in the 1970s. Yet it is our opinion that the Soviet economic system of the 1930s survives in its fundamental form to the present day and that the description of Soviet resource allocation found in the first edition does not require major amendment.

The chief organizational changes of the second edition are the omission of the lengthy discussion of socialist economic theory (the socialist controversy), the explicit treatment of Soviet military power, and the increased attention to foreign trade. The historical sections have been updated to include recent studies of the tsarist period and the 1920s, and a brief discussion of World War II has been added. The cited data have been updated to 1979 and 1980 where possible. We seek to summarize the Western and Soviet literatures on the Soviet economy, but our survey must be selective and will omit valuable studies conducted by Western and Soviet scholars. For this reason, we have sought to include more references in the selected bibliographies at the end of each chapter.

This book is developed around four central themes and is subdivided into three parts: (1) the evolution of the Soviet economic system (economic history), (2) the process of resource allocation in the Soviet economy, (3) reform of the Soviet command economy, and (4) the economic performance of the Soviet economy. We have attempted to make each part as self-contained as possible, which has necessitated a small amount of repetition; but in view of the length of the book, this practice seemed desirable. It is assumed throughout that the reader has a knowledge of economic theory equal to that normally acquired in a standard introductory course. The more advanced concepts have been relegated to footnotes and appendixes.

The authors would like to acknowledge and thank a large number of scholars for their direct and indirect participation in this project. In the latter category, Abram Bergson and David Granick must be singled out for their guidance during our years of graduate study, and the Harvard University Russian Research Center must be noted as having provided the intellectual stimulation that played an important role in the project's conception. In the direct participation category, thanks are due to Carl McMillan, Franklyn D. Holzman, Holland Hunter, Keith Bush and H. Peter Gray, all of whom kindly commented on some aspect of the first edition of this study. Valuable suggestions for revision of the first edition were supplied by James Millar, Thomas Wolf, Edward Hewett, Earl Brubaker, Vladimir Treml, Gertrude Schroeder Greenslade, Frank Durgin, Anna Kuniansky, and Susan Linz. For the conception, development, and presentation of this work, the authors bear sole responsibility.

PAUL R. GREGORY
ROBERT C. STUART

Introduction

The Russian Revolution ushered into being what would become the first important experiment with centrally planned socialism. Russia in 1917 was a large, economically promising land, populated by 144 million people of diverse ethnic backgrounds engaged primarily in agrarian pursuits. Its economic development had been retarded by the social unrest, political instability, feudal vestiges, and low educational achievement of the tsarist period. Russia would provide a rigorous test of the viability of the socialist experiment.

SUCCESSES AND FAILURES
OF SOVIET SOCIALISM

Russia became a socialist economy with the October Revolution of 1917 and instituted central planning in 1928 under the First Five Year Plan. Thus we have a sufficiently long time period for viewing the Soviet system in perspective. Yet unbiased evaluation of Soviet economic performance is difficult, since many in the West are unsympathetic to the Soviet political system. Nevertheless, amidst a degree of contention, there is substantial agreement concerning the following achievements of the first 65 years of Soviet government.

Possibly the most notable achievement from the Soviet viewpoint is a political one—the expansion of communism. The magnitude of this achievement becomes evident when one compares the tenuous control exercised by the Bolshevik regime over the former Russian Empire in 1918—encircled by unfriendly capitalist countries and plagued by civil war, foreign intervention, and a shaky economy—with the current situation in which roughly one-third of the world's population lives under some form of communism. The Soviet Union is no longer encircled by unfriendly capitalist countries; rather it has fashioned a bloc of (sometimes reluctant) socialist allies in Eastern Europe to act as buffers between itself and the capitalist world. The limits to the expansion of the communist system remain to be determined and will depend upon the course of Eurocommunism in Western Europe, the Soviets' willingness to use military force in the Third World, and the attraction of the communist system to developing countries. Ironically the major political threat to the Soviet Union—The People's Republic of China—comes from within the socialist world.

Second, the Soviet command economy has failed to succumb to alleged internal contradictions after more than a half century of operation, though at one time some prominent Western economists saw such a result as inevitable. We use the term "command economy" to indicate that resource allo-

TABLE 1 Economic Indicators—USSR and USA Comparisons, 1981

	USSR 1978	USA 1978
GNP (billion 1978 US $)	1254	2108
Population, midyear (million persons)	261	219
Per capita GNP (1978 US $)	4800	9650
Grains (million metric tons)	237	267
Milk (million metric tons)	95	55
Potatoes (million metric tons)	86	16
Meat (million metric tons)	15	25
Crude oil (thousand barrels per day)	11,200	8700
Natural gas (trillion cubic feet)	13.1	19.5
Electric power (billion kilowatt-hours)	1202	2437
Coal (million metric tons)	663	600
Primary energy production (million barrels per day of oil equivalent)	25.4	30.0
Crude steel (million metric tons)	151	124
Cement (million metric tons)	127	81
Aluminum (thousand metric tons)	2600	4360
Refined copper (thousand metric tons)	1460	1811
Iron ore (million metric tons)	244	82
Plastics (million metric tons)	3.5	16.3
Bauxite (thousand metric tons)	8500	1790
Tractors (thousands)	576	197
Automobiles (million units)	1.3	9.2
Trucks, including buses (million units)	0.8	3.7
Turbine production (million kilowatts)	19.5	27.9
Refrigerators in use (per thousand persons)	226	353
Washing machines in use (per thousand persons)	203	263
Radios in use (per hundred persons)	24	205
Television sets in use (per hundred persons)	24	62
Housing construction (square meters per capita)	0.42	1.07
Gold production (million troy ounces)	8.8	1.0

SOURCE: National Foreign Assessment Center, *Handbook of Economic Statistics, 1979*, ER79–10274, Washington, D.C., August 1979, pp. 10–20.

cation basically proceeds according to administrative orders rather than to market signals. The long-run ability of the Soviet system to function without private ownership of the factors of production and without profit motivation is no longer seriously questioned. The Soviet Union has established itself as the world's second largest economic power (the magnitude of which Table 1 readily demonstrates), and it would now be foolish to question its economic viability. Instead, the performance of the Soviet command economy relative to market economies is now the subject of contention, surely a lesser question than whether the system can operate at all.

Third, the speed with which the Soviet Union transformed itself from relative economic backwardness into industrial and military strength must be listed as a major achievement. Russia in 1917 was predominantly agricultural, with high mortality rates, especially among infants. Nearly 60 percent of the population was illiterate. The industrial sector's shares of output and labor force were quite small, and the domestic machinery sector was poorly developed, requiring heavy dependence upon the capitalist world for capital equipment. By 1937 most of the indicators had been reversed; the USSR had been transformed into an industrial economy without reliance upon foreign aid or extensive imports from the West (with the exception of industrial technology). Both during and after the period of rapid industrialization, Soviet GNP grew at high rates by international standards, all but declining in recent years. Commenting on the speed of Soviet industrialization in the 1930s, Simon Kuznets, a Nobel laureate scholar of modern economic growth, writes:

> As in all countries, economic growth in the USSR meant a decline in the shares of national product originating in, and labor force attached to, the A [agriculture] sector. But the rapidity of this shift was far greater in the USSR than in the other developed countries . . . the shift of labor force out of agriculture of the magnitude that occurred in the USSR in the 12 years from 1928 to 1940 took from 30 to 50 years in other countries . . . and the same was true of the decline in the share of the A sector in national product. A comparable shift took from 50 to 60 years in most other countries.[1]

Fourth, by devoting a larger share of resources to defense than do the United States and Western Europe, the Soviets have produced a defense capability equivalent to or superior to that of the United States. Over the past decade, the Soviet Union has outspent the United States by substantial amounts both in the aggregate and in the important areas of strategic and general purpose forces.[2] Thus the Soviets have been able to achieve military

---

[1] Simon Kuznets, "A Comparative Appraisal," in Abram Bergson and Simon Kuznets, eds., *Economic Trends in the Soviet Union* (Cambridge, Mass.: Harvard University Press, 1963), pp. 345, 347.
[2] National Foreign Assessment Center, *A Dollar Cost Comparison of Soviet and U.S. Defense Activities, 1968–78*, SR79–10004, Washington, D.C., January 1979, pp. 6–11.

parity (or even superiority) vis-à-vis the United States and Western Europe, utilizing an economic base 60 percent that of the United States and 30 percent that of the North Atlantic Treaty Organization (NATO) countries combined.[3]

On the other hand, the weaknesses exhibited by the Soviet economic system are equally well-known and are not seriously contested: the Soviet economy's inability to provide consistent increases in living standards, especially during the initial Five Year Plan periods, and its inability to produce an assortment of consumer items corresponding to the demands of the population for quantity and quality are serious problems. Second, in terms of absolute economic efficiency, the Soviets have tended to generate less output per unit of input, by their own admission, than the American and most Western European economies. This relative economic inefficiency has become more bothersome with the slackening pace of population and labor force growth, rising defense spending, and the growing reluctance of Soviet consumers to accept low-quality merchandise. Various attempts to solve the problems of consumer supply and industrial inefficiency through experiments and reform have not proven successful. Third, Soviet economic successes have often been achieved at the cost of human life, political freedom, and material deprivation, making an overall evaluation of the system extremely difficult. The most immediate cost of rapid industrialization was the establishment of dictatorial control over the population in order to implement the extreme austerity of the First Five Year Plan.

Also, the agricultural sector has thus far failed to be an adequate and reliable supplier of meat and vegetable products. In addition, the output of the major grain crops is still subject to large annual fluctuations, and the regime has been forced to negotiate long-term agreements to import substantial amounts of grain from the West. While these imports do not necessarily prove the failure of Soviet agriculture (most industrialized countries import food products), they are nevertheless a disappointment to a Soviet leadership that has devoted considerable resources to improve agricultural performance. The increased reliance on the West for basic food supplies and the periodic shortages of food staples in a large country with a high concentration of employment in agriculture point dramatically to the Soviet Union's unresolved agricultural problem.

The inability of the Soviet economy to reverse the decline in the rate of economic growth that became evident in the early 1960s must be cited as a final weakness. Although Soviet growth remains respectable by international standards, it has fallen below that of some fast-growing capitalist countries (Japan, West Germany) in the postwar era. To a country that has long cited rapid growth as a sign of the superiority of the communist system, the lagging rate of growth must be a serious disappointment.

[3] National Foreign Assessment Center, *Handbook of Economic Statistics, 1979,* ER79–10274, Washington, D.C., August 1979, p. 10.

RELEVANCE OF SOVIET ECONOMICS

Before proceeding further, it is necessary to ask what relevance a study of the Soviet economy has to contemporary problems and issues. A general answer to this question must suggest that examination of the Soviet command-type economy points toward the substitutions that are required if the market mechanism is to be replaced. Thus one can better understand not only the functions that the market performs without central direction but also the gains and sacrifices involved in its abolition. This issue has considerable relevance for the growing concern over the shortcomings of capitalism: pollution, unemployment, persistent inflation, and so on. Economies cannot function in a vacuum without a guiding mechanism, be it a market, central plan, or some combination of the two. Therefore the costs and benefits of alternative guidance mechanisms are matters worthy of continuing investigation.

Traditionally, economics is defined as the study of how scarce resources are allocated among competing uses. In the United States, for example, scarce resources (generally those that command a positive price as determined by the market) are predominantly allocated among competing uses via the interaction of supply and demand. Relative prices form the only common information required by the participants in the market (consumers and producers) to make their (consumption and production) decisions. Of course, there are major exceptions to this pattern of market allocation— such as the resources allocated by the government budget—and there are many imperfections—such as monopoly, misleading advertising, ineffective government regulation, and labor immobility—that may cause the market to perform its allocative function poorly.

The Soviet experience suggests that an economy can function by command without markets to allocate scarce resources. In fact, even the common method of defining "scarcity" is absent in such an economy because, with only minor exceptions, there are no market prices. There are, of course, exceptions to the rule of command allocation in the Soviet Union. Consumer goods, once produced in planned quantities, have generally been allocated among consumers by the market. Also, regional and occupational allocation of labor is generally achieved by the manipulation of wage differentials (in addition to a degree of physical planning). Moreover, much economic activity is carried out in the unplanned "second economy"—a subject of discussion in Part Two. Nevertheless, the most important production and allocation decisions are made not by the market but by a substitute mechanism—a *central plan*—that embodies the goals of the system's directors. Prices no longer allocate resources but serve instead largely as accounting units. The party specifies the economic objectives of society and ensures that they are enforced by means of party control over the economic and political hierarchy.

In sum, by showing how an economy operates in the absence of a market and by revealing the substitutions that must be made for it, the Soviet command economy provides insights into the operation of our own market system. In making such comparisons, however, one must guard against the fallacious technique of comparing the problems of planning reality with the elegance of the theoretical market model, or for that matter comparing perfect planning with market imperfections.

The relevance of alternative economic systems—private enterprise or centrally planned socialism and combinations thereof—to the problems of developing countries provides a second area of relevance to contemporary issues. Should a developing country emulate the Soviet or the Western market pattern to break out of the vicious circle of stagnation and poverty? Or should it combine features of both models?

The USSR was able to transform itself into an industrialized economy within a short period of time largely with minimal reliance on market forces, thus freeing central planners to maximize the speed of industrialization. Whether this rapid and comprehensive transformation could have been handled within a market context remains an open question. For it was the combination of planning and political dictatorship that permitted the realization of high investment ratios and the rapid expansion of the quantity and quality of industrial labor that, in large measure, determined its pace. The Soviet model channeled investment into selected economic sectors (neglecting domestic consumption) to develop a domestic base for heavy industry—with minimum dependence on foreign trade. The major phases of industrialization were accomplished within one decade. Would this Soviet-style industrialization "work" for developing economies in the same way, or are there crucial differences that mitigate against the use of the Soviet model and that require the adoption of the more evolutionary "aid and trade" path? Answers can emerge only from an in-depth study of Soviet economic development—a central objective of this work.

The international arms race and the general instability of world peace provide a third area of relevance. It is common to equate economic and military power, although the relationship has become more tenuous in this age of nuclear weapons, mob anarchy, and guerrilla warfare. Yet despite obvious exceptions, the equation still holds at base: for economic capacity eventually imposes limits on military capability as defense and domestic interests compete for available capital resources. These limits may take a variety of forms; for example, an inflation that the public is unwilling to accept, or the failure to meet investment and consumption objectives as resources are diverted from the civilian ecnomy.

Thus the current and future economic potential of the Soviet Union is important as it ultimately relates to military power. Questions that are relevant in this regard are: Can the Soviets return to the high growth rates of the early postwar era? Will lagging economic performance affect the Soviet stance toward arms limitation negotiations? Will the Soviet Union be forced into greater reliance on (and cooperation with) the West? Will the Soviets lose their self-sufficiency in oil production and be pushed into the struggle for Mideastern oil? How these questions are resolved will have a crucial impact on world affairs for the remainder of this century.

A fourth reason for studying the Soviet economy is that we perhaps have something to learn regarding the operation of our own public sector. The Russians have had more than 61 years of experience with the operation of state enterprises and industrial ministries in which profit maximization has not been the primary motivation. While the appropriate scope of government activity remains a subject of continuing debate in our economy, there is general agreement that government must supply certain goods and services many of which are not subjected to a "market test" but which should ideally be provided at a minimum cost of scarce resources. Can we learn from the Soviet experience (and mistakes) in the field of public enterprises, for example, to encourage cost efficiency in government enterprises (for instance, the proposed federal agency to develop synthetic fuels) and in cost-plus pricing defense industries? We would probably agree that the problems faced by the Soviet state enterprise and by our public enterprises and government agencies are similar, which suggests that we could benefit from the Soviet experience in this area, especially if government activities continue to expand into problem and crisis management areas, such as energy production and allocation, housing construction and finance, and so on.

Market economies could perhaps benefit from Soviet experience in yet another crucial area in which the unregulated market fails to provide satisfactory results. Whether we consider pollution and other environmental problems to be functions of the type of economic system or, more likely, characteristics of the industrialization process itself, it behooves us to consider how a socialist command economy copes with ecological problems. Time may not be adequate to find answers by experimenting within a particular system; therefore the experiences of other systems should provide invaluable data upon which to base policy decisions.

A final reason for learning about the Soviet economy relates to the growth of trade between East and West, with the West supplying wheat and industrial technology in return for the natural resources of the USSR. The development of the complex machinery for implementing trade and economic relations in general between command socialist and market economies—with their concomitants of credit mechanisms, currency valuations, and cooperative arrangements—must rest upon the mutual understanding of how each economic system functions.

Although trade with the Soviet Union remains relatively small, it nevertheless can have a significant effect on Western economies in specific areas. Soviet wheat purchases have markedly affected food prices in the

Western world; Soviet sales of gold on the world market exert a significant impact on gold prices; and the multimillion dollar contracts that particular companies have with the Soviet Union affect the earnings of these companies in a significant way.

The present study attempts to provide answers to some of these questions, more specifically: (1) How and with what level of efficiency does the Soviet command economy function? (2) What is the relevance of the Soviet development model to developing economies? (3) What has the Soviet growth record been in the past and what are its future prospects? (4) How does the Soviet economy regulate and control state enterprises and resolve the resource allocation problem through extramarket means?

THE ROLE OF VALUE JUDGMENTS

Discussions about the Soviet economy inevitably turn to value considerations: is a predominately private enterprise economy, such as we have in the United States and much of Western Europe, somehow superior or inferior to the Soviet economy? Although the question is legitimate, we maintain that the answer must ultimately reflect subjective individual biases (personal value judgments) and cannot rest on objective grounds.

The question of the ends or goals of a society serves as an illustration. It is generally assumed that the economic goal of a private enterprise society is the satisfaction of consumer wants concerning the production and distribution of goods and services. In other words, consumer satisfaction is the end of such an economy, and *consumer sovereignty* is said to prevail. As a general rule, if the demand for a particular product increases, more of that commodity will be produced, probably at a slightly higher price. The important point is that consumers (assuming a given set of supply relationships) determine the output mix of the economy by exerting effective demand in the marketplace. This pure case must be modified, however, to be applied to real market economies: as governments—through their monetary and fiscal powers—can alter both the current output mix and the distribution of present output between current consumption and investment and as advertising can—to some extent—mold consumer preferences directly.

The ends of society in a centrally planned socialist economy are generally pictured quite differently. The goal of such a society is said to be the satisfaction of *planners' preferences*. A central plan, which administratively determines the current output mix and then distributes it between current consumption and investment, substitutes planners' preferences for consumers' preferences. This does not necessarily mean that consumer desires will be wholly neglected. In fact, it is theoretically possible for the planning agency to plan output to fit consumers' preferences by employing a complex market research network. In practice, however, there generally has been a dichotomy between consumers' and planners' preferences. In fact, a basic rationale for the planners' preferences system is that it enables the planners to do as they, not the consumers, see fit.

Can we judge the superiority of one economic system over the other on the basis of the goals of the two societies? The answer, we think, is no—for to do so would require a weighting system that could gauge the relative importance of the goals of each so that the aggregate achievement of one society could be compared with that of the other society. Pure objectivity in either direction is impossible, because the weighting itself implies a preference for one set of goals over the other. Insofar as value judgments differ among individuals, there is no scientific or objective basis for such a conclusion.

Using strictly economic criteria, the superiority of one economic system over another can only be demonstrated when one or more individuals feel themselves "better off" and no one feels "worse off" under the one system relative to their perceptions of their own welfare under the other system. But such cases are not likely to be found in the real world.[4] One might argue that the Soviet system involves a reduction in current welfare since Soviet planners have generally opted for high investment and low consumption ratios; therefore, the private enterprise system provides higher levels of welfare and is thus superior. The Soviets could reply to this contention that the welfare of future generations has been enhanced as a result of their investment policy and that their system is superior. The whole argument would then hinge on whose welfare should be valued more highly: the welfare of the present generation or of future generations—which again would involve a value judgment.

An alternative approach would be to evaluate economies according to whether they derive maximum output from their limited resources. To do so would be to judge an economic system solely on the basis of its *technical efficiency*—with the goals of the society accepted as givens.[5] Even this cri-

---

[4] For a discussion of welfare criteria and their applicability to comparing economic systems, see, for example, Abram Bergson, "Market Socialism Revisited," *Journal of Political Economy*, vol. 75, no. 5 (October 1967), 655–672; and Maurice Dobb, *Welfare Economics and the Economics of Socialism* (Cambridge: Cambridge University Press, 1969).

[5] The matter of economic priorities can be illustrated using the familiar Production Possibilities Schedule (PPS). The graph below pictures a hypothetical economy that produces two types of goods: (1) producer and defense goods, and (2) consumer goods. This economy is endowed with a fixed stock of land, labor, and capital, which producers employing the available technology convert into output. Insofar as total resources are limited, the economy cannot produce unlimited quantities of output; instead, it must choose among a large number of maximum combinations of goods that the economy can produce. A technically efficient economy, which generates a maximum amount of output from its stock of inputs, is said to be operating on its "Production Possibility Schedule." Let us say that a consumer-oriented economy would choose point A and a planned socialist economy would

terion can be objected to on the grounds that a technically efficient economy producing that mix of output designated either by planners or consumers can have an extremely "poor" distribution of income among the members of society and is therefore "inferior" to a less efficient economy having a "better" distribution of income. This, of course, brings us back to close the circle—in that "better" or "inferior" distributions of income can only be determined by specific value judgments.

We are not suggesting that value judgments should not be made in comparing economic systems; rather, we are pointing out that such judgments must be made with the explicit understanding that they *are* value judgments and should be treated as such. For example, the substitution of planners' for consumers' preferences in the USSR was accomplished by imposing a dictatorship that subjected the Soviet population to considerable suffering and discomfort during the 1930s. Moreover, democratic political principles—defined in the Western sense of the word—remain foreign to the modern Soviet system. Any reader might find these facts personally objectionable. Nevertheless, such an objection rests upon personal value judgments, and it should be recognized that others (Soviet planners, for example) may subjectively argue that dictatorship (the "dictatorship of the proletariat") and deprivation were the necessary price of building a socialist society.[6] It is difficult to prove one viewpoint right or wrong on purely objective grounds.[7] Some might find this proposition difficult to accept in

---

choose point B on the PPS. One cannot say that A is superior to B or that B is superior to A because both statements would be personal value judgments, which vary according to individual preferences and prejudices.

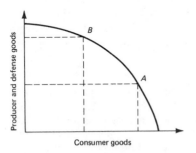

[6] For instance, the official Soviet text, *Political Economy*, argues that such suffering and sacrifice were required to overcome the economic backwardness of Russia. *Political Economy: A Textbook*, 4th ed. (East Berlin: Dietz Verlag, 1964), p. 383.

[7] For a discussion of criteria for comparing economic systems, see Bela A. Belassa, "Success Criteria for Economic Systems," in Morris Bornstein, ed., *Comparative Economic Systems, Models and Cases*, rev. ed. (Homewood, Ill.: Irwin, 1969), pp. 2–18; for more detailed treatments, see Alexander Eckstein, ed., *Comparison of Economic Systems* (Berkeley: Uni-

view of what they consider to be obvious deficiencies of the Soviet economic and political system.

PURPOSE AND SCOPE

This work is designed to serve as a basis for introductory courses in Soviet economics, comparative economic systems, and the economics of socialism. In the latter two courses, this book on Soviet planned socialism would be combined with readings on other models of socialism.

This work assumes a level of sophistication generally acquired in a one-year introductory economics course. The more rigorous theoretical concepts have been relegated to appendices and footnotes, thus providing the instructor with the option of teaching at different levels of sophistication. We emphasize the broad issues in the operation of the Soviet planned economy without lingering over its institutional aspects, which are quite complex at the introductory level and which change rather frequently. A basic understanding of the working arrangements of the Soviet economy is deemed more important: in what manner and how effectively are resources allocated by the Soviet command economy? This question can be answered only by relying extensively upon theoretical abstraction. Thus central tendencies are described without concentrating on the numerous deviations from these tendencies. This is the only way to develop an ordered framework to view the economy of the Soviet Union in its entirety.

This work consists of three parts. Part One, entitled "Origins of the Soviet Economy," focuses on the economic history of the Soviet Union from the tsarist period to the development of the central planning apparatus and collectivization during the 1930s. Chapter 1 recounts the nature and extent of Russian economic development prior to the Revolution of 1917. The objectives of this chapter are to determine the nature of the economic base inherited from the tsars, to facilitate an evaluation of the achievements of the Soviet period, and to allow comparisons with the developing countries.

Chapter 2 deals with the period from 1918 to 1928, that is, War Communism and the New Economic Policy. This chapter examines the two Soviet economic organizations of this period and their roles in the evolution of the Soviet planned economy.

Chapter 3 describes the Soviet Industrialization Debate that preceded the adoption of the First Five Year Plan in 1928. The outcome of the debate is evinced by a discussion of the vast institutional and structural changes that occurred during the 1930s once the all-out industrialization decision had been made.

---

versity of California Press, 1971), pp. 25–240; Morris Bornstein, "Comparing Economic Systems," in Morris Bornstein, ed., *Comparative Economic Systems, Models and Cases*, 4th ed. (Homewood, Ill.: Irwin, 1979), pp. 3–18; and John M. Moutias, *The Structure of Economic Systems* (New Haven and London: Yale University Press, 1976), chap. 4.

Chapter 4 deals with the foundations of the Soviet planned economy by considering the evolution of central planning in the Soviet Union during the late 1920s and early 1930s and the introduction of collective agriculture into the Soviet countryside. In this chapter, only the immediate impact of collectivization upon agricultural performance is discussed—the long-run implications are considered in later chapters. A brief discussion of the economic impact of World War II on the Soviet economy closes out the chapter.

Part Two, "How the Soviet Economy Operates," focuses on the process of resources allocation in the Soviet command economy. Chapter 5 deals with the functioning of the Soviet economy in terms of institutions, industrial planning, and price setting. The informal "second economy" is also discussed. Chapter 6 continues this topic in a discussion of decision-making by the Soviet manager, of labor allocation, and of the investment decision.

Chapter 7 discusses resource allocation in Soviet agriculture. First, the characteristics of Soviet collectivized agriculture are considered. Second, the role of collectivized agriculture as a part of, and contributor to, the industrialization process is analyzed. Third, the long-run performance of Soviet agriculture in terms of output growth and productivity is discussed.

In Chapter 8, attention is drawn to the Soviet foreign trade sector. The institutional planning and operation of foreign trade is first considered both in terms of the Soviet foreign trade monopoly and of the Council for Mutual Economic Assistance (COMECON) organization. The results of the Soviet foreign trade sector are then examined, especially as they bear upon the important question of the role of foreign trade in the course of Soviet industrialization and its impact upon economic integration within the Soviet bloc.

Part Three deals with economic reform, growth, and performance. Chapter 9 turns to the topic of economic reform in the Soviet Union and relates the results of economic reform to date. In particular, the Liberman reform discussions are analyzed along with the various reform experiments. Most attention however is devoted to the September 1965 reform, to its implementation and demise.

Chapter 10 considers Soviet economic performance in terms of a series of performance indicators: economic growth, dynamic efficiency, static efficiency, income distribution, consumer welfare, and economic stability. Chapter 11 continues the evaluation of Soviet performance by considering further indicators: military power, technological performance, economic development, and environmental quality. Chapter 12 analyzes the Soviet economy as it enters the 1980s, its accomplishments and its problems. The lagging economic performance of the 1970s is described, and the problems that confront the Soviet leadership in the forthcoming decade are discussed.

Part One

Origins of the Soviet Economy

Chapter I
Economic History of Russia to 1917

The achievements of the Soviet period cannot be evaluated in proper perspective without some conception of the economic base that the Bolsheviks inherited from the tsars. If economic development during the tsarist period had been extensive, then the rapid industrialization of the 1930s becomes merely a continuation of past development. If, on the other hand, the Bolsheviks inherited a backward and stagnant economy, their achievements must be gauged differently.

Both the rate and the level of Russian economic development prior to 1917 are matters of some controversy. Lenin proclaimed tsarist Russia as the "weakest link" in the capitalist chain; current Soviet ideology argues that the economic backwardness inherited from the tsarist period made the sacrifices of the 1930s necessary; Alexander Gerschenkron stresses the discontinuous industrialization spurt of the 1890s; and W. W. Rostow dates the Russian "take-off" into sustained growth to the 1890–1914 period.[1] The resolution of these questions has been difficult without a generally accepted definition of economic development that could be verified empirically.

Our approach to the question of Russian economic development is to consider a series of development indicators, while implicitly incorporating fairly wide margins of error into our conclusions. We first consider the development of industry and agriculture during the last half century of tsarist rule, and then we turn to other factors, such as growth of per capita GNP,

[1] *Political Economy: A Textbook*, 4th ed. (East Berlin: Dietz Verlag, 1964), p. 383: Alexander Gerschenkron, *Economic Backwardness in Historical Perspective* (Cambridge, Mass.: Harvard University Press, 1962), chap. 1; W. W. Rostow, *The Stages of Economic Growth* (Cambridge: Cambridge University Press, 1965), p. 67; W. W. Rostow, *The World Economy: History and Prospect* (Austin and London: University of Texas Press, 1978), pp. 426–429; and M. E. Falkus, *The Industrialization of Russia, 1700–1914* (London and Basingstoke: MacMillan, 1972), pp. 1–25.

changes of industrial structure and demographic characteristics, suggested by Simon Kuznets as being indicators of "modern economic growth."[2]

INDUSTRIAL GROWTH UNDER THE TSARS

Though it is usually difficult to trace the development of the industrial sector in a country as ancient as Russia, the reign of Peter the Great (1698–1725), an important turning point in Russian economic history, provides us with a convenient place to begin.

Peter the Great, impressed by the technology and industrial expertise he observed during his extensive early travels in Western Europe, determined to industrialize Russia by importing Western technology and technicians en masse. Military considerations played an important role in this decision. Thus, the initial impetus was provided to move the backward Russian economy toward the development of an increasingly modern industrial sector, by eighteenth-century standards. As a result, eighteenth-century Russia acquired a nascent industrial capacity that, when combined with its vast natural and manpower resources, enabled it to compete militarily with the West for nearly two centuries despite a succession of less vigorous Russian tsars. After Peter the Great, however, a gap began to widen between the Russian economy and its industrializing Western European competitors, especially during the nineteenth century.[3] In fact, during this period, industrialization came to be regarded in Russia as a threat to the autocracy. Tsarist authorities feared that railroads would spread egalitarianism and that the growth of factory towns would spawn a rebellious proletariat.[4] One of history's great ironies was the firm entrenchment during the reign of Peter the Great of feudalism—a retrogressive social institution that later was to become a great obstacle to long-term economic development. Serfdom was used by Peter the Great to finance his military ventures and, indeed, he staffed his new factories, mines, and postal system with serf labor to implement his progressive industrial policies.

The Crimean War (1854–1856) forced Russian leaders to realize the relative industrial backwardness of Russia vis-à-vis the industrializing Western powers. The potential dangers of this gap were painfully obvious, especially to an empire conscious country accustomed to respect as a formidable military power. As a result, the Russian government began to promote in-

---

[2] Simon Kuznets, *Modern Economic Growth* (New Haven, Conn.: Yale University Press, 1966), chap. 1.

[3] Arcadius Kahan, "Continuity in Economic Activity and Policy During the Post-Petrine Period in Russia," in William L. Blackwell, ed., *Russian Economic Development from Peter the Great to Stalin* (New York: New Viewpoints, 1974), pp. 51–70.

[4] Alexander Gerschenkron, "Russian Agrarian Policies and Industrialization, 1861–1917," *Continuity in History and Other Essays* (Cambridge, Mass.: Harvard University Press, 1968), pp. 144–147.

dustrialization in a reversal of its earlier anti-industrialization stance, especially under the forceful leadership of Count Sergei Witte, the minister of finance from 1892 to 1903. Industrial development was fostered by the government in a variety of ways. The state sponsored massive railroad construction, spurred by the obvious military importance of railway transport in a land as massive as the Russian Empire. In 1860, the Russian rail network consisted of 1,600 kilometers of track. By 1917, 81,000 kilometers had been built.[5] This new transportation network opened up the iron and coal resources of the Ukraine, which soon overtook the Ural region as the metallurgical center of the Russian Empire. In addition, it opened up world markets for Russian wheat. Russian exports of wheat products increased five times between the 1860s and 1900, competing with North American wheat, which had also been made available to the world market by the railroads.[6] The state acted as guarantor of bonds, thereby promoting the widespread participation of foreign capital in industrial development. Domestic heavy industry was promoted by a series of measures such as high protective tariffs, profit guarantees, tax reductions and exemptions, police help in labor disputes, and government orders at high prices to ensure adequate demand for domestic production. In addition, the state actively recruited foreign entrepreneurs for Russian industry. The military objectives of the state are seen in the Ministry of Finance's one-sided promotion of heavy industry at the expense of small-scale light industry during this period.[7]

The result of this state activity was a monumental spurt in Russian industrial growth during the 1880s. A prominent scholar of Russian economic history, Alexander Gerschenkron, has proposed the relative backwardness hypothesis to explain this spurt.[8] He suggests that whenever the gap between economic potential and economic actuality of a nation becomes too great, that is, whenever a nation with great economic promise as measured by its total resource endowment becomes backward relative to other countries (as Russia was around 1860), tension is created, new institutions are substituted for missing preconditions, and a spurt of industrial growth occurs. In the case of Russia, the tension was great, the resulting industrial spurt was significant, and the Russian state, which acted as a substitute for

---

[5] P. A. Khromov, *Ekonomicheskoe razvitie Rossii* [The economic development of Russia] (Moscow: 1967), p. 280.

[6] *Ibid.*, pp. 361–362; M. E. Falkus, "Russia and the International Wheat Trade, 1861–1914," *Economica*, vol. 33, no. 132 (November 1966), 416–429; and Jacob Metzer, "Railroad Development and Market Integration: The Case of Tsarist Russia," *Journal of Economic History*, vol. 34, no. 3 (September 1974), 529–550.

[7] Alexander Gerschenkron, "The Early Phases of Industrialization in Russia: Afterthoughts and Counterthoughts," in W. W. Rostow, ed., *The Economics of Takeoff into Sustained Growth* (New York: St. Martin's Press, 1963), pp. 152–154; and John P. McKay, *Pioneers for Profit: Foreign Entrepreneurship and Russian Industrialization, 1885–1913* (Chicago: University of Chicago Press, 1970).

[8] Gerschenkron, *Economic Backwardness*, chap. 1.

missing entrepreneurial resources and deficient demand, was the instigator of industrialization.

Between 1880 and 1900, industrial production more than tripled, accelerating again between 1906 and 1914 after the depression at the turn of the century and the political instability of the 1905 revolution.[9] The extent of Russian industrial progress between 1861 and 1913 is shown in Table 2, which indicates that by 1913, Russia had risen to become the world's fifth largest industrial power, behind the United States, England, Germany, and France, and had succeeded in narrowing the gap between itself and the leading producers of key industrial products.

These aggregate figures mask the low per capita output of Russian industry, which can be inferred from the population and output figures in Table 2. Despite the considerable growth of industrial output, Russia on the eve of World War I belonged to the group of poor Western European countries (Spain, Italy, and Austria-Hungary) in terms of industrial output per capita.

Russian industrial growth between 1880 and 1913 was rapid, and the industrial gap between Russia and the more advanced industrialized countries, although it remained significant, was narrowed. For this reason, economic historians who have concentrated on Russian industrial development prior to 1917 have traditionally taken a fairly sanguine view of Russian economic development during the last three decades of tsarist rule.

Is this conclusion justified? While significant industrial development is a necessary condition, it is not sufficient in itself to produce overall economic development. Insofar as the growth of GNP (industry, agriculture, services) and per capita GNP—not industrial growth alone—are the most generally accepted indicators of the rate of economic development, we must focus upon the performance of the second major sector, agriculture, during this period of rapid industrialization before a balanced picture of Russian economic development can be obtained.

RUSSIAN AGRICULTURE UNDER THE TSARS

If industrialization is to generate self-sustaining long-term growth of total output, complementary developments in agriculture must occur simultaneously. This is so because part of the agricultural labor force must be transferred to the industrial sector—for this to be possible, labor productivity in agriculture must be increased unless there is surplus labor in agriculture.[10]

---

[9] Raymond Goldsmith, "The Economic Growth in Tsarist Russia, 1860–1913," *Economic Development and Cultural Change*, vol. 9, no. 3 (April 1961), 462–463; and Alexander Gerschenkron, "The Rate of Growth in Russia Since 1885," *Journal of Economic History* (supplement), vol. 7 (1947), 144–174.

[10] For a detailed discussion of the labor surplus economy, see John C. Fei and Gustav Ranis, *Development of the Labor Surplus Economy* (Homewood, Ill.: Irwin, 1964), chaps. 3 and 4.

Second, agriculture's output of raw materials must increase to meet industry's growing demand. Third, insofar as agriculture is the dominant sector initially, it must provide savings to finance industrialization, especially in the absence of foreign aid or credits. Fourth, agriculture must produce surpluses for export to pay for the machinery imports required to sustain industrial development until a domestic machinery industry is established. Finally, agriculture may be called upon to provide a market for the expanding output of industry.[11]

The agricultural revolutions that accompanied the industrialization of Western Europe and England were generally preceded by the breakdown of feudalism, which prepared the way for a modern agriculture unfettered by traditional cultivation methods and restrictions. Feudalism developed rather late in Russia, at a time when this institution was declining or extinct in the more advanced Western nations. Perhaps as a result of its late emergence, feudalism in Russia embodied particularly odious forms of servitude in which serfs were bound to the soil, could be deported to Siberia, were conscripted virtually for life into the army, and sold on the open market by their masters. Depending upon the region of the country, Russian serfs were either required to provide labor services on the landlord's land (*barshchina*) or to make payments in kind from their crops (later money) for the use of their allotted land (*obrok*). In addition, peasant land was held communally and was periodically redistributed by the village elders, who constituted a form of village self-government.

Russian feudal agriculture provided little incentive for the individual peasant. Serf labor was so inefficient that it became customary to call *barshchina* "all that is done slowly, incorrectly, and without incentive."[12] Mobility from the countryside to the town was limited. A peasant working in the town not only had to pay a large portion of his earnings to his master but also had to return to his village if so ordered, unlike the earlier Western European practice whereby serfs could gain their freedom by living in the town.

The Emancipation Act of 1861, which freed the serfs and divided the land holdings of the landed aristocracy (the gentry) between the peasant and the gentry, was a significant watershed, for it provided a unique opportunity to establish the foundations for a modern Russian agriculture. However, the primary objective of the Russian emancipation, initiated by the

---

For a critical view of the existence of zero marginal product of labor, see Theodore W. Schultz, *Transforming Traditional Agriculture* (New Haven, Conn.: Yale University Press, 1964), chap. 4.

[11] For a more detailed discussion of the role of agriculture in the development process, see B. F. Johnston and R. W. Mellor, "The Role of Agriculture in Economic Development," *The American Economic Review,* vol. 51, no. 4 (September 1961), 566–593.

[12] M. V. Dovnar-Zapol'skii, *Na zare krestianskoi svobody* [At the daybreak of peasant emancipation] (Kiev: 1911), p. 179.

TABLE 2 Selected Economic and Social Indicators, Russia and Other Countries, 1861 and 1913

	Population (millions)	National Income, 1913 Rubles (millions)	Per Capita National Income	Grain Output (100 metric tons)	Coal Output (million metric tons)
1861					
Russia	74	5,269	71	41,500	0.38
U.K.	20	6,469	323	n.a.	85.0
France	37	5,554	150	26,220	9.4
Germany	36	6,313	175	28,706	18.7
U.S.	32	14,405	450	39,318	13.3
Netherlands	3	n.a.	n.a.	1,292	n.a.
Norway	2	331	166	802	n.a.
Sweden	4	449	112	1,265	0.03
Italy	25	4,570	183	6,455	0.03
Spain	16	n.a.	n.a.	n.a.	0.35
Austria-Hungary	35	n.a.	n.a.	20,745	2.5
1913					
Russia	171	20,266	119	123,000	36.1
U.K.	36	20,869	580	8,948	292.0
France	39	11,816	303	30,870	40.8
Germany	65	24,280	374	85,445	277.3
U.S.	93	96,030	1,033	146,100	517.0
Netherlands	6	2,195	366	3,686	1.9
Norway	2	918	659	1,076	n.a.
Sweden	6	2,040	340	4,979	0.36
Italy	35	9,140	261	13,128	0.7
Spain	20	3,975	199	9,025	3.9
Austria-Hungary	50	9,500	190	38,953	54.2

	Pig Iron (1000 metric tons)	Crude Steel[a] (1000 metric tons)	Raw Cotton (1000 meters)	Rail Network (1000 km)	Infant Mortality (per 1000)
1861					
Russia	320	7	43.0	2.2	239[b]
U.K.	3,772	334	457.0	14.6	148
France	967	84	110.0	9.6	190
Germany	592	143	74.0	11.5	260
U.S.	830	12	213.0	50.3	n.a.
Netherlands	n.a.	n.a.	3.6	0.34	196
Norway	0	n.a.	n.a.	0.07	113
Sweden	170	9	7.7	0.57	124
Italy	27	0	12.0	2.8	232
Spain	67	n.a.	27.0	2.9	174
Austria-Hungary	315	22	44.0	3.2	264
1913					
Russia	4,641	4,918	424	70.2	237
U.K.	10,425	7,787	988	32.6	108
France	5,207	4,687	271	40.7	112
Germany	16,761	17,609	478	63.4	151
U.S.	34,700	31,800	1,458	400.0	115
Netherlands	n.a.	n.a.	36	3.2	91
Norway	n.a.	0	n.a.	3.1	64
Sweden	730	591	22	14.3	70
Italy	427	934	202	18.9	138
Spain	425	242	88	15.1	155
Austria-Hungary	2,381	2,611	210	23.0	190

SOURCE: Paul R. Gregory, *Russian National Income, 1885–1913*, unpublished manuscript, 1979, pp. 181–182.
n.a. denotes figure not available.
[a] 1871.
[b] average 1867–1869.

tsar himself, was not to promote economic development, but to prevent further peasant revolts and preserve the autocracy while retaining a form of
agriculture that could still be controlled. The vested land interests were favored. While the peasants received their juridical freedom, they were allotted plots of gentry land to be "redeemed" by the holder. The remaining
gentry land (well over 50 percent) was retained by its original owners. The
peasants were generally dissatisfied with the size of their plots; many were
too small to provide earnings for the redemption payments due to the state
(which had purchased the land from the gentry).

Some peasants accepted "beggar's allotments"—small plots of land
free from all obligations—and became small freeholders. The state peasants
received land as well, under more generous terms, but as late as 1877, the
crown and the state treasury still owned almost 50 percent of the land in
European Russia.

Let us now consider the principal features of the Emancipation Act of
1861 as analyzed by Gerschenkron.[13] While the reform did contain certain
positive elements—an increase in the large estates that created export surpluses, the introduction of a money economy into the countryside via redemption payments, and the psychological impact of emancipation—the
overall balance was negative: the emancipation neither promoted productivity increases nor facilitated the transfer of labor out of agriculture into
industry. Communal agriculture was retained, as a means of control over
the rural population in the institution of the *mir* or *obshchina* (the village
communal organizations). The agricultural communes were held responsible for the debts of their individual members; therefore, the more prosperous commune members were liable for the defaults of the poorer. With this
feature, there was little incentive to accumulate wealth within the commune.[14] The peasant family could not officially withdraw its land from the
commune until all debts on the land were met and then only with a two-
thirds vote of the membership. Nor could the peasant leave agriculture permanently for the city until his land was free of obligations—the rigid internal passport system was supposed to ensure peasant compliance. In addition, the land was to be redistributed periodically within the commune,
thereby reducing incentives to improve a particular plot. In short, the
Emancipation Act made it difficult for the peasant to develop both a sense
of private property and an interest in long-term productivity improvements, factors that had proven crucial in the agricultural revolutions of
other countries.

[13] The following discussion is based primarily upon Gerschenkron, "Russian Agrarian Policies," pp. 140–256. Recent criticisms of Gerschenkron's highly pessimistic view of Russian
agriculture after 1861 are discussed at the end of this section.

[14] Olga Crisp argues that this provision served to introduce a form of income tax, graduated
according to ability to pay within the commune. Olga Crisp, *Studies in the Russian Economy Before 1914* (London and Basingstoke: Macmillan, 1976), essay 3.

According to Gerschenkron, the guiding principles of the Russian agrarian program between 1861 and 1906 were:

> to preserve the *obshchina* until the liquidation of the redemption debt, to prolong the amortization of that debt so as to protect the *obshchina*, and at the same time to continue to hold the peasantry in the vise of ruinous aggregate taxation.[15]

Gerschenkron believes (along with Lenin and Soviet scholars) that massive peasant dissatisfaction with the Emancipation Act was a significant cause of the Revolution of 1905. Peasant unrest during this period bordered on spontaneous armed rebellion in the countryside, which prompted the state to enact measures to improve the lot of the peasant: joint responsibility was abolished in 1903 and 50 percent of peasant indebtedness was forgiven in 1906, and finally canceled fully in 1907. From the point of view of long-run economic development, the Stolypin Reforms of 1906 and 1910 were significant government measures because they sought to weaken communal agriculture in favor of the emergence of a class of small peasant proprietors. Their principal provision facilitated the exit of individual peasants from the commune, which—combined with the reduced indebtedness of the peasantry—opened the way for private agriculture in Russia. Heads of households could demand their portion of commune land and withdraw from the commune. They could further demand consolidation of their land into a single area.

It is difficult to predict what impact the Stolypin Reforms would have had on the Russian economy had they been given sufficient time to take effect. Most authorities agree that they would have strengthened Russian agriculture. Western authorities (Gerschenkron, Lazar Volin, Jerome Blum, and G. T. Robinson) have joined tsarist and Soviet scholars in emphasizing the poor performance of Russian agriculture after 1861. These authorities point to a possible decline in per capita grain availability between 1870 and the 1890s, accounts of appalling poverty in the Russian village,[16] rising peasant tax arrears, and the increasing number of mortgaged estates as evidence of an "agrarian crisis." Moreover, the existence of an agrarian crisis

---

[15] Gerschenkron, "Russian Agrarian Policies."

[16] We relate a couple examples of rural poverty in Russia during the 1870s and 1880s. In the Kazan province, it was estimated that the yield per *desiatin* on fertile land was about 1.9 rubles. Obligations (taxes, redemption payments, etc.) per *desiatin*, however, were 2.8 rubles, which means that the peasant had to make up the difference by gainful employment either in industry or as a hired hand. Yu. Yanson, *Opyt statisticheskogo isledovaniia o krestianskikh nadelakh i platezhakh* [Experience of statistical investigations of peasant plots and payments] (St. Petersburg: 1877), pp. 75–85. A study of the Novgorod province revealed that total peasant income was 8.8 million rubles, of which 70 percent was earned outside agriculture. Bread purchases, taxes, and other obligations came to 6.3 million rubles, leaving a remainder of 2.6 million rubles, or 12 rubles per household for other consumption items. A. A. Kornilov, *Krestianskaia reforma* [The peasant reform] (St. Petersburg: 1905), pp. 194–195.

provides a convenient explanation for the revolution of 1905 and support for the Gerschenkron proposition that the burden of industrialization was borne by the Russian peasant.[17]

In recent years, this entirely pessimistic picture of Russian agriculture has come to be questioned. Internal passport data have been analyzed to demonstrate that the Russian peasant was relatively free to go to the city or to outlying provinces, despite official restrictions on such movements. Analyses of peasant taxes reveal that the growing arrears may not be indicative of the exhaustion of the tax-paying capacity of the Russian village.[18] Most importantly, recent studies demonstrate that the output and marketing performance of Russian agriculture may have been much better than the established literature has suggested.[19]

ECONOMIC GROWTH IN RUSSIA: AN OVERVIEW

Russian industrial growth was more rapid than that of her European neighbors after 1880. Russian agricultural performance, according to recent evidence, may have been better during the industrialization era than had been thought by earlier historians. To provide some perspective on the issue of modern economic growth in Russia, an assessment of Russian economic performance relative to that of the industrialized countries is required. In such an assessment, the position of the Russian Empire at the beginning of the "modern era" (1861) and on the eve of World War I must be established, and the Russian record of economic growth and structural change must be considered.

Data on population, national income, and various output series have been assembled (see Table 2) for Russia and other countries for the years 1861 and 1913. These figures allow one to draw a general picture of the Russian economy at the end of the tsarist era and to trace its progress from the emancipation to the eve of World War I.

On the eve of the war, Russia was one of the world's major economic powers, but the dichotomy between the country's aggregate economic power, as dictated by the magnitude of the Russian Empire, and its relative poverty on a per capita basis is striking. Russia began its modern era with a

---

[17] In the first edition of this book, this viewpoint was presented without reservation. We believe that evidence that has come to light since then raises serious questions about the traditional interpretation of Russian agricultural performance.

[18] Crisp, *Studies in the Russian Economy*, essays 1 and 3; and James Simms, "The Crisis in Russian Agriculture at the End of the 19th Century," *Slavic Review*, vol. 36, no. 3 (September 1977), 377–398.

[19] Paul R. Gregory, "Grain Marketings and Peasant Consumption, Russia, 1885–1913, *Explorations in Economic History*, vol. 17, no. 2, (April 1980) 135–164. Apparently, S. G. Wheatcroft and Arcadius Kahan have come to similar conclusions concerning the per capita output and marketing performance of Russian agriculture, although their findings have not yet been published.

population twice as large as its next most populous neighbor (France) and ended the era three times as large as its largest European neighbor (Germany). This increase indicates the more rapid growth of population in Russia than in Europe.[20]

With such a large population, exceptionally low per capita output levels would be required to prevent Russia from being one of the world's major economic powers. This point is confirmed by the national income rankings, for by 1913 Russia's national output was above France's, equal to England's, 80 percent that of Germany, and twice that of Austria-Hungary. In relative terms, the only decline between 1861 and 1913 was vis-à-vis the United States, a country that experienced a rapid growth of population and national output during this period.

Russia's economic power was concentrated in agriculture. In 1861, Russia produced more grain than any other country and was surpassed only by the United States in 1913. On a per capita basis, however, Russia ranked well behind the more advanced grain-producing countries, such as the United States and Germany, but was roughly on a par with countries such as France and Austria-Hungary. Russia's position as a major industrial power was less well-established. In 1861, Russia was a minor producer of major industrial commodities (coal, iron, and steel) and had only a rudimentary transportation system, despite its vast territory. By 1913, Russia's relative position had improved somewhat, especially relative to France and Austria-Hungary, but Russia still lagged seriously behind the major industrial powers. It was only in textiles that Russia occupied a position roughly equivalent to Germany, the continent's largest industrial producer.

The relative backwardness of the Russian economy is masked by aggregate figures but is evident from per capita comparisons. Russia began its modern era with a per capita income one-half France's and Germany's, one-fifth England's, and 15 percent that of the United States. By 1913, Russia's relative position had declined, due primarily to rapid population growth and slow output growth until the 1880s. Russia's 1913 per capita income was less than 40 percent that of France and 33 percent that of Germany, still one-fifth England's, and one-tenth that of the United States. On a per capita income basis, 1913 Russia was a poor European country, ranking well below Spain, Italy, and Austria-Hungary.

Russia's most important relative achievement was the development of a rail network that was Europe's largest by 1913 and was comparable on a per capita basis to countries like Italy and Austria-Hungary. The one social indicator in Table 2, infant mortality, shows that the advances in public health experienced in other countries were not shared by the masses in the

[20] Russian population growth was much like that in the European offshoots, Australia and North America, with a crucial difference. Russia's rapid population growth was due entirely to high rates of natural increase, while immigration played an important role in North America and Australia.

TABLE 3   Patterns of Russian Growth (percent per annum)

	NNP	Population	Per Capita NNP	Labor Force	NNP per Worker (1–4)
1861–1863 to 1881–1883	1.8	1.1	0.7	1.9	0.1
1883–1887 to 1909–1913	3.3	1.6	1.7	1.7	1.6

SOURCES: The 1861–1883 figures are for the 50 European provinces and are from Paul R. Gregory, "Economic Growth and Structural Change in Tsarist Russia: A Case of Modern Economic Growth?" *Soviet Studies*, vol. 23, no. 1 (January 1972), 422. The 1883–1913 figures are for the Russian Empire and are from Paul R. Gregory, "Economic Growth and Structural Change in Tsarist Russia and the Soviet Union: A Long-Term Comparison," in Steven Rosefielde, ed., *Economic Welfare and the Economics of Soviet Socialism* (Cambridge: Cambridge University Press, 1981).

Russian village. Russia entered its modern era with a rate of infant mortality not much different from that of Western Europe. Yet 50 years later, infant mortality was virtually unchanged in Russia, while in other countries it had declined significantly.

Growth of Per Capita NNP

A distinctive feature of modern economic growth (MEG) is accelerated and sustained growth of per capita output. This rapid growth contrasts with the secular stagnation of the premodern period. Decadal rates of growth of Russian net national product (NNP), population, and per capita NNP are given in Table 3. These figures suffer from several weaknesses, yet they should be accurate within a reasonable margin of error.

The growth of Russian NNP was relatively slow from the emancipation to the early 1880s, but this was prior to the establishment of a modern transportation system. Between 1861 and 1883, the growth rate of per capita income was negligible and labor productivity apparently failed to increase. However, in assessing tsarist economic growth, one should focus on the "industrialization era" from the mid 1880s and compare Russian growth performance with that of the industrialized countries.

During Russia's industrialization era, the growth of Russian national income was above average when compared to other countries during the same period. The Russian growth rate of 3.3 percent per annum was equaled or surpassed by only four countries and exceeded the growth rate of the two other "follower" countries, Italy and Japan.[21] Russian growth was similar to that of the European offshoots, North America and Australia, which also experienced rapid population growth.

[21] Paul R. Gregory, "Economic Growth and Structural Change in Tsarist Russia and the Soviet Union: A Long-Term Comparison," in Steven Rosefielde, ed., *Economic Welfare and the Economics of Soviet Socialism* (Cambridge: Cambridge University Press, 1981).

TABLE 4   Russian Economic Structure During the Industrialization Era

	Shares in National Product by Producing Sector (Percentages)		
	Agriculture	Industry, Construction, Transportation, and Communication	Trade and Services
1883–1887	57.5	23.5	19.0
1909–1913	51.0	32.0	17.0

	Shares in National Product by Final Use (Percentages)		
	Personal Consumption	Government	Net Domestic Investment	Net Foreign Investment
1885–1889	83.5	8.1	8.1	0.3
1909–1913	79.6	9.7	12.1	−1.5

SOURCE: Paul R. Gregory, "Economic Growth and Structural Change in Tsarist Russia and the Soviet Union: A Long-Term Comparison," in Steven Rosefielde, ed., *Economic Welfare and the Economics of Soviet Socialism* (Cambridge: Cambridge University Press, 1981).

On a per capita and per worker basis, Russian output growth was average relative to the industrialized countries. Thus Russia's above average output growth was largely the consequence of relatively rapid population and labor force growth. Russian economic growth was therefore of a largely "extensive" character, that is, was caused principally by the growth of inputs rather than the growth of output per unit of input. The less reliable evidence on tsarist capital stock suggests that roughly two-thirds of Russian output growth was accounted for by the growth of conventional labor and capital inputs.[22] Again, the Russian experience is similar to that of the European offshoots, which also grew "extensively" during this period.

The conclusion follows from this evidence that after 1885, the Russian Empire grew at total, per capita, and per worker rates that were at least average relative to those of the industrialized countries. Although Russian growth over the entire 1861 to 1913 period was indeed relatively slow,[23] this was due to the slow growth until the 1880s. During the industrialization era, Russian growth appears to take on the classical features of modern economic growth.

Structural Change

Another means of establishing whether Russia was indeed undergoing the initial stages of MEG after the mid-1880s is to compare Russian structural change with that of the industrialized countries during the early phases of MEG. In Table 4, shifts in the structure of Russian national income both by

[22] *Ibid.*
[23] Goldsmith, "The Rate of Growth in Tsarist Russia," 441–443.

TABLE 5   Illiteracy Rates: Russia in 1897 and 1913—United States in 1900 (percent of total population over ten years of age)

		Urban	Rural	Total
Russia	1897	55[a]	83[a]	72
	1913	–	–	60
U.S.	1900	–	–	11

[a] Percent of entire population.
SOURCE: A. G. Rashin, *Formirovanie rabochego klassa v. Rossii* [The formation of the working class in Russia] (Moscow: 1958), pp. 579–581.

producing sector and by final use are shown. These shifts reveal the expected MEG pattern of structural change—rising shares of industry, falling shares of agriculture, rising shares of net investment, and falling shares of personal consumption.

One way to assess these changes is to compare them with the structural shifts experienced by the industrialized countries during their first 30 years of MEG. Utilizing data from Kuznets,[24] one finds that the amount of structural change experienced in Russia during its industrialization era was about average (or perhaps slightly below average) for a country undergoing the initial stages of MEG. Thus the evidence on structural change supports the proposition that Russia was in the process of embarking upon a path of MEG during its industrialization era.

Investment in Human Capital

Between the emancipation and the 1880s, labor productivity failed to increase; thereafter, it grew at an average rate relative to the industrialized countries. One possible explanation for the initiation of productivity growth is the increased public and private investment in human capital after 1880. There is little firm evidence on literacy rates prior to 1897, but data on the literacy rates of military recruits and in St. Petersburg and Moscow show that the increase in literacy was barely perceptible prior to the early 1880s.[25] From the mid-1880s on, however, the growth of literacy rates accelerated. Between 1884 and 1904, the literacy rates of military recruits more than doubled, from 26 percent to 56 percent. For the country as a whole, the 1897 illiteracy rate was 72 percent (see Table 5), with urban lit-

[24] These results are reported in Gregory, "Economic Growth and Structural Change in Tsarist Russia and the Soviet Union: A Long-Term Comparison."

[25] Data on investment in schooling in Russia are summarized in Olga Crisp, "Labor and Industrialization in Russia," *Cambridge Economic History of Europe*, (Cambridge: Cambridge University Press, 1978), vol. 7, part 2, pp. 387–399; and in Arcadius Kahan, "Capital Formation During the Period of Early Industrialization in Russia," in the same volume, pp. 293–295.

eracy almost three times rural literacy. Between 1897 and 1913, further progress was made in providing education to the population, and a rough estimate places Russian illiteracy in 1913 at 60 percent of the over-ten-years-old population. For comparison, we note that U.S. illiteracy in 1900 was only 11 percent of the over-ten population.

The low literacy rates of the Russian population prior to the Revolution is a fairly convincing indicator of the relative backwardness of the economy. As studies of the development process have demonstrated, there is a close link between the quality of the labor force (as measured by educational achievement) and the level of economic development.[26] In the Russian case, the limited pool of educated workers constrained overall industrialization and may have forced Russian industry to adopt capital intensive production techniques to utilize more efficiently the limited supply of skilled industrial laborers (some of whom were imported from abroad).[27] The extremely low rural literacy rates show that while the pool of rural labor was substantial, it was not perhaps suited for employment under modern factory conditions without considerable training.

Demographic Patterns

MEG has characteristic demographic patterns as well. As Kuznets notes, the dominant MEG trend in birthrates is downward throughout the modern period, although changes in premodern institutional practices may create initial increases in birth rates.[28] The death rate declines rapidly during MEG, being the principal factor behind the acceleration of population growth. The most conspicuous benefactors of the declining death rate are the younger age groups, owing to increased control over infant mortality. Comparing premodern and modern rates, Kuznets notes that premodern birthrates varied substantially among countries, ranging from highs of 55 per 1000 to lows of 31 per 1000. The average premodern death rate was around 30 per 1000 in Western Europe and somewhat lower in the areas of European settlement in North America and Australia. From these initial

[26] F. Harbison and C. Myers, *Education, Manpower and Economic Growth* (New York: McGraw-Hill, 1964), chaps. 1 and 2.

[27] Gerschenkron writes "... [the] labor supply to Russian industry was inadequate in quantity and inferior in quality.... Therein lies the explanation for the paradoxical situation that a country, so poor in capital and holding much of its accumulated wealth in hands that would not make it available for industrial venture, contrived to build up ... a modern industrial structure ... [which] compared favorably with those of economically advanced countries." In Gerschenkron, "Russian Agrarian Policies," *op. cit.*, pp. 210–211. For a contrary interpretation, see Paul Gregory, "Some Empirical Comments on the Theory of Relative Backwardness: The Russian Case," *Economic Development and Cultural Change*, vol. 22, no. 4 (July 1974), 654–65.

[28] Kuznets, *op. cit.*, pp. 40–51.

TABLE 6 **Birthrates, Death Rates, and Rates of Natural Increase: 50 European Russian Provinces, 1861–1913 (per 1000)**

	Birthrate	Death Rate	Rate of Natural Increase
1861–1865	51	37	14
1866–1870	50	37	12
1871–1875	51	37	14
1876–1880	50	36	14
1881–1885	51	36	14
1886–1890	50	35	16
1891–1895	49	36	13
1896–1900	50	32	17
1901–1905	48	31	17
1906–1910	46	30	16
1910–1913	44	27	17

SOURCE: A. G. Rashin, *Naselenie Rossii za 100 let* [The population of Russia for 100 years] (Moscow: Sotzekizdat, 1956), p. 155.

levels, birth and death rates declined, the death rate approaching a lower limit of around 10 per 1000 in recent times.

Russia began the postemancipation development in 1861 with a demographic base like that of Western Europe and North America some 75 to 100 years earlier (see Table 6). The Russian birthrates of the early 1860s were exceeded only by the U.S. rates of the 1790–1800 period. The Russian 1861 death rate was well above the eighteenth-century Western Europe average of approximately 30 per 1000. The Russian death rate began to decline steadily during the late 1890s but remained high relative to Western European standards. The 1913 Russian death rate of 27 per 1000 was still more than double the Western European average of 13 per 1000 for that same year.

The high Russian death rate can be explained by the high rate of infant mortality—27 deaths per 100 during the 1867–1871 period and 24 deaths per 100 in 1911. This limited decline over a 40-year period indicates the meager success that tsarist Russia had in reducing infant mortality.[29]

The Russian birthrate hovered around 50 per 1000 from 1860 to 1900, after which it declined steadily, but in 1913 it was still twice the Western European average of the same year. Thus, although Russian birth and death rates began to conform to MEG patterns around the turn of the century, they still roughly corresponded to premodern levels at the time of the Revolution.

[29] In 1886, the average life-span was 29 years for males and 32 for females, which shows the marked effect of the high rate of infant mortality on age structure. See A. G. Rashin, *Naselenie Rossii za 100 let* [The population of Russia for 100 years] (Moscow: Sotzekizdat, 1956), p. 205.

RUSSIA'S DEPENDENCE UPON THE WEST FOR CAPITAL

As a final note, we consider tsarist Russia's economic dependence on the more developed countries of the West. This topic was to assume considerable importance during the Soviet industrialization debates of the 1920s (Chapter 3) in which the proper role of the Soviet Union in the world economy was discussed and the role of foreign capital, in particular, was a central question. The extent of Russia's dependence on foreign capital bears significantly on our discussion of Russia's economic development because heavy dependence is accepted as an indicator of underdevelopment.[30] As an economy develops, it becomes able to produce domestically the capital equipment that it had been required to import earlier (import substitution) and thus to reduce its dependence on foreign capital.

To determine Russia's dependence on foreign capital, one must first consider its domestic production of capital equipment. A possible rough indicator of Russia's domestic machinery-producing capacity was the relative importance of metal products (engineering) in the tsarist Russian economy. In 1913, metal products accounted for 10 percent and 12 percent of manufacturing net output and labor force, respectively. During that same period, the average manufacturing product share of engineering in England, the United States, and Germany was 21 percent.[31] Thus, Russia in 1913 probably devoted less than half as much of its manufacturing resources to machinery as did the major industrial powers of the West. Inasmuch as Russia in 1913 devoted a much smaller proportion of total resources to manufacturing than the three major industrial powers, the share of total resources devoted to the production of capital equipment was even smaller.

This conclusion is perhaps surprising in view of the apparent zeal with which the Russian state one-sidedly promoted the investment goods industries at the expense of consumer goods industries during the 1890s, which, according to Gerschenkron, resulted "in the relative top-heaviness of the Russian industrial structure as well as its relative concentration upon producer goods."[32]

Given the weakness of the Russian machinery industry, one would expect extensive Russian dependence on foreign capital after 1880 in view of the rapid growth rate of Russian industry during this period. Russia was in fact a large debtor country during the 1880 to 1913 period, receiving significant capital inflows from France, England, and Belgium. Foreign capital

---

[30] See in particular Hollis Chenery, "Patterns of Industrial Growth," *American Economic Review*, vol. 50, no. 4 (September 1960), 624–653.

[31] Paul Gregory, *Socialist and Nonsocialist Industrialization Patterns* (New York: Praeger, 1970), pp. 28–29, 34, 171–174.

[32] Gerschenkron, "The Early Phases of Industrialization in Russia," pp. 152–154. For a study that seeks to demonstrate that Russian industry was not top heavy in heavy industry, see Gregory, "Some Empirical Comments."

likely accounted for 40 percent of industrial investment, 15 to 20 percent of total investment, and about 2 percent of NNP at the end of the tsarist era.[33]

As a frame of reference, one might compare the Russian experience with that of two other large countries, the United States and Japan, both of which were debtor countries at early stages of their economic development. Foreign capital accounted for about one percent of United States GNP and 10 per cent of investment during the mid-1880s, when U.S. dependence on foreign capital was at its peak. It accounted for 0.2 percent of Japanese GNP between 1887 and 1896, rising briefly to a high of 4 percent between 1897 and 1906, after which Japan became a capital exporter.[34] This comparison suggests that tsarist Russia was more dependent upon foreign capital in both magnitude and duration than were either the United States or Japan during their dependency periods. The inability of the domestic economy to meet the needs of industrialization and the resulting extensive dependence on foreign capital left a deep impression on the Bolshevik leaders and played an important role in Stalin's industrialization and collectivization decisions of 1928 and 1929 (Chapter 3).

WAS RUSSIA UNDERDEVELOPED IN 1914?

Our survey of the Russian economy prior to 1914 indicates that Russia probably began to experience the initial phases of modern economic growth during the industrialization era after the early 1880s. Prior to this, the rate of growth of national output was quite slow in aggregate and per capita terms and labor productivity was not increasing. During the industrialization era, the growth of national output was rapid relative to the industrialized countries, while per capita and per worker growth rates were average vis-à-vis the industrialized countries. Suggested causes of the improvement in Russian growth performance are the creation of a modern transportation network and the growing investment in human capital. In addition to the acceleration in growth rates and efficiency characteristic of modern economic growth, Russia experienced between the 1880s and 1913 the structural shifts typical of MEG.

Despite this sustained progress over a 30-year period, the tsarist economy was still relatively backward on the eve of World War I. Russia's per capita income ranking placed her among the poorest countries of Europe. The sheer size of the Russian Empire and the magnitude of Russian agricultural output masked the per capita weakness of industrial outputs. The

[33] These figures are from Bernd Bonwetsch, "Das ausländische Kapital in Russland" [Foreign capital in Russia], *Jahrbücher für die Geschichte Osteuropas* [Yearbooks for the History of Eastern Europe], Band 22, Heft 3, 1974, pp. 416–418; and Paul Gregory, "The Russian Balance of Payments, the Gold Standard, and Monetary Policy," *Journal of Economic History*, vol. 39, no. 2 (June 1979), 379–399.
[34] Kuznets, *Modern Economic Growth*, pp. 332–334.

peasant, not the industrial worker, was still the dominant figure in the Russian economy. A minority of the population—and therefore the labor force—was literate, indicating poorly developed human capital; illiteracy was nearly complete among the vast, underemployed peasant population. Russia's demographic pattern was still roughly comparable to that of the developed countries during their premodern periods. Birthrates, death rates, and, especially, rates of infant mortality remained stubbornly high. Industrialization remained dependent upon foreign capital.

The formidable task of creating a modern industrialized economy still lay ahead when the Bolsheviks came to power in 1917. The Soviets directed themselves to their task in 1928, after recovery from the ravages of World War I and the civil war (1917 to 1920), and came to grips with the universal economic and political problems of economic development that the developed countries had faced before them. The Soviet response to this task was distinctive in that the Soviets chose to combine nonmarket forces with political dictatorship to generate rapid development, whereas other countries chose to rely primarily upon market forces and some form of political representation. We shall call this response the "Soviet development model." It serves as a recurring theme throughout this book and is dealt with specifically in Chapter 4.

The assessment of economic performance during the late tsarist era is important for two reasons. The first is that it permits us to evaluate economic performance during the Soviet era. Without knowing the economic base and the growth tradition inherited by the Soviet leadership, one cannot judge properly the achievements of the Soviet period. For this reason, we shall return to the tsarist period base in our assessment of Soviet economic performance (Chapter 10). The second reason is that one cannot judge the relevance of the Soviet development model for use by contemporary less developed countries (LDCs) without knowing the starting point of the Soviet experiment. Did the Soviet leadership launch its industrialization drive in 1928 from an economic base superior to that of today's LDCs?

In many respects, the similarities between the Russian economy in 1914 and the contemporary LDCs are striking: the low literacy rates, the high rates of birth and infant mortality, the concentration of the labor force in agriculture, and the dependence on foreign capital. Yet despite these features of relative backwardness, the evidence suggests that the Russian economy did have a substantial head start when compared to that of today's LDCs.

First, Russia in 1914 was a much richer country on a per capita income basis than most LDCs today. In 1914, Russian per capita income was some 33 to 40 percent that of its richest European neighbors, whereas per capita incomes in contemporary LDCs are only a small fraction of those in the industrialized countries. Although one cannot compare income levels of countries 65 years apart, it is nevertheless informative to note that 1913

Russian per capita income in 1978 U.S. dollars was in the range of $450 and $800,[35] figures that would place it in the middle range of contemporary LDCs. Moreover, 1913 Russian per capita income was not notoriously high or low compared with the MEG starting points in Europe and North America.[36]

A second advantage vis-à-vis the contemporary LDCs relates to agricultural marketings. During the industrialization era, Russian agriculture tended to market a fairly substantial portion of its output outside of villages. For grain, the marketed portion averaged a fairly steady 25 percent from the 1880s to 1913.[37] Thus Russian agriculture was able to produce a marketed surplus, available for export, industrial raw materials, and feeding the urban population—a crucial requirement for successful economic development. In the poorer LDCs, agriculture tends to operate closer to peasant subsistence levels and is unable to provide the margin so crucial to industrial development.

A third advantage inherited by the Soviet regime was the Russian experience with rapid industrial growth and infrastructure investment, especially after 1880. In fact, we have argued that the beginnings of modern economic growth can be discerned during this period. This industrialization provided the nucleus of a factory labor force and management personnel, and the rail network served as a valuable asset for an industrializing country. Few LDCs can launch industrialization from such a favorable base.[38]

SELECTED BIBLIOGRAPHY

Non-Soviet Sources

William Blackwell, ed., *Russian Economic Development from Peter the Great to Stalin* (New York: New Viewpoints, 1974).

Jerome Blum, *Lord and Peasant in Russia* (New York: Atheneum, 1965).

Olga Crisp, *Studies in the Russian Economy Before 1914* (London and Basingstoke: Macmillan, 1976).

M. E. Falkus, *The Industrialization of Russia, 1700–1914* (London and Basingstoke: Macmillan, 1972).

---

[35] Stanley Cohn, *Economic Development in the Soviet Union* (Lexington, Mass.: Heath, 1970), p. 111; National Foreign Assessment Center, *Handbook of Economic Statistics 1979*, ER 79–10274, Washington, D.C., August 1979, pp. xi, 27.

[36] Simon Kuznets, *Economic Growth of Nations* (Cambridge, Mass.: Harvard University Press, 1971), p. 24.

[37] S. G. Wheatcroft, "The Reliability of Russian Prewar Grain Output Statistics," *Soviet Studies*, vol. 26, no. 2 (April 1974), 157 180; Gregory, "Grain Marketings and Peasant Consumption."

[38] Charles Wilber, *The Soviet Model and the Underdeveloped Countries* (Chapel Hill: University of North Carolina Press, 1969), disagrees with this assessment. He argues that the combined populations of LDCs with economic bases at least equal to the Soviet Union's 1928 base number more than 900 million. This conclusion is based upon physical indicators—literacy, wheat yields, energy consumption, and so on.

Alexander Gerschenkron, "Russian Agrarian Policies and Industrialization, 1861–1917," *The Cambridge Economic History of Europe*, vol. 6 (Cambridge: Cambridge University Press, 1965), pp. 706–800.

Alexander Gerschenkron, "The Early Phases of Industrialization in Russia: Afterthoughts and Counterthoughts," in W. W. Rostow, ed., *The Economics of Takeoff into Sustained Growth* (New York: St. Martin's Press, 1963).

Alexander Gerschenkron, "The Rate of Growth in Russia Since 1885," *Journal of Economic History* (supplement), vol. 7 (1947), 144–174.

Dietrich Geyer, ed., *Wirtschaft und Gesellschaft in vorrevolutionären Russland* [Economy and Society in Prerevolutionary Russia] (Cologne: Kiepenheuer & Witsch, 1975).

Raymond Goldsmith, "The Economic Growth of Tsarist Russia, 1860–1913," *Economic Development and Cultural Change*, vol. 9, no. 3 (April 1961), 441–476.

John P. McKay, *Pioneers for Profit: Foreign Entrepreneurship and Russian Industrialization, 1885–1913* (Chicago: University of Chicago Press, 1970).

Jürgen Nötzold, *Wirtschaftspolitische Alternativen der Entwicklung in der Ära Witte und Stolypin* [Economic Political Alternatives in the Era of Witte and Stolypin] (Berlin: Duncker & Humblot, 1966).

Roger Portal, "The Industrialization of Russia," *The Cambridge Economic History of Europe*, vol. 6 (Cambridge: Cambridge University Press, 1965), pp. 801–872.

M. M. Postan and Peter Mathias, eds., *The Cambridge Economic History of Europe*, vol. 7, part 2 (Cambridge: Cambridge University Press, 1978), section on Russia.

G. T. Robinson, *Russia Under the Old Regime* (New York: Macmillan, 1949).

M. I. Tugan-Baranovsky, *The Russian Factory in the 19th Century*, translated by A. and C. Levin (Homewood, Ill.: Irwin, 1970).

Lazar Volin, *A Century of Russian Agriculture* (Cambridge, Mass.: Harvard University Press, 1970).

Theodore von Laue, *Sergei Witte and the Industrialization of Russia* (New York: Columbia University Press, 1963).

Soviet Sources

P. A. Khromov, *Ekonomicheskoe razvitie Rossii* [The economic development of Russia] (Moscow: 1967).

P. A. Khromov, *Ekonomicheskoe razvitie Rossii v 19. i 20. vekakh* [The economic development of Russia in the 19th and 20th centuries] (Moscow: Gospolitizdat, 1950).

V. I. Lenin, *Razvitie kapitalizma v Rossii* [The development of capitalism in Russia] (Moscow: 1952).

P. I. Lyaschenko, *History of the National Economy of Russia to the 1917 Revolution* (New York: Macmillan, 1949).

A. G. Rashin, *Formirovanie rabochego klassa v Rossii* [The formation of the working class in Russia] (Moscow: Sotseklitizdat 1958).

A. G. Rashin, *Naselenie Rossii za 100 let* [The population of Russia for 100 years] (Moscow: Sotzeklitizdat 1956).

Chapter 2

The Economic Precedents of the Twenties: The Soviet Economy Under War Communism and the New Economic Policy (1918-1928)

This chapter considers the events of the period from 1918 to 1928 and their impact upon later Soviet economic policies. During this period, the economy operated under two quite different administrative regimes—War Communism and the New Economic Policy (NEP)—that provided experience to assist in making the final choice of comprehensive central planning (1928) and collectivization of agriculture (1929).

The lessons of War Communism and the New Economic Policy provide insights into the evolution of the Soviet economic system. The Soviet planning system did not appear from a vacuum—rather, it emerged gradually as a response to the practical economic problems of earlier periods. Our emphasis of the precedents of the 1920s is not meant to deny the important impact of the early Five Year Plan period (the 1930s) and World War II upon the evolution of the current system. These topics are dealt with in Chapter 4.

WAR COMMUNISM (1918–1921)[1]

In general terms, War Communism was an abortive attempt on the part of the inexperienced Bolshevik leadership to attain full communism directly without going through any preparatory intermediate stages: the use of money was virtually eliminated, private trade was abolished, workers were

[1] The following discussions of War Communism and NEP are largely based upon the following sources: Alec Nove, *An Economic History of the USSR* (London: Penguin, 1969), chaps. 3 and 4; Eugene Zaleski, *Planning for Economic Growth in the Soviet Union, 1918–1932* (Chapel Hill: University of North Carolina Press, 1971), chap. 2; Maurice Dobb, *Soviet Economic Development Since 1917*, 5th ed. (London: Routledge & Kegan Paul, 1960), chaps. 4–9; E. H. Carr and R. W. Davies, *Foundations of a Planned Economy, 1926–1929*, vol. 1, part 2 (London: Macmillan, 1969), chaps. 33–35. M. Lewin, *Russian Peasants and Soviet Power* (London: Allen & Unwin, 1968), chaps. 1–15; Y. Avdakov and V. Borodin, *USSR State Industry During the Transition Period* (Moscow: Progress Publishers, 1977); L. Szamuely, *First Models of the Socialist Economic Systems* (Budapest: Akademiai Kiado, 1974); V. A. Vinogradov et al., eds., *Istoriia sotsialisticheskoi ekonomiki SSSR* [His-

militarized and paid virtually equal wages in kind, and farm output was requisitioned. Were these war measures the product of the ideological intent of the Bolshevik leadership to establish full communism directly, or were they forced responses to the civil war? The most generally accepted view, as postulated by the well-known British authorities on War Communism, Maurice Dobb and E. H. Carr,[2] is that War Communism was forced upon the Bolshevik leadership by the Russian civil war and that the various theoretical arguments posited by the Bolshevik leadership in support of War Communism were "no more than flights of leftist fancy."[3] In fact, Lenin—and Leon Trotsky—often referred to War Communism as the measures of a "besieged fortress." The opposite view, postulated by Paul Craig Roberts,[4] argues that Lenin originally conceived War Communism—with its elimination of market institutions and its introduction of administrative controls—as a necessary step in the socialist revolution. In Roberts's view, War Communism was adopted for ideological reasons as a product of Marxian ideas (as interpreted by Lenin), not as a forced response to the wartime emergency. We can provide no final answer to this controversy; instead, we shall attempt to outline as objectively as possible the basic features of War Communism.

The roots of War Communism can be traced to the October Revolution. One of the first actions of the fledgling Bolshevik regime was to nationalize the remaining large estates (the Land Decree of November 8, 1917) and to sanction the distribution of this land among the peasants. This action legalized in part the spontaneous appropriation of land by the peasantry, a process that had already taken place to a large degree. Irrespective of its causes, this change in land tenure was to have a far-reaching impact upon economic policy throughout the 1920s. In their enhanced capacity as full proprietors, the peasants were no longer obligated to deliver a prescribed portion of their output either to the landlord (as a rental payment) or to the state (as a tax or principal payment). Now they, not the state or landlord, made the basic decisions about how much to produce and what portion of this output would be sold. Thus the total agricultural output and the *marketed portion* thereof became dependent for the first time upon the Russian peasant.

---

tory of the socialist economy of the USSR], (Moscow: Nauka, 1976), vols. 1 and 2; V. P. Diachenko, *Istoriia finansov SSSR* [History of USSR finance], (Moscow: Nauka, 1978), chaps. 2–4.

[2] Dobb, *Soviet Economic Development*, chaps. 4–9.

[3] *Ibid.*, p. 122.

[4] Paul Craig Roberts, *Alienation and the Soviet Economy* (Albuquerque: University of New Mexico Press, 1971), chap. 2. The position that Lenin adopted War Communism for ideological reasons is also supported by the Hungarian authority Szamuely, *First Models of the Socialist Economic Systems*, pp. 7–62. This interpretation is bitterly opposed by current Soviet ideology. For a typical attack on "bourgeois falsifications," see Vinogradov et al., *Istoriia sotsialisticheskoi ekonomiki SSSR*, vol. 1, pp. 251–252.

There was a revival of the *mir* during and after the Revolution. The *mir* was the institution that had confiscated and redistributed the land of the gentry, and it remained the principal voice of legal and administrative authority within the village during the early years of Soviet rule. The village assembly settled most of the questions of interest to the peasants and was able to steer a course independent of the *selsovet*, the local administrative arm of the Bolshevik government. However, as M. Lewin writes, one should not overemphasize the socialist instincts of the peasants.[5] The peasants remained attached to their village communities, and in their eyes, the purpose of the Revolution was to give them their own farms. That the land was nationalized and belonged to the *mir* did not detract from the peasants' conviction that the land was theirs to farm and manage as they saw fit.

The initial Bolshevik attitude toward private industry was cautious and restrained, since an uneasy truce between Bolshevik and capitalist was required to prevent a drop in industrial output. Workers' Committees in privately owned enterprises were given the right to supervise management, but, at the same time, the proprietor received the executive right to give orders that could not be countermanded by the Workers' Committees. Also, the Workers' Committees were denied the right to take over enterprises without the permission of higher authorities. Only enterprises of key importance—such as banking, grain purchasing and storage, transportation, oil, and war industries—were nationalized, establishing a form of state capitalism based upon state control of key positions in the economy, mixed management of enterprises, and private ownership of agriculture, retail trade, and small-scale industry.

The uneasy truce between the Bolsheviks and the capitalists and the peasants did not last long. By 1918, the Bolsheviks were locked in a struggle for survival with the White Russian forces supported in part by foreign powers. The Germans were in possession of the Ukraine, while the White Russian armies occupied the Urals, Siberia, North Caucasus, and other economically important regions. Poland invaded in May of 1920. At one time, the Bolsheviks retained only 10 percent of the coal supplies, 25 percent of the iron foundries, less than 50 percent of the grain area, and less than 10 percent of the sugar beet sources of the former Russian Empire.[6] At one point, three-quarters of USSR territory was occupied by opponents of Soviet authority.

To divert industrial and agricultural resources from private into military uses, the Bolsheviks, lacking a domestic tax base and access to foreign aid, resorted to printing money. This expansion of the money supply combined with shrinking supplies of consumer goods created hyperinflation. On November 1, 1917, the amount of money in circulation was 20 billion

[5] Lewin, *Russian Peasants and Soviet Power*, pp. 26–28.
[6] Dobb, *Soviet Economic Development*, p. 98; Vinogradov et al., *Istoriia sotsialisticheskoi ekonomiki SSSR*, vol. I, p. 236.

rubles. The rate of monetary emission accelerated thereafter, and by July 1, 1921, 2.5 trillion rubles were in circulation. Supplies of consumer goods offered for sale dwindled as materials were diverted to military uses, and prices rose more rapidly than the rate of growth of the money supply. Between 1917 and 1921, prices increased 8000 fold.[7]

The hyperinflation resulted in the near destruction of the market exchange economy. Peasants were reluctant to exchange their products for depreciating money, as were manufacturers and artisans. The economy increasingly employed barter to effect transactions, and this led to what the Soviets call the "naturalization" (demonetization) of the economy. This naturalization process was welcomed by the left wing of the Bolshevik party, which termed the government printing press "that machine gun which attacked the bourgeois regime in its rear, namely, through its monetary system."[8] The naturalization of the economy created, however, an immediate crisis for the Soviet leadership. The central government found itself powerless to obtain through the market those goods, food supplies in particular, that it needed to fight the war.

War Communism Policies

The Bolshevik leadership under Lenin responded by introducing War Communism, a system by which the leaders attempted to substitute administrative for market allocation to marshal resources for the war. The crux of War Communism was its policy of forcibly requisitioning agricultural surpluses. Police (the *Cheka*) and party activists were sent into the countryside to collect the "surpluses" of the rich and middle peasantry—a policy that severed the existing market link between industry and agriculture. In theory at least, the link was to be maintained by state allocation of manufactured products to the peasants and barter transactions for the remaining agricultural output. In fact, the peasants received only from 12 to 15 percent of prewar supplies of manufactured goods.[9] Initially, the regime had hoped to preserve the market link with agriculture by setting aside manufactured commodities to promote exchange with the countryside, but the peasants failed to respond. On May 9, 1918, the system of requisitioning (called the *prodrazverstka*) was initiated, and the commissar for food was invested with extraordinary powers to confiscate food products from the farm population. Thus a "food dictatorship" was established, and the Bolshevik government took over the task of collecting and distributing agricultural products.

Nationalization of the economy was the second major policy of War

---

[7] Szamuely, *First Models of the Socialist Economic Systems*, p. 21; Diachenko, *Istoriia finansov SSSR*, pp. 54–55.

[8] A statement of E. Preobrazhensky quoted in Zaleski, *Planning for Economic Growth*, p. 20.

[9] Dobb, *Soviet Economic Development*, p. 117.

Communism. The sugar industry was the first to be nationalized in the spring of 1918, and by the autumn of 1920, the 37,000 enterprises had been nationalized, of which roughly half were small-scale businesses that did not use mechanical power. This pervasive nationalization of industry may be regarded in part as a crisis response, for a large number of former industrial proprietors had gone over to the White Russian side, and there was widespread fear of German take-overs of German-owned enterprises. Also, nationalization from below by workers had been proceeding at a rapid pace despite government attempts to control unauthorized worker take-overs. On the other hand, the excessive nationalization from above down to enterprises employing only one worker may perhaps be regarded as an ideological response not to be justified by the crisis situation. Nominally, the nationalized enterprises were subject to central direction by the state budget and national industrial boards. In actual practice, centralized coordination was generally lacking.

The abolition of private trade was the third cornerstone of War Communism policy. Private trade was regarded as incompatible with the War Communism system of centralized requisitioning and allocation. Government trade monopolies and monopsonies (mainly the Commissariat of Supply and the Commissariat of Agriculture) were set up to replace private organizations and concentrate commodity distribution in the hands of the state. In November 1918, all private internal trade was abolished, and the state ostensibly became the sole supplier of consumer goods to the population. In fact, the black market continued to supply a significant portion of total consumption goods and was unofficially tolerated by the authorities.[10] In the most critical moments of 1918, the Soviet government made it legal for workers to purchase up to 20 kilograms of grain directly from peasants, but this provision was quickly rescinded when it threatened to disrupt government requisitioning.[11]

Semimilitary controls over industrial workers became a major means of labor allocation. The movement of industrial workers was restricted, and they could be mobilized for special work. In some cases, army personnel were used for special projects. Labor deserters received severe penalties according to a decree of November 28, 1919, which placed the employees of state enterprises under military discipline.

The mobilization of labor was managed in large part by Leon Trotsky, the organizer of the Red Army. Trotsky's intention was to create a system of universal labor mobilization, and by the end of 1918, his mobilization plans were being put into effect. Labor was decreed to be compulsory for all

---

[10] Nove, An Economic History of the USSR, p. 62. Estimates of the period suggest that in the large towns only 31 percent of all food came through official channels (1919). Szamuely, First Models of the Socialist Economic Systems, p. 18, supplies similar estimates showing that most consumption requirements were satisfied in the free (black) market.

[11] Vinogradov et al., Istoriia sotsialisticheskoi ekonomiki SSSR, vol. I, p. 374.

able-bodied persons, compulsory labor service was declared for the peasantry, labor armies (one under the leadership of Stalin in the Ukraine) were created by delaying demobilization, and the Commission for Universal Labor Service was created with Trotsky at its head.[12] In 1920, railway workers, firemen, miners, construction workers, metal workers, and shipbuilders were mobilized. The Siberian labor army was engaged in coal mining, forestry, and rail construction; and the Caucasian labor army was charged with rail construction and crude oil extraction.[13]

The War Communism system of distribution attempted to apply class and social principles to distribution. Under the "class ration," introduced in 1918, wages were to be based upon the type of work being done. Since money wages had lost most of their meaning as a consequence of hyperinflation, the highest ration (wage) would go to workers performing heavy work under dangerous conditions; the lowest, to the free professions and the unemployed. The highest category was to receive a ration four times that of the lowest category. The wartime chaos of the period made it difficult for the state to adhere to these class ration principles because in most regions state supply agencies were doing well to keep the population above subsistence. Special rations were used, however, to supply the workers of priority industries, and in 1919, 30 categories of workers were placed on preferential rations.[14]

The final feature of War Communism was the naturalization of economic life. The procurement of agricultural products through requisitioning and confiscation replaced the market link between the city and countryside. Every citizen had to be registered with a state or cooperative shop to obtain legal rations. Settlements among state enterprises were made via bookkeeping transactions that had little real meaning. In 1920, postal services, housing, gas, electricity, and public transportation were made available free of charge, and it was decided that foodstuffs supplied through the Food Commissariat should also be free of charge.[15]

An Evaluation of War Communism

Any evaluation of War Communism must emphasize a frequently neglected point made by the Soviet literature: War Communism did enable the Bolsheviks to muster sufficient resources to win the civil war. In this sense, War Communism may be viewed as an important political and military success. It is easy to overlook this basic point and to concentrate instead on the system's many weaknesses. We seek rather to evaluate War Communism in

[12] Richard Day, *Leon Trotsky and the Politics of Economic Isolation* (Cambridge: At the University Press, 1973), chap. 2.
[13] Szamuely, *First Models of the Socialist Economic Systems*, pp. 12–14.
[14] *Ibid.*, pp. 14–17.
[15] *Ibid.*, pp. 17–18.

terms of the question: was War Communism a viable economic system for coping with the long-term problems of economic growth and development facing the Soviet regime during the 1920s?[16]

As one might expect, War Communism's replacement of market exchange by administrative resource allocation created several serious problems. First, there was a sharp decline in both agricultural output and marketings to the state during the 1918 to 1921 period, even after adjustment for war devastation. Peasants were holding back grain in storage, were planting less, and were selling to private traders. The area of Siberia sown in wheat was halved and in the Volga and Caucasus regions was reduced to as little as one-quarter of previous levels. Actual sowing concealed from authorities was reported to be as high as 20 percent of the sown area in some regions.[17] Since agricultural surpluses in excess of family subsistence were requisitioned, there was no incentive to produce a surplus. Instead, the peasants, if they could not conceal their surplus from the authorities, restricted output to the subsistence needs of their family. Thus, War Communism's agrarian policy estranged Russian peasants from the Bolshevik regime and encouraged them to engage in dysfunctional behavior, such as restricting output and hoarding or concealing surpluses during a period of agricultural shortages.

Soviet industry was also faced with serious problems. Almost all enterprises, with the exception of certain small-scale handicraft shops, had been nationalized without first establishing a suitable administrative structure to coordinate their activities. The industrial census of 1920 showed over 5000 nationalized enterprises employing only one worker.[18] The abolition of private trade, which was to be superceded by state rationing, removed the existing market link between consumer and producer. Producers, except those selling to the black market, therefore were no longer directed by the market in their production decisions.

Ostensibly, large-scale industry was to be coordinated by the Supreme Council of the National Economy (VSNKh), which was broken up into departments (*Glavki*), each of which was to direct a particular industry. The *Glavki* were usually grouped into trusts. For example, the mining trust contained six *Glavki*. By 1920, there were over 50 *Glavki* charged with controlling production and distribution.[19] In addition, the provincial economic

---

[16] Soviet doctrine depicts War Communism as a genial tactical victory by Lenin to win the civil war, while conceding that the USSR was not yet prepared for the elimination of capitalist vestiges. On this, see Vinogradov et al., *Istoriia sotsialisticheskoi ekonomiki SSSR*, vol. I, pp. 244–246.

[17] Dobb, *Soviet Economic Development*, p. 117.

[18] Nove, *An Economic History of the USSR*, p. 70.

[19] For accounts of the organization of the War Communism economy, see Zaleski, *Planning for Economic Growth*, pp. 27–29; and Samuel Oppenheim, "The Supreme Economic Council, 1917–21," *Soviet Studies*, vol. 2, no. 1 (July 1973), 3–27.

councils (*Gubsovnarkhozy*) were the local organs of VSNKh. This arrangement bordered on chaos. In 1920, there were over 37,000 nationalized enterprises. The *Glavki* possessed insufficient information about local enterprises to direct them effectively—to such a degree that an investigative committee of 1920 found that many *Glavki* not only "do not know what goods and in what amounts are kept in warehouses under their control, but are actually ignorant even of the numbers of such warehouses."[20] As a result, the directives that the *Glavki* issued to the local authorities rarely corresponded to local capacities and requirements, causing a prolonged struggle between central and local administrations. Often, local authorities merely gave formal compliance to directives from above and then countermanded them, knowing they could do so with impunity.

VSNKh was the principal champion of centralized control during War Communism, and under its influential chairman, Aleksei Rykov, it fought against the "Left Communist" contingent, which favored workers' control of factories. Rykov also attacked the concept of trade union control of enterprises, citing Lenin's opposition to workers' control and Lenin's support of rational one-man management. Nevertheless, VSNKh's success in establishing centralized control was modest. Individual industries were being run independently by the *Glavki* and local authorities with virtually no centralized coordination. Various national and local organizations had overlapping and conflicting responsibilities concerning the distribution of consumer and producer goods. Primitive plans were drawn up for particular industries, but these plans were not presented in the form of a national plan to be approved by government. The first effort at national economic planning was the general electrification plan (GOELRO), completed in December of 1920.

In sum, War Communism industry operated essentially without direction, either from the market or from planners. Bottlenecks were eliminated by employing "shock" (*udarny*) methods, which meant that whenever congestion in a particular sector became alarming, it would receive top priority in the form of adequate supplies of fuels, materials, and rations. The shock system provided a means of establishing priorities and was beneficial in this sense. However, while the concentration of resources in the shock industries allowed them to surge ahead and overcome the original bottleneck, the nonshock industries had in the process fallen behind and had created new bottlenecks, which would then be attacked by additional shock methods. In this manner, some weak sense of general direction was supplied to the economy to replace total chaos. The shock system was somewhat effective as long as it remained undiluted, which meant that the number of shock industries at one time had to be limited. As time went by, the agitation for widening the shock categories became so intense that even-

[20] Dobb, *Soviet Economic Development*, p. 112.

tually even the manufacture of pens and pencils was included, thus destroying the whole purpose of the shock method—to set up a system of priorities.

Finally, the lack of an adequate system of incentive wages led to industrial labor supply problems. The government controlled the legal distribution of consumer commodities among members of the industrial labor force, thereby controlling a significant portion of real industrial wages. The Bolshevik Party never officially subscribed to a utopian view of income distribution according to need; instead, it was realized that wage differentials were important in attracting labor in skilled and/or arduous jobs. For example, the Ninth Congress of the Communist Party in 1920 resolved that the food supply system should give preference to the industrious worker, and the Third Trade Union Conference of the same year proposed incentive premiums in kind to be paid to diligent workers.

The result however contradicted the intention and was one reason Trotsky referred to War Communism wage policy as the measure of a "beseiged fortress." In fact, wages were rationed out to industrial workers on a fairly equal basis because first, shortages were so severe that local supply authorities were content to keep the working force at subsistence and, second, it proved too complex to devise a system of incentive wages to be paid in kind.

The result of this egalitarianism was an insufficient pool of qualified labor in industry. Instead of being drawn into factories, labor was flowing out of them during War Communism. The number of townspeople declined from 2.6 million in 1917 to 1.2 million in 1920.[21] Morale was poor, worker sabotage was rampant, absenteeism was high, and the tenuous loyalty of specialists was slipping. These developments were especially ominous in view of the dearth of skilled industrial laborers during this early period. Strikes became quite common during the latter part of 1920.

The Soviet regime had succeeded in solidifying its position by the end of 1920. A peace treaty had been signed with Poland, and the White Russian army had been driven out of the crucial industrial and agricultural regions that it had occupied earlier. The crisis under which War Communism had come into existence had been overcome, and the dangers of continuing that economic policy were growing more apparent. The still powerful trade unions were revolting against the crippling centralization of industry and the conscription of labor. The alienated peasant population called for abolition of the state grain monopoly. Industrial workers were restive, the military was in a rebellious mood, and the Soviet regime was in danger of falling victim to internal discontent. Factory output had fallen to less than 15 percent of its prewar level.[22] The final blow was the Kronstadt Uprising of

---

[21] Nove, *An Economic History of the USSR*, pp. 66–67.
[22] *Ibid.*, p. 94.

March 1921, when the sailors of the Kronstadt naval base revolted in support of the Petrograd workers. The Soviet leadership moved quickly to dispel this discontent by replacing War Communism with the New Economic Policy (NEP) in March of 1921.

THE NEW ECONOMIC POLICY (1921–1928)

Just as War Communism may have been thrust upon the Soviet regime by the civil war in 1918, the New Economic Policy was forced upon the Soviet leadership by the excesses of War Communism. For whatever its reasons, the Soviet leadership at the time took pains to stress the temporary nature of both periods. Lenin declared that "War Communism was thrust upon us by war and ruin. It was not, nor could it be, a policy that corresponded to the economic tasks of the proletariat. It was a temporary measure."[23] In the same vein, Lenin described NEP as a temporary step backward (away from socialism) in order later to take two steps forward. From the viewpoint of the Bolshevik leadership, NEP was a transitional step backward because of the important roles that "antisocialist" institutions, such as private ownership, private initiative, and capitalist markets, were allowed to play during this period.

The most striking feature of NEP was its attempt to combine market and socialism: agriculture remained in the hands of the peasant, the management of industry (with the exception of the "commanding heights") was decentralized. Market links between industry and agriculture and between industry and consumer replaced state control of production and distribution. Most industrial enterprises were denationalized. But many of the largest enterprises—the so-called commanding heights—remained nationalized and encompassed about three-quarters of industrial output. In this manner, it was thought that the state could provide general guidance by retaining direct control of the commanding heights of the economy—heavy industry, transportation, banking, and foreign trade—while allowing the remainder of the economy to make its own decisions.

The political basis of NEP was the *Smychka,* or alliance, between the Soviet regime (representing the urban proletariat) and the peasant. An important political objective of NEP was to regain the political and economic support of the peasant. Thus the War Communism policy of requisitioning

---

[23] Quoted in Dobb, *Soviet Economic Development,* p. 130. According to Roberts, *Alienation and the Soviet Economy,* pp. 36–41, this quote is not reflective of Lenin's true position during War Communism. Instead, Lenin tended to view War Communism as a basically correct movement in the direction of revolutionary socialism, which he was forced to back away from by the strikes and civil unrest of 1920. Roberts points out the pains taken by Lenin during this period to justify the abandonment of War Communism on ideological grounds, which would have been unnecessary if War Communism had simply been a temporary wartime measure.

agricultural surpluses had to be abandoned, for the peasants would never ally themselves with a regime that confiscated their surpluses. Market agriculture had to be reestablished in its place, freeing the peasant both to sell surpluses freely and to buy industrial products freely.

The *Smychka* strategy represented a significant concession from the Bolshevik leaders, whose freedom of action was accordingly severely restricted because they were limited to policies that would not alienate the peasant. This at times placed them in the tenuous position of having to choose between the support of the peasantry and the attainment of basic party objectives. However, there was even a more fundamental contradiction. The reestablishment of market agriculture would serve to create a commercially minded peasantry and an environment that would reward success and penalize failure. The very success of NEP would require increasing economic differentiation among the agricultural population, and the emergence of a class of relatively prosperous peasants, who would produce the critical market surpluses. Marx had condemned the wealthy and middle peasant as adamant opponents of socialism, but NEP would serve to promote this class. Thus the ideological concession underlying NEP was apparently very great.[24]

NEP Policies

The cornerstone of NEP was the proportional agricultural tax (the *prodnalog*) introduced in March of 1921 to replace the War Communism system of requisitions. First paid in kind, and by 1924 in money, it was a single tax, based upon a *fixed proportion* of each peasant's *net produce*. The state now took a fixed proportion production, and the peasant again had an incentive to aim for as a large a surplus as possible. The *prodnalog* was differentiated according to income level (as dictated by the size of the landholding) and by family size. In 1923, for example, the *prodnalog* varied from 5 percent (landholdings less than one-quarter hectare) to 17 percent (more than three hectares) of annual income. Throughout the NEP period, the burden of the *prodnalog* was shifted increasingly to the middle and upper peasants, and it accounted for some one quarter of state revenues during NEP.[25]

The agriculture tax was the first step in reestablishing a market economy; it, in turn, necessitated further measures. Unless the peasants could dispose profitably of their after-tax surplus, they would have little incen-

---

[24] A quote from Stalin on this point (from the late 1920s, after he adopted his antipeasant stance): "What is meant by not hindering *kulak* farming? [The term *kulak* refers to the prosperous peasant.] It means setting the *kulak* free. And what is meant by setting the *kulak* free? It means giving him power." I. V. Stalin, *Sochinenia* [Collected works] (Moscow: 1946–1951), vol. XI, p. 275. Quoted in Alexander Erlich, *The Soviet Industrialization Debate, 1924–1928* (Cambridge, Mass.: Harvard University Press, 1960), pp. 172–173.

[25] Vinogradov et al., *Istoriia sotsialisticheskoi ekonomiki SSSR*, vol. 2, pp. 37–38.

tive to produce above subsistence. Therefore the state granted the peasants commercial autonomy to sell their output to the buyer of their choice, be it the state, a cooperative, or a private dealer. This measure required the legalization of private trade, which was again permitted to compete with state and cooperative trade organizations. Now the peasants could market their after-tax surplus at terms dictated by market forces, not by a state monopoly. The resurgence of private trade provided a further incentive for peasants to market their surplus, for they no longer faced a state supply monopoly, rationing out industrial products to them. Finally, peasants were allowed to lease land and to hire farm laborers, both of which had been forbidden under War Communism.

Within one year, private activity dominated Soviet retail trade and restored the market link between consumer and producer. In 1922–1923, nine-tenths of all retail trading outlets were private, and they handled over three-quarters of the value of all retail trade turnover, with state and cooperative outlets handling the balance.[26] The private trader, or *Nepman* as he was called, was less strongly entrenched in wholesale trade, which remained dominated by state and cooperative organizations.

NEP also brought about significant changes in Soviet industry. The majority of industrial enterprises were permitted to make their own contracts for the purchase of raw materials and supplies and for the sale of their output; during War Communism, the state had performed these functions. Small enterprises employing 20 persons or less were denationalized, and a small number of them were returned to their former owners. Others were leased to new entrepreneurs, thereby re-creating a class of small-scale capitalists. The Bolsheviks even granted a limited number of foreign concessions. (The lessee typically signed a contract of six year's duration obligating the enterprise to sell a prescribed portion of its output to the state.) Denationalization was limited to small-scale enterprises, and the overwhelming portion of industrial production during NEP was turned out by nationalized enterprises. The industrial census of 1923 showed that private enterprises accounted for only 12.5 percent of total employment in "census" establishments.[27] In addition, only 2 percent of the output of large-scale industry was produced by the private sector in 1924–1925.[28]

While much of large-scale industry remained nationalized, decision-making throughout industry was decentralized to a great extent. Nationalized enterprises were divided into two categories: the commanding heights

[26] Dobb, *Soviet Economic Development*, p. 143.

[27] *Ibid.*, p. 142. Census establishments were those employing 16 or more persons along with mechanical power or 30 or more without it. G. W. Nutter, *The Growth of Industrial Production in the Soviet Union* (Princeton, N.J.: Princeton University Press, 1962), pp. 187–188.

[28] Nove, *An Economic History of the USSR*, p. 104.

of the economy—fuel, metallurgy, war industries, transportation, banking, and foreign trade—were not separated from the state budget and remained dependent upon centralized allocations of state supplies. The remaining nationalized enterprises were granted substantial financial and commercial autonomy from the state budget. The latter enterprises were instructed to operate commercially, that is, to maximize profits and to sell to the highest bidder, be it state or private trade. Most important, they were not obligated to deliver output according to production quotas to the state, as under War Communism.

The nationalized enterprises of this second category were allowed to federate into trusts, which soon became the dominant form of industrial organization during NEP. By 1923, the 478 chartered trusts accounted for 75 percent of all workers employed in nationalized industry.[29] These trusts were given the legal authority to enter into independent contracts. They were to be supervised loosely either by VSNKh or by the *Sovnarkhozy* (the regional economic council), but their commercial independence was protected in that the state was not allowed to acquire the property or products of a trust except by contractual agreement. In light industry, the trusts were largely independent of state control other than the usual forms of fiscal and monetary intervention. In some key sectors of heavy industry, VSNKh exercised much stricter controls over trusts in the form of specific production and delivery targets. The profits of trusts were subject to property and income taxation in the same manner as private enterprises. The monopoly State Bank controlled trust commercial credit. Although the commanding heights enterprises remained within the state budget, they also were instructed to operate as profitably as possible to eliminate reliance on subsidies. Emphasis on capitalist-type cost accounting was the order of the day.

NEP was not a command economy. Planning authorities generally provided trusts with "control figures," which were to be used as forecasts and guides for investment decisions. Mandatory output plans were drawn up only in the case of a few key sectors in heavy industry. The limited physical planning and distribution was carried out through the Committee of State Orders (representing the commissariats), which placed orders through VSNKh, which in turn negotiated the order with the producer trusts. During the major part of NEP, the most important force of economic control and regulation was the Peoples Commissariat of Finance (*Narkomfin*), which exerted its influence through the budget and credit system (the so-called dictatorship of finance). Planning during the NEP period was carried out by a variety of organizations—VSNKh, the State Planning Committee (*Gosplan*, established in 1921), the commissariats, and local authorities. Until the late 1920s, planners limited themselves primarily to forecasting

[29] Dobb, *Soviet Economic Development*, p. 135.

trends as dictated by market conditions. Also, there was a notable lack of coordination among the various planning agencies until *Gosplan* established itself as the dominant coordinating planning body after 1927.[30]

One basic notion of a way to guide the economy during NEP was to amalgamate producing enterprises in order to simplify control and coordination. An important phenomenon was the amalgamation of trusts into syndicates, initially for the purpose of coordinating industry sales. In addition to easing the planning burden, trusts and syndicates were favored by the Soviet leadership's ideological preference for large-scale industry.[31] By the late NEP period, the syndicates came to dominate the sales of state industry, accounting for 82 percent of state industry sales in 1927–1928 and for all sales of ferrous metal.[32] The trusts and syndicates acquired considerable commercial autonomy. Syndicates were allowed to enter directly into foreign trade agreements (without permission of the state foreign trade monopoly) and had the right to receive credit from credit institutions located in the Soviet Union and in some instances from foreign banks. The growing autonomy of trusts and syndicates had its disadvantages for the Soviet leadership, particularly when the trusts attempted to charge monopoly prices for their products, as we shall discuss below.

Use of money had been virtually eliminated during War Communism as a result of hyperinflation and had been replaced by a system of barter and physical allocation. Such a system however would have been too clumsy for the new market system of NEP. To avoid this obstacle, the Soviets reintroduced the use of money with the reopening of the State Bank in 1921 for the expressed purpose of aiding the development of the economy. Both public and private enterprises were encouraged to deposit their savings in the State Bank: limitations on private bank deposits were removed and safeguards were established to protect such deposits from state confiscation. A new stabilized currency, the *chervonets*, was issued by the State Bank in 1921, a balanced budget was achieved in 1923–1924, a surplus in 1924–1925, and the old depreciated paper ruble was withdrawn from circulation in the currency reform of May 1924. Thereby a stable Soviet currency was created, which for a time was even quoted on international exchanges. Money transactions between state enterprises replaced earlier barter transactions.

NEP also witnessed an attempt to reestablish relatively normal trading relations with the outside world.[33] A state monopoly over foreign trade had

[30] Carr and Davies, *Foundations of a Planned Economy*, pp. 787–836.

[31] Avdakov and Borodin, *USSR State Industry*, chaps. 3 and 4.

[32] *Ibid.*, p. 339.

[33] For discussions of NEP trade policy, see Michael R. Dohan, *Soviet Foreign Trade in the NEP Economy and Soviet Industrialization Strategy*, unpublished doctoral dissertation, Massachusetts Institute of Technology, 1969; Leon M. Herman, "The Promise of Economic Self-Sufficiency under Soviet Socialism," in Morris Bornstein and Daniel Fusfeld, *The So-*

been established shortly after the Bolshevik takeover, and foreign trade virtually disappeared during the civil war. During NEP, the Soviet leadership was reluctant to become dependent upon capitalist markets, which they believed would suffer from increasingly severe crises. Rather, the NEP strategy of trade was enunciated in Lenin's dictum of "learning from the enemy as quickly as possible." Thus the trading monopoly aimed at the importation of capitalist technology (and foreign experts) and of equipment that could not be produced at home. With this strategy in mind, foreign concessions were granted and credits from the capitalist world were sought. It was thought that in their scramble for Russian markets, the capitalist countries would mute their political hostility to the Soviet regime, which had repudiated tsarist Russia's foreign debt.

The volume of foreign trade grew rapidly during NEP from 8 percent of the prewar level in 1921 to 44 percent in 1928.[34] Yet unlike the production figures that showed a recovery to prewar levels, the volume of foreign trade throughout NEP remained well below half that of the prewar level. Credits from the capitalist nations were not forthcoming and foreign policy failures made them even less likely. The concessions program never got off the ground; at the end of NEP, there were only 59 foreign concessions, accounting for less than one percent of the output of state industry.

The Economic Recovery of NEP

Just as War Communism provided the means for waging the civil war, NEP provided the means for recovery from the war, and, in this sense, it was an important strategic success for the Soviet leadership. The economic recovery during NEP was impressive (see Table 7).

In 1920, production statistics (Table 7) indicate the low level of economic activity that existed at the end of War Communism. Industrial production and transportation were both only one-fifth of the prewar level. The shortage of fuel threatened to paralyze industry and transportation, and industry was living on dwindling reserves of pig iron. The food shortage led to the exhaustion and demoralization of the labor force. Agricultural production was 64 percent of the prewar level. Foreign trade had virtually disappeared.

In 1928—on the eve of the First Five Year Plan and at the end of NEP—the statistics provide a striking contrast: both industry and transpor-

---

viet Economy: A Book of Readings, 3rd ed. (Homewood, Ill.: Irwin, 1970), pp. 260–290; Werner Beitel and Jürgen Nötzold, Deutsch-Sowjetische Wirtschftsbeziehungen in der Zeit der Weimarer Republik [German-Soviet economic relations in the time of the Weimar Republic] (Ebenhausen: Stiftung Wissenschaft und Politik, 1977).

[34] Michael Kaser, "A Volume Index of Soviet Foreign Trade," Soviet Studies, vol. 20, no. 4 (April 1969), 523–526.

TABLE 7   Production and Trade Indexes, USSR: 1913, 1920, 1928 (1913 = 100)

	Industry	Agri-culture	Trans-portation	Exports	Imports
1913[a]	100	100	100	100.0	100.0
1920	20	64	22	0.1	2.1
1928	102	118	106	38.0	49.0

[a] The 1913 figures refer to interwar territory of the USSR.
SOURCES: G. W. Nutter, "The Soviet Economy: Retrospect and Prospect," in David Abshire and Richard V. Allen, eds., *National Security: Political, Military, and Economic Strategies in the Decade Ahead* (New York: Praeger, 1963), p. 165; Michael Kaser, "A Volume Index of Soviet Foreign Trade," *Soviet Studies*, vol. 20, no. 4 (April 1969), 523–526.

tation had moderately surpassed their prewar levels, while agriculture was almost 20 percent above its prewar level. Foreign trade remained well below prewar levels but had recovered substantially from the negligible War Communism volumes. Although the NEP recovery was impressive, one should note that high rates of growth during recovery periods are to be expected once a suitable economic environment is established. NEP policies provided this suitable framework for recovery.

The End of NEP

According to Soviet statistics, the highest level of NEP is usually dated to 1926, when prewar production levels were generally surpassed.[35] The absolute growth of the nonagricultural private sector stopped in 1926.[36] At that time, all seemed to be going well; yet two years later, NEP was abandoned in favor of the radically different system of state central planning, collectivization of agriculture, and nationalization of industry and trade. This radical turn of events seems puzzling in view of the impressive NEP successes. Why was NEP abandoned? Several considerations stimulated the decision.

First, a large number of party members viewed NEP as a temporary and unwelcome compromise with class enemies. Now that the state was stronger, they argued, the offensive against class enemies could be resumed.[37] Second, the Soviet authorities feared that economic policy might become dominated by the growing numbers of prosperous peasants and

[35] Nove, *An Economic History of the USSR*, p. 94. Recent recalculation of the Soviet figures for the 1913 to 1927–1928 period show that they may overstate the speed of recovery during the NEP period. See on this M. E. Falkus, "Russia's National Income, 1913: A Revaluation," *Economica*, vol. 35, no. 137 (February 1968), 61. This position is also supported in Paul R. Gregory, *Russian National Income, 1885–1913*, unpublished manuscript, 1979, chap. 12.
[36] Nove, *An Economic History of the USSR*, p. 137.
[37] *Ibid.*, p. 138.

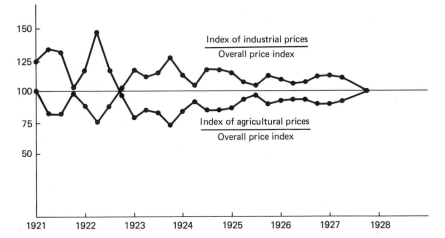

Figure 1   The Scissors Crisis. (Source: A. L. Vainshtein, *Tseny i tsenoobrazovanie v SSSR v vosstanovitel'ny period* [Prices and price formation in the USSR in the transition period] [Moscow: Nauka, 1972], pp. 158–167.)

Nepmen. Increasingly, policies were being dictated to suit the needs of the peasants, not the objectives of the state. A prime example of this was the "Scissors Crisis" of 1923, which forced the Soviet regime into the paradoxical stance of favoring private agriculture over socialist industry. The Scissors Crisis merits a slight digression at this point.

According to Soviet figures, the total marketed surplus of agriculture in 1923 was 60 percent of the prewar level, with grain marketings falling even below this figure. On the other hand, industrial production was only 35 percent of the prewar level.[38] The more rapid recovery of agriculture placed upward pressure on industrial prices relative to agricultural prices. The different sectoral recovery rates were not the sole determinants of relative price movements. A portion of the already limited output of industry was being withheld from the market by the industrial trust and syndicates, who were using their monopoly power to restrict trust sales to raise prices. The net result was an even more rapid rise of industrial prices relative to agricultural prices. The relative price movements between early 1922 and late 1923 (Figure 1) take on the shape of an open pair of scissors, from whence came the term "Scissors Crisis."

The Soviet authorities viewed the opening price scissors with alarm, for they expected the peasants to react by refusing to market their surpluses as their terms of trade with the city fell. During the prewar period, Russian peasants marketed (outside of the village) on the average 30 percent of their

---

[38] Cited in Dobb, *Soviet Economic Development*, pp. 161–162.

output. In early 1923, before the price scissors had opened sharply, they marketed about 25 percent, and Soviet authorities feared a further drop.[39] It is uncertain what did happen to peasant marketings as the scissors opened, since statistics for this early period are difficult to find. A student of the scissors crisis, James Millar, suggests that the Bolsheviks mistakenly *expected* peasant marketings to decline as agricultural prices fell in relative terms.[40] In fact, Millar argues, the peasants had traditionally responded to a decline in the terms of trade with the city by selling more to the city in order to maintain their standard of living. The Millar argument is supported by evidence showing that prewar grain marketings were not significantly affected by the terms of trade.[41] Grain marketing statistics for the Ukraine do, however, suggest a reduction in peasant marketings between 1923 and 1925, but such evidence is quite fragmentary,[42] and it is difficult to determine whether Millar's or the Soviets' perception of peasant behavior is correct.

Rightly or wrongly, the Soviet government viewed this development as a threat to the NEP recovery, for the industrial worker had to be fed and light industry required agricultural raw materials. The regime's reaction to a similar problem in 1918 had been to requisition agricultural surpluses, which resulted in a costly reduction of agricultural output; a return to requisitioning would jeopardize the progress made by NEP between 1920 and 1923. Further, influential party officials, particularly Nikolai Bukharin, feared (probably irrationally) an insufficient aggregate demand if the Scissors Crisis continued: if the peasants refused to market their output, peasant demand for industrial commodities would shrink, thereby causing an eventual glut of industrial commodities, which would also threaten the industrial recovery.

In essence, the Scissors Crisis forced the Soviet leadership to choose between two alternatives: to abandon NEP and return to requisitioning, or to retain NEP and to favor agriculture over industry to preserve the tenuous peace with the peasantry.

A third source of dissatisfaction with NEP was the conviction at that time that economic recovery had reached its limits and that further advances could be achieved only by expanding the capacity of the economy, that is, by accumulating capital. NEP statistics revealed that much capacity had been lost as a result of World War I and the civil war: the capital stock of heavy industry as of 1924 was estimated to be 23 percent below its 1917

---

[39] *Ibid.*, p. 162.

[40] James R. Millar, "A Reformulation of A. V. Chayanov's Theory of Peasant Economy," *Economic Development and Cultural Change*, vol. 18, no. 2 (January 1970), 225–227.

[41] Paul R. Gregory, "Grain Marketings and Peasant Consumption, Russia, 1885–1913," *Explorations in Economic History*, vol. 17, no. 2 (April 1980), 135–164.

[42] Jerzy F. Karcz, "Thoughts on the Grain Problem," *Soviet Studies*, vol. 18, no. 4 (April 1967), 407.

peak, and this capital equipment was on the whole old and outmoded. In 1924, the output of steel, a principal component of investment equipment, was 23 percent of 1913 output.[43] Thus industrial capacity had been lost between 1917 and 1924 and little had been done to replace it, although the building of socialism in the Soviet Union and expansion of military capacity were priority objectives of the Soviet state. After eight years of Soviet rule, investment and military commodities accounted for the same proportion of industrial output as they had prior to the Revolution. For example, 28 percent of manufacturing net output was devoted to heavy industry in 1912, and this share had only risen to 29 percent by 1926.[44] To a regime already committed to the ideological primacy of large-scale heavy industry, this was an unacceptable outcome.

In spite of their dissatisfaction with the course of industrial development during the 1920s, the Soviet leadership viewed its hands as tied as long as NEP was retained. They feared that a drive to increase industrial capacity—that is, to increase the share of heavy industry—would reduce the availability of and consequently raise the prices of manufactured goods in the short run and would further turn the terms of trade against agriculture, thus creating an additional agricultural supply crisis that would impede industrialization.

Fourth, the NEP period demonstrated to the Soviet leadership its inability to make policy in a market environment. The handling of the Scissors Crisis described above is a classic case in point. Although the scissors probably would have closed by themselves when (and if) the peasants reduced their marketings, the Soviet government intervened directly to improve the peasants' terms of trade. First, maximum selling prices were set for industrial products and price cuts for selected products were ordered. Second, imports of cheaper industrial commodities were allowed to enter the country. Third, the State Bank restricted the credit of the industrial trusts to force them to unload excess stocks. VSNKh even began to use quasi antitrust measures against the syndicates, and some were abolished.[45] The substantial closing of the scissors (Figure 1) by mid-1925 indicates the apparent success of these measures.

However, the setting of maximum industrial selling prices in a period of rising wage income had an important side effect: an excess demand for industrial products was soon created, which could not be eliminated through price increases, as ceilings had been set. Despite this excess demand and its resulting shortages, no formal rationing system was in effect, which meant that lucrative profits could be made by the *Nepmen* by selling at prices in excess of ceiling prices. This general shortage of industrial com-

[43] Erlich, *The Soviet Industrialization Debate*, pp. 105–106.

[44] Paul R. Gregory, *Socialist and Nonsocialist Industrialization Patterns* (New York: Praeger, 1970), p. 28.

[45] Avdakov and Borodin, *USSR State Industry*, pp. 196–198.

modities has been called the "goods famine," and the peasants—because of their isolation from the market—were hit especially hard.[46] Despite the efforts of the Peoples' Commissariat for Trade to sell in the village at the established ceiling prices, the peasants had to buy primarily from the *Nepman*, who sold at much higher prices. Thus the peasants, despite the nominal closing of the scissors, still lacked incentive to market their surplus. In fact, there is some evidence to suggest that grain marketings were falling as the scissors were closing.[47] The *net* marketings of grain in 1926–1927 were between 50 and 57 percent of prewar levels, although grain output was close to the prewar level.[48]

The state's pricing policy had another serious side effect that eventually destroyed the market orientation of NEP. Initially, two sets of industrial and agricultural prices coexisted side by side: the higher prices of the *Nepmen*, who sold to a great extent in the villages, and the official state ceiling price. In 1927, prices in private stores were 30 percent higher than in State Stores. By the end of 1928, they were 63 percent above official state prices.[49] The *Nepman* soon came to be regarded as a black marketeer and an enemy of the state. Beginning in late 1923, policies were adopted to systematically drive out the *Nepmen* and widen the state's control over trade. This objective was pursued through the control of industrial raw materials and goods produced by state industry, surcharges on the rail transport of private goods, and taxes on profits of *Nepmen*. In 1926, it became a crime punishable by imprisonment and confiscation of property to make "evil intentioned" increases in prices through speculation.[50] Finally, in 1930, private trade was declared a crime of speculation. Similar phenomena can be noted in agriculture. After 1926–1927, the state lowered grain procurement prices (which eventually caused peasants to divert production to higher priced crops and livestock), and a larger gap between state procurement prices and private purchase prices developed. The peasants responded by refusing to market their grain to state procurement agencies, creating the "grain procurement crisis" discussed in Chapter 4. Again the private purchaser was systematically forced out of the agricultural market by the state. This trend culminated in 1929, when compulsory delivery quotas replaced the agricultural market system.

Such actions effectively signaled the end of NEP, for the market upon which NEP primarily depended was no longer functioning. Prices were set

[46] Karcz, "Thoughts on the Grain Problem," 419.

[47] The marketed share of grain for the Ukraine between 1923 and 1926 was: 1923–1924, 26%; 1924–1925, 15%; 1925–1926, 21%.

[48] R. W. Davies, "A Note on Grain Statistics," *Soviet Studies*, vol. 21, no. 3 (January 1970), 328. The controversy over grain marketings during the late 1920s will be discussed in Chapter 4.

[49] *Statisticheski spravochrik SSSR za 1928* [The USSR Statistical handbook 1928], (Moscow: Ts.S.U, 1929), p. 727.

[50] Nove, *An Economic History of the USSR*, pp. 137–138.

by the state, acting through the *Glavki,* trusts, and syndicates, and they no longer reflected supply and demand. The economy was without direction either from market or plan—a situation that was not to be tolerated long.

The high unemployment rate of the mid and late 1920s was yet another reason for official dissatisfaction with NEP. Rising unemployment was supposed to be a problem that troubled only capitalist societies; yet rural underemployment was estimated to be between 8 and 9 million, and there were well over a million unemployed in the cities.[51] The existence of such high unemployment was not only ideologically embarrassing to the Soviet leadership, but the social unrest it engendered represented a real political threat to the regime.

A final source of dissatisfaction with NEP relates to national security problems. The fear of imperialist conspiracies, England's breaking off of diplomatic relations in 1927, and concern over Japanese activities in the Far East, prompted the Soviet leaders to realize that rapid industrialization would be required to meet the security needs of the Soviet Union and that NEP was not well-suited to generate such rapid industrialization. The Soviet leadership in 1927 expected a war with the capitalist West, and panic purchases by the population worsened the supply situation.[52]

THE PRECEDENTS OF THE 1920s

During the 1920s, the economic problem of resource allocation was dealt with by using two radially different economic systems. The first—War Communism—relied heavily upon command elements, whereas the second—NEP—attempted to combine market and command methods. The experiences of this early period tended to establish precedents that had a visible and lasting impact upon the eventual organizational structure of the Soviet planned economy. These precedents are introduced at this point as recurring themes throughout the ensuing chapters.

First, we emphasize the Soviet experiences with central planning during the 1920s. War Communism indicated that the market cannot be eliminated by fiat, for unless an enforceable plan is introduced in its place, the economy will be without direction other than that provided by the "sleepless, leather-jacketed commissars working round the clock in vain effort to replace the market."[53] To use Trotsky's apt description: "Each factory resembled a telephone whose wires had been cut."[54] The "paper" planning of

---

[51] L. M. Danilov and I. I. Matrozova, "Trudovye resursy i ikh ispol'zovanie" [Labor resources and their utilization], in A. P. Volkova et al., eds., *Trud i zarabotnaia plata v SSSR* [Labor and wages in the USSR] (Moscow: Nauka, 1968), pp. 245–248.

[52] Michal Reiman, *Die Geburt des Stalinismus* [The Birth of Stalinism] (Frankfurt/Main: EVA, 1979), chap. 2.

[53] Nove, *An Economic History of the USSR,* p. 74.

[54] Quoted in Szamuely, *First Models of the Socialist Economic Systems,* p. 97.

War Communism was shown to be virtually no plan at all, and unless planners have detailed and coordinated information from the enterprise level and up and the political and economic muscle to ensure compliance, planning will be ineffective. A further precedent in the area of planning was the importance of shock tactics in a world of deficient information and imperfect control. Thus the concentration of resources on priority projects to eliminate bottlenecks was seen as a way to give guidance to the planned economy in accordance with politically determined priorities. It was also noted that the success of shock tactics depended upon their limited application. This precedent can be seen in the "storming" tactics and the practice of singling out a few key branches for preferential treatment that persist until today. The 1920s also introduced the issue of central versus regional direction, which was to become a recurring theme throughout later periods. The friction between central and regional planning authorities (the *Glavki*, the *Sovnarkhozy*, and local authorities) throughout the 1920s revealed an imperfect harmony of national and regional interests that persists to the present period. Thus the vacillation between ministerial and regional planning, a particularly important issue during the Khrushchev years, had its roots in the 1920s. The NEP period also witnessed the growing reliance on amalgamations of state enterprises into trusts and syndicates. These amalgamations, forerunners of the modern Soviet industrial associations, served as a link between the central administrators and the producing enterprises and thus eased the burden on the administrators.

Second, the Soviet leadership's experiences with peasant agriculture during the 1920s also set important precedents. It was widely feared that peasant agriculture could be a thorn in the side of rapid industrialization, for the success of industrialization was seen as being dependent upon peasant marketings. It was thought that attempts on the part of the state to extract surpluses from the peasantry without offering economic incentives in return would be met by reductions in agricultural output and/or marketings. The Soviet leaders' apprehension was the impetus for the introduction of force into the countryside with the collectivization of agriculture in 1929 and provides an explanation for the continuing reluctance of the leadership to reinstate individual peasant farming (other than the small household plot), despite the often disappointing performance of collective agriculture.

The third important precedent of this early period was the development of an ingrained mistrust of the market that persists to the present. Most of the experiences with the market during the late NEP period were negative. The predominant trusts utilized their monopoly power to restrict output and withhold stocks. The *Nepmen* sold at high market prices despite the efforts of state pricing authorities to set limits on industrial prices. The peasants withheld their output whenever they deemed market incentives insufficient. For these and other reasons, the market was virtually abolished after 1929, with only such minor exceptions as the collective farm market, the "second economy," and, in part, the labor market. It is in this context that one can better understand the Soviet leadership's inbred opposition to fluctuating prices, output and input decisions based on profit maximization, and other market phenomena that persists to the present. Yet both War Communism and NEP convinced the Soviet leadership of the inevitability of an uneasy truce between the market and the central authorities. Throughout the transition period, the bulk of consumer goods continued to be supplied by private markets, even during periods when market transactions of this type were proscribed. During War Communism, the Soviet state continued to print money, whose use was proscribed in legal transactions, knowing full well that it was destined for illegal private markets. During NEP, the *Nepmen* were tolerated because the state knew that it would be unable to supply populations living in remote areas.

Viewing this antimarket bias in perspective, one could perhaps argue that it was irrational and stemmed from an insufficient understanding of the forces of supply and demand. On the other hand, the bias might be viewed as a rather keen perception of a development problem not always realized: often during periods of rapid industrialization, the interests of the state may conflict with the interests of individual consumers and producers—especially if the state lacks the means and expertise to manipulate the market; the individual wishes to consume, while the state wishes to save, for example. Could not one then argue that the most rational course of action is to eliminate or, at the minimum, substantially modify the market during early phases of development?

A fourth precedent, which can be related directly to the experiences of War Communism labor policies, was the evident necessity of freedom to choose occupations. If workers are to be productive, they must be allowed to choose their occupation on the basis of economic incentives. The militarization of labor that was attempted under War Communism proved to be an ineffective tool for allocating labor. Not only must wages be differentiated, but the resultant money income must have meaning in terms of real purchasing power, that is, a consumer goods market must exist. The labor experiences of War Communism set an important precedent in favor of free occupational choice—a precedent followed in subsequent periods except when temporarily abandoned during the late 1930s and 1940s in response to the tremendous turnover of the inexperienced factory labor force and wartime emergency.

A final precedent was the need to establish state control over the trade unions and other worker groups. During both War Communism and NEP, powerful forces within the party favored worker or trade union control over enterprises and trade union protection of worker interests. Opponents of these positions argued for the "statization" of the trade unions, for example, that the trade union should be the representative of state interests and that there should be "one man management" in the enterprise. By the end of

NEP, the statization of the trade unions was virtually complete and the doctrine of one man management was firmly entrenched. The reasons for party distrust of independent trade unions and worker councils are clear. Immediately after the Revolution, the central authorities had been unable to restrain wildcat nationalizations and worker takeovers. Moreover, in the absence of a coordinated central planning system, worker-dominated enterprises were operated in the interests of local workers, not in the interests of the party.

The year 1928 found the Soviet Union on the eve of the Five Year Plan period—about to embark on an ambitious program of forced industrialization. It was during this period that the Soviet command system evolved in large part into its present form. The period that we have just discussed—from the Revolution to the First Five Year Plan—is important because of its impact on this command system. One might in fact argue that War Communism and NEP represented a practical learning experience for the Soviet leadership. The next chapter describes another (more theoretical) learning experience that also had a significant impact on the evolution of the Soviet command system—the Soviet Industrialization Debate.

SELECTED BIBLIOGRAPHY

Non-Soviet Sources

Werner Beitel and Jürgen Nötzold, *Deutsch-Sowjetische Wirtschaftsbeziehungen in der Zeit der Weimarer Republik* [German-Soviet Economic Relations in the Time of the Weimar Republic] (Ebenhausen: Stiftung Wissenschaft und Politik, 1977).

E. H. Carr and R. W. Davies, *Foundations of a Planned Economy, 1926–1929,* vol. 1, parts 1, 2 (London: Macmillan, 1969).

Richard Day, *Leon Trotsky and the Politics of Economic Isolation* (Cambridge: At the University Press, 1973).

Maurice Dobb, *Soviet Economic Development Since 1917,* 5th ed. (London: Routledge & Kegan Paul, 1960), chaps. 4–9.

Alexander Erlich, *The Soviet Industrialization Debate, 1924–1928* (Cambridge, Mass.: Harvard University Press, 1960).

M. Lewin, *Russian Peasants and Soviet Power* (London: Allen & Unwin, 1968).

Alec Nove, *An Economic History of the USSR* (London: Penguin, 1969), chaps. 3–6.

Samuel Oppenheim, "The Supreme Economic Council, 1917–21," *Soviet Studies,* vol. 25, no. 1 (July 1973), 3–27.

Michal Reiman, *Die Geburt des Stalinismus* [The Birth of Stalinism] (Frankfurt/Main: EVA, 1979).

Paul Craig Roberts, *Alienation and the Soviet Economy* (Albuquerque: University of New Mexico Press, 1971).

L. Szamuely, *First Models of the Socialist Economic Systems* (Budapest: Akademiai Kiado, 1974).

Eugene Zaleski, *Planning for Economic Growth in the Soviet Union, 1918–1932* (Chapel Hill: University of North Carolina Press, 1971), chaps. 1 and 2.

Soviet Sources

Y. Avdakov and V. Borodin, *USSR State Industry During the Transition Period* (Moscow: Progress Publishers, 1977).

V. P. Diachenko, *Istoriia finansov SSSR* [History of USSR finance] (Moscow: Nauka, 1978).

E. G. Gimpel'son, *Veliki Oktiabr i stanovlenie sovetskoi sistemy upravleniia narodnym khoziastvom* [The great October and the creation of the Soviet system of regulation of the national economy] (Moscow: Nauka, 1977).

S. G. Strumilin, *Na planovom fronte* [On the planning front] (Moscow: Nauka, 1963).

V. A. Vinogradov et al., eds., *Istoriia sotsialisticheskoi ekonomiki SSSR* [History of the socialist economy of the USSR], vols. 1–3 (Moscow: Nauka, 1976).

Chapter 3
The Soviet Industrialization Debate (1924-1928)[1]

An extraordinary debate on how to initiate economic development took place in the Soviet Union between 1924 and 1928 that anticipated Western discussion on the same topic by some 25 years. Its participants ranged from leading party theoreticians to nonparty economists, and its audience included almost everyone of political and intellectual importance in the Soviet Union. The most remarkable feature of this debate was that it raised a multitude of questions concerning development strategy—issues of balanced growth versus unbalanced growth, agricultural savings, the proper scope of planning, taxation, and inflation to promote development—that are still widely debated among Western students of economic development.[2] The debate focused upon the alternative development strategies open to the Soviet economy in the late 1920s. An important point to note is that Stalin, who actually made the eventual choices of central planning and collectivization in 1928 and 1929, respectively, was an observer of and a participant in this debate.

---

[1] Our discussion of the Soviet Industrialization Debate is drawn primarily from the following sources: Alexander Erlich, *The Soviet Industrialization Debate, 1924–1928* (Cambridge, Mass.: Harvard University Press, 1960); Nicolas Spulber, *Soviet Strategy for Economic Growth* (Bloomington: Indiana University Press, 1964); Nicolas Spulber, ed., *Foundations of Soviet Strategy for Economic Growth* (Bloomington: Indiana University Press, 1964); Alexander Erlich, "Stalin's Views on Economic Development" in Ernest Simmons, ed., *Continuity and Change in Russian and Soviet Thought* (Cambridge, Mass.: Harvard University Press, 1955), pp. 81–99; M. Lewin, *Russian Peasants and Soviet Power* (London: Allen & Unwin, 1968), chaps. 6–9; Stephen F. Cohen, *Bukharin and the Bolshevik Revolution* (New York: Knopf, 1973); Michal Reiman, *Die Geburt des Stalinismus* [The Birth of Stalinism] (Frankfurt/Main: EVA, 1979); Alec Nove, "A Note on Trotsky and the 'Left Opposition,' 1929–31," *Soviet Studies*, vol. 29, no. 4 (October 1977), 576–589; James R. Millar, "A Note on Primitive Accumulation in Marx and Preobrazhensky," *Soviet Studies*, vol. 30, no. 3 (July 1978), 384–393; Richard Day, "Preobrazhensky and the Theory of the Transition Period," *Soviet Studies*, vol. 27, no. 2 (April 1975), pp. 196–219.

[2] Erlich, *The Soviet Industrialization Debate*, p. xv.

In the present chapter, we consider the major issues of the Soviet Industrialization Debate, without undue emphasis on details and biographical information. The Marxist-Leninist legacy provides the ideological foundation of the debate and is discussed first. We limit ourselves to the views of spokesmen for three important factions: Lev Shanin and N. I. Bukharin representing different views within the right wing of the Bolshevik party, and E. A. Preobrazhensky, the economic spokesman of the left wing of the party. We omit mention of significant contributors such as Bazarov, Rykov, Groman, Sokolnikov, and many others not because they are unimportant but because of space limitations and because the three views presented cover a broad spectrum of the debate, subsuming many of the ideas of other participants. A mathematical appendix at the end of the chapter summarizes the three programs and supplements the textual exposition.

THE SETTING OF THE SOVIET INDUSTRIALIZATION DEBATE

The rate of economic recovery of NEP reached its peak in 1926. The extensive loss of industrial capacity during World War I had not been recovered by the limited industrial investment during NEP. Therefore, industrial capacity during the late 1920s was probably below prewar levels. The economic instability of the 1920s—the Scissors Crisis and the goods famine, the desire for rapid industrialization, and concern with defense—pointed to the need for massive capital accumulation in industry.[3] Yet could this capital accumulation occur without ruinous inflation? This was the inflationary imbalance dilemma that initially sparked the Soviet Industrialization Debate.

The Soviet inflationary imbalance of the 1920s can be described in terms of some elementary macroeconomic concepts: the rapid NEP recovery had brought aggregate demand back close to the capacity limits of the economy. In fact, given the loss of industrial capital stock and the limited net investment of the 1920s, the fact that industrial output had regained prewar levels indicates that industrial capacity was probably already being overtaxed by the recovery of the mid-1920s. If, in this situation, considerable industrial investment was undertaken to raise industrial capacity, additional income would be created through the investment multiplier, thereby generating severe inflationary pressures. This was the Soviet inflationary imbalance in a nutshell: industrial investment was required to raise industrial capacity, yet the capacity-creating effect of investment would be felt only after a period of time. The income-generating effect of investment

---

[3] The growth models developed during this period by V. A. Bazarov and V. G. Groman predicted a declining growth rate as the Soviet economy approached its prewar equilibrium. For a discussion of these models, see Leon Smolinski, "The Origins of Soviet Mathematical Economics," in Hans Raupach et al., eds., *Yearbook of East-European Economics*, Band 2 (Munich: Gunter Olzog Verlag, 1971), p. 144.

however would be felt almost immediately, thus creating an inflationary problem.

If this inflation were to occur, the peasant would again be alienated by the increasing prices of manufactured goods, which would rise rapidly as capacity was diverted to producing investment goods. The terms of trade would again move against agriculture and another Scissors Crisis would ensue. The *Smychka* basis of NEP would be jeopardized, and some alternative system would have to be substituted to feed the industrial workers.

The second alternative, a slow rate of capital accumulation, would avoid excessive inflation and preserve the alliance with the peasant. On the other hand, the basic problem—the low capacity of the economy—would not be met, thereby keeping the economy on the brink of inflation without achieving long-run objectives.

This inflationary imbalance dilemma was the spark that ignited the Soviet Industrialization Debate in 1924. The scope of the debate then broadened to include far-reaching discussions of the long-run development alternatives available to a growing economy. The fact that the relevance of the issues raised by the Soviet Industrialization Debate is not limited to the Soviet Union of the 1920s strengthens our conviction that the problems facing developing economies are similar, irrespective of the nature of the economic system utilized during the development process.

The political background of the debate should be outlined as well.[4] After Lenin's death in January of 1924, the leadership of the Communist Party was split by a bitter factional debate. The "united opposition" of the left, led by Leon Trotsky, Grigory Zinoviev, and Lev Kamenev, opposed the NEP concessions to the peasant and to private trade and was a persistent critic of the foreign policies of the party leadership. The left opposition advocated "super-industrialization," harsh discriminatory measures against the more prosperous peasants, and resisted the notion of "building socialism in one country."[5] The party leadership consisted of a coalition between the Bolshevik "moderates"—Nikolai Bukharin, the editor of *Pravda*, who was a recognized Marxist theoretician and a popular revolutionary figure; Mikhail Tomsky, the trade union leader; and Aleksei Rykov, the head of the government bureaucracy—and Joseph Stalin, the general secretary of the Communist Party. This ruling coalition favored the continuation of NEP, the avoidance of a super-industrialization drive, the preservation of the *Smychka*, and efforts toward rapprochement with the capitalist world.

Thus the leadership coalition had a vested interest in the success of the

[4] For discussions of the political setting, see Cohen, *Bukharin and the Bolshevik Revolution*, chaps. 7–9; Reinman, *Die Geburt des Stalinismus*, chaps. 1–6; Lewin, *Russian Peasants and Soviet Power*, chaps. 6–12.

[5] The debate over "socialism in one country" refers to the issue of whether socialism could be achieved in an isolated socialist country (the Soviet Union) or whether a world socialist revolution would first be required. This issue is discussed in the next section.

NEP experiment and the policy of rapprochement with the West. The latter policy was important because through it they hoped to attract foreign credits to bolster the NEP recovery. Serious setbacks occurred on both fronts in 1927: voluntary grain marketings fell well below government targets, and the government suffered serious foreign policy setbacks—the British broke off diplomatic relations, there were troubles in Poland, and Chiang Kai-shek turned on the Chinese communists. The Soviet Union was gripped by a war scare, and it was felt that a major war with the capitalist West was imminent. Sensing a weakening in the political base of the ruling coalition, Trotsky and the left opposition chose to challenge the leadership, a challenge that was successfully repulsed and resulted in the expulsion of Trotsky from the party in December of 1927.

This recitation of the political setting of the mid-1920s is relevant to a discussion of the Industrialization Debate because it shows that the debated issues were the very ones that divided the leadership of the Communist Party. Thus the debate was much more than an abstract theoretical discussion concerning development alternatives. Rather, it was a debate that dealt with the most pressing political issues of the day.

THE MARXIST-LENINIST LEGACY

The participants in the Soviet Industrialization Debate addressed themselves to the proper way to industrialize the Soviet economy. The debate centered to a great extent on sectoral growth strategies, that is, on whether industry (the "state sector") or agriculture (the "private sector") should be favored or whether sectoral growth should be balanced.[6] This same question has been widely discussed by Western economists in the postwar period and has been called the "balanced versus unbalanced growth controversy."

The Soviet Industrialization Debate of the mid-1920s drew heavily upon the theoretical legacies of Marx and Lenin. All participants in the debate had as their goal the "building of socialism," all agreed the state (society) should own the means of production at least in industry, and all used appropriate quotations from Marx and Lenin to support their programs.

Marx

The Marxist legacy consists of Marx's (and Friedrich Engel's) limited instructions concerning the shape of the future socialist society and of Marx's

[6] The discussion of sectoral priorities can be cast in terms of either industry and agriculture or the state sector and the private sector. During the debate, industry (in particular, heavy industry) was owned primarily by the state and agriculture had private owners. It may be more accurate to picture the debate over priorities as a battle between the state-owned and the private sectors. On this, see Millar, "A Note on Primitive Accumulation," pp. 387–392.

model of expanded reproduction, a model that states the conditions for a growing economy.[7] Marx's expanded reproduction scheme is of direct relevance to the Industrialization Debate, for it provided a conceptual model for determining sectoral priorities. A further Marxist legacy that was to achieve considerable prominence in the debate was Marx's notion of primitive capitalist accumulation, the process by which capital initially came to be controlled by the capitalist class. The primitive capitalist accumulation notion was important to the debate insofar as Soviet socialist thinkers sought after Socialist parallels to primitive capitalist accumulation.

Let us begin with Marx's instructions concerning the shape of future socialist societies. They are quite brief because Marx believed that the details of the future communist society were unforeseeable. According to the Marxian dialectic, societies must inevitably evolve into higher order economic systems. Feudalism must inevitably replace slavery, capitalism must inevitably replace feudalism, and socialism must inevitably replace capitalism, for each system possesses internal contradictions that eventually explode into qualitative changes, that is, the rapid transition from one economic system to the other. The basic contradiction of capitalism, the class struggle between the worker and the capitalist, would inevitably lead to the violent overthrow of capitalism and the establishment of a socialist society. The first phase of the new socialist society would consist of a transition period that would vary from society to society depending upon the legacy of the preceding stage of capitalism. Only when communism, the final stage of social evolution, had been reached would differences among societies be eliminated. Thus Marx had remarkably little to say about the critical period of transition from capitalism to communism.

Marx believed that the socialist revolution would occur in the advanced capitalist countries, in societies that had already developed a powerful productive apparatus. The new socialist government could therefore take charge of this productive apparatus and free it from the wastes of capitalist crises and costly imperialist competition. Thus the period of transition to communism, the stage of abundance where members of society can be rewarded according to wants and needs, would not be too long in duration. In the meantime, the transition period would be characterized by the distribution of goods to individuals according to their contribution to the productive process. Those who contribute more in terms of labor services should receive more back from society. A planning system would replace the market; workers would receive vouchers from society indicating the amount of work they had performed. The workers would then be entitled to

[7] This discussion is based upon Paul M. Sweezy, *The Theory of Capitalist Development* (New York: Modern Reader Paperbacks, 1968), chaps. 5 and 10; Day, "Preobrazhensky and the Theory of the Transition Period," pp. 196–199; Friedrich Engels, *Anti-Dühring* (Moscow: Progress Publishers, 1975).

withdraw from society's production a value of goods (after deductions for investment, depreciation, etc.) equivalent to their contribution to society's output. The distribution of income would therefore remain unequal during the transition period, a defect inevitable during the first phase of communist society, but this system is fair in that it involves an exchange of equivalent values (labor for labor).[8]

During the transition period, the objective of socialist planners should be to accelerate the rate of economic growth and thus shorten the waiting time for the abundant communist society. In his model of expanded reproduction, Marx described the necessary relationship among economic sectors required to bring about economic growth. It might be noted that these are physical relationships, independent of the society's economic system; therefore they would hold in socialist as well as capitalist societies. The condition for economic growth (expanded reproduction) can be illustrated by beginning with a stationary economy that is not growing (simple reproduction).[9]

Marx divided the economy into two broad sectors: Sector I, in which the means of production are produced, and Sector II, in which consumer goods are produced. For our purposes, we equate Sector I with heavy industry and Sector II with agriculture and light industry. Using Marx's labor theory of value, which states that the value of output will equal the value of direct and indirect labor inputs plus surplus value (profits), the value of each sector's output can be written as:

$$V_1 = c_1 + v_1 + s_1$$
$$V_2 = c_2 + v_2 + s_2 \tag{1}$$

where the V's denote the value of sector output; the c's denote fixed capital costs and depreciation; the v's refer to the variable costs, primarily labor costs; and the s's denote the surplus value (or profits) of each sector. The 1's refer to Sector I; the 2's to Sector II.

In a stationary economy, the output of I (investment goods) equals the depreciation requirements of I and II, or:

$$V_1 = c_1 + c_2 \tag{2}$$

and this is Marx's condition of simple reproduction. On the other hand, the economy will grow if the fixed capital stock of the economy expands, and this occurs when the output of I exceeds the depreciation expenses of I and II, or:

$$V_1) > c_1 + c_2 \tag{3}$$

[8] The reader is referred to Marx's own discussion of these matters in Karl Marx, *Critique of the Gotha Program* (Moscow: Progress Publishers, 1971), pp. 9–21.
[9] Sweezy, *The Theory of Capitalist Development*, pp. 75–95, 162–169.

This is Marx's condition of expanded reproduction.

For the economy to be in equilibrium (an equilibrium of supply and demand for Sector I's output), capital accumulation (saving) equal to $V_1 - c_1 - c_2$ must take place. In capitalist societies, Marx assumed that workers (the recipients of v) would be at subsistence and would thus not be a source of capital accumulation. The capitalists, the recipients of surplus value s, would therefore be the source of capital accumulation. Marx did not expand upon the sources of capital accumulation during the transition period—a topic of heated controversy during the Industrialization Debate, but he did describe the process of capital accumulation during the early phases of capitalism, called "primitive capitalist accumulation."[10]

In the Marxian schema, the notion of primitive capitalist accumulation is used to explain how capital came to be controlled by a capitalist class in the first place. Marx rejected the argument that capitalists acquired capital through their own (or their ancestors') abstinence from consumption. Instead, he argued that their process occurred primarily through expropriation of the property of the weak (the serfs, the urban workers, etc.) by the strong (the state, the church, robber barons, the merchants). In this manner, the poorer segments of society were divorced from the means of production and were forced to offer their labor to the capitalist class.

What directions could the new Soviet leadership draw from the Marxist legacy in preparing their blueprints for the new socialist society? The first directive is that during the period of transition to communism, distribution should be according to one's contribution to production. The second is that some form of planning should replace the anarchy of capitalist markets. The third instruction follows from Marx's model of expanded reproduction; namely, that growth can be accelerated by giving priority to the investment goods sector over the consumer goods sector. One may care to read a final directive into Marx concerning the initial stages of capital accumulation in a new socialist state. Insofar as capitalists initially gained control of capital by expropriation (primitive capitalist accumulation), the socialist state may adopt the same method to expropriate capital from the remaining capitalists (primitive socialist accumulation).

Lenin

Lenin, in his theoretical writings, had to reconcile the socialist revolution in Russia with Marx's clear prediction that it would occur in the advanced capitalist countries. Lenin's explanation represents a basic revision of Marxism in that he argued that the socialist revolution would occur, for a variety of reasons, in the "weakest link" in the capitalist chain and that

[10] This discussion of primitive capitalist accumulation is based primarily upon Millar, "A Note on Primitive Accumulation," pp. 384–392.

Russia was that weakest link.[11] Russia's economic backwardness presented further theoretical problems for Lenin, for Marx felt that the task of making the transition from capitalism to communism would be eased by the inheritance of an advanced industrialized economy. This was not the case of Russia in 1917.

Lenin's writings on the strategy of the transition period represent an important contribution to Marxist-Leninist doctrine, although they are of less immediate relevance to the Industrialization Debate.[12] Lenin argued that the backward nature of the Russian economy required a transition period between capitalism and socialism, which he called state capitalism. In Lenin's view, a strong Soviet state would be required to capture the commanding heights of the economy. By having the state nationalize and control banking, transportation, utilities, and heavy industry, the Soviet state would be in a position to exercise control over the nonstate sector (light industry and agriculture), which would remain temporarily in private hands. With this strategy, the Soviet government would obtain the many benefits that capitalism had to offer (the services of specialists, foreign concessions, private trade) while exercising grand control over economic affairs. The enormous productive potential of capitalism, admired by Marx, would thus be put to the benefit of the working classes. In advocating state capitalism, Lenin was opposed by Nikolai Bukharin, who argued that the state should be "smashed," for Bukharin feared that a strong state might lead to the restoration of capitalism.

The failure of the Russian socialist revolution to spark the world revolution predicted by Marx presented Lenin with further doctrinal difficulties.[13] Was it possible to "build socialism in one country" (in relatively backward Russia), or would socialism in Russia have to wait on a successful socialist revolution in the advanced capitalist countries? This was a doctrinal issue that split the Bolshevik leadership. On the one side, Leon Trotsky argued for a "permanent revolution," maintaining that Russia could not hope to build socialism successfully without the assistance of more advanced socialist nations. Nikolai Bukharin (and later Stalin) opposed Trotsky by arguing that the Soviet Union's resource base and potential economic power were sufficiently strong to build socialism in Russia, isolated from the outside capitalist world. Lenin failed to make a definitive state-

[11] For a discussion of Lenin's revision of Marx in light of the Russian experience, see Paul R. Gregory and Robert C. Stuart, *Comparative Economic Systems* (Boston: Houghton Mifflin, 1980), chap. 3.

[12] In addition to the references already cited in this chapter, see H. Ray Buchanan, "Lenin and Bukharin on the Transition from Capitalism to Socialism: The Meshchersky Controversy, 1918," *Soviet Studies*, vol. 28, no. 1 (January 1976), 66–82.

[13] For a most detailed discussion of this controversy, see richard Day, *Leon Trotsky and the Politics of Economic Isolation* (Cambridge: At the University Press, 1973).

ment in this controversy, although he appeared to believe that the success of the Soviet experiment would eventually depend upon the spread of the revolution to the advanced nations. He did however argue that "breathing spells" would be required to allow consolidation of revolutionary gains before the permanent revolution could continue. Thus, contrary to Trotsky, Lenin did not believe that the world socialist revolution would be a continuous process.

Defining Lenin's legacy to the participants in the Industrialization Debate is difficult because Lenin, as a practical politician, was forced to justify Marxist theory to a wide range of conflicting policies. In the early months after the Revolution, Lenin laid out his blueprints for the fledgling Soviet regime (the "April theses"), in which the basic features of state capitalism were outlined. Shortly thereafter, he was obliged to justify War Communism and then three years later to explain the advent of NEP. For this reason, the participants in the debate found it possible to cite Lenin in support of their own programs by referring to different periods of Lenin's writings.

Having dealt with the Marxist-Leninist legacy, we now turn to the Soviet Industrialization Debate, a debate that began in earnest shortly after the death of Lenin. To a great extent, the debate was about the type of economic system—NEP or a War Communism-like system—that would be best suited to building socialism. Thus when NEP was abandoned in 1928, the outcome of the debate was clear.

PREOBRAZHENSKY—UNBALANCED GROWTH OF INDUSTRY

E. A. Preobrazhensky, the vocal spokesman of the left wing of the Bolshevik Party, took up where Marxian expanded reproduction left off and argued that a discontinuous spurt in the output of investment goods was required in order to attain rapid industrialization.[14] Preobrazhensky envisioned two possible courses of action at the end of the 1920s: the Soviet economy could either continue to stagnate or even retrogress to lower levels of capacity, or a "big push" to expand capacity could be undertaken. In taking this latter step, which he supported, halfway measures would not be advisable, for a spurt below the crucial minimum effort of investment would be self-defeating.

Preobrazhensky based this conclusion upon several factors. It was his opinion that the inflationary imbalance had two causes: the low capacity of the industrial sector, and a loss of saving ability—the latter being a consequence of institutional change in agriculture. Prior to the Revolution, the peasants had been forced to "save" in real terms a substantial portion of

[14] Preobrazhensky's views are outlined in his famous work, *Novaia ekonomika* [The new economics], which is available in English translation. See E. A. Preobrazhensky, *The New Economics*, Brian Pierce, trans. (Oxford: Oxford University Press, 1964).

their output, which was delivered either to the state or to the landlord.[15] This saving limited their capacity to purchase industrial products. The Revolution however established them as free proprietors. Rent payments were eliminated and agricultural taxes (in 1924–1925) were less than one-third of prewar obligations.[16] The peasants became accustomed to receiving industrial commodities in return for the sale of their agricultural surplus. According to Preobrazhensky, this caused a "drastic disturbance of the equilibrium between the effective demand of the village and the marketable output of the town."[17] That is, the effective demand of the peasant had increased substantially without a substantial increase in industrial capacity—thus creating an inflationary gap.

Preobrazhensky suggested that net investment in industry must be raised significantly to close the gap between effective demand and capacity and that the inflationary effects of this action must be neutralized by altering the structure of demand significantly: away from consumption and toward saving. Once the new industrial capacity had been created, private consumption could again be free to approach its previous position.

As far as the sectoral allocation of this net investment was concerned, Preobrazhensky argued for unbalanced growth to favor industry in general and heavy industry in particular on the grounds that the short-run benefits of investment in agriculture and light industry would be well outweighed by the long-run benefits of investment in capacity-expanding heavy industry. Thus he emphasized that investment goods and consumer goods industries must be arranged in "marching combat order," in keeping with the Marxian theory of economic dynamics.[18]

[15] This view is supported by Alexander Gerschenkron's analysis of the objectives of the 1861 Emancipation Act (see Chapter 1).

[16] Erlich, *The Soviet Industrialization Debate*, p. 35.

[17] *Ibid.*, p. 35.

[18] This conclusion follows the Fel'dman growth model of 1928. Employing Marxian definitions and accepting Marx's division into an investment goods sector (Department A) and a consumption goods sector (Department B), G. A. Fel'dman developed a mathematical model for the USSR State Planning Commission that made a stronger case for unbalanced growth in favor of Department A than the original Marxian model of expanded reproduction outlined above. Fel'dman made several implicit and explicit assumptions in deriving his model: (1) that the state had the power to control the division of total investment between Department A and Department B; (2) that once investment had been made in one sector, this capital could not be shifted later for use in the other sector; (3) that the economy was closed to trade with the outside world; (4) (implicitly) that the state controlled aggregate consumption and saving rather than individuals (given a particular aggregate investment goal, the state could make saving equal that amount); and (5) that capital was the sole limiting factor of production and that labor was overabundant.

Given these assumptions, Fel'dman concluded that the rate of growth of GNP in the long-run depends upon the proportion of output of the investment goods sector that is ploughed back into that sector. If a substantial portion of the Department A output goes into the consumer goods sector, then the rate of growth of total output will be small. The long-term rate of growth of consumption also depends upon reinvestment in the invest-

In arguing in favor of a big push, Preobrazhensky stressed that moderate increases in the capacity of the capital goods sector would be self-defeating: the technological gap between the USSR and the advanced capitalist powers had become so wide that it was now impossible to adopt advanced technology gradually. Second, he echoed a view widely held at the time that the replacement arrears of the Soviet economy had become so immense that a significant increase in investment was required just to keep industrial capacity from falling.

According to Preobrazhensky, foreign trade could, to some extent, act as a substitute for domestic capital production by importing foreign capital. However, the Soviets' capacity to import was limited by the lack of foreign credits (which would probably not be offered by the capitalist foes of the

---

ment goods sector. A high reinvestment ratio will yield high rates of growth of consumption in the long-run, whereas a low reinvestment ratio will yield a relatively high short-term rate and a relatively low long-term rate of growth of consumption. That is, current consumption must be scarificed in order to obtain a maximum rate of growth of both output and consumption in the long-run. In sum, Fel'dman's model concludes that the bulk of investment must flow into the capital goods sector at the expense of consumer goods sectors if the growth rate of consumption and GNP is to be maximized in the long run. The partial derivation of the Fel'dman model is given below:

Symbols: I: total investment
   I^1:   investment allocated to A
   C: total consumption
   α: portion of I allocated to A
   V_1:   capital coefficient of A
   V_2:   capital coefficient of B
   t: time subscript

Model:

$$I_t^1 = \alpha I_t \tag{1}$$

$$I_t - I_{t-1} = \frac{\alpha I_{t-1}}{V_1} \tag{2}$$

$$I_t = \left(1 + \frac{\alpha}{V_1}\right) I_{t-1} \tag{3}$$

$$= I_o \left(1 + \frac{\alpha}{V_1}\right)^{t-1} \tag{4}$$

$$C_t - C_{t-1} = \frac{(1 - \alpha)I_{t-1}}{V_2} \tag{5}$$

$$C_t - C_{t-1} = \frac{I_o(1 - \alpha)\left(1 + \frac{\alpha}{V_1}\right)^{t-2}}{V_2} \tag{6}$$

See Evsey Domar, "A Soviet Model of Growth," *Essay in the Theory of Economic Growth* (New York: Oxford University Press, 1957), pp. 223–261.

.USSR) and by the small size of the exportable agricultural surplus. However feasible, he argued that a foreign trade monopoly would be essential to ensure that machinery and not luxuries would be imported. In any case, considering the massive capital requirements of the Soviet economy in the 1920s, Preobrazhensky felt that the foreign sector could only play a limited role in the Soviet capacity buildup.[19]

The long-run payoff of Preobrazhensky's policy of one-sided reinvestment in the capital goods sector would be an enhanced capacity to produce manufactured consumer goods and industrial farm machinery. Yet he recognized that it would take years for this to happen:

> . . . a discontinuous reconstruction of fixed capital involves a shift of so much means of production toward the production of means of production, which will yield output only after a few years, that thereby the increase of the consumption funds of the society will be stopped.[20]

To dampen the interim inflationary pressures, Preobrazhensky proposed the system of primitive socialist accumulation, which was to replace the market so as to force the economy to save more for capital investment than it would have had the market prevailed. Instead of the market, state trade monopolies would set prices. By purchasing at low delivery prices and then selling at higher retail prices, the state would be able to generate a form of profit or forced saving (effecting a downward shift in the consumption function in real terms) that would reduce inflationary pressures. Preobrazhensky further suggested that during the period of primitive socialist accumulation, the main burden of industrialization should be placed on the peasantry in the form of low state purchase prices and high manufactured consumer goods prices, thereby extracting forced saving through a reduced peasant living standard.

In addition to his ideological preference for state industry, Preobrazhensky chose to burden the peasants because of the high potential of their saving capacity as exhibited prior to the Revolution and because of peasant

---

[19] Apparently, Preobrazhensky's view of the role of foreign trade did not coincide with the views of the political leader of the left wing, Trotsky. Trotsky's belief in the inability of the Soviet Union to build socialism on its own forced him to argue that the USSR remain integrated in the world economy. He felt that economic and political events would be dictated by events in the outside world and that Russia's economic weakness could be ameliorated by exchange with the more advanced world, especially when capitalist crises forced the advanced capitalist countries to compete for the Russian market. For these reasons, Trotsky attacked the trade policies of the ruling coalition as being too autarkic. Preobrazhensky may have agreed with Trotsky on these points, but he felt that a major capitalist crisis was imminent and that this crisis would destroy the Soviet industrialization drive if the USSR were integrated into the world economy. For discussions of Trotsky's views on economic integration, see Day, *Leon Trotsky and the Politics of Economic Isolation*, part 2; Nove, "A Note on Trotsky," pp. 582–584.

[20] Quoted in Erlich, *The Soviet Industrialization Debate*, pp. 56–57.

agriculture's ability to be independent of industry. The overall purpose of primitive socialist accumulation was to let the state, not private individuals, decide how much would be saved. In doing so, the state would try to equate real saving (composed of both voluntary and involuntary savings) with the output of the capital goods sector (real investment).

Preobrazhensky's notion of primitive socialist accumulation contained ideological as well as economic motives. On the ideological front, the battle would be waged between the state sector (nationalized heavy industry) and the private sector (agriculture and handicraft manufacturing), and Preobrazhensky believed that the state must ensure the victory of the socialist sector. Primitive socialist accumulation would transfer resources out of the private sector (primarily agriculture) and into the state sector by imposing "nonequivalent exchanges" between the city and countryside. The exchange of industrial and agricultural commodities would be nonequivalent because of the state's manipulation of agricultural prices. Once the state had eliminated the private sector as a viable threat, the socialized sector would become the source of capital accumulation.[21]

Preobrazhensky clearly recognized the dangers inherent in primitive socialist accumulation. Given the large volume of savings that had to be extracted from agriculture, extremely low agricultural purchase prices would have to be set. The peasant would again be faced with deteriorating terms of trade and would withdraw from the market, alienated from the Soviet regime. In Bukharin's words, primitive socialist accumulation would "kill the goose [agriculture] that laid the golden eggs." This was the weakest point of his program and proved the focus for strong attacks by his opponents. How was the industrialization drive to be sustained if agricultural supplies were not available? The platform of the left wing did call for increased emphasis on collective and state farming, but the development of socialized agriculture would be a slow evolutionary process.[22]

SHANIN—UNBALANCED GROWTH OF AGRICULTURE

Lev Shanin, a representative of the extreme right wing of the Bolshevik Party, favored a program of unbalanced growth of agriculture within an

---

[21] Lewin, *Russian Peasants and Soviet Power*, pp. 146–152; Millar, "A Note on Primitive Accumulation," pp. 387–393.

[22] Stalin's solution to this dilemma—collectivization of the peasantry, which eliminated the peasant's freedom to dispose of surpluses—did not occur to Preobrazhensky. Several years after the collectivization decision, Preobrazhensky declared in a speech: "Collectivization—this is the crux of the matter! Did I have this prognosis of the collectivization? I did not." Quoted in Erlich, *The Soviet Industrialization Debate*, p. 177. Erlich adds to this: "He [Preobrazhensky] was careful not to add that neither did Stalin at the time when the industrialization debate was in full swing. And he was wise not to point out that the decision to collectivize hinged not on superior intellectual perspicacity but on the incomparably higher degree of resolve to crush the opponent. . . ."

essentially free market environment. The inflationary imbalance of the mid-1920s also provided the point of departure for Shanin. In view of this imbalance, Shanin thought that the Soviet economy should adopt a short-term horizon in planning policy. If massive investments were made in heavy industry with its long gestation periods, demand-creating income would be released without a parallel increase in capacity except in the long run, and by that time it would be too late. Thus, Shanin emphasized the income-generation side of capital investment, whereas Preobrazhensky emphasized its capacity-creating aspect.

The difficult transition from NEP recovery to new construction of capacity could be smoothed, according to Shanin, by adopting an agriculture-first policy. There were several reasons for this conclusion.

First, Shanin argued that the short-term increment in real output to be derived from an additional ruble of investment (the marginal output-capital ratio) in agriculture far exceeded that of industry, especially in view of agriculture's surplus population and its low capital intensity.[23]

Second, Shanin believed that there was a higher propensity to save in agriculture than in industry. According to this assumption, aggregate saving (a crucial factor in an inflation prone economy) would be enhanced by a re-distribution of money income in favor of agriculture.[24] Using these two assumptions, Shanin derived his agriculture-first policy.

Shanin presented his arguments by contrasting two alternative investment programs: one channeling investment into industry, the other channeling investment into agriculture. By investing a given amount in agriculture, a relatively large increase in capacity would be generated because of agriculture's low marginal capital-output ratio. In addition, the increased investment in agriculture would increase agricultural incomes, and because of the high marginal propensity to save in agriculture, this increase in income would create a relatively large amount of incremental saving and inflationary pressures would be reduced. On the other hand, an equivalent amount of investment in industry would not only generate a smaller increase in capacity but would also fail to create as large an increase in saving because of the high marginal propensity to consume of the industrial worker.[25]

---

[23] Lev Shanin, "Questions of the Economic Course," in Nicolas Spulber, ed., *Foundations of Soviet Strategy for Economic Growth* (Bloomington: Indiana University Press, 1964), p. 219.

[24] *Ibid.*

[25] The accompanying graphs illustrate Shanin's argument: Part A shows the consumption function of industrial workers (C_I), with a high marginal and average propensity to consume out of personal income. Industrial personal income in the mid-1920s is represented by IY^0, which yields a consumption level of IC^0 for industry. The consumption function of agriculture (C_A) in Part B is drawn to have a low marginal but high average propensity to consume at the initial agricultural income level (AY^0) of the mid-1920s. The agricultural consumption level is AC^0.

The aggregate personal income of the economy in the mid-1920s is Y^0 (in Part C), which is the sum of IY^0 and AY^0 (from Parts A and B). Aggregate consumption is C^0, which is the sum of IC^0 and AC^0 (from Parts A and B). This consumption level is assumed to equal the real output of consumer goods of the two sectors operating at full capacity, which is denoted by K^0.

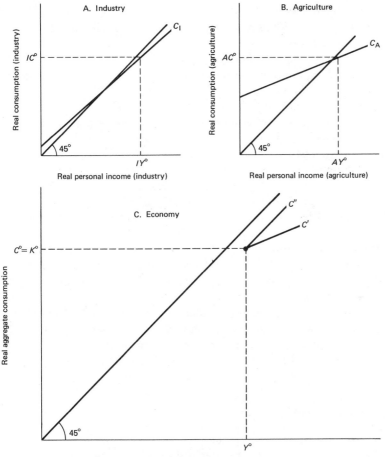

The graphs can be used to support Shanin's invest-in-agriculture policy: because of agriculture's smaller marginal capital-output ratio, agricultural investment would tend to raise capacity (K) more than would industrial investment. In this manner, inflationary pressures in the consumption goods sector would be eased, for the additional investment would raise personal income and consequently consumption—hence the necessity to raise capacity. Second, because of the lower marginal propensity to consume within the agricultural sector, more savings could be generated by investing in agriculture, thereby raising agricultural income. As agricultural income rose, the economy would expand along the C' consumption function (which tends toward agriculture's marginal propensity to consume). If investment were made in industry, the economy would expand along C'', which tends

According to Shanin, two benefits would be derived from investment in agriculture. First, the capacity of the economy would be increased by a larger amount and in a shorter period of time, thereby ameliorating the short-term inflationary imbalance. Second, the creation of additional income in agriculture would generate a larger amount of incremental saving that could be used to finance additional investment without inflation.

Finally, Shanin emphasized the benefits to be gained from foreign trade. By trading according to its comparataive advantage in agriculture, the Soviet Union could exchange agricultural products for industrial capital equipment, thereby building up the capital stock of industry while at the same time avoiding the inflation that would have occurred had the investment initially been in industry.[26]

Shanin envisioned that his policies would have to be carried out within an essentially free market environment to ensure the support of the peasantry and thereby the efficient utilization of investment in agriculture. He was sufficiently realistic to see that his proposals would have to be altered in the case of an imminent military threat, which would require the short-run enhancement of industrial capacity irrespective of the economic consequences. He also saw that certain industrial investments—such as in transportation—would be required in order to carry out his agricultural programs.[27] Therefore, industrial investment could not be neglected entirely. Another circumstance mitigating against the full-scale adoption of his agriculture-first program would be the exhaustion of foreign markets for Soviet agricultural products. Nevertheless, he minimized the importance of these exceptions and did not allow them to materially alter his main conclusions.

In the long run, after the initial inflationary imbalance had been eliminated, Shanin proposed a shift in emphasis toward industry, a shift toward reinvesting in capital goods that could be now accomplished free of inflationary pressures. At this time, the building of socialism could begin in earnest, unhindered by short-term inflationary problems.

BUKHARIN—BALANCED GROWTH

Nikolai Bukharin was the official spokesman of the right wing of the Bolshevik Party. A close personal associate of Lenin and possessing credentials as a leading Marxist theoretician, Bukharin remained a potent individual force in Soviet politics until the Stalin purges of the 1930s.[28] Prior to NEP, Bukharin's ideas were closely attuned to those of the left wing of the party,

---

toward industry's higher marginal propensity to consume. In this manner, Shanin's invest-in-agriculture policies would allow the economy to expand through additional investment and without inflation.

[26] Erlich, *The Soviet Industrialization Debate*, pp. 140–141.

[27] *Ibid.*, p. 132.

[28] Cohen, *Bukharin and the Bolshevik Revolution.*

and he even co-authored a standard textbook on communism with Preo-brazhensky. But NEP brought about a significant change in Bukharin's thinking. Throughout the NEP period, he remained an influential supporter of the NEP economic system and acted as its advocate in the face of attacks from the left wing.

Whereas Preobrazhensky felt that the victory of socialist ownership over private property had to be engineered by the state through unequal exchanges between the city and countryside, Bukharin felt that this out-come would be ensured by the natural superiority of socialist ownership.[29] The proletariat was in a position to exercise political control over the coun-try and would thus be able to contain the antisocialist tendencies of the peasant, but market relations between the city and countryside would en-sure that harmony between the peasant and the industrial worker (the *Smychka*) would be maintained. Any effort to introduce nonequivalent ex-changes would destroy the foundation of economic development.

Unlike the left wing, Bukharin and his followers felt that socialized in-dustry did not require discriminatory government action to assert its superi-ority. Rather, state industry would naturally grow more rapidly than the rest of the economy, and its share would inevitably increase. In this manner, the superiority of socialist ownership would be demonstrated to those out-side the state sector, and they would gradually be attracted to join the state sector on a voluntary basis. The peasants would increasingly join consumer and producer cooperatives, and the state would encourage agricultural co-operation through favorable credit terms granted by the State Bank. Even-tually, the peasants would join collective farms voluntarily. This action, however, would have to be noncoercive, for it would be counterproductive to impose collectivization on the peasantry before the peasants themselves were convinced of the superiority of the socialist form.

So much for the political side of the Bukharin program. On strictly eco-nomic grounds, he argued in favor of the balanced growth of industry and agriculture, granting that socialized industry would grow more rapidly than the economy as a whole. According to Bukharin, any investment policy that one-sidedly favors agriculture over industry or vice versa, or one branch of industry over another, will fail because of the interdependence of economic sectors.[30] First, industry cannot function successfully without agricultural supplies: the productivity of the industrial worker depends upon the avail-ability of marketed agricultural foodstuffs. Further, industrial capacity will be reduced greatly if agricultural raw materials are not available for sale. Industry requires sophisticated capital equipment, which it initially cannot produce domestically and which cannot be purchased abroad if agricultural surpluses are not exported to finance such imports. Agricultural producers

---

[29] Lewin, *Russian Peasants and Soviet Power*, pp. 132–142.
[30] Erlich, *The Soviet Industrialization Debate*, pp. 82–83.

on the other hand depend upon industry for hand tools, agricultural machinery, and manufactured consumer goods. If these goods are not forthcoming, the peasants will retaliate by not supplying agricultural products for industry.

Bukharin recognized the need for capital accumulation but argued that it should be kept within manageable proportions. The overextension of one sector or subsector of the economy at the expense of other sectors would create critical bottlenecks—steel shortages, deficits of vital agricultural raw materials, insufficient foreign exchange earnings—that would inevitably retard overall economic development. According to Bukharin, any formula calling for maximum investment in heavy industry without a corresponding expansion of light industry would not only aggravate the goods famine—owing to the channeling of investment resources into time-consuming capital goods industries—but would also threaten to undermine the NEP recovery.

Because he emphasized economic interrelationships, Bukharin's program called for the gradual expansion of all sectors simultaneously. The critical link between agriculture and industry would be maintained by creating a favorable atmosphere for peasant agriculture. Instead of setting low agricultural delivery prices and high industrial prices, the state should do the opposite: first, to provide an incentive for the peasant to produce and market a larger output, and second, to pressure state enterprises to lower costs. It would not be necessary to force saving from agriculture as Preobrazhensky proposed; instead, only a stable economic environment free of the uncertainties of War Communism and NEP would be needed. In such a situation, the peasants would return to their traditional frugality, creating the savings to finance further expansion of capacity. Bukharin's advice to the peasant was to "get rich," a slogan from which Stalin carefully disassociated himself.[31]

To resolve the incongruency between limited industrial capacity and his call for moderate capital investment spread fairly evenly among economic sectors, Bukharin proposed a series of measures to economize and utilize the available capital more fully. Small-scale manufacturing and handicrafts were to undergo a technological "rationalization" and be transformed into supposedly more efficient producers' cooperatives. Large-scale investment projects were to be made more efficient by better planning and more efficient construction work. Maximum attention was to be accorded to the speedy completion of investment projects. The available capital equipment was to be used more exhaustively by employing multiple shifts. Attention was to be given to appropriate factor proportions, that is, capital was not to be invested in areas where labor could do the job as efficiently.

---

[31] *Ibid.*, pp. 86–87.

The state pricing policy should stimulate cost economies and more efficient use of available resources by eliminating monopoly profits.[32] Nevertheless, Bukharin was forced to admit that balanced growth meant steady but slow progress toward socialism. His own expression was "progress at a snail's pace," a phrase that was used against him in his struggles against the left wing and then later with Stalin.[33]

Although Trotsky had criticized the foreign trade strategy of the right wing as too autarkic, the trade policies advocated by Bukharin and his associates recognized the Soviet Union's initial dependence upon the advanced capitalist powers.[34] Bukharin argued that during the early stages of industrialization, the USSR must import large quantities of industrial equipment from abroad and pay for those commodities with agricultural exports. Yet the long-term goal must be independence from the capitalist world and the "building of socialism in one country." Thus the Soviet Union's dependence upon foreign imports should be of limited duration, lasting only until domestic industry would be capable of producing the necessary capital equipment at home.

In sum, Bukharin favored the balanced expansion of both industry and agriculture under a general policy of moderate capital accumulation financed by the voluntary saving of the peasantry. This balanced growth was to be fostered by an environment that would encourage the peasantry to produce and sell their surplus to the city. State pricing policy would be used to gain the favor of the peasants by setting low industrial and high agricultural prices. By fostering methods to increase the efficiency of capital utilization, a return to the goods famine of the 1920s could be avoided without resorting to the massive industrialization drive favored by the superindustrialists of the left wing. The foreign sector would play an important role in that it would provide the foreign machinery to sustain the growing capacity of industry.

THE OUTCOME OF THE SOVIET INDUSTRIALIZATION DEBATE

In a series of adroit political maneuvers, Stalin consolidated his power within a rather brief period of time after Lenin's death in 1924. First, he allied himself with the right wing of the party (Bukharin, Rykov, and Tomsky) to purge the leftist opposition led by Trotsky from positions of power—a phase completed in late 1927. Then Stalin turned his attention to the "right deviationist" Bukharinites, who were denounced by the Central Committee of the Communist Party in November of 1928. This occurred just one

[32] *Ibid.*, pp. 84–86.
[33] Lewin, *Russian Peasants and Soviet Power*, p. 139.
[34] Day, *Leon Trotsky and the Politics of Economic Isolation*, chap. 7.

month after Stalin's adoption of the more ambitious alternative draft of the First Five Year Plan, which was supportive of the original left-wing industrialization program.[35]

The variant of the First Five Year Plan adopted in 1928 and formally approved in April 1929 staggered the imagination of even the superindustrialists. The low capacity of the Soviet industrial sector was to be subjected to an all-out attack: the Soviet fixed capital stock was to double within five years to provide the industrial base for building socialism. The First Five Year Plan also called for a 70 percent expansion of light industry, which was quite unrealistic in vew of the limited industrial capacity in 1928.[36]

Stalin's changeover from his alliance with the Bukharinites and their pro-NEP policies to an acceptance of the program of the already purged left wing should be described.[37] During the Industrialization Debate, Stalin was clealy aligned with the Bukharin position. Stalin emphasized the achievements of NEP and ridiculed the left's superindustrialization proposals and the left's demand that "tribute" (primitive socialist accumulation) be paid by the peasants. Although Stalin underscored the advantages of large-scale farming, he made it clear that any movement in the direction of collective farming would be gradual and voluntary. Throughout the Industrialization Debate, Stalin refrained from making independent contributions that could later be attributed to him alone, and even the doctrine that socialism could be built in one country that is generally credited to Stalin was in reality Bukharin's contribution.

The foreign policy setbacks and the grain collection problem of 1927 emboldened Trotsky and the left opposition to challenge the ruling coalition. Stalin, allied with the moderates, was able to repulse the attack, but he came to believe that the left had correctly foreseen the crises encountered in 1927, in particular the problem of state grain collections from a reluctant peasantry. To increase grain collections, Stalin came to rely more and more on coercion and emergency measures, personally directing state grain collections in Siberia. The coalition with Bukharin was kept intact by carefully timed concessions to the right wing concerning the lifting of force in the countryside. Stalin came away from his experiences in 1927 with the conviction that force was the answer to the agrarian problem, for primitive socialist accumulation without the power to force peasant deliveries would not work. From this point on, Stalin ceased to serve as a defender of the NEP system and began instead to criticize lagging NEP performance and to call for a superindustrialization drive. Moreover, he began to reiterate

[35] *Ibid.*, chap. 9. It was not until the Stalin purges in the late 1930s that this political process was complete. Preobrazhensky, Shanin, and Bukharin all lost their lives in the purges.
[36] *Ibid.*, p. 166.
[37] Accounts of Stalin's move to the left are found in Erlich, "Stalin's Views on Economic Development," pp. 81–99; Reiman, *Die Geburt des Stalinismus*, chaps. 5–8; Lewin, *Russian Peasants and Soviet Power*, chaps. 9–17.

Trotsky's call for tribute from the peasants and to warn of *kulak* sabotage of grain collections. Encouraged by Stalin's move to the left, former Trotskyites such as Preobrazhensky returned to the party fold, only to perish later in the purges.

The First Five Year Plan was adopted in October of 1928, amidst a new grain collection crisis that was to have a crucial impact upon subsequent events. According to Stalin, the success of the industrialization program was clearly jeopardized, for it was dependent upon an increasing supply of food products and agricultural raw materials from the countryside. As long as the peasants refused to turn over such deliveries to the city, they held the power to halt the entire industrialization program.[38] The peasants' reluctance to sell their output to the state was understandable in light of the low purchase prices paid by the state and the increasing use of coercion to collect grain.

Stalin's answer to the crisis he perceived was to mount a counteroffensive designed to break once and for all the peasants' hold over the pace of industrialization. In the autumn of 1929, he ordered the wholesale collectivization of agriculture. Peasant landholdings and livestock were forcibly amalgamated into collective farms, which were obligated to deliver to the state planned quotas of farm products at terms dictated by the state.

The ensuing turmoil was great not only in the countryside, which burst into open rebellion, but also in Soviet cities, which received a vast influx of workers from the countryside and saw a significant redistribution of labor among industrial branches as enterprises attempted to fulfill their taut production targets.

The actual Soviet industrialization pattern that emerged after 1928 (Panels A, B, and C, Table 8) bears a close resemblance to Preobrazhensky's industrialization proram: Soviet economic growth between 1928 and 1940 was heavily biased in favor of industry in general and of heavy industry in particular. Industrial production grew at an annual rate of 11 percent, whereas agricultural production grew at an annual rate of only one percent between 1928 and 1937 (C3 and 4). The negative rate of growth of livestock graphically indicates the impact of collectivization upon agricultural performance. The same trends are apparent in the differential rates of growth

---

[38] According to Jerzy Karcz, there was no real agricultural crisis during this period. The grain collection "crisis" was precipitated by the lowering of state grain procurement prices in 1926–1927, while procurement prices for animal products were raised. Peasants shifted their attention to animal products, fed grain to livestock, and held grain in stock, waiting for grain prices to be increased. Total agricultural sales did not fall during this period. Thus the "crisis" was caused not by the weakness of peasant agriculture but by the ineptitude of state pricing policy. In addition, Karcz raises the question of deliberate falsification of grain statistics by Stalin to gain support for collectivization. Jerzy F. Karcz, "Thoughts on the Grain Problem," *Soviet Studies,* vol. 18, no. 4 (April 1967), 399–434. For a different view, see R. W. Davies, "A Note on Grain Statistics," *Soviet Studies,* vol. 21, no. 3 (January 1970), 314–329. This controversy will be discussed in detail in Chapter 4.

**TABLE 8   Outcome of the Soviet Industrialization Debate:
The Industrialization Drive of 1928–1940**

	1928	1933	1937	1940
A. CHANGES IN MANUFACTURING				
1. Heavy manufacturing ÷ overall manufacturing				
Net product share (1928 prices)	31	51	63	—
Labor force share	28	43	—	—
2. Light manufacturing ÷ overall manufacturing				
Net product share (1928 prices)	68	47	36	—
Labor force share	71	56	—	—
B. CHANGES IN MAJOR ECONOMIC SECTORS, STRUCTURE OF OUTPUT				
1. Share in net national product (1937 prices)				
Agriculture	49	—	31	29
Industry	28	—	45	45
Services	23	—	24	26
2. Share in labor force				
Agriculture	71	—	—	51
Industry	18	—	—	29
Services	12	—	—	20
C. RATES OF GROWTH (1928–1937) AND CAPITAL STOCK				
1. GNP (1937 prices)			4.8%	
2. Labor force				
Nonagricultural			8.7%	
Agricultural			−2.5%	
3. Industrial production (1937 prices)			11.3%	
4. Agricultural production (1958 prices)			1.1%	
Livestock			−1.2%	
5. Gross industrial capital stock (1937 prices, billion rubles)	34.8	75.7	119	170
D. CHANGES IN THE STRUCTURE OF GNP BY END USE (1937 PRICES)				
1. Household consumption ÷ GNP	80	—	53	49
Annual growth rate (1928–1937)			0.8%	
2. Communal services ÷ GNP	5	—	11	10
Annual growth rate (1928–1937)			15.7%	
3. Government administration and defense ÷ GNP	3	—	11	21
Annual growth rate (1928–1937)			15.6%	
4. Gross capital investment ÷ GNP	13	—	26	19
Annual growth rate (1928–1937)			14.4%	
E. FOREIGN TRADE PROPORTIONS				
1. Exports + imports ÷ GNP	6%[a]	4%	1%	—

TABLE 8   (*Continued*)

	1928	1933	1937	1940
F. SHARES OF THE SOCIALIST SECTOR IN				
1. Capital stock	65.7%	—	99.6%	—
2. Gross production of industry	82.4%	—	99.8%	—
3. Gross production of agriculture	3.3%	—	98.5%	—
4. Value of trade turnover	76.4%	—	100.0%	—
G. PRICES				
1. Consumer goods prices (state and cooperative stores, 1928 = 100)	100	400	700	1000
2. Average realized prices of farm products (1928 = 100)	100	—	539	—

SOURCES: Panel A: Paul R. Gregory, *Socialist and Nonsocialist Industrialization Patterns* (New York: Praeger, 1970), pp. 28–29, 36. Heavy manufacturing is defined according to the International System of Industrial Classification as ISIC 30–38. Light manufacturing is defined as ISIC 20–29. Panel B: Simon Kuznets, "A Comparative Appraisal," in Abram Bergson and Simon Kuznets, eds., *Economic Trends in the Soviet Union* (Cambridge, Mass.: Harvard University Press, 1963), pp. 342–360. Panel C: Bergson and Kuznets, *ibid.*, pp. 36, 77, 187, 190, 209. Panel D: Abram Bergson, *Real Soviet National Income and Product Since 1928* (Cambridge, Mass.: Harvard University Press, 1961), pp. 217, 237. Panel E: Bergson and Kuznets, *Economic Trends*, pp. 288–290. Panel F: *Narodnoe khoziaistvo SSSR v 1958 g.* [The national economy of the USSR in 1958], p. 57. Panel G: Franklyn D. Holzman, "Soviet Inflationary Pressures, 1928–1957: Causes and Cures," *Quarterly Journal of Economics*, vol. 74, no. 2 (May 1960), 168–169.
[a] 1929.

of the agricultural and nonagricultural labor forces between 1928 and 1937 (C2): the former declined, while the latter expanded rapidly at an annual rate of almost 9 percent.

The structural transformations resulting from these differential sector growth rates are impressive (Panel B). Agriculture's shares of net national product and labor force declined from 49 percent and 71 percent, respectively, in 1928 to 29 percent and 51 percent, respectively, in 1940, whereas the increase in industry's product and labor force shares was from 28 percent and 18 percent, respectively, to 45 percent and 29 percent, respectively, during the same period.

The most remarkable feature of the 1930s was the extent to which the pro-heavy industry bias asserted itself (as Preobrazhensky said it should). Between 1928 and 1937, heavy manufacturing's net product share of total manufacturing more than doubled from 31 percent to 63 percent; whereas light manufacturing's product share fell from 68 percent to 36 percent.

The impact of this production program upon real consumption levels in the absence of significant foreign trade (the ratio of imports plus exports to GNP sank to one percent by 1937, Panel E) had already been foreseen by Preobrazhensky. Between 1928 and 1937, household consumption scarcely grew (at an annual rate of 0.8 percent), and the share of consumption in GNP (in 1937 prices) declined markedly from 80 percent to 53 percent.

During the same period, gross capital investment grew at an annual rate of 14 percent and the ratio of gross investment to GNP doubled from 13 percent to 26 percent. If we define total consumption expenditures to include both private consumption and communal services, and nonconsumption expenditures to include investment, government administration, and defense, then total consumption fell between 1928 and 1937 from 85 percent of GNP to 64 percent of GNP (Panel D).

The changing institutional setting within which these transformations

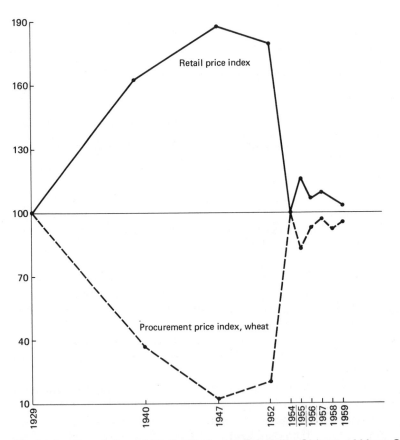

Figure 2   Correlation of State Wholesale Prices for Objects of Mass Consumption and Purchase Price of Wheat (USSR 1929 = 100). (Sources: A. N. Malafeev, *Istoriia tsenoobrazovaniia v SSSR* [The history of price formation in the USSR] [Moscow: 1964], p. 286. These figures are not directly comparable to those in Figure 1, which relate an index of agricultural prices to an index of all prices, because of the vast change in agricultural prices after 1929, when procurement prices began to diverge significantly from the retail prices of agricultural commodities, and because Figure 2 refers only to wheat prices, not to a more general farm price index.)

were occurring should also be noted (Panel F): between 1928 and 1937, the socialist sector share of total capital stock, industry, agriculture, and trade expanded sharply, so that by 1937 the socialist sector totally dominated all economic activity.

Panel G has special relevance to the outcome of the industrialization debate. Consumer prices rose by 700 percent between 1928 and 1937 and probably would have risen even faster without the extensive formal and informal rationing of the period. Average realized prices of farm products, which are weighted averages of the extremely low state procurement prices, the above-quota state delivery prices, and collective farm market prices, on the other hand, rose by 539 percent, which indicates a reopening of the price scissors against agriculture between 1928 and 1937. An examination of some partial data (Figure 2) suggests that, in fact, the scissors did reopen and were not closed again until the mid-1950s, with a resultant squeeze upon the agricultural sector in terms of low procurement prices.

In sum, the left opposition program was apparently the model for the Soviet industrialization drive. The pro-industry and pro-heavy industry bias of the first two Five Year Plans is clearly shown in Table 8 and was implemented at the expense of the agricultural sector and the consumer. The expected deterioration in the agricultural terms of trade occurred, but it did not halt the industrialization drive, possibly owing to the forced collectivization of agriculture.

In retrospect, the Soviet industrialization drive must be seen as a remarkable and rapid shift of the Soviet economic structure. However, as we examine this process in greater detail, it will become even more apparent that like any approach to economic development, the "Soviet development model" is not without cost. Thus, the costs and benefits of alternative development models must always be carefully considered. We shall return to this issue in Chapter 4.

APPENDIX TO CHAPTER 3

MATHEMATICAL MODELS OF THE SOVIET INDUSTRIALIZATION DEBATE[39]

• *Introduction.* The models of Preobrazhensky, Shanin, and Bukharin, that have been described verbally in the text, can also be shown in terms of a fairly basic mathematical growth model. Such a model is developed in this appendix, which shows how, by varying the assumptions, the policy conclusions of all three were derived.

In keeping with the original debate, the model consists of two sectors—industry and agriculture—and allows for differences in sectoral capital-output ratios and savings functions. The allocation of investment between industry and agriculture is treated as the principal policy variable of the model. The initial assumptions are: (a) the economy is closed; (b) capital is the sole limiting factor of production in both sectors; and (c) all variables are in real terms. Other less crucial assumptions are: (d) the average and marginal capital-output ratios are equal; (e) the average and marginal propensities to save are equal; (f) the initial allocation of investment does not change over the planning period; and (g) the initial sector capital ratio is equal to the constant investment allocation factor.

List of Symbols

m marginal capital-output ratio of agriculture (assumed equal to the average capital-output ratio), e.g., $m = dka/dYa = Ka/Ya$

bm marginal capital-output ratio of industry (assumed equal to the average capital-output ratio), e.g., $bm = dKi/dYi = Ki/Yi$

s marginal propensity to save of agriculture (assumed equal to the average propensity), e.g., $s = dSa/dYa = Sa/Ya$

$s - e$ marginal propensity to save of industry (assumed equal to the average propensity), e.g., $s - e = dSi/dYi = Si/Yi$

S savings (real)

I investment (real)

Y real income (output)

K capital stock (real)

g ratio of income allocated to industry

$1 - g$ ratio of income allocated to agriculture

a subscripts refer to agriculture

i subscripts refer to industry

f ratio of investment allocated to agriculture

$1 - f$ ratio of investment allocated to industry

$DY = dY/dt$

[39] We are indebted to Thomas A. Wolfe for his correction of an error in the version of this model in the first edition.

• *Derivation of the Model.* The derivation of the model begins with the allocation of investment between industry and agriculture, from which an investment equation is developed. The equilibrium condition requires equality of savings and investment. The savings equation is derived by starting with a particular allocation of income between industry and agriculture (how this allocation is determined will be considered later). In the familiar Harrod–Domar manner, the savings equation is set equal to the investment equation, and then solved for the growth rate of the economy. The steps are as follows.

Investment is allocated by the state between agriculture and industry:

$$I_a = f \cdot I \tag{1}$$
$$I_i = (1 - f)I \tag{2}$$

Investment Sector

$$DY = \frac{fI}{m} + \frac{(1 - f)\,I}{bm} \tag{3}$$

$$I = \left[\frac{bm}{(bf - f + 1)} \right] DY \tag{4}$$

Savings Sector

$$Y_a = (1 - g)Y \tag{5}$$
$$Y_i = gY \tag{6}$$
$$S = s(1 - g)Y + (s - e)gY$$
$$= (s - eg)Y \tag{7}$$

Equilibrium of Savings and Investment

$$S = I \tag{8}$$

$$\frac{bm}{(bf - f + 1)} = (s - eg)Y \tag{9}$$

$$\frac{DY}{Y} = \frac{(bf - f + 1)(s - eg)}{bm} \tag{10}$$

It is now necessary to determine how the allocation of income between industry and agriculture (the factor g) relates to the allocation of investment between industry and agriculture (the factor f). Because capital is the sole scarce factor of production, one would expect intuitively that the allocation of investment between sectors will determine the allocation of income between sectors. By equating the income of each sector with the output of that sector (as determined by the sector capital stock and the average sector capital-output ratio), the model can be completed with the following steps:

Determination of g

$$Y_a = (1 - g)Y \tag{11}$$

$$Y_a = \frac{K_a}{m} = \frac{fK}{m} \tag{12}$$

$$(1 - g)Y = \frac{fK}{m} \tag{13}$$

$$g = 1 - \left(\frac{f}{m}\right)\left(\frac{K}{Y}\right) \tag{14}$$

$$\frac{Y}{K} = \frac{f}{m} + \left(\frac{1-f}{bm}\right) \tag{15}$$

$$g = 1 - \left[\frac{\left(\frac{f}{m}\right)}{\left(\frac{f}{m} + \frac{1-f}{bm}\right)}\right] \tag{16}$$

This new expression of g (equation 16) is then substituted into the growth equation (10):

$$\frac{DY}{Y} = \frac{1}{m}\left[s\left(f + \frac{(1-f)}{b}\right) - e\frac{(1-f)}{b}\right] \tag{17}$$

Thus the growth rate of the economy has been related to the structural parameters (s, b, me, e), which are taken as given, and to the policy variable f. As one might expect, the growth equation (17) reduces to the familiar Harrod–Domar equation $(DY/Y = s/m)$ if the sector capital-output ratios and savings propensities are equal ($b = 1$, $e = 0$).

• *Policy Implications.* Shanin's policy conclusions can be derived easily from equation 17. His crucial assumptions were: (a) the industry capital-output ratio was larger than in agriculture ($b>1$), and (b) the marginal propensity to save in agriculture was greater than in industry ($e>0$). Differentiating the growth equation 17 with respect to the policy variable f, we get:

$$\frac{\partial (DY/Y)}{\partial f} = \frac{1}{m}\left[\frac{s(b-1) + e}{b}\right] \tag{18}$$

Under Shanin's two assumptions, the expression (18) is *positive*, and the higher the allocation of investment to agriculture, the higher the growth rate of the economy.

To derive Preobrazhensky's policy conclusions from the above model, we follow his assumptions that (a) the state can control the aggregate real saving rate by primitive socialist accumulation and that (b) the industry capital-output ratio (after a big push) is smaller than in agriculture ($b<1$). Thus a different savings equation must be substituted:

$$S = wY \qquad (19)$$

for equations 5–7, where w is the state controlled saving rate. The growth equation now becomes:

$$\frac{DY}{Y} = \left(\frac{w}{bm}\right)(bf - f + 1) \qquad (20)$$

Taking the partial derivative of the growth rate with respect to f, one gets:

$$\frac{\partial(DY/Y)}{\partial f} = \frac{w}{m} - \frac{w}{bm} \qquad (21)$$

which is *negative* under Preobrazhensky's assumptions, and the higher the allocation of investment to agriculture, the lower the growth rate of the economy. Thus Preobrazhensky's conclusions.

Bukharin's policy conclusions are even easier to derive from the model. If one accepts Bukharin's assumption that owing to the rigid interrelationships between industry and agriculture, investment must be allocated between them in roughly fixed proportions, f is no longer a policy variable but is, instead, a constant determined by technology. The growth rate of the economy can now be raised either (a) by more efficient utilization of sector capital (reducing m) or (b) by raising the marginal propensity to save (raising s), which is exactly what Bukharin proposed: to create a stable environment in agriculture, to promote peasant saving, and to lower capital-output ratios in industry by amalgamation, multishift operations, and industrial price setting.

SELECTED BIBLIOGRAPHY

Nikolai Bukharin, *The Politics and Economics of the Transition Period,* Kenneth Tarbuck, ed., (London: Routledge & Kegan Paul, 1979).

Stephen F. Cohen, *Bukharin and the Bolshevik Revolution* (New York: Knopf, 1973).

Richard Day, *Leon Trotsky and the Politics of Economic Isolation* (Cambridge: At the University Press, 1973).

Maurice Dobb, *Soviet Economic Development Since 1917,* 5th ed. (London: Routledge & Kegan Paul, 1960), chap. 8.

Friedrich Engels, *Anti-Dühring* (Moscow: Progress Publishers, 1975).

Alexander Erlich, "Stalin's Views on Soviet Economic Development," in Ernest Simmons, ed., *Continuity and Change in Russian and Soviet Thought* (Cambridge, Mass.: Harvard University Press, 1955), pp. 81–99.

Alexander Erlich, *The Soviet Industralization Debate, 1924–1928* (Cambridge, Mass.: Harvard University Press, 1960).

Naum Jasny, *Soviet Economists of the Twenties: Names to be Remembered* (Cambridge: At the University Press, 1972).

V. I. Lenin, *Imperialism, the Highest Stage of Capitalism* (Moscow: Progress Publishers, 1970).

M. Lewin, *Russian Peasants and Soviet Power* (London: Allen & Unwin, 1968), chaps. 6–9).

Karl Marx, *Critique of the Gotha Program* (Moscow: Progress Publishers, 1971).

James R. Millar, "A Note on Primitive Accumulation in Marx and Preobrazhensky," *Soviet Studies,* vol. 30, no. 3 (July 1978), 384–393.

Alec Nove, "A Note on Trotsky and the 'Left Opposition,' 1929–31," *Soviet Studies,* vol. 29, no. 4 (October 1977), 576–589.

Alec Nove, *An Economic History of the USSR* (London: Penguin, 1969), chap. 5.

Michal Reiman, *Die Geburt des Stalinismus* [The Birth of Stalinism] (Frankfurt/Main: EVA, 1979), chaps. 3–9.

Nicolas Spulber, ed., *Foundations of Soviet Strategy for Economic Growth* (Bloomington: Indiana University Press, 1964).

Nicolas Spulber, *Soviet Strategy for Economic Growth* (Bloomington: Indiana University Press, 1964), chaps. 1–4.

Paul M. Sweezy, *The Theory of Capitalist Development* (New York: Modern Reader Paperbacks, 1968).

Robert C. Tucker, ed., *The Lenin Anthology* (New York: Norton, 1975).

Chapter 4

The Foundation of the Soviet Planned Economy: Planning and Collectivization (1928-1945)

We have already described the precedents of the 1920s and the impact of the Soviet Industrialization Debate upon the course of Soviet industrialization during the 1930s. Our focus of attention now turns to the historical evolution of the Soviet command economic system during the early plan era, specifically to the development of a coordinated central planning apparatus and to the introduction of forced collectivization into the countryside. This brief chapter concludes our historical survey of the Soviet economy. Part Two will describe in detail how the Soviet command economic system allocates resources.

The 1920s witnessed two significant struggles over the nature of economic planning in the Soviet Union. The first was the debate over the theory of planning in a socialist economy—the debate between the so-called *genetic* and *teleological* schools of planning. The second was the struggle among the various planning bodies in existence during the 1920s for ascendancy in the planning hierarchy—a battle eventually won by *Gosplan* (the State Planning Committee). Let us first turn to the planning debate.

THE PLANNING DEBATE:
THE GENETICISTS VERSUS THE TELEOLOGISTS[1]

During NEP, an important controversy arose in the 1920s concerning the proper role of economic planning in the Soviet Union. The debate centered largely around the issue of whether planning was to be directed (and limited) by market forces or molded by the will of planners, unconstrained by market forces and limited only by the physical constraints of the economy. The so-called *geneticists* advocated the first approach to planning, the most

[1] Our discussion of the planning debate of the 1920s is based on the following sources: E. H. Carr and R. W. Davies, *Foundations of a Planned Economy, 1926–1929*, vol. 1, part 2, (London: Macmillan, 1969), pp. 787–801; Nicolas Spulber, *Soviet Strategy for Economic Growth* (Bloomington: Indiana University Press, 1964), pp. 101–111.

notable being N. D. Kondratiev (the prominent Russian authority on business cycles), V. A. Bazarov, and V. G. Groman, the latter two being *Gosplan* economists. The geneticists basically argued that economic planning should be directed by consumer demand, which would dictate to planners the needed direction of change in the economy. Thus, the principal function of the planner would be to forecast and project market trends to aid central and local administrators in their decision-making, that is, the geneticists envisioned a form of *indicative* planning, as it is called today. In drawing up such plans, authorities should always make sure of their internal consistency, for the geneticists viewed the economy as a vast complex of interrelated sectors (a general equilibrium system), the balance of which would be severely disturbed if planners neglected sectoral interrelationships. For example, to expand the heavy industry sector without concern for the resulting impact on the equilibrium of other interrelated sectors would create serious disproportions that would impede overall development. Thus the geneticists advocated a form of planning that was largely consistent with the precepts of NEP, in view of the dominant role that market forces would be allowed to play in the planning process. The advocates of genetic planning therefore were supportive of NEP and were associated with the party's right wing.

The *teleological* approach to planning, as advocated by S. Strumilin, G. L. Pyatakov, V. V. Kuibyshev, and P. A. Fel'dman, stated that the economic plan should be consciously formulated by social engineers and shaped by national goals established by the state. Such planning should seek to *overcome* market forces, rather than be directed by them as the geneticists argued. The market and finance, according to the teleologists, should *follow* the plan rather than dictate the plan. Planning should begin only after national economic goals have been set by the political authorities. Then the planners should form economic strategy, largely in terms of binding targets for basic industries, limited only by the availability of investment, and such investment should be allocated to meet the needs of industry independently of market forces.

In drawing up output and investment plans, the teleologists argued that planners need not be constrained by the need to preserve the general equilibrium of the economy, for to do so would be to subject the growth of the economy to the spontaneous forces of the market. Instead, the concept of equilibrium should be denounced as an unnecessarily severe constraint on the flexibility of planners. As stated by one teleologist, to accept the direction of the market meant acceptance of the "genetical inheritance" of 300 years of tsarism.[2]

According to the teleologists, the actual process of plan construction

---

[2] Statement of P. Vaisburg in *Planovoe khoziaistvo* [The Planned economy], no. 4 (1928), p. 167. Quoted in Carr and Davies, *Foundations of a Planned Economy*, p. 793.

should proceed according to a system of "successive approximations," that is, first plans for the leading branches (namely, heavy industry) were to be drawn up; then the plans for other sectors (light industry, agriculture, trade, etc.) would be molded into the framework of the first set of plans. In this manner, the plans of lower priority sectors would be predetermined by the plan for heavy industry, not by the market.

The late 1920s witnessed the conclusive victory of the teleological viewpoint. As the NEP system was gradually abandoned, the advocates of the genetic approach, tied as it was to a market-directed system of planning, saw their support within the party deteriorate. From the summer of 1927, actual planning paid little attention to market equilibrium and financial stability as advocated by the geneticists. Instead, attention turned to physical planning involving a "ferocious straining of effort," the outcome of which would be "decided by struggle."[3] The teleological approach to planning is obviously consistent with the superindustrialization notions of the left adopted by Stalin in 1928. Eventually, the geneticists came to be accused of counterrevolution and right-wing Menshevism. The advocates of the teleological approach, namely Strumilin, Krzhizhanovsky and others, remained prominent in the *Gosplan* apparatus during the 1930s and played a guiding role in the planning for rapid industrialization.

THE EVOLUTION OF THE PLANNING STRUCTURE[4]

A variety of agencies dealt with planning problems throughout the 1920s—VSNKh (the Supreme Council of the National Economy), the People's Commissariat of Finance, the People's Commissariat of Transportation, *Gosplan* USSR (State Planning Committee of the USSR), the regional *Gosplans,* the *Sovnarkhozy,* local authorities, and many others. However, of these agencies, only *Gosplan* was explicitly and exclusively concerned with economic planning. *Gosplan's* duties (according to a 1922 decree) were "the preparation not only of a long-range plan but also of an operational plan for the current year."[5]

From modest beginnings in February of 1921 (in 1925, *Gosplan* employed only around 50 economists and statisticians[6]), *Gosplan* gradually

[3] *Pravda,* September 14, 1927. Quoted in Carr and Davies, *Foundations of a Planned Economy,* p. 818.

[4] Our discussion is based on the following sources: Carr and Davies, *ibid.,* chaps. 33–35; Alec Nove, *An Economic History of the USSR* (London: Penguin, 1969), pp. 212–215, 263–267; Maurice Dobb, *Soviet Economic Development Since 1917,* 5th ed. (London: Routledge & Kegan Paul, 1960), chap. 13; Eugene Zaleski, *Planning for Economic Growth in the Soviet Union, 1918–1932* (Chapel Hill: University of North Carolina Press, 1971), pp. 40–73; Y. Avdakov and V. Borodin, *USSR State Industry During the Transition Period* (Moscow: Progress Publishers, 1977).

[5] Zaleski, *Planning for Economic Growth,* p. 41.

[6] Carr and Davies, *Foundations of a Planned Economy,* p. 802.

came to be accepted by the late 1920s as the planning agency in charge of coordinating economic planning for the entire economy. Much of this recognition emerged as a consequence of *Gosplan's* work on the annual *control figures*, or tentative output targets, for the various branches of the economy. The first control figures were prepared covering the year 1925–1926, and while they did not initially prove important in directing economic activity, the figures were used to establish the principle that economic policy should be guided on an annual basis by control figures prepared by *Gosplan*. In this manner, *Gosplan* came to play a supervisory role in the preparation of plans by other administrative bodies. The early control figures had a definite geneticist flavor, as they were designed to forecast rather than manipulate. The growing importance of *Gosplan's* control figures is clear: by 1926, the control figures were the first order of business of the Central Committee meeting of the party. In 1927, the party gave full compulsory status to the 1927–1928 control figures, which had taken on a strong teleological character.

While *Gosplan's* role as the coordinator of all planning was developing, it had little to do with the actual operational planning of the economy, especially at the enterprise and trust levels. Such work was primarily performed by the central planning staff of VSNKh and by the *Glavki* planning offices of VSNKh. In this manner, annual plans, including production and financial targets known as *promfinplans*, were drawn up. Gradually, the *promfinplans* drawn up by VSNKh were merged into the control figures compiled by *Gosplan*. Beginning in 1925, VSNKh was instructed to prepare its *promfinplans* on the basis of *Gosplan's* 1925–1926 control figures. By 1926–1927 VSNKh was in the habit of compiling a comprehensive *promfinplan* for all industry, to be scrutinized by *Gosplan* and the Peoples Commissariat of Finance, and it was established that the *promfinplan* was clearly dependent upon the control figures.

During this period, the machinery for physical planning was also being developed—the system of *material balances*. As certain basic industrial commodities grew scarce as early as 1925 and the administrative allocation of commodities increased, planning bodies began compiling balances for critical industrial materials. In 1925, a balance for the production and uses of iron and steel was compiled, and in 1927, an energy balance of fuel and power consumption was drawn up. The balance system was extended to building materials in 1928.[7] In charge of coordinating these balances through the *promfinplan* and control figure system were VSNKh and *Gosplan*, but initially this coordination proved too complex in the absence of detailed statistical information, and most of these early material balances were poorly prepared.

Thus the plan period began with the adoption of the First Five Year

---

[7] Carr and Davies, *Foundations of a Planned Economy*, pp. 830–831.

Plan in 1928, with the following planning principles established: first, *Gosplan* was to be the central coordinating planning body to which all other planning bodies were to submit their proposals. Second, the annual control figures prepared by *Gosplan* were to provide the general direction for the economy on an annual basis. Third, the actual detailed operational plans for industries and for enterprises (the *promfinplans*) were to conform to the control figures prepared by *Gosplan*. Fourth, materials were to be allocated through a system of balances, compiled from the control figures and *promfinplans*, which would elaborate the supplies and uses of basic industrial materials.

Gosplan's elevation to full planning authority came in 1932 with the development of the ministerial system. Between 1928 and 1932, the functions of VSNKh had grown increasingly complex and confused, and in 1932, VSNKh was in effect dissolved as a central coordinating agency for industry. Its chief departments, the *Glavki*, which later became ministries, were allowed to take direct power over planning and administering their enterprises. Earlier, VSNKh had served to coordinate the activities of the industrial departments—a role that *Gosplan* now inherited.

Soviet authorities recognized the need for long-range planning to serve as a guide for annual plans.[8] After some experimentation with long-range sectoral plans (for metals, industrial branches, transportation, and agriculture), *Gosplan* assumed responsibility in 1925 for drawing up Five Year Plans for the national economy. The five-year period was chosen because major construction projects in industry, transportation, and construction were felt to have a five-year gestation period and because annual fluctuations in agriculture could be smoothed out over this time interval. After some experimental efforts at five-year planning, *Gosplan* initiated the practise of developing the long-range plan in two variants: a minimum variant based upon cautious assumptions, and a bold maximum variant.

The maximal variant of the plan for 1928–1933 (the First Five Year Plan) was formally adopted by the party in April of 1929 and reflected the teleological thinking of Stalin. It was a 2000-page document, authored by leading proponents of the teleological approach, G. M. Krzhizhanovsky and S. Strumilin, and it called for the industrialization of the country at a maximum pace as was discussed in the previous chapter.

The manner in which Five Year Plans were to be broken down into annual operational segments and the enforcement and implementation of economic plans were resolved as well during the early Five Year Plan era. One lesson that was learned early on was that Five Year Plans cannot be written in stone, for circumstances change over a five-year period. Thus, the Five Year Plans could not be neatly divided into five annual plans. Instead, the Five Year Plan had to be constantly revised, so that the end result often

---

[8] Zaleski, *Planning for Economic Growth*, pp. 29–73.

bore little resemblance to the original targets. As Eugene Zaleski describes it, the Five Year Plan represented "a vision of growth, itself at the service of development strategy."[9] As the objectives of the long-range and annual plans were not necessarily compatible, it was decided that the state agencies controlling material supplies and credits were the ones to determine what parts of the "vision" were to be realized. For example, the First Five Year Plan (maximum variant) called for a quadrupling of investment in state industry, an 85 percent increase in consumption expenditures, a 70 percent increase in real wages, and a 30 percent increase in peasant incomes. These targets represented the planners' vision, but it was the responsibility of the economic administrators in charge of material allocations to ensure that priority targets (industrial investment) were fulfilled.

This period also witnessed the evolution of a centralized administration for the setting of prices. Extensive centralized price setting and regulation, introduced during the early plan era, proved to be a complex task involving issues well beyond the setting of prices per se and requiring the expansion of administrative arrangements.[10] Although the setting of prices was largely decentralized during the NEP period (typically reflecting cost-price relationships of the pre-Soviet period), the Commission for Internal Trade and VSNKh gained increasing authority toward the end of NEP. This tendency toward the centralization of price formation and related functions was greatly enhanced after the introduction of comprehensive central planning in 1928. Not only were internal prices subsequently shielded from world prices through the creation of a state monopoly in foreign trade, but also, a series of decrees in the late 1920s and early 1930s harnessed the price system toward the achievement of state goals; price discrimination in state purchases (buying the same product at different prices—determined by factory costs of production—and then selling at one set price) was introduced as were mmultiple pricing (charging different retail prices for the same product), profit margin controls, and differentiated sales taxes (the so-called turnover tax)—the latter serving as a primary mechanism for generating state revenues.

The early 1930s witnessed the significant expansion of the number of administrative organs concerned directly or indirectly with price formation; although during the 1930s, there was a measure of consolidation with VSNKh and later with the ministries that became the main price setting bodies.[11] This period also witnessed the tightening of financial controls over enterprises. Commercial credits between enterprises were forbidden, and

[9] Eugene Zaleski, *Stalinist Planning for Economic Growth, 1933–1952* (Chapel Hill: University of North Carolina Press, 1980), p. 483.
[10] The discussion here is based upon Raymond Hutchings, "The Origin of the Soviet Industrial Price System," *Soviet Studies*, vol. 13, no. 1 (July 1961), 1–22.
[11] For details of the organizational arrangements, see *ibid.*, 13–14.

Gosbank (the state bank) and various specialized banks controlled all credit operations. Moreover, direct grants for the state budget became a major source of investment finance.

THE DECISION TO COLLECTIVIZE

Developments in the agricultural sector during the late 1920s were as significant in the evolution of the Soviet planned economy as was the formation of the centralized planning structure. Our examination of War Communism and NEP pointed, above all, to the crucial nature of the relationship between the peasant and the state. This relationship, the subject of continuing discussion in the 1920s, was abruptly formalized by the Communist Party under Stalin's leadership when the historic collectivization movement (the forcing of the collective farm, the *kolkhoz*, on the countryside) was begun in 1929.

Our purpose here is to examine the decision to collectivize (i.e., the decision to introduce a significant command element into the Soviet countryside) and in particular to understand the reasons for collectivization as perceived by the Soviet leadership at that time. In addition, it is important that we examine the process of collectivization as it was in fact carried out, and finally, the impact of this process upon immediate postcollectivization agricultural performance. With this background, we will be in a position to consider long-run agricultural organization and the nature of the *kolkhoz* and its performance in Chapter 7.

The reader should be aware that the collectivization decision and the forces underlying that decision have only recently been the subject of in-depth research. A full understanding, therefore, must await further investigation when, hopefully, our presently limited picture can be significantly expanded.[12]

[12] In the present section, we rely heavily upon the following sources: Jerzy F. Karcz, "From Stalin to Brezhnev: Soviet Agricultural Policy in Historical Perspective," in James R. Millar, ed., *The Soviet Rural Community* (Urbana: University of Illinois Press, 1971), pp. 36–70; Jerzy F. Karcz, "Thoughts on the Grain Problem," *Soviet Studies*, vol. 18, no. 4 (April 1967), 399–434; M. Lewin, *Russian Peasants and Soviet Power* (London: Allen & Unwin, 1968); James R. Millar and Corinne A. Guntzel, "The Economics and Politics of Mass Collectivization Reconsidered: A Review Article," *Explorations in Economic History*, vol. 8, no. 1 (Fall 1970), 103–116; Alec Nove, "The Decision to Collectivize," in W. A. Douglas Jackson, ed., *Agrarian Policies and Problems in Communist and Non-Communist Countries* (Seattle: University of Washington Press, 1971), pp. 69–97; Erich Strauss, *Soviet Agriculture in Perspective* (London: Allen & Unwin, 1969), chaps. 5–6; Lazar Volin, *A Century of Russian Agriculture* (Cambridge, Mass.: Harvard University Press, 1970), chaps. 10–11; R. W. Davies, "A Note on Grain Statistics," *Soviet Studies*, vol. 21, no. 3 (January 1970), 314–329; S. G. Wheatcroft, "The Reliability of Russian Prewar Grain Output Statistics," *Soviet Studies* vol. 26, no. 2 (April 1974), 157–180; Arvind Vyas, "Primary Accumulation in the USSR Revisited," *Cambridge Journal of Economics*, vol. 3 (1979), 119–130.

Underpinnings of the Collectivization Decision

The focus of the Soviet Industrialization Debate of the 1920s was the strategy of industrialization, the desire to industrialize not being a matter of contention among the participants. From this discussion and the fact that the Soviet Union was in the 1920s primarily an agricultural economy, it is not surprising that alternative roles for the agricultural sector in the development process would be a point of focus for the participants.

Recall that Preobrazhensky had argued that the rate of saving had to be increased as industrial investment rose. The peasant, according to Preobrazhensky, should bear the burden of this increase in the savings rate through the system of primitive socialist accumulation, whereby savings would be extracted from the countryside by setting low agricultural prices. How to ensure the critically needed peasant marketings under such a system was a question that Preobrazhensky was unable to answer. Bukharin, on the other hand, argued that any system designed to extract involuntary savings from the peasants would destroy any positive relationship between peasant and state and lead to active peasant resistance in the form of reduced peasant marketings. Instead, Bukharin argued, it would be better to adopt a slower rate of economic growth and set prices to favor the peasant. The perceived behavior of the peasants during the Scissors Crisis was thought to underscore this view—that is, the falling trend in peasant marketings as relative agricultural prices dropped.[13]

Against this background, it should be pointed out that Lenin had long stressed the need to take advantage of economies of scale in agricultural production. Although there was experimentation with various forms of agricultural collectives in the 1920s, these were largely unsuccessful.[14] It was evident that the peasants would not join collective farms voluntarily in the short run. Although both wings of the party favored the growth of agricultural collectives, leading party officials realized that voluntary collectivization would be at best a slow and evolutionary process. The right wing of the party was not distressed by the fact that the regime would have to rely on peasant farming in the near term, for it was felt that a workable alliance (*Smychka*) with the peasant could be maintained. The left wing, on the contrary, was alarmed by the growing reliance upon peasant farming, especially upon the prosperous *kulak*, who was regarded as a dangerous counter-

---

[13] As was pointed out in Chapter 2, there is some controversy surrounding the Scissors Crisis and the traditional interpretation of the Russian peasant's response to falling agricultural prices.

[14] The reader interested in the agricultural collectives of the 1920s should consult D. J. Male, *Russian Peasant Organization Before Collectivization* (Cambridge: Cambridge University Press, 1971); Robert F. Miller, "Soviet Agricultural Policy in the Twenties: the Failure of Cooperation," *Soviet Studies*, vol. 27, no. 2 (April 1975), 220–244; and Robert G. Wesson, *Soviet Communes* (New Brunswick, N.J.: Rutgers University Press, 1963).

revolutionary threat.[15] Thus in 1928, collectivization was regarded by the different party factions as a desirable long-term solution to the agrarian problem, but few could have foreseen (or would have supported) the forced collectivization drive that was to follow shortly.

To what extent Stalin was personally responsible for the collectivization decision and all its ramifications is unclear.[16] He did however use as a major justification for instigating collectivization the *grain procurement crisis* of 1928, a matter that merits further attention.

Although the output of the Soviet agricultural sector had declined sharply during the Revolution and World War I, prerevolutionary levels were generally met or exceeded by 1928, although yields remained poor and fluctuations from year to year in major crops made agricultural performance uncertain (see Table 9). Indeed, by 1928, gross agricultural production had reached 124 (1913 = 100) while crop production had reached 117 and livestock products 137.[17]

Stalin, however, in a now-famous presentation made in May 1928, put forward data to suggest that *grain* output (considered a critical indicator by the Soviet leadership) had declined between 1913 and 1926–1927, but most important, that the *marketed share* of grain had declined much more rapidly.[18] According to the data presented by Stalin, between 1913 and 1926–1927 gross output of grain declined slightly, but the marketed share declined by roughly 50 percent. In addition, while grain production and marketings by the *kulaks* fell sharply (both had declined to less than one-third of prewar levels), output and marketings of the middle and poor peasants had expanded. For Stalin, this was evidence of the need to move against the *kulaks*. The talk of moving against the *kulaks* made for good window dressing, but Stalin was well aware that the bulk of grain supplies was in the hands of the middle peasants. In the turmoil that followed, it was therefore necessary to blur the distinction between the *kulak* and the middle peasant (the *seredniak*). In fact, in the heat of the collectivization campaign, a *kulak* became any peasant who resisted collectivization.

There are, however, two important reservations to Stalin's data. First, as Jerzy Karcz has pointed out, Stalin's grain data was ". . . completely misleading and presents an exceedingly distorted picture of the relation be-

---

[15] Class stratification played an important role in the thinking about collectivization and its actual implementation. Although census data from the 1920s suggest that the wealthy peasants (*kulaks*) were a very small proportion of the total peasant population, they were nevertheless seen as politically unreliable at best and enemies of the Soviet industrialization program at worst. For a detailed discussion of the problems of class stratification in this case, see Lewin, *Russian Peasants and Soviet Power*, chaps. 2 and 3.

[16] Millar and Guntzel, "Economics and Politics of Mass Collectivization," 112.

[17] Strauss, *Soviet Agriculture*, p. 303.

[18] For details of Stalin's argument and related data, see Karcz, "Thoughts on the Grain Problem," 399–402.

TABLE 9   Gross Production of Major Agricultural Products, 1913–1933 (millions of metric tons)

Year	Grain	Raw Cotton	Sugar Beets	Sunflower Seeds	Flax	Potatoes	Meat[b]	Milk	Eggs[c]
1913[a]	76.5	0.74	10.9	0.74	0.33	23.3	4.1	24.8	10.2
1923	56.9	0.14	2.6	—	0.22	—	—	—	—
1924	51.8	0.36	3.4	—	0.30	—	—	—	—
1925	72.5	0.54	9.1	2.22	0.30	38.6	—	—	—
1926	76.8	0.54	6.4	1.54	0.27	43.0	—	—	—
1927	72.3	0.72	10.4	2.13	0.24	41.2	—	—	—
1928	73.3	0.82	10.1	2.13	0.32	46.4	4.9	31.0	10.8
1929	71.7	0.86	6.3	1.76	0.36	45.6	5.8	29.8	10.1
1930	83.5	1.11	14.0	1.63	0.44	49.4	4.3	27.0	8.0
1931	69.5	1.29	12.0	2.51	0.55	44.8	3.9	23.4	6.7
1932	69.9	1.27	6.6	2.27	0.50	43.1	2.8	20.6	4.4
1933	68.4	1.32	9.0	—	0.56	—	2.3	19.2	3.5

SOURCE: Erich Strauss, *Soviet Agriculture in Perspective* (London: Allen & Unwin, 1969), pp. 304–305. The 1933 grain figure is from Alec Nove, *An Economic History of the USSR* (London: Penguin, 1969), p. 239.
[a] All data apply to pre-1939 boundaries.
[b] Meat and milk production in millions of tons.
[c] Eggs in billion units.

tween 1913 and 1926–1927 grain marketings."[19] According to Karcz, these data, when appropriately reconstructed as grain balances for these years, suggest that in fact gross grain output had, by 1928, all but recovered to prewar levels and that the problem was the definition of marketings. Thus in the data brought forth by Stalin, *gross marketings* were presented for 1913 while *net marketings* were given for 1926–1927.[20] With two sets of data, quite incomparable, Stalin's case for collectivization as the answer to the marketing problem appeared to be strong.

A second and related factor, according to Karcz, was the role of government policy in bringing about the grain procurement "crisis." In a few years immediately preceding collectivization, net grain marketings did decline precisely because the state lowered grain procurement prices in 1926–1927, naturally encouraging peasants to market their grain through other than state channels—that is, where prices were more attractive—and to hold back their grain in anticipation of higher prices. At the same time, peasant taxes were lowered, as were the prices of manufactured goods, thus stimulating peasant demand. Also, in the face of lower state grain procurement prices, peasants were encouraged to shift into the production of meat and related products, the prices of which were generally rising. Thus, although peasant marketings of grain were falling, the output and marketings

[19] *Ibid.*, 403.
[20] *Ibid.*, 403–409. Gross marketings include sales to other peasants within the village. Net marketings include only sales outside of agriculture.

of *other* farm products were rising in response to more favorable prices and were offsetting the declining grain marketings.

The immediate justification for collectivization may therefore have been based upon inadequate statistical information and the will to impose adverse state policy on the peasants, in addition to ideological underpinnings and the drive for large-scale production units.[21] As S. G. Wheatcroft has shown, comparisons of output and marketings of the twenties with prewar figures will be subject to wide margins of error; so the controversy over Stalin's statistics will probably never be resolved. However, from the vantage point of the state, the grain crisis was real. State grain collections from the peasants (*zagotovki*) were alarmingly low (the peasants were selling on the private market), and the government had to undergo the humiliating experience of importing grain.[22] Even Bukharin became convinced that harsher methods were necessary. At this time, Stalin unleashed an emergency campaign to increase state grain collections, dispatching trusted party officials to supervise the campaign. Grain supplies were confiscated, road blocks were set up, and peasants holding grain were charged as speculators. Stalin suspended these emergency measures in 1928 to quiet down the alarmed Bukharinites, but he came away from the experience convinced that force and coercion could be applied successfully in the countryside once the Bukharinites were destroyed.

THE COLLECTIVIZATION PROCESS

While the discussion of collectivization and Stalin's arguments on its behalf were well under way in 1928, it was not until mid-1929 that central control over existing cooperatives was substantially strengthened and the system of grain procurements changed—in short, the beginning of the process of mass collectivization.[23] By the latter part of 1929, an all-out drive for collectivization had been initiated by the Communist Party, becoming in large measure an organized movement against the *kulaks* and the middle peasants.

There were significant regional differences in the speed of collectivization and also a continuing debate over the precise organizational form to be utilized. The data in Table 10 suggest however that the overall speed of collectivization was rapid. Between July 1, 1929, and March 1, 1930, for example, the proportion of peasant households in collective farms increased from 4 to 56 percent.[24]

[21] Karcz's analysis of grain marketings and agricultural performance during the late 1920s has been disputed by R. W. Davies. Thus we cannot know for sure whether Stalin's analysis of the agricultural "crisis" was erroneous. For example, Davies estimates that the 1926–1927 net grain marketings were slightly more than one half of prewar marketings—a figure close to Stalin's. See Davies, "A Note on Grain Statistics," 328.

[22] Lewin, *Russian Peasants and Soviet Power*, pp. 214–244.

[23] *Ibid.*, p. 409.

[24] Volin, *A Century of Russian Agriculture*, p. 222.

TABLE 10   Expansion of the Collective Farm Sector, 1918–1938 (selected years)

Year	Collective Farms (in thousands)	Households in Collectives (in thousands)	Peasant Households Collectivized (percentage)
1918	1.6	16.4	0.1
1928	33.3	416.7	1.7
1929	57.0	1,007.7	3.9
1930	85.9	5,998.1	23.6
1931	211.1	13,033.2	52.7
1932	211.1	14,918.7	61.5
1935	245.4	17,334.9	83.2
1938	242.4	18,847.6	93.5

SOURCE: Lazar Volin, A Century of Russian Agriculture (Cambridge, Mass.: Harvard University Press, 1970), p. 211.

Although the fiction was maintained that the collectivization movement was a spontaneous action on the part of the peasantry, resisted only the "kulak saboteurs," there can be little doubt that collectivization was imposed on an unwilling peasantry by brutal force. Vague definitions of what constituted a kulak household were employed to permit the arrest and deportation of peasants resisting collectivization. Militia and the secret police (then called the GPU) were sent into the countryside to force peasants into collectives along with thousands of armed party faithful from the city. The "dekulakization" drive resulted in the flight, execution, deportation, and resettlement of millions of peasants and provided the initial manpower for a vast army of penal labor. According to one estimate, 3.5 million peasants became a part of the gulag penal labor force, 3.5 million were resettled, and another 3.5 million died during forced collectivization.[25] There is considerable controversy over the number of victims of collectivization, but there is little doubt that it numbered in the millions.

Although Stalin, in a famous speech in March 1930, warned against proceeding too rapidly and blamed local party leaders for the excesses that had occurred, in fact the pace of collectivization remained rapid, and by the mid-1930s the process was basically completed.[26] The role of the Communist Party in the countryside was formally strengthened when in 1933 political departments (Politotdely) were established in the machine tractor stations. The machine tractor stations (MTS) had themselves been estab-

[25] S. Swianiewicz, Forced Labor and Economic Development (London: Oxford University Press), p. 123.
[26] Volin, A Century of Russian Agriculture, pp. 228–229.

lished in 1930, and in addition to serving as a mechanism for supplying machinery and equipment to the collective farms (for which payment in kind would be made to the state), they were to play a significant role in the management of collective farms.[27] Informal party control in the countryside had also been strengthened considerably by collectivization, through the party's placing of "reliable" men in the posts of collective farm chairman.

THE IMMEDIATE IMPACT OF COLLECTIVIZATION

In Chapter 7 we will examine the role of collectivization and the collective farm system in Soviet agriculture. At this juncture, our interest is in the immediate impact of the collectivization process upon agricultural output, human lives in the rural sector, and the agricultural capital stock.

The most immediate result of collectivization was a decline in agricultural output. Although there were year to year fluctuations, the general decline is unmistakable (see Table 9). The index of gross agricultural production (1913 = 100) declined from a precollectivization high of 124 in 1928 to an immediate postcollectivization low of 101 in 1933.[28] In large part this can be accounted for by a sharp decline in gross production of livestock products from 137 in 1928 (1913 = 100) to 65 in 1933.[29] Although grain output declined in the initial years of collectivization (1928 through 1932, with the exception of 1930), both gross and net marketings of grain increased between 1928–1929 and 1931–1932, due to some extent to a sharp decline in the number of cattle for which grains for fodder were now not necessary.[30] The worsening of agricultural performance during the First Five Year Plan (1928–1932) plus the losses from state reserves were major factors contributing to the famine that reached a peak in 1932–1933.

The loss of lives (especially severe in grain-producing regions) from both the collectivization process *per se* and the famine thereafter (the famine being the major factor) has been the subject of considerable discussion, but very little hard data are available by which to assess its severity. The most frequently quoted estimate of lives lost is five million, although the reader should be cautioned that other estimates vary from one to ten million.[31]

---

[27] For a detailed account of the history and functions of the MTS, see Robert F. Miller, *One Hundred Thousand Tractors* (Cambridge, Mass.: Harvard University Press, 1970), especially chap. 2.

[28] Strauss, *Soviet Agriculture*, p. 303.

[29] *Ibid.*

[30] Karcz, "From Stalin to Brezhnev," p. 42.

[31] For detailed discussion of various estimates, see Dana G. Dalrymple, "The Soviet Famine of 1932–1934," *Soviet Studies*, vol. 15, no. 3 (January 1964), 250–284.

TABLE 11   Numbers of Livestock in the Soviet Union, 1928–1935 (in millions of head)

Year	Cattle (total)	Cows	Pigs	Sheep	Goats	Horses
1928[a]	60.1	29.3	22.0	97.3	9.7	32.1
1929	58.2	29.2	19.4	97.4	9.7	32.6
1930	50.6	28.5	14.2	85.5	7.8	31.0
1931	42.5	24.5	11.7	62.5	5.6	27.0
1932	38.3	22.3	10.9	43.8	3.8	21.7
1933	33.5	19.4	9.9	34.0	3.3	17.3
1934	33.5	19.0	11.5	32.9	3.6	15.4
1935	38.9	19.0	17.1	36.4	4.4	14.9

SOURCE: Erich Strauss, *Soviet Agriculture in Perspective* (London: Allen & Unwin, 1969), p. 307.
[a] Borders of the Soviet Union as of 1939.

In addition to the loss of life and the decline in agricultural production, there was a sharp decline in agricultural capital stock, most notably caused by the mass destruction of animal herds as the peasants vented their hostility toward the collectivization process by slaughtering their livestock rather than bringing them into the collective farms. The impact of this development can be observed in Table 11. In addition, Naum Jasny, one of the research pioneers in this area, has indicated that other forms of capital stock—notably buildings and machinery—simply disappeared during the turmoil of collectivization.[32] The impact of collectivization upon per capita incomes of the farm population was predictable: they fell sharply to perhaps one-half the 1928 level.[33]

Collectivization was indeed a unique "solution" to what Soviet leaders apparently viewed as an intractable problem. In Chapter 7 we will examine the organizational structure of the collective farm and the means by which it was to extract a "surplus" from the countryside. It did of course have both costs and benefits, and a proper evaluation of collectivization can only be cast in a long-term framework, with due consideration for potential alternatives. These matters we leave for further discussion in Chapter 7.

[32] Naum Jasny, *The Socialized Agriculture of the USSR* (Stanford, Calif.: Food Research Institute, 1949), p. 323.
[33] Naum Jasny, *Essays on the Soviet Economy* (New York: Praeger, 1962), p. 107. Jasny's figures on per capita income of the Soviet farm population in constant prices reveal the following picture:

1928	100
1932–33	53
1936	60
1937	81
1938	63

THE SOVIET ECONOMY DURING WORLD WAR II[34]

The impact of World War II upon the Soviet economy must be considered, not because it brought about fundamental and lasting changes in the manner the economy was operated, but because of the enormous loss of resources during the war. The war also served as a test of the proposition that a command-type system, like that put in place during the 1930s, would be best suited to marshalling resources for war.

The resource losses were undisputably large. The direct loss of life, including civilian casualties, was in the neighborhood of 20 million people, that is, some 10 percent of the prewar population. These figures do not include the millions of Soviet prisoners of war who chose not to be repatriated, those repatriated POWs who entered the *gulag* camps, and those who remained in poor health due to wartime injuries and malnutrition. According to official Soviet statistics, national income declined by one-third between 1940 and 1942, and 1943 agricultural output was only 40 percent of the 1940 level. These drastic reductions were primarily due to the German occupation in 1942 of some one-third of Soviet territory, including the prime agricultural and metal producing regions of the Ukraine. Although the official Soviet claim is that the war cost the USSR "two five-year plans," the actual loss of production lay between three and six years of earnings, before even counting the staggering loss of human life.[35]

What changes in the system of planning and resource allocation that emerged in the 1930s were made during the war years? According to Eugene Zaleski, the wartime planning system was essentially that of the 1930s with some important differences.[36] First, a series of new agencies with extraordinary powers were superimposed on the existing planning system, the most important being the State Committee for Defense (headed by Stalin) and the Evacuation Committee, charged with the relocation to the east of factories and the work force. Second, less emphasis was placed upon compiling national economic plans and more emphasis was put on specific plans for war-related activities. According to Zaleski, this move was dictated by the danger of having imprecise general plans with conflicting goals, which would leave the choice of plan fulfillment to lower agencies. The more limited number of specific, defense-related plans allowed planners to control

---

[34] This discussion of World War II is based largely on the following sources: Nove, *An Economic History of the USSR, op. cit.,* chap. 10; Zaleski, *Stalinist Planning for Economic Growth,* chaps. 14 and 15; James R. Millar, "Financing the Soviet Effort in World War II," *Soviet Studies,* vol. 32, no. 1 (January 1980); James R. Millar and Susan J. Linz, "The Cost of World War II to the Soviet People," *Journal of Economic History,* vol. 38, no. 4 (December 1978), 959–962; N. A. Voznesensky, *Soviet Economy During the Second World War* (New York: International Publishers, 1949), translated from the Russian.

[35] Millar and Linz, "The Cost of World War II," p. 961.

[36] Zaleski, *Stalinist Planning for Economic Growth,* chap. 14.

defense production more closely. The rest of the economy was guided not only by general plans and was regulated more by the state budget and state rationing powers than by economic planners per se. Third, *Gosplan* and the war-related ministries and special commissions gained more power through the increased importance of material balances. At the height of the war effort, central plans were being drawn up for 30,000 materials and supplies to be allocated among 120 large users.[37]

The shift of resources into the defense sector was dramatic. The share of national income devoted to the war effort increased from about 10 percent in 1940 to slightly under one-half in 1943.[38] Insofar as personal consumption had to be kept at subsistence levels, this meant the wholesale sacrifice of capital investment resources—a forced shift away from the traditional priority of capital accumulation.

On the labor front, there was a return to the militarization of labor. Direct mobilization of labor was introduced in December of 1941, and draconian measures were initiated to ensure strict labor discipline. These measures, which remained nominally in effect until 1955, will be discussed in Chapter 6. The measures were dictated by severe manpower shortages due to mobilization and to the occupation of a considerable part of Soviet territory. The civilian labor force dropped from 31 million in 1940 to 18 million in 1942.[39] Faced with the growing scarcity of consumer goods, the state attempted to preserve an equilibrium between the supply and demand for consumer goods by introducing a strict wage policy. However, the labor shortage caused spontaneous wage increases that could not be controlled by the government. Rationing of consumer goods was introduced during successive stages, with higher rations for workers in special categories. A flourishing private market trade existed throughout the war years, especially in the collective farm markets; collective farm prices in 1943 were higher than state rationed prices by a factor of 14.[40] Financial authorities sought throughout the war to recover the excessive earnings of collective farmers by imposing special income taxes on the farm population.

To a greater extent than its allies, the Soviet Union financed the war effort through direct taxes, thus reversing the trend toward dependence upon indirect taxes established during the 1930s. As James Millar writes: "the governments of Britain and the U.S. were perhaps more cautious about increasing tax rates than the Soviet government. They were concerned, for instance, to maintain an effective system of pecuniary incentives . . . and they may have been concerned for more purely political reasons as well."[41] In the Soviet case, Stalin felt that labor discipline could be maintained by

---

[37] *Ibid.*, p. 287.
[38] Millar, "Financing the Soviet War Effort," Table B.
[39] Zalski, *Stalinist Planning for Economic Growth*, p. 311.
[40] *Ibid.*, p. 326.
[41] Millar, "Financing the Soviet War Effort."

strict legislation, and he had little reason to be concerned about political consequences.

On the basis of the available evidence, can conclusions be drawn concerning the advantages of a command economic system in times of war? The answer to this question is beyond the scope of this study, but several preliminary comments can be made. The first is that the Soviet economic effort during the war must be rated as a great accomplishment. The USSR was ill-prepared for war and suffered devastating losses of manpower and territory. Yet as Alec Nove has indicated, the Soviet Union produced the bulk of its own war materiel, with the Western allies making up the weakness in road transport vehicles.[42] Second, Stalin's dictatorship was in a position to militarize labor rapidly and thus compensate for severe manpower shortages. Third, one cannot determine whether these achievements are a consequence of the command economic system that was in place at the outbreak of the war. It should be noted that the capitalist protagonists in the war also introduced significant command elements into their economies, and the relevant question is whether these economies functioned as effectively as the Soviet economy in supplying the resources required to wage world war. Only a vast comparative study of the various war economies could answer this question.

CONCLUSIONS: SOVIET ECONOMIC HISTORY TO 1945

We have outlined in capsule form the events from the Revolution to World War II that played a role in influencing the evolution of the Soviet command economic system. The operation of the Soviet planned economy during World War II was the final topic in this historical section. By 1945, the evolution of the Soviet economic system was essentially complete; it is a system that remains remarkably intact to the present day. We have sought to show how this system developed from the relatively backward economy inherited by the Bolsheviks in 1917, from the experiences of War Communism and NEP, from the Soviet Industrialization Debate, and from the experiences of World War II. In Part Two, we turn from economic history to a discussion of actual resource allocation practices in the Soviet Union.

SELECTED BIBLIOGRAPHY

Y. Avdakov and V. Borodin, *USSR State Industry During the Transition Period* (Moscow: Progress Publishers, 1977).

E. H. Carr and R. W. Davies, *Foundations of a Planned Economy, 1926–1929* (London: Macmillan, 1969), vol. 1, parts 1 and 2.

R. W. Davies, *The Industrialization of Russia*, vols. 1 and 2 (Cambridge, Mass.: Harvard University Press, 1980).

---

[42] Nove, "The Decision to Collectivize," pp. 274–275.

Maurice Dobb, *Soviet Economic Development Since 1917*, 5th ed. (London: Routledge & Kegan Paul, 1960).

Alexander Erlich, *The Soviet Industrialization Debate, 1924–1928* (Cambridge, Mass.: Harvard University Press, 1960).

Naum Jasny, *Soviet Industrialization, 1928–1952* (Chicago, Ill.: University of Chicago Press, 1961).

Naum Jasny, *The Socialized Agriculture of the USSR* (Stanford, Calif.: Food Research Institute, 1949).

Jerzy F. Karcz, "From Stalin to Brezhnev: Soviet Agricultural Policy in Historical Perspective," in James R. Millar, ed., *The Soviet Rural Community* (Urbana: University of Illinois Press, 1971), pp. 36–70.

Jerzy F. Karcz, "Thoughts on the Grain Problem," *Soviet Studies*, vol. 18, no. 4 (April 1967), 399–434.

M. Lewin, *Russian Peasants and Soviet Power* (London: Allen & Unwin, 1968).

M. Lewin, "The Immediate Background of Soviet Collectivization," *Soviet Studies*, vol. 17, no. 2 (October 1965), 162–197.

James R. Millar, "Financing the Soviet Effort in World War II," *Soviet Studies*, vol. 32, no. 1 (January 1980).

Alec Nove, *An Economic History of the USSR* (London: Penguin, 1969), chaps. 7–10.

Alec Nove, *Economic Rationality and Soviet Politics* (New York: Praeger, 1964), pp. 17–40.

Leon Smolinski, "Planning Without Theory, 1917–1967," *Survey*, no. 64 (July 1968), 108–128.

Leon Smolinski, "Soviet Planning: How It Really Began," *Survey*, no. 64 (April 1968), 100–115.

Nicolas Spulber, ed., *Foundations of Soviet Strategy for Economic Growth* (Bloomington: Indiana University Press, 1964).

Nicolas Spulber, *Soviet Strategy for Economic Growth* (Bloomington: Indiana University Press, 1964).

V. A. Vinogradov et al., eds., *Istoriia sotsialisticheskoi ekonomiki SSSR* [History of the socialist economy of the USSR], vols. 1–5 (Moscow: Nauka, 1976).

Lazar Volin, *A Century of Russian Agriculture* (Cambridge, Mass.: Harvard University Press, 1970), chaps. 9 and 10.

N. A. Voznesensky, *Soviet Economy During the Second World War*, translated from the Russian edition (New York: International Publishers, 1949).

Eugene Zaleski, *Planning for Economic Growth in the Soviet Union, 1918–1932* (Chapel Hill: University of North Carolina Press, 1971).

Eugene Zaleski, *Stalinist Planning for Economic Growth, 1933–1952* (Chapel Hill: University of North Carolina Press, 1980).

Part Two

How the Soviet Economy Operates

Chapter 5
How the Soviet Economy Operates: Planning and Pricing

INTRODUCTION TO SOVIET RESOURCE ALLOCATION

In this chapter, we turn from the origins of the Soviet planned economy to its actual operation. Although arrangements for allocating resources in the Soviet Union have changed over time, we shall concentrate on the Soviet economy between the First Five Year Plan (1928) and the economic reform of 1965. The pre-1928 period was discussed in Chapter 2 and the reforms of 1965 and thereafter are discussed in Chapter 9. The 1928 to 1965 period warrants special emphasis, since it illustrates the basic working principles used to industrialize the Soviet economy. In addition, it appears that the various Soviet economic reforms have at best brought about relatively minor changes in basic Soviet working arrangements. Nevertheless, the reader should be aware that some changes, primarily in the areas of industrial planning and criteria for managerial success, have occurred since 1965.

Our foremost concern in the next two chapters is to elaborate how resources are allocated in the Soviet Union, in particular by what arrangements goods and services are produced and distributed and how the major factors of production (labor and capital) are allocated. Particular attention will be given to both the formal and informal means through which resource allocation is achieved. To analyze the matter of goods production, we consider in this chapter the planning apparatus, the relationship between the planners and enterprises, and the process of price formation. We approach the latter question of factor allocation in Chapter 6 by examining the Soviet manager, the labor market, and the allocation of scarce capital among competing uses.

First, however, it is necessary to outline the institutional framework in which the Soviet economy operates, since these institutions—the state economic hierarchy and the Communist Party—provide much of the direction and control generally exerted by the market in capitalist economies.

POLITICAL INSTITUTIONS AND CONTROL
OF THE ECONOMY[1]

In the Soviet Union, the crucial economic decisions—the allocation of output among consumption, investment, and defense, and the rates of expansion of different sectors—are made administratively, not by the market. Whereas in the United States about one-quarter of GNP is allocated by administrative decisions through the public sector, in the Soviet Union, almost all output is allocated administratively.[2] In this manner, *planners' preferences* supplant *consumer sovereignty* by taking resource allocation out of the hands of the market and placing it under the control of an administrative apparatus.[3] In this section, we consider the political apparatus, the planning apparatus, and the intertwining of the two.

Nominally, the Soviet Union is governed by an elected government that is subject to the Soviet constitution. The highest organ of the state is the *Supreme Soviet,* which is comprised of directly elected deputies. Because the Supreme Soviet meets infrequently, the *Praesidium* appointed by the Supreme Soviet carries on the work of the Supreme Soviet between sessions. The *Council of Ministers* is the government bureaucracy of the USSR and is elected by the Supreme Soviet. The Soviet Union is a republic, composed of 15 union republics, and each union republic has a state apparatus that parallels the national apparatus. Beneath the union, republican governments are the provincial (*oblast'*) governments and the local (*raion*) governments.

Parallel to the state apparatus is the Communist Party of the Soviet

---

[1] Our discussion relates to institutions in the postwar period. It is based upon Jerry F. Hough and Merle Fainsod, *How the Soviet Union Is Governed* (Cambridge, Mass.: Harvard University Press, 1979); Abram Bergson, *The Economics of Soviet Planning* (New Haven, Conn.: Yale University Press, 1964), chap. 3; Paul K. Cook, "The Political Setting," in Joint Economic Committee, *Soviet Economy in a Time of Change* (Washington, D.C.: U.S. Government Printing Office, 1979) vol. 1, pp. 38–50; Alec Nove, *The Soviet Economy,* rev. ed. (New York: Praeger, 1969); Alec Nove, *The Soviet Economic System* (London: Allen & Unwin, 1977).

[2] This assertion should be interpreted with caution. While the dominant mechanism for Soviet resource allocation is the *plan,* the reader should be aware that the plan cannot be pervasive in all facets of resource allocation. As one considers how the economic system handles less important products and services or local needs, less formal arrangements or even those of the "second economy" can be important.

[3] By a system of *planners' preferences,* we mean a mechanism for guiding the economic system so that the decisions as to what to produce, how to produce, and who gets the output are made by central planners rather than by the dollar (and political) votes of consumers in the marketplace. Although theoretically under such a system planners may take full account of consumers' wishes, historically this has not typically been the case in the Soviet Union.

Union (CPSU).[4] The supreme authority over the party organization is exercised nominally by the Party Congress, made up of delegates from all levels of the party hierarchy. Party congresses are held only at infrequent intervals, and they serve to elect (often perfunctorily) the *Central Committee* of the CPSU which in turn appoints the *Politburo*—the most important policy-setting body in the Soviet Union.

At the republican, regional, and local levels, departments of the CPSU duplicate the various state agencies; thus for each state agency there is a parallel party branch. This applies even to the lowest administrative echelons. At the enterprise level, a party branch supervises enterprise operations. Unlike the state apparatus, where lines of authority generally run from the local to the provincial to the republican to the national level, all lines in the party apparatus run directly to Moscow, suggesting a significant centralization of power.

One of the principal functions of all branches of the CPSU is the control and supervision of the economy. This control is exercised in several ways. Many branches of government report directly to the party. The State Planning Committee, for example, reports directly to the Praesidium (Politburo) of the CPSU. At lower levels, building projects are first submitted to the party before being submitted to the appropriate government office. At the enterprise level, the party organization serves two functions—one, to mobilize the workers to fulfill the plan (often through the enterprise trade union that the party dominates), and the other, to check on the enterprise manager. These are just isolated examples of party supervision.

Perhaps the most potent tool used by the CPSU to direct the economy is the *nomenklatura* system.[5] The *nomenklatura* is a comprehensive list of appointments that are controlled by the party. It is the party that nominates individuals for all important posts in the CPSU, state, industry, and

---

[4] The Communist Party is, of course, a crucial mechanism in Soviet society. For a detailed treatment of party structure and functions, see Leonard Shapiro, *The Communist Party of the Soviet Union* (New York: Random House, 1971); and T. H. Rigby, *Communist Party Membership in the U.S.S.R., 1917–1967* (Princeton, N.J.: Princeton University Press, 1968). For the official Soviet view (subject to change in different editions), see *History of the Communist Party of the Soviet Union* (Moscow: Foreign Languages Publishing House, 1960). For recent evidence, see T. H. Rigby, "Soviet Commmunist Party Membership Under Brezhnev," *Soviet Studies*, vol. 28, no. 3 (July 1976), 317–337; T. H. Rigby, "Addendum to Dr. Rigby's Article on CPSU Membership," *Soviet Studies*, vol. 28, no. 4 (October 1976), 613; Aryeh L. Unger, "Soviet Communist Party Membership Under Brezhnev: A Comment," *Soviet Studies*, vol. 29, no. 2 (April 1977), 306–316. For a discussion of the more general question of political participation, see Jerry F. Hough, "Political Participation in the Soviet Union," *Soviet Studies*, vol. 28, no. 1 (Jannuary 1976), 3–20.

[5] For more detail on the *nomenklatura* system, see Bohdan Harasymiw, "Nomenklatura: The Soviet Communist Party's Leadership Recruitment System," *Canadian Journal of Political Science*, vol. 2, no. 4 (December 1969), 493–512; Jerry F. Hough, *The Soviet Prefects* (Cambridge, Mass.: Harvard University Press, 1969), pp. 114–116, 150–170.

army. At the national level, the Central Committee Cadres Department exercises this function. Party control over *nomenklatura* is crucial insofar as it is party nominees who run for elective office and become enterprise directors and farm managers. It is not surprising to find that while roughly 10 percent of the Soviet population belongs to the CPSU, very few agricultural or industrial managers are not members of the party.

The dominant role of the Communist Party in the Soviet Union is envisioned in Article 6 of the Soviet Constitution:

> The leading and guiding force of Soviet society and the nucleus of its political system, of all state organizations, is the Communist Party of the Soviet Union.[6]

We turn now from the party apparatus to the state apparatus to consider the planning and organization of the economy. Throughout most of the plan period (1928 to present), the Soviet economy has operated under a ministerial system in which individual enterprises belonging to a particular branch of the economy (aviation, chemicals, metallurgy, etc.) are subordinated to a single ministry.[7] There are three types of ministries: the *all-union ministry* runs the enterprises under its control directly from Moscow, and its enterprises are not answerable to regional authorities. The *union-republican ministry* has offices both in Moscow and in the various republics, and the enterprises under its control are subject to the dual authority of Moscow and the republican Councils of Ministers. The *republican ministry* directs enterprises within the republic and has no direct superior in Moscow. The heads of these ministries are members of the Council of Ministers of the USSR and of the republican Councils of Ministers, respectively.

The ministerial system was introduced in 1932 to replace VSNKh. Initially, three ministries were created, for the heavy, light, and timber industries. Since then, the number has fluctuated from a high of 32 in the late Stalin years, to 11 immediately after Stalin's death, to around 40 in the late 1960s. There are presently 62 ministries.[8] The ministries have at times possessed considerable power: they control a network of productive enterprises and have tended to develop their own supply and disposal agencies. Although various superior agencies have been established at different times to coordinate the activities of the ministries, this has principally been done by *Gosplan*, which has derived much of its authority from its close association with the Praesidium (Politburo) of the CPSU.

---

[6] *Constitution (Fundamental Law) of the Union of Soviet Socialist Republics* (Moscow: Novosti Press Agency Publishing House, 1978), p. 21.

[7] Industrial associations were introduced as intermediate authorities between the ministries and enterprises in the late 1960s. The associations are discussed in chapter 9. A reference on the associations is: Alice C. Gorlin, "Industrial Reorganization: The Associations," in Joint Economic Committee, *Soviet Economy in a New Perspective* (Washington, D.C.: U.S. Government Printing Office, 1976), pp. 162–188.

[8] Nove, *The Soviet Economy*, pp. 69, 110; Cook, "The Political Setting," chart 2.

Gosplan was established in 1921 and engaged primarily in nonoperational long-term planning during the 1920s. During the 1920s, the role of Gosplan as the central coordinator of national planning was challenged by the People's Commissariat of Finance (Narkomfin), by VSNKh, and the ministerial planning bodies, but by the late 1920s Gosplan was fairly well recognized as the principal planning body in the Soviet Union.[9] After its reorganization in 1928, it came to play an important coordinating function, especially after the ministerial system was introduced in 1932. Although the ministries themselves performed most of the current planning within the ministry, Gosplan was given the task of coordinating these ministerial plans by drawing up material balances, the basic planning system to be discussed shortly. The structure and functions of Gosplan have changed quite significantly during the plan period, though to relate these changes in detail would be confusing to the reader and would not add significantly to our understanding of Soviet planning.[10] The important point to note is that in spite of continuing changes in the organizational structure of planning agencies, Gosplan has played a central coordinating role throughout the plan period, especially with the application of material balance planning.

The one major organizational change in the planning apparatus that deserves mentioning is the Sovnarkhoz reform of 1957, which was in effect until 1965.[11] It was argued by then Premier Nikita Khrushchev that the ministerial system had certain deficiencies—empire building within the ministry, lack of regional coordination, and bureaucratic delays—that could be corrected by reorganizing the economy along regional lines. Thus, in 1957 the ministries were abolished (with the exceptions of the ministries supervising nuclear industries and electricity) and a system of 105 Sovnarkhozy (Regional Economic Councils) was introduced. Enterprises were to be subordinated to the Sovnarkhozy (rather than to a ministry), which was in turn subject to the republican government, which, in turn, was subject to the all-union government. In fact, throughout this period, Gosplan gen-

[9] E. H. Carr and R. W. Davies, Foundations of a Planned Economy, 1926–1929, vol. 1, part 2 (London: Macmillan, 1969), pp. 802–836.

[10] In 1948–1949, Gosplan was weakened by the establishment of what had formerly been its material allocation department, technical department, and Central Statistical Agency as separate agencies. After Stalin's death, these departments (with the exception of the Central Statistical Agency) were returned to Gosplan. In 1955, Gosplan was split into two agencies: Gosplan, which was to concentrate on long-term planning, and the State Economic Commission, which was to be concerned with short-term plans. As a result of the regionalization reforms (the Sovnarkhozy) of 1957, Gosplan took on new responsibilities. It absorbed the planning functions of the defunct ministries and was the crucial coordinating agency at the all-union level. In 1960, Gosplan was again split into the State Economic-Science Council, in charge of long-range planning, and Gosplan, in charge of current planning. On these organization changes, see Nove, The Soviet Economy, pp. 71–85.

[11] Nove, The Soviet Economy, pp. 78–81. Also, Oleg Hoeffding, "The Soviet Industrial Reorganization of 1957," American Economic Review, Papers and Proceedings, vol. 49, no. 2 (May 1959), 65–77.

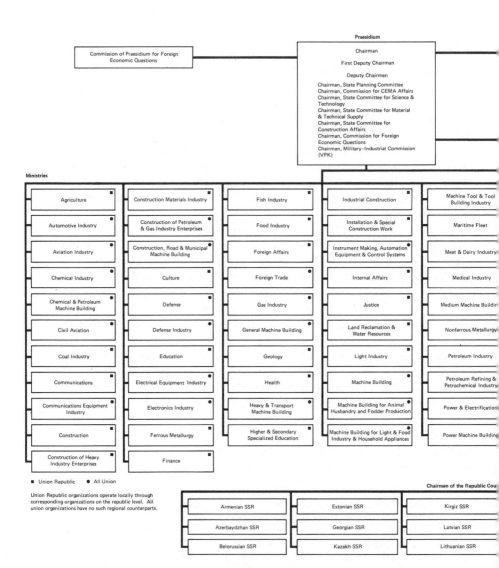

Figure 3   Central Economic Administrative Structure of the USSR as of 1979. (Source: Paul K. Cook, "The Political Setting," in Joint Economic Committee, *Soviet Economy in a Time of Change*, vol. 1 [Washington, D.C.: U.S. Government Printing Office, 1979], face p. 50, no. 2.)

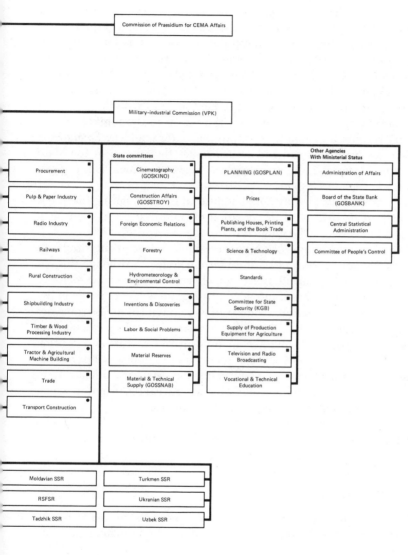

Commission of Praesidium for CEMA Affairs

Military-industrial Commission (VPK)

State committees

Other Agencies
With Ministerial Status

Procurement	Cinematography (GOSKINO)	PLANNING (GOSPLAN)	Administration of Affairs
Pulp & Paper Industry	Construction Affairs (GOSSTROY)	Prices	Board of the State Bank (GOSBANK)
Radio Industry	Foreign Economic Relations	Publishing Houses, Printing Plants, and the Book Trade	Central Statistical Administration
Railways	Forestry	Science & Technology	Committee of People's Control
Rural Construction	Hydrometeorology & Environmental Control	Standards	
Shipbuilding Industry	Inventions & Discoveries	Committee for State Security (KGB)	
Timber & Wood Processing Industry	Labor & Social Problems	Supply of Production Equipment for Agriculture	
Tractor & Agricultural Machine Building	Material Reserves	Television and Radio Broadcasting	
Trade	Material & Technical Supply (GOSSNAB)	Vocational & Technical Education	
Transport Construction			

Moldavian SSR	Turkmen SSR
RSFSR	Ukranian SSR
Tadzhik SSR	Uzbek SSR

erally bypassed the republican governments and the *Sovnarkhozy* and dealt directly with the enterprise.[12]

In 1965, after the fall of Khrushchev, who had engineered the 1957 *Sovnarkhoz* reform, Aleksei Kosygin and Leonid Brezhnev replaced regional planning with the former ministerial system. The failure of the regional system was blamed on the growing "localism" of the various *Sovnarkhozy*, which placed the needs of the region above that of the national economy, and on the difficulties of coordinating a regionally operated planning apparatus. Both of these problems had led since 1957 to the growth of national supervisory agencies. However, the return to the ministerial system in 1965 was not a complete return to the status quo. The *Sovnarkhoz* supply agencies were retained and placed under the control of the State Committee on Material-Technical Supplies (*Gossnab*), which had, prior to 1957, been a branch of *Gosplan*.

Finally, as we have already noted, industrial mergers during the 1960s were formalized in 1973 with the creation of industrial associations as a managerial level between the ministries and the enterprises.[13] The association is a "combination of enterprises under a single management, similar to a merged multiplant concern in Western terminology."[14] Although this is a complex change, the implementation of which has varied from one sector to another, the basic directions of intended change are evident. To some degree, both the enterprises and the ministries were intended to lose some decision-making power, which will rest in the associations. In particular, an attempt is being made to simplify the administrative structure and to bring similar enterprises into closer coordination in order to improve supervision, especially in the crucial area of new technology. As with other reform movements in the Soviet economy, only time will reveal the extent to which this design is implemented and improves performance.

A recent organization chart of the Soviet economic-administrative structure is provided in Figure 3 to illustrate the organization of the Soviet economy according to its ministerial system.

SUPPLY AND OUTPUT PLANNING[15]

In the Soviet Union, the most basic economic decisions are made by the Communist Party. The planning apparatus, which is a branch of the state

[12] Nove, *The Soviet Economy*, p. 76.

[13] See Gorlin, "Industrial Reorganization," Alice C. Gorlin, "The Soviet Economic Associations," *Soviet Studies*, vol. 26, no. 1 (Jannuary 1974), 3–27.

[14] Gorlin, "The Soviet Economic Associations," p. 3.

[15] We avoid detailed footnoting of sources in this section. The material presented here is largely based on the following sources: Bergson, *The Economics of Soviet Planning*, chap. 7; Nove, *The Soviet Economy*, pp. 87–96; R. W. Davies, "Soviet Planning for Rapid Industrialization," *Economics of Planning*, vol. 6, no. 1 (1966), and "Planning a Mature Economy in

government, must then draw up plans for all levels of the economy to implement the basic political and economic decisions. After the plan is formulated and each ministry, region, and enterprise receives its input and output targets, a complex control organization swings into action. The planners themselves have their own control system (described below), but the party also plays a significant role in this area. From the various national party control commissions to the enterprise party committee, party officials are given the task of making sure that all levels of the economy are observing plan directives. In this manner, the party attempts to ensure that planners' preferences are being fulfilled.

The Soviet planning apparatus must translate party directives into actual operational plans. As the reader might imagine, this is an extremely complicated task in view of the complexity of the Soviet economy, which produces millions of distinct commodities and encompasses a vast territory. Yet the Soviet economy has been directed by a comprehensive central plan since 1928, indicating that the actual Soviet planning system has somehow been able to direct the economy in spite of its complexity.

From our discussion thus far, it might seem as if the Soviet economy is totally planned and rigidly controlled. Such a conclusion would be unwarranted, for as we shall see during our discussion of the functioning of the economy, both formal and informal aspects of the system result in a good deal of both unplanned and uncontrolled activity. Indeed, one long-time observer of the Soviet economy, Eugene Zaleski, suggests that the Soviet economy might better be described as a centrally *managed* rather than a centrally planned economy. By this, Zaleski means that the construction of the plan is only the first step in the resource allocation process. The deci-

---

the USSR," *Economics of Planning*, vol. 6, no. 2 (1966); Michael Ellman, "The Consistency of Soviet Plans," *Scottish Journal of Political Economy*, vol. 16, no. 1 (February 1969). These last three are reprinted in Morris Bornstein and Daniel Fusfeld, eds., *The Soviet Economy: A Book of Readings*, 3rd. ed. (Homewood, Ill.: Irwin, 1970). See also Herbert Levine, "The Centralized Planning of Supply in Soviet Industry," in Joint Economic Committee, *Comparisons of the United States and Soviet Economies* (Washington, D.C.: U.S. Government Printing Office, 1959), pp. 151–176, reprinted in Morris Bornstein and Daniel Fusfeld, eds., *The Soviet Economy: A Book of Readings*, rev. ed. (Homewood, Ill.: Irwin, 1965), pp. 49–65; Michael Ellman, *Soviet Planning Today: Proposals for an Optimally Functioning Economic System* (Cambridge: Cambridge University Press, 1971); Gertrude E. Schroeder, "The 'Reform' of the Supply System in Soviet Industry," *Soviet Studies*, vol. 24, no. 1 (July 1972), 97–119, and "Recent Developments in Soviet Planning and Managerial Incentives," in Joint Economic Committee, *Soviet Economic Prospects for the Seventies* (Washington, D.C.: U.S. Government Printing Office, 1973), pp. 11–38; Michael Ellman, *Socialist Planning* (Cambridge: Cambridge University Press, 1979); Nove, *The Soviet Economic System;* Gertrude E. Schroeder, "The Soviet Economy on a Treadmill of 'Reforms,' " in Joint Economic Committee *Soviet Economy in a Time of Change* (Washington, D.C.: U.S. Government Printing Office, 1979), pp. 312–340; vol. 1; Eugene Zaleski, *Stalinist Planning for Economic Growth, 1933–1952* (Chapel Hill: University of North Carolina Press, 1980).

sions made during the implementation stage are just as important. Moreover, much economic activity remains out of the purview of planners and is controlled by local officials, enterprises, and even private markets. The extent of economic activity not controlled by planners has caused observers to question whether the Soviet economy is "planned" after all.[16]

Our discussion of the Soviet planning system begins with a discussion of industrial supply and output planning—the so-called system of *material balances*. This discussion will be followed by a more formal presentation of the planning problem in terms of an input-output model.

Material Balance Planning

Soviet material balance planning defies a simplified description.[17] First, the fairly frequent administrative changes in the Soviet ·planning apparatus complicate description, and second, there is the problem of differentiating between the idealized version of Soviet planning described in Soviet texts on planning and its actual operation.[18] In discussing Soviet material balance planning, we avoid further reference to administrative changes and describe Soviet planning under the ministerial system prior to the economic reforms of 1965. In our later evaluation of Soviet planning, the problem of theory versus practice will be given further scrutiny.

Our discussion begins with the construction of the annual plan.[19] The key to Soviet success in dealing with the enormous complexities of planning is that only a limited number of commodities are centrally planned and distributed by *Gosplan SSSR*. Even then, industrial supply and distribution

[16] John Wilhelm, "Does the Soviet Union Have a Planned Economy?" *Soviet Studies*, vol. 31, no. 2 (April 1979), 268–274; Igor Birman, "From the Achieved Level," *Soviet Studies*, vol. 30, no. 2 (April 1978), 153–172.

[17] For a discussion of the historical development of material balance planning in the late 1920s, see Carr and Davies, *Foundations of a Planned Economy*, pp. 829–836.

[18] As an example, see A. N. Efimov et al., *Ekonomicheskoe planirovanie v SSSR* [Economic planning in the USSR] (Moscow: 1967).

[19] This chapter deals only with annual plans, which are the operational plans in the Soviet economy, and omits long-term "perspective planning," since historically there seems to have been little relationship between the perspective and annual plans. See Naum Jasny, *Essays on the Soviet Economy* (New York: Praeger, 1962), essay 6. In theory at least, annual plans should be compiled on the basis of the five- or seven-year perspective plans, in such a manner that at the end of five (or seven) annual plans, the perspective plan targets are met. This was not generally the case for the first eight Five [Seven] Year Plans. The Ninth and Tenth Five Year Plans (1971–1980) apparently sought to remedy this situation by upgrading the role of the long-range plan by requiring more conformity between it and the annual operational plans. Although there was pressure during the 1970s to improve long-term planning, it is not clear that substantial gains were made. For evidence on this, see Schroeder, "Recent Developments in Soviet Planning," pp. 13–15, and Schroeder, "The Soviet Economy on a Treadmill of 'Reforms,' " pp. 318–319.

plans compiled by *Gosplan* have been known to total 70 volumes of almost 12,000 pages and to deal with well over 30,000 commodities.

The most important industrial products—such as steel, cement, machinery, building materials—are called *funded commodities. Gosplan SSSR* is in charge of drawing up output and distribution plans for these funded commodities, which are specifically approved by the USSR Council of Ministers. Between 1928 and the present, *Gosplan* has developed annual balances for between 277 and 2390 separate funded product groups. Currently, *Gosplan* prepares some 2000 balances. Output and distribution plans are also drawn up for two other categories of industrial products. *Planned commodities* are those industrial products jointly planned and distributed by *Gosplan,* the State Committee for Material-Technical Supply, and the All-Union Main Supply and Sales Administrations—under the approval of the heads of these organizations. In recent years, several thousand commodities have been planned according to this system. Finally, *decentrally planned* commodities are planned and distributed by the territorial administrations of the State Committee for Material-Technical Supply and by the ministries without the explicit approval of higher organs. In recent years, over 50,000 industrial products have been planned according to this system.

In addition to these three categories, the ministries plan and allocate "nonplanned" industrial commodities, largely for internal use. In 1970 for example, the ministries allocated 26,000 products in this category.

An idealized version of *Gosplan's* planning of funded commodities through the industrial supply and output planning system would appear as follows (the breakdown into distinct steps is somewhat arbitrary, for there is considerable overlapping).

1. The first step in the planning process is for the party (the Politburo or the Central Committee) to establish its priorities for the forthcoming planning period. This is usually done in the spring preceding the planning period. The party expresses its priorities by setting output targets (generally in the form of desired rates of growth) for a number of crucial funded commodities.

2. These output targets are sent down through the state apparatus to *Gosplan,* which has been active gathering data on past plan fulfillment and bottlenecks. *Gosplan* then formulates a preliminary set of. *control figures* (tentative output targets) for 200 to 300 product groups that fulfills the priorities set by the party. *Gosplan* also tentatively estimates, on the basis of past performance, the inputs required to achieve the control figures. At this stage, the planning departments of the ministries aid *Gosplan* in the formulation of the full set of control figures and project input requirements—a process that involves considerable negotiation and friction as the ministries bargain for reasonable targets and sufficient resources.

3. These control figures are then sent down through the planning hier-

archy via the ministerial organizations until they reach the individual enterprises. As the control figures progress through the planning hierarchy, they are disaggregated into specific tasks. For example, the all-union ministry will receive its control targets, which are then disaggregated by branches within the ministry, and so on, until each enterprise under the purview of the ministry receives its own control figures. At this stage, the planning branch of the ministry will prepare a list of tentative input requirements, based on the ministry's control figures, for internal use by each enterprise.

4. Information now begins to flow up the planning hierarchy from the enterprise to *Gosplan*. The enterprise will relate its input requirements to its immediate superior, which in turn will aggregate the requirements of all enterprises under its control. These will be related to its superior, and so on, up to the ministry and then to *Gosplan*. At each stage in this process, the requested inputs are compared with estimated input needs and the so-called *correction principle* is used to adjust for differences between the two (after considerable bargaining among the various levels).

5. At this point in the process, *Gosplan* must check the consistency of the control figures, that is, determine whether a *material balance* exists. A material balance is achieved when the planned supplies of each commodity equal its targeted material input requirements and final uses. Assuming a total of 2000 funded commodities to be balanced, a material balance is achieved when:

Exhibit 1

$$S_1 = D_1$$
$$S_2 = D_2$$
$$\cdot$$
$$\cdot$$
$$\cdot$$
$$S_{2000} = D_{2000}$$

where the S's refer to the planned supplies and the D's refer to the estimated demands for the (2000) materials.

The planned supply of the first commodity (S_1), for example, is the sum of its planned output (the control figure), which is denoted as X_1, available stocks (V_1), and planned imports (M_1). The total demand for the first commodity (D_1) is the sum of its intermediate (interindustry) demands $(X_{11}, X_{12}, X_{13}, \ldots X_{1\,2000})$[20] and its final demand (investment, household demand, and exports), which is denoted as Y_1. From Exhibit 1, it is noted that a consistent

---

[20] The X_{ij} refer to interindustry demands. For example, X_{13} would refer to the quantity of commodity 1 required to produce the planned output of commodity 3. In more general terms, X_{ij} would refer to the quantity of commodity i required to produce the planned output of commodity j. Such input requirements are also called *intermediate* inputs.

set of control figures requires that:

Exhibit 2

$$Sources \qquad\qquad Distribution$$

$$X_1 + V_1 + M_1 = X_{11} + X_{12} + \cdots + X_{1,2000} + Y_1$$
$$X_2 + V_2 + M_2 = X_{21} + X_{22} + \cdots + X_{2,2000} + Y_2$$

$$X_{2000} + V_{2000} + M_{2000} = X_{2000,1} + X_{2000,2} + \cdots + X_{2000,2000} + Y_{2000}$$

In most cases, planned production (the X_1) is the most important supply source, accounting for as high as 95 percent of the total supply of funded materials. On the other hand, imports are usually an insignificant source of supply. It is *Gosplan's* task to ensure that a material balance exists.

A simplified hypothetical material balance consisting of four product categories—coal, steel, machinery, and consumer goods—is provided in Table 12 to illustrate the concepts of intermediate demand, final demand, balance, and so on.

Usually when *Gosplan* first compares supplies and demands, it finds a tendency for demands to exceed supplies because of large interindustry requirements and taut planning in general. *Gosplan* must then equate supplies and demands by adjusting their different components (Exhibit 2). To illustrate this process in the simplest possible manner, assume that a material balance has been achieved with the exception of the first commodity, which is, say, steel—that is, the supplies of all other commodities equal their demands, but the demand for steel exceeds its supply. This material imbalance can be equilibrated in five different ways:

a. *Gosplan could order an increase in the planned output of the deficit commodity (raise X_1).* This approach, however, could throw the remaining sectors out of balance because additional coal, electricity, and other inputs used to make steel would be required, and their targets would have to be increased accordingly, which would in turn require increased outputs of commodities used in producing them, and so on. If an output target is changed to achieve a material balance, a chain of *secondary effects* is set off that affects balances in other sectors. For this reason, Soviet planners have generally been reluctant to use this approach to achieve a balance, finding it difficult to adjust for the secondary impacts of such changes. When Soviet planners have used this approach, they have tended to adjust only for secondary effects in obvious cases.[21] A more common approach has been to call

---

[21] In practice, Soviet planners have generally adjusted only for *first-order relationships* when output targets are changed because of the tremendous amount of time required to make the necessary computations. By first-order changes, we mean the additional coal, electricity, ore, and other commodities required to produce the additional steel in our example above. No account is taken of the additional resources required to produce the extra coal, electricity, and ore. For a detailed discussion of this point, see Levine, "The Centralized Planning of Supply," in Bornstein and Fusfeld, pp. 55–57.

TABLE 12 A Sample Material Balance

	Sources			Intermediate Inputs Required By:				Final Use	
	Output	Stocks	Imports	Coal Industry	Steel Industry	Machinery Industry	Consumer Goods Industry	Exports	Domestic Uses
Coal (tons)	1000	10	0	100	500	50	50	100	210
Steel (tons)	2000	0	20	200	400	1000	300	100	20
Machinery (units)	100	5	5	20	40	10	20	10	10
Consumer goods (units)	400	10	20	0	0	0	100	100	230

Demonstration that a balance exists:
sources of coal: 1010 tons = uses of coal: 1010 tons
sources of steel: 2020 tons = uses of steel: 2020 tons
sources of machinery: 110 units = uses of machinery: 110 units
sources of consumer goods: 430 units = uses of consumer goods: 430 units

for increased production without raising planned inputs, thus pressuring enterprises to economize on inputs and increasing the tautness of planning.

b. *Gosplan could increase imports* (M_1) *of the deficit commodity.* The major drawback of this approach is that it would make the consistency of the material balance dependent on foreign suppliers and would require use of essential foreign exchange reserves (if imported from the West). Even utilizing trade connections within the communist bloc would be an uncertain alternative because of the risk of delivery deadlines not being met. This second approach has generally been of limited importance in Soviet material balance planning, although during the First Five Year Plan (1928–1932), it was used to make up deficits of certain types of machinery; during the postwar period, it has been used to import grain and, in recent years, advanced technology products from the West.

c. *Gosplan could reduce interindustry demands for the deficit commodity (the X_{1j}s).* This could be done by directing enterprises to use substitutes not in short supply or by reducing their overall inputs. The danger inherent in this approach is that by reducing planned intermediate inputs or by forcing enterprises to use inferior substitutes, the affected enterprises may not be able to meet their own output targets, thus creating further bottlenecks.

d. *Gosplan could reduce final demands for the deficit commodity* (Y_1). This could be done by reducing either exports, household demand, or investment demand. The positive feature of this approach is that household demand (such as for coal for home heating) in particular can be treated as a residual in the planning process, with little impact upon interindustry balances. Its negative feature is that such final demands are required to meet the material needs of the populace and could tend to be too readily sacrificed simply to achieve a balance of interindustry demands.

e. *Gosplan could draw upon stocks of the deficit commodity* (V_1). This approach is generally impractical because of either the lack of adequate stockpiles or the unwillingness of planners to draw down strategic supplies, and it has been used only rarely.

Gosplan has historically favored the third and fourth balancing techniques and has generally applied them within the context of a priority system, which has limited the flow of inputs to low-priority industrial branches (generally consumer goods) and has restricted the availability of final consumer goods. In the former case, planners have assumed that the neglect of low-priority consumer goods branches will not jeopardize plan fulfillment in the high-priority heavy industry branches, which tend to be fairly independent of the consumer good branches. For example, if a garment-producing enterprise were to fall short of its output goal owing to inadequate materials, this failure would not jeopardize plan fulfillment in the steel industry. In the latter case, if coal were in deficit, a simple balancing method would be to reduce coal available for household heating, which would have little immediate impact on the crucial interindustry balance. Over time (especially during the 1920s), the consumer sector has tended to be neglected for the sake of achieving a material balance, so much so that it has at times been called the "buffer" sector of the Soviet economy.

This neglect can be seen from the evidence presented in Table 13. For example, if one examines official Soviet estimates for plan achievement in producer and consumer goods for the period 1928 through 1975, the achievement in producer goods has been substantially greater than that in consumer goods. Although in recent years there has been continuing emphasis upon the need to improve both the quantity and the quality of consumer goods, plan adjustments and shortfalls still seem to predominate in the consumer goods sector.

After *Gosplan* achieves (or approximates) the material balance, the final version of the plan is submitted to the Council of Ministers for approval (and sometimes modification), after which the finalized targets are sent down the hierarchy to the individual firm. In its final form, the enterprise plan is called the *techpromfinplan* (the technical-industrial-financial plan) and establishes enterprise output targets as well as input allocations, supply plans, delivery plans, financial flows, wage bills, and many other targets.

The final stage of material balance planning occurs during the actual operation of the finalized plan. During this stage, *Gosplan* checks plan fulfillment at the various levels and gathers information upon which next year's plan will be based. An important element of the plan fulfillment stage is the response of *Gosplan* and the ministries to bottlenecks, that is, their manipulation of available resources to ensure fulfillment of priority targets.

It would be a mistake to think that the process of resource allocation is completed with the approval of the final version of the plan. Rather, important shifts of resources occur during the course of plan fulfillment as the planning agencies respond in a pragmatic manner to the various crises and bottlenecks that arise. The national economic plan is only the first stage of Soviet resource allocation. The real process of resource allocation commences with plan fulfillment. As bottlenecks develop, it becomes evident that certain targets must be sacrificed, and it is at this stage that centralized management supercedes centralized planning. As Table 13 indicates, plan fulfillment can vary dramatically by sector, even when one deals with broad aggregates. Those who control the flow of resources during plan implementation therefore play a crucial role in determining economic outcomes.

The Planning Problem—An Input-Output Framework

We have presented a sanitized version of Soviet material balance planning. Our description neglects what goes on behind the scenes as all the interested parties (*Gosplan*, the ministries, regional and local authorities, the enterprises, and party officials) struggle, bargain, and cajole for resources.

TABLE 13 Fulfillment of Principal Goals of Soviet Five Year Plans (5YPs), 1928–1980 (percent fulfillment)

	1st 5YP (1928–1932)	2nd 5YP (1933–1937)	4th 5YP (1946–1950)	5th 5YP (1950–1955)	7th 5YP (1959–1965)	8th 5YP (1966–1970)	9th 5YP (1971–1975)	10th 5YP (1976–1980)
NATIONAL INCOME								
Official estimate	92	96	119		98	101	95	95[E]
Western estimates	70	67	84–90	94				
INDUSTRIAL OUTPUT								
Official estimates	101	103	117		102	101	97	93[E]
Western estimates	60–70	76–93	84–95	97				
PRODUCER GOODS								
Official estimates	128	121	128		106	100	100	
Western estimates	72	97	97	94				
CONSUMER GOODS								
Official estimates	81	85	96		99	103	92	
Western estimates	46	68	81	103				
AGRICULTURAL PRODUCTION								
Official estimates	58	63–77	90		77	97	92	98[E]
Western estimates	50–52	66–78	76–79	80				
LABOR PRODUCTIVITY								
Official estimates	65		101				96	
Western estimates	36–42	86	81	85				
RETAIL TRADE								
Official estimates	39	54	86	109		106	96	91[E]
Western estimates								

SOURCES: Naum Jasny, *Essays on the Soviet Economy* (New York: Praeger, 1962), p. 266; Eugene Zaleski, *Stalinist Planning for Economic Growth: 1933 to 1952* (Chapel Hill, University of North Carolina Press, 1980), p. 503; Alec Nove, *An Economic History of the USSR* (London: Penguin, 1969), p. 353; Department of Commerce, *State Five Year Plan for the Development of the USSR National Economy for the Period 1971–1975*, JPRS 56970–1, Washington, D.C., September 1972, part 1, p. 65, part 2, pp. 356–358; Donald Green, et al., "An Evaluation of the 10th Five-Year Plan Using the SRI-WEFA Econometric Model of the Soviet Union," in Joint Economic Committee, *Soviet Economy in a New Perspective* (Washington, D.C.: U.S. Government Printing Office, 1976), p. 305; *Narodnoe khoziaistvo SSSR v 1979 G.* [The national economy of the USSR in 1979], (Moscow: Statistika, 1980).
[E] denotes estimated plan fulfillment.

As this process remains behind the scenes and out of Soviet textbooks, the Western observer can only imagine its intensity.

Soviet material balancing is carried out largely independently of the theoretically powerful input-output approach to planning, which could provide an alternative for Soviet plan formulation. An examination of input-output planning facilitates understanding of present Soviet planning practices and will help us to assess future improvements in Soviet planning procedures.[22]

Conceptually, the basic problem of plan formulation is quite simple. In the Soviet case, the planner (*Gosplan*) receives plan directives from the Communist Party. At this level, plan objectives·must be highly aggregated and require that the planner disaggregate them to an operational level. The planner might begin the task of plan formulation from a list of final demands for various products to be produced in various sectors of the economy. The planner must then prepare a plan relating inputs to outputs and bearing in mind two important considerations.

First, the plan must be *feasible*, that is, it must be capable of being achieved, given existing resource availabilities and the state of technology. Second, it would be desirable that the plan be *optimal*. Among all plan variants that are feasible, the *best* should be chosen. A plan that is best would be one that achieves the maximum level of output for a given input—or what amounts to the same thing, a minimum input for a given level of output. The maximum level of output is that which yields the greatest level of "satisfaction" to the political authorities of the USSR. The implication here is that a number of variants of the plan should be prepared and the best variant (as defined above) be chosen. Given the fact that the preparation of a plan for an economy the size of the USSR is a massive task, the application of mathematical techniques capable of computer manipulation has obvious appeal. Indeed, the basic planning problem as we have outlined it is the classic case of maximization under constraints, for which a large body of techniques is available. Let us turn to the input-output model, examining first the basic model, second its application to the Soviet case, and finally, the implications for future applications in Soviet planning procedures.

A basic input-output table such as Exhibit 3 is in essence a graphic presentation of the national accounts of an economic system, showing the interrelationships among the producing and the using sectors. The rows consist of producing sectors (in our simple example, industry, agriculture, and other sectors are shown) while the columns are consuming sectors. Each producing sector will generate output, some of which will be used as an *intermediate input* for the production of more output by that sector and by

---

[22] For an introductory discussion on planning, see Paul R. Gregory and Robert C. Stuart, *Comparative Economic Systems* (Boston: Houghton Mifflin, 1980), pp. 135–141. For a discussion of the basic input-output model and its application to Soviet planning, see Michael P. Todaro, *Development Planning* (Nairobi: Oxford University Press, 1971).

EXHIBIT 3

Hypothetical Input-Output Table

Columns:	1	2	3	4	5	6	7	8	9
Input: Consuming Sectors ╱ Outputs: Producing Sectors	Industry	Agriculture	Other sectors	Total intermediate production	Consumption (C)	Exports (E)	Government and defense (G)	Total final demand (D)	Total gross output (GO)
1 Industry	x_{11}	x_{12}	x_{13}	Σx_{1j}	C_1	E_1	G_1	D_1	$D_1 + \Sigma x_{1j}$
2 Agriculture	x_{21}	x_{22}	x_{23}	Σx_{2j}	C_2	E_2	G_2	D_2	$D_2 + \Sigma x_{2j}$
3 Other sectors	x_{31}	x_{32}	x_{33}	Σx_{3j}	C_3	E_3	G_3	D_3	$D_3 + \Sigma x_{3j}$
4 Total intermediate use	Σx_{i1}	Σx_{i2}	Σx_{i3}	$\Sigma\Sigma x_{ij}$	ΣC	ΣE	ΣG	$D_1 + D_2 + D_3$	
5 Labor	L_1	L_2	L_3	ΣL_j	L_C	L_E	L_G	ΣL	
6 Capital	K_1	K_2	K_3	ΣK_j	K_C	K_E	K_G	ΣK	
7 Land	LA_1	LA_2	LA_3	ΣLA_j	LA_C	LA_E	LA_G	ΣLA	
8 Total inputs	I_1	I_2	I_3	ΣI_j	I'_C	I'_E	I'_G	$\Sigma I'$	

NOTES: $D_i = C_i + E_i + G_i$; $I_j = L_j + K_j + LA_j$; $I'_C = L_C + K_C + LA_C$, etc.

131

the other sectors. The remaining output will be used to satisfy the various components of final demand, such as consumption, exports, government, and so on. The table is divided into four quadrants. The interindustry transactions quadrant (upper left), for example, shows the amount of industrial output that is needed to produce agricultural output (X_{12}), a relationship that can be expressed as a technical coefficient (a_{ij}).[23] Such a coefficient can be computed for each cell of this quadrant and indicates the amount of item i that is needed to produce one unit of j. This technical relationship is crucial in the development of a plan, a point to which we will return shortly.

The final use quadrant (upper right) shows the distribution of production to final use, while the value-added quadrant (lower left) shows the contribution of the primary inputs (land, labor, and capital) to output. Finally, the direct factor purchase quadrant (lower right) shows the distribution of primary inputs to final users.

The matrix of technical coefficients is derived from the interindustry transactions quadrant and provides the planner with crucial information, namely how much intermediate input is necessary to produce a unit of a particular output. The use of the input-output model is limited (unless the I–0 table is recomputed regularly) insofar as it assumes constancy of these coefficients. Thus it is assumed that the production function underlying the relationship exhibits constant returns to scale and is without factor substitution. Although such assumptions may seem unduly restrictive, there has been considerable support for the use of this method of planning, at least in the short run. Let us return to the Soviet case, illustrating how a feasible plan could be formulated using the input-output approach.

Assuming that Soviet planners have a matrix of technical coefficients (A) derived from past performance, the plan process would begin with the specification by the planner of the final demands (Y) to be produced in the forthcoming plan year. The next step, matrix inversion, provides the planner with a list of gross outputs of each sector (X) that will, if produced, satisfy the planners demand for final output.[24] The power of this model lies in

[23] The technical coefficients are computed as follows:

$$a_{ij} = \frac{X_{ij}}{X_j}$$

where a_{ij} = the amount of commodity i required to produce one unit of commodity j

X_{ij} = the amount of good i actually used by industry j
X_j = the gross output of industry j

[24] If the matrix of technical coefficients is known, and the input-output table is entirely in physical units, then the consistency of a set of control figures can be checked almost immediately by using the formula:

$$(I - A)X = Y \tag{1}$$

where X is the proposed vector of control figures (in gross output terms), A is the familiar the fact that within reason, even for an economy disaggregated into a considerable number of producing and using sectors, the computation of sectoral outputs can be computerized. Furthermore, the matrix inversion process takes into account both initial *and* second round effects (something material balancing cannot do), a feature crucial to the development of a balanced plan.

If the planner decides to increase the output of steel, obviously it will be necessary to increase the output of electricity, since electricity is used in the production of steel. However, when the output of electricity is increased, more inputs used in the generation of electricity will be needed, and so on. The process of matrix inversion is powerful in the sense that it can take into account all these "second round" effects and with the aid of a computer permit the rapid calculation of a number of feasible plan variants. It is in this capability that the real power of the input-output method lies. The process of adjustment to changing outputs can be captured and the feasibility of numerous variants checked. If adjustments are necessary, the alternatives can be calculated quickly. The process of plan formulation is iterative or sequential. The input-output approach facilitates the rapid execution of a complicated iterative process.

If the input-output approach were the theoretical basis of material balance planning, it would provide a powerful basis for plan formulation. Why is it not then the basis of Soviet planning practice? There are a number of basic problems with the input-output approach, all of which have tended to limit its practical application in the Soviet case.[25]

Leontief matrix of technical coefficients, I is the identity matrix, and Y is the vector of final outputs. An inconsistency in the proposed control figures would be indicated by a negative Y element, or by a Y element that is unacceptably small in light of planned investment, consumption, and exports. Thus the internal consistency of alternative vectors of control figures could be readily determined simply by matrix multiplication.

If on the other hand, Soviet planners desired to compute the vector of gross outputs (X) required to produce a proposed vector of final output targets (Y), then the following formula can be used:

$$(I - A)^{-1}Y = X \qquad (2)$$

where $(I - A)^{-1}$ is the inverse of $(I - A)$ and X is the set of required gross outputs. The feasibility of producing Y would be determined by considering the primary factor requirements (such as labor, capital, etc.) of the various programs relative to their availabilities.

[25] To what extent is input-output analysis actually used in the USSR? For a recent discussion and analysis of this point, see Albina Tretyakova and Igor Birman, "Input-Output Analysis in the USSR," *Soviet Studies*, vol. 28, no. 2 (April 1976), 157–186; Vladimir G. Treml, "A Comment on Birman-Tretyakova," *Soviet Studies*, vol. 28, no. 2 (April 1976), 187–188. For more background material, see Vladimir G. Treml, "Input-Output Analysis and Soviet Planning," in John P. Hardt et al., *Mathematics and Computers in Soviet Planning* (New Haven, Conn.: Yale University Press, 1967), pp. 68–120; Herbert Levine, "Input-Output Analysis and Soviet Planning," *American Economic Review*, vol. 52, no. 2 (May 1962); John Michael Montias, "On the Consistency and Efficiency of Central Planning," *Review of Economic Studies*, vol. 29, no. 81 (October 1962); Benjamin N. Ward, *The*

First, there has always been an element of ideological bias against such methods, a bias that was particularly strong during the Stalin era but that has slackened in recent years. In the early years when economic laws and the notion of balance and equilibrium were rejected, one can understand official distrust of input-output procedures. Furthermore, the input-output framework as we have outlined it suggests that land and capital are scarce factors, for which scarcity prices exist.[26] This thinking is (or was) contrary to the labor theory of value.

Second, the present Soviet system of data gathering does not adapt itself well to input-output technology. Data is gathered on an administrative basis rather than on the product basis required to compute input-output tables. Material balances are prepared on an industrial branch basis and result in concrete plans for the various industrial ministries. Yet these ministries tend to produce internally a broad range of products (steel, machinery, and consumer goods in one ministry, for example) that should show up in different commodity categories in an input-output table. A far more serious data problem is the generally poor and unreliable data base underlying both

---

Socialist Economy (New York: Random House, 1967), chap. 3; Vladimir G. Treml et al., "Interindustry Structure of the Soviet Economy," in Joint Economic Committee, *Soviet Economic Prospects for the Seventies,* (Washington, D.C.: U.S. Government Printing Office, 1973), pp. 246–269; Vladimir G. Treml et al., "The Soviet 1966 and 1972 Input-Output Tables," in Joint Economic Committee, *Soviet Economy in a New Perspective* (Washington, D.C.: U.S. Government Printing Office, 1976), pp. 332–376; Dimitri M. Gallik et al., "The 1972 Input-Output Table and the Changing Structure of the Soviet Economy," in Joint Economic Committee, *Soviet Economy in a Time of Change* (Washington, D.C.: U.S. Government Printing Office, 1979), vol. 1, pp. 423–471.

[26] If the matrix B represents a matrix of primary resource coefficients, where b_{kj} represents the amount of the k_{th} primary factor (land, labor, capital, etc.) required to produce one unit of output of commodity j, then:

$$B(I - A)^{-1} = T$$

is the matrix of full primary resource coefficients. Each element of T (t_{kj}) indicates the amount of primary factor k required *both directly and indirectly* to produce one unit of commodity j. The price of j would therefore be computed by multiplying the p_k by the t_{kj} where p_k is the price of the k_{th} primary factor and summing over the k's:

$$p_j = \sum_{k=1}^{n} p_k t_{kj}$$

(assuming n primary factors).

The "optimality" problem could be solved by determining all the Y vectors that meet the following condition:

$$TY = Z$$

where Z is the vector of primary resource availabilities. These Y vectors would represent a "production possibilities schedule" from which the *optimal* vector could be chosen as defined by the planners' objective function.

the construction of input-output balances and industrial planning. This tends to result in what one Soviet economist has termed "natural calamities"[27] when the technological coefficients are actually estimated.

Third, it has proven difficult to compute complete input-output tables in physical terms. As one might expect, certain products are heterogeneous and must be aggregated in value terms. This leads to further problems. Because of the distortive impact of the turnover tax (different users pay different prices), it is difficult to convert from the value figures (for example, rubles of steel) to the physical figures (for example, tons of steel) of primary concern to supply planners. Also, the computed input-output tables reflect in value terms the existing nonscarcity industrial prices and are therefore of dubious value.

Fourth, material balance planners have traditionally derived balances for between 300 and 2000 materials. At the distribution stage, they have planned about ten times the higher figure. Yet the Central Statistical Agency's 1959 national input-output table was a 73 by 73 matrix, and the 1966 and 1972 tables were 110 by 110.[28] Work has been done on a 600-branch national table by the Academy of Sciences (Siberian branch).[29] Input-output tables of much larger dimensions would have to be developed to preserve the current level of disaggregation of the material balance system. Given the current data-gathering capacity and computational sophistication of the Soviet Union, this would probably prove to be too complicated a task. Thus, the input-output tables used for planning would have to be at a higher level of aggregation than the material balance and industrial supply system. This aggregation would be done in value terms, and the technical coefficients would be weighted averages of disaggregated coefficients. To be useful for Soviet planning purposes, some method of meaningful disaggregation would have to be devised, which is an extremely thorny problem.

An Evaluation of Material Balance Planning

The input-output approach is a powerful theoretical base for material balance planning. However, for a number of important reasons that we have discussed, planning practice is really material balance planning. What are the strengths and weaknesses of the material balance approach? On the pos-

[27] Statement of S. Shatalin quoted in Treml et al., "Interindustry Structure of the Soviet Economy," p. 249.

[28] *Narodnoe khoziaistvo SSSR v 1969 g.* [The national economy of the USSR in 1969], (Moscow: Statistika, 1970) pp. 50–75; Treml et al., "The Soviet 1966 and 1972 Input-Output Tables."

[29] F. Baturin and P. Shemetiv, "Activities of Siberian Economists," *Problems of Economics: A Journal of Translations*, vol. 7, no. 7 (November 1969), 69. Translated from *Voprosy ekonomiki* [Problems of economics], no. 5 (1969).

itive side, by placing severe pressure on enterprises in the form of taut tar-gets designed to strain enterprise capacity, Soviet supply planning has brought about rapid growth of industrial output in selected priority sectors and has presided over the vast and rapid transformation of the Soviet econ-omy. Thus the major strength of Soviet planning seems to be its ability to direct resources into areas selected by planners with more speed and force than can a market-directed economy. An example is the ability of Soviet planners to direct resources to the military effort.

The material balance system works in an indirect sense to equate sup-ply and demand within the priority system. That is, although taut output targets often exceed enterprise capacities and create supply shortages, ulti-mately the administration can equate supplies and demands by directing available resources into higher priority enterprises. The Soviets themselves stress this very point: their planning system is seen to replace the "anarchy of the market" by rational direction of resources into socially necessary ends.[30] In fact, Soviet planners recognized from the very outset of the indus-trialization drive that taut planning would result in severe strains and pressures on the economy, but they considered the risks well worth taking. Taut (*naprazhennye*) plans continue to be demanded by the Soviet leader-ship and remain a basic fact of industrial planning up to the present. For example, *Gosplan* was directed by the Central Committee of the CPSU to undertake three separate revisions of the Ninth Five Year Plan (1971–1975) so as to uncover further "hidden reserves" of the economy—a euphemism for increasing the tautness of the plan.

One reason for taut planning was its role in helping to maintain plan discipline. As has been pointed out by Western students of Soviet plan-ning,[31] the greater the degree of slack in the economy, the greater the flexi-bility exercised by managers at the local level and the greater the likelihood that production may stray from strict adherence to the priority system. In other words, taut planning is required to enable central authorities to maintain strict control over the economy.

Second, arguments can be made for Soviet-style taut industrial plan-ning on other grounds, using the theories of Western development econom-ics. The argument here is that by setting taut (often unattainable) targets rather than setting moderate targets that avoid bottlenecks, enterprises will be forced to expand to the limits of their production possibilities and the economy will be pulled up to higher production levels in the process. This pressure, combined with an appropriate degree of administrative flexibility,

[30] Mikhail Bor, *Aims and Methods of Soviet Planning* (New York: International Publishers, 1967), chap. 6.
[31] Richard D. Portes, "The Enterprise Under Central Planning," *Review of Economic Stud-ies*, vol. 36, no. 106 (April 1969), 197–212. Also see Michael Keren, "On the Tautness of Plans," *Review of Economic Studies*, vol. 39, no. 4 (October 1972), 469–486.

could lead to more rapid economic development than would have occurred under more "rational" balanced planning.[32]

On the negative side, it is also recognized that excesses result from the Soviet material balance system.[33] First, the pressured Soviet system often forces Soviet managers to engage in dysfunctional forms of behavior. Faced with overambitious targets and lacking flexible access to supplies, managers have frequently engaged in excessive stockpiling. They strive to build up emergency stocks as "safety factors," which they can use for future plan fulfillment or for trading, by overstating input requirements to their immediate superiors. As a result of such actions, which are often required to make the system work, the economy loses on two counts: scarce materials tend to stand idle (resources are wasted) and planners receive inaccurate information. On another score, the overtaut planning system has created a definite sellers' market, which has meant that managers can generally unload their output irrespective of its quality and design. This feature has been an important source of the quality problems so widely noted in the Soviet press. The economic reforms of the 1960s—with their emphasis on profitability, sales, and interest charges—aimed at correcting these problems.

A second weakness of Soviet planning is that as long as the consumer sector is used as a buffer, personal incentives and productivity suffer, and productivity increases are most important as the major source of growth as the economy becomes more mature. The Soviets have relied heavily on using material incentives to promote labor productivity, but if consumer goods are not available in the desired quantities and qualities (because they have been sacrificed for heavy industry), the incentive system will be less effective.

As we argued earlier, it is apparent that the consumer sector was a buffer for plan imbalances during the Stalin years. To what extent this is still the case is a difficult question to answer. Although consumption grew at very respectable rates during the 1950s and 1960s, this growth slipped steadily in the 1970s, and the share of consumption in gross national prod-

[32] Holland Hunter, "Optimum Tautness in Developmental Planning," *Economic Development and Cultural Change*, vol. 9, no. 4, part 1, (July 1961), 561–572. A similar argument has been made by Albert Hirschman, *The Strategy of Economic Development* (New Haven, Conn.: Yale University Press, 1958), pp. 29–33. Hunter is careful to recognize that there is a level of "optimal tautness" and that Soviet planning may have exceeded this optimal limit. Western experts concluded that the Ninth Five Year Plan, for example, went well beyond this optimal limit and that serious shortfalls in metals, timber, and electricity hindered its implementation. On this, see J. Noren and F. Whitehouse, "Soviet Industry in the 1971–75 Plan," in Joint Economic Committee, *Soviet Economic Prospects for the Seventies* (Washington, D.C.: U.S. Government Printing Office, 1973), pp. 207, 239–242.

[33] Hunter, "Optimum Tautness," 567–571; and Herbert Levine, "Pressure and Planning in the Soviet Economy," in Henry Rosovsky, ed., *Industrialization in Two Systems: Essays in Honor of Alexander Gerschenkron* (New York: Wiley, 1966), pp. 266–285. Reprinted in Morris Bornstein and Daniel Fusfeld, eds., *The Soviet Economy: A Book of Readings* (Homewood, Ill.: Irwin, 1970), pp. 64–82.

uct declined steadily in the past 15 years. Thus while there was substantial rhetoric in the 1970s about the need to expand consumer goods output, the attention paid to quality, imports, better food products, and so on may not have kept pace with the growing expectations of the average Soviet citizen.

Third, material balance planning is quite cumbersome and slow. Enterprises invariably get their finalized targets well into the operating year (often as late as March) and must work without clear knowledge of what their targets actually are. When the targets are received, enterprises often desperately attempt to meet production targets at the end of each period by engaging in what the Soviets called *Shturmovshchina*—"storming"—a fairly inefficient method of scheduling production. Informal methods have been developed to get around this problem. One, the "correction principle," involves the use of advance estimates at each stage of the planning process prior to receipt of the information on the current production targets. Another device is the "advance fund allotment," which gives enterprises about one-quarter of the previous period's input allotments to tide them over until the final plan is received. A further device used by the ministries is "reserving," whereby ministries reserve a portion of enterprise material allotments to aid in combatting bottlenecks.[34] With the tendency toward planning delays and the use of informal methods, Soviet administrators have found that planning is less of a problem when targets change only marginally from year to year. Thus there is a built-in tendency in the Soviet planning system to avoid dramatic change. At the enterprise level, the manager is reluctant to introduce new technologies that require a restructuring of established supply channels. In general, the introduction of new technology and of new ways of doing things are retarded by the material balance system.[35]

Fourth, the Soviet planning system, with its stress on output goals, generates dysfunctional behavior at various planning levels. The enterprise will pursue output targets even if they lead to clearly irrational results.[36] The ministry tends to be primarily concerned with the success of enterprises under its own control and places the input needs of its own enter-

[34] Levine, "Pressure and Planning in the Soviet Economy," in Bornstein and Fusfeld, p. 73.

[35] One finds frequent complaints in the Soviet press from enterprises that have attempted to introduce new products and new technologies but were unable to obtain necessary supplies. *Pravda* (December 25, 1971, p. 2) reported on the tribulations of two electrical engineers, attempting to produce new torch lamps, whose efforts were foiled by their inability to obtain detailed parts. *Ekonomicheskaia gazeta* [The economic gazette], no. 39 (1969), reported on the problems of a plant processing motor vehicle transmissions, which was unable to obtain the necessary measuring instruments to produce a new design.

[36] In the oil industry, drilling enterprises are given targets in thousands of meters to be drilled. Theoretically, a dry hole is treated the same as a gusher. Enterprises therefore refuse to move their drilling equipment and continue to drill in the established fields. On this, see: "Soviet Oil Expert Warns of Reliance on Old Fields," *The New York Times*, February 13, 1980.

prises over those of enterprises outside its control. The same was true under the *Sovnarkhoz* reforms (1957–1964), when the regional authorities were concerned primarily with the success of regional enterprises. The planning system is also responsible for a lack of concern for the environment, because enterprise managers are judged on the basis of output target fulfillment, not on the basis of how well the environment is protected from air and water pollution and depletion of natural resources. Also, the uncertainties of the material supply system have caused enterprises to adopt peculiar production patterns. Soviet enterprises have been known to integrate vertically as many operations as possible to provide their own material inputs—it is not rare in the Soviet Union for machinery-producing enterprises to fabricate their own steel.[37] Thus vital specialization of production is limited by the planning system. In this light, one may ultimately come to recognize the frequent organizational shuffling of the Soviet planning system as an attempt to solve such problems of supply and specialization by finding an "optimal" Soviet planning structure.

A fifth and frequent criticism of central economic planning is the notion that it requires a very large bureaucracy to generate and implement the plan. The theme of a rapidly growing cadre of administrative personnel is a subject of continuing complaint in the Soviet press.[38] At the same time, Western evidence, and indeed Soviet official statistics, do not support the view that the administrative apparatus is especially large. A study by Gur Ofer, attempting to assess the size of the Soviet service sector, comes to the conclusion that the size of the administrative aparatus is smaller than one would expect, based upon the evidence of development patterns in other countries.[39] Ofer's results have been challenged, but they suggest at a minimum that fears of a cancerous growth of the Soviet bureaucracy have not been upheld.

Finally, one can evaluate Soviet material balance planning in terms of its *consistency* and *optimality*. A consistent plan is one in which supplies

[37] David Granick, *Soviet Metal Fabricating and Economic Development* (Madison: University of Wisconsin Press, 1967), pp. 159–160; Schroeder, "The Soviet Economy on a Treadmill of 'Reforms,' " p. 336.

[38] Leon Smolinski, "What Next in Soviet Planning?" *Foreign Affairs*, vol. 42, no. 4 (July 1964), 604.

[39] This evidence can be found in Gur Ofer, *The Service Sector in Soviet Economic Growth* (Cambridge, Mass.: Harvard University Press, 1973). For more recent evidence, see Frederic L. Pryor, "Some Costs and Benefits of Markets: An Empirical Study," *Quarterly Journal of Economics*, vol. 91 (February 1977), 81–102. For additional discussion of this theme, see Frank A. Durgin, "What Is Left for the Market in Our Market Economy," *ACES Bulletin*, vol. 16, no. 3 (Winter 1974), 41–51; Gertrude E. Schroeder, "A Critique of Official Statistics on Public Administration in the USSR," *ACES Bulletin*, vol. 18, no. 1 (Spring 1976), 23–44; Frank A. Durgin, "A Commentary on Gertrude Schroeder's 'Critique of Official Statistics on Public Administration in the USSR,' " *ACES Bulletin*, vol. 19, no. 1 (Spring 1977), 109–116; and Gertrude E. Schroeder, "Reply," *ACES Bulletin*, vol. 19, no. 1 (Spring 1977), 117–118.

and demands of funded commodities are equal. It is obvious that consistency is one of the main objectives of the Soviet material balance system. From the point of view of Soviet planners, consistency is a desirable goal: if the plan were highly inconsistent, that is, if targeted material requirements were allowed generally to exceed available supplies, plan fulfillment would become a competitive struggle for deficit inputs that the planner would have difficulty in controlling, even with the priority system. Instead, connections, prestige, and ability to maneuver (already important factors in plan fulfillment) would primarily determine who would be able to fulfill the target—a definitely undesirable situation in a controlled economy.

On the other hand, *optimality* should also be a desirable goal in a planned economy. To illustrate the concept of optimality, consider a situation where five different sets of control figures are consistent. From the point of view of the state, it would be desirable to be able to choose the "best," or optimal figures; to do otherwise would be to misallocate scarce resources.[40] This kind of choice is usually beyond the reach of Soviet planners, however, because the Soviet material balance system works so slowly that planners are fortunate if they approximate just one consistent plan variant in the allotted planning period. Current Soviet balancing techniques, time, and manpower are inadequate to find several consistent plan variants from which to choose the optimal one, and the Soviet's disregard of the importance of optimality must be seen as a major weakness of material balance planning.[41]

Our evaluation of the Soviet industrial planning reveals an apparent paradox to which we shall return in Part Three, namely, that the material balance system has been effective in generating rapid growth of industrial output and military power. In fact, it has presided over the elevation of the Soviet Union to a world power. On the other hand, the deficiencies of the Soviet planning system are striking: the excessive stockbuilding, the quality problems, the consumer sector buffer, the lack of emphasis on optimality, and so on. Which view of Soviet planning is correct? We will come back to this question later.

MONEY IN THE SOVIET ECONOMY

In market economic systems, money plays a crucial role in coordinating the activities of the economic actors, namely, enterprises, households, and the

---

[40] The optimal set of control figures could be defined in technical terms as the one that yields the maximum value of all consistent sets when entered into the planners' objective function, that is, the consistent set of control figures that the planners regard as the "best" in terms of their preferences and biases.
[41] Schroeder, "Soviet Economy on a Treadmill of 'Reforms,'" pp. 319–322, discusses the computerization of Soviet planning. About one-half of the calculations involved in the 1978 plan were aided by computers.

government.[42] The reader may be puzzled to note that our discussion of Soviet planning has thus far focused solely upon input and output determination in physical terms. We turn now to an examination of the financial side of Soviet planning. We begin with a brief discussion of money in the Soviet economy, followed by an examination of its role in the running of an enterprise, and, finally, its role in the public sector. We reserve discussion of the household sector for the following chapter.

In a basic sense, money in the Soviet economy plays a role similar to that in other systems, namely as a store of value, a medium of exchange, and a unit of account. There is however a very basic difference between the role of money in the Soviet economy and its role in market economic systems. Although the precise role of money is the subject of considerable debate in both systems, money is assumed to influence real economic activity in the market system, and thus under the general rubric of monetary policy falls a long list of ways in which the nature of economic events is thought to be influenced by changes in monetary events. In the case of the Soviet economy, no such connection between monetary and real phenomena is argued, and money is generally thought to play a *passive* role in the execution of economic activity. Thus money should not be a factor that either encourages or inhibits the economic activity of enterprises.

The present-day Soviet monetary system derives in large part from the credit reforms of 1930–1932 and subsequent modifications, especially in 1947. In the Soviet economy, there are three basic economic units—the enterprise, the state, and the household. Although enterprises are owned by the state, they are nevertheless separate entities, the accounts of which are kept in value terms, under the *khozraschet* (economic accounting) system.

There are two monetary channels in the Soviet economy—the enterprise and the household. Money in both channels arises from the provision of credit to enterprises through the state bank. This credit is closely controlled through a credit plan and provides for the financing of capital investment in the case of the enterprise and for the payment of other expenses—notably, the wages of labor. Both flows are closely monitored, although the rules for each flow differ. In general, however, state-granted and -controlled credit provides the means for financing enterprise activity. That activity in turn provides revenue for the state budget through profits taxes, where under strict state control, the redistributive function can take place. Thus in the Marxian schema, surplus value is redistributed by the state. We turn now to an examination of the components of this system.

[42] Our discussion of the role of money in the Soviet economy is based upon George Garvy, *Money, Financial Flows, and Credit in the Soviet Union* (Cambridge, Mass.: Ballinger, 1977), and Adam Zwass, *Money, Banking, and Credit in the Soviet Union and Eastern Europe* (White Plains, N.Y.: M. E. Sharpe, 1979). For a history of money in the Soviet Union, see for example Z. V. Atlas, *Sotsialisticheskaia denezhnaia sistema* [Socialist Monetary System] (Moskva: Finansy, 1969).

THE ENTERPRISE PLAN AND FINANCIAL CONTROLS

Our previous discussion of material balance planning emphasized supply planning in physical terms. Let us now turn to the financial side of the enterprise. The enterprise *techpromfinplan* (technical-industrial-financial plan) includes, as its name suggests, a pervasive financial plan as well as physical input and output indicators. This financial plan parallels the physical section of the industrial supply and output plans and acts as a check on enterprise performance. The financial plan consists of a wage bill, planned cost reductions, credit plans for purchasing inputs, along with many other targets. The amount of detail contained in the financial plan has varied over the years. Reforms sought in 1965 to reduce the number and specificity of financial controls, but financial targets continue to serve as the monetary counterparts of enterprise's output and input targets.

Soviet managers have tended to regard the fulfillment of financial plans (cost reduction targets, wage bills, credit plans, etc.) as less important than output plans (especially prior to 1965) and have tended to sacrifice the former as a result. Despite this, financial targets have remained important to the planners because they serve to enhance the planners' control over enterprise operations. In the Soviet terminology, this is called *ruble control* (*kontrol' rublem*), a system that works as follows: because the financial plan is the monetary counterpart of a firm's input and output plans, deviations from the financial plan should signal deviations from the physical plan. If a firm's labor input plan calls for the employment of 500 workers, the enterprise can draw only enough cash from its bank account to pay that number. If the input plan calls for ten tons of steel, the enterprise can draw upon its funded input account only enough for that particular transaction, nothing in excess. If the firm is in need of working capital, short-term credit will be granted only if the transaction is called for in the plan. Reinforcing the system of ruble control is the fact that all (legal) interfirm transactions are handled by *Gosbank* (the State Bank), which supervises all such transactions and is the sole center for the settling of accounts. However, the reforms of the 1960s have tended to increase the share of profits that can be retained for use by the enterprise, as opposed to the share that must be returned to the state budget. Though limited in scope, this direction of change is important for enterprise decision-making.[43]

The Soviet manager, in response to this system of financial supervision, has developed informal sources of supply that do not require bank clearing operations and other informal devices to circumvent many financial controls.[44] Also, successful firms are often not strictly held to their financial

---

[43] See Garvy, *Money, Financial Flows, and Credit*, pp. 101–105.

[44] For an analysis of informal sources of supply, see Aron Katsenelinboigen, "Coloured Markets in the Soviet Union," *Soviet Studies*, vol. 29, no. 1 (January 1977), 62–85.

plans. Financial controls are used primarily to detect significant deviations from planned activities, and desired corrections are normally made administratively. Despite the flexibility and circumventions of financial controls, ruble control remains an important monitoring device in the Soviet planning system.

PUBLIC FINANCE AND FINANCIAL PLANNING IN THE SOVIET UNION

The major allocation decisions in the Soviet Union are reflected in the annual budget of the USSR, which determines the allocation of total output by end use among private consumption, investment, public consumption, defense, and administration. The annual budget of the USSR is a consolidated budget, which encompasses the all-union budget, the state budgets of the republics, and the local budgets of provinces, regions, and districts.[45] It is a much more comprehensive system of accounts than the budget of the United States, which encompasses only federal receipts and expenditures.

As one might expect, a much larger portion of the Soviet GNP flows through its state budget than is the case with the American GNP. Between 1929 and the present, 10 to 20 percent of American GNP has been channeled through government budgets (including state and local government). In the Soviet Union, the cumulative average for the postwar period has been about 45 percent.[46] The relatively greater importance of the state budget in the Soviet economy derives from the financing of most investment directly from the state budget and because communal consumption (public health, education, and welfare) represents a larger share of total consumption in the Soviet Union. Thus the scope of *public* goods is broader in the USSR than in the United States. In a sense, one could argue that all products produced by the Soviet economy are public because they are produced by state or collective enterprises with land and capital provided by the state. However, in dealing with the Soviet economy, the convention is normally observed that if the enterprise operates on its own accounting system, independently of the state budget, it is not considered as a public enterprise.

The budget of the USSR directs resources into consumption, investment, defense, and administration in the following manner: the state collects revenues from sales taxes (the so-called turnover tax), deductions from

[45] M. V. Condoide, *The Soviet Financial System* (Columbus: Bureau of Business Research of Ohio State University, 1951), pp. 78–79; Nove, *The Soviet Economic System*, chap. 9. For a Soviet textbook on the subject, see M. K. Shermenov, ed., *Finansy SSSR* [Finances of the USSR], (Moscow: Finansy, 1977).

[46] Abraham Becker, *Soviet National Income, 1958–1964* (Berkeley: University of California Press, 1969), pp. 92–93. The measure used in both cases is the ratio of expenditures (plus budget surplus) to GNP.

enterprise profits, direct taxes on the population, and from social insurance contributions (see Table 14). The first two alone have consistently accounted for over 60 percent of total revenues throughout most of the plan period. These revenues are then directed through the national budget, the republican budgets, and through provincial and local budgets to various uses: to finance investment in the form of grants, which at various times has accounted for between 33 percent and 64 percent of total expenditures (the "National economy" category in Table 14); to finance communal consumption ("Social and cultural undertakings"), which has accounted for from 14 to 36 percent of the total; and to finance defense and administration.

Once the overall allocation of budget resources into nonprivate consumption uses (investment, communal consumption, defense, and administration) is made and the physical outputs of consumer goods are specified by *Gosplan*, financial authorities (the State Bank and the Ministry of Finance) must ensure that a macroequilibrium of supply and demand exists.

The objective of Soviet financial planning at the macro level is to balance the aggregate money demand for consumer goods with the aggregate supply at established prices. This is done centrally, because planning authorities must ensure the compatibility of the output of consumer goods at established prices with employment levels and wage rates. The smaller the planned output of consumer goods and the larger the number employed and the higher the wages, the more likely that aggregate money demand will exceed available supply at established prices.

TABLE 14   The Budget of the USSR, 1931–1978 (selected years)

RECEIPTS (PERCENT OF TOTAL)	1931	1934	1937	1940	1950	1960	1970	1978
Turnover tax	46	64	69	59	56	41	32	32
Deductions from profits	8	5	9	12	10	24	35	30
Social insurance	9	10	6	5	5	5	5	5
Taxes on population	4	7	4	5	9	7	8	8
Other revenue	33	14	12	19	20	23	20	25
EXPENDITURES (PERCENT OF TOTAL)								
National economy	64	56	41	33	38	47	48	54
Social and cultural undertakings	14	15	24	24	28	34	36	34
Defense	5	9	17	33	20	13	12	7
Administration and justice	4	4	4	4	3	2	1	1
Other expenditures	13	16	14	6	11	4	3	4

SOURCES: *Narodnoe khoziaistvo SSSR v 1970 g.* [The national economy of the USSR in 1970] (Moscow: Statistika, 1971), p. 731; M. V. Condoide, *The Soviet Financial System* (Columbus: Bureau of Business Research of Ohio State University, 1951), pp. 84–87; *Narodnoe khoziaistvo SSSR v 1978 g.* [The national economy of the USSR in 1978], (Moscow: Statistika, 1979), p. 534.

A simple algebraic example illustrates this relationship.[47] Assume that the output plan calls for enterprises to produce Q_1 "units" of consumer goods and Q_2 "units" of producer goods. The planners determine through the use of labor input coefficients that L_1 man-years of labor are required to produce Q_1 and L_2 man-years are required to produce Q_2, and these employment levels are accordingly targeted by *Gosplan*. These workers are paid the prevailing wage rates in the consumer and producer goods sectors, respectively, and average annual wages are denoted in the two sectors as W_1 and W_2 respectively. In this manner, an annual wage income of $W_1L_1 + W_2L_2$ is created (we consider only wage income and ignore the income earned by collective farmers and others).

The total demand for consumer goods, therefore, is that portion of total wage income that is not taxed away or saved. If personal taxes are denoted by T and personal savings by R, the total money demand (D) for consumer goods is:

$$D = W_1L_1 + W_2L_2 - T - R$$

The total supply of consumer goods at established prices (S) is total value of all consumer goods (denoted as P_1Q_1):

$$S = P_1Q_1$$

where P_1 denotes the existing consumer price level.

The task of the financial authorities is to strike an appropriate balance between consumer demand and supply at prevailing prices, that is, between $W_1L_1 + W_2L_2 - T - R$ and P_1Q_1.

Balancing Techniques

We illustrate the various balancing techniques used by Soviet planners by reviewing their handling of the inflationary pressures of the 1930s. The setting was as follows: the industrialization drive of the early 1930s had created severe inflationary pressures on both the supply and demand sides of the consumer market. On the supply side, the structure of the economy had shifted drastically during this period in favor of producer goods and away from consumer goods, and the output of consumer goods had declined in real terms.[48] At the same time, Soviet planners were practicing "overfull" employment planning by confronting enterprises with output goals that were obviously unattainable with the targeted enterprise labor force.

[47] This algebraic approach is a modification of the model used by Howard Sherman, *The Soviet Economy* (Boston: Little, Brown, 1969), chap. 10, appendix A.

[48] Per capita real consumption (not including communal services) declined at an annual rate of −0.3 percent between 1928 and 1937. Janet G. Chapman, "Consumption," in Abram Bergson and Simon Kuznets, eds., *Economic Trends in the Soviet Union* (Cambridge, Mass.: Harvard University Press, 1963), pp. 238–239.

This forced enterprise managers to compete vigorously among themselves for labor, and average wages were bid up in the process. Although wage rates were centrally determined, managers could still offer higher wages by upward reclassification of workers and by setting low piece rate norms. During the First Five Year Plan, for example, average annual industrial wages were initially planned to increase from 690 rubles to 934 rubles (a substantial increase). In fact, they rose to 1427 rubles. For the 1928 to 1937 period as a whole, average industrial wages rose at an annual rate of 17.7 percent.This wage inflation exerted upward pressure on industrial wholesale prices and was a major factor in forcing up retail prices to an index of 200 (1928 = 100) in 1933 and 700 in 1937.[49]

The rising industrial wages were only one inflationary force driving up the demand for consumer goods. Labor was also being drawn at rapid rates out of agriculture into higher paying industrial jobs, thereby raising average wages for the entire economy as well—a further inflationary factor on the demand side.[50] Another complication was the rapid expansion of the full-time labor force, due mainly to the rising participation rates of women and to the decline in part-time agricultural employment. Thus while the supply of consumer goods was declining and producer goods prices were rising, both average wages and employment were rising, generating substantial increases in money incomes. An indication of the scope of the rise in money wages was the increase in currency in circulation (used almost exclusively for wage payments) from 3 billion rubles in 1930 to about 16 billion rubles in 1940.[51] The inflationary implications of these trends are obvious.

As the algebraic example shows, several methods could have been used to deal with the growing inflationary problem.[52] One obvious approach would have been a wage freeze (the W's in the equation) enforced by strict limitations on the amount of cash that an enterprise could draw for wage payments. On the other hand, a system of flexible wages was required to attract labor into high priority sectors and to maintain incentives. The above cited figures on industrial wage increases during the 1930s show clearly that this approach was not followed, for these very reasons. A second approach would have been to increase personal taxes (T), thereby reducing personal disposable income, but high tax rates also would have reduced labor incentives and retarded industrialization. However, increasing taxes would not have stopped the Soviet inflation of the 1930s, since it largely originated in

[49] Franklyn D. Holzman, "Soviet Inflationary Pressures, 1928–1957: Causes and Cures," *Quarterly Journal of Economics*, vol. 74, no. 2 (May 1960), 177.
[50] *Ibid.*, 176.
[51] *Ibid.*, 180.
[52] For a detailed discussion of the alternative methods of financing Soviet economic development, see Franklyn D. Holzman, "Financing Soviet Economic Development," in Moses Abramovitz, ed., *Capital Formation and Economic Growth* (Princeton, N.J.: Princeton University Press, 1955), pp. 229–287.

the labor market through excessive expenditures of managers. The increased taxes could at best merely mop up the excess purchasing power after it had already done its damage. A further complication was that inflationary pressures were so great during the early 1930s that extremely high tax rates (perhaps as high as 60 percent of personal income) would have been required, and such high rates would have had a demoralizing impact on work incentives.

A third alternative would have been to encourage personal savings (R)—a difficult feat during a period of rapid inflation. The Soviets did make government bond purchases compulsory (as automatic payroll deductions) between 1930 and 1957—a policy that did create some resentment and tended to reduce work incentives. The Soviets also established a network of savings banks to encourage voluntary savings, but it proved difficult to persuade people to save during the inflationary 1930s.[53]

A fourth method for balancing supply and demand would be to raise consumer retail prices (P_1) to soak up the excess consumer demand, and this is exactly what the Soviets did in large measure. The *turnover tax* was the formal device used. The turnover tax was a differentiated sales tax levied primarily on consumer products and will be discussed in detail in the section on prices. This tax was the difference (after wholesale and retail trade margins) between the average cost of production (plus a planned profit margin) and the retail sales price. As the state determined retail prices, excess demand for a commodity could be eliminated quite simply by raising the turnover tax and hence the retail price. The extent to which this method was used can be seen from the much more rapid increase of retail prices between 1928 and 1937 than average costs of production, as measured by material costs (wholesale prices of industrial commodities) and wage costs. For example, wholesale prices of basic industrial commodities increased 75 percent. Average industrial wages increased 430 percent, but retail prices of consumer goods rose 700 percent between 1928 and 1937. These differential rates illustrate the increasing role of the turnover tax, which averaged 22 percent of the retail price in 1928–1929 and 64 percent in 1935.[54] For example, in 1934 the state sold rye for 84 rubles per centner, of which 66 rubles was turnover tax, and wheat for 104 rubles per centner, of which 89 rubles were turnover tax.[55]

Thus inflation via increased indirect taxation was used to soak up excess consumer demand during the 1930s. A prominent authority on Soviet taxation, Franklyn Holzman, postulates that Soviet tax authorities preferred indirect commodity taxes (the turnover tax) over direct income taxes because the former would have less of a disincentive effect on workers. It was

---

[53] *Ibid.*, pp. 230–238.
[54] Holzman, "Soviet Inflationary Pressures," 168, 173.
[55] Alec Nove, *An Economic History of the USSR* (London: Penguin, 1969), p. 210.

hoped that industrial workers would pay more attention to increases in their money wages than to the reduction in their real wages, which resulted as retail prices rose faster than money wages (the so-called money illusion), and that incentives would be maintained. In addition, the turnover tax was administratively easier to collect and administer than direct taxation in a populous, semiliterate agricultural country.[56] To this day, the turnover tax remains an important source of government revenue in the Soviet Union.

The final balancing method employed heavily by the Soviets in the 1930s was *repressed inflation.* What this means is that Soviet authorities simply allowed some of the excess consumer demand to persist. Despite rapidly rising retail prices during the 1930s, consumer demand still exceeded supply with the possible exception of 1937, which was a good crop year, with relatively abundant food supplies for purchase. Soviet authorities were therefore called upon to ration consumer goods either formally or indirectly during most of the 1930s. Such rationing proved necessary because Soviet financial authorities found it difficult to keep prices high enough to eliminate inflationary pressures in the face of the numerous unplanned wage increases and shortfalls in plan fulfillment in the consumer sector.

Rationing of essential consumer goods was introduced in the winter of 1928–1929, first on foodstuffs and then on manufactured consumer goods.[57] To maintain labor incentives, to preserve the effectiveness of wage differentials, and to reward special groups, Soviet pricing authorities sanctioned a complex system of multiple prices during the early 1930s.[58] They consisted of: (1) retail prices of rationed goods sold in state and cooperative stores ("normal-fund" prices); (2) the so-called prices of the "commercial fund," which were higher than the "normal fund" prices (yet even these were often available only in "closed shops," open only to special groups); (3) *Torgsin* shop prices of items, which could only be bought with precious metals and foreign currency; (4) free market prices (primarily on the collective farm markets); and (5) several other prices, including inflated black market prices.[59] The collective farm markets where peasants could sell their private produce were especially useful in siphoning off the excess purchasing power of industrial workers and in preserving industrial incentives, for extra earned income could be used to buy scarce food products in these markets.

While prices in state and cooperative stores doubled between 1928 and

[56] Holzman, "Financing Soviet Economic Development," pp. 231–237.

[57] On rationing in the 1930s, see V. A. Vinogradov et. al., eds., *Istoriia sotsialisticheskoi ekonomiki SSSR* [History of the socialist economy of the USSR], (Moscow: Nauka, 1978), vol. 4, chap. 13.

[58] On pricing, see A. L. Vainshtein, *Tseny i tsenoobrazovanie v SSSR v vostanovilel'ny period* [Prices and price formation in the USSR in the transition period], (Moscow: Nauka, 1972).

[59] Nove, *An Economic History of the USSR*, pp. 203–207.

1932, collective farm market prices, the only free market prices in the Soviet Union, rose 30 times, a clear indication of the extent of repressed inflation during this period. After 1932, this differential was reduced and nearly closed in 1937, but it was opened again by the outbreak of World War II. Because of the complex multiple price system, it is difficult to gauge trends in the general price level during the 1930s. What is known for sure however is that retail prices rose substantially, but not by enough to eliminate the excess consumer demand entirely—as is witnessed by the long queues and the multiple prices of the 1930s.

The Soviet's use of inflation during the industrialization drive of the 1930s provides a case study of how inflation can be used to allocate resources out of consumer goods into investment goods while seeking to preserve industrial incentives.

Financial Planning in the Postwar Period

In recent years, there has been a growing Western interest in Soviet financial planning. This interest focuses in general on the role of pecuniary variables in a centrally planned socialist economy. However, there is specific interest in the extent to which (and the reasons why) the Soviet economy may have been able to avoid the rapid inflation experienced in recent years by other countries. To what extent can the Soviet economic system shield itself from the impact of such external shocks as the rise of OPEC in the 1970s and 1980s? What can we learn from an examination of the Soviet postwar financial record?

The traditional Western view has held that the Soviet economy has been relatively free of overt inflation but that it has probably suffered from an unknown degree of repressed inflation.[60] Let us consider the available evidence on each of these points.

The main evidence in support of the view that overt inflation has been effectively controlled is the official Soviet index of retail prices. This index, after a substantial decline in the immediate postwar years, has remained roughly constant since then.[61] What factors might explain such a pattern?

First, although there have been a number of major revisions of wholesale prices in recent years, these revisions have probably had a limited impact upon retail prices, with some notable exceptions. In the case of agricultural products, for example, where wholesale purchase prices have been raised to make farm production profitable, retail prices of these products have not been raised, the difference being absorbed by the state as a sub-

---

[60] We define inflation as an upward trend in the price level; repressed inflation, as persistent excess demand at prevailing prices.
[61] *Narodnoe khoziaistvo SSSR v 1978 g.* [The national economy of the USSR in 1978] (Moscow: Statistika, 1979), p. 447.

sidy. In other instances, the turnover tax rate has been reduced, thus allowing wholesale prices to increase without commensurate increases at the retail level. The important exception is where the prices of what planners consider to be luxuries (for example automobiles, coffee, tea, jewelry) have been raised sharply. In this pattern lies a basic element of Soviet price policy, namely, to attempt to keep the prices of "necessities" stable, while increasing the prices of "luxuries" sufficiently to absorb excess purchasing power.

Second, although the average monthly money wage has grown steadily since the 1950s, so too has the output of consumer goods and services. This issue will receive greater attention when we consider the overall performance of the Soviet economy.

Third, one could argue that in the postwar years planners have been better able to control inflationary forces than was the case in the 1930s. Methods of control used by *Gosbank* have improved, and the use of overfull employment planning may have lessened. No longer can enterprises draw excess funds for wage payments from their *Gosbank* accounts, and state control over wage payments has increased. The upshot of these changes is that average annual wage increases have been held to modest rates (by Western standards) throughout the postwar era. Wage inflation, a major source of inflationary pressure in the 1930s, has been kept under control in the postwar years.

The picture presented thus far seems to support the view that inflation has not been a serious problem in the postwar Soviet experience. However, this picture has recently been challenged in a number of ways, all of which deserve our attention. What is the evidence that there may in fact be a problem with inflation in the Soviet economy?

First, it has been pointed out that lack of detailed knowledge about Soviet price indices, along with the traditional problems with such measures, could lead one to question the validity of the official retail price index as an accurate measure of retail prices.[62] However, an alternative retail price index computed by Gertrude Schroeder and Barbara Severin, while showing generally declining retail prices in the 1950s and 1960s, suggests only modest growth of retail prices in the early 1970s—at an average annual rate of approximately 1.5 percent.[63]

[62] For a discussion of Soviet price indices, see Morris Bornstein, "Soviet Price Statistics," in Vladimir G. Treml and John P. Hardt, eds., *Soviet Economic Statistics* (Durham, N.C.: Duke University Press, 1972), pp. 355–396. The argument has been made that over time, there has been a systematic and continuing disappearance of the lower price variants of a particular product, thus effectively raising the average retail price.

[63] This index is from Gertrude E. Schroeder and Barbara S. Severin, "Soviet Consumption and Income Policies in Perspective," in Joint Economic Committee, *Soviet Economy in a New Perspective*, (Washington, D.C.: U.S. Government Printing Office, 1976), pp. 620–660. For a discussion of this and other evidence on inflation, see Joyce Pickersgill, "Soviet Inflation: Causes and Consequences," *Soviet Union* vol. 4, part 2 (1977), 297–313; see also Joyce

Second, it has been argued that a number of indirect indicators point to the existence of repressed inflation. The case for repressed inflation rests upon (1) the observation that collective farm market prices (where market forces prevail) have risen more rapidly than retail prices, which are controlled by the state; (2) the reports of persistent shortages of consumer goods; and (3) the rapid rise of savings deposits in recent years. It is true that collective farm market prices rose more rapidly than state retail prices in the late 1960s and the 1970s, though the differential is quite modest. While the average propensity to save has risen from the very low levels of the 1950s, this may only reflect the fact that Soviet citizens have little else to do with funds not spent on consumption.[64] All of this evidence seems to point to a conclusion that although the official Soviet retail price index may be biased on the downward side, the extent of inflation has been quite limited.

The arguments above focus primarily upon the possibility that open inflation may exist in the Soviet economy. However, in an economic system where controls are used, a possible variant of inflation would be repressed inflation, where at prevailing prices, excess demand persists. How can one discover the presence of repressed inflation?

The approach to answering this question has been the development and application to the Soviet case of a disequilibrium model of household behavior. This model, developed by R. J. Barro and H. I. Grossman, suggests that both labor supply responses and savings responses will be influenced by the availability of consumer goods. Thus in a case of repressed inflation (excess demand), it is argued that an increase in the availability of consumer goods will lead to a decrease in savings and an increase in labor supplied.[65] This model, with modifications, has been applied to the Soviet case by D. H. Howard.[66] Howard finds that the Barro-Grossman model fits the Soviet case quite well, thus supporting the view of a disequilibrium situation in which there is repressed inflation.[67] However, these results have been challenged by Barbara Katz and by Machiko Nissanke, who criticize the nature and the

Pickersgill, "Soviet Household Saving Behavior," *The Review of Economics and Statistics,* vol. 58, no. 2 (May 1976), 139–147. More generally, see M. Yves Laulan, ed., *Banking, Money and Credit in the USSR* (Brussels: NATO Directorate of Economic Affairs, 1973); M. Yves Laulan, ed., *Economic Aspects of Life in the USSR* (Brussels: NATO Directorate of Economic Affairs, 1975).

[64] For the development of these views, see Pickersgill, "Soviet Household and Saving Behavior," pp. 139–147.

[65] R. J. Barro and H. I. Grossman, "A General Disequilibrium Model of Income and Employment," *American Economic Review,* vol. 61, no. 1 (March 1971), 83–93.

[66] For a complete statement, see David H. Howard, *The Disequilibrium Model in a Controlled Economy* (Lexington, Mass.: Heath, 1979).

[67] David H. Howard, "The Disequilibrium Model in a Controlled Economy: An Empirical Test of the Barro-Grossman Model," *American Economic Review,* vol. 66, no. 5 (December 1976), 871–879.

measurement of the variables examined and the econometric difficulties of applying the Barro-Grossman model to the Soviet case.[68] Also, it should be noted that the application of the disequilibrium approach to the East European case by Richard Portes and others does not lend support to the hypothesis of repressed inflation.[69] In view of the differences between the Soviet Union and Eastern Europe, one does not know whether these results can be applied to the USSR. Finally, we should note that Joyce Pickersgill finds that the savings behavior of Soviet households can be accounted for by rational consumer behavior and that the increase in household savings of the postwar era does not necessarily suggest repressed inflation.

In the next chapter, we will return to the question of labor supply. For the present, we must conclude that the evidence does not seem to support the existence of significant inflation in the Soviet Union. Open inflation has probably been greater than the official index of retail prices would suggest. However, even if Western estimates more accurately capture the reality of Soviet inflation, even this does not suggest that inflation has been rapid. The application of the disequilibrium approach to the Soviet case does promise to shed light on the existence of consumer market disequilibrium there. However, this research is in its formative stage—as the controversy surrounding its application attests. Therefore, it would be unwise to draw firm conclusions from the evidence at this point.

In Chapter 10, we will return to the issue of Soviet inflation, both in the wholesale and the retail markets, and make some international comparisons.

THE SOVIET BANKING SYSTEM

The Soviet banking system plays an integral role in the planning process. Soviet banking is quite unlike its Western counterpart, for it is dominated by a single bank, *Gosbank*, which is a monopoly bank in its purest form. As a monopoly bank, *Gosbank* combines the functions of central and commercial banking, but owing to the absence of money and capital markets, some

---

[68] Barbara Katz, "The Disequilibrium Model in a Controlled Economy: Comment," *American Economic Review*, vol. 69, no. 4 (September 1979), 721–725; Machiko K. Nissanke, "The Disequilibrium Model in a Controlled Economy: Comment," *American Economic Review*, vol. 69, no. 4 (September 1979), 726–732; David H. Howard, "The Disequilibrium Model in a Controlled Economy: Reply and Further Results," *American Economic Review*, vol. 69, no. 4 (September 1979), 733–738.

[69] See, for example, Richard Portes, "The Control of Inflation: Lessons from East European Experience," *Economica*, vol. 44, no. 174 (May 1977), 109–130; Richard Portes and David Winter, "The Demand for Money and for Consumption Goods in Centrally Planned Economies," *The Review of Economics and Statistics*, vol. 60, no. 1, (February 1978), 8–18; Richard Portes and David Winter, "The Supply of Consumption Goods in Centrally Planned Economies," *Journal of Comparative Economics*, vol. 1, no. 4, (December 1977), 351–363.

traditional banking functions (open market operations, commercial paper transactions, etc.) are not performed by *Gosbank*.

The tremendous scope of *Gosbank's* organization is difficult to conceptualize: it has more than 150,000 employees and more than 300 main offices, about 3500 local branches, and 2000 collection offices. *Gosbank's* customers include approximately 250,000 enterprises, 40,000 collective farm accounts, and nearly one-half million government organizations. Since 1954, *Gosbank* has been independent of the Ministry of Finance, and its director has ministerial status in the government. Since 1963, the savings bank system (with over 70,000 branches) has been incorporated into *Gosbank's* operations. The only other banks in the Soviet Union are the specialized banks—the Investment Bank (*Stroibank*) and the Foreign Trade Bank (*Vneshtorgbank*). The former is concerned with the disbursing of funds budgeted for capital investment, and the latter handles international transactions; neither competes with *Gosbank*.[70]

Throughout its history, *Gosbank* has had two primary functions: first, to make short-term loans for the working capital needs of enterprises. In the process, it creates money (it is the only money-creating institution in the Soviet Union) by creating cash for consumers and workers as firms draw on cash accounts for wage payments and noncash accounts for interenterprise transactions. Its second purpose is to oversee enterprise plan fulfillment and to monitor payments to the population by acting as the center of all accounts in the Soviet Union. Let us now consider how these two objectives are pursued.

Each Soviet enterprise deals directly with a local *Gosbank* branch. It is dependent upon *Gosbank* for short-term credit to finance inventories and working capital. Its receipts are automatically deposited at *Gosbank*, and it draws cash for wage payments at the discretion of the branch bank. In addition, the portion of its own profits that the enterprise is allowed to retain (a factor that has increased in importance since the 1965 reforms) remains on deposit at, and under the supervision of, *Gosbank*. *Gosbank* is the sole legal grantor of short-term credit. Interfirm credit is forbidden, and a strict discipline on payments is enforced in interfirm transactions to prevent spontaneous interfirm lending. In addition, all transactions between firms involving funds in enterprise accounts are handled by, and are subject to, the supervision of *Gosbank* (with the exception of small payments).

As far as the control function of *Gosbank* is concerned, its supervision of enterprise accounts and its short-term lending operations are important.

---

[70] George Garvy, *Money, Banking and Credit in Eastern Europe* (New York: Federal Reserve Bank of New York, 1966); Paul Gekker, "The Banking System of the USSR," *Journal of the Institute of Bankers*, vol. 84, part 3, (June 1963), 189–197; Garvy, *Money, Financial Flows, and Credit*; Zwass, *Money, Banking, and Credit*.

As the single clearing agent for the economy and the sole source of short-term credit, *Gosbank* is in a unique position to monitor the activities of enterprises. In drawing up short-term credit plans and in controlling enterprise accounts, *Gosbank* plays a largely passive role in the planning process by providing the monetary resources required to implement the physical plan. In making short-term loans for working capital, *Gosbank* has tended to grant production credit for specific purposes: if a particular transaction is called for in the input plan, the firm is automatically granted credit for this specific purpose. Not only is credit granted for specific purposes, but all interfirm transactions are cleared by *Gosbank*, and *Gosbank* must receive evidence of the transaction—such as a lading bill—before the clearing operation is completed.[71] In this way, as the enterprise financial plan is the monetary counterpart of the physical plan, deviations from the physical plan will reveal themselves as deviations from the financial plan. This is a further extension of *ruble control*. Even if an enterprise builds up excess balances at *Gosbank*, this liquidity still does not represent a command over producer goods unless thay are specifically called for in the plan.[72]

As the social accounting center monitoring cash payments to the population, *Gosbank* plays a role in the macroeconomic planning described above. It provides financial authorities with data on disposable income—information that is vital in macroplanning. In case of a projected imbalance, *Gosbank* will act to limit the flow of wage payments to the population as much as possible, within the limits of the plan. This is accomplished primarily by restricting the convertibility of enterprise accounts into cash for wage payments and by permitting wage payments in excess of the planned wage bill only if the output target is overfulfilled.

The monopoly powers of *Gosbank* are seldom used to influence the flow of production. Instead, *Gosbank's* audit operations serve primarily to reveal to planning authorities deviations from planned tasks, which are then corrected by the planners. Throughout its history, *Gosbank* has tended to automatically meet the credit needs of the economy (as specified in the plan) instead of regulating the flow of money and credit on a discretionary basis in order to direct the level of economic activity.

THE SOVIET PRICE SYSTEM

In our discussion of Soviet central planning, it was noted that the planning hierarchy is responsible for the allocation and distribution of resources in the Soviet Union. One may rightly be puzzled over the role that prices play, insofar as they, not central planners, carry the primary allocative responsibilities in market economies.

[71] Reforms since 1965 have resulted in the granting of credit for more general purposes rather than restricting the use of credit for very specific purposes.
[72] Garvy, *Money, Banking and Credit in Eastern Europe*, pp. 122–136.

At this juncture, a warning set forth in the Introduction is worth re-stating: namely, one must avoid comparing the ideal form of one economic system with the real world form of another. This is especially true of prices, where the tendency is to contrast price formation in an abstract, competi-tive market system with the realities of price formation in the Soviet Union—a temptation we shall try to avoid.

In this section, we consider the Soviet price system. First, the actual system of industrial wholesale, retail, and agricultural price setting is dis-cussed. Second, the role that prices are supposed to play in the Soviet eco-nomic system—allocation, control, measurement, and income distribu-tion—is considered. Last, we provide an evaluation of the Soviet price system.

Price Setting in the Soviet Union

Most prices in the Soviet Union are fixed by central authorities, rather than by the interaction of supply and demand. Price setting responsibilities have at various times been shared by the Price Bureau of *Gosplan SSSR*, the Ministry of Trade, the Ministry of Finance, the Union-Republican Councils of Ministers, and various republican and *oblast'* authorities.[73] The most im-portant prices established by the forces of supply and demand have been the collective farm market prices. It is useful to discuss price setting in the Soviet Union in terms of four different types of prices, for the principles ob-served in each case are quite different: (1) industrial wholesale prices, (2) retail prices, (3) agricultural procurement prices, and (4) collective farm market prices.[74]

INDUSTRIAL WHOLESALE PRICES

Industrial wholesale prices perform less of an allocative function than other Soviet prices. Contrary to retail price setting, where an attempt is generally made to set market-clearing prices, industrial wholesale prices tend to serve primarily as accounting prices, used to add together heterogeneous inputs

[73] Philip Hanson, *The Consumer Sector in the Soviet Economy* (Evanston, Ill.: Northwestern University Press, 1968), pp. 175–176.

[74] For general treatments of Soviet pricing policies, the reader is referred to the following sources: Morris Bornstein, "Soviet Price Theory and Policy," in Morris Bornstein and Dan-iel Fusfeld, eds., *The Soviet Economy: A Book of Readings* (Homewood, Ill.: Irwin, 1970), pp. 106–137; Hanson, *The Consumer Sector*, chap. 8; Morris Bornstein, "The Soviet Price Reform Discussion," *Quarterly Journal of Economics*, vol. 78, no. 1 (February 1964), pp. 15–48; Bergson, *The Economics of Soviet Planning*, chap. 8; Morris Bornstein, "The Soviet Debate on Agricultural Prices and Procurement Reforms," *Soviet Studies*, vol. 21, no. 1 (July 1969), pp. 1–20; Morris Bornstein, "The Administration of the Soviet Price System," *Soviet Studies*, vol. 30, no. 4 (October 1978), pp. 466–490; Morris Bornstein, "Soviet Price Policy in the 1970s," in Joint Economic Committee, *Soviet Economy in a New Perspective* (Washington, D.C.: U.S. Government Printing Office, 1976), pp. 17–66.

and outputs. That industrial wholesale prices play no real allocative role should come as no surprise, in view of our earlier discussion of industrial supply planning.

At the wholesale level, there are two important types of prices. First, the *factory wholesale price* is the price at which the industrial enterprise sells its product to the wholesale trade network. Second, the *industry wholesale price* is the price at which goods are sold to buyers outside the industry. In the latter case, a turnover tax will likely be included (on the average, about 8 percent of the industry wholesale price in heavy industry).[75] In the former case, there is seldom a turnover tax. Although the rules of price setting have changed somewhat over time, generally speaking, this function has tended to remain centralized. Thus agencies in the planning hierarchy establish wholesale prices on the basis of *average branch cost* of production plus a small profit markup (generally 5–10 percent). Included in enterprise costs are wage payments, costs of intermediate materials, depreciation, insurance, and payments to overhead. Interest and rental charges are not normally included in costs, and depreciation charges do not include charges for obsolescence. While market prices in a competitive market system tend toward marginal costs, they are in the Soviet case average cost prices. Using average branch costs means that many enterprises will in fact take losses at the established prices because the cost figures are averages of low and high cost producers, and historically such has been the case. The consequences of such losses in the Soviet system have generally been small.

During the early years of planning, the prices of important industrial inputs were purposely kept low, and many industrial enterprises were operated under state subsidies. Since enterprise survival is not based on profits or losses, as in a market system, such losses are of little particular importance, since subsidies are granted almost automatically to enterprises to cover operating losses. In these cases, minimization of losses (which might be a short-run objective for a capitalist firm) becomes a long-run criterion of operation and price setting in the Soviet Union.

In the context of recent reform discussions about the role of profits in the Soviet Union, the important point is this: profit calculations have always existed in the Soviet schema; they simply have not been an important criterion of enterprise performance—at least not until 1965—and the presence or absence of profits has therefore not been the basis for action by Soviet planning authorities. A fundamental reason for this is the inability of pricing authorities to establish "fair" prices, under which the level of profits serves as a true indication of enterprise performance.

In some cases—especially the extractive industries, in which marked cost variations among producers occur—so-called accounting prices have

[75] Bornstein, "Soviet Price Theory and Policy," p. 110; *Narodnoe khoziaistvo SSSR v 1978 g.* [The National economy of the USSR in 1978], p. 141.

been used. Then producers in effect receive different prices (depending upon cost differences) while all buyers pay the same price, with the state providing the intermediate cushion. Thus, the low-cost producers are in effect paying a differential rent to the state.

In rare cases, attempts have been made by pricing authorities to adjust the prices of close substitutes for differences in "use value," the most notable cases being the pricing of fuel oil and coal, and nonferrous metals and ferrous metals. In both instances, it was determined that the "use values" of fuel oil and nonferrous metals were higher than those of coal and ferrous metals, respectively, therefore prices in excess of average branch costs were set for fuel oil and nonferrous metals (the difference between average branch costs and the wholesale prices being the turnover tax). Nevertheless, such instances are rare because generally it is difficult to distinguish among industrial commodities according to their "use values."

Further problems are created by the treatment of "new" products and of products bought and sold in Western markets.[76] If the labor theory of value is to be observed, "new" products produced by a new technology that results in labor savings should be priced relatively low. The enterprise director who therefore takes the risk of introducing new labor-saving technology faces the prospect of having what would have been increased profits passed on to the users of his product in the form of price reductions. The reader can understand that such a pricing formula would not be conducive to technological innovation, and Soviet pricing authorities have (without great success) sought ways to exempt such "new" products from the labor theory of value formula. Cases of large differentials between domestic wholesale prices and world market prices have also been troublesome to pricing authorities. In the case of imports, planners may have to pass on to the Soviet enterprise at a low domestic price equipment that has been purchased at a high price in the world market. In the case of exports (oil, for example), the product may sell for a much higher price in the world market than the producing enterprise receives at home. Because of these discrepancies, there has been an increased tendency in recent years to adjust Soviet domestic prices on the basis of movements in world prices.

A major problem of industrial price setting is that owing to the administrative complexities of price reform, industrial prices have seldom conformed to average branch costs. It has proven too difficult to change prices regularly along with costs. Instead, industrial prices have tended to remain rigid over long periods. As a result, general subsidies have often been re-

[76] The problems of pricing "new" products and the impact of world prices on Soviet prices are discussed in Joseph S. Berliner, *The Innovation Decision in Soviet Industry* (Cambridge, Mass.: MIT Press, 1976), part 2; Vladimir G. Treml, "Foreign Trade and the Soviet Economy: Changing Parameters and Interrelationships," in Egon Neuberger and Laura Tyson, eds., *Transmission and Response: The Impact of International Disturbances on the Soviet Union and Eastern Europe* (New York: Pergamon Press, 1980).

quired as the wholesale prices of many commodities gradually fell below rising costs. Industrial wholesale prices remained roughly constant between 1929 and 1936, despite rapidly rising wage costs, and by 1936 subsidies were the rule rather than the exception. A price reform in spring of 1936 sharply increased prices to cover costs, while in 1949 another large general price increase was required to eliminate subsidies. Despite the general rule that prices should cover costs, industrial prices remained virtually unchanged from the 1955 price reform to the 1966–1967 price reform despite changing wage costs and changing technology.[77] Since 1966–1967, there have been only modest official adjustments in industrial wholesale prices, and familiar complaints that the 1966–1967 prices did not reflect current costs were already being heard shortly after the reform was completed. The next general price reform is slated for 1982.

As in the case of retail prices, official Soviet industrial wholesale price indexes indicate a very modest degree of inflation throughout the postwar era, but there is reason to suspect that the official indexes suffer from the same deficiencies as the retail price indexes. Yet Western recalculations also fail to reveal significant inflation in the industrial wholesale price sphere.[78]

RETAIL PRICES

At the retail level, most prices are also formed by state planning authorities. They are basically designed to *clear the market* (to equate supply and demand), although this standard is often not met. This basic policy is in line with the Soviet policy of market distribution of consumer goods to preserve the incentive to work: for wage differentials to be meaningful, it is essential that they represent a differential command over consumer goods. In reality, retail prices have often tended to be somewhat below market clearing levels, and thus queues have often served in part as a rationing device.

The retail price is simply the industry wholesale price, plus the retail margin (and costs, where additions to the product are generated at the retail level), plus the turnover tax. Unlike Western sales taxes, where consumers are generally aware of the tax rate they are paying, the Soviet turnover tax is included in the retail price without the purchaser knowing how large it is. The level of the tax is a function of supply and demand conditions in the given market and of the prevailing industry wholesale price. Where the price without turnover tax is below the market clearing level, a tax sufficient to raise the retail price to the clearing level is added. In Figure 4, if

---

[77] Abram Bergson, Roman Bernaut, and Lynn Turgeon, "Basic Industrial Prices in the USSR, 1928–1950," The Rand Corporation, Research Memorandum RM-1522, August 1, 1955; *Narodnoe khoziaistvo SSSR v 1969 g.* [The national economy of the USSR in 1969], (Moscow: Statistika, 1970), p. 190.

[78] For Western recalculations of industrial prices, see Abraham Becker, "The Price Level of Soviet Machinery in the 1960s," *Soviet Studies,* vol. 26, no. 3 (July 1974), 363–380; James E. Steiner, *Inflation in Soviet Industry and Machine Building and Metalworking,* SRM78–10142, Office of Strategic Research, Washington, D.C., 1978.

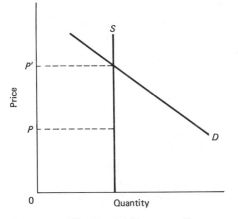

Figure 4   The Soviet Turnover Tax.

the industry wholesale price is *OP* and the resulting equilibrium price *OP'*, the turnover tax will be *PP'* (or slightly below if the price is set below clearing levels).[79] Thus the level of taxation is price determined rather than price determining.

At this point, the reader might well ask, what happens if the industry wholesale price is greater than *OP'?* Obviously, in such a case there will be no turnover tax, and unless there is a subsidy that permits the setting of the retail price *below* the industry wholesale price, surplus unsold stocks will result. Two comments are in order. First, throughout much of the plan period, a sellers' market has prevailed—obviating the subsidy problem at the retail level. Second, the matter of unsold stocks is more fundamental than simply a question of price setting. In particular, as economic development proceeds and greater attention is given to consumer goods in the Soviet Union, one would expect the sellers' market to subside. Such indeed has been the case—for example, in the clothing industry and more recently in the consumer durables area.[80] In these cases, there have been unsold stocks

[79] The supply schedule in Figure 4 is drawn to be perfectly inelastic. This is done under the assumption that the quantity of output is determined by the state plan, irrespective of price. This would apply largely to enterprises producing a single homogeneous product. For a multiproduct firm attempting to fulfill a gross output target, the supply schedule would likely be less than perfectly inelastic, that is, would have a positive slope.

[80] For example, sales of clothing and leather footwear grew at an annual rate of around 8 percent between 1968 and 1971. During the same period, clothing and footwear stocks grew at an annual rate of around 19 percent, largely because the types of goods produced failed to correspond to the wishes of the consumer. *Planovoe khoziaistvo* [The planned economy], no. 10 (1972), pp. 5–7. This growing selectivity also applies to consumer durables. For example, the "Baku" refrigerator proved to be of such low quality that Azerbaijan SSR consumers refused to buy it. The quick-witted manager in charge of its production then changed the name and appearance and released it as a new model. For an account of this, see *Sotsialisticheskaia industria* [Socialist industry], no. 14 (1969), p. 2.

in recent years, unlike the old sellers' market where producers could be unresponsive to consumers without losing sales. Thus the current problem is a combination of matching output to consumer tastes and setting appropriate prices. In recent years, the simultaneous existence of surpluses of some commodities and shortages of others have demonstrated the magnitude of this structural problem. There are also financial implications involved: if stocks are unsold, the state is not able to collect the turnover tax—an important source of revenue. A fundamental problem of economic reform revolves around this question: when the sellers' market subsides, how can producers be made responsive to the consumer if the price system fails to provide effective information concerning consumer wants? What was not so much a problem in the past may well be an increasing problem in the future.

If retail prices are to serve as mechanisms to transmit consumer preferences to producers, fundamental changes will be necessary. In this regard, the two-tiered price system shown in Figure 4 is an obstacle. Because retail prices are essentially demand determined and factory wholesale prices are cost determined, it may happen that *relative* retail prices diverge significantly from *relative* factory wholesale prices. Yet producers will be more responsive to the relative wholesale prices that they receive rather than to the retail prices paid by consumers, which reflect consumer preferences. Thus, the signal sent by the consumer in the form of a market-clearing retail price is not received by the producer, who is paid a different factory wholesale price. For some products, the two-tiered system is being gradually and automatically eliminated—namely, in food processing and in clothing and textiles. Their retail prices have been held roughly constant in recent years whereas their factory wholesale prices have risen along with rising wage and material costs, thus squeezing out the turnover tax.

Although there has been a continuing effort to vary prices on a zonal basis and to change them over time, this sort of variability has been highly restricted, given the magnitude of the administrative task involved. One can expect this problem to become more difficult in the future, as the economy grows more complex and the product range widens. Finally, it might be noted that the level of turnover tax (as one would expect) has varied widely among products and is as high as 80 percent of price on some products. The average light industry turnover tax in 1970 was 23 percent of wholesale price.[81] As we have seen, the revenue from this tax accounts for a substantial portion of state budgetary revenues, and therefore remains an important consideration in both financial planning and price setting.

AGRICULTURAL PROCUREMENT PRICES

Turning to agricultural pricing, we note that until 1958 (and again for grain after 1965), there existed a two-level pricing system for state purchases of

[81] *Narodnoe khoziaistvo SSSR v 1970 g.* [The national economy of the USSR in 1970], (Moscow: Statistika, 1971), p. 178.

agricultural products from collective farms. For compulsory deliveries, a low fixed price was paid, while for sales to the state above the compulsory level, a higher fixed price was established. Unlike pricing in the industrial sector, these prices until recently bore little relation to the production costs of the collective farm. There was no cost accounting whatsoever on collective farms until the mid-1950s, at which time initial cost studies revealed that for most collective farms, production costs were substantially above even the above-quota prices. In this manner, state pricing policy was placing the collective farms in a most difficult financial position by purchasing output at less than cost. At the same time, the state farms, operating essentially as industrial enterprises, were receiving subsidies from the state to compensate them for the low procurement prices and were not financing their own capital investment, as were the collective farms.

The two-level system was abandoned in 1958 and, although revived in 1965 for grain and then some other products, the differential between the below- and above-quota grain prices has been small relative to earlier differentials. Most notably, however, throughout the 1950s and 1960s purchase prices were raised substantially, so that for many products, average purchase prices covered production costs.[82] This latter development is in line with the agricultural policy of recent years; namely, that collective farm production should be "profitable" in the general sense of revenues covering costs. This policy remains in a state of active debate, since the problem of agricultural land rental charges remains unresolved. Finally, there has been a preliminary effort to revise agricultural purchase prices not only in terms of their levels but also in terms of their flexibility over time and in regions.

COLLECTIVE FARM MARKET PRICES

The most significant example of a true market price in the Soviet economy is the collective farm market price. In these markets, the collective farmers sell their produce (from private plots and after meeting state targets) at prices determined by demand and supply. While these prices fluctuate, they have generally been substantially above the level of state food prices, a phenomenon explained in part by quality differentials and by the maintenance of state prices at artificially low (below equilibrium) levels. For example, collective farm market prices were on the average more than double state retail prices in 1940. After considerable variation throughout the postwar period, collective farm market prices were 63 percent greater than state retail prices in 1972.[83] The collective farm markets have been especially important in large cities, where standard sources of supply—the state trade network for example—have been inadequate. How important are

[82] Thus a squeeze is put on food processing establishments, which are forced to make planned losses as the line is held on retail food prices.

[83] David W. Bronson and Barbara S. Severin, "Consumer Welfare," Joint Economic Committee, *Economic Performance and the Military Burden in the Soviet Union* (Washington, D.C.: U.S. Government Printing Office, 1970), p. 381.

these markets? Although measurement is rather complex, collective farm markets accounted for 13.9 percent of aggregate food sales in 1960 and for 8.8 percent in 1978. However, for certain products, these markets are of much greater significance. In 1957, for example, when the aggregate collective farm market share of food sales was 18.2 percent, they accounted for 63 percent of potato sales, 48 percent of egg sales, and 35 percent of meat sales. In 1970, they accounted for 67 percent, 54 percent, and 35 percent, respectively, of sales of these products.[84]

The Functions of Soviet Prices

Our discussion of the Soviet price system suggests that Soviet prices are formed quite differently from their market economy counterparts. However, to evaluate Soviet prices we must consider them in the context of the various roles that prices are supposed to play in the Soviet command economy. To judge the Soviet price system exclusively as an instrument for allocating resources (as is sometimes done) would be a mistake, for Soviet authorities have generally not intended it to be used as such. Instead, industrial supply and output planning are supposed to allocate resources, with prices playing other roles. Soviet prices can be considered in terms of four possible functions: (1) allocation, (2) control, (3) measurement, and (4) income distribution. A biased picture of Soviet prices would inevitably be drawn if one were to concentrate only on the first function.

ALLOCATION
In any economic system, prices can reflect relative scarcities on the basis of which economic decisions are made. As any standard economics textbook will explain, the profit maximizing producer will employ inputs so as to equate marginal factor outlays and marginal revenue products. The utility maximizing consumer will purchase goods and services so as to equate marginal utilities per dollar, and so on. In this manner, supply and demand schedules arise, and prices that reflect *relative scarcities* are determined. Under ideal conditions, such an arrangement will result in a maximum output produced at a minimum cost irrespective of the economic system and is, in this sense, optimal.[85] It is only necessary for the consumer and producer to be aware of relative prices to respond correctly in such a system; no planner is required to tell either how to behave.

[84] Data from *Narodnoe khoziaistvo SSSR v 1978 g.* [The national economy of the USSR in 1978], p. 433; Jerzy F. Karcz, "Quantitative Analysis of the Collective Farm Market," *American Economic Review,* vol. 54, no. 4, part 1 (June 1964), 315–333, see especially the discussion on page 315.
[85] See for example, F. Bator, "The Simple Analytics of Welfare Maximization," *American Economic Review,* vol. 47, no. 1 (February 1957), 22–59. Of course, this definition of optimality (called Pareto Optimality) does not take the optimality of the distribution of income into consideration.

Such price allocation is scarcely to be found in either planned or market economies in the real world, since imperfect competition, price controls, public goods, government regulations, and so on prevail almost everywhere.

What we have in the real world is a mixture of price allocation and administrative allocation. In the United States, for example, resource allocation is accomplished primarily through the price mechanism, though not necessarily in the optimal manner described above. In the Soviet Union, administrative planning bears the primary responsibility for allocation, although prices do play a limited role. Thus, while both systems have scarce resources to be marshaled toward the achievement of given (although different) goals—for which the price system might be utilized—the fundamental differences are, first, the extent to which prizes are utilized for these purposes and, second, the manner in which price formation is executed.

Soviet industrial wholesale prices, being centrally determined and based on the ideological definition of average branch costs, do not represent relative scarcities—as Soviet planners are well aware. This is one of the reasons why the administrative planning structure remains so much in charge of resource allocation and why there is so little price allocation in the Soviet Union. Like any generalization, there are exceptions. In the labor sector, differential wages are used largely to allocate labor. Also, retail prices are used largely to distribute *available* consumer goods among the population, although such prices generally play an unimportant role in the decision to produce such goods. The most striking feature of the Soviet economic system remains the minor role that prices play in the allocative process.

That Soviet prices generally fail to reflect relative scarcities is important despite their lack of use as allocative instruments, since Soviet prices do play other roles. This may sound rather abstract, but it is important. The Soviets have chosen administrative allocation over price allocation. Yet it is difficult to administratively allocate resources on a day-to-day basis without knowing relative scarcities, and it is even more difficult to relegate decision-making to lower echelons without scarcity prices. How to introduce a degree of price allocation into such a system and how to make the prices themselves more "rational" are recurrent themes in the reform discussions in the Soviet Union and Eastern Europe.

To determine what functions Soviet prices are designed to perform if not allocation, one must consider the control, measurement, and income distribution functions of prices in the Soviet Union.

CONTROL

The control function of prices is perhaps the most important in the Soviet context. Even in a centralized economy, some delegation of authority and responsibility is required, ranging from the central planning agencies to the enterprises. This necessitates a mechanism for control of subordinates. In market economies, the profit mechanism and variants thereof can act as a control device as well as an allocative device. In the Soviet case, however, profits have played virtually no allocative role in the industrial enterprise (at least prior to 1965). Nevertheless, many of the directives of higher planning authorities must be stated and verified in value terms—for example, rubles of steel output rather than tons. Thus the extensive use of value categories—the most famous being *valovaia produktsia* or *val* (gross production)—in Soviet planning means that prices have been used in a control function to evaluate and assess performance at all levels. However, value indicators have been largely used to indicate *deviations* from planned activities. Actual control has been carried out mainly through physical controls and directives.

MEASUREMENT

The measurement role of Soviet prices is also important and is similar to the control function in various aspects. Prices are required to measure the results of economic activity, especially if one's scope extends beyond individual products: the measurement of economic activity requires the aggregation of dissimilar products, and aggregation requires valuation. Without prices, one cannot determine at what rate the economy is growing, whether the capital-output ratio is rising or falling, and so on, and these are important variables in the planning process. For example, the total output of the economy ("gross material product" as the Soviets call it) must be valued to be measured, and in an important sense, the results of this measurement will depend upon the nature of the prices used. For example, the Soviets used 1926–1927 "constant" prices until the 1950s to measure Soviet total output. Over such a long period of time, these prices came to reflect prevailing prices and costs less and less, and eventually, because of their questionable economic significance, they were abandoned for a more up-to-date price base.

This illustration points out an important potential conflict among the various roles that a price system can play in the Soviet command economy, and this applies to both the control and the measurement functions. Control and measurement are more easily carried out when prices are not changed frequently. However, if prices remain unchanged, after awhile they will not reflect current cost relationships and therefore will be even less useful as a guide to allocation. Soviet authorities have been reluctant to change prices for two basic reasons. First, it is administratively difficult to gather the mass of wage and cost data required for a reform of prices. Second, it has proven a complex task to plan and evaluate when prices are in the process of change. In such a case, value targets must be stated in two variants—one for the old, the other for the new prices—and general confusion tends to reign until the new prices are firmly established.

INCOME DISTRIBUTION

Finally, Soviet prices play an important role in the distribution of income. In addition to the centrally determined wage scales that of course affect the distribution of income, pricing authorities can influence the distribution of real income through retail prices. In fact, some Soviet pricing policies can be partially explained in terms of their impact on income distribution. For example, low housing rents have been charged (despite a severe housing shortage) throughout the plan period, and below equilibrium prices have generally been charged in state and cooperative shops for basic food products.[86] In line with these price-setting policies has been the practice of charging nothing or only nominal prices for health care and education.[87]

One can view the Soviet policy of setting low prices for necessities such as basic food products and health and education as an attempt to improve the distribution of real income. It is noteworthy that the most direct method of equalizing the distribution of income—the leveling of wage income—has not been used on the grounds that this would weaken the incentive system.

The Reform of Soviet Prices

Most present-day Soviet economists would probably argue in favor of some sort of reform of the price system. There are however substantial differences among the reform advocates. These differences reflect more than simple differences over the mechanics of price formation—in large part they imply substantially different roles for prices. Let us consider three broad schools of thought among Soviet economists:

1. Prices should be based upon value as defined in an appropriate Marxian framework.
2. Prices should be based upon scarcity and should be derived as the logical result of an optimizing mathematical model.
3. Prices should reflect scarcity and should be determined by the forces of supply and demand.

1. For those who adhere to the Marxian framework, there are several schools of thought on price formation, the details of which need not detain

[86] Political factors have also been important in maintaining low prices on basic foods such as meat and dairy products. In the post-Stalin era, the Soviet leadership risked popular discontent and sometimes civil unrest when such prices were raised. An example of this was the 30 percent increase in meat and butter prices in 1962. On this see Hanson, *The Consumer Sector*, pp. 171–177.

[87] While charges for such services are generally very low, they do appear more substantial when considered as a portion of family income. Also, it is possible to contract some services—for example, those of a doctor—privately. In such cases, charges will be higher. For a discussion of this point, see Robert J. Osborn, *Soviet Social Policies: Welfare, Equality, and Community* (Homewood, Ill.: Dorsey Press, 1970), pp. 89–94.

us here.[88] The question revolves around the law of value and its operation in a socialist society. While Stalin's view of a restricted role for the law of value in socialist societies left little room for discussion during the 1930s, such has not been the case in the post-Stalin era. In general, Soviet economists define value as the sum of labor expenditure (v), capital used in the productive process (c), and surplus product (s) as in the traditional Marxian formula:[89]

$$Value = c + v + s$$

In terms of traditional Marxian theory, the principles of price formation are clear. The problem arises however in the use of this formula as a practical guide to price setting. If price is to equal value, then for each commodity it is necessary that price equal $c + v + s$. How is each component to be determined? The problem here is basically one of circularity. Even if we assume that c and v are known, s will not be known, since surplus product in the socialist economy would be indicated by gross national product less the aggregate wages bill. To derive gross national product, however, valuation is involved. If we assume such a valuation and derive surplus product for the entire economy, how will it be distributed among individual commodities? Those Soviet economists adhering to this general line of price formation have differed as to how this distribution should take place; some have suggested that it should be distributed in proportion to c, others have said in proportion to v, and some have argued for proportionality to $c + v$.

These formula are all *cost* oriented and neglect demand as an element of the creation of value. However, those advocating this sort of price formation are not arguing in favor of an allocative role for prices and thus are willing to neglect demand, for allocation would generally remain the responsibility of the central planning agencies. Another problem for those pursuing the Marxian framework concerns the measurement of costs. According to Marx, labor (either in its direct or congealed form) is the sole source of value; therefore the elements that should enter into costs are only those that require or have required labor expenditures: wages, intermediate materials, overhead, and depreciation (the amount of previously expended labor being used up in the production process with the wear and tear on capital). There is no room for a rental charge on capital or land. In addition, it is difficult to include a charge for obsolescence.[90]

[88] In addition to sources already cited, see Robert W. Campbell, "Marx, Kantrovich and Novozhilov: Stoimost' Versus Reality," *Slavic Review*, vol. 20, no. 3 (October 1961), 402–418.

[89] For a discussion of the Marxian position, see, for example, Alexander Balinky, *Marx's Economics* (Lexington, Mass.: Heath, 1970).

[90] There are numerous representatives of this cost-oriented approach to be found largely among the ranks of planners. For examples, see V. Batyrev, "Voprosy teorii stoimosti pri sotsializme" [Question of the theory of value under socialism], *Voprosy ekonomiki* [Problems of economics], no. 2 (February 1967), 36–47; and A. Gusarev, "Tsena-Instrument

The 1966–1967 reform accepted the principle that profits should be related to the value of assets, defined as fixed and working capital, though as Morris Bornstein has pointed out, no single (uniform) profit rate was established.[91]

2. The scarcity approach to pricing is of a fundamentally different nature. The main advocates of scarcity type pricing are the mathematical economists, the most notable of whom are V. S. Nemchinov, V. V. Novozhilov, and L. V. Kantorovich, the latter being one of the originators of linear programming techniques in 1938.[92] According to a representative scheme proposed by Kantorovich, a set of relative prices would be generated by the dual of a linear programming model in which the final bill of goods (determined by the state, presumably) would be produced with a cost minimizing combination of inputs with existing factor endowments and technology.[93] There are several variants of this basic approach. Their unifying feature is the maximization of an objective function (often the "consumption fund" of the economy), with the scarce factors of production (which are fixed in the short-run) acting as the principal constraints. Factor prices are then computed as "shadow prices" (the ratio of the change in the value of the objective function to the change in the factor).[94] In theory, such a set of prices would parallel those generated in a competitive market model (they would be scarcity prices) and would therefore be capable of performing an allocative role in the economy. While there are tremendous practical problems in the generation and continuing utilization of such a set of prices, Soviet criticism of this approach has more typically been on the basis of its apparently non-Marxian character (its reliance on bourgeois theories of marginal utility).[95]

plana" [Prices-Instrument of the plan], *Ekonomicheskaia gazeta* [The economic gazette], no. 40 (October 1969), 5–6.

[91] Morris Bornstein, "Soviet Price Policy in the 1970s," p. 20.

[92] These three mathematical economists were awarded the coveted Lenin Prize in 1965. Kantorovich's original contribution to linear programming techniques can be found in a monograph entitled *Matematicheskie metody organizatsii i planirovaniia proizvodstva* (Leningrad, 1939), translated as "Mathematical Methods of Organizing and Planning Production," *Management Science*, vol. 4, no. 4 (July 1960), 366–422.

[93] This schema can be found in L. V. Kantorovich, *Ekonomicheskii raschet nailucheskogo ispol'zovania resursov* (Moscow, 1959). This volume was translated by P. K. Knightsfield, and under the editorship of G. Morton published as *The Best Use of Economic Resources* (Cambridge, Mass.: Harvard University Press, 1965).

[94] One can find numerous examples of this approach in current Soviet economic literature. See for example the translation of the N. Fedorenko and S. Shatalin survey, "The Problem of Optimal Planning of the Socialist Economy," *Problems of Economics: A Journal of Translations*, vol. 7, no. 7 (November 1968), 3–29.

[95] Batyrev, "Voprosy teorii stoimosti," 36–37. For an ideological defense, Soviet mathematical economists couch their models in appropriate Marxian terminology. See Aron Katsenelinboigen, *Studies in Soviet Economic Planning* (White Plains, N.Y.: M. E. Sharpe, 1978), chap. 4.

From a theoretical standpoint, the Soviet mathematical school has demonstrated that such a system of price formation would lead to optimization, since these prices do represent relative scarcities. Apart from the ideological problems, however, the data requirements, necessary computational facilities, and the need for spatial and temporal price flexibility would create significant problems if prices were actually set in this manner. Nevertheless, as a direction of change, the notion of scarcity prices derived from mathematical models may be of great importance to future changes in the Soviet economy.

3. The proponents of the third approach argue that prices should be determined by the forces of supply and demand and that prices should be allowed to fluctuate without central direction as socialist industrial enterprises engage in microeconomic competition among themselves for supplies. Thus the market (presumably a viable wholesale market for producer goods) would determine prices, not a mathematical model as proposed by the mathematical school. The two approaches are similar, however, in that they both propose that prices should reflect scarcity.[96]

An economic system is a mechanism for the allocation of resources to achieve socially desired ends. In any such system, prices play an important role, and accordingly it is essential that these prices be formulated in such a manner that they do in fact serve the ends to which they are devoted. Indeed, one can argue that the price system as a means of transmitting information becomes increasingly important as the economic system grows and becomes more complex. If this is the case, we can expect the discussion of price formation to continue in the future.

An Evaluation of Soviet Prices

Thus far we have described the operation and functions of the Soviet price system. We now turn to a partial evaluation of Soviet pricing. Is the Soviet price system really unsatisfactory and "irrational," as many Western observers claim?[97] It is, of course, difficult to answer this question because the response depends to a great extent upon the criteria used to judge Soviet prices. If one accepts the criterion that "good" prices should smoothly allocate scarce resources among competing goals by equating supply and demand, then the Soviet price system will show up poorly. If, on the other hand, one judges the price system on the basis of how well it leads to the

---

[96] The Soviets refer to this approach as "market socialism" and attribute such views to less orthodox East bloc (primarily Czech) economists. Judging from the vehemence of Soviet attacks on market socialism, it is apparent that such unorthodox views are shared by some Soviet economists. For a fairly typical critique of market socialism, see A. Eremin, "On the Concept of 'Market Socialism,'" *Problems of Economics: A Journal of Translations*, vol. 13, no. 4 (August 1970), 3–20.

[97] For this view, see Bergson, *The Economics of Soviet Planning*, pp. 166–170.

accomplishment of goals desired by leaders (say, Soviet planners), then the judgment may be quite different. While we cannot hope to provide conclusive answers to the relative "goodness" of Soviet prices, some plausible generalizations are in order.

First, it is probably true that many Western economists tend to idealize the price system as it is supposed to operate in perfectly competitive markets. However, the conditions of perfect competition are rarely met in the real world. What is worse, the competitive pricing model tells us little about the relative merits of market pricing when the conditions of perfect competition are only partially met.[98] In addition, there are cases where even the perfectly competitive model fails to provide a "good" system of prices—the cases of public goods, such as national defense and highways, and externalities (air and water pollution, for example). Thus it is difficult to evaluate the "goodness" or "badness" of Soviet prices in *relative* terms, for what are being compared are imperfect real-world alternatives.[99]

Second, we must recognize that when one judges the Soviet price system in absolute terms, it has become apparent to both Soviet and Western observers that the Soviet price system does not perform its postulated functions especially well. This dissatisfaction among observers on both sides is reflected in the long-standing Western criticisms of the lack of scarcity pricing and price inflexibility, and in the Soviet's own criticisms along these same lines. In particular, the conflict between the price flexibility required for scarcity pricing and smooth distribution of goods, and the price inflexibility required for effective control and measurement has led to numerous problems. The absence of an interest charge on capital (prior to 1965) caused managers to treat capital as a free good, with ensuing capital wastage. For many years, natural gas was allowed to disappear into the air as a by-product of oil production. There are many more examples. Perhaps most disturbing have been the strict limitations imposed by the inflexible Soviet price system on the devolution of decision-making through decentralization.

Third, to truly evaluate Soviet prices, one must determine to what extent the Soviet price system has promoted or retarded the attainment of the long-run economic, military, and political goals of the Soviet leadership. For example, has the Soviet price system furthered the Soviet economic

[98] The standard reference here is R. G. Lipsey and K. Lancaster, "The General Theory of Second Best," *Review of Economic Studies*, vol. 24, no. 63 (1956), 11–32.

[99] On this point, Philip Hanson writes in *The Consumer Sector:*

Nowadays the Soviet press provides lists of defects in the Soviet economic system ready-made for Western commentators. The description that has been given of the difficulties in the working of feedbacks from demand to supply is a compilation of the grumbles that are aired by Soviet reform-mongers. So what? Anyone who made a study of . . . the distributive trade press in the U.K. could make a long list of faults in British arrangements . . . (p. 193).

goal of rapid industrialization? In this regard, we encounter a controversy that will be discussed in Part Three—namely, are the traditional microeconomic concepts of economic rationality—scarcity prices, cost minimization, internal rates of return, etc.—short-run static concepts that have little meaning during the course of economic development? In other words, is economic development perhaps to be promoted by not observing static rules of efficiency as dictated by current scarcity prices? Soviet planners' refusal to allow the price system to play an important role in the resource allocation process and their relegation of prices primarily to control, measurement, and income distribution roles may be viewed in this light as entirely rational.

THE SECOND ECONOMY OF THE SOVIET UNION

The major "unplanned" component discussed to this point has been the private plot of the farm population. State regulations govern (or seek to govern) the size of such plots and the proportion of work time devoted to private farming, but such activity is legal according to Soviet law—as is the practice of selling private plot produce at market prices. Yet hidden from view is a broad range of private, unplanned, and generally illegal economic activities, called the "second economy" or "counter economy" by students of this phenomenon.

The second economy has been analyzed extensively by Gregory Grossman, Vladimir Treml, Dimitri Simes, and Aron Katsenelinboigen.[100] It consists of a number of market-type activities of varying degrees of legality, all involving "unplanned" exchange. According to Grossman, second economy activities must fulfill at least one of the two following tests: (1) the activity is for private gain; (2) the activity knowingly contravenes existing law.

Examples of secondary economy activities are easily found in the press, court reports, and émigré interviews. A physician or dentist may treat private patients for higher fees. A salesperson may set aside high-quality merchandise for customers who offer large tips (bribes). A manager of a manufacturing firm sets aside the highest quality production for sale to the black market. A collective farmer may divert collective farm land and supplies to

[100] See Katsenelinboigen, "Coloured Markets in the Soviet Union," *op. cit.;* Dimitri K. Simes, "The Soviet Parallel Market," *Economic Aspects of Life in the USSR* (Brussels: NATO Directorate of Economic Affairs, 1975), pp. 91–100; Gregory Grossman, "The 'Second Economy' of the USSR," *Problems of Communism*, vol. 26 (September–October 1977), 25–40; Gregory Grossman, "Notes on the Illegal Private Economy and Corruption," in Joint Economic Committee, *Soviet Economy in a Time of Change* (Washington, D.C.: U.S. Government Printing Office, 1979), vol. 1, pp. 834–855; and Vladimir G. Treml, "Production and Consumption of Alcoholic Beverages in the USSR: A Statistical Study," *Journal of Studies on Alcohol*, vol. 36 (March 1975), 285–320; Gertrude E. Schroeder and Rush Greenslade, "On the Measurement of the Second Economy in the USSR," *ACES Bulletin*, vol. 21, no. 1 (Spring 1979), 3–22.

his private plot ("theft of socialist property"). Black marketeers in port cities deal in contraband merchandise. Owners of private cars transport second economy merchandise. In many cases, official and second economy transactions are intertwined. A manager may divert some production into second economy transactions to raise cash to purchase unofficially supplies needed to meet the plan. The official activities of an entire enterprise may serve as a front for a prospering second economy undertaking. Workers may engage in private production on the job (repairing private automobiles in state garages). Private construction teams may build structures for private individuals. Information sellers (apartment brokers) may provide information on the availability of apartments or imported goods. The list could be expanded indefinitely. An important area of second economy activity is bribery and corruption—influence buying, purchasing favors that only state and party officials can provide.

According to available accounts, second economy activities are concentrated in collective farms and in the transportation network. Apparently, the supervision of collective farms is more lax, and they therefore serve as better fronts for the second economy. Transportation enterprises are also critical to the second economy, for second economy merchandise must be transported somehow. The increase in private ownership of automobiles has apparently enhanced the operation of the second economy and has led to a growing market in stolen gasoline.

We cannot establish how important the second economy is, say, as a percent of retail sales or GNP, but those who have studied the second economy argue that it is quite significant. Exact estimation of the importance of the second economy will never be possible, for measurement of an illegal activity is a virtually impossible task. To take one isolated example where estimates are available: in 1970, one-fourth of all alcohol consumed in the Soviet Union was produced and supplied through the second economy. In 1972, 500 million liters of stolen gasoline is estimated to have been sold by the second economy. The most reliable information on the scope of the second economy comes from the émigré surveys, conducted by Gur Ofer and Aaron Vinokur in Israel, which show that earnings derived from an activity other than that in the main place of employment account for some 10 percent of earnings.[101] The magnitude of the second economy would come as no surprise, for the official planning system has assigned low priority to "nonessential" services (beauty shops, appliance repairs, and so on), and expenditures on these items typically rise with rising income. Moreover, the official supply system has failed to offer the Soviet consumer sufficient supplies of quality merchandise, and the second economy would serve as a

[101] Gur Ofer and Aaron Vinokur, *Family Budget Survey of Soviet Immigrants in the Soviet Union* (Jerusalem: Soviet and East European Research Center, Hebrew University, June 1977), table 14.

means of channeling available quality merchandise to the highest bidder. Moreover, the Soviet taxation system imposes almost confiscatory marginal tax rates on professionals who are legally licensed to carry out private professional activity. As in many Western countries, the tax system of the Soviet Union drives professionals into the second economy. The immense power over resources placed in the hands of officials is another reason for the existence of the second economy. Rather than the market, officials allocate many of the scarce commodities treasured by the Soviet consumer— automobiles and auto licenses, apartments, building permits, and so on. This situation opens up the possibility of bribery and corruption, much as it does in the West.

The second economy has its advantages and disadvantages as far as the planners are concerned. It helps to preserve incentives because higher wages and bonus payments can be spent in the second economy. Moreover, the second economy serves to reduce inflationary pressures in the official economy. On the negative side, the second economy diverts participants in the economy from planned tasks and loosens planners' control over the economy. The Soviets do not publish data on currency in circulation, and it is likely that second economy transactions are conducted largely in cash. For this reason, studies of savings based on savings account deposits (see previous section) may be biased. The brisk market in jewelry and precious metals also provides the participants in the second economy with a means of storing value.

SELECTED BIBLIOGRAPHY

Political Institutions and Control of the Economy

Jerry F. Hough and Merle Fainsod, *How the Soviet Union Is Governed* (Cambridge, Mass.: Harvard University Press, 1979).
Alec Nove, *The Soviet Economic System* (London: Allen & Unwin, 1977).
Leonard Shapiro, *The Government and Politics of the Soviet Union* (Essex: Hutchison Publishing Group, 1978).

Supply and Output Planning

Abram Bergson, *The Economics of Soviet Planning* (New Haven, Conn.: Yale University Press, 1964), chap. 7.
Philippe Bernard, *Planning in the Soviet Union* (Oxford: Pergamon Press, 1966).
Mikhail Bor, *Aims and Methods of Soviet Planning* (New York: International Publishers, 1967).
R. W. Davies, "Planning a Mature Economy," *Economics of Planning*, vol. 6, no. 2 (1966), 138–153.
R. W. Davies, "Soviet Planning for Rapid Industrialization," *Economics of Planning*, vol. 6, no. 1 (1966), 53–67.
Michael Ellman, "The Consistency of Soviet Plans," *Scottish Journal of Political Economy*, vol. 16, no. 1 (February 1969), 50–74.

Michael Ellman, *Socialist Planning* (Cambridge: Cambridge University Press, 1979).

Herbert Levine, "The Centralized Planning of Supply in Soviet Industry," *Comparisons of the United States and Soviet Economies* (Washington, D.C.: U.S. Government Printing Office, 1959).

Michael Manove, "A Model of Soviet-Type Economic Planning," *American Economic Review*, vol. 61, no. 3, part 1 (June 1971), 390–406.

Jan Marczewski, *Crisis in Socialist Planning, Eastern Europe and the USSR* (New York: Praeger, 1974).

John Michael Montias, "Planning with Material Balances in Soviet-Type Economies," *American Economic Review*, vol. 49, no. 5 (December 1959), 963–985.

Gertrude E. Schroeder, "Recent Developments in Soviet Planning and Managerial Incentives," in Joint Economic Committee, *Soviet Economic Prospects for the Seventies* (Washington, D.C.: U.S. Government Printing Office, 1973), pp. 11–38.

Gertrude E. Schroeder, "The 'Reform' of the Supply System in Soviet Industry," *Soviet Studies*, vol. 24, no. 1 (July 1972), 97–119.

Gertrude E. Schroeder, "The Soviet Economy on a Treadmill of 'Reforms,' " in Joint Economic Committee, *Soviet Economy in a Time of Change*, (Washington, D.C.: U.S. Government Printing Office, 1979), vol. 1, pp. 312–340.

Eugene Zaleski, *Stalinist Planning for Economic Growth* (Chapel Hill: University of North Carolina Press, 1980).

The Soviet Price System

Alan Abouchar, ed., *The Socialist Price Mechanism* (Durham, N.C.: Duke University Press, 1977).

Abraham Becker, "The Price Level of Soviet Machinery in the 1960s," *Soviet Studies*, vol. 26, no. 3 (July 1974), 363–380.

Abram Bergson, *The Economics of Soviet Planning* (New Haven, Conn.: Yale University Press, 1964), chap. 8.

Morris Bornstein, "The Administration of the Soviet Price System," *Soviet Studies*, vol. 30, no. 4 (October 1978), 466–490.

Morris Bornstein, "The 1963 Soviet Industrial Price Revision," *Soviet Studies*, vol. 15, no. 1 (July 1963), pp. 43–52.

Morris Bornstein, "The Soviet Debate on Agricultural Prices and Procurement Reforms," *Soviet Studies*, vol. 21, no. 1 (July 1969), 1–20.

Morris Bornstein, "Soviet Price Policy in the 1970s," in Joint Economic Committee, *Soviet Economy in a New Perspective* (Washington, D.C.: U.S. Government Printing Office, 1976), 17–66.

Morris Bornstein, "The Soviet Price Reform Discussion," *Quarterly Journal of Economics*, vol. 78, no. 1 (February 1964), 15–48.

Morris Bornstein, "Soviet Price Theory and Policy," in M. Bornstein and D. Fusfeld, eds., *The Soviet Economy*, 3rd ed. (Homewood, Ill.: Irwin, 1970), pp. 106–137.

Robert W. Campbell, "Marx, Kantrovich and Novozhilov: Stoimost' Versus Reality," *Slavic Review*, vol. 20, no. 3 (October 1961), 402–418.

Philip Hanson, *The Consumer Sector in the Soviet Economy* (Evanston, Ill.: Northwestern University Press, 1968), chaps. 7 and 8.

David H. Howard, "The Disequilibrium Model in a Controlled Economy: An Empirical Test of the Barro-Grossman Model," *American Economic Review*, vol. 66, no. 5 (December 1966), 871–879.

Raymond Hutchings, "The Origins of the Soviet Industrial Price System," *Soviet Studies*, vol. 13, no. 1 (July 1961), 1–22.

Alec Nove, *The Soviet Economic System* (London: Allen & Unwin, 1977), chaps. 2 and 3.

Joyce Pickersgill, "Soviet Household Saving Behavior," *The Review of Economics and Statistics*, vol. 58, no. 2 (May 1976), 139–147.

Gertrude E. Schroeder, "The 1966–67 Soviet Industrial Price Reform: A Study in Complications," *Soviet Studies*, vol. 20, no. 4 (April 1969), 462–477.

Public Finance and Financial Planning in the Soviet Union

V. P. Diachenko, *Istoriia finansov SSSR* [History of USSR finance] (Moscow: Nauka, 1978).

George Garvy, *Money, Financial Flows, and Credit in the Soviet Union* (Cambridge, Mass.: Ballinger, 1977).

Franklyn D. Holzman, "Financing Soviet Economic Development," in Moses Abramovitz, ed., *Capital Formation and Economic Growth* (Princeton, N.J.: Princeton University Press, 1955), pp. 229–287.

Franklyn D. Holzman, "Soviet Inflationary Pressures, 1928–1957: Causes and Cures," *Quarterly Journal of Economics*, vol. 74, no. 2 (May 1960), 167–188.

Franklyn D. Holzman, *Soviet Taxation: The Fiscal and Monetary Problems of a Planned Economy* (Cambridge, Mass.: Harvard University Press, 1955).

M. Yves Laulan, ed., *Banking, Money and Credit in the Soviet Union and Eastern Europe* (Brussels: NATO Directorate of Economic Affairs, 1975).

Frederic L. Pryor, *Public Expenditures in Communist and Capitalist Nations* (Homewood, Ill.: Irwin, 1968).

Adam Zwass, *Money, Banking, and Credit in the Soviet Union and Eastern Europe* (White Plains, N.Y.: M. E. Sharpe, 1979).

Second Economy in the Soviet Union

Gregory Grossman, "Notes on the Illegal Private Economy and Corruption," in Joint Economic Committee, *Soviet Economy in a Time of Change* (Washington, D.C.: U.S. Government Printing Office, 1976), pp. 834–855.

Gregory Grossman, "The 'Second Economy' of the USSR," *Problems of Communism*, vol. 26 (September–October 1977), 25–40.

Aron Katsenelinboigen, "Coloured Markets in the Soviet Union," *Soviet Studies*, vol. 29, no. 1 (January 1977), pp. 62–85.

Dimitri K. Simes, "The Soviet Parallel Market," *Economic Aspects of Life in the USSR* (Brussels: NATO Directorate of Economic Affairs, 1975), pp. 91–100.

Gur Oter and Aaron Vinokur, *Family Budget Survey of Soviet Immigrants in the Soviet Union*, (Jerusalem: Soviet and East European Research Center, Hebrew University, June 1977).

Chapter 6

How Resources Are Allocated in the Soviet Union—The Soviet Manager, Labor, and Capital

THE SOVIET MANAGER

In market economies there is much "automaticity" to the managerial system: in attempting to maximize profits (or some variant thereof), the manager will automatically respond to changing prices and technology without the prompting of central directives. In the Soviet Union, where such automaticity has not generally existed, the question may be asked: How can one construct a managerial environment that achieves desired social ends (as formulated by party and state authorities)?

The attention that we devote to the managerial structure of the Soviet command economy is to be justified on two grounds, and indeed, it is these two grounds that largely distinguish the Soviet planned system from market-oriented systems.

First, managers in a market system tend to take their instructions from the signals of the market—generally in the form of price information—upon which they base their production and distribution decisions (plans). Under Soviet planning, such instructions derive directly from the *plan*. A plan is in fact a set of instructions telling a manager how to behave—often irrespective of market signals. Hence our focus upon the variables that tell the manager what the enterprise goals are (as stated in the plan) and how the manager's behavior is oriented by the incentive system toward the achievement of those goals.

Second, in market economies, capacity expansion of the enterprise (capital investment) is largely a function of planning within the firm in response to market phenomena (discount rates, anticipated returns, risk, etc.). In the Soviet planned system, capacity changes are decided by plan directives, emanating from agencies outside of the firm. At the same time, the past performance of the enterprise and the external authorities' appraisal of its future capabilities are the basis of plan formation, thus making information from the firm important in both the formulation and execution stages of planning.

In this chapter, we deal explicitly with the Soviet managerial system—the parametric framework in which the manager operates, the managerial personnel, and the managers' responses to enterprise goals under the established system of incentive and behavioral constraints.

Enterprise Planning and the Soviet Manager

The operation of the Soviet industrial enterprise is governed in most every respect by the *techpromfinplan* (technical-industrial-financial plan). This plan is the annual (semiannual, quarterly, monthly) subplan of long-term (five- to seven-year) "perspective" plans (although we have noted the link between the two is often difficult to find) and is itself composed of subplans, each comprising a number of appropriate indicators or targets pertaining to the operation of the enterprise. In its broadest sense, the *techpromfinplan* sets forth the social goals—in the Soviet case, planners' preferences—that the enterprise is to implement. In a narrow sense, the *techpromfinplan* specifies output levels (in quantity and value terms), output assortment, labor and other inputs, productivity indexes, profit norms, and so on, which the enterprise is expected to observe.

The most important component of the *techpromfinplan* has been the production plan. Based upon the capacity of the enterprise (normally defined as past performance plus some increment to incorporate planned capacity expansion), expected resource utilization, and estimated productivity increases, the production plan has typically specified the ruble value of output (*valovaia produktsia*), the commodity assortment, and the delivery schedule of this output.[1]

In addition to the production plan, the *techpromfinplan* includes a number of other component plans, the most important of which are the financial plan (the monetary expression of the physical plan), the plan of material and technical supply, the delivery plan, the plan of plant and equipment utilization, the plan of labor and wages, and finally, indexes of labor productivity.

In the above plans, state goals and the means for their achievement are elaborated, and within the plan framework, the enterprise is exhorted by the state and party to perform all these tasks at the best possible levels.

One might conclude from this formal version of Soviet planning that

[1] Enterprises producing homogeneous products often have their output targets stated in physical units rather than value terms—such as tons of cement, square meters of textiles, or tons of plastic—with a specified assortment. It is here that the reform of 1965 sought to make a substantial impact by moving away from gross output toward sales as an important success indicator.

the Soviet managers' freedom to make decisions is severely restricted. The *techpromfinplan* governs their choice of enterprise inputs and outputs, and they are morally and legally obligated to implement the plan, with bonuses geared to motivate them in this direction. Looking beneath the surface, however, one unearths a significant area of managerial flexibility. Due in large part to the inability of central organs to specify and control all details of local enterprise operation, Soviet managers do have a sphere of decision-making freedom. To understand management in the Soviet context, one must first understand the nature of this flexibility; second, the manner in which it is exercised; and third, its consequences.

Plan Execution by the Soviet Manager

Both formally and informally, one of the most important functions of the factory manager is the translation of state goals into daily tasks. If one considers the enterprise plan, it is readily apparent that the Soviet manager is confronted with both multiple targets (outputs, cost reduction, innovation, deliveries, etc.) and multiple constraints. Yet the enterprise plan fails to specify formally either the nature of the maximand (enterprise goal) or, for that matter, the nature of the trade-offs among possibly competing goals. The plan does not tell the manager which goals are more important than others, except informally—through party campaigns, bonuses, word of mouth, and other means. The manager is thus faced with a dilemma. If all plan indicators cannot be simultaneously and harmoniously achieved,[2] which ones should be met and which sacrificed and to what degree in each case?[3] This question is resolved in the capitalist enterprise by the use of

[2] A common conflict under conditions of ambitious output targets occurs between profit maximization and output target fulfillment. The graph below illustrates how this conflict may arise. The enterprise's output target is Q', which it produces at an average cost above the price that it receives (and thus makes losses denoted by the area of the loss rectangle). To maximize enterprise profits, the enterprise would restrict its output to Q (and fail to fulfill its output target) but would maximize profits denoted by the profit rectangle.

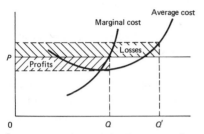

[3] For a discussion of the "success indicator" problem in Soviet industry, see Alec Nove, "The Problem of Success Indicators in Soviet Industry," in *Economic Rationality and Soviet Politics* (New York: Praeger, 1964), pp. 83–98.

profit as an enterprise goal and a set of scarcity prices such that the trade-offs among various objectives are readily apparent.

While profits have always formally been a part of the economic calculus of the Soviet enterprise, their maximization has generally not been an important enterprise goal either in theory or practice.[4] In fact, quite apart from the meaning of profit in the light of Soviet prices, profits have tended to be of minimal importance in the operation of an enterprise. What then replaces profits in the Soviet managerial calculus? In essence, the plan, the formal and informal constraints, and the managerial incentive structure have made *gross output*—and more recently, refinements such as "realized" gross output, in other words, sales—the most important indicator of enterprise performance. In short, managers have been rewarded primarily for the achievement of output targets, and accordingly, those targets not directly related to output have tended to be of secondary importance.

A frequent misconception should be cleared up at this point. Soviet enterprises do operate on an independent "economic accounting" (*khozraschet*) system, which is often taken to mean that Soviet enterprises operate to maximize profits. The *khozraschet*, or official managerial accounting system of the Soviet industrial enterprise, cannot, however, be understood to imply that profit and other monetary variables are of prime importance. Enterprise profits are calculated, but the *khozraschet* system simply guarantees that enterprises have financial relations with external organs such as *Gosbank*, and further, that their operations are elaborated and evaluated in terms of value indicators using official prices. The minimal practical significance of *khozraschet* to the Soviet economy must be understood, for in the first instance, the structure of Soviet prices makes such calculations suspect, and in the second, the result of such value calculations have had little impact upon the present and future direction of enterprise activities. Future production targets are generally not a function of current profits. This aspect of the Soviet managerial system should be emphasized, in view of the crucial role of profits in market economies.

The Success Indicator Problem

The choice of gross output instead of profits as the crucial "success indicator" of managerial performance generates a series of problems. In most cases, maximands relating to output (whether in value or quantity terms) cannot be defined in perfect detail by central authorities, and in the Soviet case in particular, gross production "success indicators" have led to considerable managerial freedom and often distortion. Where the weight of the

---

[4] The enhanced role of profits in the Soviet enterprise after 1965 as a consequence of the September 1965 economic reform will be discussed in Chapter 9. The reform theoretically increased the importance of two performance indicators: "realized" output (sales) and enterprise profits.

output has been the success indicator in the production of castings, for example, castings tend to be made heavier than necessary, thus wasting scarce inputs. Where size has been the indicator, in the production of cloth, for example, managers favor large sizes and largely ignore assortment goals. These distortions are only a part, however, of what has been described as the problem of success indicators in Soviet industry.[5]

We noted that the planners estimate plant capacity—a crucial aspect of plan formulation—as a direct function of past performance plus allowances for productivity improvements. At the enterprise level, however, managers face a dilemma: if they significantly overfulfill output targets in the current year, they may receive a sizable bonus, but in subsequent years, targets will be substantially increased (the "ratchet effect"), thereby diminishing the likelihood of bonus earnings in the immediate future. As a result, managers will tend to be cautious about overfulfilling plan targets even if overfulfillment is well within their grasp. Another problem arises from the stress upon the expansion of output in combination with a bonus system that reinforces this narrow production-oriented conception of performance. A rapid expansion of physical output this year is unambiguously "good" according to the success indicator, irrespective of poor performance in other areas. Thus technological change, cost reduction, and on-time deliveries, all very important indicators for the Soviet economy as a whole, tend to be secondary considerations as far as the manager is concerned.

In addition to these basic structural difficulties, there are dysfunctional characteristics of the managerial system. Soviet managers are faced by continual pressure from above in the form of taut production targets. Therefore management must rely heavily on the efficient functioning of the material and technical supply system, a system over which management has little formal control. Yet enterprise output depends to a great extent upon the availability of appropriate inputs in the proper quantity, quality, and at the appropriate time. In the absence of a genuine wholesale market, the enterprise must rely upon all other supplier enterprises to meet their plan obligations, and a failure by a single enterprise can cause continuing reverberations throughout the system.[6] The supply system is crucial to enterprise

[5] Nove, "The Problem of Success Indicators," p. 88. A striking example of the possible distortion as pictured by the Soviet humor magazine *Krokodil* and cited by Nove is the nail factory whose gross output target is specified in *weight*. The month's output is one gigantic nail being hauled away with a crane. See Alec Nove, *The Soviet Economy*, rev. ed. (New York: Praeger, 1969), p. 174.

[6] Enterprise failures to meet delivery targets are generally not severely punished. Fines tend to be nominal and difficult to collect, and generally enterprises do not bother to pursue those who break contracts. Because of the lack of coordination of supply plans between the State Committee for Material-Technical Supply (*Gossnab*), *Gosplan*, and the ministries, no particular agency has been willing to take the responsibility for contract violations. For Soviet discussions of these problems, see *Planovoe khoziaistvo* [The planned economy], no. 6, 1978, 101–109; *Pravda*, February 18, 1978.

plan fulfillment; yet its manifold weaknesses outlined above continue to impede enterprise target fulfillment.[7]

Informal Behavior Patterns

The emphasis on taut production targets has led to certain informal behavior patterns by enterprise management, some of which have had negative economic consequences. First, there has been an inevitable tendency for the enterprise manager to resurrect a practice utilized under War Communism—namely, *priorities*—using plan directives, the bonus system, informal and formal communications from the party, and simple intuition as indicators of the nature of the priority structure.

On the one hand, the priority system indicates the predominance of output performance over other plan targets. The priority awareness of Soviet managers relates to two aspects of enterprise operations. First, the priority system directs them to emphasize output performance over other plan targets, with the resulting neglect of costs, innovations, quality, and so on, as described above. Second, the priority system relates to managers the relative importance of the various enterprises with whom they conduct business. If managers find themselves unable to meet delivery obligations to both enterprises X and Y, they must rely on their priority awareness to make their choice.

The major reason for the important role of priorities in the world of the Soviet manager is the existence of supply uncertainty, which itself is due to the tautness of planning and to planning errors. The priority system does have its positive aspect, because in an imperfect system, it ensures that planners get their high-priority targets irrespective of planning errors and supply deficiencies; yet it does force managers to seek informal sources of supply and to engage in dysfunctional practices.

A second informal behavior pattern is the *safety factor* phenomenon. The combination of ambitious targets, uncertain supply, and substantial re-

---

[7] In recent years, attempts have been made to develop *direct supply links* between enterprises to make the supply system more reliable. Also some so-called free sales of some commodities are being allowed. Nevertheless, most material supplies are still centrally allocated, and often the central supply organs seek to disrupt the direct supply links and force a return to centralized allocation. For a discussion of the direct links system, see for example V. Dymshits, "Sluzhba snabzheniia segodnia i zavtra" [Supply services, today and tomorrow], *Ekonomicheskaia gazeta* [The economic gazette], no. 28 (1969), 4–5; V. Ivanov, "Material'notekhnicheskoe snabzhenie v novykh usloviiakh khoziaistvovaniia" [Material-technical supply under new circumstances of management], *Voprosy ekonomiki* [Problems of economics], no. 5 (May 1969), 40–47; Gertrude E. Schroeder, "The 'Reform' of the Supply System in Soviet Industry," *Soviet Studies*, vol. 24, no. 1 (July 1972), 105–107; Gertrude E. Schroeder, "The Soviet Economy on a Treadmill of 'Reforms,'" in Joint Economic Committee, *Soviet Economy in a Time of Change* (Washington, D.C.: U.S. Government Printing Office, 1979), vol. 1, pp. 323–224.

wards for fulfillment of priority targets causes the manager to search for organizational slack, or a *safety factor*, as it is called in the Soviet parlance. This search leads the manager into patterns of dysfunctional behavior, for example the hoarding of material supplies (especially those most likely to be in short supply), thus immobilizing scarce resources. This stockpiling is not totally dysfunctional, for the Soviet manager will use his *tolkach*[8] (expediter) to barter and exchange stockpiled materials with other enterprises. Nevertheless, this informal supply system operated by the *tolkach* (and tolerated by planning and legal authorities) results in a weakening of centralized control over material allocation—a definitely undesirable feature from the planning authorities' point of view. Yet the toleration of the informal supply system indicates that the authorities have reluctantly accepted it as a necessary evil, required by the frequent breakdowns in the official supply system.

Third, under the existing priority system there is a tendency for managers to avoid change, for the manager tends to expect a negative impact from both process and product innovation. Such innovations are considered risky because they might endanger plan fulfillment during the current period, and they carry little potential reward because output targets will simply be ratcheted upward if the innovations are successful. The innovation problem will be discussed in detail in Chapter 11. At the same time, quality, which is typically very difficult to incorporate effectively into quantitative indicators, has tended to be of secondary importance to the manager, who—at least prior to 1965—was judged on the basis of *production*, not sales. Also, in a sellers' market, those searching for supplies will be less likely to complain about inferior quality. In this case, the economic facts of life dictate against the use of legal and other channels to seek redress of supply grievances pertaining to quality or quantity.

Fourth, the bonus structure has tended to produce no rewards for 99 percent fulfillment, but substantial rewards for 101 percent fulfillment. This discontinuous aspect of the bonus sytem, plus the other characteristics outlined above (especially supply inadequacy), lead to *storming*, or the production of a substantial portion of the monthly output in the final few days of the month. The result of *storming* is a reinforcement of other dysfunctional features—irregular delivery on supply contracts, improper utilization of capacity, poor quality, and so forth.[9]

---

[8] The figure of the *tolkach* has become a commonplace of Soviet life. They travel around the country at factory expense on factory assignments, often vacationing at government expense. A Soviet article describes the crowding of Soviet hotels on weekends by the *tolkachi*, leaving no rooms for vacationing families. See V. Varvarka, "Otpusk v kommandirovke" [Vacation during a business trip], *Ekonomichesksaia gazeta* [The economic gazette], no. 14 (1969), 16.

[9] Raymond Hutchings, *Seasonal Influences in Soviet Industry* (London: Oxford University Press, 1971), pp. 187–195.

From what we have said, it is apparent that the reward system for enterprise managers influences both the selection of priority targets and, further, attainment of these targets. Let us now examine the managerial incentive structure in greater detail to determine how this comes about.

Soviet Management and Incentives[10]

The basic problems of management are not peculiar to the Soviet industrial enterprise; their counterparts can be found for the most part in capitalist industrial enterprises. Given a set of goals (whether from a board of directors or a central planner), and given that appropriate information for both plan formulation and execution is held largely at local levels (in the branch plant of a capitalist enterprise, for example), how is a managerial environment and incentive structure to be constructed such that (1) managers know precisely what is expected from them, and (2) they are motivated to fulfill these expectations?

The Soviet answer to these questions is a peculiar managerial framework, in the sense that it combines a relatively high degree of centralization of decision-making within a rather formal bureaucratic structure on the one hand with a significant degree of managerial freedom through informal decentralization on the other. Thus the hierarchical centralized planning structure implies that managers respond to "rules" while, at the same time, the *khozraschet* enterprise system implies that managers have a degree of local freedom and initiative in the operation of the enterprise.

It must be recognized that in almost any organization, there will exist both a formal and an informal sphere of managerial decision authority. In a sense, the latter oils the operation of the former. In the Soviet case, to the degree that the latter does not smooth the operation of the former, there exists a myriad of internal and external enterprise controls to reorient enterprise behavior along desirable paths. These controls will be examined as we consider both the positive and negative aspects of the Soviet managerial reward structure.

[10] The discussion of Soviet management is based primarily upon the following works: Joseph S. Berliner, *Factory and Manager in the USSR* (Cambridge, Mass.: Harvard University Press, 1957)—a study of the early years of Soviet management experience based primarily upon émigré interviews; David Granick, *Management of the Industrial Firm in the USSR* (New York: Columbia University Press, 1954)—an in-depth study of industrial management of the 1930s, based primarily upon a detailed reading of the Soviet local and specialized press; Barry M. Richman, *Soviet Industrial Management* (Englewood Cliffs, N.J.; Prentice-Hall, 1965)—a general survey of material similar to that discussed by Berliner and Granick. More recent material on the Soviet as compared with other industrial managers can be found in David Granick, *Managerial Comparisons of Four Developed Countries: France, Britain, United States, and Russia* (Cambridge, Mass.: MIT Press, 1972). For treatment of the Soviet managerial system in the language of organization theory, see David Granick, *Soviet Metal Fabricating and Economic Development* (Madison: University of Wisconsin Press, 1967), chap. 7. The Soviet manager and innovation are treated in Joseph S. Berliner, *The Innovation Decision in Soviet Industry* (Cambridge, Mass.: MIT Press, 1976), part 3.

Managerial Personnel and Rewards

Before considering the Soviet managerial reward system, let us consider the profile of a Soviet industrial management. From the evidence gathered by Western authorities on Soviet management,[11] we know that the typical Soviet manager is probably well-educated (usually at the college level)—most likely in the field of engineering, with minimal emphasis on finance and what we would describe as "business" courses. This is an interesting deviation from the American pattern where, for example, the manager has to be primarily conversant with financial and sales matters. Instead, the Soviet managers' engineering training prepares them more for technological production problems. While Soviet managers are typically not from a working-class background, they will during the course of their educational experience, and also throughout the period of managerial advancement, receive more practical training than their American counterparts.

The rewards for successful managerial performance can be significant. Although data in this area are limited, it is probably safe to generalize that the typical Soviet manager earns a base pay substantially higher than the average Soviet worker, and further, that monetary bonuses are a significant portion of total earnings. Bonus payments have varied substantially both over time and by regions. In 1934, the share of bonus earnings in managerial incomes averaged 4 percent, rising to 11 percent by 1940. It was allowed to rise to 33 percent under wartime pressures but declined after the war to 12–15 percent in the mid-1950s. In 1961, the share dropped to 8 percent. The renewed emphasis on material incentives after 1961 caused the relative importance of managerial bonuses to rise again, to 16 percent in 1965 and to 35 percent in 1970.[12] Thus bonus earnings are important for the Soviet factory manager, although as a portion of aggregate managerial earnings, they were of no greater importance in the Soviet Union than in the United States in the 1960s.[13] It should be noted however that while participation in bonus schemes is generally universal for Soviet managerial personnel, such is not the case in the United States.

Executive bonuses in the United States tend to be paid for achievement of both short- and long-run objectives. For example, the American manager is expected to strike a proper balance between short-run and long-run profitability. In addition, bonus arrangements in the United States are more likely to be based on subjective evaluations of performance.[14] In the Soviet Union, however, bonus payments tend to be for short-run, rather clearly de-

---

[11] Notably, Berliner, *Factory and Manager;* Granick, *Management of the Industrial Firm;* Granick, *Managerial Comparisons of Four Developed Countries;* Richman, *Soviet Industrial Management.*

[12] Richman, *Soviet Industrial Management,* pp. 134–135; Berliner, *The Innovation Decision,* pp. 478–484.

[13] Granick, *Managerial Comparisons of Four Developed Countries,* chap. 9.

[14] Granick, *Managerial Comparisons of Four Developed Countries,* chap. 9.

fined tasks, such as the quantitative fulfillment of a specific output target or specific cost reductions. The short-run nature of Soviet bonuses tends to create an environment of pressure, and this in itself becomes a mechanism through which short-run priorities can readily be identified by managers. It is in this sense that some longer-run targets, such as quality, innovation, and so forth, may well be set aside in favor of more rewarding short-run achievements.

In the Soviet case, the monetary bonus awards are normally awarded on a short-run basis (i.e., monthly), while the nonmonetary rewards are in greater measure long-run rewards, although they too can be thought of as defining priority goals and delineating the sphere of informal managerial behavior. Enterprises may for example provide the manager with living quarters and an automobile, the latter most likely with a driver. Both are significant amenities in present-day Soviet society when one considers the shortage of housing space (and the lack of a formal market for the purchase of same) and the prestige and convenience of an automobile. Finally, the enterprise manager can anticipate participation in local, state, and party organs, adulation in the press for particularly good performance, and also upward mobility to positions of greater prestige and reward.

While the Soviet manager's position is one of potentially significant monetary rewards, it is also one of significant risk. First, in an environment of uncertainty where the manager lacks decisive control over all inputs (for example, the delivery of material supplies to the enterprise on time), the manager is clearly in danger of not being able to meet priority targets. There are two possible consequences of such failure: loss of bonus, which represents a substantial portion of total income, or loss of job. A third consequence, execution or imprisonment, was widespread during the 1930s, when failures to fulfill targets were seen to be the work of saboteurs. Fortunately, Soviet managers no longer work under this threat.[15] Executive turnover was very high in the 1930s, although it is clear that this pattern has changed significantly in recent years. Thus for the postwar years, turnover of Soviet managerial personnel at both the middle and upper levels has been substantially less than that of comparable managerial personnel in American corporations. This represents significantly increased job security for Soviet managers of the 1960s and 1970s as opposed to those of the 1930s.[16]

External Constraints upon Soviet Managers

Numerous internal and external constraints upon managerial flexibility make the job of the Soviet manager even more difficult. The planning and

---

[15] One can better understand the dysfunctional behavior of Soviet managers and their search for the "safety factor" by remembering that these practices originated during the 1930s, when managers faced severe consequences if they failed to meet plan obligations.

[16] Granick, *Managerial Comparisons of Four Developed Countries*, chap. 8.

administrative bodies external to the firm also have targets to meet, which depend upon the performance of subordinate enterprises. Regional and ministerial authorities are therefore interested in forcing enterprises under their control to exert themselves to the maximum. This relationship is significant, whether industry is arranged on a territorial or ministerial basis, for higher bodies will place pressure upon the subordinate enterprises to ensure fulfillment of their own targets. The ministry practice of holding back enterprise supply allotments ("reserving") and of planning enterprise targets to exceed the aggregate ministry target are part of this pressure. In this manner, managers are subjected to increased pressure from their immediate supervisors. In addition, while the *khozraschet* system of management implies a degree of autonomy for the enterprise, it also suggests the establishment of financial rewards and connections with the State Bank—a further form of external control. The system of "ruble control" implies that the funds of the enterprise must be deposited in the bank, and the bank will exercise control over enterprise funds.

While the trade union does not play an important role in wage scale determination, it may be of importance in nonwage matters—for example, in overseeing working conditions, sick leave, vacation benefits, and the manager's authority to fire workers—which, in turn, limits managerial flexibility. Finally, the Communist Party may serve on the one hand to define priorities in the industrial sector for the manager and on the other hand to limit managerial decision-making freedom by the elaboration of "inadequacies"—revelation of deceptive statistical reporting and other undesirable behavior patterns of managers. While the precise role of the party in managerial affairs remains to be fully understood, its influence would seem to be pervasive within the enterprise and it most likely could be described as an alter ego to the manager.

Prospects for Change

The frequent organizational shifts in past years would indicate a degree of dissatisfaction within the Soviet leadership with managerial arrangements in recent use. The Soviet press abounds with reports of dissatisfaction over the operation of the managerial system. The system operates to allocate resources as directed by planning authorities, but it is generally conceived to work inefficiently. Poor quality, lack of innovative activity, and the continuation of illegal activities in the performance of enterprise duties are evidence of a system characterized by a good deal of dysfunctional (in terms of goal achievement) behavior.

Soviet leaders have long been aware of the problem of the inefficient performance of their industrial enterprises. In fact, most of the problems noted in this section—excessive stockpiling, informal supply arrangements, inflated material requests—were already apparent to the planning authorities as early as 1929.[17] It is only recently that Soviet authorities have attempted to correct deficiencies in the planning structure and the managerial incentive system through the process of economic reform, a topic dealt with in Chapter 9. Why have Soviet administrators waited so long to deal with these problems? Largely because the existing system tends to respond relatively well to the priority goals of planners, and in this manner, the planners are assured that they control the direction of the economy. Whether alternative arrangements can guarantee the same degree of control is questionable, hence the willingness to bear the obvious deficiencies of the existing system for so long.

LABOR ALLOCATION IN THE SOVIET UNION

We now consider the allocation of labor in the Soviet economy, which is accomplished through a combination of administrative controls and market forces. The latter, in the form of voluntary responses to wage differentials, primarily affect the supply of labor in various occupations and regions, whereas administrative controls have been used to affect both the supply and demand sides of the Soviet labor market, with the mix of market forces and administrative controls changing over time. In describing labor allocation, we first concentrate on general long-run trends, after which consideration will be given to periods when labor allocation has diverged distinctly from the central tendency. Given the important role played by the market in labor allocation, we shall consider both the demand and supply of labor in the Soviet economy. Let us consider first the determination of enterprise demand for labor through the planning system.

Labor Planning in the Soviet Union

In the Soviet Union, the amount of labor required by an industrial enterprise is decided largely outside of the firm by superior authorities. In fact, the determination of enterprise labor staffing is an integral part of the general planning process. The enterprise *techpromfinplan* contains not only enterprise output and material input targets but also instructions on labor inputs. The amount of detail on labor staffing has varied over the years—reforms in 1965 reduced the number of external labor staffing directives—however, throughout most of the plan era, *techpromfinplan* labor staffing instructions have tended to be quite detailed, specifying the enterprise wage bills, the distribution of enterprise labor force by wage classes, average wages, planned increases in labor productivity, and so on. As one might recognize from our discussion of the Soviet manager, the manager has

---

[17] E. H. Carr and R. W. Davies, *Foundations of a Planned Economy, 1926–1929* (London: Macmillan, 1969), pp. 833–834.

tended to exercise some discretion in the area of labor staffing within the constraints of the *techpromfinplan;* nevertheless, enterprise labor staffing is basically a decision made by planning authorities in accordance with the production plans that they also determine.

Gosplan derives a balance for the Soviet labor force just as it derives balances for material inputs. The most important part of such Soviet manpower balancing is the estimation of available manpower resources, which is carried out by *Gosplan* with the help of regional and local governments and planning authorities. This is not an easy task, for the reserve labor force in agriculture must be estimated along with the potential reserves among the female population, in addition to existing urban labor resources. Also, demographic factors such as birth and death rates and migration rates between regions and between the countryside and towns must be considered.

Once the available supply (both actual and potential) off labor resources has been estimated, *Gosplan* must estimate the demands for labor resources. The labor requirements of the various economic branches are determined in much the same manner as material input requirements. The planning authorities estimate in detail (after considerable bargaining and consultation with lower echelons)—on the basis of coefficients (norms) relating labor inputs to outputs—the labor staffing required to produce the given output targets. As in the case of material inputs, enterprises and lower planning echelons have commonly exaggerated their labor staffing needs for the purpose of adding to their safety factor, and planning authorities have had to allocate labor resources below enterprise requests to balance supplies and demands. Another complication is the fact that labor productivity tends to increase over time, meaning that the relationship between enterprise outputs and labor inputs varies over time—adding another variable to the problem of estimating required labor inputs.[18]

Once the planning authorities draw up the balance of labor resources, a second problem arises: how are they to bring the appropriate amount of labor into the various enterprises, or to use the Soviet terminology, how are they to "guarantee the labor requirements of the national economy"?[19]

---

[18] Detailed discussions of *Gosplan's* labor balances can be found in A. N. Efimov et al., *Ekonomicheskoe planirovanie v SSSR* [Economic planning in the USSR], (Moscow: 1967), chap. 6 and in Y. Dubrovsky, ed., *Planning of Manpower in the Soviet Union*, translated from the Russian (Moscow: Progress Publishers, 1975). For discussions of the construction of the labor balance for the 1971–1975 plan, see Murray Feshbach and Stephen Rapawy, "Labor Constraints in the Five-Year Plan," in Joint Economic Committee, *Soviet Economic Prospects for the Seventies* (Washington, D.C.: U.S. Government Printing Office, 1973), pp. 485–507; Murray Feshbach and Stephen Rapawy, "Soviet Population and Manpower Trends and Policies," in Joint Economic Committee, *Soviet Economy in a New Perspective* (Washington, D.C.: U.S. Government Printing Office, 1976), pp. 113–154.

[19] Efimov et al., *Ekonomicheskoe planirovanie*, p. 171.

Population Growth—the Supply Side

The supply of labor to the Soviet economy is a function of the population base from which it is derived and the manner in which members of households decide to participate in the labor force. Both sets of forces are interrelated, but first we examine some salient features of Soviet population dynamics, turning thereafter to incentive arrangements.

Although it would not be possible to do justice to the subject of Soviet population in the limited space available, we can note that excellent sources are available.[20] We limit our coverage here to broad trends throughout the plan era.

The Soviets inherited from the tsars a population that had been growing rapidly since the 1860s due to high fertility and declining mortality. Despite enormous losses during the first and second world wars, high rates of natural increase and territorial annexations caused the population of the USSR to grow at an annual rate of slightly over one percent between 1928 and 1961. During the early postwar period, Soviet population growth was especially rapid (1.7 percent per annum between 1951 and 1966). Since the early 1960s, there has been a sharp and continuing decline in the rate of growth of the Soviet population due to declining Soviet fertility.[21] Although expansion of the labor force has continued due to the continuing growth of population in the able-bodied ranges (16 through 54 years for women and 16 through 59 years for men), this growth will largely end in the 1980s. At the same time, overall labor force participation rates are very high, suggesting limited if any addition to the labor supply from this source. Although there has been a serious female/male imbalance in the Soviet population resulting from the impact of World War II, this imbalance has been declining, along with the general aging of the population.

Beyond the basic demographic patterns outlined above, there are other factors that affect labor supply. In the Soviet case, regional redistribution has been important, most notably the outmigration from rural to urban areas.[22] While serving as a major source of industrial labor in the past, the

[20] Warren W. Eason, "Labor Force," in Abram Bergson and Simon Kuznets, eds., *Economic Trends in the Soviet Union* (Cambridge, Mass.: Harvard University Press, 1963), pp. 38–95; Ansley Coale et al., *Human Fertility in Russia Since the Nineteenth Century* (Princeton, N.J.: Princeton University Press, 1979); *Narodnoe khoziaistvo SSSR v 1978 g.* [The national economy of the USSR in 1978] (Moscow: Statistika, 1979), p. 7; Feshbach and Rapawy, "Soviet Population and Manpower Trends and Policies"; Murray Feshbach, "Employment Trends and Policies in the U.S.S.R.," paper prepared for the 14th International CESES Seminar, Rapallo, Italy, September 1978.

[21] This discussion is based upon Feshbach and Rapawy, "Soviet Population and Manpower Trends and Policies," *op. cit.*

[22] For an examination of migration patterns see Feshbach and Rapawy, "Soviet Population and Manpower Trends and Policies," pp. 124–127. For an attempt to measure the impact of various forces on rural-urban movements, see Robert C. Stuart and Paul R. Gregory, "A Model of Soviet Rural-Urban Migration," *Economic Development and Cultural Change,*

importance of the rural sector as a supplier of labor to urban areas has declined due to the aging of the rural population, the need to maintain the growth of agricultural output, and the difficulty of accommodating rural migrants in already crowded Soviet cities. Regional migration must be used to alleviate regional labor shortages, although Soviet past experience in this area suggests limited potential. In the case of Siberia, for example, higher wages have attracted new workers, but high turnover rates inhibit the development of a stable productive labor force. In Central Asia, the one region of the Soviet Union where the rate of growth of population remains high (and well above that prevailing in European Russia), migration of the able-bodied population has not been significant.[23]

Soviet policies have been modified to encourage the greater overall participation of younger and older people. For example, students are used to offset seasonal imbalances and for short-term needs in agriculture. Rules have been modified to enable older persons (specifically pensioners) to return to work yet still retain pension benefits.

All of these measures can make a contribution to increasing the Soviet labor supply and improving the regional distribution of labor. However, at the present level of labor productivity, the Soviet economy has a significant labor shortage. According to existing demographic projections, this problem will persist through the 1980s (Chapter 12). But it is one thing to have people available and another to have them participate in the larbor force at the appropriate level and with the maximum effort. Let us examine this aspect of the labor supply decision.

There are a number of alternative means by which eligible participants could be induced to contribute effectively to the labor effort. First, administrative means could be used. In an extreme form, the state could conscript (or incarcerate) labor and assign it to particular regions and particular sectors of the economy. A second alternative would be the use of material and moral rewards, differentiated to attract labor to those regions and sectors where it is needed most. Finally, as a long term variant, the supply of labor could be influenced through manpower training, education, and organized recruitment.

In the Soviet case, all of these mechanisms have been used. In times other than collectivization of war, emphasis has been placed upon the use of

---

vol. 26, no. 1 (October 1977), 81–92. For a recent analysis of the regional aspects of the Soviet labor force, see Stephen Rapawy, "Regional Employment Trends in the U.S.S.R.: 1950–1975," in Joint Economic Committee, *Soviet Economy in a Time of Change* (Washington, D.C.: U.S. Government Printing Office, 1979), vol. 1, pp. 600–617.

[23] For an examination of this case, see Murray Feshbach, "Prospects for Outmigration from Central Asia and Kazakhstan in the Next Decade," in Joint Economic Committee, *Soviet Economy in a Time of Change* (Washington, D.C.: U.S. Government Printing Office, 1979), vol. 1, pp. 656–709.

market-type mechanisms—wages, education, and training—to influence household decision-making. We view relative wages as the most important force influencing Soviet labor force allocation. At the same time, market forces have been constrained in a number of ways—such as closed cities, the passport system, and labor mobilization.[24] Let us examine each of the allocational mechanisms in greater detail.

Differential Wages in the Soviet Union

Soviet wage-setting authorities have long recognized the allocative function of differential wages, and the principle has been accepted that wage determination should be governed by the needs of labor allocation rather than by considerations of equality.[25] Problems of poverty and income inequality should therefore be corrected by the social security system, not by the manipulation of wage differentials. Wage authorities point out that the "wrong" set of wage differentials will adversely affect labor productivity and promote excessive labor turnover. Ideologically, wage differentials are justified by the socialist distribution principle of "equal pay for equal work" and by Lenin's admonition against "equality mongering." Differentials are justified by Marx's labor theory of value, which recognizes that different types of labor must be converted into a common denominator. The Soviets call this the "principle of the reduction of labor." Insofar as labor consists of six dimensions—the length of time worked, the skill required, the region, the industry, the enterprise in which the work is performed, and working conditions—a socialist wage scale must differentiate among workers according to these dimensions.

Industrial wages are set by central authorities in the Soviet Union. Various agencies have over time participated in wage scale determination—the ministries, the Council of Ministers, the Central Council of Trade Unions, the State Committee on Labor and Wages, and many others—but the trend since 1956 has been toward uniformity in regulating wages by increasing centralization and standardization. A nationwide reform of industrial wages ongoing from 1956 to 1965, but largely completed between 1958 and 1960, established a more simplified uniform system of industrial wages for the Soviet labor force.[26] A new round of reforms between 1972 and 1976 extended

[24] Victor Zaslavsky and Yuri Luryi, "The Passport System in the USSR and Changes in Soviet Society," *Soviet Union*, vol. 6, no. 2 (1979), 137–153.

[25] This discussion is based upon Alastair McCauley, *Economic Welfare in the Soviet Union* (Madison: University of Wisconsin Press, 1979), pp. 174–186.

[26] Leonard J. Kirsch, *Soviet Wages: Changes in Structure and Administration Since 1956* (Cambridge, Mass.: MIT Press, 1972), pp. 1–8; Janet G. Chapman, "Labor Mobility and Labor Allocation in the USSR," paper presented at the joint meeting of the Association for the Study of Soviet-Type Economics and the Association for Comparative Economics, Detroit, Mich., December 1970, p. 3; Janet G. Chapman, "Soviet Wages Under Socialism," in Alan Abouchar, ed., *The Socialist Price Mechanism* (Durham, N.C.: Duke University Press, 1977), pp. 246–281; McCauley, *Economic Welfare in the Soviet Union*, chap. 8.

the earlier reforms to other economic branches and continued the process of standardization of wage scales.

Industrial wage rates are set in the following manner: in each industrial branch, base rates (*stavka*) specifying the absolute wage of the lowest paid occupation are established. Then for each branch, a schedule (*setka*) is designated, which gives the wages of higher grade occupations as percentages of the lowest grade rate.[27] By altering the base rate, the state can direct labor into and out of branches according to the plan. In this manner, high average wages in high priority sectors such as machinery, metallurgy, electricity, and coal were used to effect the dramatic shifts of labor out of agriculture and light industry into heavy industry during the early plan era. During NEP, average wages in the consumer goods sector exceeded those in heavy industry. Beginning with the First Five Year Plan, average wages in heavy industry grew more rapidly than in light industry, with a resulting shift of labor.[28] In the postwar period, a close correlation still persists between average branch wages and the national importance of the branch,[29] although recent statements suggest that wage authorities are now attempting to reduce differentials between light and heavy industries.[30]

By manipulating the *setka*, the state can encourage workers to acquire the skills that it requires. Thus, Stalin established schedules in 1931 that heavily favored skilled workers, to encourage the then untrained labor force to acquire industrial skills. As a result of the Stalin wage policy, large differentials arose between the earnings of skilled and nonskilled industrial workers. In fact, some evidence suggests that industrial wage differentials during

---

[27] Prior to 1956, this system was extremely complex. In all, there existed around 1900 different *setka* schedules and about 1000 different *stavka* assignments. In the 1957–1961 system there were 10 *setka* schedules and 50 different *stavka* assignments. The 1972–1976 reforms reduced the number of *setka* to 3 and the number of *stavka* to 17. On this, see B. M. Sukharevsky, "Zarabotnaia plata i material'naia zainteresovannost" [The wage and material incentives] in A. P. Volkova et al., eds., *Trud i zarabotnaia plata v SSSR* [Labor and wages in the USSR], (Moscow: 1968), p. 302; see also Kirsch, *Soviet Wages*, table 4–2, p. 75; McCauley, *Economic Welfare in the Soviet Union*, p. 202.

[28] Emily C. Brown, "The Soviet Labor Market," *Soviet Trade Unions and Labor Relations* (Cambridge, Mass.: Harvard University Press, 1966), pp. 11–37, reprinted in Morris Bornstein and Daniel Fusfeld, eds., *The Soviet Economy: A Book of Readings*, 3rd ed. (Homewood, Ill.: Irwin, 1970), pp. 217–220.

[29] Abram Bergson, *The Economics of Soviet Planning* (New Haven, Conn.: Yale University Press, 1964), p. 115. Soviet labor experts have noted in recent years that this system tends to create excessive turnover problems in branches having low base rates. In the eastern regions during the 1960s, turnover was highest in the food industry, where wages were lowest, and lowest in ferrous metals, where wages were highest. Attempts are being made to reduce the turnover problem in consumer branches by raising the minimum wage (in 1968 and 1971). On this, see Chapman, "Labor Mobility," p. 13; McCauley, *Economic Welfare in the Soviet Union*, pp. 200–207.

[30] Sukharevsky, "Zarabotnaia plata," p. 292; McCauley, *Economic Welfare in the Soviet Union*, pp. 206–207.

the 1930s were larger than in the United States.[31] With the growing level of education of the labor force, the extreme differentials of the 1930s have been gradually reduced since World War II, especially after 1956; and between 1956 and 1976, new ratios were established that set the rates of the most skilled categories at a maximum of 2.1 times those of unskilled categories—as opposed to the 4:1–8:1 ratios of the 1930s and 1950s. Two other factors have contributed to the leveling of industrial wages in the postwar period: minimum wage rates have been increased dramatically (they doubled between 1957 and 1968 and then were raised another 17 percent in 1971) and the numbers (and percentage) of workers making low wages have declined markedly.[32]

Industrial wages are also differentiated by region to encourage labor mobility into such rapidly growing areas as Siberia, Kazakhstan, Central Asia, and the Far North, which have harsh climates and lack the cultural amenities of European Russia. Such regional differentials are computed by means of a uniform system of coefficients, which are multiplied by the standard wage rates to yield regionally differentiated wages. For example, the coefficients used to compute wages in the Far North range from 1.5–1.7;[33] that is, wages between 50 percent and 70 percent higher than the standard rates are paid to workers in the Far North for performing the same basic tasks as workers in European Russia. Supplements are also used, which bring the basic wage rate in the Far North to as high as 2.8 times that in European Russia.[34] As of 1968, there were ten regional coefficients used to establish regional wage differentials—a much simplified system from the ninety regional coefficients that existed prior to 1956.[35] In addition to regional differentiation, some higher rates are provided in cases of dangerous work and work performed under arduous conditions. For example, underground mining occupations receive basic monthly wages 14 to 33 percent higher than those for above ground occupations. In the chemicals industry, work performed under especially hot, heavy, and unhealthy conditions re-

---

[31] Abram Bergson, *The Structure of Soviet Wages* (Cambridge, Mass.: Harvard University Press, 1944), chap. 8; Sukharevsky, "Zarabotnaia plata," p. 291.

[32] McCauley, *Economic Welfare in the Soviet Union*, p. 201; Kirsch, *Soviet Wages*, chap. 4; Murray Yanowitch, "The Soviet Income Revolution," *Slavic Review*, vol. 22, no. 4 (December 1963), reprinted in Morris Bornstein and Daniel Fusfeld, *The Soviet Economy*, 2nd ed. (Homewood, Ill.: Irwin, 1966), pp. 228–241. See also Sukharevsky, "Zarabotnaia plata," p. 196.

[33] Brown, "The Soviet Labor Market," p. 219; Sukharevsky, "Zarabotnaia plata," p. 302.

[34] Chapman, "Labor Mobility," p. 23. Even these differentials have not proven sufficient to maintain an adequate labor force in the Far North and Siberia. Recent Soviet studies have suggested that the established regional differentials are not sufficient to compensate for cost of living differentials, not to mention the low level of services (child care, health, education) available in these regions. On this, see *ibid.*, pp. 13–16.

[35] Sukharevsky, "Zarabotnaia plata," p. 302; McCauley, *Economic Welfare in the Soviet Union*, p. 202.

ceives payment 33 percent above that for work performed under normal conditions.[36]

The *total* wage of Soviet industrial workers is actually the sum of two components. On the one hand, the worker receives the basic wage computed according to the *setka* and *stavka* system described above. This component does not vary relative to the performance of the individual or the enterprise, and is guaranteed by the state. In addition, the worker receives a variety of supplementary bonus and incentive payments that vary with performance. These supplementary payments are in the form of bonuses for overfulfillment of plan norms, of premia paid from the wage fund or material incentive fund of the enterprise, and of supplements for special working conditions. For example in 1957, 56 percent of the average industrial worker's full wage was the basic wage, the remaining 44 percent being incentive payments of one kind or another. Of the latter, about 29 percent was for overfulfillment of norms, 6 percent was from premia payments, and 15 percent was supplements for region and special working conditions. In 1972, the figures were as follows: the basic wage accounted for 59 percent; bonuses, for 20 percent; premia for norm overfulfillment, for 11 percent; and regional and special working conditions differentials, for 10 percent of average monthly earnings in industry.[37]

Prior to the general reform of wages that began in 1956, bonuses and incentive payments made up a larger share of industrial wages owing to the greater importance of piece rates and incentive schemes. During the early 1950s, such payments accounted for slightly more than 40 percent of average industrial incomes. As a result of the 1956–1965 wage reform, bonuses and supplements now account for around 30 percent of industrial wage income. This decrease is a consequence of the substantial decline in the percentage of workers paid according to piece rates, which dropped from two-thirds to one-third of all industrial workers between 1957 and 1961.[38]

The common current in the Soviet wage policy has been that wage rates should be set to equate supply and demand for labor. If the state wants an increase of employment in metallurgy, for example, wage rates should be raised to attract additional labor into metallurgy. If the state wants to develop the Far North, it must take labor supply factors into account and set a highly differentiated wage to overcome the workers' aversion to the region. As Leonard Kirsch has pointed out, in actual practice, the equation of supply and demand has been accomplished by combining centralized wage setting with enterprise flexibility in the area of incentive payments.[39] Thus if the basic wage rates established by central authorities create labor short-

---

[36] Sukharevsky, "Zarabotnaia plata," p. 292; Kirsch, *Soviet Wages*, Table 6-1, p. 125.
[37] McCauley, *Economic Welfare in the Soviet Union*, p. 248.
[38] Sukharevsky, "Zarabotnaia plata," pp. 297–302; Kirsch, *Soviet Wages*, chap. 2.
[39] Kirsch, *Soviet Wages*, chap. 8.

ages or surpluses at the enterprise level, managers have made needed adjustments at the local level by raising or lowering incentive payments. According to Kirsch, the trend toward more simplicity and national uniformity in wage rates may therefore result in a loss of flexibility and a weakening of central control over labor allocation.

Extramarket Controls over Labor Allocation

That wage-setting authorities have attempted to establish market-clearing wage rates through the system of basic and incentive wage payments does not imply that they have been content to rely entirely on the market to allocate labor. Instead, planning authorities have actively sought to influence supply conditions in labor markets within this context of voluntarism through education, organized recruitment, controls over labor mobility, penal labor, and *nomenklatura*.

EDUCATION

In the Soviet Union, one of the most important sources of control over labor allocation in the long-run is the educational system. It is important to note that the avowed objective of Soviet education is to meet the needs of the national economy.[40] In this regard, *Gosplan*, the Council of Ministers, and (since 1966) the All-Union Ministry of Education plan the numbers of students to enter particular areas of study and the types of educational facilities to be provided. Such decisions are supposedly made to accord with the manpower needs of the country as stated in the economic plan. The close relationship between education and the economy is maintained at the regional and local levels as well as at the national level. At the local level, educational authorities work with planning authorities and local enterprises to relate their activities to the needs of the local economy. Of course, the coordination is less than perfect, and one often finds complaints of a lack of coordination of labor and education planning.[41]

Graduates of secondary schools are often placed in local enterprises by local authorities on a quota basis. Local military commisariats are entrusted

[40] Nicholas DeWitt, "Education and the Development of Human Resources: Soviet and American Effort," in Joint Economic Committee, *Dimensions of Soviet Economic Power* (Washington, D.C.: U.S. Government Printing Office, 1962), pp. 235–236. Because Soviet leaders see a direct and planned link between, say, higher education and the needs of the economy, the Soviet perception of higher education and the absence of the "liberal arts" notion differ significantly from thinking in the United States. For more recent developments in Soviet education, see David Carey, "Developments in Soviet Education," in Joint Economic Committee, *Soviet Economic Prospects for the Seventies* (Washington, D.C.: U.S. Government Printing Office, 1973), pp. 594–637; National Foreign Assessment Center, *USSR: Trends and Prospects in Educational Attainment 1959–85*, ER79–10344, Washington, D.C., June 1979; Dubrovsky, *Planning of Manpower*, chap. 9.

[41] Chapman, "Labor Mobility," p. 4.

with placement of discharged military personnel in the local economy. Graduates of vocational schools are directed to positions by regional authorities, and graduates of specialized secondary and higher educational institutions are directed by special commissions to jobs in accordance with plans approved by *Gosplan* and the Council of Ministers. By placing new entrants in the labor market in this fashion, planning authorities influence the allocation of labor within the economy. There seems to be little official compulsion to force graduates to accept their assigned jobs, although specialized and higher education graduates are obligated to work for three years where the state places them.[42]

ORGANIZED RECRUITMENT

A second source of state control over labor allocation is organized recruitment, which was a more important factor during the 1930s than in the postwar period.[43] During the 1930s, *Orgnabor*—the Administration for Organized Recruitment of Labor—facilitated the vast transfer of labor from the countryside to the city by supplying industrial enterprises with new laborers from collective and private farms. In this manner, some three million peasants were transferred from the village to the city through *Orgnabor* contracts. After World War II, *Orgnabor* became more involved in the transfer of workers among industrial enterprises than from agriculture to industry, and by the late 1950s, *Orgnabor's* role in supplying industrial labor was a limited one. Its major role, instead, became the recruiting of labor for vast construction projects and new industries in the east and north. In this task, *Orgnabor's* efforts were supplemented by appeals of the *Komsomol* organization, designed to recruit younger workers.[44]

CONTROLS OVER LABOR MOBILITY

The competitive bidding for industrial workers plus the vast influx into the cities of untrained peasants from the countryside created excessive job turnover during the 1930s. This forced the state and the enterprises to adopt additional extramarket controls over labor mobility. To take one example, the average worker in the food industry changed jobs on the average of three times a year in 1930 and 1931, and for the economy as a whole, the average industrial worker changed jobs more than once per year.[45] One can imagine the negative impact that such high turnover had on labor productivity. In fact, labor productivity remained well below planned levels dur-

---

[42] Brown, "The Soviet Labor Market," pp. 206–210; and F. D. Romma and K. P. Urzhinsky, *Pravovye voprosy podbora rasstanovki kadrov* [Legal questions concerning the selection and arrangement of cadres], (Moscow: 1971).

[43] For a discussion of controls, see Edmund Nash, "Recent Changes in Labor Controls in the Soviet Union," in Joint Economic Committee, *New Directions in the Soviet Economy*, part 3 (Washington, D.C.: U.S. Government Printing Office, 1966), pp. 849–871.

[44] Brown, "The Soviet Labor Market," pp. 210–212.

[45] Chapman, "Labor Mobility," p. 8.

ing the First Five Year Plan, a factor that contributed to the wage inflation of the period.

During the 1930s, a series of measures was adopted to reduce the excessive turnover: absenteeism was deterred by severe penalties (eviction from factory housing and loss of social insurance benefits), "closed shops" were used to reward select groups of reliable workers, and enterprise control over limited housing was used as leverage to promote labor stability. After 1938, such controls became even more severe: labor books (in which a person's work record would be recorded) were issued to all employed persons, an internal passport system was used to monitor the movements of population, and permission was required to change jobs (failure to comply being a criminal offense). These were only a few of the administrative measures employed. Such measures can perhaps be viewed as preparations for war, but they were also a part of the purges of the late 1930s. Administrative controls over labor increased during the war with the mobilization of specialists, the lengthening of the workday, the making of absenteeism a criminal offense, and the establishment of labor reserve schools. Most of the laws pertaining to labor control during the war were passed in 1940. They were quite severe and resulted in numerous instances of criminal prosecution and imprisonment.[46] They remained on the books until their full repeal in 1956, although they had actually fallen into disuse during the early 1950s. In 1956, the workday was shortened, criminal liability for leaving work without permission and for absenteeism was abandoned, and social benefits were raised. As an immediate response to this liberalization, turnover in industry rose to 38 percent in 1956, after which it declined to a fairly steady 20–22 percent, which is below comparable turnover rates in manufacturing in the United States.[47] Nevertheless, the problem of "rolling stones" (workers who change jobs too frequently) remains a source of official concern, especially in the outlying republics where labor is quite scarce. This concern has been sufficiently serious for the state to introduce a series of measures—special bonuses for uninterrupted employment (1965), a new labor code giving reliable workers special privileges and priority in job advancement (1971), and experimental programs in various urban areas to reduce job turnover—designed to combat what the state perceives as excessive job turnover.

PENAL LABOR[48]

The most glaring deviation from the principle of a free labor market was the creation of a large penal labor force in the Soviet Union between 1929

---

[46] For a detailed discussion of labor controls from the mid-1930s to 1956, see Alec Nove, *An Economic History of the USSR* (London: Penguin, 1969), pp. 195–198, 260–263.

[47] Chapman, "Labor Mobility," pp. 7–8; Feshbach and Rapawy, "Labor Constraints," p. 539.

[48] This discussion is based on the following references: Steven Rosefielde, "How Reliable Are Available Estimates of Forced Concentration Camp Labor in the Soviet Union?" *So-*

and 1956. The number of prisoners in Soviet concentration camps (the *gulag* population) during this period cannot be estimated with precision, but disparate sources—an occasional official reference, comparisons of official labor force figures with the able-bodied population, accounts of ex-prisoners, the materials published by Alexander Solzhenitsyn—all point to astonishing numbers of forced laborers. The sources agree that the *gulag* population was around two million in 1931 and was between four and five million in 1933. During World War II, the estimates diverge substantially, but the true figure probably lies within the range of seven to fifteen million. This number probably remained fairly constant until the death of Stalin, after which it declined. The official abolition of the *gulag* by Khrushchev in 1956 did not immediately spell the end of the large *gulag* population, the size of which may have been as high as four million in 1959. The proportion of workers in concentration camps was probably 5 percent in the mid-1930s and rose to over 10 percent during the war years.[49]

The legal foundation for mass political internments was provided by Article 58 of the 1926 Soviet criminal code, which declared actions directed toward weakening state power a crime against the state. Falling under this classification were a wide variety of offenses—including sabotage, propaganda, agitation, conscious failure to carry out one's duties, subversion of industry, and suspicion of espionage. Collectivization provided the initial manpower for the *gulag* population, as peasants who resisted collectivization were deported or sent directly to concentration camps. The political purges of the late 1930s provided a second wave of *gulag* entrants. Ex-prisoners of war, resettled minorities, citizens of occupied territories, and many other groups were incarcerated during the war years.

It would be difficult to justify the internment of large percentages of the population and labor force in forced labor camps on moral and economic grounds. One may classify the *gulags* as the product of an irrational Stalin and his associates and not regard the *gulags* as being consciously designed for economic purposes. The *gulag* population was put to work principally in mining and on construction projects in harsh climates to which free labor could not be attracted. Apparently the state did seek to derive economic benefit from forced labor. However, the costs of this penal labor were immense. The high death rates in the concentration camps caused a substantial loss of population. The 1959 population census revealed 15 million "unexplained" civilian casualties as of 1950, presumably the conse-

viet Studies, vol. 32, no. 4 (October 1981); David Dallin and Boris Nicolevsky, *Forced Labor in Soviet Russia* (New Haven, Conn.: Yale University Press, 1947); Naum Jasny, "Labor and Output in Soviet Concentration Camps," *Journal of Political Economy*, vol. 59, no. 5 (October 1951), 405–419; Alexander Solzhenitsyn, *The Gulag Archipelago* (New York: Harper & Row, 1973 and 1974); vols. 1 and 2; S. Swianiewicz, *Forced Labor and Economic Development* (London: Oxford University Press, 1965).
[49] The various estimates are summarized by Rosefielde, "How Reliable Are Estimates?", Tables 1 and 4.

quence of high mortality in the *gulags*. Moreover, the sense of alienation of former prisoners and their families (along with deteriorated health) would not render them enthusiastic "builders of socialism" after their release. Furthermore, it is likely that forced labor is less productive than free labor. The diversion of labor from the labor market into concentration camps more than likely caused a loss of output due to a general lowering of labor productivity.

NOMENKLATURA CONTROLS

A final source of extramarket control over labor is the control over appointments, promotions, and dismissals exercised by the Communist Party through the *nomenklatura procedure*. As was pointed out in Chapter 5, the *nomenklatura* is a list from which the party nominates responsible individuals for posts in industry, agriculture, the state apparatus, and the army. In this manner, the party is able to control the staffing of important managerial and other administrative positions.

An Evaluation of Soviet Labor Policy

One way to evaluate Soviet labor policy would be to consider its role in the process of resource allocation. How well have Soviet authorities utilized available labor resources? Are there notable labor shortages or surpluses either by occupation or by region? Has aggregate unemployment been avoided? How well does the system correct structural unemployment? This is the criterion of *allocative efficiency*.[50] Although the allocative efficiency of the Soviet labor market is an important criterion, a broader criterion may also be in order. The effectiveness of Soviet labor policy may also be evaluated in light of its contribution to the economic and social goals of the state, which we denote as *goal achievement efficiency*.[51] Although these two efficiency measures are not necessarily incompatible, they may be in some cases. The restrictive labor policies during War Communism, the late 1930s, and World War II, for instance, definitely reduced the allocative efficiency of the Soviet labor market in order to achieve the political, economic, and military objectives of the state. On the other hand, the labor mobility of the early 1930s may have promoted allocative efficiency, yet been detrimental to goal achievement efficiency—namely, rapid industrialization. A final criterion—the equity of Soviet wage policy is discussed in Part Three.

Let us consider first the contribution of Soviet labor policy to the major

[50] Our approach to allocative efficiency is quite intuitive and should not be confused with a formal development of Pareto optimality. The optimality of Soviet labor policy in terms of the Pareto conditions is discussed by Bergson in *The Economics of Soviet Planning*, pp. 118–126.

[51] A similar standard is suggested by Kirsch, *Soviet Wages*, chap. 8.

economic goal of the Soviet state between 1928 and the present, namely the achievement of rapid industrial growth. The discussion here will concentrate on the initial industrialization period of the 1930s. To achieve the long-run objective of rapid industrialization, labor policy had to accomplish several things: (1) the industrial labor force had to expand at a rapid rate; (2) within the industrial sector, a transfer of labor out of light industry into heavy industry was required; (3) the quality of the industrial labor force had to be improved to enable it to work with modern technology; and (4) a regional distribution of labor compatible with the distribution of natural resources had to be achieved. Soviet labor policy seems to have performed these functions reasonably well, with the possible exception of the last function.

QUANTITATIVE AND STRUCTURAL CHANGES

Despite the slower population growth after the Revolution, the Soviets were able to expand their total labor force at an annual rate of 2.5 percent between 1928 and 1937,[52] a quite high rate by international standards.[53] Even more important than the overall rate of growth in employment was its sectoral distribution. In keeping with the state policy of rapid industrial transformation, the nonagricultural labor force expanded at an annual rate of nearly 9 percent while the agricultural labor force contracted at an annual rate of −2.5 percent (Table 8, Chapter 3). Commonly in the course of industrialization, agriculture suffers a *relative* decline in labor force, with the *absolute* decline coming much later. In the Soviet case, there was an immediate sharp absolute decline, and this transfer of labor out of the rural sector was a significant "contribution" of agriculture to development. The trends within the industrial subsectors were in keeping with the state policy of industrial expansion in favor of heavy industry. Light industry suffered a decline in its labor force between 1928 and 1937 that was as dramatic as the shift of labor out of agriculture (Table 8, Chapter 3).

How did Soviet labor policy effect these shifts? The rapid growth of the total labor force can in part be explained by the large rise in the participation rate (the percentage of total population employed on a full-time basis).[54] Without such an increase in participation rates, the rapid rate of expansion of the Soviet labor force would have been difficult to achieve in

[52] Richard Moorsteen and Raymond Powell, *The Soviet Capital Stock, 1928–1962* (Homewood, Ill.: Irwin, 1966), pp. 643, 648.

[53] Simon Kuznets, *Economic Growth of Nations* (Cambridge, Mass.: Harvard University Press, 1971), p. 74.

[54] One finds varying estimates of trends in the Soviet labor participation rate. The reason is that prior to 1928, the major portion of the Soviet labor force was engaged in agriculture and, by definition, just about all in agriculture are considered employed, even if they only work part-time. Thus the measure cited here is for full-time labor equivalents. See Eason, "Labor Force," pp. 53–56.

view of the slow overall population growth. During the First Five Year Plan alone (1928–1932), the number of workers and employees more than doubled according to official Soviet figures.[55]

Which particular labor policies contributed to the high participation rate? First, the policy of establishing subsistence or below subsistence wages in agriculture, coupled with the organized recruitment of able-bodied workers in agriculture (*Orgnabor*), resulted in the wholesale transfer of labor out of agriculture, where days worked per year were few relative to industry (owing to seasonal and other factors). Second, in the city, the authorities introduced moral and legal, as well as economic, inducements for all able-bodied individuals to work. "Parasitism" was subject to severe penalties, and only women with young children were exempt from work obligations, with young mothers being encouraged to work where day care facilities were available. Such pressures increased throughout the 1930s and peaked in the late 1930s (during the Stalin purges) when cases are recorded of nonworking mothers with newborn infants being criminally prosecuted for "parasitism."[56] In addition to moral and legal incentives, economic incentives also contributed to the rising participation rate. The low real wages of the 1930s made it necessary for both husband and wife to work to make ends meet.[57] Thus in 1939, 71 percent of all women between the ages of 16 and 59 were members of the labor force.[58]

This increase in the overall participation rate is even more remarkable in view of the significant decline in the participation rate of the younger and older age groups during the 1930s. In 1926, 59 percent of the young people between ages of 10 and 15 worked. In 1939, this number had been reduced to 24 percent, and by 1959, it was 12 percent. This decline was the result of the spread of universal education in the Soviet Union. Not only did the participation rate of the younger age groups decline, but also the participation rates of the older age groups fell during the 1930s. In 1926, 54 percent of the Soviet population over 60 years of age participated in the labor force; by 1939, this number had been reduced to 49 percent.[59]

Soviet wage policy was also used to effect the distribution of labor within industry. In particular, the setting of higher relative wages in heavy industry than in light industry, the use of "closed shop" privileges to reward workers in high priority branches, and the setting of low piece rate norms to allow large supplemental earnings in heavy industry encouraged the rapid transfer of labor into priority branches. As far as the trends in intersectoral

---

[55] L. M. Danilov and I. I. Matrozova, "Trudovye resursy i ikh ispol'zovanie" [Labor resources and their utilization], in A. R. Volkova et al., eds., *Trud i zarabotnaia plata v SSSR* [Labor and wages in the USSR], (Moscow: 1968), p. 247.

[56] Nove, *An Economic History of the USSR*, p. 262.

[57] Chapman, "Labor Mobility," p. 31.

[58] Eason, "Labor Force," p. 57.

[59] *Ibid.*, p. 57.

wage differentials during the rapid industrialization period are concerned, of 17 industrial branches, average wages in coal and in iron and steel ranked tenth and thirteenth, respectively, in 1924. By 1940, they ranked first and second, respectively.[60] On the other hand, the rankings of the consumer goods branches declined generally. These dramatic shifts in relative wages go a long way toward explaining the radical shift of labor within industry.

THE REGIONAL DISTRIBUTION OF LABOR

In recent years, regional differentiation in wage rates has come to play an increasingly important role in the development of Siberia and the Far East. This is an important aspect of overall Soviet development policy in view of the vast oil and gas, timber, and hydroelectric power resources of these regions. Despite generally higher nominal wages and income supplements in these areas, Soviet authorities have been hard pressed to keep these regional economies supplied with highly mobile, skilled, and younger workers owing to the low real standard of living in these areas. To counter this trend, additional fringe benefits have been granted, such as longer paid vacations, earlier retirement programs, improved child care facilities, and so forth. Nevertheless, studies show that despite all these added benefits, per capita real family income in the eastern regions scarcely differed from the average level in the Russian Republic owing to higher prices, harsher climate, inadequate housing, and lack of cultural facilities.[61] Thus it seems as if the regional distribution of labor in the Soviet Union remains one of the most problematic areas of Soviet labor policy, and the Soviet state, despite all its efforts to be contrary, is still unable to achieve a net increase in population beyond the Urals.

QUALITATIVE CHANGES

Not only was Soviet labor policy successful in bringing about significant quantitative and structural (if not regional) changes in the Soviet labor force, but in addition, the qualitative changes were equally dramatic. Any evaluation of Soviet labor policy would be incomplete without mention of Soviet manpower policy.

A cursory examination of the educational level of the Russian population prior to the Soviet period indicates how poorly equipped the Soviet labor force was to meet the needs of all-out industrialization. The last major census of the tsarist period in 1897 showed 78 percent of the over-15-year-old population as illiterate, with only 1.4 million having education beyond

[60] Bergson, *The Economics of Soviet Planning,* p. 115.
[61] Chapman, "Labor Mobility," pp. 14–28; Feshbach and Rapawy, "Soviet Population and Manpower Trends and Policies," pp. 539–541; Gertrude E. Schroeder, "Regional Income Differentials: Urban and Rural," in NATO Economic Directorate, *Regional Development in the USSR: Trends and Prospects* (Newtonville, Mass.: Oriental Research Partners, 1979), pp. 35–37.

the seventh grade out of a population of 126 million and only 93,000 with completed higher education. The immediate preindustrialization figures of the 1926 census show considerable improvement preparatory to the industrialization drive: the illiteracy rate had dropped to 56 percent, six million had received education beyond the seventh grade, and roughly half a million had completed higher education.[62]

The major spurt in educational achievement, however, occurred during the industrialization drive of the 1930s. By 1939, the illiteracy rate had dropped to 20 percent, 14 million had completed education beyond the seventh grade, and more than one million had completed higher education.[63] Thus, the Soviet educational system did a very significant job in meeting the manpower needs of a modernizing economy.

Soviet labor policy contributed to this modernization of Soviet manpower in several ways: first, labor codes were put into effect forbidding the employment of younger people, a factor that enhanced the effectiveness of the universal education decrees. Most important, large wage differentials were established between skilled and unskilled laborers, providing positive incentives for laborers to acquire highly rewarded skills. Stalin in 1931 cast aside "left equalitarianism" and introduced large incentives for skilled occupations. Wage differentials widened substantially between 1928 and 1934 and continued to increase throughout the 1930s.[64] The wage revision beginning in 1956 narrowed wage differentials, a policy made possible by the vast increases of skilled labor during the prewar period. For example, the number of graduates of specialized secondary institutions (*technicum*) increased from 1.3 million in 1926 to 3.3 million in 1939, whereas the total population only increased by 17 percent. By 1959, the number had risen to 7.9 million[65] and in 1977 it was 19.6 million.

Further Evaluation of Soviet Labor Policies

So far we have evaluated Soviet labor policy on the basis of its contribution to the long-run objective of rapid industrialization. Our conclusion is that its contribution was considerable. Thus far the evaluation has been primarily on the basis of the goal achievement efficiency of Soviet labor policy. Now we turn to some aspects of its allocative efficiency.

SOVIET FULL EMPLOYMENT POLICIES

As one might expect, aggregate unemployment has probably not been high in the Soviet Union throughout the plan period. Insufficient aggregate de-

[62] DeWitt, "Education and the Development of Human Resources," p. 244.
[63] *Ibid.*, p. 243.
[64] Bergson, *The Structure of Soviet Wages*, chaps. 8 and 14. Also see Sukharevsky, "Zarabotnaia plata," pp. 291–292; and Kirsch, *Soviet Wages*, pp. 174–179.
[65] DeWitt, "Education and the Development of Human Resources," p. 244; National Foreign Assessment Center, *USSR: Trends and Prospects*, p. 14.

mand should not be a problem in a centrally planned economy where investment, public consumption, defense, and administration are supposedly balanced so as to fully utilize available labor. In this manner, the demand for labor as determined in the national balances has generally been sufficient or more than sufficient to employ fully all those willing to work at established wage rates. This was not always so: immediately prior to the First Five Year Plan (1927–1928), unemployment averaged over 8 percent of the nonfarm labor force.[66] The overfull employment planning of the 1930s actually created an excess demand for labor that reduced unemployment to minimal proportions. Unfortunately, unemployment data were no longer gathered during the 1930s, with the official Soviet claim that unemployment had been liquidated.[67] One can assume with some degree of safety that unemployment owing to insufficient aggregate demand has not been a serious problem during the plan period.

The lack of published unemployment figures signals both the strength and weakness of Soviet labor policy. It could indicate the absence of large-scale aggregate unemployment; yet it raises questions about the existence of significant frictional and structural unemployment in view of the official lack of attention to unemployment problems. Underemployment also seems to be a growing problem, as managers are reluctant to let unneeded workers go. Thus it is probably safe to assume that unemployment, while not a pressing national problem, has not been liquidated entirely as a social problem. For instance, younger people are reported to have difficulties in finding jobs. There has tended to be little coordinated job information, and job placement services have only been recently established. Local employment exchanges were abolished during the 1930s with the "liquidation" of unemployment. Although numerous agencies have been known to aid in the placement of workers—local governments, the trade unions, the *Sovnarkozy*—unemployed workers have been forced to find new jobs primarily through informal means such as word of mouth, bulletin boards, newspaper and radio ads, and "open-door days" at factories. A 1962 survey of the chemicals industry showed that 84 percent of jobs were obtained as hires at

---

[66] Bergson, *The Economics of Soviet Planning*, p. 105.

[67] The Soviet figures on the liquidation of unemployment are:

Year	Unemployed (in thousands)
1922	407
1924	1344
1929	1741
April 1930	1081
October 1930	240
December 1930	no unemployment

SOURCE: Danilov and Matrozova, "Trudovye resursy," pp. 245–248.

the factory gates.[68] This is an area where ideology has seemed to lead to a less efficient solution than possible. In 1967, a national employment service was established—being located within *Gosplan*—called the State Committee on Labor Resource Utilization. Also regional and local employment offices have been established in larger cities. In addition, vocational guidance programs are now being emphasized in the schools.[69] Thus the period since 1967 has witnessed something of a turnabout in Soviet attitudes toward labor exchanges, which were originally viewed as necessary only under capitalism. Now such agencies seem to be well-accepted instruments of labor allocation, with roughly one-half of all industrial jobs mediated by an employment agency.[70]

LABOR UNIONS IN THE SOVIET UNION[71]

In the labor market of the Soviet Union, there should be little monopolistic behavior—often said to be a major source of allocative inefficiency in market economies. Enterprise managers must take the basic wage rates determined by superior planning agencies as given and must respond to them accordingly, although they do have some flexibility in determining actual wages through their controls over bonuses and job classifications. In turn, trade unions play no real role in the wage-setting function. Therefore, the workers themselves cannot directly affect wage rates via collective bargaining with the state. Instead of acting as bargaining agents for their memberships, Soviet trade unions concern themselves primarily with encouraging the membership to meet their planned tasks, enforcing labor discipline, protecting workers from dismissals, and enforcing labor codes.

Thus, the major inefficiencies resulting from monopolistic behavior in labor markets on the part of employers and employee organizations have been avoided for the most part in the Soviet Union. This does not mean, however, that one should expect perfectly efficient behavior on the part of management in labor staffing problems. First, management is highly restricted by its wage bill and employment staffing plans and therefore lacks necessary flexibility. Second, the pressure to fulfill output targets causes management to ignore potential ways to economize on labor cost in many cases. Instead, managers are inclined to keep superfluous workers in case they are needed later.[72] Finally, managers have often lacked the authority

---

[68] Murray Feshbach, "Manpower in the USSR," in Joint Economic Committee, *New Directions in the Soviet Economy*, part 3 (Washington, D.C.: U.S. Government Printing Office, 1966), pp. 724–725.

[69] Chapman, "Labor Mobility," p. 4.

[70] *Ibid.*, p. 4; Romma and Urzhinsky, *Pravovye voprosy*, chaps. 1 and 2.

[71] For a more detailed discussion of this issue, see Bergson, *The Economics of Soviet Planning*, pp. 116–118; Paul Barton, "Trade Unions in the USSR," *AFL-CIO Trade Union News*, vol. 34, no. 95 (September 1979), 1–15.

[72] Chapman, "Labor Mobility," p. 5.

to fire unneeded laborers, who are protected by the trade union under the labor codes. Experiments are being undertaken to change the rules and thus to encourage management to fire superfluous workers.[73]

Third, the tremendous administrative complexity of centrally administering wage rates has tended to create anomalies throughout the plan period. Especially during the period when ministries administered wage rates, the Soviet wage structure had certain peculiarities; piece rate earnings were often allowed to dwarf basic rates, thus rendering the basic rate differentials meaningless. Also, workers in different branches performing the same work tended to be rewarded quite differently. In 1956, a cashier in nonferrous metals earned roughly twice as much as a cashier in metal processing. Such differentials were in keeping with the priority system but tended to be less than efficient—a lower wage would probably have been sufficient to attract the correct number of cashiers into the priority sector.[74] This is a further example of the sacrifice of allocative efficiency to ensure target fulfillment in priority sectors. In Siberia, wage rates in heavy industry were allowed to get far out of line with corresponding rates in light industry, thereby causing severe consumer goods supply problems that have retarded the overall development of the region.[75] In addition, the growing standardization and centralization of basic wage rates during the wage reform have tended to add inflexibility to the system, with resulting surpluses and shortages of workers in various occupations (the shortage of machine operators, for example).[76]

Fourth, we have argued that material reward is important for inducing greater participation and effort, although in the Soviet case, a mixture of both administrative and market-type allocation mechanisms are utilized. To what degree are the market-type mechanisms constrained, possibly in undesirable ways, by the particular organizational arrangements of the Soviet economic system?

The reader will recall that during our discussion of inflation and in particular of repressed inflation, it was pointed out that one might consider the labor supply response of a Soviet household within the context of a disequi-

---

[73] In this regard, the so-called *Shchekino experiment* is worthy of mention. It was introduced on an experimental basis in the Shchekino Chemical Combine in October of 1967 and allowed the enterprise to use cost savings from reduced employment to raise wages of the remaining workers. In this manner, it was hoped to encourage managers to eliminate excess staff. The results as of 1969 were that the number employed fell by 800 and average wages rose sharply. So far, the results of the Shchekino experiment are impressive, but as of 1972, the experiment had been extended to only 300 enterprises, and there were still significant pressures on management ("storming," variable production targets, need for volunteers for harvesting, and so on) to retain redundant workers. See Chapman, "Labor Mobility," p. 5; Rapawy, "Soviet Population and Manpower Trends and Policies," p. 489.

[74] Bergson, *The Economics of Soviet Planning*, pp. 117–118.

[75] Chapman, "Labor Mobility," pp. 23–25.

[76] Kirsch, *Soviet Wages*, chap. 8.

librium model. Thus, under conditions of excess demand (at prevailing prices) in the consumer goods market and with limited alternative outlets for household earnings, the labor supply decision may in part be a function of the availability of consumer goods. Although the application of formal analysis to Soviet labor supply decisions is at an early stage, initial studies have shown that allocative efficiency of the Soviet labor market may have been impeded by disequilibria in the consumer market.[77]

DISCRIMINATION BY SEX IN THE SOVIET UNION

An evaluation of Soviet labor and manpower policy would not be complete without reference to the role of women in the Soviet economy.[78] The traditional Western view prompted by Soviet writings has been that Soviet women have enjoyed relatively free access to the various occupations and professions, thus avoiding the allocative inefficiency that might derive from discrimination. This view has been supported by a rather general view of the role of women in the Soviet labor force—in particular, the high participation rates and the provision of child care and other support services to facilitate this role. In addition, it has been noted that women play an important role in key professions—for example, medicine.

In recent years, increasingly sophisticated analysis of Western labor markets and notably the role of women in these markets has led to a renewed interest in, and examination of, the role of women in the Soviet economy. Thus far, this reappraisal lends only partial support to the traditional scenario outlined above.

The overall participation rate of both men and women in the Soviet economy is very high. In recent years, women have accounted for approximately 51 percent of the labor force. However, it has been pointed out that there is an inverse relationship between the rate of pay and the proportion of women in a particular occupation or sector.[79] Thus in terms of the distribution of the labor force, women tend to predominate in sectors such as textiles and services that have low wages. For example, in 1970, while accounting for 51 percent of all workers and employees, women accounted for 85 percent of health service, 78 percent of credit and banking, 75 percent of trade, 68 percent of communication, and 61 percent of government employ-

[77] In addition to the sources cited in footnotes 65–69 in Chapter 5, see also Michael D. Harsh, "Econometric Influences in Soviet Labor Allocation," paper presented at the annual meeting of the American Association for the Advancement of Slavic Studies, New Haven, Conn., October 1979.

[78] See Norton T. Dodge, *Women in the Soviet Economy* (Baltimore, Md.: Johns Hopkins Press, 1966); D. Atkinson et. al., eds., *Women in Russia* (Hassocks, England: Harvester Press, 1978); Gail W. Lapidus, *Women in Soviet Society* (Berkeley and Los Angeles: University of California Press, 1979).

[79] For development of this theme, see William Moskoff, "An Estimate of the Soviet Male-Female Income Gap," *ACES Bulletin*, vol. 16, no. 2 (Fall 1974), 21–31.

ment.[80] Furthermore, within these sectors, women occupy a lower proportion of the technical and higher paying positions than would be true for the lesser paying positions. Thus the evidence suggests that women earn less than men due to their higher representation in lower paying sectors and occupations.

A recent study of the Soviet urban sector (based upon an émigré sample) provides strong, though rather preliminary, evidence to support the above view. This study, by Gur Ofer and Aaron Vinokur, concludes that the hourly pay for Soviet urban women is roughly 0.68–0.70 of that for men, a figure closely approximating the gap that is found for the United States.[81] Furthermore, these authors find that rather traditional factors such as the return to schooling and the role of experience are important in explaining these Soviet differences, just as they are in the United States.

Clearly, additional research will be necessary to elucidate the nature and causes of male-female earnings differentials in the Soviet Union and in other socialist countries.[82] However, the evidence presented above suggests that equality in the workplace may have to be a goal for the future.

It will take considerable effort to unravel the forces underlying this pattern. Soviet women have enjoyed substantial achievement in terms of education and participation in the labor force. These achievements have in part been the result of changing values and policies, possibly also a function of the industrialization experience. At the same time, the typical Soviet woman bears a rather high share of the household work burden.[83] High participation rates may also be in part functions of a severe labor shortage and of the impact of World War II on the Soviet population. However, it remains true that Soviet women do not participate equally with Soviet men in the better paying jobs, and in jobs of administrative responsibility—for example, enterprise director or farm head—women are almost nonexistent.[84]

[80] *Narodnoe khoziaistvo SSSR v 1970 g.* [The national economy of the USSR in 1970], (Moscow: Statistika, 1971), p. 516.

[81] Gur Ofer and Aaron Vinokur, "Earning Differentials by Sex in the Soviet Union: A First Look" (Jerusalem: Department of Economics, Hebrew University, June 1979), research report no. 120.

[82] J. R. Moroney, "Do Women Earn Less Under Capitalism?", *Economic Journal*, vol. 89, no. 355 (September 1979), 601–613.

[83] For an examination of these issues, see Michael Paul Sacks, *Women's Work in Soviet Russia* (New York: Praeger, 1976).

[84] Discussions of the role of women in the Soviet rural economy are given in Norton T. Dodge, "Recruitment and the Quality of the Soviet Agricultural Labor Force," in James R. Millar, ed., *The Soviet Rural Community* (Urbana: University of Illinois Press, 1971), pp. 180–213; Robert C. Stuart, "Women in Soviet Rural Management," *Slavic Review*, vol. 38, no. 4 (December 1979). For an examination of the role of women in industrial management, see Kathryn M. Bartol and Robert A. Bartol, "Women in Managerial and Professional Positions: The United States and the Soviet Union," *Industrial and Labor Relations Review*, vol. 28, no. 4 (July 1975), 524–534.

THE ALLOCATION OF CAPITAL IN THE SOVIET ECONOMY: THE INVESTMENT DECISION

Investment Planning

By designating the physical outputs of the economy in the process of material balance planning, authorities must plan at the same time the expansion of enterprise capacity, that is, capital investment in plant and equipment.[85] In order to meet the expansion of output called for by either current or perspective plans, the capacity of the enterprise must be expanded accordingly to ensure the consistency of the output plan. Earlier it was noted that enterprise output plans are based upon past performance plus projected increases from additional plant and equipment. Although there has at times been an imperfect meshing of output and investment plans, the latter have been primarily determined by the former.

Most of the research and development (R&D) work in the Soviet Union is conducted outside of the enterprise, although large enterprises do have R&D facilities. There are three types of R&D organizations, and R&D is more centralized than in capitalist economies.[86] First, there is the research and development institute (1700 in 1969), which conducts applied research in a specialized technological area. The second type of R&D establishment is the engineering design organization, which specializes in the design of new products and of production processes. It is called a project-making organization, and in 1964, there were approximately 1000 engineering design organizations. The third type of R&D establishment is the construction engineering organization. It determines matters such as the location of the plant, the kind of equipment, and the scale of production. In 1970, there were 1400 such organizations.

Most of these R&D organizations are attached to ministries, and they are charged with the design and implementation of innovation and the expansion of existing facilities. Unlike capitalist enterprises in which routine

---

[85] Investment choice in the Soviet Union has been discussed in a number of articles and books: Bergson, *The Economics of Soviet Planning,* chap. 11; Gregory Grossman, "Scarce Capital and Soviet Doctrine," *Quarterly Journal of Economics,* vol. 67, no. 3 (August 1953); Alfred Zauberman, *Aspects of Planometrics* (New Haven, Conn.: Yale University Press, 1967), chaps. 13 and 14; Alan Abouchar, "The New Soviet Standard Methodology for Investment Allocation," *Soviet Studies,* vol. 24, no. 3 (January 1973), 402–410; Berliner, *The Innovation Decision* chap. 21; Stanley H. Cohn, "Deficiencies in Soviet Investment Policies and the Technological Imperative," in Joint Economic Committee, *Soviet Economy in a New Perspective,* (Washington, D.C.: U.S. Government Printing Office, 1976), pp. 447–459; Stanley H. Cohn, "Soviet Replacement Investment: A Rising Policy Imperative," in Joint Economic Committee, *Soviet Economy in a Time of Change* (Washington, D.C.: U.S. Government Printing Office, 1979), pp. 230–245; Michael Ellman, *Socialist Planning* (Cambridge, Mass.: Cambridge University Press, 1979), chap. 5.
[86] Berliner, *The Innovation Decision,* chap. 2.

investment decisions and technological innovation are taken within the enterprise, such matters are handled by external R&D establishments, whose responsibility ends when the project design is completed. This explains in part the reluctance of Soviet managers to risk introducing new technology.

The task of the project-making organization is first to elaborate and then to choose among alternative projects that yield the expansion of enterprise capacity specified by higher planning authorities. In this section, we deal with how project-making organizations choose among alternative projects. In a broad sense, they actually have little to do with the basic allocation of capital among competing ends, for they are concerned primarily with allocating fixed amounts of investment in accordance with centralized directives within their own administrative unit. The allocation of capital *among* administrative units, which, after all, is the decision most basic to the allocation of capital, remains in the hands of higher planning authorities.

In the Soviet Union, an annual investment plan for the entire economy that has been formulated by *Gosplan,* the ministries, and various state committees is submitted to the Council of Ministers. Once approved, the various R&D organizations, *Gosplan,* and the ministries supervise its implementation by the project-making organizations. Just as the material balance plan has its financial counterpart, so does the investment plan. The Ministry of Finance provides a portion of the funds required to finance the various projects directly from the state budget—the financial institution directly in charge of disbursing such investment funds is the Investment Bank (*Stroibank*), with *Gosbank* providing the funds for general repairs.[87] In this manner, the financial counterpart of the investment plan is used to locate deviations from the investment plan in much the same manner as it is used to monitor other enterprise operations. An overcommitment of investment resources (a situation where the materials and equipment required for approved projects exceed available supplies) will usually result in financial authorities providing insufficient financial resources to complete the project as scheduled. This practice tends to bring investment supplies and demands into balance but builds costly delays into underfinanced investment projects. One important source of this tendency to overcommit investment resources has been the ministries' desire to get as many projects started as early as possible so as to establish a priority claim on future investment

---

[87] One of the features of the general reform introduced in 1965 was to give enterprises more control over internally generated investment funds by allowing for some decentralized investment decisions. See our discussion in Chapter 9 on the implementation of this aspect of the reform. Prior to the reform (1964), internally generated investment funds accounted for 39 percent of enterprise capital investment. By 1968, this figure had risen to 45 percent. See *Finansy SSSR* [Finances of the USSR], no. 10 (1968), pp. 22–23. It should be noted that even these internally generated funds are strictly controlled by higher financial authorities.

supplies. This problem had become so serious that by 1971, 85 percent of investment projects begun the previous year were still unfinished.[88]

Problems of Investment Choice in the Soviet Economy

The choice among alternative investment projects, all of which yield the same increase in capacity, is not easy to resolve in the Soviet context. How is the project-making enterprise to choose among them? Ideally, a choice should be made that would minimize the consumption of scarce capital resources while achieving the required capacity expansion. On the surface, this seems like a simple criterion; yet for Soviet investment planners, it can be very complex.

First, there is an ideological constraint. The Marxian labor theory of value attributes all value to the current and past labor that have gone into the production of a commodity. From this, Soviet ideologists concluded during the early plan period that capital does not create value; therefore enterprises should not pay interest charges for its use—a view that prevailed until the 1965 economic reform. Thus, using interestlike calculations to rank investment alternatives seemed out of line with Marxian ideology. As Alfred Zauberman has expressed it, "where yield on capital is rejected as the motive force of the economy, its maximization could not serve as a guide for investment decisions."[89] In line with this reasoning, fixed capital from 1930 through 1965 was allocated to enterprises as an interest free grant. Enterprises therefore came to regard capital as a free factor of production, to be sought after as long as its marginal productivity remained positive. The only legitimate capital cost definitely allowable by Marxian value theory is depreciation, which supposedly compensates the state for the past labor being used up in production. There is no room in this strict Marxian framework however for technological obsolescence that does not represent a using up of past labor. As a result, the sole capital cost to enterprises, depreciation, has generally been small because of the omission of charges for obsolescence.[90]

The conflict between the strict interpretation of the labor theory of value and Soviet growth strategy is obvious. Whereas Marxian value theory dictates that capital does not create value, the basis of Soviet growth strategy has been to direct as much additional capital as possible into growth producing sectors such as electricity, machinery, and metallurgy. Rapid industrial growth is the objective of the system; yet the instrument crucial to

[88] *Voprosy ekonomiki* [Problems of economics], nos. 9 and 11 (1972). Also see Nove, *The Soviet Economy*, pp. 97–98, 231–240.

[89] Zauberman, *Aspects of Planometrics*, p. 139.

[90] Gert Leptin, *Methode und Efficienz der Investitionsfinanzierung durch Abschreibungen in der Sowjetwirtschaft* [Methods and efficiency of investment financing through depreciation in the Soviet economy], (Berlin: Osteuropa-Institut, 1961), part 2.

generating this growth was said to create no value of itself and carried a zero price. In practice, this conflict between ideology and growth strategy was resolved by having Soviet planners allocate capital administratively, according to a strict set of priorities and without reference to relative rates of return.[91]

The Soviet industrial price system represents a second problem. If more than one project yields the planned capacity increase, the project-making organization must generally evaluate the costs and benefits of alternative projects in value terms. If one of two equally expensive investment projects economizes on coal inputs while the other saves natural gas, the final choice will depend to a great extent on the relative prices of coal and gas. If these prices fail to reflect relative scarcities, then the "wrong" choice can be made. Because of the inconsistencies of the Soviet price system, one can understand the reluctance of planners to rely exclusively on value criteria in making investment decisions. Instead, most official guidelines suggest that value criteria be combined with physical indicators such as labor productivity and savings of specific material inputs, rather than relying exclusively on single value indicators.[92]

A third problem, closely related to the first, has been the lack of recognition of the importance of the time factor in capital investment decisions—a consequence of the absence of a recognized *time discount factor*, or interest rate. In market economies, investment projects that promise to yield large returns in the distant future will be ranked against projects yielding smaller but quicker returns by computing the present discounted value of each project using the interest rate as a common discount factor. A high interest rate (that supposedly reflects both society's time preferences and the scarcity of capital) will discourage long-term projects with delayed returns.

In the Soviet Union, there has historically been little recognition (at least until recently) of the time factor in choosing among alternative investment projects, and the perceived opportunity cost—either to the Soviet enterprise or to the ministry—of tying scarce resources down in long-term projects has been small. The lack of a time discount factor explains to a great extent the undue delays in the completion of investment projects (a

---

[91] For a detailed discussion of these points, see Grossman, "Scarce Capital," 311–314, reprinted in Franklyn D. Holzman, *Readings on the Soviet Economy* (Skokie, Ill.: Rand McNally, 1962).

[92] "Recommendations of the All-Union Scientific-Technical Conference on Problems of Determining the Economic Effectiveness of Capital Investment and New Techniques in the USSR National Economy," *Problems of Economics: A Journal of Translations*, vol. 1, no. 9 (January 1959), 86–90, reprinted in Holzman, *Readings on the Soviet Economy*, pp. 383–392. Also see "Standard Methodology for Determining the Economic Effectiveness of Capital Investments," *Ekonomicheskaia gazeta* [The economic gazette], no. 39 (1969), 11–12, translated in *The ASTE Bulletin*, vol. 13, no. 3 (Fall 1971), 25–36.

problem frequently referred to in the Soviet press) and the tendency to select projects with long gestation periods (the gigantomania of the early
thirties) despite the considerable scarcity of capital resources. Such behavior can be attributed in part to the expansion of planners' time horizons beyond sight during the "heroic phase of growth" during the 1930s.[93]

The Development of Investment Choice Criteria

Beginning in 1930, interest was outlawed as a capitalistic vestige no longer
required when capital is the property of the state. In keeping with the general sentiment of the early 1930s, it was argued that the economic laws of
capitalism were no longer operative and that capital should be allocated
administratively, without resort to the economic criteria of the old capitalist order. Thus, Stalin argued that the allocation of investment according to rates of return or other profitability measures would be contrary
to the interests of the state, for resources would then be directed away from
heavy industry into light industry, where profit rates would be higher. In
addition, it was argued in some quarters that the liberation from economic
rules would permit planners to choose more advanced technology than
would be justified if standard economic rules were strictly observed,
and thus the rapid industrial transformation of the Soviet Union would be
promoted.[94]

The intersectoral allocation of investment became an administrative
decision of higher planning authorities after 1930 and open discussion of investment choice criteria at the economywide level disappeared. The practical problem of allocating investment funds within specific sectors led
however—even during the barren Stalin years—to the development of informal investment allocation rules that were eventually officially formalized
between 1958 and 1960. During this early period, ministerial project-making organizations were forced to develop more specific rules for making decisions rather than simply choosing the investment variant yielding the
lowest operating costs (the only rule officially sanctioned), since the ministry had a limited capital allotment that had to be stretched as far as possible. This problem was especially troublesome in the railroad and electrical
power industries, where continuous substitutions between ever increasing
capital outlays and ever lower operating costs were possible. Thus, project-
making engineers and industry officials began to develop investment rules
for internal use that implicitly introduced rates of return and other capital
profitability criteria into the investment decision. Disguised under such
acceptable terminology as "effectiveness of investment" and "periods of

---

[93] Zauberman, *Aspects of Planometrics*, p. 139.
[94] Nove, *The Soviet Economy*, p. 233.

recoupment," these investment criteria came into fairly wide use within selected ministries by the late 1930s.[95]

The use of such interestlike calculations was officially sanctioned in 1958 by an all-union conference on capital effectiveness, after roughly three decades of pioneering work by engineers and economists.[96] The appearance of the USSR Academy of Science publication *Typical Method of Determining the Economic Effectiveness of Capital Investment and New Technology* in 1960 further substantiated the official acceptance of interestlike criteria for allocating investment within administrative units. Let us turn to the rules suggested by this 1960 publication.

Investment Decision Rules, 1960–1969

The most important decision rule suggested by *Typical Method* was the *Coefficient of Relative Effectiveness* (CRE), which was designed to evaluate the trade-offs between capital outlays and operating expenses. Such a measure was easily rationalized in terms of Marxian value theory, since operating expenses ultimately reflect labor costs, and capital should be evaluated according to how well it economizes the use of labor. To illustrate how the CRE measure operates, we assume that a project-making organization must choose between two alternative projects, both yielding the planned capacity increase. The two differ in terms of initial capital outlays (K) and resulting annual operating expenses (C), which, let us say, do not vary over time. Under normal circumstances, the higher the capital outlay, the lower the operating costs, and the CRE must evaluate this trade-off. It should be noted that a capital charge is *not* included in operating expenses—only a depreciation charge—an omission that may bias the CRE measure in favor of capital intensive projects. In our example, the CRE is given by the following formula, where the a and b subscripts refer to the two projects:

$$\text{CRE} = \frac{C_b - C_a}{K_a - K_b}$$

Thus, if project b costs one million rubles and project a costs two million rubles of capital outlay,[97] and project b's operating expenses are 0.2 million and project a's operating expenses are 0.1 million, then the CRE of project a (relative, of course, to project b) would be 10 percent. This should be inter-

---

[95] For a detailed discussion of the various techniques used during this period, see Grossman, "Scarce Capital," 315–343.

[96] "Recommendations of the All-Union Scientific-Technical Conference," 86–90.

[97] Capital outlay includes the cost of buildings, equipment, and installation, but excludes the cost of the site. Zauberman, *Aspects of Planometrics*, p. 142.

preted to mean that for every additional ruble of capital outlay on project *a*, 0.1 ruble of operating costs would be saved over project *b*.[98]

The *Typical Method* further suggested that a norm be established—the standard coefficient of efficiency—for *each* branch. If a project's CRE fell below the norm, it should be rejected unless there were special reasons for not doing so. In this manner, a minimum profitability, or capital effectiveness, rate would be established for each branch. Because these norms varied by branch (with the higher the priority, the lower the profitability norm for a given branch), capital profitability rates would not equalize among branches, as had been advocated by several prominent Soviet economists and many Western economists.[99] This result, however, was to be expected, in view of the state's desire to promote priority industrial and military sectors independently of restrictive economic criteria. Although there is no definite evidence, the CRE norms actually established were most likely not high enough to equate the supply and demand for capital, and administrative capital rationing remained the primary mechanism for investment allocation, despite the CRE.[100]

Although the CRE was just one of many rules suggested between 1960 and 1969, it became the most important and most widely used. It is important to note how crude a measure it actually was, for it failed to come to grips with varying patterns of capital expenditures, different service lives of projects, risk differences, and different time spacing of operating cost economies, as well as a host of other problems.

An important question raised by the CRE criterion was whether a single, uniform standard coefficient should be established for the entire economy, promoting eventual equalization of marginal rates of returns on investment projects in all branches.[101] The *Typical Method* was clearly in favor of differentiated standard branch norms. For the state to surrender its control over investment allocation and to replace it by a uniform mechanical rule was judged as contrary to the long-range vision of the Soviet leadership. The 1958 all-union conference on capital effectiveness leading up to the publication of the *Typical Method* was quite clear on this point: "Some

---

[98] An equivalent test would be: Let E be the "standard coefficient of efficiency." Then the projects should be compared by comparing their full costs—including an imputed interest cost:

$$C_i + EK_i = \text{minimum}$$

The project with the lowest *full* cost would be chosen. See Bergson, *The Economics of Soviet Planning*, p. 254.

[99] Bergson, *The Economics of Soviet Planning*, pp. 225–265; Judith Thornton, "Differential Capital Charges and Resource Allocation in Soviet Industry," *Journal of Political Economy*, vol. 79, no. 3 (May–June 1971), 545–561.

[100] Bergson, *The Economics of Soviet Planning*, pp. 262–263.

[101] See *ibid.*, p. 258, for a demonstration that a uniform norm will result in the equalization of the marginal productivities.

projects with smaller effectiveness may be approved . . . because they accelerate the solution of the basic economic problem, and are necessary for defense, political and other reasons . . ." and further, "capital investments are made on the basis of the economic laws of socialism which require the preferential development by the means of production. . . ."[102] An important point often overlooked in these discussions of the CRE is that the suggested rules generally pertain to the internal allocation of fixed sums of investment within a branch, and that only those investment alternatives would be evaluated that yield the planned increases in capacity. Also, the norms were generally not set to equate supply and demand, thus requiring a continuation of administrative rationing independently of the suggested rules. Thus, the leadership's acceptance of interestlike calculations in 1960 really represented no significant deviation from the centrally planned nature of the Soviet economy. Instead, the objective throughout was to make the allotted investment more effective and efficient within the context of planned .choice.

Another common current running through official pronouncements during this period was the reluctance of planning authorities to rely too heavily upon a single criterion. For example, the 1958 conference report made it quite clear that while the conference favored the CRE measure, it was to be used in combination with a number of other indicators when the situation required. If industrial prices failed to reflect relative scarcities, physical indicators were to be used along with the CRE criterion. The possibilities of substantial delays in project completion were also to be considered, as well as the interrelation of the project with other branches. Social factors such as the workers' safety were to enter into the calculation as well.[103]

Revised Investment Rules, 1969

In September of 1969, a new methodology for evaluating the relative effectiveness of investment projects was approved. The new *Standard Methodology for Determining the Economic Effectiveness of Capital Investments*[104] (referred to here as *Standard Methodology*) is identical to the CRE method, except for the acceptance of a *uniform* standard norm to apply to all branches of the economy. The measurement suggested to compare alternative investment projects is the *Comparative Economic Effectiveness of Capi-*

---

[102] "Recommendations of the All-Union Scientific-Technical Conference," 88.
[103] *Ibid.*, 88–89.
[104] "Standard Methodology for Determining the Economic Effectiveness of Capital Investments," translated in *The ASTE Bulletin*, vol. 13, no. 3 (Fall 1971), 25–36. It originally appeared in *Ekonomicheskaia gazeta* [The economic gazette], no. 39 (1969), 11–12

tal Investments, referred to here as the CEE. The CEE measure requires that investment projects be selected so that:

$$C_i + E_n K_i = \text{minimum}$$

where: C_i represents the current expenditures of the ith investment variant, K_i represents the cost of the investment project, and E_n is the uniform *normative coefficient of effectiveness* of capital investments, which is the same for all branches. The *Standard Methodology* suggests that this normative coefficient be set at 12 percent. Thus, the *Standard Methodology* (like the *Typical Method*) calls for evaluating investment projects on the basis of their *full* costs (operating costs plus imputed capital costs) with imputed capital costs calculated using a uniform coefficient for all branches.

An example of how the CEE method works would perhaps be helpful at this point: assume three alternative investment projects (Table 15). As one might expect, there is a trade-off between operating costs and investment outlays in our example (the higher the K, the lower the C):

In our example, the projects should refer to investment projects within a branch or in different branches. Because the normative coefficient is uniform for the entire economy, this should make no difference in the evaluation process. The CEE investment criterion calls for the selection of the project having the lowest costs, that is, the lowest *full* cost (the sum of operating expenses plus a capital charge). In the table, the project with the lowest full cost, Project 2, should be selected, for it yields the optimal trade-off between greater investment outlays and lower operating costs.[105]

In addition to establishing the CEE concept, the *Standard Methodology* provides detailed discounting procedures for evaluating in present value terms projects whose operating expenditures and capital outlays change over time. The *Standard Methodology* suggests using a discount rate of 8 percent, which it claims is in line with current depreciation procedures.

On the surface, the use of a uniform normative coefficient for the entire economy would seem to violate the branch priority principle and call for the allocation of investment strictly on the basis of rates of return. This conclusion seems to be further supported by the fact that the *Standard Methodology* calls upon the investment plan to allocate investment among branches according to a uniform coefficient of effectiveness. In fact, this may not prove to be so. First, the suggested normative coefficient (12 percent) will probably not be high enough to equate the supply and demand

---

[105] The importance of differential normative coefficients in preserving the branch priority system can be illustrated using Table 15. Suppose that Project 2 is in light industry, whereas Projects 1 and 3 are in heavy industry. Instead of using 12 percent as a norm for light industry, a higher 30 percent rate is set. The CEE of Project 2 now becomes 447.5, which eliminates it from selection.

TABLE 15 Computation of the "Comparative Economic Effectiveness" (CEE) of Three Investment Projects

Project	Operating Costs (C)	Investment Outlay (K)	Uniform Normative Coefficient	Full Costs (1 + [3 × 2])
1	300	510	12%	361.2
2	290	525	12%	353.0
3	285	590	12%	355.8

for capital—a point already noted by Soviet critics.[106] As long as this remains true, much capital allocation will be handled by administrative procedures. Second, the *Standard Methodology* states that deviations from the normative coefficient may be approved by *Gosplan* in order to stimulate technological progress, to allow for differences in wage and price levels, and to promote regional development. For example, a lower (8 percent) normative coefficient was established for the Far North, and there is talk of establishing an 8 percent norm for electrical power generation. The generally liberal allowance for exceptions to the uniform coefficient rule quickly became a matter of concern to reform-minded Soviet economists, one of whom wrote that they "open the door to the broadest degree of arbitrariness" in investment decisions.[107] Third, the *Standard Methodology* suggests that the CEE index be supplemented by further indexes—productivity of labor, capital-output ratios, capital investment per unit of output, and selected physical indexes—to "take account of the influences of the most important factors on the economic effectiveness of capital investments and to take account of the interaction of this effectiveness with other divisions of the plan.[108] Fourth, the *Standard Methodology* states that the investment plan should follow the output plan of the national economy; for example, the allocation of investment among branches is still to be predetermined by the industrial supply and output plan. This statement seems to contradict one of the key provisions of the new investment rules—namely, that capital should be allocated among branches according to a uniform normative coefficient of effectiveness.[109]

Thus, the new *Standard Methodology* was a step in the direction of investment allocation on the basis of rates of return irrespective of branch of

---

[106] V. Cherniavski, "The Measure of Effectiveness," *Problems of Economics: A Journal of Translations,* vol. 15, no. 8 (December 1972); and L. V. Kantorovich, *Essays in Optimal Planning* (White Plains, N.Y.: International Arts and Sciences Press, 1976), essays 8–10.
[107] Quoted in V. Vainshtein, "On Methods of Determining the Economic Effectiveness of Capital Investment," *Problems of Economics: A Journal of Translations,* vol. 15, no. 3 (July 1972), 12.
[108] "Standard Methodology," p. 31.
[109] Abouchar, "The New Soviet Standard Methodology," 407.

production, but it clearly did not call for a clear break with investment allocation according to the priority principle. We emphasize that efficiency indexes are brought into play only *after* the basic investment allocation decisions are made in the investment plan. Investment funds are allocated in the investment plan. The efficiency indexes play a relatively minor role: they assist in selecting that investment project which yields the capacity expansion called for in the investment plan.

Proposals of Soviet Mathematical Economists

An influential group of Soviet mathematical economists that includes such prominent academicians as L. V. Kantorovich, V. V. Novozhilov, and V. S. Nemchinov argues that the CEE criteria can be effectively used only if based upon a rational system of underlying prices.[110] "Objectively determined prices," they argue, should be generated by using linear programming techniques. Although the methods proposed by the mathematical school differ, there is a unifying thread among them: the basic resource allocation problem is seen as choosing among the large number of alternative activities, whose usage levels are limited by resource availabilities, in such a manner as to optimize the economy's objective function. For example, the objective function may be the total cost of producing a planned bill of final output targets, with the goal being to minimize the total cost. In the course of finding the optimal combination of economic activities, a set of "objectively determined prices" would emerge as the solution to the dual linear programming problem, which could then be used as rational resource prices. Importantly, an "objectively determined" price of capital would also be generated, which would be rational in the sense that this price would equate the supply and demand for capital, which the Soviet mathematical economists propose to use as the normative coefficient of effectiveness.

An Evaluation of Investment Choice

Investment choice in the Soviet Union has been far from perfect throughout the plan period. The gigantomania[111] of the early 1930s and the large percentage of uncompleted construction projects today may be cited as the most visible wastes of the current system. There is much to criticize about investment choice throughout the plan period: the lack of a capital charge until recently, the reluctance of planners to rely on profitability criteria,

---

[110] V. S. Nemchinov, ed., *The Uses of Mathematics in Economics* (Cambridge, Mass.: MIT Press, 1964); and L. V. Kantorovich, *The Best Use of Economic Resources* (Cambridge, Mass.: Harvard University Press, 1965).

[111] Leon Smolinski, "The Scale of Soviet Industrial Establishments," *American Economic Review*, supplement, vol. 52 (1962), 138–148.

and the overtaut investment planning. In the past, Western criticism of investment planning has centered on the use of differentiated branch norms that resulted in differentiated rates of return among sectors. All of these have been cited as major sources of inefficiency in the Soviet economy.[112]

However, when one considers the *relative* inefficiency of investment choice in the Soviet Union, the issue becomes much more complex, especially in the context of rapid economic development. Some Western development economists stress that investment choice based upon capitalist marginal rules in developing economies is inefficient, owing to the existence of externalities and interdependencies.[113] For example, marginal efficiency calculations might necessitate the rejection of a vital road, canal, or factory that planners working with an integrated plan and a long time horizon might accept.[114] Thus, the issue of the relative efficiency of Soviet investment choice under conditions of rapid industrialization is very cloudy, and we are unable to provide a clear answer. The ultimate answer depends upon the compatibility of static and dynamic efficiency. What we suggest here is that the reader avoid drawing hasty conclusions until we take up this matter again in Part Three.

The external signs are that Soviet investment choice has not been particularly good. As we shall point out in Chapters 10 and 11, the rate of growth of capital productivity has been negative throughout most of the plan era, and in recent years the rate of decline has accelerated. The Soviet technology gap vis-à-vis the West has not been narrowed in the past 20 years, and Soviet managers and investment planners appear to prefer costly repairs of existing capital to replacement with new equipment.[115] Soviet investment policy has been geared to replacing capital much more slowly than in the West. Thus, most evidence points to deficiencies in investment decision making in the Soviet Union that have not been corrected by the introduction of efficiency formulae.

SUMMARY: RESOURCE ALLOCATION IN THE SOVIET UNION

In the last two chapters, we have surveyed how resources are allocated in the Soviet economy. With several significant exceptions, resources are allo-

---

[112] Bergson, *The Economics of Soviet Planning,* p. 334; Judith Thornton, "Differential Capital Charges and Resource Allocation in Soviet Industry," *Journal of Political Economy,* vol. 79, no. 3 (May–June 1971), 545–561.

[113] For example, see P. N. Rosenstein-Rodan, "Problems of Industrialization of Eastern and South Eastern Europe," *Economic Journal,* vol. 53, no. 210 (June–September 1943), 202–211.

[114] In the new *Standard Methodology,* it is clearly pointed out that a broad view of costs and benefits must be taken, which should extend far beyond the project itself. Questions should be asked such as: how will the proposed project affect transportation facilities, related industries, labor supplies, etc.?

[115] Cohn, "Soviet Replacement Investment," pp. 230–245.

cated administratively by the central plan. Material balance planning is used to allocate industrial supplies almost without reference to their prices, which are designed to equal average branch costs of production. Throughout the planning process, financial authorities and party officials monitor plan fulfillment, the former through the use of "ruble control." Soviet managers are supposed to direct their enterprise in accordance with the *techpromfinplan*, which has been formulated by superior planning agencies. In fact, managers do exercise some discretion in the operation of the enterprise, and, in this area, they are motivated by the managerial reward system, which has tended to be output oriented. The enterprise's investments are determined external to the enterprise, with the basic allocation of investment funds being determined administratively in the investment plan.

The major exceptions to administrative allocation are the labor and the consumer goods market. In the Soviet Union, labor has been allocated primarily by differential wages, supplemented by other controls such as organized recruitment, placement of selectively educated graduates, and other administrative arrangements. Consumer goods, once produced in planned quantities, have primarily been allocated to consumers through the market. Thus retail prices have tended to approach market clearing prices, just as wage rates have tended toward market clearing rates.

SELECTED BIBLIOGRAPHY

Soviet Enterprise Management

Joseph S. Berliner, *Factory and Manager in the USSR* (Cambridge, Mass.: Harvard University Press, 1957).

Joseph S. Berliner, *The Innovation Decision in Soviet Industry* (Cambridge, Mass.: MIT Press, 1976).

Joseph S. Berliner, "Managerial Incentives and Decisionmaking: A Comparison of the United States and the Soviet Union," in M. Bornstein and D. Fusfeld, eds., *The Soviet Economy*, 3rd ed. (Homewood, Ill.: Irwin, 1970), pp. 165–195.

David Granick, *Management of the Industrial Firm in the USSR* (New York: Columbia University Press, 1954).

David Granick, *Managerial Comparisons of Four Developed Countries: France, Britain, United States, and Russia* (Cambridge, Mass.: MIT Press, 1972).

David Granick, *The Red Executive* (Garden City, N.Y.: Doubleday, 1960).

David Granick, *Soviet Metal Fabricating and Economic Development* (Madison: University of Wisconsin Press, 1967), chap. 7.

Alec Nove, *Economic Rationality and Soviet Politics* (New York: Praeger, 1964), chap. 5.

Barry M. Richman, *Management Development and Education in the Soviet Union* (East Lansing: Michigan State University, 1967).

Barry M. Richman, *Soviet Industrial Management* (Englewood Cliffs, N.J.: Prentice-Hall, 1965).

Labor Allocation in the Soviet Union

Abram Bergson, *The Economics of Soviet Planning* (New Haven, Conn.: Yale University Press, 1964), chap. 6.

Abram Bergson, *The Structure of Soviet Wages* (Cambridge, Mass.: Harvard University Press, 1944).

Emily Clark Brown, *Soviet Trade Unions and Labor Relations* (Cambridge, Mass.: Harvard University Press, 1966).

Janet G. Chapman, "Labor Mobility and Labor Allocation in the USSR," paper presented at the joint meeting of the Association for the Study of Soviet-Type Economics and the Association for Comparative Economics, Detroit, Mich., December 1970.

Janet G. Chapman, *Real Wages in Soviet Russia Since 1928* (Cambridge, Mass.: Harvard University Press, 1963).

Janet G. Chapman, "Soviet Wages Under Socialism," in Alan Abouchar, ed., *The Socialist Price Mechanism* (Durham, N.C.: Duke University Press, 1977), pp. 246-281.

Warren W. Eason, "Labor Force," in Abram Bergson and Simon Kuznets, eds., *Economic Trends in the Soviet Union* (Cambridge, Mass.: Harvard University Press, 1963).

Murray Feshbach and Stephen Rapawy, "Labor Constraints in the Five-Year Plan," in Joint Economic Committee, *Soviet Economic Prospects for the Seventies* (Washington, D.C.: U.S. Government Printing Office, 1973).

Murray Feshbach and Stephen Rapawy, "Soviet Population and Manpower Trends and Policies," in Joint Economic Committee, *Soviet Economy in a New Perspective* (Washington, D.C.: U.S. Government Printing Office, 1976), pp. 113-154.

Arcadius Kahan and Blair Ruble, eds., *Industrial Labor in the USSR* (New York: Pergamon, 1979).

Leonard J. Kirsch, *Soviet Wages: Changes in Structure and Administration Since 1956* (Cambridge, Mass.: MIT Press, 1972).

Alastair McAuley, *Economic Welfare in the Soviet Union* (Madison: University of Wisconsin Press, 1979).

Mary McAuley, *Labor Disputes in Soviet Russia 1957-1965* (Oxford: Oxford University Press, 1969).

Stephen Rapawy, "Regional Employment Trends in the U.S.S.R.: 1950 to 1975," in Joint Economic Committee, *Soviet Economy in a Time of Change* (Washington, D.C.: U.S. Government Printing Office, 1979), vol. 1, pp. 600-617.

The Investment Decision

Alan Abouchar, "The New Soviet Standard Methodology for Investment Allocation," *Soviet Studies*, vol. 24, no. 3 (January 1973).

Abram Bergson, *The Economics of Soviet Planning* (New Haven, Conn.: Yale University Press, 1964), chap. 11.

Frank A. Durgin, "The Soviet 1969 Standard Methodology for Investment Allocation Versus 'Universally Correct' Methods," *The ACES Bulletin*, vol. 19, no. 2 (Summer 1977), 29-54.

P. Gregory, B. Fielitz, and T. Curtis, "The New Soviet Investment Rules: A Guide to Rational Investment Planning?" *Southern Economic Journal,* vol. 41, no. 3 (January 1974).

Gregory Grossman, "Scarce Capital and Soviet Doctrine," *Quarterly Journal of Economics,* vol. 67, no. 3 (August 1953).

Gert Leptin, *Methode und Efficienz der Investitionsfinanzierung durch Abschreibungen in der Sowjetwirtschaft* [Methods and efficiency of investment financing through depreciation in the Soviet economy] (Berlin: Osteuropa-Institut, 1961).

Alfred Zauberman, *Aspects of Planometrics* (New Haven, Conn.: Yale University Press, 1967), chaps. 13 and 14.

Alfred Zauberman, *Mathematical Theory in Soviet Planning* (New York: Oxford University Press, 1976), chap. 4.

Chapter 7

Soviet Agriculture

The history of Soviet agriculture forms a very important part of the overall story of Soviet economic development. This importance stems in part from the traditionally significant role played by the peasant in Soviet society; it also stems, from the Soviet experience—being a most interesting case study of the role of agriculture in a developing economy and, in particular, of the unique Soviet solutions to development problems.

We have already examined important facets of Soviet agricultural development in the period prior to the introduction of planning in 1928, and in addition, have discussed the drive to collectivization and the immediate impact of that historic event upon the institutions and performance of Soviet agriculture. In this chapter, we turn first to a consideration of the organization and operation of Soviet agriculture in the postcollectivization period and, in particular, focus upon the collective farm (*kolkhoz*), the state farm (*sovkhoz*), and their roles in the Soviet agricultural sector.

Second, from the point of view of the Soviet experience with economic development, it is important to understand the extent to which agriculture in fact "contributed" to this development—we can then formulate more accurately the role of agriculture in the Soviet development experience. Finally, although the immediate impact of collectivization upon agricultural output was negative, it remains necessary to examine Soviet agricultural output and productivity performance in a long-run framework, which is done in the concluding section of this chapter.

THE ORGANIZATION OF SOVIET AGRICULTURAL PRODUCTION: THE KOLKHOZ AND THE SOVKHOZ

Although various forms of collective production organizations had existed earlier in the Soviet Union, the predominant form—comprising 91.7 percent of all collectivized land by 1931—became the agricultural *artel*, or *kolkhoz.*[1] In addition, initially playing a subservient role, was the state farm, or *sovkhoz.* The state farm might well be described as a factory in the countryside insofar as important features of its organization and operation are very similar to the industrial enterprise. The *kolkhoz* however was, and in some measure remains, a form of organization unique to the Soviet bloc countries. Organizational aspects of Soviet agriculture are summarized in Table 16.

The Kolkhoz

The *kolkhoz* is in theory a cooperative organization in which the peasants voluntarily join to till the soil, using means of production contributed initially by those who join, but now owned jointly by all in the *kolkhoz.* Under the *kolkhoz* charter of 1935 (since 1969 there has been a new charter), the means of production are said to be "*kolkhoz*-cooperative" property, belonging to the *kolkhoz* in perpetuity.[2] In addition to the socialized sector of the *kolkhoz* (land, equipment, buildings, etc.), the use of which is governed by the chairman and management board, each peasant is entitled to own a limited number of animals and to cultivate a private plot. These plots and private holdings have been very important in terms of their contribution to Soviet agricultural output, although they have been subjected to a considerable degree of restriction over the years.[3]

In reality, the voluntary aspects of *kolkhoz* membership have been absent. *Kolkhoz* members who depart for the city do not in fact receive the equity that they have contributed to the farm. In addition, the internal passport system has limited peasant labor mobility both within the rural sector

---

[1] The reader interested in the discussion of the different organizational forms might consult D. J. Male, *Russian Peasant Organization Before Collectivization* (Cambridge: Cambridge University Press, 1971); Robert G. Wesson, *Soviet Communes* (New Brunswick, N.J.: Rutgers University Press, 1963).

[2] As we shall see, the organizational and operational features of the typical *kolkhoz* have changed quite significantly over time. The new *kolkhoz* charter, finally published in 1969, in large measure served only to formally codify changes already made and authorized during the intervening years. Thus with the increased size of the *kolkhoz*, an expanded managerial structure was authorized, limited new autonomy for management was enacted— confirming earlier trends—and the labor day (*trudoden*) as a method of calculating payments to labor was abandoned in favor of a wage system. Also, the designation "*kolkhoz*-cooperative" was dropped in the new charter. For a discussion of these changes, see Robert C. Stuart, *The Collective Farm in Soviet Agriculture* (Lexington, Mass.: Heath, 1972).

[3] Although the presence of the private sector has been ideologically unpalatable to the regime, the importance of its product contribution relative to its input usage has been sufficiently great to ensure its preservation. Over time however, the official attitude toward the private sector has tended to fluctuate. The major work on this sector is Karl-Eugen Wädekin, *The Private Sector in Soviet Agriculture*, George Karcz, ed., Keith Bush, translator (Berkeley: University of California Press, 1973).

TABLE 16 The Organization of Soviet Agriculture (selected indicators)

	1928	1932	1940	1953	1957	1960	1965	1970	1978
Number of collective farms (in thousands)	33.3	211.7	236.9	97.0	78.2	44.9	36.9	33.6	26.7
Sown area of collective farms as a portion of total sown area (%)	1.2	70.5[a]	78.3	83.9	68.4	60.6	50.2	47.9	44.2
Number of state farms	1407	4337	4159	4857	5905	7375	11,681	14,994	20,500
Sown area of state farms as a portion of total sown area (%)	1.5[b]	n.a.	7.7	9.6	25.7	33.1	42.6	44.4	51.2
Sown area of the private sector as a portion of total sown area (%)[c]	97.3	n.a.	13.0	4.4	3.8	3.3	3.2	3.2	3.0[d]

SOURCES: Selected volumes of *Narodnoe khoziaistvo SSSR* [The national economy of the USSR]; *Sel'skoe khoziaistvo SSSR* [Agriculture of the USSR]; and *SSSR v tsifrakh* [The USSR in figures.]

[a] Based upon aggregate sown area for 1933.

[b] Includes state farms and other state agricultural enterprises.

[c] The private sector consists of three parts: (1) private plots of collective farm members; (2) private plots of workers in industry and other state organizations; (3) the private peasant economy. The last was of minimal importance after the 1930s.

[d] 1975.

225

and between the rural and urban sectors, although collective farm peasants were recently included in the passport system.

The highest organ of administration in the *kolkhoz* is the general meeting, or in some instances since 1958, meetings convened in the basic production units within the *kolkhoz*—the brigades. In theory, the general meeting elects the chairman of the *kolkhoz*, although in reality this position is generally filled by a party appointee through the *nomenklatura* procedure, and the vote is perfunctory. In addition to the chairman, the general meeting selects a management board that normally consists of the chairman and other leading personnel (specialists, brigadiers, etc.).[4] Again, although theoretically elected, in practice the board is generally chosen by the chairman and secretary of the party committee. Finally, the revision commission, an auditing body, is similarly selected.[5] In addition to such personnel matters, the general meeting is also supposed to exercise powers relating to membership matters, discipline, general approval of plan documents, and other administrative matters.

No discussion of the administrative structure of the *kolkhoz* would be complete without reference to the roles of the Communist Party and, prior to 1958, the Machine Tractor Stations (MTS). Within the *kolkhoz* there may exist one or more party organizations (a Primary Party Organization and possibly a candidate group or Party-Komsomol group).

It is difficult to know with any precision the impact of the party apparatus on the decision-making of the *kolkhoz*. However, the party organizations and their members are, as "leaders of the masses," responsible for the appropriate direction of state and party policies. More than this, however, the party is concerned with the immediate operation of the farm, insofar as managerial personnel are typically party members and, in addition, will work closely with the secretary of the party organization.

In addition to a general leadership role, the party is directly concerned with what we would call personnel matters—selection and dismissal, work conditions, general morale, and so on. The party also organizes and runs

---

[4] The management board is relatively small (7–15 persons), thus making it suitable for operational management. In practice, there may be division of labor within this body—the chairman may be responsible for the field crop sector, the vice-chairman for the cattle sector, etc. Normally, this body may convene once a week or more frequently; meetings may last several hours. As we shall see later, the substantially increased size of the *kolkhoz* since the early 1950s has measurably increased the role of the brigade—especially that of the brigadier—and brigade meetings as a focus of decision-making activity. In addition, there has been a tendency to expand the presence of advisory bodies capable of supplying technical information to the decision-making centers. See Stuart, *The Collective Farm*, chap. 2.

[5] *Ibid.* The auditing commission has proven to be a very ineffective body, partly due to the nature of its tasks and possible conflicts with party personnel, and also the lack of personnel adequately trained in auditing matters. A knowledge of economic matters has never been a prerequisite for any position in a *kolkhoz*.

campaigns to promote better farm performance. In short, the party is an all-pervasive force in the agricultural, just as it is in the industrial, enterprise.

We have already noted in Chapter 4 that the MTS were established in 1930, basically to act as mechanisms of state control in the countryside and also to serve as a device to allocate the usage of machinery and equipment among the collective farms. From their beginning, the MTS were powerful instruments of state control in the Soviet countryside in that they had a monopoly over agricultural specialists (until the early 1950s) and over most major farm equipment—both of which were absolutely essential to the success of the individual *kolkhoz*. But more than this, the director of the MTS, along with the chairman of the *kolkhoz*, was responsible for the execution of economic activity within the *kolkhoz*—thus the MTS played a decisive and continuing role in the day-to-day operations of the *kolkhoz* and bore responsibility for its results. Under these circumstances, one can readily understand the close tutelage under which the *kolkhoz* fell. In fact, it was described by Khrushchev in the 1950s as the presence of "two bosses" in the countryside—an intolerable situation that ultimately led to the dissolution of these stations in 1958 and to the sale of their equipment directly to the *kolkhoz*.

The Sovkhoz

The second major form of production enterprise in Soviet agriculture is the state farm, or *sovkhoz*. Unlike the *kolkhoz*, the *sovkhoz* is structurally similar to Soviet industrial enterprises. This means that the *sovkhoz* is a budget-financed organization, operating within the guidelines of the *khozraschet* managerial-financial system and paying wages to its workers. Managerial selection is similar to that of an industrial enterprise, as is the role of the Communist Party.

It is evident from the data assembled in Table 16 that the importance of the *sovkhoz* has increased significantly since collectivization. As we pursue our discussion of Soviet agricultural policy in this chapter, the reasons for this change will become clearer. At this point, suffice it to say that the growing role of the *sovkhoz* can be attributed to its favored ideological position in the Soviet system and its superior budget-financing status. Finally, the *sovkhoz* has a position within the state economic and administrative structure as a form of enterprise that can be controlled directly by the state for the implementation of policy, whether that policy be the conversion of weak *kolkhozy*, the provision of large cities with agricultural supplies, or the organizational transformation of the farm unit into an agroindustrial complex. Since the early 1950s, the *sovkhoz* has been the organization used by the state to carry out the state policies and campaigns described later in this chapter.

AGRICULTURAL PLANNING: THE KOLKHOZ

The *kolkhoz* is not, in substance, an independent cooperative, for its most important decisions are planned from above. Like other economic entities in the Soviet system, the *kolkhoz* and the *sovkhoz* have an annual plan drawn up by planning organs and integrated with the overall national economic plan. Within the *kolkhoz*, this plan is broken down into short-run targets; although like the industrial enterprise, priority is primarily placed on the *gross output* target. The distribution of this planned output is also predetermined by the plan insofar as the *kolkhoz* is required to meet certain compulsory deliveries at fixed prices set by the state. The remainder of the output can either be sold to the state at higher, "above quota" prices (the famous "two-level" price system, which was largely abandoned in 1958), sold in collective farm markets, or delivered to the collective farm members as partial in-kind payment for their labor services.[6] At the same time, input configurations are established within the plan, leaving little room for flexibility: land and equipment utililzation (prior to 1958) were determined by the MTS, and labor was distributed by a system of norms specifying compulsory minimum participation rates for collective farm members in the socialized sector of the farm.[7] Capital funds may be obtained from retained earnings, in which case the portion of gross income to be set aside and the utilization of such funds are both spelled out in the plan, with only limited room for the manager to shift funds from one to another.[8] In the case of the *sovkhoz*, the bulk of capital funds is provided through budget financing.

Although long-term planning has always existed in Soviet agriculture, it has had little operational meaning. Crop patterns, land usage, labor distribution, and other important microeconomic decisions have largely been made on a short-run basis by administrative planning organs external to the *kolkhoz*. These organs, though establishing plan targets in conjunction with

[6] The two-level price system was formally abolished in 1958, although thereafter farms were actively encouraged to deliver more than the state quotas. The two-level system was partially restored for grain in 1965. The whole matter of agricultural procurement has been the subject of ongoing discussion. For a survey of various positions, see Morris Bornstein, "The Soviet Debate on Agricultural Prices and Procurement Reforms," *Soviet Studies*, vol. 21, no. 1 (July 1969), 1–20. In large measure, the two-level price system could be abandoned as the Soviet Union grew richer and the agricultural sector declined in relative importance. For many years however, this price system tended to institutionalize the Scissors Crisis of the 1920s.

[7] Following the demise of the MTS in 1958, machinery and equipment were sold to the *kolkhozy* and the managerial functions of the MTS eliminated.

[8] *Kolkhoz* investment, unlike other agricultural and industrial investment in the Soviet system, is not budget financed. Capital investment must, therefore, be met from funds generated within the *kolkhoz* or by the use of loans from *Gosbank*. For a discussion of *kolkhoz* financing, see James R. Millar, "Financing the Modernization of *Kolkhozy*," in James R. Millar, ed., *The Soviet Rural Community* (Urbana: University of Illinois Press, 1971), pp. 276–303.

the *kolkhoz* management board, have been concerned primarily with satis-
fying immediate superiors. Under this sytem, the familiar industrial problem of success indicators—the problems of defining capacity, achievement,
and so on—has also plagued *kolkhoz* operations, worsened by the normal
unpredictability of the natural environment in which agricultural production takes place.[9]

Distribution of Kolkhoz Output

The most crucial aspect of the *kolkhoz* has been its system of output distribution and labor payment, for this system has, over the years, ensured the
steady flow of agricultural products to the state, in spite of spotty overall
agricultural performance. As we shall see, this was the Soviet way of forcing
agriculture to perform the necessary support role to industry that is required in the course of economic development.

Until 1958, as noted, the *kolkhoz* operated under a two-level price system. The state paid a fixed price for compulsory deliveries of important
crops (grains, technical crops, etc.), which until the early 1960s was not adjusted to even cover gradually rising costs of production in the *kolkhoz.*
These deliveries were not based upon output performance, but rather upon
sown area—thus shifting the burden of the unpredictability of agricultural
returns onto the agricultural sector and away from the state.[10] Produce left
over after the compulsory sales and after in-kind payment for MTS services
could be either sold to the state at higher above quota prices or in the collective farm markets at retail prices. The latter have been the primary outlet for the produce of the private plots and a major source of money income
for the peasant family.[11] Such a system might have worked more smoothly

---

[9] The problem of setting appropriate targets based upon a realistic assessment of capacity
has been peculiarly difficult in agriculture. Planners have tended to use various measurement techniques, such as on-site inspection, past performance, and so on. In general, the
ratchet effect has been prevalent, thus inducing *kolkhoz* management to hide production
capability as inspectors search for a basis upon which to increase targets. The absence of
significant long-term planning in agriculture has had a negative impact upon this process.
For an extended discussion, see Stuart, *The Collective Farm*, chap. 6. Since the mid-1960s, a
major effort has been made to increase the importance of long-term planning and to stabi-
lize production targets within the Five Year Plan horizon.

[10] The state farm was not well-suited to carry the burden of agricultural output fluctuations. In the case of crop failures, the state would cover losses in that it would have to meet
the wage bill by subsidizing the state farm from the state budget. Therefore, resources
would flow back into, not out of, agriculture. This explains why primary reliance was
placed on the *kolkhoz* and not on the *sovkhoz* during the 1930s.

[11] The private sector has been and remains an important source of peasant family income.
In 1953, for example, 45.7 percent of aggregate family income was derived from the private
subsidiary economy. By 1963, this proportion had declined relatively little, to 42.9 percent.
See V. P. Ostrovskii, *Kolkhoz'noe krest'ianstvo SSSR* [*Kolkhoz* peasants of the USSR] (Saratov: Saratov University, 1967), p. 93.

were it not for the dismal state of agricultural planning throughout much of the plan era, plus the normal problems of variability in this sector. In fact, farm capacity was frequently not known by planners, and targets were constantly ratcheted upward in the expectation of improved performance. Thus achieving success was often limited to a one-time opportunity, for the level of state exactions increased accordingly, so that the collective farmers had no better standing than they had had initially.

Finally, an essential feature of the *kolkhoz* has been the method of labor payment—the labor day, or *trudoden*, which was formally abandoned in 1966 in favor of a wage payment system as used in state farms and industrial enterprises. The labor day was not a measure of labor time and bore no necessary relationship to the workday—rather, it was an arbitrary unit by which all farm tasks were rated. A given task, for example ploughing a field, might yield the collective farmer a certain number of labor days, the value of which was uncertain because only at the end of the year could the *value* of the labor day—in money and in kind—be determined by dividing any remaining product and income (after compulsory state exactions) by the number of labor days earned by the *kolkhoz* as a whole. Then and only then could each person's labor day earnings be established.

To ensure the state of a first and guaranteed claim upon output, this system was unique in that the collective farmer bore the burden of crop fluctuations by having the value of labor days shrink. Indeed, with labor earning a residual, there could be little incentive for managers to use labor effectively, let alone for the laborers to devote significant effort to production in the socialized sector of the *kolkhoz*. From other standpoints, however, the system was even less appropriate. First, the labor day was itself a largely arbitrary measure of work input. From farm to farm, region to region, and over time, the number of labor days granted for a given task could vary widely and with little relation to the actual or perceived effort required to complete a given task. In addition, income distributions to the peasants were small and very infrequent, since the value of the labor day was not calculated until the termination of the year (advances were introduced in the 1950s, a matter to be discussed later), and thus the peasant was expected to expend effort for an unknown reward in the distant future. In this light, the relative promise of labor devoted to the private plot and the lack of incentive to exert oneself in the socialized sector can be appreciated. Throughout the plan era, these private plots have occupied a small portion of peasants' work time but have produced roughly one-half of their aggregate family income, plus a significant contribution to agricultural output.[12]

---

[12] For a discussion of the contribution of the private sector see, for example, Karl-Eugen Wädekin, "Kolkhoz, Sovkhoz, and Private Production in Soviet Agriculture," in W. A. Douglas Jackson, ed., *Agrarian Policies and Problems in Communist and Non-Communist Countries* (Seattle: University of Washington Press, 1971), pp. 106–137.

Finally, the labor day system of distribution prevented the use of cost accounting. It is little wonder that cost accounting did not exist on collective farms until the mid-1950s, at which point state farm wage rates were frequently utilized to value the labor component of *kolkhoz* production costs. Such a system must have made the cost information that went into decision-making virtually worthless and thus hindered the efficient utilization of farm inputs.

CHANGING PATTERNS IN SOVIET AGRICULTURE: THE KHRUSHCHEV ERA

Collectivization was a social transformation of the first magnitude. It not only produced a great social upheaval in its initial stages but it also served to create a unique institutional structure that has lasted to the present day as a cornerstone of Soviet agrarian policy, despite its apparently negative impact upon incentives and efficiency. In the postwar period, however, there have been important changes in the agricultural sector. Although the impact of World War II upon agricultural production was severe, agricultural gross production had generally recovered to its prewar level by the late 1940s.[13] As we shall discuss shortly, however, agricultural performance was not promising in terms of yields, costs, seasonality of production, and so on. Although Stalin did devote attention to agriculture during the early postwar period, he did so primarily in terms of two rather grandiose schemes—first, the effort to achieve productivity gains through massive amalgamation of collective farms into gigantic complexes, and second, the so-called Stalin Plan for Transforming Nature, the essence of which was a vast irrigation network for the country.[14] Both were subsequently the subject of severe criticism by Khrushchev, and indeed, the path to higher productivity in Soviet agriculture was rather different in the Khrushchev era.

The Twentieth Congress of the Communist Party in 1953 devoted extensive time to a discussion of agricultural problems in the Soviet Union. In fact, Khrushchev was to stake—and perhaps ultimately end—his career on

[13] The reader interested in the details of the war period might read Erich Strauss, *Soviet Agriculture in Perspective* (London: Allen & Unwin, 1969), chap. 7; Lazar Volin, *A Century of Russian Agriculture* (Cambridge, Mass.: Harvard University Press, 1970), chap. 12. Useful sources in Russian would be the multivolume official history, P. N. Pospelov, ed., *Istoriia velikoi otechestvennoi voiny sovetskogo soiuza* [History of the great patriotic war of the Soviet Union], (Moscow: Voenizdat, 1945); I. A. Gladkov, ed., *Sovetskaia ekonomika v periode velikoi otechestvennoi voiny* [The Soviet economy in the period of the great patriotic war], (Moscow: Nauka, 1970), chaps. 5–6; Iu. V. Arutiunian, *Sovetskoe krestianstvo v gody velikoi otechestvennoi voiny* [Soviet peasants in the years of the great patriotic war], 2nd ed., (Moscow: Nauka, 1970); I. E. Zelenin, *Sovkhozy SSSR (1941–1950)* [Sovkhozy of the USSR, 1941–1950], (Moscow: Nauka, 1969).

[14] The postwar developments in Soviet agriculture and the role of V. R. Williams and T. D. Lysenko, both interesting figures in the history of Soviet agriculture (and science), are discussed in Volin, *A Century of Russian Agriculture*, chap. 13.

his many attempts to revitalize the agricultural sector on a long-run basis.[15] The changes of the Khrushchev era were by almost any judgment extensive and important, though not all successful. We shall classify the policies of this period into three broad groups: (1) agricultural compaigns, (2) organizational changes, and (3) economic adjustments. Although these classifications are somewhat arbitrary, they will assist in developing an understanding of the period and of its importance for the future.

Agricultural Campaigns[16]

Khrushchev associated himself with three main agricultural campaigns: the virgin lands program, the corn program, and the "plow-up" campaign.[17] Let us consider each briefly.

The virgin lands campaign was an effort to cultivate (using state farms) a large tract of land in Siberia and Kazakstan, the purpose of which would be the expansion of grain output. Begun in 1954, the goal was initially quite modest—namely, the reclamation of 13 million hectares (one hectare is 2.47 acres) of land by 1955. In fact, the scheme proved to be more grandiose, and by 1960, 42 million hectares had been seeded, representing roughly 20 percent of all sowings by all farms in that year. However, if the vision was grandiose, the results were less so. Although substantial (yet inadequate) amounts of funds were invested in this program, the marginal nature of the virgin lands soils, the highly variable climate (with a short growing season), and the scarcity of other production inputs—notably irrigation—meant that for the most part yields remained low, and total output, although never very high, fluctuated significantly from year to year.[18] In retrospect, it

---

[15] For a useful survey of this period, see Jerzy F. Karcz, "Khrushchev's Agricultural Policies," in Morris Bornstein and Daniel Fusfeld, eds., *The Soviet Economy: A Book of Readings*, 3rd ed. (Homewood, Ill.: Irwin, 1970), pp. 223–259. For a discussion of agricultural policy-making under Khrushchev, see Sidney I. Ploss, *Conflict and Decision-Making in Soviet Russia: A Case Study of Agricultural Policy, 1953–1963* (Princeton, N.J.: Princeton University Press, 1965); Werner G. Hahn, *The Politics of Soviet Agriculture, 1960–1970* (Baltimore, Md.: Johns Hopkins University Press, 1973). For a survey of the post-Khrushchev years, see Roger A. Clarke, "Soviet Agricultural Reforms Since Khrushchev," *Soviet Studies*, vol. 20, no. 2 (October 1968), 159–178. See also the discussion by Alec Nove, W. A. Douglas Jackson, and Jerzy F. Karcz in *Slavic Review*, vol. 29, no. 3 (September 1970), 379–428.

[16] For a survey of these campaigns, see Joseph W. Willett, "The Recent Record in Agricultural Production," in Joint Economic Committee, *Dimensions of Soviet Economic Power* (Washington, D.C.: U.S. Government Printing Office, 1962), pp. 91–113.

[17] In addition, Khrushchev fostered a program in the late 1950s encouraging increased agricultural production in an effort to overtake the United States in the per capita production of selected products.

[18] It should be noted that this type of performance is not especially unusual for dryland farming. For a discussion, see Carl Zoerb, "The Virgin Land Territory: Plans, Performance, Prospects," in Roy D. Laird and Edward L. Crowley, eds., *Soviet Agriculture: The Perma-*

would seem that the continuation of the program was primarily a result of the buoyancy created by the few good crop years. Finally, while the virgin lands territory was of questionable long-run viability, with given technology and funding, the scheme did provide a short-run expedient to delay the import of large supplies of grain. In this sense, the program was successful in that the average annual output of grain gained from the expansion of sown area was roughly 15 million tons for the period 1958–1963, thus allowing Khrushchev to gain political ascendancy and allowing the regime to buy time.[19] It was not until 1971 that the Soviet Union was forced to import vast quantities of grain from the West.

The second major program initiated by Khrushchev was the corn program. Started in 1955 and based primarily upon adulation of corn production in the United States (under radically different conditions, it might be noted) and the fact that corn gives more fodder per acre than other types of feed, this program increased the sown area of corn from 4.3 million hectares in 1954 to 37 million hectares by 1962. The purpose of the corn program was to solve the continuing fodder problem and thus enhance the production of meat and related products.

The corn program, much like the virgin lands program, was ill-conceived insofar as it was modeled on American success with corn yields, yet neglected important differences between the Soviet Union and the United States. In particular, corn production requires a warm and humid climate—the Corn Belt of the United States—a type of climate basically absent from most of the Soviet countryside. In addition to planting the corn in clearly marginal areas without associated inputs—fertilizer, for example— Soviet leaders neglected to consider the many years of scientific effort devoted to the development of special hybrids suitable for the conditions of American agriculture but not readily transferable to Soviet conditions. Corn has however become an important component of the Soviet fodder supplies.

Finally, Khrushchev's "plow-up" campaign, begun in 1961, was designed to eliminate the grassland system of crop rotation prominent under Stalin and thus drastically cut the area of land devoted to fallow. The purpose of fallow is of course to give the land a rest between crops and to allow

---

nent Crisis (New York: Praeger, 1965), pp. 29–44; Frank Durgin, "The Virgin Land Programme, 1954–60," Soviet Studies, vol. 12 (1961–1962), 255–280. For a recent assessment, see Martin McCauley, Khrushchev and the Development of Soviet Agriculture: The Virgin Lands Programme 1953–1964 (New York: Holmes and Meier, 1976).

[19] This suggestion was made by Strauss, Soviet Agriculture in Perspective, p. 172. The production of the virgin lands was not unimportant. The average annual contribution of roughly 15 million tons represents approximately 13 percent of the official average annual output of grains in the Soviet Union (1956–1965). For details, see Douglas B. Diamond, "Trends in Output, Inputs, and Factor Productivity in Soviet Agriculture," in Joint Economic Committee, New Directions in the Soviet Economy, part 2B (Washington, D.C.: U.S. Government Printing Office, 1969), p. 369.

a rebuilding of its nutrients. Undoubtedly such a scheme would be expected to yield short-run results, but its long-run effects would be uncertain, depending upon whether rational programs were instituted to replace the fallow program.

These schemes all reflected certain basic flaws in Khrushchev's agricultural policy. First, they "bought time" in the sense that they were to a great extent directed toward the achievement of short-run gains at the expense of the long-run health and productivity of the agricultural sector. Second, they were, without exception, unrealistic. All were carried out without sufficient planning, and accordingly, there was insufficient recognition of the demands that success in each campaign would place upon the available resources—manpower, fertilizers, capital investment, and so on. Third, Khrushchev was for the most part willing to ignore the weight of scientific evidence on fundamental questions such as crop selection and rotation. Fourth, these campaigns, which perhaps had their respective merits had they been applied selectively on a moderate scale, were discontinuously applied on a nationwide scale, thereby proving disruptive rather than beneficial to the farm sector.

Organizational Changes

While the flamboyancy of the above programs tended to hold the spotlight during the 1950s and early 1960s, there were at the same time some important and far-reaching organizational changes in progress. Most important, the nature of the *kolkhoz* and the administrative organs external to the *kolkhoz* underwent substantial readjustment.

While the *kolkhoz* and its related administrative organs had been relatively untouched by organizational change during the Stalin era, the late 1940s and early 1950s witnessed the beginning of a long-term campaign of amalgamation and conversion—collective farms were brought together to increase their size, and at the same time, many were converted into state farms. Between 1940 and 1969 the number of *kolkhozy* declined from 236,900 to 34,700, while socialized sown area in such collective farms increased from approximately 500 hectares to 2800 hectares per *kolkhoz*.[20] The pace of amalgamation varied, as did the regional impact. However, the general trends were similar throughout the country and have persisted in the 1970s. First, the amalgamation reflected a persistent trend in Soviet economic thinking, dating back to Lenin—namely the belief that large-scale operations (known in industry as gigantomania) are most efficient. If

[20] *Strana Sovetov za 50 let* [Country of the Soviets during 50 years], (Moscow: Statistika, 1967), p. 121; *Narodnoe khoziaistvo SSSR v 1969 g.* [The national economy of the USSR in 1969], (Moscow: Statistika, 1970), pp. 404–405. Further discussion of the amalgamation campaign can be found in Stuart, *The Collective Farm*, chap. 4.

one examines closely the process of amalgamation, it is apparent that the number of *kolkhozy* and the number of brigades have tended to decline at roughly the same rate over time. Thus *kolkhozy* were simply being brought together under a single administrative structure, and what was formerly a single small *kolkhoz* became a brigade, and as such a subunit of a large *kolkhoz*. On balance, this pattern has probably been one of the centralization of decision-making, although generalizations are inadvisable in view of the changing nature of the brigade as a basic production unit.

THE ENHANCED ROLE OF THE BRIGADE

In the past, the brigade was in many cases simply a short-term amalgamation created to complete a specific task such as harvesting. The current trend is toward a brigade of the "complex" type—that is, a long-term production unit to which land and labor are permanently attached (and since 1958, machinery and equipment as well). Thus the role of the brigadier (brigade manager) has assumed new importance, since the brigade has become a permanent production unit, with its own plan a component part of the overall *kolkhoz* plan and its own land, equipment, labor supplies. In addition, the trend has been toward the introduction of *khozraschet*, or economic accounting, at the brigade level. In many of the larger and well-established *kolkhozy*, the tendency has been to create "departments" in which crop and animal sections will be subsumed, most probably using the link as a method for the organization of labor.[21] This pattern closely resembles that utilized in the state farms. Although the amalgamation campaign had all but ceased by the mid-1960s, the ultimate patterns, especially the future of the *kolkhoz* as an organizational form, remain unclear. The changing characteristics of the typical *kolkhoz* have made it increasingly similar to the *sovkhoz* and thus less reminiscent of the unique organizational form introduced during the collectivization era.

CHANGING DECISION-MAKING PATTERNS

Within the *kolkhoz*, decision-making patterns have changed in recent years, and in addition, the quality of managerial personnel has been improved. During the past 25 years, there has been a continuing attempt to maintain a delicate balance between decision-making by the individual farm management—the upper-level managers and the production brigades—and by the regional agricultural authorities. While the annual production targets formulated by external economic planners remain the fundamental force directing economic activity within the *kolkhoz*, certain important changes

---

[21] The link is the smallest organized work unit in the collective farm and exists within a brigade. The concept of the link and its relevance in Soviet agriculture has been the subject of long-standing discussion in the Soviet Union. For details, see Dimitry Pospielovsky, "The 'Link System' in Soviet Agriculture," *Soviet Studies*, vol. 21, no. 4 (April 1970), 411–435.

have taken place that have tended to increase decision-making freedom within the *kolkhoz.*

Since the mid-1950s, for example, there has been a tendency toward targeting output and letting the individual farm decide how best to produce it, rather than basing the expected yield on the land area to be planted. In addition, since the late 1960s, there has been a renewed effort to introduce serious long-term planning and thus remove one of the major complaints of farm managers—the year-to-year manipulation of targets by state authorities that forces managers to engage in a guessing game with the state.[22]

On the matter of input determination, there has also been some relaxation of controls. Prior to the mid-1950s, the proportion of farm income to be devoted to capital investment was determined centrally, with only minimal regional variation; now this is basically a matter to be decided within the farm, although naturally there is pressure to increase investment. Nevertheless, the proportion of farm income reinvested now varies quite widely from farm to farm.

The abolition of the MTS in 1958 meant the dissolution of a powerful external managerial force, though doubtless some of this power remains in the hands of the state and party through regional agricultural and party authorities. Nevertheless, in the early 1950s, the agricultural specialists were removed from the MTS and placed in the collective farms themselves—an important move to improve the quality of collective farms' decisions—and finally in 1958, the machinery and equipment were shifted to the farms—and especially to the brigade level, in the form of complex mechanized brigades.

Insofar as decision-making *levels* are important, the impact of the changes in the postwar period is less than clear. As we have noted, the amalgamation process has substantially increased the average size of the collective, and yet along with changing decision rules for managers, there have been important changes in the organization of the farm itself.

As of 1956, election procedures (to the extent that these are meaningful) were frequently decentralized to the brigade meeting. In addition, the charter or basic operating document of the farm was to be formulated by the farm itself, and while there were external controls on this matter, it seems nevertheless to represent a measure of relaxation. The abolition of the MTS did, of course, help to remove the second of the famous "two bosses" referred to by Khrushchev.

If the brigade increased in importance during the 1950s and 1960s, it also grew in size, to closely resemble the *kolkhoz* of earlier years. At the same time, there was a continuing effort to infuse the party apparatus deeper into the farm, not only by changing the organizational structure of

---

[22] For a recent comment on this, see Kenneth R. Gray, "Soviet Agricultural Specialization and Efficiency," *Soviet Studies,* vol. 31, no. 4 (October 1979), 545.

the party within the farm but also by enhancing the party status of managerial personnel.[23] Thus in 1952, 79.4 percent of collective farm chairmen were party members, while by 1960, the proportion had increased to 95.3 percent.[24]

THE CHANGING QUALITY OF FARM MANAGEMENT

If one can measure managerial quality in terms of formal educational achievement, then the quality of *kolkhoz* managers has increased quite significantly in the past 25 years.[25] The same can be said for assistant chairmen, although the proportion of brigade leaders with higher and/or secondary specialized education has *not* increased notably.

Apart from the *level* of education, the *type* of training received by managerial personnel is important. We have noted that in the industrial sector of the Soviet economy, there is a tendency to favor managers trained in technical skills (especially engineering) as opposed to those trained in economics and administrative skills. The pattern in collective agriculture has been markedly similar. Although data on the type of training are scarce, we can generally conclude that training in an agricultural discipline—agronomy, for example—along with party reliability are both most important for the potentially successful manager.

It is instructive to note that in 1955, Khrushchev conducted a campaign to divert from industry sufficient managerial personnel to replace approximately 25 percent of existing collective farm chairmen. This program reflected the importance attached to farm management by Khrushchev and, in addition, served to improve significantly the educational levels of the top management group.[26] At the same time, the educational level of collective farm specialists has been and remains high, substantially higher in fact than that of managerial personnel. In 1966, 91 percent of all zootechnicians and 94.6 percent of all agronomists in collective farms had completed higher or secondary specialized education. At the same time however, only 10.9 percent of brigade leaders had received similar levels of education.[27]

From the standpoint of managerial decision-making in the *kolkhoz*, it is important to note that there has been a virtual absence of training in eco-

---

[23] For a discussion of the party in the *kolkhoz* during the 1950s and 1960s, see Stuart, *The Collective Farm*, chap. 2.

[24] *Narodnoe khoziaistvo SSSR v 1959 g.* [The national economy of the USSR in 1959], (Moscow: Statistika, 1960), p. 452.

[25] For a discussion of collective farm managerial personnel, see Stuart, *The Collective Farm*, chap. 8.

[26] For a discussion of this campaign, see Jerry F. Hough, "The Changing Nature of the Kolkhoz Chairman," in James R. Millar, ed., *The Soviet Rural Community* (Urbana: University of Illinois Press, 1971), pp. 103–120; Robert C. Stuart, "Structural Change and the Quality of Soviet Collective Farm Management, 1952–1966," in J. Millar, *The Soviet Rural Community*, 121–138.

[27] Stuart, *The Collective Farm*, p. 182.

nomics, accounting, and related subjects. For accounting personnel themselves, the picture has been bleak; in January of 1960, 47.4 percent of all *kolkhoz* accounting workers had had no bookkeeping training whatsoever.[28] With this record, it is little wonder that the auditing commission discussed earlier was such an ineffective body in the *kolkhoz*.

Economic Adjustments

If Soviet agricultural development of the past can be described as "extensive" in character, Soviet authorities since Stalin have recognized the need to increase output not only by expansion of inputs but also by better use of those inputs. In Soviet parlance, the drive for greater efficiency in agricultural production falls under the rubric of "intensification."

During the Khrushchev era, new emphasis was placed upon monetary incentives and, in general, upon the introduction of *khozraschet* into collective farms.[29] The initial cost data on collective farms after cost accounting was introduced in the mid-1950s indicated that costs were very high and that prices (average state purchase price) did not cover costs for most agricultural products. To take an extreme example, the procurement price of potatoes did not even cover the *kolkhoz*'s cost of transporting them to the delivery point. Although agricultural cost calculations were suspect—given the nature of the labor day and the absence of charges for land and capital—the general conclusion was that prices had to be raised if farms were to support increasing money distributions to peasants and at the same time set aside funds for capital investment.

The matter of agricultural price reform has been one of continuing debate throughout the postwar period. The debate has been concerned with much broader problems than simply the magnitude of prices. Questions such as regional price differentiations, price flexibility in the face of harvest fluctuations, methodology of price formation, and so on have been discussed. In spite of considerable indecision on these issues, one important pricing trend has prevailed—namely, increasing the level of prices vis-à-vis costs.[30] Between 1952 and 1956, average procurement prices of wheat were

---

[28] *Ibid.*, p. 185.

[29] For a discussion of these trends, see Frank A. Durgin, Jr., "Monetization and Policy in Soviet Agriculture Since 1952," *Soviet Studies*, vol. 15, no. 4 (April 1964), 381–407.

[30] The importance of price increases in Soviet agriculture cannot be underestimated. After the introduction of cost accounting in 1956, studies revealed that for many products, not even the above quota prices covered average costs of production. This pattern was reversed by price increases that for some products were very large. On the question of pricing reform, see Bornstein, "The Soviet Debate." On the question of cost-price comparisons, see Nancy Nimitz, "Soviet Agricultural Prices and Costs" in Joint Economic Committee, *Comparisons of United States and Soviet Economies* (Washington, D.C.: U.S. Government Printing Office, 1959), pp. 239–284; Stuart, *The Collective Farm*, chap. 7; Alec Nove, *The Soviet Economic System* (London: Allen & Unwin, 1977), pp. 190–197.

raised 630 percent; potatoes, 810 percent; and beef, 500 percent.[31] By the mid-1960s, agricultural prices in general covered production costs (with the exception of animal products on state farms), though with markedly differing levels of profitability. In addition to price increases, other financial concessions were made to the farm sector: tax payments were lessened, the two-level price system (paying higher prices for above quota deliveries) was abandoned in 1958 (though partially reconstituted in 1965), and payments on debts to the MTS for machinery and equipment were at first delayed and finally partially written off. In sum, these measures significantly improved the financial health of the *kolkhozy*.

In addition to measures designed to improve the financial position of farms, further steps were taken to improve peasant incentives. Both the *form* and the *frequency* of payment of peasant earnings changed, thus partially offsetting the more negative aspects of the labor day system prior to its abandonment in 1966. First, in the mid-1950s, a decree recommended the introduction of monthly cash payments to stimulate greater productivity. Of the total annual payment received by a peasant, the cash portion increased, and in addition, it came to be paid throughout rather than at the end of each year. In 1957, only 22.4 percent of *kolkhozy* made money advances ten or more times per year, while in 1963, the corresponding figure was 52.5 percent.[32]

One of the most dramatic aspects of the monetization process has been the very sharp upturn of the level of rural incomes in the post-Stalin era. From 1953, the year of Stalin's death, through 1967, the total income of the agricultural population from farm wages and private plot activity more than doubled, while the number of farm workers declined by approximately 10 percent.[33] This pattern had a substantial impact upon rural-urban wage differentials and was designed in part to stem the outflow of productive labor from the rural sector and to improve the standards of living within the rural sector, and thus motivate peasants toward greater participation and effort in the socialized sector of Soviet agriculture.[34]

[31] Nove, *The Soviet Economic System*, p. 191.

[32] G. Ia. Kuznetsov, *Material'noe stimulirovanie truda v kolkhozakh* [Material stimulation of labor in collective farms], (Moscow: Mysl', 1966), p. 29.

[33] For a discussion of rural income levels since the early 1950s, see David W. Bronson and Constance B. Krueger, "The Revolution in Soviet Farm Household Income, 1952–1967," in James R. Millar, ed., *The Soviet Rural Community* (Urbana: University of Illinois Press, 1971), pp. 214–258; Gertrude E. Schroeder and Barbara S. Severin, "Soviet Consumption and Income Policies in Perspective," in Joint Economic Committee, *Soviet Economy in a New Perspective* (Washington, D.C.: U.S. Government Printing Office, 1976), pp. 620–660; Karl-Eugen Wädekin, "Income Distribution in Soviet Agriculture," *Soviet Studies*, vol. 27, no. 1 (January, 1975), 3–26; Karl-Eugen Wädekin, "Labor Remuneration in the Socialized Agriculture of Eastern Europe and the Soviet Union," *Studies in Comparative Communism*, vol. 11, nos. 1 and 2 (Spring, Summer 1978), 96–120.

[34] If one looks at average annual money wages, the rural-urban differential has declined significantly. For example, in 1950, the average annual ruble money wage of collective farm-

The culmination of the monetization trend came in 1966, when the *kolkhozy* were directed to abandon the labor day as an accounting device. *Kolkhozy* were instructed to pay wages in accordance with rates prevailing on nearby *sovkhozy*, and when financial conditions did not allow the *kolkhozy* to meet these levels, the state bank was to provide appropriate loans. This did not mean however that payment would subsequently be entirely in monetary form, for peasants would still have to rely upon forage from the socialized sector to feed animals in the private sector.[35]

In addition to the improved income position of the peasants, available evidence suggests a decisively improved income position for managerial personnel. For agricultural specialists, tractor drivers, and others who formerly worked outside the *kolkhoz* but who became members of *kolkhozy*, relative earnings were maintained at or above the level previous to the transfer. In 1961, a tractor driver earned 2.57 times more per workday than a collective farmer in the fields. In recent years, agricultural specialists (agronomists, zootechnicians, etc.) earned 70 to 100 rubles per month, depending upon level of education, experience, and so on. Despite relatively small bonus earnings, these personnel come close to earning the average monthly wage of the industrial sector.

The collective farm chairman has traditionally earned little more than the average peasant and turnover has been high.[36] In recent years, the basis of calculating managerial income has changed. Rather than a myriad of performance indicators such as sown area, size of herds, and so forth, the prevailing pattern now emphasizes production performance per se—more output at lower cost. Available evidence suggests that collective farm chairmen now earn two, three, or more times the level of average peasant earnings. Unlike the industrial managers, however, farm managers have traditionally received only minimal bonuses, and even these have varied regionally and over time to quite a degree.

On balance, one would expect that the improved income position of

---

ers, state agricultural workers, and nonagricultural workers was 42.8, 459.8 and 830.1, respectively. By 1975, the comparable figures were 1027.8, 1528.8, and 1780.7. For details of computation, see Schroeder and Severin, "Soviet Consumption," p. 629.

[35] Although the private sector in the collective farm represents a very small portion of farmland, it represents an important portion of livestock. Since the private plots are not suitable for the growing of forage crops in any quantity, forage has normally been a part of the peasant's income (in-kind) received for working in the socialized sector of the farm. Income from the private plot as a portion of *kolkhoz* family income has fallen from roughly 36 percent in 1965 to 25 percent in 1978. For details, see *Narodnoe khoziaistvo SSSR v 1978 g.* [The national economy of the USSR, 1978], (Moscow: Statistika, 1979), p. 392.

[36] For a discussion of managerial incentives, see Alec Nove, "Incentives for Peasants and Administrators," in *Economic Rationality and Soviet Politics* (New York: Praeger, 1964), pp. 186–205; Robert C. Stuart, "Managerial Incentives in Soviet Collective Agriculture During the Khrushchev Era," *Soviet Studies*, vol. 22, no. 4 (April 1972), 540–555.

managerial personnel in combination with higher peasant income would enhance the participation and effort of both groups in the socialized agricultural sector. While we do not have a measure for effort as such, we have noted that participation has not in fact increased. In 1953, for example, men devoted 75 percent of their work time to the socialized sector of the collective farm, 9 percent to the private plot, and 16 percent to external work. The figures for women during the same year were 59 percent, 10 percent, and 31 percent for the three sectors, respectively. By 1963, a year for which similar data are available, there had been virtually no change, with the exception of a slight expansion of the proportion of time spent by women in the private sector of the *kolkhoz*.[37]

CHANGING PATTERNS IN SOVIET AGRICULTURE: THE BREZHNEV YEARS

We have devoted considerable attention to the development of Soviet agriculture under the leadership of Nikita Khrushchev largely because the years of his leadership represent the first major attempt to modernize Soviet agriculture. This attempt focused upon the need both for more resources in agriculture and for better utilization of those resources already available.

Although the flambuoyant style of Khrushchev came to an end with his replacement in 1964, the emergence of Leonid Brezhnev as the spokesman for Soviet agriculture signaled a continuation of the modernization effort in both old and new directions.

At a Plenum of the Central Committee of the Communist Party in March of 1965, Brezhnev spelled out the future directions of Soviet agricultural policy.[38] The main thrust of this policy during the Brezhnev years has been a serious and generally continuing commitment to increasing the inputs to agriculture and to achieving greater growth in agricultural productivity.

The infusion of more resources into Soviet agriculture became evident in several directions. Investment in agriculture, which during the 1950s had been roughly 16 percent of total Soviet investment, increased to some 25 percent of total investment in the 1970s. This growth of investment was in part to rectify earlier neglect through the expansion of fertilizer inputs and the continued improvement of machinery, equipment, and land (especially in the northwest of the Russian Republic). Financial improvement of the

[37] I. F. Suslov, *Ekonomicheskoe problemy razvitiia kolkhozov* [Economic problems of the development of collective farms], (Moscow: Ekonomika, 1967), p. 193.

[38] For a survey, see David M. Schoonover, "Soviet Agricultural Policies," in Joint Economic Committee, *Soviet Economy in a Time of Change* (Washington, D.C.: U.S. Government Printing Office, 1979), pp. 87–115.

farms was also guaranteed by other policy measures. For some poor collective farms, long-term debts were written off, and for all collectives, guaranteed wages (roughly at state farm levels) were introduced. Farm purchase prices were raised significantly to ensure profitability and to stimulate any lagging sectors, notably meat production. Price differentials of 50 percent were also introduced for above quota deliveries—initially, for those of grain and then for meat. After many years of unfavorable cost-price ratios in Soviet agriculture, pricing policies must have exerted a positive effect on farm incentives, but they also have resulted in a large state subsidy to agriculture, whereby retail prices (for example, in the case of meat) have been held well below the wholesale prices paid by the state.

In addition to these economic changes, the Brezhnev years have also witnessed a continuation of organizational changes. Within farms, an effort has been made to simplify plan targets and to maintain these targets at levels known in advance to the farms. Increasingly, *khozraschet* has been introduced into state farms. There has been a renewed emphasis upon the important role to be played by trained agricultural specialists, a theme of the Khrushchev years.

While state farms have continued to replace the collective farms in a formal sense (see Table 16), many of the policy initiatives begun under Khrushchev and continued under Brezhnev have effectively eliminated the important differences between these two institutions. However, the most important program of organizational change has been the serious implementation of agroindustrial integration.[39] Although various forms of interfarm cooperation are by no means new, the recent thrust has been the creation of large integrated complexes that combine both collective and state farms with processing and other industrial-type facilities. This program of integration is the basis of a long overdue attack on the problem of lagging meat production and on the historical neglect of the fodder base in the meat producing sector.[40]

Although not all of these policies have been successfully implemented, especially with the climatic reverses of the 1970s, they nevertheless represent a fairly rational and stable direction for Soviet agricultural policy. Furthermore, discussion of plans for the 1980s at a July 1978 Party Plenum pointed to a continuation of these policies and, in particular, to the allocation of more resources to the agricultural sector.

[39] For a discussion of this program, see Arcadius Kahan, "The Problems of the 'Agrarian-Industrial Complexes' in the Soviet Union," in Zbigniew Fallenbuchl, ed., *Economic Development in the Soviet Union and Eastern Europe*, vol. 2 (New York: Praeger, 1976), pp. 205–222; Robert C. Stuart, "Aspects of Soviet Rural Development," *Agricultural Administration*, vol. 10, no. 2 (1975), 165–178.

[40] For a summary, see Michael D. Zahn, "Soviet Livestock Feed in Perspective," in Joint Economic Committee, *Soviet Economy in a Time of Change*, (Washington, D.C.: U.S. Government Printing Office, 1979), pp. 165–185. For additional discussion and references to the literature, see Schoonover, "Soviet Agricultural Policies," pp. 104–106.

SOVIET AGRICULTURE AND ECONOMIC DEVELOPMENT

Thus far, the focus of this chapter has been on the organization and operation of Soviet agriculture. Emphasis has been placed upon the introduction and development of the collective farm as unique features of the Soviet experience. In this section, we turn to an examination of the performance of the Soviet agricultural sector. Initially, the focus will be upon the role of agriculture in the long-term Soviet development experience, followed by an examination of the recent trends in such performance indicators as output, input, and productivity.

Since we are concerned with the role of agriculture in the development process, the supportive functions of the agricultural sector in the course of economic development bear repetition at this juncture:[41]

1. Provision of manpower for industry
2. Expansion of output and marketings to supply foodstuffs for the expanding nonagricultural sector and raw materials for industry
3. Provision of agricultural products for export to earn foreign exchange to pay for importation of machinery and equipment
4. Assistance to capital accumulation in the industrial sector by the transfer of savings from the rural to the industrial sector

As far as the first supportive role is concerned, Soviet agriculture did without a doubt provide a vast amount of manpower to industry within a relatively brief amount of time. Between 1926 and 1939 alone, the urban population increased from 26.3 million to 56.1 million—a net gain of some 30 million—and by 1959, this figure had increased to 100 million—a net overall increase of over 73 million, of which 43.4 million (well over one-half) can be accounted for by migration from rural to urban areas.[42] This internal migration along with the increasing participation rates of the urban population sustained an average annual rate of growth of the nonagricultural labor force of 8.7 percent between 1928 and 1937, while the agricultural labor force declined at an annual rate of −2.5 percent during the same period. This vast transformation was effected by both market and nonmarket forces: first, a substantial gap between urban and rural incomes was created, thereby promoting movement out of agriculture; second, massive recruitment campaigns were carried on in the countryside to facilitate the transfer.

How well Soviet agriculture performed the second supportive function during the crucial early years of industrialization is the subject of some con-

---

[41] For a detailed discussion of the role of agriculture in economic development, the reader is referred to J. W. Mellor, *The Economics of Agricultural Production* (Ithaca, N.Y.: Cornell University Press, 1966).

[42] Warren W. Eason, "Labor Force," in Abram Bergson and Simon Kuznets, eds., *Economic Trends in the Soviet Union* (Cambridge, Mass.: Harvard University Press, 1963), pp. 72–73.

**TABLE 17   Average Annual Grain Output and Marketings
(millions of tons; 1927-1928 = 100)**

Period	Grain Output	Index	Grain Marketing, Gross[a]	Net[b]	Index Gross	Net
1927–1928	72.8	100	16.1	8.3	100	100
1928–1929	72.5	100	15.7	8.3	98	100
1929–1930	77.6	107	19.5	10.2	121	123
1930–1931	76.5	105	22.6	17.9	140	216
1931–1932	69.7	96	23.7	18.8	147	226
1932–1933	79.8	110	19.4	13.7	120	165
1933–1937	72.9	100	27.5		171	
1938–1940	77.9	107	32.1		199	
1954–1958	110.3	152	43.5		270	
1960–1963	126.0	173	50.0		311	
1964–1967	148.0	203	59.2		368	
1968–1970	172.9	237	65.9		409	
1971–1973	190.6	262	71.5		444	
1974–1978	198.5	273	75.9		471	

SOURCES: Output data through 1958 from Erich Strauss, *Soviet Agriculture in Perspective*, (London: Allen & Unwin, 1969), pp. 304–305; grain marketing data from 1927–1928 through 1932–1933 from Jerzy F. Karcz, "Khrushchev's Agricultural Policies," in Morris Bornstein and Daniel D. Fusfeld, eds., *The Soviet Economy: A Book of Readings*, 3rd ed. (Homewood, Ill.: Irwin, 1970), p. 44; grain marketing data from 1933–1937 through 1954–1958 from Charles K. Wilber, "The Role of Agriculture in Soviet Economic Development," *Land Economics*, vol. 45, no. 1 (February 1969), 87–96; data for the 1960s and 1970s from selected volumes of *Narodnoe khoziaistvo SSSR* [The national economy of the USSR] and *SSSR v tsifrakh* [The USSR in figures].
[a] Gross marketings are all off-farm sales other than those within agriculture as such. They are defined as state purchases for the period 1960–1970.
[b] Net marketings are obtained from gross marketings by subtracting grain that is repurchased by the agricultural population or by farms through retail trade or government allocations.

troversy. Although statistics on marketings of all agricultural products external to the village are not readily available, the figures on grain marketings (Table 17) provide valuable insights.

The evidence presented here suggests that the rate of increase of both gross and net grain marketings during the early collectivization years was substantially faster than the increase in grain production. Possibly more important, although gross marketings increased at a respectable pace over the precollectivization levels, net marketings (defined as gross marketings less repurchases by the rural sector) more than doubled between the years 1927–1928 and 1930–1931 from 8.3 to 17.9 million tons respectively. Jerzy Karcz has attempted to show that the entire increase in gross grain marketings between 1928 and 1933 can be accounted for not by the ability of the state to gather additional grain per se from *kolkhozy*, but by the reduction in animal herds—that would otherwise consume grains—that took place during collectivization.[43] However, one may question this conclusion in the light of the large state exactions during poor harvest years that exacerbated the famine of 1932–1934. Also the drastic decline in peasant living standards during the 1930s might be cited as counterevidence to Karcz's conclusions. Thus in the absence of a broader analysis of all agricultural products over a longer period of time, it is difficult to make an overall evaluation of the product contribution of the agricultural sector to economic development.

As far as the third function is concerned, Soviet agriculture did contribute to overall economic development during the First Five Year Plan by earning crucial foreign exchange to pay for machinery imports from the West. Between 1929 and 1931, Soviet imports increased by over 60 percent (in volume terms) despite the worsening terms of trade resulting from the collapse of agricultural prices in the world market during this period. In fact, Soviet imports were severely limited by balance of payments constraints—given the Western countries' unwillingness to grant long-term credits to the fledgling communist regime. The Soviet government's sole recourse therefore was to continue to market abroad the traditional Soviet export commodities—grain and wheat, timber, and petroleum. Between 1929 and 1931, Soviet exports expanded somewhat less than 50 percent, and this expansion was spearheaded by an increase in the proportion of the total domestic output of agricultural products exported. In 1928, for example, less than one percent of the domestic output of grain, wheat, and corn was exported; yet by 1931, 14 percent of the output of grain, 18 percent of wheat, and 2 percent of corn was exported. In this manner, agricultural exports were used to finance machinery and ferrous metals imports, which rose from one-third of total Soviet imports in 1928 to almost three-quarters by the end of the First Five Year Plan.[44] The costs of maintaining agricultural exports were considerable, for they worsened the famine of 1932–1934. As one student of this famine writes:

> The immediate cause was not poor harvests but the requisitioning of grain from moderate harvests in such quantities that not enough was left for the peasants themselves. The main reasons for this drastic policy appear to have been, first the attempt to maintain exports of agricultural produce and hence imports of machinery. . . .[45]

[43] Jerzy F. Karcz, "From Stalin to Brezhnev: Soviet Agricultural Policy in Historical Perspective," in James R. Millar, ed., *The Soviet Rural Community* (Urbana: University of Illinois Press, 1971), p. 42.

[44] Franklyn D. Holzman, "Foreign Trade," in Abram Bergson and Simon Kuznets, eds., *Economic Trends in the Soviet Union* (Cambridge, Mass.: Harvard University Press, 1963), pp. 294–295.

[45] Philip Hanson, *The Consumer Sector in the Soviet Economy* (Evanston, Ill.: Northwestern University Press, 1968), p. 36.

The most controversial rule of Soviet agriculture in economic development relates to the fourth function—namely the transfer of savings from the countryside to the city. On the surface, it would appear that the Preobrazhensky model of primitive socialist accumulation was indeed used successfully in forcing savings from the rural population during the early years of industrialization. While estimates of the extent of decline must be quite crude, Naum Jasny has estimated that per capita income of the farm population had fallen to 53 percent of the 1928 level by 1932–1933, which perhaps is not too unrealistic in view of the fact that the peasants' standard of living during the best prewar year for the Russian peasantry (1937) was still only 81 percent of 1928.[46] Although it would appear from such figures that Soviet agrarian policies succeeded in marshaling forced savings from the rural sector, such a judgment may, at this juncture, be premature for reasons discussed below. The burden of industrialization was also borne by the urban sector. Mindful of the significant decline in urban living standards during the 1930s, Abram Bergson notes the following:

> Contrary to a common supposition, the industrial worker fared no better than the peasants under Stalin's five year plans. Indeed, he seemingly fared worse, although I believe he was able to maintain in some degree the margin he enjoyed initially in respect to consumption per capita.[47]

It may be as well that the decline in both urban and rural standards during the First Five Year Plan has been underestimated, so that the savings "forced" from the Soviet population were indeed quite significant.[48]

However, the fundamental issue here is the role of collectivization in the extraction of a surplus from the countryside to form the basis of the industrial expansion of the Soviet economy in the 1930s and thereafter. That savings were forced via reductions in living standards is not at issue, for investment rates (saving rates) did explode during the early 1930s as a consequence of transferring income from individuals to the state. The issue instead is: was the collective farm responsible? Although the Western assessment of collectivization has generally been negative, especially in a long-run perspective, the *kolkhoz* has been credited by some as being the mechanism that served to extract a surplus from the countryside and hence played a crucial role in the accumulation process.[49]

[46] Naum Jasny, *The Soviet Economy During the Plan Era* (Stanford, Calif.: Food Research Institute, 1951), p. 107.
[47] Abram Bergson, *The Real National Income of Soviet Russia Since 1928* (Cambridge, Mass.: Harvard University Press, 1961), p. 257.
[48] Steven Rosefielde, "The First Great Leap Forward Reconsidered: The Lessons of Solzhenitsyn's Gulag Archipelago," *Soviet Studies*, forthcoming, 1980.
[49] In addition to earlier writings by Maurice Dobb, the most recent exposition of this viewpoint is: Michael Ellman, "Did the Agricultural Surplus Provide the Resources for the Increase in Investment in the USSR During the First Five Year Plan?" *Economic Journal*, vol. 85, no. 4 (December 1975).

Although it has proven difficult to achieve precision in defining and measuring an agricultural surplus, evidence provided by the Soviet economist A. A. Barsov and analyzed by James Millar appears to demonstrate that during the crucial period of the First Five Year Plan, Soviet agriculture was a net *recipient* of resources.[50] In order for surpluses to be transferred from agriculture to industry, the flow of deliveries from agriculture to industry must exceed the flow of deliveries from industry to agriculture (grain for tractors, if you will). As these are flows of physical commodities, the outcome will depend upon the prices applied. Millar uses the prices of 1928 (which place a low relative valuation on agriculture) and finds an inflow to agriculture on a net basis. Michael Ellman uses modified 1913 prices (which place a higher relative valuation on agriculture prices) and obtains a net outflow. But the crucial point is that both Millar and Ellman find that the advent of collectivization failed to alter the magnitude of the surplus, however it is measured. Thus one cannot argue that collectivization was responsible for any significant change in the surplus. Millar summarizes his view as follows:

> Ultimately, therefore, although the state did succeed in raising real resources from the peasantry for investment purposes, the destruction occasioned by resistance to collectivization obliged it to turn around and use those resources for replacement investment in agriculture. This inflow, together with the net inflow to the private sector that was financed by the favorable change in the terms of trade with the nonrural population, caused the agricultural sector taken as a whole to become a net recipient of resources during the First Five Year Plan. Whatever its merits may have been on other grounds, mass collectivization of Soviet agriculture must be reckoned as an unmitigated economic policy disaster.[51]

If the argument that collectivization provided the surplus for industrial development cannot be sustained, are there other arguments for the collective farm? The most obvious one is that the introduction of the *kolkhoz* and *sovkhoz* into the countryside allowed the regime to consolidate its power in the countryside and to eliminate what it considered to be the most dangerous opponents of Soviet rule. From the vantage point of the Soviet leadership, the benefits derived in the political sphere were likely substantial and worth the costs of collectivization. Another argument is made by Arvind

---

[50] For a summary of the evidence and appropriate references, see James R. Millar, "Mass Collectivization and the Contribution of Soviet Agriculture to the First Five Year Plan: A Review Article," *Slavic Review*, vol. 33, no. 4 (December 1974), 750–766; James R. Millar, "Soviet Rapid Development and the Agricultural Surplus Hypothesis," *Soviet Studies*, vol. 22, no. 1 (July 1970). For the original data and discussion, see A. A. Barsov, *Balans stoimostnykh obmenov mezhdu gorodom i derevnei* [Balance of the value of the exchange between the city and the country], (Moscow: Nauka, 1969); see also Arvind Vyas, "Primary Accumulation in the USSR Revisited," *Cambridge Journal of Economics*, vol. 3, no. 3 (1979), 119–130.

[51] Millar, "Mass Collectivization," 764.

Vyas and echoed by Ellman, namely, that collectivization was required to generate an adequate flow of labor off the farm into the city.[52] Collectivization's contribution to this flow was the securing of an adequate flow of foodstuffs (wage goods) for the city and the reduction of collective farm living standards to such an extent to force peasants off the *kolkhoz* into industry at high rates.

Millar's response to this position is that traditionally industrializing countries have had no difficulty in obtaining adequate labor supplies from the countryside. In fact, in some instances the problem has been to prevent urban overpopulation during the early phases of industrialization.[53] Second, Millar questions whether less drastic (and less costly means) could have been employed to facilitate this transfer.

As the above discussion reveals, there is considerable controversy surrounding the role of collective agriculture during the early years of industrialization. The immediate negative consequences of collectivization have been noted: the destruction of livestock, the loss of the more efficient farmers, the stagnation of crop output. Moreover, as David Granick has argued,[54] rapid collectivization policies, pursued to meet the perceived urgent need for rapid accumulation, may have resulted in the sharp deterioration in the stock of intangible capital, especially in organizational capital. The short-term consequences of collectivization will remain controversial, but its long-term consequences are less disputable and will be the subject of the following section. Jerzy Karcz has argued that one must consider as a cost of the Stalin era the negative consequences of "command farming"—poor incentives, inadequate specialization, and distortion of decision-making patterns.[55]

PERFORMANCE OF THE AGRICULTURAL SECTOR

In Table 18 we present official Soviet and Western calculated indexes of Soviet agricultural performance for the period 1913 through 1978. It is apparent that for the early years of collectivization, Soviet agriculture performed rather poorly, gross output growing at an average annual rate of one

[52] Vyas, "Primary Accumulation," 128. Thus on the matter of the contributions of the peasants and workers, Vyas concludes that ". . . the contribution of the two classes to accumulation can be put very simply: the peasantry provided the food and labour power, while the working class was engaged in the production of capital goods." (p. 129).

[53] James R. Millar, "Two Views on Soviet Collectivization of Agriculture," mimeograph, 1980.

[54] David Granick, *Soviet Metal Fabricating and Economic Development* (Madison: University of Wisconsin Press, 1967), chap. 4 and pp. 365–366.

[55] Karcz, "Khrushchev's Agricultural Policies," p. 68. For a development of the command model, see Jerzy F. Karcz, "An Organizational Model of Command Farming," in Morris Bornstein, ed., *Comparative Economic Systems*, rev. ed. (Homewood, Ill.: Irwin, 1969), pp. 278–299.

TABLE 18   USSR Indexes of Gross Agricultural Output, 1913–1978 (official and calculated)

	Total		Crops		Livestock	
	Official	Calculated	Official	Calculated	Official	Calculated
TERRITORY OF 1939 (1913 = 100)						
1913	100	100	100	100	100	100
1928	124	116	117	117	137	120
1933	101	—	121	—	65	—
1937	134	127	150	161	109	108
1940	156	122	172	145	116	99
PRESENT TERRITORY (1940 = 100)						
1940	100	100	100	100	100	100
1950	99	99	95	92	109	109
1952	101	101	95	96	113	109
1954	109	110	99	98	134	125
1956	137	142	130	136	155	151
1958	156	161	147	144	180	184
1959	157	155	140	131	191	198
1962	167	168	149	138	207	218
1965	180	179	161	153	223	228
1968	206	207	195	185	244	244
1970	221	226	204	190	265	271
1972	214	208	185	172	273	265
1974	242	234	212	190	305	303
1976	242	233	225	206	290	277
1978	261	—	235	—	322	—

SOURCES: D. Gale Johnson, "Agricultural Production," in Abram Bergson and Simon Kuznets, eds., *Economic Trends in the Soviet Union* (Cambridge, Mass.: Harvard University Press, 1963), p. 208; Abraham S. Becker, *Soviet National Income, 1953–1964* (Berkeley and Los Angeles: University of California Press, 1969), p. 241; Douglas B. Diamond and Constance Krueger, "Recent Developments in Output and Productivity in Soviet Agriculture," in Joint Economic Committee, *Soviet Economic Prospects for the Seventies* (Washington, D.C.: U.S. Government Printing Office, 1973), p. 336; various issues of *Narodnoe khoziaistvo SSSR* [National economy of the USSR], *SSSR v tsifrakh* [the USSR in figures]; Douglas B. Diamond and W. Lee Davis, "Comparative Growth in U.S. and U.S.S.R. Agriculture," in Joint Economic Committee, *Soviet Economy in a Time of Change*, (Washington, D.C.: U.S. Government Printing Office, 1979), vol. 2, p. 47.

percent or slightly less between 1928 and 1937 (the latter a good crop year). Also, the production of livestock products declined during these years primarily due to the destruction of animal herds by peasants resisting the collectivization of agriculture.

In view of our discussion of change in the Khrushchev years, it is notable that Soviet agriculture grew most rapidly between 1952 and 1958, the early years of experimentation with the virgin lands, abolition of the MTS, increased farm prices, and limited decentralization of decision-making. During this period, Soviet agriculture (as measured by the official index of gross agricultural output) grew at an average annual rate of around 9 per-

TABLE 19   Output of Selected Agricultural Products—USSR (millions of tons, average annual basis)

Period[a]	Grain	Cotton	Sugar Beets	Potatoes	Meat (slaughter weight)	Milk	Eggs (billion units)
1909–1913	65.2	.68	9.7	22.4	3.9	42.1	9.5
1924–1928	69.3	.58	7.9	41.1	4.2	29.3	9.2
1936–1940	77.4	2.50	17.1	49.4	4.0	26.5	9.6
1946–1950	64.8	2.32	13.5	80.7	3.5	32.3	7.5
1951–1955	88.5	3.89	24.0	69.5	5.7	37.9	15.9
1956–1960	121.5	4.36	45.6	88.3	7.9	57.2	23.6
1961–1965	130.3	4.99	59.2	81.6	9.3	64.7	28.7
1966–1970	167.6	6.10	81.1	94.8	11.6	80.6	35.8
1971–1975	181.6	7.67	76.0	89.8	14.0	87.4	51.4
1976–1978	218.9	8.51	95.6	84.9	14.5	93.0	60.6

SOURCES: Data up to and including 1965 from *Narodnoe khoziaistvo SSSR v 1968 g.* [The national economy of the USSR in 1968], (Moscow: Statistika 1969), 314–315; data for 1966 through 1978 from *SSSR v tsifrakh v 1978* [The USSR in figures in 1978], (Moscow: Statistika, 1979), 108–109.
[a] Data up to and including the series for 1936–1940 are based upon borders of the Soviet Union prior to September 17, 1939.

cent but decelerated considerably thereafter to an average annual rate of less than 3 percent between 1959 and 1978. According to the official index, agricultural output increased at an average annual rate of 2.3 percent between 1970 and 1978. Long-run individual crop figures are given in Table 19 and they tell essentially the same story, although as five-year averages, annual fluctuations are removed. Thus it would seem that the growth of agricultural output in the Soviet Union has over the long-run been quite uneven and has been declining since the early 1960s; although one can argue that in comparison with other developing economies, the Soviet performance has been respectable.[56]

Certainly any evaluation of Soviet agricultural performance must consider factor productivity performance, that is, trends in output per unit of input, for it is important to determine whether the above growth was brought about largely by expansion of inputs (such as sown acreage) or by increased output per unit of input. In Table 20, we present estimates of factor productivity for three important and possibly representative periods. The first, from 1928 to 1938, should shed light upon agricultural productivity performance during the crucial initial years of the industrialization drive. The second, from 1950 to 1960, should reflect the performance of the

[56] Charles K. Wilber, "The Role of Agriculture in Soviet Economic Development," *Land Economics*, vol. 45, no. 1 (February 1969), 39 ff., argues that when compared with other countries over various historical periods, the growth rate of Soviet agricultural output has been good.

agricultural sector during the years of the Khrushchev experiments, when land and capital inputs to agriculture were expanding. The third period (broken down into two subperiods), 1960 to 1977, captures the more recent performance of Soviet agricultural productivity.

Between 1928 and 1938, output per man-day actually declined (col. 7), whereas output per number engaged rose (not shown). The reason for this divergence is that while the number engaged in agriculture declined markedly, the number of man-days of those remaining increased as the shift was made from part-time to full-time agricultural employment. Trends in output per man-day are more reflective of the labor productivity performance of Soviet agriculture in that they show better the true labor input, and output per man-day did decline.[57] As far as output per unit of total inputs (land, labor, capital, materials) is concerned, it declined between 1928 and 1938. It is interesting to note that capital inputs to agriculture actually declined between 1928 and 1938 (col. 1), contrary to the vision of the Soviet leadership, which foresaw the vast mechanization of Soviet agriculture through the auspices of the MTS. On the whole, one would have to conclude that the productivity performance of Soviet agriculture during the early period of collectivized agriculture was disappointing.

In contrast, the productivity performance of Soviet agriculture was much better during the second period (1950 to 1960). Output per man-day and per unit of total factor input grew at a respectable pace (at greater than 3 percent annually). The capital stock of agriculture grew at a much more rapid rate than labor inputs, indicating substitutions of capital for labor and the increased mechanization of Soviet agriculture. The impact of the virgin

[57] The reader should note that the measurement of factor productivity is complex, and especially so in the Soviet case. The results are particularly sensitive to the indicators chosen and the weights used in aggregating those indicators. For a discussion of problems relating to Soviet agricultural statistics, the reader is referred to D. Gale Johnson, "Agricultural Production," in Abram Bergson and Simon Kuznets, eds., *Economic Trends in the Soviet Union* (Cambridge, Mass.: Harvard University Press, 1963); Arcadius Kahan, "Soviet Statistics of Agricultural Output," in Roy D. Laird, ed., *Soviet Agricultural and Peasant Affairs* (Lawrence: University of Kansas Press, 1963), pp. 134–160; Roger E. Neetz, "Inside the Agricultural Index of the USSR," in Joint Economic Committee, *New Directions in the Soviet Economy* (Washington, D.C.: U.S. Government Printing Office, 1966), pp. 483–493; Vladimir G. Treml and John P. Hardt, eds., *Soviet Economic Statistics* (Durham, N.C.: Duke University Press, 1972), part 4. For a discussion of trends and prospects through 1975, see Douglas B. Diamond and Constance Krueger, "Recent Developments in Output and Productivity in Soviet Agriculture," in Joint Economic Committee, *Soviet Economic Prospects for the Seventies* (Washington, D.C.: U.S. Government Printing Office, 1973), pp. 316–339, and F. Douglas Whitehouse and Joseph Havelka, "Comparisons of Farm Output in the US and USSR, 1950–1971," in Joint Economic Committee, *Soviet Economic Prospects for the Seventies* (Washington, D.C.: U.S. Government Printing Office, 1973), pp. 340–374. For trends through 1977, see Douglas B. Diamond and W. Lee Davis, "Comparative Growth in U.S. and U.S.S.R. Agriculture," in Joint Economic Committee, *Soviet Economy in a Time of Change* (Washington, D.C.: U.S. Government Printing Office, 1979), vol. 2, pp. 19–54.

lands campaign on acreage is seen in the substantial rise in the land index. Thus on both an output and a productivity basis, the 1950s were the "golden age" of Soviet agriculture.

A less optimistic picture emerges after 1960 for both output and output per unit of input. The annual growth rate of output declined from 4.9 percent in 1950–1960, to 3.0 percent in 1960–1970, and then to 1.9 percent in 1970–1977. Inputs to agriculture however grew at roughly equivalent rates in the 1950s and 1960s, and declined somewhat during the 1970s. Capital inputs continued to be infused into agriculture at rapid rates throughout the 1960s and 1970s, contrary to the common notion that Soviet agriculture has been starved of capital resources. The major difference between resource patterns of the 1950s and those thereafter has been the absence of another virgin lands campaign to again expand sown acreage in a significant manner. The emerging productivity picture is disappointing to say the least. During the 1950s, output per unit of input grew at 2.1 percent, declining to 0.9 percent in the 1960s and then to 0.4 percent between 1970 and 1977. Thus in the 1970s, agricultural productivity scarcely improved, and vast infusions of capital and material inputs (fertilizers) were required to obtain advances in output.

Attempts to compare the productivity of Soviet agriculture on a relative basis with Western European agriculture have produced some rather surprising results—for the measures seem to point toward rather higher Soviet productivity levels than one might have anticipated. Thus, Soviet farm output per man-hour has been estimated to be above that of Italy and, depending upon the price weights chosen, at or only slighly below the level of France and West Germany.[58] Such results are quite contrary to the traditional picture of Soviet agriculture as being inefficient relative to the agriculture sector in advanced Western countries, but they date to 1960. From the evidence cited in Table 20, one would think that the Soviet position has deteriorated since 1960.

Finally, to what extent can Soviet agricultural improvement be observed where it counts most, in the diet of Soviet citizens? The data in Table 21 provide us with a summary picture of changes in the Soviet diet. While these numbers—and especially the concept of a norm—must be interpreted with caution, they nevertheless reflect a pattern of dietary change typical of a country experiencing economic development. Per capita consumption of protein foods such as meat has increased, while the per capita consumption of starchy foods such as potatoes has decreased. Thus in terms of both the volume and the mix of available food products, there has been improvement in the Soviet diet, although in a number of cases, established norms have not been met (particluarly the norm for meat).

---

[58] Earl R. Brubaker, "A Sectoral Analysis of Efficiency under Market and Plan," *Soviet Studies*, vol. 23, no. 3 (January 1972), 440.

TABLE 20 Growth Indexes of Inputs and Factor Productivity in Soviet Agriculture, 1928–1977 three year averages, 1950–1977

	(1) Capital	(2) Land	(3) Labor (man-days)	(4) Current Purchases	(5) Total Inputs (weighted average) of cols. 1, 2, 3, 4	(6) Agricultural Output	(7) Output per Man-Day (col. 6 ÷ col. 3)	(8) Output per Land Input (col. 6 ÷ col. 2)	(9) Total Output per Unit of Input (col. 6 ÷ col. 5)
(1928 = 100)									
1928	100	100	100	100	100	100	100	100	100
1938	97	125	112	590	141	104	93	83	74
(1950 = 100)									
1950	100	100	100	100	100	100	100	100	100
1960	256	129	94	221	130	161	171	125	124
(1960 = 100)									
1960	100	100	100	100	100	100	100	100	100
1970	234	102	96	211	123	134	140	131	109
(1970 = 100)									
1970	100	100	100	100	100	100	100	100	100
1977	203	104	90	156	111	114	127	110	103

SOURCE: D. Gale Johnson, "Agricultural Production," in Abram Bergson and Simon Kuznets, eds., *Economic Trends in the Soviet Union* (Cambridge, Mass.: Harvard University Press, 1963), pp. 216–218; Diamond and Davis, "Comparative Growth," p. 50.

TABLE 21   USSR Annual Per Capita Consumption of Selected Foods, 1950–1978 (kilograms)

Food Item	Soviet Norm	1950 Actual	1960 Actual	1970 Actual	1978 Actual
Meat & fat	82.0	26.0	40.0	48.0	56.0
Fish & fish products	18.6	7.0	9.9	15.4	16.9
Milk & milk products[1]	405.0	172.0	240.0	307.0	320.0
Eggs (number)	292.0	60.0	118.0	159.0	230.0
Sugar	40.0	11.6	28.0	38.8	43.0
Vegetable oil	9.1	2.7	5.3	6.8	8.2
Potatoes	97.0	241.0	143.0	130.0	120.0
Grain[2]	110.0	172.0	164.0	149.0	140.0
Vegetables & melons	146.0	51.0	70.0	82.0	90.0
Fruit & berries	113.0	11.0	22.0	35.0	41.0

SOURCE: U.S. Department of Agriculture, *The Agricultural Situation in the Soviet Union: Review of 1975 and Outlook for 1976* (Washington, D.C.: USDA, Economic Research Service, Foreign Agricultural Economic Report, no. 118, April 1976), p. 23; *SSSR v tsifrakh v 1978 g.* [The USSR in figures in 1978], (Moscow: Statistika, 1979), p. 204.
[1] Includes the milk equivalent of butter.
[2] Flour equivalent.

SOVIET AGRICULTURE: AN OVERVIEW

There is probably no sector in the Soviet economy that has been the subject of more discussion both within the Soviet Union and in other countries than agriculture. Western economists have typically been very critical of Soviet agriculture; they point to such persistent problems as output fluctuations, poor yields, high costs, and inadequate investment. One can however rationalize much of Soviet behavior in the agricultural sector in terms of a particular type of development strategy—albeit a strategy that concentrated largely on short-run gains. However, to develop at a rate such as the Soviet Union has in the past 60 years and to the level it now enjoys are achievements of major significance. If the rural sector paid disproportionately for this pace of development, we must, when appraising the Soviet model as a development alternative, consider this price as opposed to other means of promoting development.

The role of agriculture in the Soviet strategy of economic development remains a matter of some controversy. On the one hand, we have noted that agriculture seems to have made a contribution to the development process—possibly smaller than originally thought—and yet for much of the plan era, agricultural performance has not been good, requiring in recent years substantial injections of state funds to modernize the sector.

But, what of the future? While this is not the place to speculate about possible future agricultural performance, a few general comments are in order. It must be noted that Soviet agriculture has been, and will continue to be, plagued by unfavorable natural conditions. The regional diversity of the Soviet countryside defies generalizations— 47 percent of the territory is under permafrost, the north and northwest have an overabundance of moisture, while the south has very little moisture. Climatic factors have led to great instability in year-to-year production.[59]

At the same time, the Russian peasant has been drawn rapidly and reluctantly into a modern industrial society, as the rural sector continues to decline in relative importance. Such a transformation, and in a relatively short span of time, inevitably creates difficulties of organization and motivation.

The prevailing attitude of Soviet leaders toward the agricultural sector contains several important threads. First, Soviet reconstruction of rural life is dedicated in the long-run to a planned, nonmarket type of solution to economic problems. To resolve organizational problems, the state farm is utilized; to resolve problems of labor force distribution and utilization, the state injects industrial processing into the countryside, and so on. There is no evidence to suggest that this pattern of thinking will change. Indeed, it is worth noting that for many of these programs (the virgin lands, the development of specialized farms around cities, and so on), the *sovkhoz* has been the basic organizational mechanism. Although Soviet agriculture remains dominated by the *kolkhoz*, which still accounts for almost 54 percent of agricultural employment, the *sovkhoz* has gained substantially in importance throughout the postwar period (from 8 percent to 45 percent of agricultural employment between 1950 and 1978)[60] and may continue to grow in relative importance as new state programs are implemented through the *sovkhoz*.

Second, the Soviet view of the apparently "successful" capitalist countries (for example, the United States and Canada) suggests that even in these cases, the state is destined to play an important (if different) role in agriculture, and yet it sees a fundamental similarity—the necessity of the industrial sector eventually to subsidize in one form or another the inherently less profitable agricultural sector. In fact, since 1965, the Soviets have been forced to pay large subsidies to agriculture—largely meat and milk subsidies—as procurement prices have risen above retail prices. These subsidies have become enormous (perhaps equal to 40 percent of the national income produced in agriculture in 1978).[61] One should note however an important distinction between Western and Soviet agricultural subsidies. Soviet farm subsidies are the result of the state's decision to hold retail food prices

[59] There is some meteorological evidence that unfavorable climatic conditions will extend into the 1980s. Central Intelligence Agency, *USSR: The Impact of Recent Climate Change on Grain Production*, ER76–10577U, Washington, D.C., October 1976.
[60] *Narodnoe khoziaistvo SSR v 1978* [The national economy of the USSR in 1978] (Moscow: Statistika, 1979), p. 287.
[61] Vladimir G. Treml, *Agricultural Subsidies in the Soviet Union* (Washington, D.C.: Foreign Demographic Analysis Division, Foreign Economic Report, no. 15, 1978).

below clearing levels, which when combined with rising procurement prices require a farm subsidy. Agricultural subsidies in the West are, on the other hand, largely a result of state decisions to maintain agricultural prices above market clearing levels, thus requiring state purchases of excess food products.

Third, the 1970s was a period when the Soviet Union was willing (and, within important constraints, able) to abandon its posture as a net grain exporter to become a net grain importer.[62] Although severe harvest disruptions in the 1970s were major factors influencing this policy, the recognition of the need to improve the Russian diet was also an important element. The future of this posture will depend upon Soviet trade policy, the attitudes of the major grain exporting countries, and the behavior of the world grain market.[63]

There appear to be no dramatic new programs on the horizon for Soviet agriculture, such as increased freedom for private agriculture. Instead, the blueprints of the Soviet leadership for the 1980s and 1990s call for continuation of the policies of the 1960s and 1970s. The foundation of Soviet agriculture will continue to be the *kolkhoz* and *sovkhoz*, with relative gains for the latter. Long-range plans call for the continued infusion of capital and fertilizer inputs into agriculture at the high rates that have prevailed throughout the postwar era, perhaps with greater emphasis on the quality of such inputs.[64] Deficient performance will continue to be blamed upon waste and the poor performance of individuals rather than upon the basic system of organization and incentives. The major campaign of the 1980s may be the development of the "nonblack earth zone of the Russian Republic," a vast region less subject to significant annual fluctuations in precipitation. Thus agricultural investments are being targeted specifically to the development of this region, and the success of this program will have a significant effect on agricultural performance in this decade.

If the performance of Soviet agriculture is to improve markedly, the transformation from an extensive to an intensive pattern of growth is es-

---

[62] During the 1960s, the Soviet Union exported grain at an average annual rate of approximately 57 million metric tons and imported grain at an average annual rate of approximately 3 million metric tons. Between 1971 and 1977, the average annual rate of import was 14.7 million metric tons, and exports were 3.5 million metric tons. The import rate remained high through 1979, clouded only by the embargo on U.S. grain sales to the Soviet Union announced by President Jimmy Carter in January of 1980, in response to the Soviet invasion of Afghanistan. For details, see Judith G. Goldich, "U.S.S.R. Grain and Oilseed Trade in the Seventies," in Joint Economic Committee, *Soviet Economy in a Time of Change* (Washington, D.C.: U.S. Government Printing Office, 1979), vol. 2, pp. 133–164.

[63] National Foreign Assessment Center, *USSR: Long-Term Prospects for Grain Imports*, ER79-10057, Washington, D.C., January 1979.

[64] David W. Carey and Joseph Havelka, "Soviet Agriculture: Progress and Problems," in Joint Economic Committee, *Soviet Economy in a Time of Change* (Washington, D.C.: U.S. Government Printing Office, 1979), vol. 2, pp. 70–82.

sential. The Soviet leadership has been injecting capital and fertilizer resources into Soviet agriculture, but as we have seen, output per unit of input has been declining, with only a slight increase in the late 1970s. Part of this problem may be resolved by traditional means, such as improving the quality of inputs (better imported farm equipment, improvements in fertilizers), but we would have to question whether traditional solutions will yield hoped-for results.

Finally, we must emphasize that some of the problems of Soviet agriculture cannot be blamed upon the economic system of command farming. Soviet agriculture operates under unfavorable natural conditions, and the farm population is an aging one. Moreover, agriculture is a declining industry in many industrialized countries that at one time had a vibrant agricultural economy (France and West Germany, for example). Despite these reservations, it is our opinion that the economic system of command farming is the major ingredient in the disappointing performance of Soviet agriculture.

SELECTED BIBLIOGRAPHY

David W. Carey, "Soviet Agriculture: Recent Performance and Future Plans," in Joint Economic Committee, *Soviet Economy in a New Perspective* (Washington, D.C.: U.S. Government Printing Office, 1976), pp. 575–599.

Roger A. Clarke, "Soviet Agricultural Reforms Since Khrushchev," *Soviet Studies*, vol. 20, no. 2 (October 1968), 159–178.

Douglas B. Diamond, "Trends in Output, Inputs, and Factor Productivity in Soviet Agriculture," in Joint Economic Committee, *New Directions in the Soviet Economy* (Washington, D.C.: U.S. Government Printing Office, 1969), pp. 339–381.

Douglas B. Diamond and Constance Krueger, "Recent Developments in Output and Productivity in Soviet Agriculture," in Joint Economic Committee, *Soviet Economic Prospects for the Seventies* (Washington, D.C.: U.S. Government Printing Office, 1973), pp. 316–339.

Maurice Dobb, *Soviet Economic Development Since 1917*, rev. ed. (New York: International Publishers, 1961).

Evsey D. Domar, "The Soviet Collective Farm as a Producer Cooperative," *American Economic Review*, vol. 56, no. 4, part 1 (September 1966), 734–757.

Frank A. Durgin, Jr., "Monetization and Policy in Soviet Agriculture Since 1952," *Soviet Studies*, vol. 15, no. 4 (April 1964).

M. Fallenbuchl, "Collectivization and Economic Development," *The Canadian Journal of Economics and Political Science*, vol. 3, no. 1 (February 1967), 1–15.

W. A. Douglas Jackson, ed., *Agrarian Policies and Problems in Communist and Non-Communist Countries* (Seattle: University of Washington Press, 1971).

Naum Jasny, *The Socialized Agriculture of the USSR* (Stanford, Calif.: Stanford University Press, 1949).

Joint Economic Committee, *Soviet Economy in a Time of Change* (Washington, D.C.: U.S. Government Printing Office, 1979), vol. 2, part 3.

Jerzy F. Karcz, "An Organizational Model of Command Farming," in Morris Bornstein, ed., *Comparative Economic Systems: Models and Cases*, rev. ed. (Homewood, Ill.: Irwin, 1969).

Jerzy F. Karcz, ed., *Soviet and East European Agriculture* (Berkeley and Los Angeles: University of California Press, 1967).

Jerzy F. Karcz and V. P. Timoshenko, "Soviet Agricultural Policy, 1953–1962," *Food Research Institute Studies*, vol. 4, no. 2 (May 1964).

Roy D. Laird, ed., *Soviet Agricultural and Peasant Affairs* (Lawrence: University of Kansas Press, 1963).

Roy D. Laird and Edward L. Crowley, eds., *Soviet Agriculture: The Permanent Crisis* (New York: Praeger, 1965).

Roy D. Laird, Joseph Hajda, and Betty A. Laird, eds., *The Future of Soviet Agriculture in the Soviet Union and Eastern Europe* (Boulder, Col.: Westview Press, 1977).

Martin M. McCauley, *Khrushchev and the Development of Soviet Agriculture: The Virgin Lands Programme 1953–1964* (New York: Holmes and Meier, 1976).

James R. Millar, ed., *The Soviet Rural Community* (Urbana: University of Illinois Press, 1971).

Robert F. Miller, *One Hundred Thousand Tractors* (Cambridge, Mass.: Harvard University Press, 1970).

Walter Y. Oi and Elizabeth M. Clayton, "A Peasant's View of a Soviet Collective Farm," *American Economic Review*, vol. 58, no. 1 (March 1968), 37–59.

David M. Schoonover, "Soviet Agricultural Policies from Development to Maturity," *Soviet Union*, vol. 4, part 2 (1977), 271–296.

Erich Strauss, *Soviet Agriculture in Perspective* (London: Allen & Unwin, 1969).

Robert C. Stuart, "Aspects of Soviet Rural Development," *Agricultural Administration*, vol. 2 (1975), 165–178.

Robert C. Stuart, *The Collective Farm in Soviet Agriculture* (Lexington, Mass.: Heath, 1972).

Lazar Volin, *A Century of Russian Agriculture* (Cambridge, Mass.: Harvard University Press, 1970).

F. Douglas Whitehouse and Joseph Havelka, "Comparison of Farm Output in the US and USSR, 1950–1971," in Joint Economic Committee, *Soviet Economic Prospects for the Seventies* (Washington, D.C.: U.S. Government Printing Office, 1973), pp. 340–374.

Agricultural Performance and Economic Development

R. W. Davies, "A Note on Grain Statistics," *Soviet Studies*, vol. 21, no. 3 (January 1970).

Kenneth R. Gray, "Soviet Agricultural Specialization and Efficiency," *Soviet Studies*, vol. 31, no. 4 (October 1979), 542–558.

Arcadius Kahan, "The Collective Farm System in Russia: Some Aspects of Its Contribution to Soviet Economic Development," in Carl Eicher and

Lawrence Witt, eds., *Agriculture in Economic Development* (New York: McGraw-Hill, 1964), pp. 251–271.

Jerzy F. Karcz, "Back on the Grain Front," *Soviet Studies,* vol. 22, no. 2 (October 1970), 262–294.

Jerzy F. Karcz, "From Stalin to Brezhnev: Soviet Agricultural Policy in Historical Perspective," in James R. Millar, ed., *The Soviet Rural Community* (Urbana: University of Illinois Press, 1971), pp. 36–70.

Jerzy F. Karcz, "Thoughts on the Grain Problem," *Soviet Studies,* vol. 18, no. 4 (April 1967), 399–434.

James R. Millar, "Mass Collectivization and the Contribution of Soviet Agriculture to the First Five-Year Plan: A Review Article," *Slavic Review,* vol. 33, no. 4 (December 1974), 750–766.

James R. Millar, "Soviet Rapid Development and the Agricultural Surplus Hypothesis," *Soviet Studies,* vol. 22, no. 1 (July 1970), 77–93.

James R. Millar and Corinne A. Guntzel, "The Economics and Politics of Mass Collectivization Reconsidered: A Review Article," *Explorations in Economic History,* vol. 8, no. 1 (Fall 1970), 103–116.

Alec Nove, "The Agricultural Surplus Hypothesis: A Comment on James R. Millar's Article," *Soviet Studies,* vol. 22, no. 3 (January 1971), 394–401.

W. F. Owen, "The Double Developmental Squeeze on Agriculture," *American Economic Review,* vol. 56, no. 1 (March 1966), 43–70.

Harry G. Shaffer, ed., *Soviet Agriculture: An Assessment of Its Contributions to Economic Development* (New York: Praeger, 1977).

Charles K. Wilber, "The Role of Agriculture in Soviet Economic Development," *Land Economics,* vol. 45, no. 1 (February 1969).

Chapter 8

Soviet Foreign Trade

In this chapter, we examine the role of the foreign sector in the Soviet economy. We begin with a discussion of trade in the Soviet planned economy—in particular, the state trade monopoly and the trade planning instruments utilized throughout the plan era. In addition to developing an understanding of how trade is conducted, it is necessary to examine both the volume and the structure of Soviet trade, and especially its distribution among various trading partners in the world—notably among capitalist countries (developed and underdeveloped) and socialist bloc member countries of the COMECON organization. These trends can give us a picture of how Soviet trade policies have functioned in practice.

Finally, we examine the role of foreign trade in economic development and especially its role in the Soviet development experience.

TRADE IN THE SOVIET PLANNED ECONOMY

The Organization of Foreign Trade[1]

The organizational mechanisms used to conduct Soviet foreign trade are numerous, and over the years they have grown in number and complexity.

---

[1] For a general discussion of foreign trade in centrally planned economies, see Franklyn D. Holzman, *International Trade Under Communism* (New York: Basic Books, 1976); and Alan A. Brown, "Towards a Theory of Centrally Planned Foreign Trade," in Alan A. Brown and Egon Neuberger, eds., *International Trade and Central Planning* (Berkeley and Los Angeles: University of California Press, 1968), pp. 57–93. for a survey of the literature and basic issues, see Franklyn D. Holzman, *Foreign Trade Under Central Planning* (Cambridge, Mass.: Harvard University Press, 1974), chap. 1. For details of organizational arrangements, see V. P. Gruzinov, *The USSR's Management of Foreign Trade* (White Plains, N.Y.: M. E. Sharpe, 1979). For details of recent organizational changes, see Scott Bozek, "The U.S.S.R.: Intensifying the Development of Its Foreign Trade Structure," in Joint Economic Committee, *Soviet Economy in a Time of Change* (Washington, D.C.: U.S. Government Printing Office, 1979), vol. 2, pp. 506–525.

Altogether, these organizations comprise the foreign trade monopoly of the Soviet Union. The basic organization responsible for the conduct of foreign trade is the Ministry of Foreign Trade, which itself is subordinate to *Gosplan,* and the USSR Council of Ministers (see Figure 5). The operative trade units, that is the organizations that actually do the buying and selling in foreign markets, are Foreign Trade Organizations (FTOs)—or the All-Union Import-Export Associations, as they are described in Soviet parlance. These foreign trade organizations are usually subordinate to the Ministry of Foreign Trade and are financially independent, operating on a *khozraschet* basis. Most of the FTOs are organized by product. Thus the FTO *Avtoeksport* ("auto export") deals in automobiles and *Mezhdunarodnaia kniga* ("international book") deals in books. These organizations may handle imports, exports, or both. Reforms of the late 1970s were directed toward combining both the import and the export tasks within a single FTO. In addition to those FTOs dealing with specific products, others exist for the servicing of foreign trade and conducting trade on a regional basis. An exam-

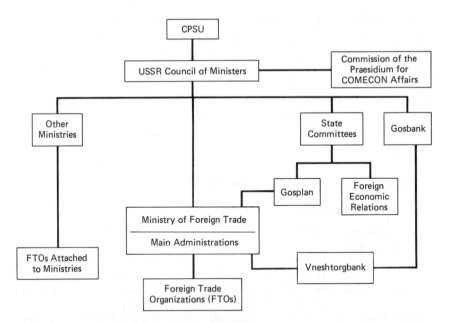

Figure 5   The Organization of Soviet Foreign Trade. (Source: Compiled from V. P. Gruzinov, *The USSR's Management of Foreign Trade* [White Plains, N.Y.: M. E. Sharpe, 1979], pp. 26, 75, 79; Edward A. Hewett, "Most-Favored Nation Treatment in Trade Under Central Planning," *Slavic Review,* vol. 37, no. 1 [March 1978], 28; Paul K. Cook, "The Political Setting," in Joint Economic Committee, *Soviet Economy in a Time of Change* [Washington, D.C.: U.S. Government Printing Office, 1979], vol. 1, face p. 50, no. 2.)

ple of the former would be *Vneshtorgreklama* ("foreign trade advertising"), which handles advertising in foreign trade. An example of the latter would be *Vostokintorg*, which is the Eastern Trade Association.

The FTOs have within them the means of conducting foreign trade, and they provide necessary technical and financial services. Their revenue is calculated as a percentage of their foreign trade turnover (exports plus imports). In addition to the individual FTOs, the Ministry of Foreign Trade is divided into main administrations or branches that are concerned with a wide range of issues relating to foreign trade. These administrations provide technical and financial services, including research on foreign trade.

The financial arrangements for Soviet foreign trade are handled by a special bank, *Vneshtorgbank*.[2] Though traditionally under the jurisdiction of *Gosbank*, the *Vneshtorgbank* has had significantly expanded powers and functions since the early 1960s. It now operates under policy guidance from *Gosbank*, but in close cooperation with the main foreign exchange administration of the Ministry of Foreign Trade. In addition to a large number of correspondent banks in foreign countries, *Vneshtorgbank* also operates through Soviet-owned banks abroad—for example, the Moscow Narodny Bank of London.

There are other more specialized organizations for the conduct of trade, the importance of which has been growing in recent years. A number of special FTOs do not fall under the jurisdiction of the Ministry of Foreign Trade. *Intourist*, the FTO responsible for Soviet tourism, falls within the jurisdiction of the administration for foreign tourism under the Council of Ministers. Another example is SOOC (Soviet Olympic Organizing Committee), operating independently of the Ministry of Foreign Trade and the FTOs but fully empowered to sign agreements with foreign firms for the conduct of the 1980 Olympic Games held in Moscow. Finally, the Soviet Union has Joint Stock Companies, for example, Belarus Machinery Inc., which sells and services Belarus tractors in the United States.

The Planning of Foreign Trade

Soviet foreign trade, like other sectors of the Soviet economy, is managed as an integral part of the system of material balance planning.[3] Soviet foreign

---

[2] For more detail on financial arrangements, see George Garvy, *Money, Financial Flows, and Credit in the Soviet Union* (Cambridge, Mass.: Ballinger, 1977), pp. 152–155.

[3] This discussion is based upon Lawrence J. Brainard, "Soviet Foreign Trade Planning," in Joint Economic Committee, *Soviet Economy in a New Perspective* (Washington, D.C.: U.S. Government Printing Office, 1976), pp. 695–708; Vladimir G. Treml, "Foreign Trade and the Soviet Economy: Changing Parameters and Interrelationships," in Egon Neuberger and Laura Tyson, eds., *Transmission and Response: The Impact of International Disturbances on the Soviet Union and Eastern Europe* (New York: Pergamon Press, 1980); Herbert Levine, "The Effects of Foreign Trade on Soviet Planning Practices," in Alan A.

trade planners have tended to use imports and exports as balancing items in the national economic plan (imports where there were shortages and exports where there were surpluses). Planners have sought to avoid heavy reliance on trade to balance the plan for reasons discussed later in this chapter. In trade with COMECON countries,[4] Soviet authorities planned for trade to play a more important role, namely, to promote the integration of these countries with the Soviet economy. Specifically, the Soviet Union was to serve as the basic source of raw materials for Eastern European development, with manufactured products supplied in return.

In recent years, a combination of reforms in the Soviet foreign trade sector plus a new Soviet posture in foreign trade (the greater use of Western imports to stimulate economic performance and a more aggressive export posture to pay for imports) have led to the evolution of an increasingly sophisticated foreign trade planning structure, but the main features of foreign trade planning have remained basically intact since the 1930s.

Trade objectives are expressed in three plans, these being (1) an import-export plan, (2) a plan for support materials and services for Soviet projects outside the Soviet Union, and (3) a balance of payments plan. These plans are segregated according to region, and in the case of trade with COMECON, they are supposed to be coordinated with the general (and trade) plans of each member country. This coordination function is supported by long-range programs to promote joint planning among COMECON members—efforts to plan integration on a five-year time horizon in terms of industrial branches, projects, and joint ventures.

The foreign trade plans contain detailed plan targets. The import-export plan indicates the regional distribution of exports and imports, the tasks of each organization involved (the Foreign Trade and other ministries, the FTOs), and the schedule of deliveries. The balance of payments plan is developed by the Ministry of Foreign Trade in conjunction with the Ministry of Finance and shows both payments and receipts (on both a current and a credit basis) for various categories of goods and services distinguished by currency type—for example, by specific convertible currencies and transferable rubles. The transferable ruble (or *valuta* ruble) is used as an accounting tool and often has little relationship with internal ruble prices. In addition to the balance of payments plan, a capital plan is also prepared by the Ministry of Finance, *Gosplan,* and the *Vneshtorgbank.* It summarizes claims and credits on an annual basis.

The integration of the foreign trade plans and the national economic

Brown and Egon Neuberger, eds., *International Trade and Central Planning* (Berkeley and Los Angeles: University of California Press, 1968), pp. 255–276.
[4] The Council for Mutual Economic Assistance, called COMECON, or alternatively, CMEA, is the Soviet bloc's equivalent to the European Common Market and will be discussed in this chapter. The member countries, in addition to the USSR, are Bulgaria, Hungary, East Germany, Cuba, Mongolia, Poland, Rumania, and Czechoslovakia.

plan is incomplete in that there is no comprehensive plan that translates foreign trade flows into domestic prices. The trade plans are expressed in terms of foreign trade rubles, whose relationship to domestic prices is unclear. This separation of financial plans into those in *valuta* rubles and in domestic rubles has complicated Soviet economic planning; yet no solution has been offered to this point.

The apparatus for the conduct of Soviet foreign trade is fundamentally different from that of a market economy. The most basic difference is that the foreign trade monopoly serves to isolate Soviet internal producers and consumers of export and import items, respectively, from direct contact with the outside world. From this basic difference stems a set of arrangements in international trade that are very different from those typically observed in the West.

The operative unit for carrying out the foreign trade plan is the FTO. While the FTOs have been the focus of substantial attention and reform effort in recent years, their basic function remains to connect the internal producer or consumer with the external world. The FTO purchases authorized export items from the Soviet producer at internal ruble prices and sells them in foreign markets at agreed upon (typically, world market) prices. Within COMECON, the sale will be transacted in transferable rubles.[5] Likewise, an FTO will purchase authorized items in foreign markets at negotiated or world market prices, and the internal Soviet consuming firm will be charged the internal ruble price for the imported item. The financial side of these transactions is the responsibility of the various financial organs involved with foreign trade, along with the Ministry of Foreign Trade. If the imported item is sold to the using enterprise at a higher price than that paid by the FTO, a surplus is created for the state budget. In the late 1970s, surplus earnings accounted for some 10 percent of state revenues.[6]

Soviet Foreign Trade Policy

Thus far we have examined only the mechanisms for organizing Soviet foreign trade and how foreign trade is included in the national economic plan. But what are the rules that determine the level and distribution of Soviet foreign trade? We turn now to a discussion of Soviet foreign trade policy.

Western observers have noted that the volume of Soviet foreign trade has been significantly less than one would find in market economies at simi-

---

[5] As we shall see below, the pricing of goods and services in Soviet foreign trade is a matter of great complexity. The influence of world market prices is only a beginning point in the discussion.

[6] Treml, "Foreign Trade." This surplus is the consequence of overvalued exchange rates used to translate *valuta* ruble prices into domestic prices and the rise in the world prices of Soviet raw material exports.

lar levels of economic development.[7] This pattern is said to demonstrate a Soviet bias against trade or a "policy of trade aversion." Data on the volume of Soviet trade and trade proportions are given in Table 22. What factors explain the Soviet bias against trade?

From the earliest days of the Soviet regime, the prevailing Marxist-Leninist ideology called for rejection of traditional Western arguments concerning the benefits to be gained from international trade—the thesis of *comparative advantage*—just as it has called for the rejection of other Western "economic laws." Western markets were viewed as subject to chaotic fluctuations that could jeopardize the planned nature of the Soviet economy. Moreover, it was argued that "socialism in one country" was possible due to the vast resources of the Soviet Union. These matters were discussed in Chapter 3.

A second major factor explaining the Soviet policy of trade aversion was the early perception (and, in large part, reality) of a "hostile capitalist encirclement," which encouraged the Soviet regime to avoid reliance upon foreign markets for its economic development. Events over the years have tended to bolster Soviet distrust of Western markets. In the immediate postwar era, the United States spearheaded a movement to restrict credits and the flow of "strategic" goods to the USSR. The United States has also used cutoffs of high technology trade and, in January 1980, of grain to punish the Soviets for political misdeeds.

Third, as a sector to be incorporated into an already complex planning system, foreign trade as a priority sector might significantly complicate the overall planning process—in particular by introducing outside forces not directly controlled by Soviet planners and thus increasing the degree of plan uncertainty. One can find the tendency to avoid reliance on outsiders at all levels of the Soviet economy,[8] and this reluctance is intensified when foreign suppliers (even ideologically friendly suppliers from COMECON) are involved. It is noteworthy that Soviet trade potential within COME-

---

[7] For empirical evidence on this point, see for example Paul R. Gregory, *Socialist and Nonsocialist Industrialization Patterns* (New York: Praeger, 1970), pp. 119–120, and Frederic L. Pryor, *The Communist Foreign Trade System* (Cambridge, Mass.: MIT Press, 1963), chap. 1. According to Treml, "Foreign Trade," the Soviets in the 1970s abandoned their "policy of trade aversion" and now have a trade share of national income of 21 percent. The confusion lies in the manner of translating Soviet trade data in *valuta* rubles into domestic prices, and there is much controversy over this issue. On this controversy, consult Treml, *ibid.*, footnote 1.

[8] The tendency toward self-reliance (autarky) on the part of Soviet enterprises and ministries has been chronicled by Gertrude E. Schroeder, "The Soviet Economy on a Treadmill of 'Reforms,' " in Joint Economic Committee, *Soviet Economy in a Time of Change* (Washington, D.C.: U.S. Government Printing Office, 1979), vol. 1, pp. 335–336 and by David Granick, *Soviet Metal Fabricating and Economic Development* (Madison: University of Wisconsin Press, 1967).

TABLE 22   Real Volume of Imports and Exports of the USSR (1913 =100) and Trade Ratios

Year	Exports Composite Index	Imports Composite Index	Exports as Percent of National Income	Year	Exports Composite Index	Imports Composite Index	Exports as Percent of National Income
1913	100.0	100.0	10.4	1948	51.1	64.3	
1917	6.9	176.3		1949	58.2	72.4	
1918	0.5	7.7		1950	80.7	82.0	
1919	0.0	0.2		1951	94.6	101.4	
1920	0.1	2.1		1952	114.2	123.4	
1921	1.3	15.3		1953	120.0	133.1	
1922	5.4	19.6		1954	132.6	154.4	
1923	14.3	10.4		1955	142.3	149.2	3.0
1924	22.2	18.9		1956	150.7	173.8	3.0
1925	25.1	37.8		1957	179.2	186.7	3.6
1926	32.2	33.8		1958	184.2	223.8	3.1
1927	34.7	38.9		1959	242.9	264.7	3.9
1928	37.7	49.4		1960	242.6	290.1	3.7
1929	44.4	48.3	3.1	1961	265.7	299.4	3.9
1930	57.0	72.1	3.5	1962	311.8	334.6	4.3
1931	61.4	82.4	3.0	1963	321.7	364.3	4.4
1932	53.7	59.1	2.6	1964	333.9	378.9	4.4
1933	49.8	31.9	2.3	1965	371.5	401.5	4.5
1934	43.2	24.0	1.8	1966	422.9	396.3	4.6
1935	38.0	26.3	1.3	1967	458.0	423.0	5.0
1936	28.6	30.3	0.8	1968	503.4	479.5	5.9
1937	30.0	27.8	0.5	1969	558.8	514.1	6.0
1938	26.2	32.3		1970	590.8	552.9	6.3
1939	10.6	20.4		1971	608.5	586.1	6.4
1940	21.8	27.7		1972	626.3	685.6	5.7
1941	14.4	29.1		1973	714.9	785.1	6.0
1942	4.8	17.6		1974	809.3	812.8	6.5
1943	4.3	15.5		1975	833.0	962.1	6.3
1944	6.6	16.5		1976	898.0	1022.9	6.5
1945	15.5	20.0		1977	980.7	1039.5	
1946	27.2	49.4		1978	1028.0	1194.3	
1947	30.0	43.9					

SOURCES: Michael Kaser, "A Volume Index of Soviet Foreign Trade," *Soviet Studies,* vol. 20, no. 4 (April 1969), 523–526; *Vneshnaia torgovlia SSSR v 1978 g.* [USSR foreign trade 1978], (Moscow: Statistika, 1979), p. 16; Franklyn D. Holzman, "Foreign Trade," in Abram Bergson and Simon Kuznets, eds., *Economic Trends in the Soviet Union* (Cambridge, Mass.: Harvard University Press, 1963), p. 290; Vladimir G. Treml, "Foreign Trade and the Soviet Economy: Changing Parameters and Interrelationships," in Egon Neuberger and Laura Tyson, eds., *Transmission and Response: The Impact of International Disturbances on the Soviet Union and Eastern Europe* (New York: Pergamon Press, 1980).

CON remains "underutilized," although there can be no ideological objections to such trade.

Fourth, the Soviets stress that the capitalist countries have erected barriers against trade with the Soviet Union, beginning with the embargoes following the 1917 Revolution to the present-day restrictions on lending, failure to grant tariff reductions, and controls on strategic commodities.

Fifth, and possibly most important, the very mechanisms for the conduct of Soviet foreign trade have themselves served to complicate the conduct of foreign trade, to limit Soviet participation in the international financial community, and to necessitate peculiar arrangements that inhibit foreign trade. We turn to these arrangements in the following section.

Internal Barriers to Foreign Trade

We have already noted that the arrangements for conducting foreign trade and for the pricing of traded commodities have isolated Soviet enterprises from foreign market influences. If there is a difference between the internal ruble price and the foreign price of a particular product, this difference appears as a subsidy or as a revenue source in the state budget, with no immediate implications for the internal Soviet enterprise. This isolation of the Soviet enterprise both as a producer and as a consumer sets it apart from capitalist enterprises, which enter directly into foreign trade arrangements and can respond more readily to foreign markets. The isolation of Soviet producing enterprises makes it difficult for them to be competitive in world markets by not knowing what the changing world market requires. The Soviets' inability to compete in capitalist markets in the areas of manufactured goods and in the service fields is in part accounted for by this isolation.[9] The weak Western market for Soviet manufacturers has limited Soviet foreign exchange earnings over the years, which has in turn restricted Soviet imports from the West.[10] The Soviet Union has been unable (or unwilling) to expand its exports of petroleum products and other raw materials to offset its expanding import requirements from the West. Trade deficits vis-à-vis Western countries therefore have had to be financed with credits granted by capitalist countries.[11]

[9] Paul G. Ericson, "Soviet Efforts to Increase Exports of Manufactured Products to the West," in Joint Economic Committee, *Soviet Economy in a New Perspective* (Washington, D.C.: U.S. Government Printing Office, 1976), pp. 709–727; H. H. Kravalis et al., "Soviet Exports to the Industrialized West: Performance and Prospects," in Joint Economic Committee, *Soviet Economy in a Time of Change* (Washington, D.C.: U.S. Government Printing Office, 1979), vol. 2, pp. 414–462.

[10] Franklyn D. Holzman, "Some Theories of the Hard Currency Shortages of Centrally Planned Economies," in Joint Economic Committee, *Soviet Economy in a Time of Change* (Washington, D.C.: U.S. Government Printing Office, 1979), vol. 2, pp. 297–316.

[11] Paul G. Ericson and Ronald S. Miller, "Soviet Foreign Economic Behavior: A Balance of Payments Perspective," in Joint Economic Committee, *Soviet Economy in a Time of Change* (Washington, D.C.: U.S. Government Printing Office, 1979), pp. 208–243.

Existing arrangements for conducting trade inhibit trade in other ways. First, the Soviet ruble is an inconvertible currency, not listed on world currency markets and not accepted by (or available to) trading partners. Ruble inconvertibility, along with the Soviet system of centralized planning and price setting, means that the Soviet prices used in foreign transactions (*valuta* rubles) bear little relation either to relative scarcities in the domestic economy or to world market prices. There is therefore no common scale of value through which the potential advantages or disadvantages of trade can be measured. In the absence of an effective way to assess the costs and benefits of trade, bilateral agreements have to be negotiated between the Soviet Union and its trading partners, balanced usually in terms of some approximation of world market prices. The use of bilateral arrangements is almost inevitable, given Soviet internal controls over trade flows, the nature of Soviet prices, and the lack of meaning of the ruble (or any other socialist currency) in world markets.

Since the ruble is not a convertible currency, its real value in terms of other currencies (its exchange rate) is not known.[12] The exchange rate set administratively by the Soviet government tends to be arbitrary and not necessarily reflective of the relative purchasing power of the ruble. Thus the exchange rate as a means to assess the benefits from trade is of little use in this case.

Unlike capitalist economies, where the gains from trade are obvious from comparisons of domestic and foreign prices, what goods should be traded and with what countries is not clear in the Soviet case. Internal Soviet prices (as we have shown in Chapter 5) themselves may not reflect domestic relative scarcities, and internal prices are difficult to compare with foreign prices due to the lack of appropriate rates of exchange. The absence of firm information on relative foreign and domestic costs and prices explains in part the depressed levels of Soviet trade. Even if there were substantial gains to specialization of production and exchange (say, trading Soviet machines for Bulgarian consumer goods) due to large differences in costs of production, this would likely not be evident to foreign trade planners. Thus, in the Soviet Union, an important pressure in favor of trade expansion is absent, namely, a clear appreciation of the fact that certain products can be obtained abroad with less sacrifice of resources than if produced domestically.

Soviet trade authorities (along with their COMECON counterparts) have sought to remedy this situation by developing criteria—Foreign Trade Efficiency Indexes (FTEI)—for evaluating on a rational basis exports and

[12] For a discussion of the long-term impact of exchange rate prices, see Franklyn D. Holzman, "The Ruble Exchange Rate and Soviet Foreign Trade Pricing Policies, 1929–1961," *American Economic Review*, vol. 57, no. 4 (September 1968), 807–812. For a discussion of how ruble-dollar exchange rates are presently determined, see Garvy, *Money, Financial Flows, and Credit*, chap. 7.

imports.[13] The FTEI have been in use within COMECON since the mid-1960s and seek to provide rules for calculating the ratios of domestic to foreign costs of potential export and import items. The general principle underlying these formulae is that foreign trade prices should be translated into domestic prices by calculating the amount of domestic production required to earn the foreign exchange (*valuta* rubles) needed to purchase the foreign item (in the case of the FTEI index, for imports). Although these formulae bear a certain resemblance to the relative cost comparisons made by capitalist economies, the approximation is very rough. To be an accurate index of the opportunity costs of domestic production versus foreign production, internal prices must reflect domestic relative scarcities, and the implicit exchange rates used in the indexes must indicate the relative purchasing power of the foreign exchange accounting units. These conditions are not met in most instances. Moreover, the FTEIs are used only as an aid for foreign trade planners. Most trading decisions are made administratively—without consulting foreign trade efficiency indexes as a part of long-term agreements—and are often based upon political decisions.

The second important consequence of Soviet trade arrangements is the difficulty of devising appropriate financial arrangements to handle the financing of trade imbalances. Specifically, since a nonconvertible currency cannot be used in payment for goods and services, Soviet trade with each

[13] For discussions of FTEIs, consult: Lawrence J. Brainard, "Soviet Foreign Trade Planning," pp. 701–707; Carl H. McMillan, "Some Recent Developments in Soviet Foreign Trade Theory," *Canadian Slavonic Papers*, vol. 12, no. 3 (Fall 1970), 243–272; Andrea Boltho, *Foreign Trade Criteria in Socialist Economies* (Cambridge: Cambridge University Press, 1971).

Typically, FTEIs are calculated separately for potential exports and imports. In simplified form the *import index* is:

$$X_{ie} = \frac{Z_i X_{i \cdot eq}}{V_i}$$

Where: X_{ie} is the index of import effectiveness of the product.

V_i is the foreign exchange cost of one unit of the product.

Z_i is the domestic cost of producing one unit of the product.

$X_{i \cdot eq}$ is the ratio of foreign exchange receipts from the country in question from exported goods to the domestic cost of producing these goods.

The import effectiveness index is easy to understand except for $X_{i \cdot eq}$, which plays the role of a crude exchange rate. The Z's represent the internal ruble prices of imported items and the V's represent foreign prices expressed in transfer (*valuta*) rubles. These transfer rubles are determined administratively and will vary for each of the USSR's trading partners. The problem is translating these foreign prices into domestic prices—a role played by exchange rates in capitalist countries. For this purpose, a form of opportunity cost measure is calculated for each trading partner. For this import index, this is the average domestic cost of producing goods domestically to earn the foreign exchange necessary to import the item from the particular country. This is calculated by taking the foreign exchange earnings from Soviet exports to that country and dividing by the domestic cost of producing these goods for export.

partner must balance. If not, the Soviet Union must pay in gold or convertible Western currencies or arrange credit. In contrast, if the United States were to purchase more goods and services from Canada than Canada buys from the United States, there would be no immediate problem, since Canada would be willing to accept U.S. dollars either for purchases in the United States or for use in other countries where dollars are readily acceptable at the established rate of exchange. Thus, the U.S. trade deficit with Canada is automatically financed, and a trade imbalance is possible. This cannot be done in the case of Soviet transactions with other countries, for currency inconvertibility leads to "commodity inconvertibility." If the Soviet Union were to have a trade deficit with Poland, for example, the Soviet Union could not automatically finance the deficit by paying in rubles. Insofar as Poland cannot use rubles to freely purchase what it wants from the Soviet Union or another country, they are of no value to the Polish trade authorities. The tendency therefore is to balance transactions with all countries, even though a "rational" trading plan would call for surpluses or deficits vis-à-vis individual trading partners. In this manner, trade is restricted to the amount that one trading partner is willing to accept from the other, a form of barter transaction. Within COMECON, trade imbalances must be cleared by hard currency payments, and, in rare instances, credits are granted to finance deficits.

THE EXTERNAL ENVIRONMENT: THE SOCIALIST COUNTRIES

In terms of geographical distribution, the Soviet Union distinguishes between its trade with socialist countries (COMECON and other) and capitalist countries (developed and underdeveloped). The Council for Mutual Economic Assistance, COMECON, was established in 1949 on the initiative of the Soviet Union for the expressed purpose of integrating the socialist planned economies of Eastern Europe with the Soviet Union through the specialization of trade and production among member countries.[14] Trade with COMECON members has accounted for more than 50 percent of Soviet foreign trade throughout the postwar era (see Table 23), and the Soviet Union is in many respects the dominant partner in this organization. Although there have been some changes in the trading arrangements and

[14] The members of COMECON are Bulgaria, Cuba (since 1972), Czechoslovakia, the German Democratic Republic, Hungary, Poland, Rumania, Mongolia, and the Soviet Union. For a more extensive discussion of bloc trade, see Michael Kaser, *COMECON, Integration Problems of the Planned Economies*, 2nd ed. (London: Oxford University Press, 1967); Frederic L. Pryor, *The Communist Foreign Trade System* (Cambridge, Mass. MIT Press, 1963); Jozef M. van Brabant, *East European Cooperation: The Role of Money and Finance* (New York: Praeger, 1977); Edward A. Hewett, *Foreign Trade Prices in the Council for Mutual Economic Assistance* (Cambridge: Cambridge University Press, 1974).

TABLE 23 Soviet Foreign Trade—Geographic Distribution in Selected Postwar Years (percentages)

	1946	1950	1953	1956	1959	1962	1965	1970	1975	1978
1. Socialist countries[a]	54.5	81.1	83.2	75.7	75.3	70.2	68.8	65.2	56.3	59.8
COMECON member countries	40.6	57.4	59.3	49.6	52.0	57.5	58.0	55.6	51.7	55.6
2. Capitalist countries	45.5	18.9	16.8	24.3	24.7	29.8	31.2	34.7	43.6	40.1
Industrial	38.4	15.1	14.5	16.8	15.9	18.1	19.3	21.2	31.2	28.0
LDCs	7.1	3.8	2.3	7.5	8.8	11.7	11.9	13.5	12.4	12.1
Total (lines 1 and 2)	100.0	100.0	100.0	100.0	100.0	100.0	100.0	100.0	100.0	100.0

[a] Includes China, Cuba, Vietnam, North Korea, and Yugoslavia.
SOURCE: Compiled from official Soviet foreign trade handbooks, in particular from annual editions of *Vneshnaia torgovlia SSSR* [Foreign trade of the USSR] and *Statisticheski ezhegodnik Stran-chlenov S.E.V.* [Statistical yearbook of the member countries of S.E.V.].

cooperative agreements among COMECON countries since the 1960s, only a relatively limited degree of integration among these countries has been achieved for a number of basic reasons.[15]

First, in spite of Soviet economic and political pressure for integration, the countries of Eastern Europe have focused upon developing their own diversified industrial economies, including an adequate base of heavy industry.[16] During the postwar era, the COMECON countries have not been content to specialize in specific product lines as desired by the USSR, for they have viewed this as a loss of national economic independence. This stance is buttressed by the fact that COMECON possesses no supranational authority over its members. Each member has veto power, and various Soviet efforts to give COMECON supranational powers have been successfully opposed by other members.

Second, although some coordination has been developed, there has been less effective development of integrated planning arrangements, and only preliminary steps have been taken to develop common yardsticks (such as common costs and prices, and a convertible COMECON trading currency) to direct specialization and to achieve a more optimal pattern of bloc trade.[17] The most important effort to date to promote COMECON integration is the Comprehensive Program of 1971, to be implemented by 1990. The Comprehensive Program is a series of bilateral agreements for bilateral economic and scientific cooperation and for joint economic planning among individual COMECON members.

Since the economic mechanisms and pricing arrangements are similar among the bloc countries (with the exception of Hungary, where major reforms have been undertaken), the USSR's COMECON trading partners conduct trade much like the Soviet Union does. Intrabloc trade is conducted largely on a bilateral basis, with five-year and one-year planning

[15] For discussions of the degree of integration of the COMECON countries, see Joseph Pelzman, "Trade Integration in the Council for Mutual Economic Assistance: Creation and Diversion, 1954–1970," *ACES Bulletin*, 18 (Fall 1976), 39–60, and Josef van Brabant, "Trade Creation and Trade Diversion in Eastern Europe: A Comment," *ACES Bulletin*, vol. 19, no. 1 (Spring 1977), 79–98.

[16] For a discussion of one particular but important case, see John Michael Montias, *Economic Development in Communist Rumania* (Cambridge, Mass.: MIT Press, 1967), chap. 4. Also see John Michael Montias, "Socialist Industrialization and Trade in Machinery Products," in Alan A. Brown and Egon Neuberger, eds., *International Trade and Central Planning* (Berkeley and Los Angeles: University of California Press, 1968), pp. 130–158.

[17] For a discussion of recent developments in the process of integration, see Morris Bornstein, "East-West Economic Relations and Soviet-East European Economic Relations," in Joint Economic Committee, *Soviet Economy in a Time of Change* (Washington, D.C.: U.S. Government Printing Office, 1979), vol. 1, pp. 291–311; Arthur Smith, "The Council for Mutual Economic Assistance in 1977: New Economic Power, New Political Perspectives, and Some Old and New Problems," in Joint Economic Committee, *East European Economies Post-Helsinki* (Washington, D.C.: U.S. Government Printing Office, 1977), pp. 152–173.

horizons. To facilitate multilateral clearing, the Bank for International Co-operation (IBEC) was created in 1964. However, most intra-COMECON trade is conducted in transferable rubles, a nonconvertible currency used basically in bilateral arrangements.[18] Trade in hard currencies is small, and multilateral clearing is minuscule, perhaps 5 percent of the total.[19] Where there is a bilateral deficit, it is normally settled by adjusting future plan targets or by the shipment of "soft goods" (goods that are relatively unattractive because they are overpriced in COMECON relative to world market prices). Preference would be for "hard goods" that would have a market in the West, but hard goods are typically not offered to correct imbalances.

As with Soviet trade, the trade of bloc members is determined by their national planning agencies and with little or no cost-benefit frame of reference. The pricing of traded commodities in intrabloc trade has been complicated by the absence of a set of internal prices (say, USSR ruble prices) suitable for valuing transactions among member countries. As a general rule, the pricing principle for intrabloc trade is to begin by determining what the commodity would have cost in the world market. Such calculations are not easy to make in the case of machinery and equipment not sold in the West, since authorities can only guess at the price the commodity would command in world markets. This ambiguity has led to controversy between the Soviet Union and its COMECON partners over whether the terms of trade are "fair" and to claims that the USSR pays too little for manufactured imports from other COMECON countries.

Prior to 1975, COMECON prices were fixed over the life of long-term national plans. According to the pricing formula agreed upon in Bucharest in 1958, the world market prices of 1957 were applied to intrabloc transactions until 1965. For the planning period 1966–1970, average 1961–1965 world market prices were used, and then average world prices of 1966–1970 were used for the period 1971–1975.[20] The explosion of energy and other raw material prices in the 1970s caused the USSR to change this pricing formula, as the Soviet Union is the dominant supplier of energy to Eastern Europe. COMECON adopted in 1975 a new "sliding pricing formula," whereby average world market prices of the preceding five years are used. Thus rising energy prices are passed on to COMECON partners gradually over time. Also, provision was made to pay for Soviet energy deliveries

[18] For an in-depth discussion, see van Brabant, *East European Cooperation*, chaps. 3 and 4.
[19] Martin Kohn and Nicholas Lang, "The Intra-CMEA Foreign Trade System: Major Price Changes, Little Reform," in Joint Economic Committee, *East European Economies Post-Helsinki* (Washington, D.C.: U.S. Government Printing Office, 1977), p. 137.
[20] For a detailed discussion of these issues, see Raimond Dietz, "Price Changes in Soviet Trade with CMEA and the Rest of the World Since 1975," in Joint Economic Committee, *Soviet Economy in a Time of Change* (Washington, D.C.: U.S. Government Printing Office, 1979), vol. 1, pp. 263–299; Bornstein, "East-West Economic Relations," pp. 299–308.

above targeted levels in hard currencies at prevailing world market prices. These changes are projected to lead to a 30 to 40 percent improvement in the USSR's terms of trade with Eastern Europe during 1980.

In spite of attempts at reform of institutional arrangements, the basic problems of integrating the COMECON countries remain. It has proven especially difficult to integrate the industrialized members (the USSR, East Germany, and Czechoslovakia) with the less industrialized countries (Bulgaria and Rumania), due to the unwillingness of the latter to specialize in low technology products and agriculture. Disputes among these countries have arisen, and with East European products finding a growing market in the West and with increasing hard currency credits, imports of more advanced technology from the West (rather than from the Soviet Union) have become increasingly attractive. It is from this basic pattern that the problem of an expanding COMECON hard currency debt has arisen, an issue we will examine below.

SOVIET TRADE WITH CAPITALIST COUNTRIES

Soviet trade with capitalist countries has increased significantly during the postwar years. If one excludes the atypical immediate postwar period, Soviet trade with capitalist countries as a portion of total Soviet foreign trade has increased from roughly 19 percent in 1950 to roughly 40 percent in 1978 (see Table 23). This expansion in trade with capitalist countries has been accompanied by a reduction of trade with socialist countries (especially with the People's Republic of China).

The expansion of Soviet trade with capitalist countries can be divided into two different components: Soviet trade with the industrialized West (North America, Western Europe, and Japan) and with the less developed countries (LDCs). Let us examine each in turn.

Soviet trade with the LDCs has expanded from minuscule levels in the early 1950s but has not expanded as a share of Soviet trade since the early 1960s, stabilizing at about 12 percent of trade turnover. The composition of Soviet trade with the LDCs is markedly different from that with the industrialized West. The Soviet Union exports primarily machinery and equipment to LDCs, along with some raw materials and petroleum (for "client" states). Whereas the USSR has difficulty marketing its heavy industry manufactures in the West, an LDC market does exist for such exports.

A dominant theme of Soviet relations with LDCs is its economic and military aid. The thrust of Soviet assistance to LDCs is broadly political and concentrates upon a limited number of strategic nations. From its inception in the mid-1950s, Soviet aid has grown in magnitude but remains well below levels of U.S. aid. Between 1956 and 1978, Soviet aid agreements totaled just under 47 billion dollars, though actual deliveries amounted to just under 33 billion dollars. This figure is about one-fifth the volume of U.S. economic and military aid for the same period.[21]

The features of Soviet aid to LDCs are distinctive when compared to those of other aid-granting nations. First, Soviet aid is dominated by military as opposed to general economic aid. For the period 1956 through 1978, 63 percent of aid agreements were military, while 77 percent of actual aid deliveries were military.[22] Second, Soviet aid is typically specific project aid combined with technical and service support provided on the site by Soviet advisers. In 1978, there were 75,000 technicians from the Soviet Union and Eastern Europe in the LDCs.[23] Third, Soviet aid is frequently repayable in the form of long-term low interest loans. Finally, Soviet aid is usually directed at a few recipients and seldom offers hard currency credits for purchases outside of the Soviet Union. From 1954 to 1978, six countries received over 60 percent of all Soviet economic aid to the LDCs.[24]

The share of Soviet trade with the industrialized West remained fairly constant at nearly 15 percent during the 1950s, then almost doubled from 1960 to 1978. Thus Soviet trade with the industrialized West has been expanding more rapidly than that with its other trading partners; yet currently, trade to the USSR accounts for only 2.5 percent of the exports of the major industrialized countries. It should be emphasized that exports to the Soviet Union still represent a relatively minor market for the industrialized West, although it looms large for selected products. Soviet trade with Western industrialized countries has been dominated by a very different set of issues. These have revolved around the nature of Soviet foreign trade arrangements in an era of growing Soviet import needs from the West (especially industrial technology and grain) and the Soviet drive to expand exports to pay for these imports. During the early 1970s, in trade with the West, the rate of growth of imports outstripped the rate of growth of exports by a significant margin, the result being a growing hard currency deficit with the West.[25] Let us examine the pattern of Soviet trade in greater detail.

The growth of imports from the industrialized West has been concen-

---

[21] For a survey of Soviet economic and military aid, see Orah Cooper and Carol Fogarty, "Soviet Economic Military Aid to the Less Developed Countries, 1954–78," in Joint Economic Committee, *Soviet Economy in a Time of Change* (Washington, D.C.: U.S. Government Printing Office, 1979), vol. 2, pp. 648–662, and especially Appendix Table 1. For worldwide data, see National Foreign Assessment Center, *Handbook of Economic Statistics 1979*, ER79–10274, Washington, D.C., August 1979, pp. 110–126.

[22] Cooper and Fogarty, "Soviet Economic Military Aid," Appendix Table 4.

[23] National Foreign Assessment Center, *Handbook of Economic Statistics 1979*, p. 125.

[24] *Ibid.*, pp. 118–119.

[25] For a discussion of theoretical issues underlying the hard currency debt, see Holzman, "Some Theories of the Hard Currency Shortages," pp. 297–316. For measurement, see Ericson and Miller, "Soviet Foreign Economic Behavior," pp. 208–243; and Bornstein, "East-West Economic Relations," p. 297.

trated in two broad areas—industrial goods and services designed to support the technological needs of the Soviet economy, and agricultural goods (largely grain and fertilizer) to offset serious climatic (and thus harvest) reverses and to stimulate agricultural productivity in general and meat production in particular.[26]

The rapid growth of Soviet imports from the West slowed substantially in the mid-1970s, but Soviet exports to the industrialized West have not kept up with the pace of imports, so the hard currency debt continues to grow. Since Soviet manufactures typically do not compete well in Western markets (they are sold primarily to socialist bloc nations and the LDCs), the result has been a growing Soviet hard currency debt estimated by various researchers to be between $9.5 billion and $12.5 billion (in net terms) in 1978.[27] The burden of this debt can be measured in two ways. The first is to determine the ratio of annual payments on hard currency debt to hard currency export earnings. In 1978, this "debt service ratio" stood at 17 percent. A second measure is to determine the ratio of gross hard currency debt to hard currency export earnings. This ratio equaled unity in 1978. Although the Soviet debt position remains within reason, it has had its costs in terms of gold sales abroad, increased reliance on Western credits, and the need to expand arms sales. Moreover, the debt position of Eastern Europe is more alarming, and Eastern Europe may someday require assistance to service its hard currency debt. The effect of this growing debt has been twofold since the mid-1970s. First, Soviet authorities have trimmed the growth of imports from the industrialized West for the purpose of regaining control over the hard currency balance, a policy that has cut the annual trade deficit substantially. The second element of Soviet trade policy of the 1970s has been the continuing campaign to increase participation in Western markets. This effort has several goals.

First, there has been a long-standing effort to improve both the political and the economic bases of trade with Western countries such as the United States.[28] The most significant breakthroughs have come in commer-

[26] For a discussion of the role of agriculture in Soviet foreign trade, see David M. Schoonover, "Soviet Agricultural Trade and the Feed-Livestock Economy," in Joint Economic Committee, *Soviet Economy in a New Perspective* (Washington, D.C.: U.S. Government Printing Office, 1976), vol. 2, pp. 813–821. For recent developments, see David M. Schoonover, "Soviet Agricultural Policies," in Joint Economic Committee, *Soviet Economy in a Time of Change* (Washington, D.C.: U.S. Government Printing Office, 1979), vol. 2, pp. 103ff, and Judith G. Goldich, "U.S.S.R. Grain and Oilseed Trade in the Seventies," in Joint Economic Committee, *Soviet Economy in a Time of Change* (Washington, D.C.: U.S. Government Printing Office, 1979), pp. 133–164.

[27] Ericson and Miller, "Soviet Foreign Economic Behavior," p. 224.

[28] For a background of U.S.-Soviet trade and commercial relations, see Holzman, *International Trade Under Communism*, pp. 159–173. For a survey of recent developments, see Hertha W. Heiss, Allen J. Lenz, and Jack Brougher, "United States-Soviet Commercial Relations Since 1972," in Joint Economic Committee, *Soviet Economy in a Time of Change* (Washington, D.C.: U.S. Government Printing Office, 1979), vol. 2, pp. 189–207.

cial relations with Western Europe and Japan, in which the USSR has gained tariff reductions and has had relatively easy access to private and government credit. United States legislation on trade with the Soviet Union remains restrictive, focusing especially upon limiting sales of "strategic" goods, restricting governmental credits, and failing to grant general trade concessions. The 1960s and 1970s were a period of considerable discussion on trade matters between the Soviet Union and the United States, culminating in the negotiation of the U.S.-USSR Trade Agreement in 1972. This agreement, which was to grant Most Favored Nation (MFN) status, was annulled in 1975 by the Soviets when it was linked with the question of Jewish emigration. The question of granting MFN status remains up in the air, a matter of substantial emotional and political (though possibly dubious economic) importance to the Soviet side, especially when China was granted MFN in January of 1980. The Soviets have argued that not being granted MFN has made their manufactured products less competitive in U.S. markets, but there is some controversy about the future effect of granting MFN on USSR exports to the United States.[29]

Second, the Soviet Union has been more aggressive in devising arrangements for increasing imports from the West without an immediate increase in exports.[30] For example, the importance of compensation agreements between the Soviet Union and the United States has increased in recent years.[31] Compensation agreements were almost nonexistent in the early 1960s but grew substantially thereafter, involving Western Europe, Japan, and the United States.[32]

The compensation agreement underscores an important problem in Soviet-Western trade, especially in the area of capital imports. Because of prohibitions against private ownership, the Soviets are denied the advantages (and avoid the disadvantages) of direct foreign investment. Foreign

---

[29] For a discussion of this issue, see Edward A. Hewett, "Most-Favored Nation Treatment in Trade Under Central Planning," *Slavic Review*, vol. 37, no. 1 (March 1978), 25–39; Helen Raffel, Marc Rubin, and Robert Teal, "The MFN Impact on U.S. Imports from Eastern Europe," in Joint Economic Committee, *East European Economies Post-Helsinki* (Washington, D.C.: U.S. Government Printing Office, 1977), p. 1427.

[30] For useful background, see Jack Brougher, "USSR Foreign Trade: A Greater Role for Trade with the West," in Joint Economic Committee, *Soviet Economy in a New Perspective* (Washington, D.C.: U.S. Government Printing Office, 1976), pp. 677–694; Ericson, "Soviet Efforts to Increase Exports, pp. 709–726.

[31] For a recent discussion of compensation agreements, see Dennis J. Barclay, "U.S.S.R.: The Role of Compensation Agreements in Trade With the West," in Joint Economic Committee, *Soviet Economy in a Time of Change* (Washington, D.C.: U.S. Government Printing Office, 1979), vol. 2, pp. 462–481.

[32] Maureen Smith, "Industrial Cooperative Agreements: Soviet Experience and Practices," in Joint Economic Committee, *Soviet Economy in a New Perspective* (Washington, D.C.: U.S. Government Printing Office, 1976), pp. 767–785; Carl H. McMillan, "East-West Industrial Cooperation," in Joint Economic Committee, *East European Economies Post-Helsinki* (Washington, D.C.: U.S. Government Printing Office, 1977), pp. 1175–1224.

companies cannot own and manage subsidiaries in the USSR. However, near substitutes have been sought, and the compensation agreement is one, for it promises the Western investor a share in the resulting output. Joint ventures, coproduction, and licensing have been used as well to promote industrial cooperation without Western ownership.

Another device for trade expansion has been direct investment by the Soviet Union in the West.[33] This phenomenon, which grew significantly in the 1970s, is diversified geographically and by type of economic activity, varying from production (on a limited basis) through trade and service organizations to banking. However, with these organizations typically wholly owned, controlled, and managed by the Soviet Union, Western nations express the usual concern that one might connect with a multinational enterprise, adding the participation of a foreign and sometimes antagonistic government.

The future of Soviet trade with the Western industrialized nations and especially with the United States will hinge upon the fruitful development of these new strategies along with the improvement of the mechanisms with which the Soviet planned economy conducts its foreign trade. However, basic problems such as restrictions on strategic goods, limitations on direct investment, product quality, and marketing difficulties—issues to which we will return at the end of this chapter—will remain dominant in the 1980s.

THE STRUCTURE AND VOLUME OF SOVIET COMMODITY TRADE

Over the years, the composition of Soviet trade has changed with the evolving requirements of the domestic economy. In 1913, imports were concentrated in three areas: raw materials (for the textiles industry), 22 percent; consumer goods, 21 percent; and machinery and equipment, 16 percent. On the export side, raw materials, grain, and animal products accounted for virtually all of Russian exports. In 1928, on the eve of the Five Year Plan era, the structure of exports and imports was much like that of the late tsarist era.[34]

The forced industrialization program of the 1930s brought about significant shifts in the structure of Soviet trade. On the import side, there was

---

[33] This discussion is based upon Carl H. McMillan, "Soviet Investment in the Industrialized Western Economies and in the Developing Economies of the Third World," in Joint Economic Committee, *East European Economies Post-Helsinki* (Washington, D.C.: U.S. Government Printing Office, 1977), pp. 625–647; Carl H. McMillan, "Growth of External Investments by the COMECON Countries," *World Economy*, vol. 2, no. 3 (September 1979), 363–386.

[34] Franklyn D. Holzman, "Foreign Trade," in Abram Bergson and Simon Kuznets, eds., *Economic Trends in the Soviet Union* (Cambridge, Mass.: Harvard University Press, 1963), pp. 291–300.

a distinct movement away from importing consumer goods and toward importing producer goods. Producer goods and consumption goods accounted for 27 percent and 7 percent of aggregate Soviet imports in 1918; by 1931, the figures were 95 percent and 5 percent for production and consumption goods, respectively.[35] Also notable during the early years of Soviet industrialization was the increasing importance of imports of machinery and equipment. From a level of 15.9 percent of imports in 1913, machinery and equipment imports grew to account for 55.2 percent of imports in 1932.[36] This pattern changed significantly after the First Five Year Plan, basically through the development of domestic capacity in key industrial sectors. Nevertheless, if we look at the portion of Soviet utilization of key industrial commodities (those of crucial importance to the industrialization effort) accounted for by imports, the result is striking and suggests that foreign technology may have been a very important element in the industrialization process.[37] In 1930, for example, 89 percent of the aggregate Soviet consumption of turbines, boilers, and generators came from imports. In 1932, 66 percent of the machine tools used in the Soviet Union were imported.[38]

Export patterns did not change radically during the early years of Soviet industrialization. Fuels, raw materials, and consumer goods remained important as a portion of aggregate export volume. Exports of grain, which had virtually disappeared by 1928, increased significantly during the First Five Year Plan but fluctuated significantly thereafter, depending upon the harvest. It is significant that grain exports were never again to regain the import role they played throughout the tsarist era.

Since the 1950s, there have been important shifts in Soviet commodity trade patterns on both the import and the export sides (Tables 24 and 25). These shifts have been a focus of concern by Soviet policy makers in the 1970s and form one of the more important arguments in support of upgrading the trade mechanism, a matter that we examined earlier in this chapter.

On the import side, there have been increases in the relative importance of machinery and equipment and of food-related items since the 1950s. On the export side, fuels have grown to a dominant position, along with the traditionally important exports of raw materials. The aggregate data however hide the important underlying issue of geographic distribution. In the hard currency markets, fuels and raw materials are dominant,

---

[35] *Ibid.*, p. 297.

[36] *Ibid.*, p. 296.

[37] It is important to recognize that the shift in trade patterns during the First Five Year Plan not only provided producer goods so necessary for the immediate expansion of output but also—and this may be the more crucial factor—provided prototypes of the best Western technology that could then be duplicated. For a discussion of the role of Western technology during the early years, see Antony C. Sutton, *Western Technology and Soviet Economic Development 1930 to 1945* (Stanford, Calif.: The Hoover Institution, 1971).

[38] Holzman, "Foreign Trade," pp. 297–298.

TABLE 24 The Structure of Soviet Exports (percentages)

	1950	1955	1960	1965	1970	1975	1977
Machinery	11.8	17.5	20.5	20.0	21.3	18.5	18.7
Fuels and energy	3.9	9.6	16.2	17.2	15.6	31.4	35.0
Metals, ores, minerals	12.3	18.6	21.6	23.2	21.5	17.0	13.1
Chemicals, fertilizer, rubber	4.0	2.7	2.9	2.8	3.5	3.5	2.8
Construction products	0.2	0.5	0.3	0.5	0.6	0.6	0.5
Forest products, paper	3.0	5.0	5.5	7.2	6.5	5.7	5.0
Fibers	11.2	10.1	6.4	5.1	3.4	3.0	3.2
Agricultural raw materials	3.8	1.9	2.0	1.3	1.0	.5	0.5
Grain and oilseed	12.9	8.6	8.6	3.4	3.3	1.6	1.1
Sugar	0.9	0.7	0.5	0.6	0.8	0.07	0.05
Other foodstuffs	3.3	2.5	3.8	4.3	4.1	2.0	1.4
Cloth, clothing, shoes	2.2	1.5	1.2	0.8	0.7	0.5	0.4
Small consumer durables	0.2	0.2	0.8	0.7	0.9	1.1	0.9
Other consumer manufacturing	2.4	1.4	0.8	0.8	1.1	1.5	1.4
Unclassified	27.7	19.0	8.8	11.8	15.5	12.9	15.7

SOURCE: Computed from Michael R. Dohan, "Export Specialization and Import Dependence in the Soviet Economy, 1970–77," in Joint Economic Committee, *Soviet Economy in a Time of Change* (Washington, D.C.: U.S. Government Printing Office, 1979), vol. 2, pp. 370–371.

TABLE 25 The Structure of Soviet Imports (percentages)

	1950	1955	1960	1965	1970	1975	1977
Machinery	21.5	30.2	29.7	33.4	35.1	33.2	37.5
Fuels and energy	11.5	8.1	4.2	2.5	2.0	3.9	3.6
Metals, ores, minerals	15.1	16.6	17.0	10.0	10.7	12.5	10.2
Chemicals, fertilizer, rubber	6.9	3.4	6.0	6.2	5.7	4.7	4.4
Construction products	1.4	0.6	0.8	0.7	0.4	0.3	0.4
Forest products, paper	3.9	3.0	1.8	1.9	2.2	2.1	1.8
Fibers	7.8	5.4	6.4	4.4	4.8	2.4	2.7
Agricultural raw materials	0.4	2.2	2.2	1.0	2.0	1.4	1.7
Grain and oilseed	1.0	0.8	1.0	5.0	1.1	7.4	3.4
Sugar	3.1	2.8	2.3	3.8	3.4	5.9	6.1
Other foodstuffs	11.9	16.3	9.7	12.0	11.1	9.1	10.2
Cloth, clothing, shoes	5.6	3.8	13.8	9.3	12.3	8.9	8.6
Small consumer durables	0.07	0.2	0.5	0.2	0.3	0.1	1.4
Other consumer manufacturing	1.7	0.8	3.0	4.7	5.7	3.9	4.2
Unclassified	6.5	5.5	1.5	5.0	3.0	4.0	5.0

SOURCE: Computed from Michael R. Dohan, "Export Specialization and Import Dependence in the Soviet Economy, 1970–77," in Joint Economic Committee, *Soviet Economy in a Time of Change* (Washington, D.C.: U.S. Government Printing Office, 1979), vol. 2, pp. 370–371.

with machinery and equipment (exported mainly to Eastern Europe and the LDCs) playing only a very small role. Unless the Soviet Union can continue to expand fuel and raw material sales in hard currency markets, trade diversification in the direction of manufactures will be essential in the 1980s and beyond.[39]

Finally, the development of Soviet foreign trade since World War II has been distinctive on several fronts, all of which deserve closer attention. The volume of trade has grown significantly—more rapidly than the economy. Thus in 1950, exports and imports accounted for 2.1 and 2.9 percent, respectively, of GNP. By 1977, these shares had grown to 6.7 and 9.2 percent.[40] The rapid growth of trade volume has caused Vladmir Treml[41] to argue that the USSR has abandoned at long last its policy of trade aversion. Does the Soviet Union still "underutilize" its trade potential, as it obviously did from the 1930s to the early 1970s? This question remains unresolved at this juncture because of the difficulty of translating foreign trade prices into domestic prices. What is clear is that the 1970s witnessed a dramatic increase in foreign trade volume, starting from extremely depressed rates in the immediate postwar period.

The structure of Soviet imports and exports has been planned largely by administrative decree throughout the era of central planning. There is no strong reason, therefore, to expect the observed Soviet pattern of trade to correspond to its relative resource endowments. It is thus interesting to find that the Soviet Union does appear to have the pattern of trade one would expect of a capitalist country having the relative resource endowments of the USSR.[42]

TRADE IN SOVIET ECONOMIC DEVELOPMENT

Western trade theory suggests that with varying resource availabilities in different countries, specialization of production and exchange with other countries can serve to promote economic development. According to such theorizing, during the early stages of modernization, an LDC should export those goods and services in which it has a comparative advantage, and it should utilize export earnings to finance imports off those goods and ser-

[39] For an elaboration, see Bozek, "The U.S.S.R.: Intensifying the Development of Its Foreign Trade Structure."

[40] Michael R. Dohan, "Export Specialization and Import Dependence in the Soviet Economy, 1970–77," in Joint Economic Committee, *Soviet Economy in a Time of Change* (Washington, D.C.: U.S. Government Printing Office, 1979), vol. 2, p. 369. There is controversy over the share of imports of national income, with Treml, "Foreign Trade," Table 1, estimating the import share much above Dohan and other researchers. The share figures cited in Table 22 are those of Treml for the years 1955 to 1976.

[41] Treml, *ibid.*

[42] Steven Rosefielde, "Factor Proportions and Economic Rationality in Soviet International Trade," *American Economic Review*, vol. 64, no. 4 (September 1974), 670–680.

vices needed for industrialization that would be produced at high relative cost domestically. As the economy grows more sophisticated over a long period of time, it will be able to substitute domestic production for imports and lessen its dependence upon trade.

The role of trade in Soviet economic development was discussed seriously in the Industrialization Debate of the 1920s, with the right wing of the party emphasizing the comparative cost advantages of international trade. The trade strategy eventually adopted by Stalin during the forced industrialization of the 1930s rejected traditional comparative advantage principles and called for a policy of isolation from the outside world. It was argued that socialism could be "built in one country," without reliance on the capitalist world, and the Soviet Union's use of trade during the 1930s represents a case study of an industrialization that had only minimal reliance on other economies. We now examine the role played by foreign trade during the early years of Soviet economic development.

A hallmark of Soviet economic development over the years has been the emphasis on self-sufficiency as a desirable economic goal. Self-sufficiency was most prominent during the 1930s, when trade proportions were negligible, but the policy of trade aversion has been continued into the postwar era. Soviet reasoning in support of self-sufficiency has already been described (capitalist encirclement, planning uncertainty, etc.), and the Soviet leadership's vision of capitalist world markets as chaotic underscored the theoretical legitimacy of trade aversion.

Possibly more important than such theoretical considerations was the Soviet development strategy of treating agriculture as a low-priority sector throughout the 1930s. Thus the very nature of Soviet development strategy prohibited extensive reliance upon foreign trade. As Bukharin had argued, a prosperous peasantry was the key to expanding trade; once the collectivization decision was made, the Soviet Union's role as a major supplier of grain and animal products to the world market was effectively terminated. Moreover, the Soviet economy of the thirties had certain basic features that could support a minimal role for the foreign sector. With a favorable and varied resource base, a political mechanism to enforce high internal saving rates, and a reasonable scale for heavy industrial development from which to begin in 1928, substantial reliance upon foreign products and capital could be avoided. In particular, the existence of a state monopoly in foreign trade enabled the Soviet authorities to avoid noncritical imports (a pressing problem for many present-day LDCs) and to focus upon those imports most crucial for economic growth—in particular, machinery and equipment and associated technology. Strict controls over the flow of exports and imports allowed the promotion of specific industrialization goals with relatively low foreign trade volumes.

Soviet trade patterns prior to 1917 were, as Franklyn Holzman has pointed out, ". . . what one would have expected from such a nation."[43] Exports were primarily agricultural products or semifabricates, while imports were mostly producers goods and raw materials. In 1913, for example, 60 percent of Russian exports were agricultural, 34.4 percent were raw materials and semifabricates, while 27 percent of imports were consumer goods, the remainder being raw materials and producer goods.[44]

Although trade was important in the period prior to 1900—for example, between 1886 and 1890, 46 percent of Russian wheat production was exported—this importance declined immediately prior to the Revolution, due in large part to the onset of World War I. In addition, what had previously been a favorable balance of payments position—commodity exports typically exceeding commodity imports offset by capital inflows—was sharply reversed by 1917. The portion of grain output exported during World War I declined sharply, as did the foreign exchange earnings on this grain, largely due to growing competition in the world grain market.[45] In addition, while imports initially declined, by 1917 they were once again increasing, thus leading to an unfavorable Russian trade position and the expansion of Russian debts abroad.

From the relatively low levels of the immediate prerevolutionary period, the volume of Soviet foreign trade increased quite significantly between 1917 and 1928. However, the prerevolutionary trade level was not regained by 1928; trade volume that year was well below 50 percent of the 1913 level (Table 22). The instigation of the industrialization drive in that year significantly altered Soviet thinking on appropriate trade patterns and levels.

During the first three years of the First Five Year Plan (1928–1933), the volume of both Soviet exports and imports increased significantly. Thus the volume of exports (1913 = 100) increased from 37.7 in 1928 to a high of 61.4 in 1931 while the volume of imports increased at a more rapid rate from 49.4 in 1928 to a high of 82.4 in 1931, declining thereafter (Table 22). The expansion of imports was directed almost exclusively to meeting the needs of heavy industry. In 1932, 66 percent of machine tools, 55 percent of metal cutting tools and 77 percent of turbines and generators were imported.[46] Equipment was imported for two purposes: to generate electricity and to build other machines. In light of this significant expansion of foreign trade during the First Five Year Plan, it may well be that Soviet planners did not in fact initially plan to pursue a deliberate policy of autarky, rather that later economic events forced them into that course. The volume of Soviet

[43] See Holzman, "Foreign Trade," p. 284.
[44] *Ibid.*
[45] *Ibid.*, p. 286.
[46] *Ibid.*, p. 290.

foreign trade declined very sharply after the conclusion of the First Five Year Plan, but this trend was in some part the result of a collapse in world markets (especially grain prices) brought on by the world depression of the 1930s.[47]

After the onset of the depression, the prices of Soviet exports and imports declined significantly, though the rate of decline of the former greatly outstripped that of the latter. The index of the prices of Soviet exports fell from 100 in 1929 to 48.7 in 1931, while the prices of Soviet imports declined from 100 in 1929 to 68 in 1931. The result of these price changes was a substantial decline in the Soviet commodity terms of trade.[48]

Although the significant increase in the volume of trade during the First Five Year Plan must be considered important to the initial industrialization effort, the decline in the terms of trade must have been an important factor—in addition to ideological and strategy considerations—in leading the Soviet economy toward a different role for the foreign sector. After the First Five Year Plan, the volume of Soviet foreign trade declined sharply and steadily, increasing again only after World War II. For example, the share of exports in national income declined from 10.4 percent in 1913 to 0.5 percent in 1937.[49] Thus at the peak of the forced industrialization drive of the late 1930s, the Soviets were operating a virtually autarkic economy. It was not until the early 1950s that the volume of trade turnover exceeded that of 1913, despite the fact that national income had been expanding at a rapid rate since 1928. Thus the Soviet Union represents a case study of a country that was able to generate rapid growth of output and substantial shifts in the structure of output in the direction of heavy industry with only modest levels of industrial imports. Since the early 1950s, there has been a moderation of the Soviet policy of autarky as practiced during the thirties, so that now it is more appropriate to speak of trade aversion rather than autarky.

SOVIET FOREIGN TRADE: PROSPECTS FOR THE FUTURE

In this chapter, we have examined the role of foreign trade in the Soviet economy. In addition to looking at the long-term role of foreign trade in the Soviet development experience, we have also investigated postwar trends in the organization and execution of foreign trade. In light of the Soviet long-term eperiences with foreign trade, what are the events and forces that will shape the Soviet foreign economy in the 1980s?[50]

---

[47] For a discussion of the role of foreign trade in the preplan and early planning years, see Michael R. Dohan, *Soviet Foreign Trade in the NEP Economy and Soviet Industrialization Strategy.* Unpublished doctoral dissertation, Massachusetts Institute of Technology, 1969.

[48] Holzman, "Foreign Trade," pp. 287–288.

[49] *Ibid.*, p. 289–290.

[50] For an examination of trends and prospects, see Lawrence J. Brainard, "Foreign Economic Constraints on Soviet Economic Policy in the 1980s," in Joint Economic Committee,

In the past, foreign trade has not been a particularly important element in the overall Soviet economy. However, Soviet institutional arrangements—in particular, the state monopoly over foreign trade—have greatly facilitated the ability of Soviet planners to direct trade toward the fulfillment of state objectives—in particular, the importation of advanced technology.

In recent years, as with other sectors of the economy, Soviet authorities have sought to improve the crude mechanisms for the conduct of trade, many of which have outlived their usefulness in an era of increasing domestic economic complexity and diversity. Soviet authorities have sought to bring more rationality into foreign trade decisions via Foreign Trade Efficiency Indexes, and there are signs of erosion of the complete control of the Ministry of Foreign Trade over foreign transactions.[51] Export manufacturers and ministries are gaining more direct access to foreign exchange and to foreign markets. If foreign trade is to be used more effectively in the future, the price may be a loosening of central control over trade and a resubjection of the Soviet domestic economy to the "chaotic" forces of capitalist markets.[52] It remains to be seen whether Soviet political authorities will be willing to pay this price. As we shall point out in Chapter 9, such efforts toward decentralization of authority have been rejected in domestic economic reform. Will they ultimately be rejected in foreign transactions as well?

There is little doubt that the events of recent years, and especially of the decade of the 1970s, represent a Soviet reappraisal of the appropriate role for foreign trade in the Soviet economy. The 1970s were a period of reform and change. In addition to the changing internal factors affecting Soviet trade, turbulent forces in the world economy—notably the sharp rise in petroleum prices—and in international affairs contributed to the Soviet reappraisal. Evidence presented by Vladimir Treml suggests that the Soviets may be in the process of abandoning their traditional policy of trade aversion. In our view, it would be premature to make this argument. From the viewpoint of Soviet authorities, there would be substantial costs to such a move. The planned Soviet economy would become increasingly subject to the ups and downs of capitalist markets and to political decisions by its adversaries to withhold products (grain, high technology) required by the plan. Yet these costs may ultimately be viewed as smaller than the alternatives—namely, significant reform of domestic industry and agriculture.

Soviet trade with some countries, notably the United States, remains small and one-sided, with little U.S. interest in Soviet goods. This experi-

---

Soviet Economy in a Time of Change (Washington, D.C.: U.S. Government Printing Office, 1979), vol. 1, pp. 98–109.

[51] Treml, "Foreign Trade."

[52] For a series of papers on this subject, see Neuberger and Tyson, *Transmission and Response.*

ence is to some degree a function of the peculiar relations between the two superpowers. It is also, however, a function of much more basic forces, the nature of which will change only very slowly in the 1980s. These forces—for example, the problems of the quality, design, serviceability, and financing of Soviet exports—are familiar to Western observers of the Soviet scene. Such problems—in addition to the traditional difficulty of Western business participation in the Soviet environment, problems of security, and so on—will limit the growth of trade in the 1980s.

Finally, the Soviet Union is itself a large and potentially rather self-sufficient nation. While the desire to stimulate better agricultural and industrial performance through trade is strong, it is at the same time balanced by the reluctance to let outside economic events influence the planned Soviet economy as Soviet political objectives are pursued in the external world. Whether or in what ways this balance may change in the 1980s will depend largely upon the ability of the Soviet leaders and their planned economy to withstand two sorts of pressures—those from outside, as world economic arrangements and realities change, and those from inside, as Soviet consumers increasingly demand that their ruble incomes be able to purchase more and better consumer goods and services. These issues, and in particular the general role of foreign trade and the impact of technology transfer from the West, will be considered in more detail in Chapter 12.

SELECTED BIBLIOGRAPHY

Gunnar Adler-Karlsson, *Western Economic Warfare: 1947–1967* (New York: Humanities Press, 1968).

Andrea Boltho, *Foreign Trade Criteria in Socialist Economies* (Cambridge: Cambridge University Press, 1971).

Josef C. Brada, ed., *Quantitative and Analytical Studies in East-West Economic Relations* (Bloomington: Indiana University Press, 1976).

Alan A. Brown and Egon Neuberger, eds., *International Trade and Central Planning* (Berkeley and Los Angeles: University of California Press, 1968).

Robert Campbell and Paul Marer, eds., *East-West Trade and Technology Transfer* (Bloomington, Ind.: International Development Research Center, 1974).

Michael R. Dohan, *Soviet Foreign Trade in the NEP Economy and Soviet Industrialization Strategy*. Unpublished doctoral dissertation, Massachusetts Institute of Technology, 1969.

Z. Fallenbuchl and C. H. McMillan, eds., *Partners in East-West Economic Relations: The Determinants of Choice* (London: Pergamon Press, forthcoming).

Marshall I. Goldman, *Soviet Foreign Aid* (New York: Praeger, 1967).

Gregory Grossman, "U.S.-Soviet Trade and Economic Relations: Problems and Prospects," *ACES Bulletin*, vol. 15, no. 1 (Spring 1973), 3–22.

V. P. Gruzinov, *The USSR's Management of Foreign Trade* (White Plains, N.Y.: M. E. Sharpe, 1979).

Edward A. Hewett, *Foreign Trade Prices in the Council for Mutual Economic Assistance* (Cambridge: Cambridge University Press, 1974).

Edward A. Hewett, "Most-Favored Nation Treatment in Trade Under Central Planning," *Slavic Review*, vol. 37, no. 1 (March 1978), 25–39.

Franklyn D. Holzman, "East-West Trade and Investment Policy Issues," *United States International Economic Policy in an Interdependent World* (Washington, D.C.: U.S. Government Printing Office, 1971), pp. 363–395.

Franklyn D. Holzman, "Foreign Trade," in Abram Bergson and Simon Kuznets, eds., *Economic Trends in the Soviet Union* (Cambridge, Mass.: Harvard University Press, 1963), pp. 283–332.

Franklyn D. Holzman, "Foreign Trade Behavior of Centrally Planned Economies," in Henry Rosovsky, ed., *Industrialization in Two Systems: Essays in Honor of Alexander Gerschenkron* (New York: Wiley, 1966).

Franklyn D. Holzman, *Foreign Trade Under Central Planning* (Cambridge, Mass.: Harvard University Press, 1974).

Franklyn D. Holzman, *International Trade Under Communism* (New York: Basic Books, 1976).

Joint Economic Committee, "Foreign Economic Activities," in *Soviet Economy in a New Perspective* (Washington, D.C.: U.S. Government Printing Office, 1976), part 3.

Joint Economic Committee, "Foreign Economic Activities," in *Soviet Economy in a Time of Change* (Washington, D.C.: U.S. Government Printing Office, 1979), vol. 2, part 4.

Joint Economic Committee, "Foreign Economic Relations," in *East European Economies Post-Helsinki* (Washington, D.C.: U.S. Government Printing Office, 1977), part 3.

Joint Economic Committee, "Foreign Economy," in *Soviet Economic Prospects for the Seventies* (Washington, D.C.: U.S. Government Printing Office, 1973), part 7.

Michael Kaser, *COMECON: Integration Problems of the Planned Economies*, 2nd ed. (London: Oxford University Press, 1967).

Anton Malish, Jr., *United States-East European Trade: Considerations Involved in Granting Most-Favored-Nation Treatment to the Countries of Eastern Europe* (Washington, D.C.: United States Tariff Commission, Staff Research Studies, no. 4, 1972).

Paul Marer, *Soviet and East-European Trade (1946–1969)*: Statistical Compendium and Guide (Bloomington: Indiana University Press, 1972).

Carl H. McMillan, ed., *Changing Perceptives in East-West Commerce* (Lexington, Mass,: Heath, 1974).

John Michael Montias, *Economic Development in Communist Rumania* (Cambridge, Mass.: MIT Press, 1967), chap. 4.

Frederic L. Pryor, *The Communist Foreign Trade System* (Cambridge, Mass.: MIT Press, 1963).

John Quigley, *The Soviet Foreign Trade Monopoly: Institutions and Laws* (Columbus: Ohio State University Press, 1974).

Glen Alden Smith, *Soviet Foreign Trade: Organization, Operations, and Policy, 1918–1971* (New York: Praeger, 1973).

Antony C. Sutton, *Western Technology and Soviet Economic Development 1917 to 1930* (Stanford, Calif.: The Hoover Institution, 1968).

Antony C. Sutton, *Western Technology and Soviet Economic Development 1930 to 1945* (Stanford, Calif.: The Hoover Institution, 1971).

Antony C. Sutton, *Western Technology and Soviet Economic Development 1945 to 1965* (Stanford, Calif.: The Hoover Institution, 1973).

Jozef M. van Brabant, *East European Cooperation: The Role of Money and Finance* (New York: Praeger, 1977).

Vladimir G. Treml, "Foreign Trade and the Soviet Economy: Changing Parameters and Interrelationships," in Egon Neuberger and Laura Tyson, eds., *Transmission and Response: The Impact of International Disturbances on the Soviet Union and Eastern Europe* (New York: Pergamon Press, 1980).

Jozef Wilczynski, *The Economics and Politics of East-West Trade* (New York: Praeger, 1969).

P. J. D. Wiles, *Communist International Economics* (Oxford: Basil Blackwell, 1968).

Thomas Wolf, *U.S. East-West Trade Policy* (Lexington, Mass.: Heath, 1973).

Part Three

Soviet Economic Reform, Growth, and Performance

Chapter 9

Soviet Economic Reform: Theory, Practice, Prospects

In Part Two, we considered how the Soviet economy "works," that is, how resources are allocated in the Soviet Union. In this connection, Soviet planning—namely, material balance planning, financial planning, and foreign trade planning—and pricing were discussed along with Soviet labor policy and managerial practices. Nowhere was the *theory* of resource allocation in a centrally planned socialist economy discussed. Instead, the emphasis was on what was actually being done. This pragmatic approach to Soviet resource allocation is not accidental, for as Alec Nove suggests, the Soviets have had "virtually no theory to guide them; and no theory of planning emerged from their activities."[1] In fact, Soviet texts on planning and resource allocation notably ignore the underlying theory,[2] other than some obligatory references to Marxian theory (largely as interpreted by Lenin) and to the fact that the so-called planning principle rather than the chaos of the market should govern resource allocation. The emphasis of such works is largely on describing what is practiced, not on the underlying theoretical principles.

The topic of this chapter is economic reform in the Soviet Union. By this, we mean reform or change of the system of centralized planning and management described in Part Two. The topic of economic reform has already been introduced peripherally. The growing use of economic accounting, the interest in "efficiency indexes" in investment and trade planning, and experiments with new worker incentive systems represent attempts to improve the system. We have yet to deal with the topic of general reform of the Soviet command economy. It will be demonstrated in this chapter that very little has been accomplished in this area and that the economic system

---

[1] V. S. Nemchinov, ed., *The Use of Mathematics in Economics* (Cambridge, Mass.: MIT Press, 1964), p. ix. Nove is the editor of this English translation.

[2] For example, *Ekonomicheskoe planirovanie v SSSR* [Economic planning in the USSR] (Moscow: 1967), Mikhail Bor, *Aims and Methods of Soviet Planning,* translated from the Russian (New York: International Publishers, 1967).

that operates in the Soviet Union today is much like that which emerged in the 1930s. In fact, many observers argue that for the time being at least, economic reform is "dead" in the Soviet Union. This does not mean, however, that economic reform is not a vital and contemporary topic. First, discussions of (and attempts to introduce) economic reforms are one indicator of the Soviet leadership's dissatisfaction with existing arrangements. Second, reform efforts call forth the ingrained sources of opposition to change in Soviet society and thus enable one to understand better how the system works. Third, the fact that significant economic reform has not been effected does not rule out the possibility that it will be attempted one day. It is important therefore to anticipate the effect of such a reform.

TWO CURRENTS IN REFORM THINKING: HISTORICAL BACKGROUND

We delineate two schools of thought about resolving the problems of centralized planning and management described in Part Two. The first school argues that the operation of the planned economy can be improved by allowing more decision-making authority at the local and enterprise levels. Routine decisions should be left to those best acquainted with the micro-situation, while broad matters affecting the national economy should be resolved by higher authorities. The second school calls for the improvement of administrative planning techniques, to ensure that the instructions to the microunits are "rational" and that monitoring procedures detect deviations from these instructions.

This dichotomy between "decentralization" and "better centralization" can be traced all the way back to the discussions of the 1920s. The supporters of NEP were in effect advocates of the first approach: let the routine day-to-day decisions be made by managers and "experts," with the state controlling the commanding heights. In the NEP environment, the bulk of economic decisions would be made at microlevels, and the task of the planners would be limited to devising grand strategy. The mechanism that would make this all possible would be the market, which would coordinate the actions of producers and consumers. In words of Stephen Cohen, the "first great reform in Soviet history was the introduction of . . . NEP in 1921."[3] The appeal of NEP as a model of reform persists, largely due to Lenin's writings in its support.

The coming demise of NEP forced Soviet planners and theorists to grapple with a different scenario, one in which the market was eliminated and resource allocation decisions were to be made administratively. The

---

[3] Stephen F. Cohen, "The Friends and Foes of Change: Reformism and Conservatism in the Soviet Union," *Slavic Review*, vol. 38, no. 2 (June 1979), 195.

guiding mechanism of the market was absent, and new methods of rational resource allocation had to be sought.

The 1920s was a productive period for theorizing about the administrative planning option. During this period, rough outlines began to emerge that probably would have eventually led to full-fledged theories of socialist resource allocation through central planning. Talented economists and statisticians were busy estimating national balances, an example being the well-known 1923–1924 balance of the national economy prepared by the Central Statistics Board under the direction of P. I. Popov.[4] Such efforts, the intellectual predecessors of input-output techniques later sophisticated by Professor Wassily Leontief in the United States, pointed the way toward the future development of mathematical planning techniques involving both balancing and optimization of resource allocation—an approach that was blocked by the harsh reaction against mathematical economics during the Stalin years. Nevertheless, such efforts (premature, given the state of knowledge at the time) were based on the premise that the socialist economy can be directed by mathematical planning models expressing input-output relationships among branches. It was not until the post-Stalin years that Soviet economists were allowed to return to their work and to develop the relatively sophisticated theories of mathematical planning in a centrally directed socialist economy.

With the establishment of the Stalinist dictatorship, discussion of the theory of Soviet planning ceased. The NEP system was anathematized, and the search for rational administrative planning procedures was halted by the brutal repression of economic science. Although the deficiencies of material balance planning and managerial behavior were likely known to the Soviet leadership, the Soviet economic system was declared infallibly directed by the planning principle. Criticism of the system became dangerous, and economic failures were attributed to individual mistakes and willful sabotage, not to the system itself. The "law of value"—supply and demand—was declared by Stalin not to operate in a socialist economy. Instead, a new economic regulator, the planning principle, had replaced the capitalist laws of supply and demand, and the tools developed by bourgeois economists to analyze capitalist economies were seen as unnecessary constraints no longer relevant to a socialist society. Such a socialist economy could be scientifically directed by technicians and engineers without

[4] On this, see V. S. Nemchinov's comments on the 1923–1924 balance in *The Use of Mathematics in Economics*, pp. 2–10. Popov's original presentation of the 1923–1924 balance is translated in Nicolas Spulber, ed., *Foundations of Soviet Strategy for Economic Growth* (Bloomington: Indiana University Press, 1964), pp. 5–19. For a discussion of the early Soviet mathematical economics school, see Leon Smolinski, "The Origins of Soviet Mathematical Economics," in Hans Raupach et al., eds., *Yearbook of East-European Economics*, Band 2 (Munich: Günter Olzog Verlag, 1971), pp. 137–154.

observing "economic laws." This view came to be more firmly entrenched and is reflected in the growing disregard for market forces displayed by economic planners in the late 1920s.[5]

By the 1930s, it had become dangerous to argue for either the positive role of market forces or the existence of economic laws in a planned socialist economy. Increasingly, planners shied away from concepts like "equilibrium" and "balanced growth" as unnecessary constraints on their freedom of action, and most economic theorizing ground to a halt.[6]

Soviet economic science entered into a dark age during the Stalin dictatorship. The economic system that emerged under Stalin was an ad hoc response to practical problems and crises, and it evolved without the benefit of a calculated blueprint. But it was the product of the party (Stalin) and as such could not be criticized. It is no wonder that serious work on defining an optimal planning system or improving the existing system was discouraged, and theorists on economic reform and mathematical planning went underground, only to reemerge after Stalin's death. The two attempts by high officials to initiate reform (in 1933 and 1947) led to the execution of the ill-fated reformers.[7]

The death of Stalin in 1953 unleashed pent-up pressure to enact economic reform. To a great extent, Khrushchev was the embodiment of the reform ethos, and his overthrow in 1964 signaled the return to a more conservative approach to reform. The resurgence of interest in economic reform assumed several forms in the 1950s. First, there was a slight shift from blaming all economic problems on human shortcomings to a willingness to experiment with organizational changes. Although the inclination to deal with problems via organizational reorganization continues to the present day, it probably reached its peak in 1957 with Khrushchev's attempted shift from a ministerial to a regional system of economic management. Second, there was a resurgence of interest in mathematical planning techniques and theories of rational planning. Prominent Soviet pioneers in this area such as L. V. Kantorovich and V. V. Novozhilov suggested that resources could be utilized much more efficiently, without loss of central control, if optimal planning procedures were used.[8] In 1959, the book *The Use of Mathematics in Economics* was published under the editorship of V. S. Nemchinov. It

---

[5] E. H. Carr and R. W. Davies, *Foundations of a Planned Economy, 1926–1929*, vol. 1, part 2 (London: Macmillan, 1969), pp. 787–801.

[6] Spulber, *Soviet Strategy for Economic Growth*, chap. 2; Gregory Grossman, "Scarce Capital and Soviet Doctrine," *Quarterly Journal of Economics*, vol. 67, no. 3 (August 1953), 311–315; R. Dunayevskaya, "A New Revision of Marxian Economics," *American Economic Review*, vol. 34, no. 3 (September 1944), 531–537; Smolinski, "The Origins of Soviet Mathematical Economics," pp. 150–151.

[7] Cohen, "The Friends and Foes of Change," p. 196.

[8] For a review of Kantorovich's and Novozhilov's contribution, see Robert W. Campbell, "Marx, Kantorovich and Novozhilov: Stoimost' Versus Reality," *Slavic Review*, vol. 20, no. 3 (October 1961), 402–418. For a general survey see Michael Ellman, *Soviet Planning*

contained the original papers of Kantorovich and Novozhilov, written during the repressive Stalin years. Since then, subsequent volumes in this series have been published, prestigious mathematical economics institutes of the Soviet Academy of Science have been established, and prominent Soviet mathematical economists have been awarded the coveted Lenin Prize. One, Kantorovich, has even received the Nobel Prize in economics.

A sign of the growing official toleration of reform discussion was the publication in obscure technical journals of papers suggesting various means to reform and improve the existing planning system by some decentralization (devolution) of decision-making authority.[9]

The official start of serious reform discussion in the Soviet Union can be dated to September 9, 1962, with the publication of the article "Plan, Profits and Bonuses" in *Pravda* by the then-obscure economist, Evsei Liberman.[10] The publication of Liberman's paper signaled official endorsement of open discussion of reform and initiated an important debate among orthodox planners, mathematical economists, and those advocating greater decision-making authority at the microlevel. We shall return to this discussion and its outcome shortly, but first we must look at the reasons behind the party decision to allow open reform discussion.

WHY THE ECONOMIC REFORM DISCUSSION?

To understand the factors behind party endorsement of reform discussion, one must return to the scenario of the late 1950s and early 1960s. The 1950s was a period of heady growth of both agriculture and industry, and the Soviet leadership was emboldened to make rash claims about overtaking the United States and creating full communism. This optimism was nurtured by the perceived economic weakness of the United States, which had suffered mild recessions and slow growth throughout the 1950s. Yet after 1958, signs of trouble began to emerge that were to temper the euphoria to the earlier period and encurge the experiment-conscious leadership to seek solutions through economic reform.

First, and possibly most important to Soviet leaders, the rate of Soviet economic growth had been declining since the late 1950s. Although still re-

---

Today: Proposals for an Optimally Functioning Economic System (Cambridge: Cambridge University Press, 1971); Alfred Zauberman, *The Mathematical Revolution in Soviet Planning* (Oxford: Oxford University Press, 1975). For an insider's view, see Aron Katsenelinboigen, *Studies in Soviet Economic Planning* (White Plains, N.Y.: M. E. Sharpe, 1978), chap. 3. Also see Leon Smolinski, ed., *L. V. Kantorovich: Essays in Optimal Planning* (White Plains, N.Y.: International Arts and Sciences Press, 1976).

[9] Evsei Liberman's reform proposals had been made in the journal *Voprosy ekonomiki* [Problems of Economics] as early as 1955.

[10] The original Liberman paper and the debate it generated are given in Myron E. Sharpe, ed., *Planning, Profit and Incentives in the USSR*, vols. 1 and 2 (White Plains, N.Y.: International Arts and Sciences Press, 1966).

spectable by international standards, the downward trend in the average annual rate of growth was unmistakable.[11] For a country whose economic superiority (by its own perception) was demonstrated by its rapid economic growth, such a pattern was clearly undesirable.[12] Further it was recognized that the period of "easy" Soviet growth was past, that is, growth based upon the shift of labor from agriculture to industry, the absorption of more advanced technology, the education of a largely illiterate population, and raising the labor participation rate. The gains from the virgin lands experiment had played out in agriculture. According to official statistics, annual economic growth, which was typically above 10 percent prior to 1958, had steadily declined, reaching a low of 4 percent in 1963.[13] Continuation of this declining trend would create serious problems for the Soviet leadership in the military and economic spheres.

Second, the Soviet capital-output ratio (k/o) had been rising since 1958.[14] Although k/o ratios had generally risen in other industrialized countries during the postwar period, the rise was more rapid in the Soviet Union. This trend was especially disturbing to the Soviets because they were able to hold down the k/o ratio during much of the 1930s and early 1950s (Chapter 11) and because with a declining growth rate, even greater capital infusions would be required to restore Soviet growth to its previous rate.

Third, there had been a distinct rise of consumer pressure in the Soviet Union in the 1950s, as evidenced by the increase in unsold inventories and signs of excess purchasing power.[15] This pressure was unlikely to subside, as Soviet planners continued to emphasize monetary incentives for workers and at the same time neglected the production or importation of high quality consumer goods. Such trends assumed added importance in combination with the declining growth rate and rising k/o ratio, for the consumer could

[11] It should be noted that the slowdown in Soviet growth rates is difficult to measure with precision due to the serious impact of the index number problem (discussed in Chapter 10) during the initial spurt of industrialization in the 1930s. Thus the severity of the slowdown will depend in large measure upon the analyst's choice of various growth estimates for the early 1930s.

[12] For example, the most prominent comparison of Soviet and American economic performance found in *Narodnoe khoziaistvo SSSR* [The national economy of the USSR] shows the Soviet economy expanding about four times as fast as the American economy during the postwar period.

[13] *Narodnoe khoziaistvo SSSR v 1975 g.* [The national economy of the USSR in 1975], (Moscow: Statistika, 1976), p. 56.

[14] Stanley H. Cohn, "General Growth Performance of the Soviet Economy," in Joint Economic Committee, *Economic Performance and the Military Burden in the Soviet Union* (Washington, D.C.: U.S. Government Printing Office, 1970), p. 12.

[15] David W. Bronson and Barbara S. Severin, "Consumer Welfare," in Joint Economic Committee, *Economic Performance and the Military Burden in the Soviet Union* (Washington, D.C.: U.S. Government Printing Office, 1970), pp. 93, 99.

no longer be neglected for the purpose of raising the investment rate. In this sense, it became especially important that the Soviets give specific attention to economic reform in the light industry sector. The depth of official concern with the existing system of the production and distribution of consumer goods was evident in the attention devoted to the trade system in the promulgation of the party program in October of 1961, which was to pave the way for the open discussion of economic reform in the Soviet Union.[16]

A fourth reason for interest in reform was the growing complexity of the Soviet economy—that is, the expanding numbers of interconnections among producers, consumers, and suppliers, which increased the difficulty of planning. Censuses of Soviet industry revealed over 50,000 distinct industrial enterprises in the USSR. In a sense, as the economy grew and the number of sectors and their product ranges broadened, the priority principle became less and less useful. Soviet planners were no longer able to put on "steel blinkers."[17] Instead, they now had to choose among steel, aluminum, and plastics, all of which in certain instances may do the same job. With the growing complexity, mistakes made in the planning process would be more serious—they would reverberate throughout the system, with less likelihood of being quickly arrested. Further, it became apparent that it would not be possible to continue to utilize buffer sectors indefinitely, as in the case of consumer goods—long used as a buffer to ensure the priority of heavy industry—for consumer pressure would increasingly deny this outlet to Soviet planners.

The resurgence of economic theorizing must have had an impact as well on the party decision to allow reform discussion. Economists representing various schools of thought (the mathematical economists, the advocates of devolution) were making claims that their method would improve the fulfillment of party objectives, while leaving the choice of social objectives to the party. As Aron Katsenelinboigen, a former professor of economics at Moscow State University, now an émigré, writes: "When there is an urgent practical need for some method . . . Soviet leaders are in fact willing to sacrifice ideology."[18] In this case, the reformers were offering to uncover enormous hidden reserves to solve economic problems while requiring relatively small ideological concessions in return. The mathematical econo-

---

[16] Jere L. Felker, *Soviet Economic Controversies* (Cambridge, Mass.: MIT Press, 1966), pp. 48–57.

[17] This was Khrushchev's often quoted criticism of planning during the Stalin years. See Marshall Goldman, "Economic Growth and Institutional Change in the Soviet Union," in P. Juliver and H. Morton, eds., *Soviet Policy-Making: Studies of Communism in Transition* (New York: Praeger, 1967), pp. 63–80, reprinted in Morris Bornstein and Daniel Fusfeld, eds., *The Soviet Economy: A Book of Readings*, 3rd ed. (Homewood, Ill.: Irwin, 1970), p. 350.

[18] Katsenelinboigen, *Studies in Soviet Economic Planning*, p. 79.

mists, in fact, cleverly presented their models in appropriate Marxian terminology, carefully concealing the close relationship of their results to neoclassical concepts of opportunity costs and utility maximization.

REFORM VERSUS ORGANIZATIONAL CHANGE

To the extent that the term *reform* is used to categorize change in both the structure and the operation of the Soviet economy, the phenomenon is not new. It is however useful to isolate two sorts of changes: first, those of a purely organizational character, not having a direct impact upon the fundamental nature of the economic system; second, those that vitally affect the resource allocation system. This categorization allows us to distinguish the myriad organizational adjustments so prevalent during the Khrushchev and Brezhnev years from reform of the second type. These organizational changes were aimed at solving basic economic problems, and yet they were probably directed away from the more fundamental resource allocation problem of decentralization of decision-making.

The concept of decentralization of decision-making is difficult to characterize with accuracy.[19] If one thinks, however, simply in terms of the administrative *levels* at which decision-making choices are exercised, the organizational changes of the 1950s and thereafter had little or no impact upon the system and should be viewed as a sideshow to the reform movement.

The chronicling of organizational change need not detain us here. The concept of regional versus hierarchical planning is of importance however, and it was emphasized in a major reform instituted by Khrushchev in 1957. As the reader will recall (Chapter 4), the ministerial system was instituted in the 1930s and involved planning the economy through industrial ministries—thus, steel output was planned by a ferrous metals ministry often thousands of miles from the steel producer and his suppliers. The major criticism of this system was the tendency of the ministry to become autarkic and to place its own interests above the interests of the economy as a whole. Given supply shortages for example, ministries would attempt to develop their own supplies and hoard where necessary.

---

[19] See, for example, Leonid Hurwicz, "Centralization and Decentralization in Economic Process," in Alexander Eckstein, ed., *Comparison of Economic Systems* (Berkeley and Los Angeles: University of California Press, 1971), pp. 79–102; Leonid Hurwicz, "Conditions for Economic Efficiency of Centralized and Decentralized Structures," in Gregory Grossman, ed., *Value and Plan* (Berkeley and Los Angeles: University of California Press, 1960), pp. 162–183; Leonid Hurwicz, "On the Concept and Possibility of Informational Decentralization," *American Economic Review, Papers and Proceedings,* vol. 59, no. 2 (May 1969), 513–524; Thomas Marschak, "The Comparison of Centralized and Decentralized Economies," *American Economic Review, Papers and Proceedings,* vol. 59, no. 2 (May 1969), 525–532.

The solution proposed was the creation, in 1957, of regional economic councils (*sovnarkhozy*) to unify the chain of command from top to bottom and to focus upon regional aspects of economic development—in Soviet parlance, the so-called territorial principle.[20] Thus the economy was reorganized on a regional basis with regional enterprises (steel, textiles, cement, etc.) being subordinated to the appropriate *sovnarkhoz*.

The *sovnarkhoz* system was abandoned by Khrushchev's successors in 1965 because, in a fundamental sense, it suffered from the same problems as the ministerial system (only on a regional basis) and lacked redeeming features. As we noted above, this sort of reform had little fundamental impact upon the system, insofar as the level of decision-making was virtually unchanged, and the myriad problems associated with centralization (success indicators, supply, and so on) remained unsolved.

The *sovnarkhoz* reform was probably the most important attempt at organizational change since the 1930s. It demonstrates also the continuity of the opposing currents in Soviet organizational thought, for the choice of territorial versus functional organization was (as noted in Part One) an important issue of the 1920s. We have singled out the *sovnarkhoz* reform as an example of organizational change, and the pervasiveness of organizational change as a response to economic problems cannot be stressed sufficiently. Virtually every Soviet economic organization (*Gosplan*, the banking system, the foreign trade monopoly, the ministries, the state committees) has had its functions redefined over the years and its position in the organization chart altered. In fact, a chart measuring 46 by 33 inches is required to sketch the changes in the administrative structure of the Soviet economy that have taken place since 1917.[21] The resort to organizational changes is by no means a thing of the past. As we shall point out below, Soviet authorities in the late Brezhnev era have again returned to organizational reshuffling rather than to economic reform to solve economic problems.

We turn now from a discussion of organizational change to the subject of economic reform. We begin with the first phase of reform, namely, the Liberman proposals of 1962 and the ensuing debate among the various reform factions. The various experimental programs are taken up next, and then we deal with the official government reforms of 1965.

ECONOMIC REFORM: DEBATE AND EXPERIMENTATION

Soviet economic reform has been the subject of a great deal of debate, both in the Soviet Union itself and in the West. Our attention to this discussion is essential, for the period since Stalin's demise in 1953 is synonymous with

---

[20] For details, see Oleg Hoeffding, "The Soviet Industrial Reorganization of 1957," *American Economic Review, Papers and Proceedings*, vol. 49, no. 2 (May 1959), 65–77.
[21] Central Intelligence Agency, *Evolution of the Central Administrative Structure of the USSR, 1917–1979*, CR79–10123, Washington, D.C., 1979.

the rebirth of discussion about economic matters. Although circumscribed in certain respects by dogma, not since the Industrialization Debate of the 1920s could one hear, for example, a discussion on price formation under socialism with views ranging from the most orthodox Marxian positions to those of the mathematical school advocating the use of scarcity prices derived from linear programming models.

Western views on Soviet economic reform have varied widely. This divergence results in large part from the difficulty of distinguishing between the intent and the actual implementation of economic reform. Time and again, what is announced by the Soviet press and what is actually done are two entirely different things. Moreover, official state policies are invariably portrayed as remarkable successes in the controlled Soviet press. Reform proposals are announced with considerable fanfare, the press features optimistic reports about the success of the reform, and then the reform (or experiment) disappears from public view. It is thus difficult to establish whether a reform has actually been implemented, whether it has been abandoned or is still in effect. Optimistic early reports about the significance of announced reforms are typically premature. Experienced Western observers have learned to study Soviet economic reform with great caution, relying on the assumption that the new reform may introduce some greater administrative flexibility into the system of planning and management without altering the Soviet economic system significantly.[22]

This chapter concentrates primarily upon *actual* rather than proposed economic reforms in the Soviet Union. The major exception to this is our discussion of the Liberman proposals, which remain largely unimplemented and superceded by the 1965 reform. It is important to distinguish between proposed reforms and actual reforms in the Soviet context—a distinction often missed in popular writings. In our view, actual economic reform in the USSR has been quite modest, whereas some proposed economic reforms are quite radical and far-reaching.

The Liberman Proposals

The proposals of Evsei Liberman, a professor of engineering economics at Kharkov University, much discussed in the West largely due to their emphasis on profits, are a convenient focus for the beginning of our reform dis-

---

[22] Examples of this cautious approach are: Abram Bergson, "Planning and the Market in the USSR: the Current Soviet Planning Reforms," in Alexander Balinky et al., *Planning and the Market in the USSR: The 1960s* (New Brunswick, N.J.: Rutgers University Press, 1967), pp. 43–64; Gertrude E. Schroeder, "The 'Reform' of the Supply system in Soviet Industry," *Soviet Studies*, vol. 24, no. 1 (July 1972), 97–119; Gertrude E. Schroeder, "The Soviet Economy on a Treadmill of 'Reforms,'" in Joint Economic Committee, *Soviet Economy in a Time of Change* (Washington, D.C.: U.S. Government Printing Office, 1979), vol. 1, pp. 312–340; Alec Nove, *The Soviet Economic System* (London: Allen & Unwin, 1977), chap. 11.

cussion. Although Liberman had been writing about enterprise performance and arguing for a reduction in the tutelage over managers since the 1920s, his ongoing research was first brought to the level of public discussion in 1962 with the publication of his article "The Plan, Profits and Bonuses" in *Pravda*.[23] Most importantly, its publication in the official party newspaper signaled an official sanctioning by the Soviet leadership of reform discussion.

Several facets of this early reform era deserve comment. First, Liberman gained prominence well out of proportion to the importance of his proposals.[24] In fact, Liberman served to some extent as the figurehead of the liberal "profit group," which included the eminent mathematical economist, V. S. Nemchinov.[25] To this day, his proposals remain largely unimplemented, and his renewed emphasis on profits—the aspect of his proposals that attracted most attention in the West—was most limited. Liberman was quite clear in pointing out that the central planning of output would be maintained in full vigor and that profits would serve as a basis for managerial rewards only after the output targets for quantity and assortment had been met. If enterprises failed to meet their output targets, they would be "deprived of the right to bonuses."[26] Thus Liberman did not propose that profits act as the fundamental guide for economic activity, but rather that profits were to have a more important role along with other success criteria and would be the source of bonus payments (if any were forthcoming). This major concession was a response to the critics of the "profit school," who argued that enterprises would cease production of important yet low profit goods.

Turning to the details of Liberman's proposals,[27] we note that Liberman suggested that bonus payments (after fulfillment of the planned output target) should be an increasing function of the profit-capital ratio, thus encouraging the expansion of profits but the reduction of capital usage. Profitability norms established for each industry would serve as the basis for evaluating managerial performance. To encourage enterprise managers to

[23] Translated in Morris Bornstein and Daniel Fusfeld, eds., *The Soviet Economy: A Book of Readings*, 3rd ed. (Homewood, Ill.: Irwin, 1970), pp. 360–366. Translations and analysis of Liberman's other writings are in Sharpe, *Planning, Profit and Incentives*, vols. 1 and 2.

[24] For a discussion of Liberman's career, see Robert C. Stuart, "Evsei Grigorevich Liberman," in George W. Simmons, ed., *Soviet Leaders* (New York: Crowell, 1967), pp. 193–200.

[25] Felker, *Soviet Economic Controversies*, pp. 58–67.

[26] Liberman, in Bornstein and Fusfeld, *The Soviet Economy*, p. 361. Also see E. G. Liberman, *Economic Methods and Effectiveness of Production* (White Plains, N.Y.: International Arts and Sciences Press, 1971).

[27] For succinct statements of the Liberman proposal and its relation to a cost-profit calculus, see Alfred Zauberman, "Liberman's Rules of the Game for Soviet Industry," *Slavic Review*, vol. 22, no. 4 (December 1963), 734–744; Felker, *Soviet Economic Controversies*, pp. 58–62; George R. Feiwel, *The Soviet Quest for Economic Efficiency* (New York: Praeger, 1972), chap. 5; Sharpe, *Planning, Profit and Incentives*, vol. 1, introduction.

set ambitious targets for themselves, rewards would be higher for successful fulfillment—or perhaps even underfulfillment—of an ambitious profitability plan than for the overfulfillment of an "easy" target.

The number of centrally planned enterprise directives would be limited to the quantity and assortment of output and its delivery. The enterprise itself would plan its own material, labor inputs, and new technology. This would prove possible under the new system, according to Liberman, because the new emphasis on profits would encourage managers to seek out cost economies and new reserves rather than build up excess stocks.

On the crucial issue of centralization versus decentralization of decision-making, Liberman remained ambiguous. All the basic instruments of central planning—price setting, the state budget, ruble control, state control of large investments—would be maintained, along with the centralized planning of material supply.[28] How this system could be made compatible with enterprises planning their own inputs was not spelled out in detail by Liberman other than by his assertion ("with reasonable confidence") that the two would prove compatible.[29] Liberman's conservatism on the issue of supply was in marked contrast to "marketeers" such as Nemchinov and A. Birman, who advocated free trade in producer goods.[30] On the crucial issue of the price system, Liberman also equivocated,[31] although he did suggest that the current Soviet price system would act as a serious impediment to the actual implementation of his proposals by giving unfair profitability advantages to some producers while discriminating against others. Nevertheless, he believed that his system would force managers to press for more rational prices.[32]

The publication of the original Liberman proposals in 1962 sparked considerable controversy and a period of open discussion in the Soviet press and academic journals between 1962 and 1965.[33] During this period, the various factions—ranging from the conservative antireformers to the Liberman supporters and the more radical reformers, especially the mathematical school—were given the opportunity to state their positions. De-

[28] Liberman, in Bornstein and Fusfeld, *The Soviet Economy*, pp. 362–363.

[29] *Ibid.*, p. 363.

[30] Nove, *The Soviet Economic System*, pp. 309–310.

[31] According to Nove, *ibid.*, p. 309, Liberman never developed a coherent pricing model. Prices, in Liberman's own words, were to be "fixed and flexible."

[32] Michael Kaser, "Kosygin, Liberman, and the Pace of Soviet Industrial Reform," in George R. Feiwel, ed., *New Currents in Soviet-Type Economies: A Reader* (Scranton, Pa.: International Textbook, 1968), p. 334.

[33] For further English translations of the major contributions to the debate, see M. E. Sharpe, ed., *The Liberman Discussion: A New Phase in Soviet Economic Thought* (White Plains, N.Y.: International Arts and Sciences Press, 1965). For chronological accounts of the 1962 to 1965 debate, see Kaser, "Kosygin, Liberman," pp. 330–343; and Felker, *Soviet Economic Controversies*, chaps. 3 and 4.

layed by a politically conservative leadership, considerable criticism over the issue of profit and its meaning in a socialist economy, and in particular, a lack of willingness to let important decisions to be made by the "anarchy" of the market, the official decision came at the party Plenum in September of 1965. Prior to the party decision, a series of experiments were undertaken to test various reform ideas on a partial basis.

Reform Experiments

Acting out of a sense of caution, the Soviet leadership authorized a series of experiments to test different reform ideas. These experiments—the NVP experiment, the light industry reform, and the transportation experiment— were carried out between 1962 and 1965, testing the ideas of the profit group and the advocates of more conservative economic reform.[34]

The conservative NVP ("normative value of processing") experiment was initiated in the Tartar Republic in 1962 and then was broadened to selected consumer goods industries in other regions. The basic notion of the NVP experiment was to improve the efficiency of enterprise operation by replacing the much maligned gross output index by the new NVP index. The reader will recall that the use of gross output as the prime enterprise success criterion encouraged enterprise managers to meet their gross output targets by increasing their use of expensive materials. Under the NVP index, enterprise performance was to be judged on the basis of planned labor costs, fuel costs, and some overhead expenses, thus removing the incentive to overemploy expensive intermediate materials. Profit performance would not be included in the NVP index, to eliminate the conservatives' reservation that enterprises would only produce high profit items. Stated in terms more familiar to Western economists, the NVP reform simply called for the substitution of enterprise value added (net output) for gross value of output. Its advocates argued that the NVP index provided a more reasonable measure of output performance. The NVP opponents argued that it was a mere palliative and did not deal with the fundamental issues of appropriate incentives, the encouragement of quality production, and the matching of consumer demands and supplies. The profit group was given its opportunity with the light industry experiments initiated in 1964.

One of the major criticisms of the Soviet planning system was the lack of a feedback mechanism between the consumer and producer—a phenomenon especially prominent in the clothing industry, where an accumulation of unsalable inventories had resulted. In a step to resolve this problem, an experimental program sanctioned by the Central Committee was begun in

---

[34] These experimental programs are discussed in Felker, *Soviet Economic Controversies*, chaps. 4 and 5; and Feiwel, *The Soviet Quest for Economic Efficiency*, chap. 5. References to the light industry experiment are supplied separately.

1964.[35] The Bolshevichka factory in Moscow and the Maiak factory in Gorky were allowed to receive their production orders directly from a selected group of retail outlets rather than being assigned quantitative output targets. Unsold stocks or returned output would detract from plan fulfillment. In particular, attention was to be paid to consumer demand as a determinant of production, with bonuses (set between 40 and 50 percent of basic pay) dependent upon fulfillment of delivery and profit plans, not output plans.

Although these experimental enterprises remained under a considerable degree of constraint from above—in particular, in the centralized control of their material supplies—their performance in this program was considered a success, and in subsequent years the program was expanded, even to heavy industry. By 1965, this reform had been extended to 25 percent of the garment factories, 28 percent of the footwear factories, 18 percent of the textile mills, and 30 percent of the leather factories.[36]

The extent to which this reform, also dubbed the "direct links" reform, was continued after 1965 is not known. In fact, these changes were subsumed by the official general (and more conservative) reform of September 1965, and thus this direction of change seems to have been blunted. Apparently there remained a general lack of willingness to free these experimental enterprises from administrative controls, and hence many of the supply, incentive, and other problems of Soviet industry continued to plague these enterprises. When this experiment was applied more broadly, the inability of the trade network to anticipate consumer demand and to coordinate orders with shifting consumer tastes became more apparent.

A third experimental program, begun in 1965, deserves brief mention. Several trucking enterprises were given the authority to seek out their own customers (especially on return hauls), to acquire trucks on their own initiative, to pay drivers bonuses for picking up extra shipments, and were encouraged to lay off unneeded workers. The thrust of this program was to interest these trucking enterprises in maximizing profits. The initial successes of this experiment caused it to be extended to other trucking firms.

THE OFFICIAL REFORM OF 1965

The most important—though most modest—economic reform in the Soviet Union was announced by Premier Alexei Kosygin in September of 1965 as a

---

[35] For a discussion of this experiment, see Goldman, "Economic Growth and Institutional Change," p. 322; Kaser, "Kosygin, Liberman," pp. 337–338; Eugene Zaleski, *Planning Reforms in the Soviet Union, 1962–1966* (Chapel Hill: University of North Carolina Press, 1967), pp. 122–140.

[36] Goldman, "Economic Growth and Institutional Change," p. 357; Feiwel, *The Soviet Quest for Economic Efficiency*, pp. 242–250.

general reform to be gradually implemented in total by 1970.[37] In light of the high expectations for significant change raised by the debates and experiments of the preceding years, the official response must have been disappointing to the proponents of decentralization of economic authority. However, the conservatism and caution of the party leadership should have been anticipated, given the power of the forces in support of the status quo. First, we consider the substance of the 1965 reform proposal, after which we evaluate its implementation in the period 1965 through 1971 and its modification thereafter.

Enterprise Planning and Management

The basic thrust of the Kosygin plan was a reduction in the number of enterprise targets to be set from above, and most important, replacement of gross output by "realized output" (sales) as the primary indicator of success for an enterprise. In addition, the number of indicators for labor planning—previously four—was to be reduced to a single indicator: the magnitude of the wage fund. Thus an enterprise manager was now to face the following eight targets established within the central plan, compared to the earlier system of twenty to thirty targets:

1. Value of goods to be sold
2. Main assortment
3. The wage fund
4. Amount of profit and the level of profitability
5. Payments to and allocations from the state budget
6. The volume of investment and the exploitation of fixed assets
7. Main assignments for the introduction of new technology
8. Material and technical supplies

Turning to the financial aspects of planning, several changes were decreed. An interest charge on fixed and working capital was proposed, to be implemented at a 6 percent rate effective in 1966.[38] In addition to this new capital charge, provisions were made for an enhanced role to be played by *Gosbank*. This new role centered upon a reduction in the importance of the state budget and, in its place, the utilization of *Gosbank* facilities for the financing of enterprise investment.

Thus a new expanded role was envisaged for *Gosbank*, especially in the

---

[37] See Alexei Kosygin, "On Improving Management of Industry, Perfecting Planning, and Enhancing Economic Incentives in Industrial Production," in Morris Bornstein and Daniel Fusfeld, eds., *The Soviet Economy: A Book of Readings*, 3rd ed. (Homewood, Ill.: Irwin, 1970), pp. 387–396.

[38] This rate could be lower for unprofitable enterprises. See Zaleski, *Planning Reforms*, p. 143.

provision of investment funds at differentiated charges depending upon usage. Also, *Gosbank* was to facilitate the clearance of debts among enterprises and between enterprises and their customers in the trade network.

The Kosygin schema also placed new emphasis upon the importance of accounting. Ties to the budget as a source of investment finance and subsidies were to be reduced and a production development fund was to be established. This fund was to be fed from three main sources: profits, amortization of equipment, and sales of unneeded equipment.

Profits and Incentives

The changing role of profits called for in the September 1965 reform was relatively modest. Prices were to be reformed to allow enterprises to be profitable under normal conditions of operation, in order to end one of the long-standing results of average branch cost pricing—a good many enterprises continually suffering losses. In addition, the role of profit was to change in two respects. First, although profit was always a part of the Soviet managerial (*khozraschet*) system in the Soviet Union, it was given a position of greater importance, along with the now more limited number (eight) of indicators of managerial success.

Second, profits were to be an important source of funds for decentralized investment by enterprise managers (a 20 percent share for decentralized investment was projected[39]) and were to be used as a source of funds for bonus payments to workers. The former would be channeled through two funds—the production development fund and the fund for social welfare and housing (to build factory-owned apartments)—while the latter would be channeled through a new material incentive fund. These three funds were to replace the old enterprise fund and were designed to enhance the importance of profits for enterprise activity in addition to giving enterprise managers greater freedom of decision-making.

Prior to the 1965 reform, worker bonus schemes had been subject to criticism not only because of the meager amounts involved but also because the funding was typically from the wages fund rather than from profits. The 1965 rules for the utilization of the new material incentive fund were complex.[40] Briefly, however, this fund was to be placed largely under the control of the enterprise itself and was to provide material incentive payments above and beyond those normally provided by the wages fund.

Two observations should be made concerning the role of profits in the 1965 reform. First, it was apparent that in terms of increasing the impor-

[39] Keith Bush, "The Implementation of the Soviet Economic Reform," *Osteuropa Wirtschaft*, no. 2 (1970), 67–90 and no. 3 (1970), 190–198.
[40] Leonard J. Kirsch, *Soviet Wages: Changes in Structure and Administration Since 1956* (Cambridge, Mass.: MIT Press, 1972), chap. 7.

tance of profits as a success indicator for management, little change was envisioned. Output (now in the form of sales) remained the all-powerful indicator, and profits remained a secondary indicator of enterprise success, along with seven other targets. In addition, where managers might enjoy a measure of freedom in the utilization of profits, for example in the case of decentralized investment or worker bonuses, in many instances other constraints were erected, such as prohibiting management to contract for material supplies or tightening centralized regulations over bonuses.

Second, the behavior of profits in the immediate aftermath of the reform serves as a partial indicator of the importance of profits. For the first three years of the reform, profits in enterprises operating under the reform grew at a more rapid pace (about 50 percent faster between 1965 and 1968) than those in the nonconverted enterprises. Decentralized investment also increased, though at a rate substantially less than that envisaged in the original reform blueprint.[41] These figures suggest increased managerial interest in profitability in the years immediately following the 1965 reform.

The Kosygin reforms continued past tradition by calling for a variety of organizational changes in the economic management and planning system.[42] Key functions were centralized in three powerful new state committees: the State Committee for Material-Technical Supply (*Gossnab*), the State Committee for Prices (*Gostsen*), and the State Committee for Science and Technology (*Gostekhnika*). Industrial enterprises were to be combined into large associations, called "production associations," and research enterprises and institutes were to be grouped into "science-production associations." The rationale given for these associations was that they would yield economies of scale, reduce the bureaucracy, and assist in the planning process. *Gossnab* was given the primary responsibility for allocating producer goods, and the ministerial supply organizations that had dominated the rationing of funded goods were largely to disappear. *Gossnab* was supposed to apply itself to the creation of a wholesale trade system based upon direct contracting arrangements among suppliers and buyers. Changes in the planning process were also proposed: there was to be an increased emphasis on long-term plans; the "scientific basis" of planning was to be upgraded through the use of computers, mathematical programming, and the like; and "complex planning" (the planning of regional complexes) was to be emphasized.

---

[41] Keith Bush, "The Soviet Economic Reform After Six Years," *Radio Liberty Report*, CRD 258/71, August 1971, p. 6; and Bush, "The Implementation of the Soviet Economic Reform."

[42] For discussions of the organizational aspects of the 1965 reform, see National Foreign Assessment Center, *Organization and Management in the Soviet Economy: The Ceaseless Search for Panaceas*, ER77–10769, Washington, D.C., December 1977.

TABLE 26   Conversion of Industrial Enterprises to New Economic System, 1966–1970 (as percentages of all industry)

At End Of:	Number of Enterprises Converted	Percentage of All Enterprises Converted	Percentage of Total Output	Percentage by Number of Staff	Percentage of Total Profit
1966	704	1.5	8	8	16
1967	7,248	15.0	37	32	50
1968	26,850	54.0	72	71	81
1969	36,049	72.0	84	81	91
1970	41,014	83.0	92	92	95

SOURCE: Keith Bush, "The Soviet Reform After Five Years," Radio Liberty Research Report, CRD 258/71, August 1971, p. 2; Nikolai Fedoryenko et al., *Soviet Economic Reform: Progress and Problems*, translated from the Russian (Moscow: Progress Publishers, 1972), p. 202.

IMPLEMENTATION OF THE 1965 ECONOMIC REFORM

Initially, two phases of implementation of the reform were anticipated. The first, or "extensive," phase was to be the phased conversion of nonagricultural enterprises to the new system. The second, or "intensive," phase, scheduled to begin in 1970, would be the one in which the true potential of the reform would be realized.[43] In terms of the original format, all industrial enterprises were to be converted to the new system by the end of 1968 and the remainder of the economy by the end of 1970. The exception was agriculture, where the introduction of full *khozraschet* into *sovkhozy* was to take place at a somewhat slower pace. The progress of the reform is summarized in Table 26. Three general comments are in order.

First, although the original timetable was not met, in a formal sense, the major proportion of industrial enterprises were in fact converted to the new system. Until 1972, little progress was made in the direction of merging converted enterprises into production associations.

Second, the reform was not implemented in some important sectors of the economy, notably in the construction industry and also in the material-technical supply system. As of 1971, only 10 percent of both construction and repair organizations and material-technical supply organizations were operating under the new system.[44] These patterns indicate some resistance to the general reform movement. Finally, it is well to remember that these figures on reform implementation are formal, and above all, they do not

---

[43] Gertrude E. Schroeder, "Recent Developments in Soviet Planning and Managerial Incentives," in Joint Economic Committee, *Soviet Economic Prospects for the Seventies* (Washington, D.C.: U.S. Government Printing Office, 1973), p. 12.

[44] *Planovoe khoziaistvo* [The planned economy], no. 5 (1971), as summarized by *ABSEES: Soviet and East European Abstract Series*, vol. 2, no. 2 (October 1971), p. 99. See also Fedoryenko et al., *Soviet Economic Reform*, pp. 199–202.

mean that where "implemented," the reform system actually operated according to the original conception outlined above. In fact, as we shall note below, the original conception of the reform itself has been significantly altered since 1965, casting more doubt on the importance of such conversion figures.

The Reform—Financial Aspects

One of the seemingly significant aspects of the September 1965 reform blueprint was the emphasis upon decentralized investment (at the enterprise level) through the newly formed production development fund and the utilization of bank credits, which had until then accounted for only a very small portion of investment in fixed capital.

The volume of decentralized investment derived from the production development fund did expand in the converted enterprises. In 1965, the share of decentralized investment was 12 percent, rising to the targeted 20 percent in 1972. Subsequently, the share of decentralized investment declined to about 12 percent in 1976.[45] More importantly, the distinction between decentralized and centralized investment quickly lost its meaning. The problem of appropriately marrying a centralized system with decentralized elements of resource allocation—especially in the crucial area of investment—was especially acute in the case of the 1965 reform. On the one hand, managers were encouraged to invest on a decentralized basis, while on the other hand, they were unable to purchase investment goods through the material supply network. These supply problems are familiar to any student of the Soviet system, and continued to exist in spite of a system of fines for nondelivery and various attempts to develop the concept of "free sales."[46] The supply system remained largely centralized and out of reach of the typical enterprise manager. A further factor limiting the manager's control over decentralized investment was the growing centralized regulation of the size and distribution of the production development fund, especially since 1972.

The envisioned expansion of the banking system as a supplier of credit did not materialize. Credits, though available, were utilized less in the converted than in the nonconverted enterprises basically because it was the profitable enterprises that invested, and they had sufficient internal reserves. It should also be noted that those enterprises converted had surplus

---

[45] National Foreign Assessment Center, *Organization and Management in the Soviet Economy*, p. 15.

[46] Goldman, "Economic Growth and Institutional Change," p. 323; Schroeder, "Recent Developments in Soviet Planning," pp. 107–111. On the lack of material supplies as a brake upon decentralized enterprise investment, see for example, D. Allakhverdian, "O finansovykh problemakh khoziaistvennoi reformy" [About the financial problems of economic reform], *Voprosy ekonomiki* [Problems of economics], no. 11 (1970), 63–74.

working capital resulting from the inability to spend production development and sociocultural and housing funds simply due to the absence of a
mechanism for decentralized investment. Bank financing of state centralized investment grew slowly, accounting for only 2.3 percent of all investment in 1973.[47]

The Reform—Labor Allocation

Clearly any economic reform that attempts to decentralize decision-making
must focus upon the enterprise management's ability to control labor
inputs. The question of labor allocation is a crucial issue of economic reform, for if a cost-profit calculus is to have real meaning, substitution of
inputs becomes a prime sphere of managerial decision-making and may
well imply the dismissal of labor by enterprises.

Nominally, the 1965 reform enhanced the manager's freedom to allocate labor by retaining only one central constraint—the wage bill—over
labor staffing, as opposed to the earlier system of detailed specifications. Of
course, the wage tariff was still centrally determined. Because the original
statement by Kosygin in 1965 placed considerable emphasis upon the reduction of the number of indicators governing the enterprise labor force,
this was originally seen by some Western observers as the main decentraliz-
ing factor of the entire reform.[48] In fact, the significance of such changes
was reduced for two reasons. For those enterprises not covered, obviously
the change was of little importance, and that applied to all changes of
course, not just labor allocation. Second and more crucial, the substance
rather than the number of indicators was the important matter to the enterprise manager. Indeed, the post-1965 system seems to have retained central control over both the wages fund and the utilization of this fund, although new freedom was supposed to exist in the latter area.[49] This result,
along with trade union pressure against the right of enterprises to dismiss
workers, left enterprise managers' decision-making power virtually unchanged from the prereform era.

[47] National Foreign Assessment Center, *Organization and Management in the Soviet Economy*, p. 15.
[48] For example, Abram Bergson argued in a 1967 article that the Soviets chose to decentralize decision-making in the area of labor staffing because wage rates happen to be the most
rational—in the sense of equating supply and demand—of all Soviet prices. Thus managers
could be trusted to make correct decisions. See Abram Bergson, "Planning and the Market
in the USSR," in George Feiwel, ed., *New Currents in Soviet-Type Economics: A Reader*
(Scranton, Pa.: International Textbook, 1968), p. 345.
[49] According to the reform plan, the wages fund was to remain centrally planned, while
enterprises were to have freedom in distributing the fund to various classes of personnel.
This freedom was in reality very limited, and thus in essence, Soviet wage determination
procedures remained substantially unaffected by the 1965 reform. See Kirsch, *Soviet
Wages*, chap. 7.

REFORM OF THE REFORM

As we have emphasized, the basic thrust of the 1965 reform program was a reduction of the tutelage of the enterprise manager by higher planning organs. Was this goal achieved in any degree? Initially, the idea was to create a system whereby managers would be encouraged to respond spontaneously to various economic "levers"—profits, bonuses, increased authority over investment, and so on—so as to make the Soviet enterprise more efficient and release "hidden reserves." For these reasons, the number of plan targets was to be reduced, reliance was to be placed upon more rational success indicators such as sales and profitability, managers and workers were to become materially interested in the outcome of enterprise performance by tying bonus funds to enterprise activity, and so on. In other words, more decision-making authority was to pass to the manager.

Between 1965 and 1971, there was evidence of greater managerial spontaneity in response to these economic levers, especially as regards the disposition of bonus funds. As managers began to exercise their newfound authority, planners and bureaucrats began to react against "undesirable" spontaneous enterprise actions and to press for amendments to the 1965 rules. During the very period when the reform was scheduled to move into its "intensive" phase, amendments and modifications were introduced that significantly altered the content of the original reform.[50] The particular shortcomings that these amendments sought to correct were the unduly large shares of new bonus funds received by managerial personnel, the lack of attention to labor productivity and quality improvement, the unwillingness of managers to request taut production targets or to economize costs, and so on—many of the very shortcomings that the 1965 reform had sought to eliminate in the first place.

Between June 1971 and January 1978, a number of changes were introduced that significantly modified the spirit of the original reform proposal. First, rigid regulations governing the size of enterprise incentive funds replaced the original more flexible system. Now the ministry, based upon limits determined by *Gosplan*, was to determine the size of enterprise incentive funds by fixing planned incentive fund targets. The size of the various incentive funds was thus to depend upon enterprise performance vis-à-vis planned indicators, basically upon the fulfillment of output, profitabil-

[50] This and the following discussion are largely based on Schroeder, "Recent Developments in Soviet Planning and Incentives," pp. 11–38; Schroeder, "The Soviet Economy on a Treadmill of 'Reforms,'" pp. 312–340; Gertrude E. Schroeder, "Post-Khrushchev Reforms and Public Financial Goals," in Z. M. Fallenbuch, ed., *Economic Development in the Soviet Union and Eastern Europe* (New York: Praeger, 1976), pp. 348–367; National Foreign Assessment Center, *Organization and Management in the Soviet Economy*, pp. 1–22; Alice C. Gorlin, "Industrial Reorganization: The Associations," in Joint Economic Committee, *Soviet Economy in a New Perspective* (Washington, D.C.: U.S. Government Printing Office, 1976), pp. 162–188.

ity, and labor productivity targets. Incentive funds were also to depend upon three additional targets: the plan for key products in physical units, the plan for consumer goods, and the plans for changes in product quality and new products. Furthermore, the size of the incentive fund was tied to the tautness of the enterprise plan: the higher the output, profitability, and labor productivity targets, the larger the potential incentive funds. The more recent restrictions on enterprise funds restore most authority to the ministries. The ministry again has the authority to determine the conditions under which incentive funds will be accumulated and disbursed. Enterprises can be punished by fund reductions for failing to meet specific targets set by the ministries.

Second, strict controls over the distribution of enterprise incentive funds have been introduced. In the new regulations, limits are placed upon the rate of growth of managerial bonuses, average wages are not allowed to increase faster than labor productivity, and regulations are established to reduce bonus differentials among branches. Significantly, managerial bonuses are tied to fulfillment of sales and profitability plans *plus* the fulfillment of the physical assortment plan, and the ministries are allowed to add additional conditions if they so desire. Ministries now set the requirements for incentive funds, limiting income growth to targeted rates. Ceilings are set on managerial bonuses as a proportion of base salary, and the ministry can deny bonuses if delivery plans are not met.

Third, the manager's control over the production development fund (for investment) has been circumscribed. Under the modified rules, the proportion of enterprise profits to be allocated to this fund is to be set by the ministry in accordance with bank credits planned for decentralized investments. The incentive effects of the enterprise investment fund have been nullified. The concept of decentralized investment has been abolished by treating expenditures from the fund like all other investments.

Finally, and perhaps most important, the number of enterprise targets has again been expanded. New targets have been reinstated since 1970: labor productivity, gross output, consumer goods assignments in heavy industry, quality targets, material and fuel economy targets, delivery obligations, new products, and the size of basic incentive funds.

Many of the administrative changes proposed by Kosygin in 1965 were not implemented as initially planned. During the early years of the reform, enterprises did not amalgamate into productive associations, but after a party-government decree in April 1973, the formation of production associations proceeded at a rapid pace. By the end of 1980, production associations are planned to account for three-quarters of industrial output. The purposes of the production association were to gain the advantages of economies of scale in management through the amalgamation of firms involved in similar lines of business and to economize on administrative personnel. In practice, the formation of industrial associations meant little more than "changing the names on doors" in Moscow; supervisory power continued to remain in the hands of the chief administrations of the ministries, and there was a 60 percent expansion in the bureaucracy between 1966 and 1977.[51] The ministries continued to be the centers of economic power, allocating materials and equipment, dictating the incentive systems of enterprises and industrial associations, and controlling investment. *Gossnab* was supposed to replace the ministerial supply organs, but in 1978, *Gossnab* handled only one-half the value of rationed producer goods.[52] The market for producer goods failed to emerge, and the traditional system of material supplies and central balances continued to function. The role of bank credits in regulating economic activity did not increase at the rate proposed by Kosygin, and most investment continued to be financed directly from the state budget rather than through bank credit. Capital was no longer granted to enterprises free of charge, but it was agreed that the low 6 percent interest charge did not promote the efficient utilization of investment resources.

The 1965 reform called for an enhanced role for long-term planning, seeking to establish the Five Year Plan as the basic operating plan of the national economy. Yet after 15 years' experience, the annual economic plan remains operative. One new feature of Soviet planning, "counterplanning," called for rewards to enterprises that adopt counterplans. If an enterprise voluntarily adopts more demanding targets than established in the Five Year Plan, its opportunities for bonuses are enhanced. Despite campaigns to promote counterplans, only 13,000 industrial enterprises were engaged in counterplanning in 1977.

In general, the period since 1965 has witnessed a reversal of official attitudes toward the solution of basic economic problems (perhaps as a result of lagging economic performance during the early phases of the reform). Rather than relying on economic "levers" at the enterprise level, attention is being increasingly directed toward improving planning methods and increasing tutelage over enterprises to improve economic performance. Thus, rather than reducing the number of plan indicators as was envisioned in 1965, they are again being increased and incentives are being tied to the fulfillment of all of them, which represents a return to the earlier system. Emphasis is now on new planning methods—increased attention to perspective planning, automated plan calculations, the formulation of new scientific norms, automated supply systems, automated information-retrieval systems, and so on—and on new organizational methods, in particular, on the formation of state committees and production associations to take over

---

[51] Schroeder, "The Soviet Economy on a Treadmill of 'Reforms,'" p. 314.
[52] *Ibid.*, p. 323.

some of the responsibilities of the ministries.[53] The Soviet planning bureaucracy has indeed embarked upon an ambitious program of computerization, with increased emphasis on computer production (annual output running at around 2000 computers in 1977) and upon the creation of computer-based "automated management systems" (ASUs). Reportedly, one-half of the calculations involved in the 1978 national plan were made by computers, *Gossnab's* inventories are now monitored by computers, the Central Statistical Administration is now largely computerized, and the ministries are developing their own systems. Grandiose plans for a nationwide system of computer centers remain unrealized. The basic problems that confront the computerization of planning and management remain inadequate computer hardware, the creation of independent and incompatible computer systems, and the underutilization of existing hardware. More sophisticated planning techniques employing input-output procedures and optimization remain adjuncts to planning, confined largely to research institutes. The "tried and true" procedures of material balance planning continue to be used, with computerization of information as a planning aid.[54] Nevertheless, there is little doubt of the real commitment of the Soviet leadership to computerization as a means of improving economic performance, and it remains to be seen how successful this effort will be.

This change in focus away from economic levers and toward improving planning techniques and organizational shuffling caused one Western authority on Soviet economic reform to write in 1973 that ". . . after seven years of the reform, economic methods, or 'levers,' have been effectively converted into administrative 'levers'. . . As a consequence, centralized planning and administration are even more entrenched. . . ."[55]

INDUSTRIAL PRICE REFORM

An implicit factor in the Soviet reform discussion was the issue of industrial prices. As was pointed out in Chapter 5, industrial prices have been set to equal average branch cost of production (capital and rental charges omitted) plus a planned profit margin without reference to demand. Such prices are not scarcity prices, in the sense that they do not equate supply and demand, nor do they reflect full marginal cost. In fact, more often than not,

---

[53] Paul K. Cook, "The Political Setting," in Joint Economic Committee, *Soviet Economic Prospects for the Seventies* (Washington, D.C.: U.S. Government Printing Office, 1973), pp. 10–11.

[54] Schroeder, "The Soviet Economy on a Treadmill of 'Reforms,'" pp. 319–322; S. E. Goodman, "Computers and the Development of the Soviet Economy," in Joint Economic Committee, *Soviet Economy in a Time of Change* (Washington, D.C.: U.S. Government Printing Office, 1979), vol. 1, pp. 524–553.

[55] Schroeder, "Recent Developments in Soviet Planning and Incentives," p. 36.

industrial prices have been allowed to diverge from costs owing to the administrative complexity of price reform, thus necessitating state subsidies for enterprises sustaining losses.

Against this background, one can understand the complexities of the decentralization issue, that is, the extent to which crucial economic decisions can be left up to enterprise managers without first having the primary information mechanism upon which such decisions are to be based—a "rational" price system. In this context, one can perhaps understand the relative willingness of Soviet authorities to give managers more discretion in the area of labor staffing, where prices tend to be based more on scarcity.

Such considerations culminated in the general reform of industrial prices during 1966-1967. Did this reform transform the Soviet price system into a more useful information mechanism for decentralization? The answer is quite simple: it did not.

The 1966-1967 price reform was conducted separately from the Kosygin reform of 1965, and, as we already noted, was not a major consideration in the earlier Liberman discussions. The goals of the 1966-1967 industrial price reform were quite modest. In view of the enhanced role of profits and monetary incentives envisioned in the Kosygin reform, it was deemed essential to set industrial prices at average cost plus a profit margin sufficient to eliminate the pattern of subsidization of unprofitable enterprises. Thus price revision did become an important vehicle for implementation of the reform. No attempt was made to set prices to equate supply and demand— if this is possible at all in a planned economy. The more radical views— especially those of the mathematical school, advocating the generation of scarcity prices through linear programming models or through an auctioning process—were rejected. Prices were raised in 1966 and 1967—though still on the basis of average costs—and they notably reduced the number of planned loss enterprises and to some degree the profitability differentials among branches of industry.[56] In addition, a new centralized organ, the State Committee for Prices (*Gostsen*) had been established, with rather broad powers, to administer the price system.

The reform of prices would be crucial to any attempt to enhance the role of profits (which, as we have seen, was not a major goal of the 1965 reform) and to resolve the problem of low quality consumer goods (which was a major goal of the reform). The price reforms of 1966-1967 and thereafter failed to confront the basic issue with regards to profitability, namely, to set prices in such a manner that enterprise profitability would reflect manage-

[56] Gertrude E. Schroeder, "The 1966-67 Soviet Industrial Price Reform: A Study in Complications," *Soviet Studies*, vol. 20, no. 4 (April 1969), 464 ff.; Morris Bornstein, "Soviet Price Policy in the 1970's," in Joint Economic Committee, *Soviet Economy in a New Perspective* (Washington, D.C.: U.S. Government Printing Office, 1976), pp. 17–67; Joseph S. Berliner, "Flexible Pricing and New Products in the USSR," *Soviet Studies*, vol. 27, no. 4 (October 1975), 525–544.

rial performance. If prices fail to include all legitimate factor payments (such as for superior equipment, locational advantages, favorable raw materials, etc.) then it is unclear whether high profits are the consequence of pricing foibles or of effective management. The 1966–1967 price reform did not come to grips with these issues and continued to use the traditional formulae for setting prices. Ministries continue to redistribute profits from profitable to unprofitable enterprises, some branches (food processing, for example) have prices that generally fail to cover average branch costs and require large subsidies. Thus the failure to effect significant changes in the manner of price formation has meant that profit-oriented reforms could not be put into practice even if the leadership were willing.

A whole series of measures was adopted after 1967 to encourage technological progress, the production of high quality consumer and producer goods, and realistic regional price differentials. The procedures for setting "limit prices," "sliding prices," and quality differentials are complex and require lengthy explanations. It is sufficient to say that such measures have not brought about significant change in the Soviet price system.

The most critical appraisal of Soviet price reform would be to evaluate Soviet prices as mechanisms for resource allocation in the fullest sense. Cast in this light, price reform seems to have left things pretty much as they were, in the sense that the familiar complaints of the past can still be heard. It should be noted, however, that prices formed in markets do not always meet desired goals, and the centralized determination of "rational" prices is a formidable (possibly impossible) task. Soviet price reform has broken some ground, especially in the ideological sphere. In the case of price setting in the extractive industries, mining for example, experiments with marginal cost pricing have been undertaken with a recognition of rental charges for natural resources. Further, the recent emphasis upon capital charges is a notable departure in Soviet thinking about price setting. In some measure, therefore, the recent price reforms may have gotten away from simply changing the level of prices and toward changing the bases upon which prices are established.

THE REFORM IN PERSPECTIVE

Economic reform is neither a recent nor a new phenomenon to the countries of the socialist bloc. In fact, most of the Eastern European countries have adopted reforms since the mid-1950s.[57] In reviewing these reforms,

[57] For accounts of economic reform in Eastern Europe, see the selection of articles in Feiwel, *New Concepts in Soviet-Type Economies*, part 2; Bela Belassa, "The Economic Reform in Hungary," *Economica*, vol. 37, no. 145 (February 1970) 1–22; J. Wilczynski, *Socialist Economic Development and Reforms* (New York: Macmillan, 1971); Morris Bornstein, "Economic Reforms in Eastern Europe," in Joint Economic Committee, *East European*

one can note that they all attempt to respond to the problems of excessive centralization, restrictive managerial behavior, and irrational price systems—which are exactly the same problems with which Soviet reformers are grappling. This suggests that the deficiencies of the Soviet economic system are not unique but are general concomitants of centrally planned socialism.

The most striking feature of economic reform in the Soviet Union is its conservative nature. Its goal throughout has been to retain the most basic features of the original economic system—centralized planning of outputs and inputs, centralized administration of prices, centralized allocation of investment—but to make it a more workable system by using "realized output" as a success indicator, reducing the number of planned targets, introducing capital charges, and so on. None of these changes however alters the basic system. Not only have the Soviet reforms been very conservative, especially compared to some of the more far-reaching reforms in Eastern Europe—notably in Hungary—but they also have been largely unimplemented in fact—for example, in the continued centralized allocation of investment—and have even been reversed, for example, the reintroduction of additional centralized plan targets and the tightening of administrative controls over bonuses.

The conservative nature of economic reform in the Soviet Union is not necessarily an indictment of such efforts, for there is no reason to believe that systemic improvements are more easily attained in market than in planned economies. In fact it is an open question to what extent marginal improvements in the Soviet system, introduced in isolation, can be effective and to what extent they will be counterproductive.[58] Also the question of timing is a difficult one. What is the proper sequence of reform? Should a general price reform precede limited decentralization of decision-making or vice versa, and so on? Such crucial questions remain largely unanswered even on theoretical terms. Many of the "solutions" may appear straightforward in theory, though certainly much less so in practice. In this sense, the appeal of the competitive market model can readily lead to overstatement of the potential of economic reform and inevitably to criticism for lack of practical achievement in the light of these overly optimistic expectations. In this context, one can perhaps understand the natural reluctance of Soviet authorities to depart on a program of radical reform.

Economies in Post-Helsinki (Washington, D.C.: U.S. Government Printing Office, 1977), pp. 102–134; Morris Bornstein, *Plan and Market: Economic Reform in Eastern Europe* (New Haven, Conn.: Yale University Press, 1973); H. Höhman, M. Kaser, and K. Thalheim, *The New Economic Systems of Eastern Europe* (London: Hurst, 1975).

[58] An example of this is the "rejection or transplants" phenomenon noted by A. Zielinski in the Polish case. Thus the system tended to reject transplants from market systems—in particular the use of a capital charge. A. Zielinski, "Economic Reform in Poland," paper presented at the CESES Seminar, Sorrento, Italy, Summer 1968.

A second argument against substantive reform of the Soviet economy stems from the Soviet view of the superiority of the "planning principle," the system by which crucial economic decisions are made by rational experts—planners—rather than by the anarchy of the market. To place more decision-making power in the hands of individual managers and consumers would subject the economy to anarchistic forces and would thus destroy the basic strength of the current system.[59]

The third explanation of the conservatism of Soviet economic reform lies in the role of vested interests. The people most directly affected by the reform—those in the ministries, the banking system, the planning organs, the party—have tended to resist significant decentralization of decision-making authority, which is tantamount to a reduction in their own decision-making power. As one authority writes: "The gradual derationing of producer goods that was a part of the 1965 program has not occurred, if for no other reason than that it would obviate the need for the bureaucrats who were supposed to carry it out."[60] The fact that the letter of the economic reform has not always been observed can also be explained by vested interests, for there have often been differences between those generating and those implementing economic reform.

Contrary to the perceptions of some Western economists, who see the reform process as being dead, Soviet authorities now picture economic reform as a continuous process. One reform after another is announced, and changes in organizational arrangements are becoming so complex they are difficult to follow and assess. For example, in July of 1979 *Pravda* announced a new "major" economic reform that again emphasized organizational reorganization.[61] Yet the reform is "dead" in the sense that Soviet authorities have turned their attention to organizational change as a means of resolving economic problems, and the few remaining advocates of significant decentralization as a means of resolving economic difficulties have gone underground. It would appear that only a major economic crisis or a radical change in the party leadership could bring about a real decentralization of economic authority.

In the meantime, the Soviet leadership has returned to the approach of using experimental programs to test reform ideas. Experiments have been conducted in industry and construction to test different forms of bonus systems and plan indicators, and the use of gross or net output indicators is still heatedly debated. The most significant ongoing experiment is the Shche-

---

[59] Goldman, "Economic Growth and Institutional Change," pp. 345–359, and G. Kosiachenko, "Important Conditions for Improvements of Planning," in Morris Bornstein and Daniel Fusfeld, eds., *The Soviet Economy: A Book of Readings*, 3rd ed., (Homewood, Ill.: Irwin, 1970), pp. 381–386.

[60] Schroeder, "The Soviet Economy on a Treadmill of 'Reforms,' " p. 324.

[61] David Dyker, "Half-Hearted Reform: The New Planning Decree," *Soviet Analyst*, vol. 8, no. 20 (October 1979), 5–8.

kino experiment, which began at the Shchekino Chemical Combine in 1967 and covered 1200 enterprises by 1978.[62] The goal of the Shchekino experiment is to encourage enterprises to meet output targets with reduced labor inputs. Participating enterprises are allowed to keep for incentive payments savings in the wages fund created by laying off redundant workers. Thus the experiment is supposed to strike at the notorious practice of labor hoarding by Soviet enterprises. Despite official support, this experiment has been slow in spreading, largely because the ministries have reacted to labor saving by confiscating excess wages funds, ratcheting up labor productivity targets for the next year's plan, and generally neutralizing the desired effect of the experiment. New rules introduced in April of 1978 seek to protect participating enterprises from such abuses, but it remains to be seen whether the experiment will spread of its own volition.

ECONOMIC REFORM ALTERNATIVES: MATHEMATICS AND THE MARKET

Soviet leaders have rejected the market model since 1928, so they should not be expected to adopt market methods in the future, except where absolutely essential. Even then, only those elements of the market will be adopted that can fit into the context of the central planning system. In this respect, the utilization of mathematical methods does hold promise for the future.[63]

To synthesize the views of the mathematical economists on economic reform, one should note that their central thesis is that resources can be allocated in a rational manner in a planned economy through the use of mathematical planning techniques. Because the basic resources available to the economy at one point in time—land, labor, capital, raw materials—are limited, the resource allocation problem becomes one of distributing these limited resources among competing uses in an optimal manner.

At the enterprise level, the enterprise has output targets and limited resources with which to produce those outputs. The allocation of enterprise resources, therefore, can be carried out in terms of an output program that falls within resource constraints and minimizes the use of scarce resource inputs while fulfilling the output target. Thus, managers would operate the

---

[62] For discussions of the Shchekino experiment, see Schroeder, "The Soviet Economy on a Treadmill of 'Reforms,' " pp. 329–330; Janet G. Chapman, "Labor Mobility and Labor Allocation in the USSR," paper presented at the joint meeting of the Association for the Study of Soviet-Type Economics and the Association for Comparative Economies, Detroit, Mich., December 1970, p. 5; Emily Clark Brown, "Continuity and Change in the Soviet Labor Market," *Industrial and Labor Relations Review*, vol. 23, no. 2 (January 1970), 171–190.
[63] For a discussion of mathematical methods in the context of Soviet planning, see John P. Hardt et al., *Mathematics and Computers in Soviet Economic Planning* (New Haven, Conn.: Yale University Press, 1967); and Ellman, *Soviet Planning Today*.

enterprise by solving linear programming problems consisting of an objective function (the output targets), resource constraints, and a system of equations expressing technological processes available to the enterprise. The optimal solution of such a model would not only instruct managers which processes and which process intensities to use but would also indirectly supply them with resource valuations in the form of *shadow prices* that would relate to them the *opportunity costs* (scarcity values) of the resources at their disposal. In this manner, both the resource allocation problem and the valuation problem would be solved simultaneously, thus enabling the enterprise to rationally allocate the resources at its disposal.[64]

Planning authorities could also avail themselves of the same mathematical techniques in developing regional and national plans. The main difference between such planning and enterprise operation would be the greater amount of detail required at the enterprise level. At the regional and national planning levels, the mathematical planning models constructed would encompass fewer commodity designations and would be at higher levels of aggregation. In all cases, the planning authorities would have specific objectives to meet (their objective functions), limited resources that could be employed to meet those objectives, and a number of technological production processes from which to choose. Thus a fixed target of outputs could be produced at a minimum cost of resources, or outputs could be maximized subject to resource constraints. As in the case of the enterprise, the scarcity values of the resources used could be indirectly computed as shadow prices from the optimal production program, and these scarcity values could then be used as a guide for planners.

Insofar as the Soviet economy produces millions of commodities, such mathematical planning techniques would drastically overtax existing computational and data gathering abilities. Well-recognizing this problem, the Soviet mathematical economists suggest the construction of a series of interrelated plans. The higher the planning agency, the higher the level of aggregation of products dealt with. Thus a national plan consisting of a relatively small number of highly aggregated and important commodities would be constructed. This would be subdivided into a series of regional plans, also dealing with a manageable number of commodities, and so on down to the individual enterprise.[65]

Proponents of mathematical planning techniques well-recognize the

---

[64] For a discussion of possible uses of programming in the operation of the Soviet enterprise, see L. V. Kantorovich, "Further Developments of Mathematical Methods and the Prospects of Their Application in Economic Planning," in V. S. Nemchinov, ed., *The Use of Mathematics in Economics* (Cambridge, Mass.: MIT Press, 1964), pp. 317–319.

[65] Kantorovich, "Further Developments of Mathematical Methods," pp. 319–321; and Benjamin Ward, "Linear Programming and Soviet Planning," in John P. Hardt et al., *Mathematics and Computers in Soviet Economic Planning* (New Haven, Conn.: Yale University Press, 1967), pp. 189–193.

limitations inherent in their approach, given the stage to which their knowledge has advanced. Yet they stress that realizable optimum plans can be developed that will result in a better utilization of society's resources. Areas where further advances are required are "better and more complete technical data, statistical indicators and methods of economic analysis as such."[66] While the use of mathematical planning techniques remains limited in the Soviet Union in actual planning,[67] the contributions of the Soviet mathematical economists should not be underrated, for they have taken the first steps toward defining the underlying theoretical model of resource allocation and valuation under central planning.

There is a practical alternative to organizational tinkering and mathematical modeling, namely, the various reform programs of the Eastern European socialist economies.[68] These programs, from the more extreme case of Yugoslavia to the notably conservative case of Bulgaria, represent a wide range of variants of socialist resource allocation. The East European systems, though presently at different stages of economic development, all began during the early 1950s, under pressure from the Soviet Union to implement the Stalinist model of industrialization. Although that pressure has not ceased, as the events in Hungary (1956) and Czechoslovakia (1968) attest, these economies have nevertheless found it necessary to implement changes in their economic arrangements. These reforms have focused on the organization of agricultural production and, most important, on the relaxation of centralized control and the implementation of planning with economic "levers": prices, costs, profits, and decentralized managerial control. They should, at least in some measure and with reservation, be a learning mechanism for the reform of Soviet planning arrangements. Outside of Yugoslavia, the most radical reform (the Hungarian "New Economic Mechanism" of 1966) has brought about significant decentralization through the abolition of output targets, the freeing up of prices, and the enhancement of the role of profits.[69] Nevertheless, even in this case, bureaucratic opposition and vested interests remain intact, and even though the Hungarian reform is now 15 years old, it remains to be seen what its long-run fate will be. Whether the Soviet Union will at some point in the future emulate the Hungarian reform remains another matter, irrespective of any success of the Hungarian program. The Soviet economy is less subject to the external pressures (to export to and import from the West) that confront a

---

[66] Kantorovich, "Further Development of Mathematical Methods," p. 320.

[67] On this, see Vladimir G. Treml, "Input-Output Analysis and Soviet Planning," in John P. Hardt et al., *Mathematics and Computers in Soviet Economic Planning* (New Haven, Conn.: Yale University Press, 1967), pp. 101–104; and Ward, "Linear Programming," pp. 193–195.

[68] For a detailed bibliography of this literature, see Bornstein, "Economic Reforms in Eastern Europe," pp. 132–134.

[69] Belassa, "The Economic Reform in Hungary," 20–22; Bela Csikos-Nagy, "The Hungarian Reform After Ten Years," *Soviet Studies*, vol. 30, no. 4 (October 1978), 540–546.

small country like Hungary, and thus it is less compelled by circumstances to adopt the Hungarian model.

SELECTED BIBLIOGRAPHY

Alexander Balinky et al., *Planning and the Market in the USSR: The 1960s* (New Brunswick, N.J.: Rutgers University Press, 1967).

Joseph S. Berliner, *The Innovation Decision in Soviet Industry* (Cambridge, Mass.: MIT Press, 1976).

Keith Bush, "The Implementation of the Soviet Economic Reform," *Osteuropa Wirtschaft*, nos. 2 and 3 (1970).

Stephen F. Cohen, "The Friends and Foes of Change: Reformism and Conservatism in the Soviet Union," *Slavic Review*, vol. 38, no. 2 (June 1979), 187–202.

Nikolai Fedoryenko et al., *Soviet Economic Reform: Progress and Problems*, translated from the Russian (Moscow: Progress Publishers, 1972).

George R. Feiwel, *The Soviet Quest for Economic Efficiency* (New York: Praeger, 1972).

Jere L. Felker, *Soviet Economic Controversies* (Cambridge, Mass.: MIT Press, 1966).

Alice C. Gorlin, "Industrial Reorganization: The Associations," in Joint Economic Committee, *Soviet Economy in a New Perspective* (Washington, D.C.: U.S. Government Printing Office, 1976), pp. 162–188.

Aron Katsenelinboigen, *Studies in Soviet Economic Planning* (White Plains, N.Y.: M. E. Sharpe, 1978).

Willem Keizer, *The Soviet Quest for Economic Rationality* (Rotterdam: Rotterdam University Press, 1971).

Alexei Kosygin, "On Improving Management of Industry, Perfecting Planning, and Enhancing Economic Incentives in Industrial Production," in M. Bornstein and D. Fusfeld, eds., *The Soviet Economy*, 3rd ed. (Homewood, Ill.: Irwin, 1970), pp. 387–396.

E. G. Liberman, *Economic Methods and the Effectiveness of Production* (White Plains, N.Y.: International Arts and Sciences Press, 1971).

National Foreign Assessment Center, *Organization and Management in the Soviet Economy: The Ceaseless Search for Panaceas*, ER77–10769, Washington, D.C., December 1977.

Alec Nove, *The Soviet Economic System* (London: Allen & Unwin, 1977), chap. 11.

Karl W. Ryavec, "Soviet Industrial Management: Challenge and Response, 1965–1970," *Canadian Slavic Studies*, vol. 2 (Summer 1972), 151–177.

Kark W. Ryavec, "Soviet Industrial Managers, Their Superiors and the Economic Reform: A Study of an Attempt at Planned Behavioral Change," *Soviet Studies*, vol. 21, no. 2 (October 1969), 208–229.

Gertrude E. Schroeder, "The 1966–67 Soviet Industrial Price Reform: A Study in Complications," *Soviet Studies*, vol. 20, no. 4 (April 1969), 462–477.

Gertrude E. Schroeder, "Recent Developments in Soviet Planning and Incentives," in Joint Economic Committee, *Soviet Economic Prospects for the Seventies* (Washington, D.C.: U.S. Government Printing Office, 1973), pp. 11–38.

Gertrude E. Schroeder, "The 'Reform' of the Supply System in Soviet Industry," *Soviet Studies*, vol. 24, no. 1 (July 1972), 97–119.

Gertrude E. Schroeder, "The Soviet Economy on a Treadmill of 'Reforms,' " in Joint Economic Committee, *Soviet Economy in a Time of Change* (Washington, D.C.: U.S. Government Printing Office, 1979), vol. 1, pp. 312–340.

Myron E. Sharpe, ed., *Planning, Profit and Incentives in the USSR*, vols. 1 and 2 (White Plains, N.Y.: International Arts and Sciences Press, 1966).

Leon Smolinski, ed., *L. V. Kantorovich: Essays in Optimal Planning* (White Plains, N.Y.: International Arts and Sciences Press, 1976).

Eugene Zaleski, *Planning Reforms in the Soviet Union, 1962–1966* (Chapel Hill: University of North Carolina Press, 1967).

Alfred Zauberman, "Liberman's Rules of the Game for Soviet Industry," *Slavic Review*, vol. 22, no. 4 (December 1963), 734–744.

Alfred Zauberman, *The Mathematical Revolution in Soviet Planning* (Oxford: Oxford University Press, 1975).

Chapter 10

Soviet Economic Growth and Performance

Our survey of the Soviet economy is virtually complete at this point; yet to fail to consider how well the Soviet economy has performed relative to other economies would be a significant omission. In fact, this is ultimately what the study of differing economic systems is all about: which economic organization seems to function the "best"? Although we recognize that it is risky to generalize from the performance of one economy to the performance of the system,[1] that is, to treat Soviet economic performance as representative of the command socialist system as a whole, we compare the performance of the Soviet command economy with that of industrialized market economies in this chapter. Of special interest are the comparisons between the USSR and the United States, despite the different levels of development of the two countries. This is not to deny that other comparisons, such as the USSR with West Germany or Japan, are just as relevant.[2] The United States and the Soviet Union are nonetheless the world's two largest economic powers, with fairly equal population sizes. Considerable research has already gone into Soviet-American comparisons, and the Soviets themselves tend to judge their economic performance relative to that of the United States. In this chapter, we emphasize long-run performance and concentrate on secular trends. The often considerable variation around the secular trend is not considered in detail.[3]

[1] Philip Hanson, "East-West Comparisons and Comparative Economic Systems," *Soviet Studies*, vol. 22, no. 3 (January 1971), 327–343. We have shown that the performance of the USSR economy is in many respects differrent from that of other planned socialist economies. See Paul R. Gregory and Robert C. Stuart, *Comparative Economic Systems* (Boston: Houghton Mifflin, 1980), chap. 10.
[2] Angus Maddison, *Economic Growth in Japan and the USSR* (New York: Norton, 1969); Abram Bergson, *Productivity and the Social System: The USSR and the West* (Cambridge, Mass.: Harvard University Press, 1978), chap. 11.
[3] The reader interested in pursuing the question of cyclical instability in socialist economic systems should consult G. J. Staller, "Fluctuations in Planned and Free Market Econo-

In comparing the economic performance of countries, there are two major problems. First, it is often difficult to measure the various economic performance criteria in an unambiguous manner. For example, measures of economic growth—frequently used performance criteria—are often dramatically affected by the choice of price weights—the index number problem. Thus direct comparisons of growth rates tend to be difficult to interpret. If it is difficult to evaluate the relative growth performance of countries, although one can narrowly define economic growth in rather specific terms, it is even more difficult to measure less easily quantifiable performance criteria, such as environmental quality or dynamic efficiency.

The second major problem is even more difficult to come to grips with. In view of the multitude of possible performance criteria—economic growth, environmental quality, efficiency of resource utilization, relative standards of living, equity of income distribution, military power, and so on—how can one rank the performance of one economy relative to another unless one economy outperforms the other in all categories? As an example, let us assume that the Soviet economy has outperformed the American economy in terms of growth and equity of income distribution, but that the United States economy has outperformed the USSR in all other categories. Which country deserves the higher overall rating? This depends of course upon the relative importance of the various performance criteria, which is a matter of individual judgment, not of objective economics.[4]

In sum, there seems to be no unambiguous way to objectively evaluate the performance of one economy relative to another except in obvious (and rare) cases where one outperforms the other in all categories. Given, however, the widespread interest in performance evaluation, what can be done? Our answer is to examine the performance of the Soviet economy and market economies in terms of what we consider the most important performance criteria; the reader can then supply his (or her) own subjective weights to aggregate the individual performance indicators. In this chapter, we deal with the "conventional" economic success indicators commonly used

---

mies," *American Economic Review*, vol. 54, no. 4, part 1 (June 1964), 385–395; Oldrych Kyn, Wolfram Schrette, and Juri Slama, "Growth Cycles in Centrally Planned Economies: An Empirical Test," Osteuropa Institute, Munich, working paper no. 7, August 1975; Josef Goldman, "Fluctuations and Trends in the Rate of Economic Growth in Some Socialist Countries," *Economics of Planning*, vol. 4, no. 2 (1964), 89–98; C. W. Lawson, "An Empirical Analysis of the Structure and Stability of Communist Foreign Trade," *Soviet Studies*, vol. 26, no. 2 (April 1974), 224–238.

[4] For a discussion of the success criteria problem, see Bela Belassa, *The Hungarian Experience in Economic Planning* (New Haven, Conn.: Yale University Press, 1959), pp. 5–24. Also see Alexander Eckstein, ed., *Comparison of Economic Systems* (Berkeley and Los Angeles: University of California Press, 1971), parts 1 and 2; John Michael Montias, *The Structure of Economic Systems* (New Haven, Conn.: Yale University Press, 1976), chap. 4.

to assess economic performance: economic growth; static and dynamic efficiency; the equity of the distribution of income; consumer welfare, including both private and public goods; and economic stability (or security). Less
conventional indicators of economic performance—military strength, environmental quality, economic development models, and technological
change—will be considered in the following chapter. The stroke of our pen
is quite broad: how well has the Soviet economy performed in each of these
areas during the era of central planning (a time span of over 50 years) vis-à-
vis the long-term performance of the industrialized capitalist countries?
The time horizon of each comparison is dictated by the availability of data,
and some series do not go back past World War II, but our objective is to
assess the entire plan era with broad data aggregates. Shorter term performance will be considered in the final chapter.

SOVIET ECONOMIC GROWTH

Although it is not widely recognized, measures of the long-term growth of
real GNP are sensitive to the choice of constant price weights. If one measures the growth rate of an economy that has successfully transformed itself
into an advanced industrial country, the computed real growth rate will
often be much higher if constant preindustrialization prices are used as
weights. This phenomenon is called *index number relativity*, or the "Gerschenkron Effect," after Alexander Gerschenkron, who analyzed it in his
study of Soviet industrial production.[5]

Although the explanation of index number relativity might seem a digression to the reader, we attempt to provide an explanation of this phenomenon because of its importance in evaluating USSR growth, especially
during the 1930s. Moreover, index number effects play important roles in
the assessment of Soviet military power (Chapter 11) and of the size of Soviet GNP relative to other countries.

An intuitive account of index number relativity would be as follows. In
the course of industrialization, a negative correlation exists between the
rates of growth of sector outputs and the rates of growth of sector prices.
The fastest growing sectors—machinery, electricity, transportation equipment—all tend to experience *relative* declines in prices (relative to the
prices of the slowly growing sectors, such as food products and textiles) as
advanced technology is introduced and economies of scale are achieved.
Thus, if constant preindustrialization prices are used, the most rapidly expanding sectors will receive large relative weights, whereas the other sec-

[5] Alexander Gerschenkron, "The Soviet Indices of Industrial Production," *Review of Economics and Statistics*, vol. 29, no. 4 (November 1947), 217–226.

tors will receive small relative weights. Conversely, if postindustrialization prices are used, the rapidly expanding sectors will receive small relative price weights (which reflect the reductions in their relative prices), and the other sectors will receive large relative price weights. The same logic would apply to comparisons of the relative size of the total output of two countries, one "industrialized," the other "backward." The industrialized country produces larger relative volumes of "advanced" goods, whose relative prices are low, and produces relatively small volumes of "traditional" goods, whose relative prices are high. The backward country produces relatively large volumes of traditional goods at relatively low prices and relatively small volumes of advanced goods at relatively high prices. If the relative output of the two countries is calculated using the prices of the advanced country, the differential will be smaller than if the prices of the backward country were used. A hypothetical example is supplied in the accompanying note to assist the reader.[6]

This may seem quite academic to the reader, but Soviet 1976 GNP was three-quarters that of the United States in *dollar* prices but one-half that of the United States in *ruble* prices. Moreover, the annual growth rate of Soviet real GNP between 1928 and 1937, as calculated by Abram Bergson, was 11.9 percent using the preindustrialization prices of 1928, and 5.5 percent when calculated in postindustrialization prices of 1937.[7] The complexity of the question is increased when one realizes that comparable estimates of American growth in preindustrialization prices, say of the 1800s, are not available.[8] What then is the "true" growth rate (or relative GNP) of the So-

[6] For example, consider a hypothetical case in which the USSR in 1928 produced 100 "units" of textiles and 50 "units" of machinery, and that is all. The 1928 per unit prices of textiles and machinery were *1 R* and *2 R*, respectively. Assume further that in 1980, the USSR produced 200 "units" of textiles and 1000 "units" of machinery, and the prices of textiles and machinery had risen to *10 R* and *10 R*, respectively. If one values both 1928 and 1980 outputs in 1928 prices, 1980 output is *11 times* 1928 output. If one values both 1928 and 1980 output in 1980 prices, 1980 output is *8 times* 1928 output. Formal analyses of the index number problem are found in Richard Moorsteen, "On Measuring Productive Potential and Relative Efficiency," *Quarterly Journal of Economics*, vol. 75, no. 3 (August 1961), 451–467; G. W. Nutter, "On Economic Size and Growth," *Journal of Law and Economics*, vol. 9, no. 2 (October 1966), 163–188.

[7] Abram Bergson, *The Real National Income of Soviet Russia Since 1928* (Cambridge, Mass.: Harvard University Press, 1961), p. 261. The 1976 relative GNP figures are from Imogene Edwards, Margaret Hughes, and James Noren, "U.S. and U.S.S.R.: Comparisons of GNP," in Joint Economic Committee, *Soviet Economy in a Time of Change* (Washington, D.C.: U.S. Government Printing Office, 1979), vol. 1, p. 378.

[8] Growth in the United States between 1834 and 1908 has been estimated in 1860 prices. See Robert Gallman, "Gross National Product in the United States, 1834–1909," *Output, Employment and Productivity in the United States After 1800* (New York and London: National Bureau of Economic Research, 1966), pp. 3–75. These estimates are not comparable with the figures in 1929 prices cited in Table 27 because the two differ on current price estimates. Thus these figures are not tests of the impact of index number relativity on the measurement of U.S. GNP.

viet Union or of the United States? There is in fact no single "true" growth rate. Instead, there are a whole series of growth rates, one for each set of price weights, which yield a *range* of growth rates. Fortunately, for purposes of intercountry comparisons, truly significant differences arise only when comparing growth rates computed using pre- versus postindustrialization prices, owing to the large structural changes that occur during industrialization. Differences between growth rates in constant postindustrialization or constant preindustrialization prices tend to be smaller. Nevertheless, index number relativity continues to operate in industrialized countries, but only to a smaller degree.

With these reservations in mind, we shall contrast "comparable" Soviet and Western growth rates; in other words, we shall concentrate on growth rates that employ "late" year (postindustrialization) price weights. This method, however, does not eliminate all biases resulting from index number problems but acts instead only as a crude adjustment. The cited Soviet growth rates have been estimated by American economists, who have recalculated Soviet GNP using Western GNP definitions[9] to ensure the comparability of Soviet and American rates.[10] For reference purposes, we include the official estimates of growth rates of Soviet *net material product*, which differs from the standard Western concept by its exclusion of services not directly connected with physical production.

In Table 27, we supply annual growth rates of tsarist GNP (1885–1913), of Soviet real GNP during the plan era (1928–1979) and of the United States between 1834 and 1979. The Soviet figures to 1950 are based on the estimates by Abram Bergson, which are the most widely accepted Western estimates of Soviet growth. Bergson's figures are available through 1958. Estimates of the Central Intelligence Agency (CIA) are available for the entire postwar era and are used to extend the Bergson series.[11]

---

[9] Of course, there is the problem of valuation of Soviet GNP, because established prices often fail to reflect costs of production owing to substantial subsidies and indirect taxes. The figures cited employ the factor cost concept, which eliminates subsidies and indirect taxes. There is still a problem in that such factor costs fail to adequately reflect capital costs, but various adjustments show that overall growth rates are not substantially altered by the inclusion of capital costs. See Bergson, *Real National Income*, p. 219. For a discussion of conceptual differences in measures of aggregate output, see John Pitzer, "Reconciliation of Gross National Product and Soviet National Income," *NATO Colloquium* (Brussels, July 1977).

[10] For studies of the availability and reliability of Soviet statistics, see Vladimir G. Treml and John P. Hardt, eds., *Soviet Economic Statistics* (Durham, N.C.: Duke University Press, 1972). Also see Abram Bergson, "Reliability and Usability of Soviet Statistics," *The American Statistician*, vol. 7, no. 3 (June–July, 1953), 19–23.

[11] The cited Bergson figures are in 1950 prices and the CIA figures employ 1959 or 1970 weights; thus, this is a mixed index. Differences that arise as a result of the mixed weighting scheme are most likely minimal. Differences between this index and one based on the Bergson 1937 price weighted figures (to 1958) are negligible. Individuals associated with

**TABLE 27   Long-term Growth of GNP in the USSR and the U.S.
(annual rates of growth)**

USSR	American Estimates	Official Soviet Estimates (net material product)
1885–1913	3.3[c]	—
1928–1940	5.4[a]	14.6[d]
1950–1960	6.0[c]	10.1
1960–1970	5.1[c]	7.0
1970–1979	4.0[c]	5.3
1928–1979	4.5[b]	8.8
1928–1979, effective years	5.1[b]	9.7
1950–1979	4.9[b]	7.6

United States	1860 Prices	1929 Prices	1958 and 1972 Prices
1834–1843 to 1879–1888	4.4	—	—
1879–1888 to 1899–1908	3.7	3.8	—
1899–1908 to 1929	—	3.4	—
1929–1950	—	—	2.8
1950–1960	—	—	3.2
1960–1970	—	—	4.0
1970–1979	—	—	3.1
1929–1979	—	—	3.1
1950–1979	—	—	3.5

SOURCES: Abram Bergson, *The Real National Income of Soviet Russia Since 1928* (Cambridge, Mass.: Harvard University Press, 1961), p. 210; Herbert Block, "Soviet Economic Performance in a Global Context," in Joint Economic Committee, *Soviet Economy in a Time of Change* (Washington, D.C.: U.S. Government Printing Office, 1979), vol. 1, p. 135; Paul Gregory, *Russian National Income, 1885–1913*, mimeograph, 1979, Table 1; A. L. Vainshtein, *Narodny dokhod Rossii i SSSR* [The national income of Russia and the USSR], (Moscow: Statiskal, 1969), p. 119; *Narodnoe khoziaistvo SSSR v 1978 g.* [The national economy of the USSR in 1978], (Moscow: Statistika, 1979), pp. 31–33; National Foreign Assessment Center, *Handbook of Economic Statistics 1979*, ER79–10274, Washington, D.C., August 1979, p. 22; *The Economic Report of the President* (selected years); *Dostizheniia sovetskoi vlasti za 40 let v tsifrakh* [the accomplishments of the Soviet regime over 40 years in numbers], (Moscow: 1957), p. 327; Robert Gallman, "Gross National Product in the United States, 1834–1909," *Output, Employment and Productivity in the United States after 1800* (New York and London: National Bureau of Economic Research, 1966), p. 26. The 1979 USSR figures are based on preliminary Soviet figures.

[a] 1950 prices.
[b] Combined index, 1950 prices 1928–1950, 1970 prices thereafter.
[c] 1970 weights.
[d] 1926–1927 prices.
[e] 1913 prices.

What conclusions can be drawn from Table 27 concerning Soviet growth performance relative to that of the United States? First, it is obvious that Soviet growth since 1928 has been more rapid than American growth during the same period. The average annual growth rate of the Soviet economy between 1928 and 1979 was 4.5 percent, whereas the rate for the United States between 1929 and 1979 was 3.1 percent. If one measures Soviet growth only during "effective years,"[12] that is, if one eliminates the war years, Soviet growth rises to 5.1 percent, almost 2 percentage points above the American annual growth rate.

Second, the Soviet growth rate during the postwar period (1950–1979) of 4.9 percent exceeded the comparable American rate of 3.5 percent (1950–1979)—a difference of almost 1.5 percentage points annually.

Third, Soviet growth in the postwar period has been declining, from a high of 6.0 percent between 1950 and 1960 to 4.0 percent between 1970 and 1979. During this latter period, the worst growth years were 1963 (2.2 percent), 1969 (2.3 percent), 1972 (2.0 percent), and 1975 (1.7 percent).[13] This declining growth rate has had a depressing effect upon the long-term Soviet growth rate, which is a combination of relatively rapid growth from 1928 to 1940 and from 1950 to 1960 and relatively slower growth after 1960. As the Soviet growth slowdown continues, the growth rate differential between the United States and the Soviet Union has declined.

Fourth, the official Soviet estimates of the growth of net material product in constant prices are much larger than the American estimates of Soviet growth using Western GNP concepts and different price weights. Such differences are greatest when comparing the 1928–1940 period, part of which is explained by the Soviets' use of preindustrialization 1926–1927 prices until 1950.[14] From the Soviet viewpoint, this is more than a matter of

---

the Rand Corporation and various governmental agencies have made contributions to the estimation of Soviet GNP using Western accounting practices. See for example, Stanley H. Cohn, "General Growth Performance of the Soviet Economy," in Joint Economic Committee, *Economic Performance and the Military Burden in the Soviet Union* (Washington, D.C.: U.S. Government Printing Office, 1970); Abraham Becker, *Soviet National Income, 1958–1964* (Berkeley: University of California Press, 1969).

[12] The practice of computing Soviet growth for "effective years" was originated by Gregory Grossman, as a suggested measure of what long-term Soviet growth might have been in the absence of the war. Gregory Grossman, "Thirty Years of Soviet Industrialization," *Soviet Survey* (October 1958). One could perhaps argue that the Great Depression should be omitted from computing the long-term United States growth rate, except that it could be argued that the business cycle is inherent to the capitalist system and should be included.

[13] Cohn, "General Growth Performance," p. 9; Herbert Block, "Soviet Economic Performance in a Global Context," in Joint Economic Committee, *Soviet Economy in a Time of Change* (Washington, D.C.: U.S. Government Printing Office, 1979), vol. 1.

[14] Bergson calculates Soviet growth between 1928 and 1937 as 11.9 percent annually in 1928 prices, compared with the official claim of 16.9 percent (Bergson, *The Real National Income of Soviet Russia*, p. 216). In recent Soviet publications, the official estimates of Soviet growth during the 1930s have been severely criticized as being unrealistic and incon-

academic interest; it is difficult to determine how much Soviet growth has actually declined in recent years because the earlier rate (1928–1940) is difficult to interpret. Another cause of the differences between American and Soviet estimates is the Soviet's omission from net material product of selected service categories (such as passenger transportation, government employees, lawyers, housing), which have been among the slowest growing sectors in the Soviet Union.

Fifth, United States growth rates during early periods of industrial transformation are closer to the Soviet plan period rates than are the twentieth-century American rates. Thus the American economy grew at 4.4 percent annually between 1834–1843 and 1879–1888, which is one percentage point less than the Soviet rate during the 1928–1940 period and is roughly equal to the Soviet 1950–1979 rate.[15] In fact, the United States growth rate of 6.6 percent during the 1869–1878 to 1879–1888 period exceeded the Soviet 1928–1940 rate.

Sixth, whereas the Soviet growth rate of 6.0 percent between 1950 and 1960 was rapid by international standards, it was by no means unprecedented among the major industrial powers during this period. The annual West German growth rate between 1950 and 1960 was 7.8 percent and the Japanese rate for the same period was almost 9 percent.[16] It may not be a coincidence that those major industrial powers that suffered the most extensive wartime destruction also experienced the most rapid growth rates in the immediate postwar period. More important, both Japan and West Germany (especially Japan) have been able to sustain high rates of growth after 1960, in contrast to the USSR's declining rate of growth. Since 1970, the USSR growth rate has been only slightly above that of Western Europe.

Seventh, Soviet growth rates during the plan era well exceeded the growth rate during the "industrialization era" of the tsarist period (1885–1913). In fact, the long-run Soviet growth rate during 1928–1979 was roughly 50 percent above the 1885–1913 rate. Thus the Soviet period has seen an acceleration of economic growth. If the decline in the Soviet growth rate continues however, the difference between the tsarist and Soviet growth rates could become negligible.

---

sistent; on this, see Vainshtein, *Narodnii dokhod Rossii i SSSR*, pp. 99–108. For a further discussion of the official Soviet figures, see Alec Nove, "1926/7 and All That," *Soviet Studies*, vol. 9, no. 2 (October 1957), 117–130.

[15] In these comparisons, we use early year price weights for the United States (1860 prices) and late year price weights for the USSR—a seeming violation of the principle stated above. Index number relativity does not show up in these calculations for the United States, probably because of different calculating methods used by Gallman (the 1860 price estimates) and Kuznets (the 1929 price estimates). Note that for the same period (1879–1888 to 1899–1908), the 1929 price weights yield a higher growth rate (Table 27).

[16] National Foreign Assessment Center, *Handbook of Economic Statistics 1979*, p. 22; World Bank, *World Tables 1976* (Baltimore, Md.: Johns Hopkins University Press, 1976), pp. 262–263.

**TABLE 28   Long-term Growth of GNP of Selected Countries
(average annual growth rate)**

United Kingdom	1855–1864 to 1978	2.2
France	1831–1840 to 1978	2.5
Belgium	1900–1904 to 1978	2.3
Netherlands	1860–1870 to 1978	2.6
Germany (West Germany after 1945)	1850–1859 to 1978	2.9
Denmark	1865–1869 to 1974	3.1
Sweden	1861–1869 to 1978	3.1
Italy	1895–1899 to 1978	2.9
Japan	1874–1879 to 1978	4.6
United States	1834–1843 to 1978	3.5
Canada	1870–1874 to 1978	3.6
USSR	1928 to 1979	4.5–5.1

SOURCES: Simon Kuznets, *Economic Growth of Nations* (Cambridge, Mass.: Harvard University Press, 1971), pp. 11–14; and Table 27, above. The Kuznets figures are updated from *Handbook of Economic Statistics 1979*, p. 22.

Eighth, Soviet growth between 1928 and 1979 exceeded the long-term growth rates of the other industrialized economies, including the United States (Table 28). Only the long-term Japanese growth rate (4.6 percent) roughly equals the Soviet 1928–1979 rate. The above comparison does however assume that the 1928–1979 Soviet rate was indeed the long-term growth rate of the Soviet economy, although it is computed using a much shorter time period than the other rates. This assumption may eventually not prove to be the case, in view of the declining Soviet growth pattern. For the other countries however, there seems to be no consistent difference between early period and late period rates,[17] so perhaps the shorter Soviet period does not distort our overall conclusion that the long-term Soviet growth rate is the highest recorded (along with Japan's). We emphasize that we are dealing with long-term rates, which conceal the fact that growth rates as high or higher than the long-term Soviet rate have been attained by many of these countries (Japan, the United States, Germany, and others) during various subperiods in the past.

Thus we conclude that Soviet economic growth during the plan era was more rapid than American growth throughout the twentieth century and was more rapid than the long-run growth of other industrialized countries—except Japan. Soviet growth during the 1950s was rapid but was surpassed by the two other major industrial powers—West Germany and Japan—which had also suffered extensive war damage. Only during its period of industrial transformation did American growth approach the Soviet rate during the plan era. Soviet growth was also above the growth rate of the tsarist economy after 1885. These conclusions are probably sufficiently

[17] Simon Kuznets, *Economic Growth of Nations* (Cambridge, Mass.: Harvard University Press, 1971), pp. 37–43.

general to not be notably affected by the index number problem and the other measurement problems mentioned above.

Let us now turn to a deeper question: to what extent was the rapid Soviet growth a consequence of the Soviet economic system per se or of other special factors unrelated to the system? This is a fundamental issue in appraising alternative systems, for we are interested in the merits of the system independent of special circumstances.[18] In this regard, certain special factors probably affected long-run Soviet growth performance. First, the Soviets industrialized late and could therefore borrow more advanced technology from the West. Second, the large Soviet population, concentrated as it was in agriculture at the beginning of the plan era, provided, as we have seen, a plentiful supply of labor for industry. Economies of scale could therefore be achieved in the course of Soviet industrialization without diminishing the marginal productivity of capital. On the negative side, Soviet agricultural resources were limited relative to population, with only a small proportion of land suitable for cultivation.[19] Although it is impossible to weigh the impact of each of these factors on Soviet growth, one can speculate that the Soviets' borrowing of more advanced technology was an important factor in explaining rapid growth, especially during the 1930s and the immediate postwar period.

Special factors aside, to what extent was the more rapid Soviet growth a product of the Soviet system of central planning and political dictatorship? It would seem that much of the superior Soviet growth perrformance can be explained by the substitution of growth-oriented planners' preferences for consumer sovereignty. In this manner, the state was able to opt for a pattern of development conducive to rapid economic growth by planning high investment and labor participation rates and by expanding the education of the labor force. In the case of educational levels for example, in 1926 only 6 percent of the over-15-year-old population (of 89 million) had received education beyond the seventh grade. By 1959, this percentage had risen to 39 percent (of 148 million).[20] The high investment ratios (Chapter 3) and labor participation rates (Chapter 6) have already been discussed.

The growth bias of Soviet planning can be illustrated by comparing the pattern of Soviet growth (the growth of household consumption vis-à-vis gross investment) with that of the United States (Table 29). The major difference between the two is the much more rapid growth of investment than

---

[18] On this point see Abram Bergson, "Comparative Productivity and Efficiency in the USA and USSR," in Alexander Eckstein, ed., *Comparison of Economic Systems* (Berkeley and Los Angeles: University of California Press, 1971), pp. 161–240.

[19] Bergson, *The Real National Income of Soviet Russia*, p. 260.

[20] Nicholas DeWitt, "Education and Development of Human Resources: Soviet and American Effort," in Joint Economic Committee, *Dimensions of Soviet Economic Power* (Washington, D.C.: U.S. Government Printing Office, 1962), p. 244.

**TABLE 29   Differential Growth Patterns, GNP by Final Use,
USSR—United States (annual growth rates)**

	Household Consumption	Gross Investment	GNP	1 ÷ 2
USSR				
1928–1937[a]	0.7	14.5	5.5	0.05
1950–1955[a]	8.7	8.7	7.6	1.00
1958–1964[b]	4.8	7.4	5.9	0.65
1965–1969[f]	6.2	6.8	4.9	0.91
1970–1978[g]	3.4	5.7	3.7	0.60
1928–1955[a]	2.8	7.9	4.8	0.35
UNITED STATES				
1834–1843 to 1879–1888[c]	4.0	6.5	4.4	0.62
1879–1888 to 1899–1908[d]	3.8	3.8	3.8	1.00
1899–1908 to 1914–1923[d]	3.1	3.0	3.1	1.03
1929–1950[e]	2.7	2.6	2.6	1.04
1950–1970[e]	3.6	2.0	3.6	1.80
1970–1978[h]	3.6	3.8	3.2	0.95
1929–1970[e]	3.2	2.3	3.1	1.39

SOURCES: Bergson, *The Real National Income of Soviet Russia*, p. 210; Abraham Becker, *Soviet National Income 1958–1964* (Berkeley: University of California Press, 1969), p. 256; Simon Kuznets, *National Product Since 1869* (New York: National Bureau of Economic Research, 1946), Table II-16; Robert Gallman, "Gross National Product in the United States, *Output, Employment and Productivity in the United States After 1800*, (New York and London: National Bureau of Economic Research, 1966), pp. 26–34; *The Economic Report of the President* (Washington, D.C.: U.S. Government Printing Office, 1979), p. 184; Stanley H. Cohn, "The Economic Burden of Defense Expenditures," in *Soviet Economic Prospects for the Seventies*, p. 151; Block, "Soviet Economic Performance," p. 136.

[a] 1937 ruble factor cost.   [e] 1958 prices.
[b] 1958 adjusted factor cost.   [f] 1955 prices.
[c] 1860 prices.   [g] 1970 prices.
[d] 1929 prices.   [h] 1972 prices.

consumption in the USSR as opposed to the more rapid growth of consumption—with the exception of the very early 1834–1888 period—in the United States. The most extreme case of this is the negligible growth of household consumption in the USSR between 1928 and 1937, a period when investment was expanding at over 14 percent annually. Although investment expanded more rapidly than consumption in the United States between 1834 and 1888, the extreme differences noted in the Soviet case were avoided. This growth orientation is also reflected in the differential growth pattern of the various originating sectors of Soviet GNP (Table 30). The consumption-oriented sectors (trade, services, and agriculture) expanded more slowly than total output in the USSR, whereas in the United States they have expanded (during the period in question) at roughly the same rate as GNP, with the exception of agriculture.

TABLE 30   Annual Rates of Growth: Major Economic Sectors

	USSR, 1928–1978		United States, 1947–1969	
	Sector Growth	Sector Growth ÷ GNP Growth	Sector Growth	Sector Growth ÷ GNP Growth
Agriculture	1.7	0.36	1.5	0.39
Industry	7.2	1.47	4.2	1.08
Construction	6.9	1.41	2.8	0.72
Transportation and communications	8.0	1.63	4.3	1.10
Trade	4.2	0.86	4.0	1.03
Services	4.0	0.82	4.0	1.03
GNP	4.9		3.9	

SOURCES: R. Moorsteen and R. Powell, *The Soviet Capital Stock, 1928–1962* (Homewood, Ill.: Irwin, 1966), pp. 622–624; Stanley H. Cohn, "General Growth Performance of the Soviet Economy," in Joint Economic Committee, *Economic Performance and the Military Burden in the Soviet Union* (Washington, D.C.: U.S. Government Printing Office, 1970), p. 17; *The Economic Report of the President*, 1969 (Washington, D.C.: U.S. Government Printing Office, 1969), p. 207; Block, "Soviet Economic Performance," p. 135.

DYNAMIC EFFICIENCY AND THE GROWTH OF PRODUCTIVITY

A second criterion for evaluating the performance of economies is *dynamic efficiency,* which "relates to the community's capacity to add to its technological knowledge and to exploit such knowledge with increasing effect."[21] We use this criterion in addition to economic growth because as we just noted, the Soviet Union deliberately adopted a rapid growth strategy of high investment rates, high labor participation rates, borrowing of more advanced technology, and rapid expansion of education and training. Thus one would be surprised if the Soviets had *not* attained relatively high rates of economic growth. This is not to detract from their growth achievement, just to place it in its proper perspective.

In such a case, dynamic efficiency might prove a useful second performance criterion, for it measures the rate at which a country is able to increase the efficiency of resource utilization over time, that is, the rate of increase of the amount of output derived from a given amount of factor inputs. Dynamic efficiency can be measured only imperfectly and indirectly. Its most common measure is the rate of growth of output per unit of *combined* factor inputs.[22] A less general measure would be the rate of

[21] Abram Bergson, *Planning and Productivity Under Soviet Socialism* (New York: Columbia University Press, 1968), p. 52.
[22] To determine the rate of growth of combined inputs—labor and capital—the individual growth rates of labor and capital, respectively, must be combined in some manner. In simi-

growth of output per unit of labor (or capital) input. One measures the rate of growth of output per unit of input by subtracting the growth rate of the input from the growth rate of output. For example, if GNP grows at 5 percent annually and combined factor inputs grow at 3 percent annually, the annual rate of growth of output per unit of combined factor input would be 2 percent.

From this description of total factor productivity, one can see that it provides only an indirect link to dynamic efficiency because one can only imperfectly measure the rates of growth of factor inputs in both qualitative and quantitative terms. For example, it is extremely difficult to measure changes in the quality of Soviet capital and labor force relative to such changes in the United States or other countries. Further, how does one measure nonconventional inputs such as management? As a result, only conventional inputs such as land, labor, and capital can be measured and generally only in quantitative terms.[23] The danger therefore is that important changes in nonconventional inputs and qualitative changes of conventional inputs will be ignored, thus distorting the estimation of the growth of output per unit of input.

In Table 31, we relate several measures of the rates of growth of factor productivity in the Soviet Union, United States, and selected other countries, both over the long-run and for the early postwar period. The table includes both the rate of growth of output per unit of combined (capital and labor) input (column 5) and also the growth of output per unit of specific factor input, namely, labor productivity (column 6) and capital productivity (column 7). More up-to-date comparisons are not possible because of the lack of updated input data for Western countries.

Looking at both the long-term trends and the 1950–1962 trends, we see

---

lar studies for Western countries, the two growth rates are generally combined by computing a weighted average, the weights being the labor and capital shares of total income. In the Soviet case, capital does not generate income; therefore there is no real "capital share" of total income. For this reason, "synthetic" factor shares have been used for the Soviet case, based largely upon factor shares found in Western countries. For examples of the use of "synthetic" factor shares, see Abram Bergson, *The Economics of Soviet Planning* (New Haven, Conn.: Yale University Press, 1964), pp. 341–343; R. Moorsteen and R. Powell, *The Soviet Capital Stock, 1928–1962* (Homewood, Ill.: Irwin, 1966), pp. 264–266. We shall return to this matter shortly.

[23] Attempts have been made to adjust for quality differences and to measure nonconventional inputs, but they rest very heavily upon rather tenuous assumptions made by the researchers themselves. See for example, Edward Denison, *Why Growth Rates Differ* (Washington, D.C.: The Brookings Institution, 1967); and Edward Denison, *Accounting for United States Economic Growth 1929–1969* (Washington, D.C.: The Brookings Institution, 1974). For an attempt to adjust Soviet inputs for quality differences, see Earl R. Brubaker, "The Age of Capital and Growth in the Soviet Nonagricultural Nonresidential Sector," *Soviet Studies*, vol. 21, no. 3 (January 1970), 350–359; and Earl R. Brubaker, "Embodied Technology, the Asymptotic Behavior of Capital's Age, and Soviet Growth," *Review of Economics and Statistics*, vol. 50, no. 3 (August 1968), 304–311.

TABLE 31   Annual Rates of Growth of Inputs and Productivity: USSR, United States, and Selected Countries

PANEL A: LONG-TERM TRENDS

	(1) Output	(2) Labor, Man-hours	(3) Reproducible Capital	(4) Combined Inputs	(5) Output Per Unit of Combined Input (1–4)	(6) Labor Productivity (1–2)	(7) Capital Productivity (1–3)
USSR (GNP) 1928–1966	5.5[a]	2.2	7.4[b]	3.5[a]	2.0	3.3	−1.9
United States (GNP) 1929–1969	3.3	0.8	2.0[b]	1.1	2.2	2.5	1.3
United Kingdom (GDP) 1925–1929 to 1963	1.9	0.8	1.8[b]	1.1	0.8	1.1	0.1
France (GDP) 1913–1966	2.3	−0.5	2.0[b]	0.2	2.2	2.8	0.3
Canada (GNP) 1926–1956	3.9	0.8	2.9[b]	1.2	2.7	3.1	1.0
Norway (GDP) 1899–1956	2.8	0.3	2.5[b]	0.7	2.1	2.5	0.3

PANEL B: POSTWAR PERIOD, 1950–1962, NATIONAL INCOME

	(1) Output	(2) Labor, Man-hours	(3) Reproducible Capital	(4) Combined Inputs	(5) Output Per Unit of Combined Input (1–4)	(6) Labor Productivity (1–2)	(7) Capital Productivity (1–3)
USSR	6.2[a]	1.4	10.1[b]	3.6[d]	2.6	4.7	-3.9
United States	3.4	0.8	3.9[c]	1.5	1.9	2.6	-0.5
Denmark	3.4	0.6	3.9[c]	1.4	1.9	2.8	-0.5
France	4.7	0.2	3.4[c]	1.0	3.7	4.5	1.3
West Germany	7.3	1.7	5.4[c]	2.7	4.5	5.6	1.9
United Kingdom	2.4	0.4	2.3[c]	0.8	1.6	2.0	0.1
Italy	6.0	0.8	2.5[c]	1.3	4.7	5.2	3.5
Norway	3.5	-.1	3.4[c]	0.8	2.7	3.6	0.1
Netherlands	4.6	0.9	4.0[c]	1.7	2.8	3.7	0.6
Japan[e]	10.0	1.7	9.8	3.8	6.2	8.3	0.2

SOURCES: Panel A: Moorsteen and Powell, *The Soviet Capital Stock*, pp. 38, 166, 315, 361–362, 365; A. Becker, R. Moorsteen, and R. Powell, *Soviet Capital Stock: Revisions and Extension, 1961–1967* (New Haven, Conn.: The Economic Growth Center, 1968), p. 11, 25, 26; Kuznets, *Economic Growth of Nations*, p. 74; Edward Denison, *Accounting for United States Economic Growth 1929–1969* (Washington, D.C.: The Brookings Institution, 1974), p. 54, p. 186; Ben J. Wattenberg, ed., *The Statistical History of the United States from Colonial Times to the Present* (New York: Basic Books, 1976), pp. 257–258. Panel B: Kuznets, p. 74; Abram Bergson, *Planning and Productivity Under Soviet Socialism* (New York: Columbia University Press, 1968), pp. 53, 94; Edward Denison and William Chung, *How Japan's Economy Grew so Fast* (Washington, D.C.: The Brookings Institution, 1976), pp. 19, 31.

[a] 1937 prices.

[b] Total fixed capital (average of net and gross stock for the USSR).

[c] Reproducible capital, average of gross and net stock.

[d] Combined using weights of 0.75 and 0.25 for labor and capital respectively.

[e] 1953–1971.

that the Soviet Union distinguishes itself from the United States and other countries by a more rapid growth of both labor and capital—2.2 percent and 7.4 percent, respectively between 1928 and 1966. Again, the exception is postwar Japan, which generated input growth rates comparable to the USSR's. This reinforces our earlier point that one would expect more rapid Soviet output growth because of the more rapid growth of inputs—thus our hesitancy to use growth as our sole performance criterion. In the USSR, about 65 percent of long-term growth (column 1 ÷ column 4, panel A) is accounted for by growth of inputs, whereas in the United States and other countries (the United Kingdom is somewhat of an exception), a much smaller portion of growth can be attributed to the growth of inputs. The significance of this pattern is that Soviet growth has tended to be quite dependent upon an expanding labor force and capital stock, rather than upon expanding output per unit of input. Thus Soviet growth has tended to be *extensive* (based upon expanding inputs) rather than *intensive* (based upon better utilization of inputs)—a rather expensive growth pattern in terms of economic costs, for capital is expanded at the expense of current consumption and labor is expanded at the cost of leisure.

Can one argue that rapid input growth forced the USSR into an extensive growth pattern? The example of Japan is instructive, for Japan was able to combine rapid input growth with a relatively intensive growth pattern. Some 60 percent of Japanese postwar growth is explained by increasing output per unit of input.

Turning to the rate of growth of output per unit of combined input (column 5), we see that the long-term Soviet rate (1928 to 1966) is perhaps somewhat below, or roughly equivalent to, the long-term productivity growth rates in the United States, France, Canada, and Norway. It is difficult to generalize on the basis of such narrow differences because the impact of wartime destruction on Soviet productivity is difficult to gauge, because such estimates are quite sensitive to measurement errors, and because the use of synthetic factor weights for the USSR requires that a margin of error be included. As far as the 1950–1962 period is concerned, while the annual rate of growth of output per unit of combined input in the Soviet Union—2.6 percent—exceeded the American rate of 1.9 percent, it was only average as far as Western Europe was concerned, being well exceeded by France, West Germany, and Italy, and dwarfed by the Japanese rate.

The same conclusion holds for the relative rate of growth of labor productivity in the Soviet Union (column 6). The long-term growth of Soviet labor productivity (3.3 percent annually) is slightly above the average rates in the other countries examined (but well above the United Kingdom). Soviet labor productivity growth in the postwar period was extremely rapid (4.7 percent annually) and far exceeded the American rate. It matched the growth in France, West Germany, and Italy but was dwarfed by the Japanese rate of 8.3 percent.

Trends in Soviet capital productivity relative to the other countries (the rate of growth of output per unit of capital input) are interesting to note. The long-term growth rate of Soviet capital productivity is −1.9 percent annually, which indicates a rising capital-output ratio over the long-run. Of the surveyed countries, none has a long-term negative rate of growth of capital productivity, although the United States and Denmark registered negative rates of small magnitude during the postwar period. The declining productivity of the Soviet capital stock could perhaps be partially explained by the law of diminishing returns (in view of the very rapid growth of Soviet capital relative to labor),[24] and it could also possibly be an indication of the inefficient capital utilization discussed in the section on investment choice (Chapter 6).

In sum, both the long-term and early postwar (1950–1962) comparisons show Soviet dynamic efficiency, as measured indirectly by the rate of growth of output per unit of combined input, to be neither exceptionally large nor small when compared to trends in the United States and other industrialized Western countries. Instead, Soviet productivity performance could be described as average. What these figures do indicate quite clearly is the extent to which the fast Soviet growth rate may be attributable to the policy of rapidly expanding inputs. The impersonal statistics of input and output growth rates veil a very significant point concerning long-term Soviet economic growth. The relatively low proportion of output growth explained by productivity growth means that Soviet growth was of the "high cost" variety. Rapid growth rates of labor and capital occasion significant sacrifice from the population in the form of lessened consumption, leisure, and "home production." If the USSR had been able to grow as "intensively" as the industrialized market economies (let us say two-thirds of output growth accounted for by productivity growth), then the same long-term rate of economic growth could have been achieved with considerably less sacrifice demanded of the population. The USSR-Japanese postwar productivity comparison is notable, for it illustrates this point well. Both countries experienced roughly comparable input growth rates (equal sacrifice); yet the Japanese output growth rate was almost 4 percentage points above that of the Soviet Union. One cannot argue *a priori* that the Japanese experience is representative of capitalism under conditions of rapid input growth (just as one cannot argue that the USSR is representative of command socialism), but the Japanese counterexample must be recognized.

Comparisons of productivity growth from the mid-1960s to the present cannot yet be made, pending a major new study of productivity growth in the West. What has happened in the Soviet Union since 1966 is a matter of record however. From 1966 to 1970, the rate of growth of output per unit of

[24] M. L. Weitzman, "Soviet Postwar Growth and Capital–Labor Substitution," *American Economic Review*, vol. 60, no. 4 (September 1970), 676–692.

combined factor input continued at around 2 percent per annum. Thereafter, productivity growth declined and became zero (or even negative) after 1973.[25] The productivity figures cited so far are for the economy as a whole and include the productivity performance of low priority sectors such as trade and services (and agriculture, which we have noted is no longer such a low priority area of the Soviet economy). It is therefore crucial to establish whether the economywide productivity pattern of the USSR applies to its top priority sector—industry—as well.

There has been a substantial debate in Western literature concerning the productivity performance of postwar Soviet industry, principally directed toward an explanation of its declining rate of growth.[26] This discussion is highly technical and involves debates over the appropriate measurement of industrial output and the specification of Soviet industrial technology (via econometric and other methods), but the crux of the debate can be summarized in a relatively simple fashion. Throughout the postwar era, industrial capital has grown at a much more rapid rate than industrial labor (from 1960 to 1970, labor at 3 percent and capital at 10 percent per annum).[27] With such divergent rates of input growth, how successfully capital can be substituted for labor depends upon the technology ("production function") of Soviet industry. If capital can be easily substituted for labor, then these divergent rates should not impair the growth of output. If, however, it becomes increasingly difficult to substitute capital for labor (the technical measure is called the "elasticity of substitution"),[28] then one

[25] National Foreign Assessment Center, *Handbook of Economic Statistics 1979*, ER79-10274, Washington, D.C., August 1979, p. 65. The figures have been reweighted in accordance with Table 31.

[26] This discussion was spurred by Martin Weitzman's seminal paper of 1970. See Weitzman, "Soviet Postwar Growth," pp. 676–692. Contributors to this debate are Padma Desai, "The Production Function and Technical Change in Postwar Soviet Industry," *American Economic Review*, vol. 66, no. 3 (June 1976), 372–381; Stanislaw Gomulka, "Soviet Postwar Industrial Growth, Capital-Labor Substitution, and Technical Changes: A Reexamination," in Z. M. Fallenbuchl, ed., *Economic Development in the Soviet Union and Eastern Europe* (New York: Praeger, 1976); Steven Rosefielde and C. A. Lovell, "The Impact of Adjusted Factor Cost Valuation on the CES Interpretation of Postwar Soviet Economic Growth," *Economica*, vol. 44 (November 1977), 381–392; Steven Rosefielde, "Index Numbers and the Computation of Factor Productivity: A Further Appraisal," *Review of Income and Wealth*, forthcoming; Abram Bergson, "Notes on the Production Function in Soviet Postwar Industrial Growth," *Journal of Comparative Economics*, vol. 3, no. 2 (June 1979), 116–126.

[27] National Foreign Assessment Center, *Handbook of Economic Statistics 1979*, p. 65; F. Douglas Whitehouse and Ray Converse, "Soviet Industry: Recent Performance and Future Prospects," in Joint Economic Committee, *Soviet Economy in a Time of Change* (Washington, D.C.: U.S. Government Printing Office, 1979), vol. 1, pp. 402–422.

[28] *A simple technical explanation of the substitution problem is as follows. The increase in output (dQ)* can be decomposed (assuming a linear homogeneous production function and other "usual" assumptions concerning the shape of the production function) into that increase due to increase in labor (*L*) and capital (*K*) inputs and a residual due to technical progress (*T*). Thus:

would expect a declining pattern of output growth. The measurement of the elasticity of substitution of Soviet industry is a complicated theoretical and econometric matter, as the debate over this issue suggests, and competing estimates have been offered, most of which suggest that Soviet industrial technology does not allow "easy" substitution of capital for labor. The whole point of this exercise is to demonstrate that the declining rate of growth of industrial output may (partially or fully) be the consequence of growing substitution difficulties rather than the result of declining productivity performance per se.

The relevant issue is: what has been the relative productivity performance of Soviet industry (the branch of highest official priority) relative to the industrialized capitalist economies? This appears to be the crucial test of the productivity performance of the Soviet planned economy. In this regard, Abram Bergson has demonstrated that even if one uses a wide range of estimates of Soviet industrial technology (encompassing all positions in the debate), the annual growth rate of productivity has been roughly equal to the disappointing records of the United States and the United Kingdom (1955–1970) and well below the other industrialized countries.[29] Insofar as the growth rate of industrial output in the USSR was higher than that of the industrialized countries,[30] this again points to a highly extensive pattern of

---

$$dQ = \frac{\delta Q}{\delta L} dL + \frac{\delta Q}{\delta K} dK + dT$$

Dividing through by Q yields:

$$\frac{dQ}{Q} = \eta_L \frac{dL}{L} + \eta_K \frac{dK}{K} + \frac{dT}{T}$$

where $\eta_L = \frac{\delta D}{\delta L} \cdot \frac{L}{Q}$ and $\eta_K = \frac{\delta D}{\delta K} \cdot \frac{K}{Q}$

are the partial elasticities of output with respect to each factor input. If the elasticity of substitution is less than unity, then it follows (Weitzman, "Soviet Postwar Growth," p. 679) that η_L will increase if K grows more rapidly than L (definitely true in the Soviet case). Thus the weight of the slower growing factor input (L) increases over time, while that of the faster growing input (K) declines. The growth rate of combined factor inputs declines over time, therefore, partially (or fully) offsetting the decline in the rate of growth of output.

[29] Bergson, "Notes on the Production Function," p. 124. For example, Bergson finds the range of possible rates of growth of factor productivity in Soviet industry (1955–1970) to run from 1.6 percent to 2.3 percent per annum, depending upon the elasticity of substitution and the method of calculating the rate of return to capital. Using the same procedures, Bergson calculates the following ranges for other countries (1955–1970):

United States	1.5 (no variation)
France	3.6–3.9
West Germany	3.2–3.6
United Kingdom	1.8–2.2
Italy	4.2–4.7
Japan	5.9–7.0

[30] National Foreign Assessment Center, *Handbook of Economic Statistics 1979*, p. 30.

growth for Soviet industry. Since 1970, the rate of growth of Soviet industrial productivity has declined even further.[31]

In sum, one would have to conclude that the rate of growth of factor productivity throughout the era of central planning has been at best average, relative to the industrialized countries. This conclusion applies to the priority industry sector as well as to the economywide figures. Insofar as the long-term growth of Soviet output has been above that of the industrialized countries (with the exception of Japan), this means that the Soviet growth advantage is the consequence of more rapid input growth and that Soviet economic growth has been much more extensive than in the capitalist West.

SOVIET STATIC EFFICIENCY

Not only is the changing efficiency of an economy over time—dynamic efficiency—a valuable performance criterion, but one might also consider its efficiency at one point in time—*static efficiency*. The two concepts are interrelated in that an economy's dynamic efficiency in the long-run will determine its static efficiency at a distant point in time, and static efficiency, in turn, may have an important impact upon dynamic efficiency in the long-run. In any case, the efficiency of the economy today is a matter of concern and interest. In this section, the focus is upon the static efficiency of the Soviet economy relative to that of the United States and selected other market economies.

Static efficiency is defined intuitively by Bergson as ". . . the degree to which *equity apart* [our italics], the community is in fact able to exploit the economic opportunities that are open."[32] The degree of static efficiency therefore will depend on the available stock of technological knowledge and on the effectiveness of its utilization, both of which serve to define the economic opportunities open to the community at a given point in time.[33]

How then is the relative static efficiency of the Soviet economy to be measured? Again, as in the case of dynamic efficiency, static efficiency can only be measured indirectly by comparing the magnitude of the output that is derived from a unit of "combined" factor inputs at one point in time. It is immediately obvious from our discussion of dynamic efficiency that such

---

[31] *Ibid.*

[32] Bergson, *Planning and Productivity*, p. 15. See also Joseph S. Berliner, "The Static Efficiency of the Soviet Economy," *American Economic Review*, vol. 54, no. 2 (May 1964), 480–490.

[33] This static efficiency concept can be illustrated in the figure below using the Production Possibilities Schedule (PPS). If the economy is operating on its PPS (Point A), then it has attained maximum static efficiency. If it operates below the PPS (Point B for example), it has failed to attain maximum static efficiency. The available stock of technological knowledge will determine the location of the schedule, and an increase in this stock will move the schedule out. Thus, with an increase in the stock of technological knowledge, Point A will

"factor productivity" comparisons measure static efficiency indirectly because inputs differ in quality and some of them cannot be measured at all. In measuring output per unit of input at one point in time, differences in climate and soil fertility (an important factor in determining agricultural productivity), scale differences, cultural factors, and many other variables that may or may not affect productivity tend to be ignored, for they cannot readily be included.[34] There is yet another problem: to compute the relative magnitudes—as opposed to rates of growth—of output per unit of combined factor inputs suitable for intercountry comparisons, both output and factor inputs must be measured in a common unit. Soviet output must either be valued in foreign prices (American prices, for example) or the output of the other country must be valued in ruble prices. The same is true of combined factor inputs (land, labor, and capital). As we have shown, index number relativity will affect such measurements because output mixes and relative prices vary among economies, and what one country produces in abundance at relatively low prices will likely be produced in smaller quantities at relatively higher prices by another country. In this manner, the relative GNP of one country valued in its own prices will be smaller than when valued in the prices of another country.[35]

A further problem in the Soviet case is that combined factor inputs (capital, land, and labor), which are measured by the total cost of such inputs, cannot be measured directly because capital and land fail to generate rent and interest—under the labor theory of value—as they do under capitalism. Therefore "synthetic" capital charges must be computed by applying an "arbitrary" rate of return to the value of net capital stock, and the choice of this rate of return can significantly affect the outcome of factor productivity comparisons.[36]

---

now be below the new PPS, and if the economy is to remain statically efficient, it must advance to a higher point on the new PPS.

[34] Hanson, "East-West Comparisons," 332–343; Bergson, *Productivity and the Social System*, pp. 95–107.

[35] An illustration and explanation of this phenomenon in American–Soviet GNP comparisons is found in Robert Campbell, "Problems of United States-Soviet Economic Comparisons," in Joint Economic Committee, *Comparisons of the United States and Soviet Economies* (Washington, D.C.: U.S. Government Printing Office, 1959), part 1, pp. 13–30.

[36] Hanson, "East-West Comparisons," 340, argues that perhaps Soviet labor was (for the period in question, the early 1960s) in "excess supply" because of labor hoarding in industry and seasonal unemployment in agriculture. A low weight should therefore be attached

TABLE 32   National Income Per Unit of Combined Factor (Labor and Reproducible Capital) Inputs, 1960 U.S. Price Weights (United States = 100)

	National Income	Industry
United States	100	100
France	63	71
West Germany	65	69
United Kingdom	64	61
Italy	47	60
USSR	41	58

SOURCE: Bergson, *Productivity and the Social System: The USSR and the West* (Cambridge, Mass.: Harvard University Press, 1978), pp. 101, 111.

Despite all the shortcomings noted above, we relate Abram Bergson's estimates of national income per unit of combined factor (labor and reproducible capital) input in American prices to the Soviet Union, the United States, and several European countries in 1960 (Table 32). The United States price weighted index was chosen because Soviet factor productivity makes its best showing using this variant.

The calculations of national income per unit of factor input show that the Soviet economy in 1960 derived slightly less than 50 percent as much output per unit of combined input as did the American economy, about 65 percent as much as France, West Germany, and the United Kingdom, and slightly below the output per unit of input in Italy. When the comparison is for industry alone, the Soviet productivity ratios improve (this is reflective of the relatively poor performance of agriculture and services). USSR factor productivity in 1960 was roughly equal to that of Italy and the United Kingdom and was 80 percent that of France and West Germany. Although it is possible that a substantial portion of the computed productivity differentials could be accounted for by input quality differences[37] and by omitted factor inputs, such as land or entrepreneurship, this seems unlikely.[38]

Thus one would have to conclude that the level of output per unit of combined capital and labor input in the Soviet Union was low relative to

---

to labor and a high weight to capital. This would raise Soviet factor productivity considerably relative to the United States because the Soviet labor force is larger than the American labor force.

[37] Bergson has made adjustments for quality differences in the Soviet and American labor forces—as indicated by the larger Soviet female labor force and lower educational levels of Soviet workers. These adjustments, which are admittedly very crude, raise Soviet factor productivity relative to the United States by about 10 percentage points but fail to alter the overall conclusion of the relatively low productivity of the Soviet economy. Bergson, *The Economics of Soviet Planning*, p. 342.

[38] The major source of the low factor productivity of the Soviet economy seems to be the low productivity of the commerce and service sectors. On this, see Earl R. Brubaker, "A Sectoral Analysis of Efficiency Under Market and Plan," *Soviet Studies*, vol. 23, no. 3 (January 1972), 443.

the other countries surveyed (except Italy) in 1960. These productivity rankings have changed significantly since 1960 (The West German ratio is likely equal to that of the United States in 1980), but the Soviet Union's ranking, as we have shown above, has not changed appreciably relative to the industrialized capitalist countries. The potential sources of low Soviet productivity have been described in Chapters 5 and 6—the managerial bonus system, irrational prices, deficient investment allocation criteria, lack of incentives to innovate and to introduce new technology—and may be more severe than the sources of economic inefficiency in the industrialized West. It is interesting to note that Soviet estimates show Soviet industrial efficiency (output per production worker) to be slightly above one-half that of American industry.[39]

Just what does the low Soviet output per unit of input tell us about static efficiency in the Soviet Union? Can one attribute low productivity to weaknesses in the Soviet economic system or are factors independent of the economic system involved? On the one hand, it might be argued that low output per unit of input and low levels of economic development tend to go together, and the Soviet Union, like Italy—whose factor productivity is also low—is less developed (in terms of development indicators like per capita income and percentage of rural population) than the other countries in Table 32. Thus the Soviet productivity deficit should perhaps be regarded as a function of the low level of development of the Soviet Union and not as an indicator of its static inefficiency.[40] To determine the extent to which low Soviet static efficiency is a product of the stage of economic development requires firm information on the relationship between efficiency levels and economic development. Moreover, if one attempts to make hypothetical adjustments for the level of development, the outcome in the Soviet case depends upon which development indicator one employs. After examining this matter, Bergson concludes that "the low Soviet factor productivity does

[39] Gertrude E. Schroeder, "The Economic Reform as a Spur to Technological Progress in the USSR," *Jarbuch der Wirtschaft Osteuropas* [Yearbook of Eastern European Economics] Band 2 (Munich: Gunter Olzog Verlag, 1971), p. 346.

[40] The problem of comparing the productivity performance of two countries at different levels of development is illustrated in the figure below using the Production Possibilities Schedule (PPS). The country at a higher level of development would have a higher PPS (*aa*) than the country at a lower level of development (*bb*). Thus both countries may be operating at maximum static efficiency (at points A and B), yet the computed productivity at A will be greater than at B.

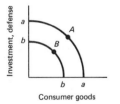

not seem fully explicable in such terms."[41] It is also not clear whether Soviet static efficiency should improve (in relative terms) as the stage of development advances, for the ability of the command economy to deal with the growing complexities of a modern economy remains to be demonstrated. The growth of Soviet factor productivity over time (Table 31) has been only average when compared with other industrialized countries; therefore the Soviet Union does not seem to have reduced its productivity gap as it gradually closed its development gap—a result that one would expect if low productivity were solely the result of low economic development.

The low level of static efficiency in the Soviet Union has evoked considerable discussion among Western students of the Soviet economy. We summarize briefly two representative points of view. On the one side, Alec Nove and Peter Wiles,[42] both English economists, argue that the Soviets deliberately sacrificed static efficiency to achieve their long-run political objectives—the restructuring of the economy, the transformation of property relations, the expansion of military power, and rapid economic growth. Static efficiency, they argue, could have been achieved only at the expense of these goals, by adopting a more gradual marginalist approach and by eliminating political control over economic decisions. Thus the static inefficiency of the Soviet economy today can be viewed as a deliberate policy decision, just as the rapid Soviet growth rate can be considered a deliberate policy choice of the Soviet leadership—with static inefficiency as the price that the Soviet leadership willingly paid for rapid economic development.

In opposition to this line of reasoning, Abram Bergson[43] argues that rapid economic development and static efficiency are not necessarily incompatible, as Nove and Wiles maintain, for an economy with greater static efficiency will produce a larger output and consequently a larger volume of savings (with the same savings rate), which will promote economic growth. Bergson does grant, however, that in a centrally planned economy, the state may opt to promote growth by autonomously increasing the savings rate through the introduction of forced savings, administrative economic controls, collectivization, and autarky—measures that may reduce static efficiency yet generate growth. If the state does so, however, it is at the expense of reduced living standards, which is in itself a significant cost to be considered in evaluating the performance of economies. According to Bergson, the basic question, therefore, should be: to what extent could similar rates of growth or slightly lower rates have been attained in the Soviet case through maximum utilization of resources (static efficiency) without sacrificing living standards?

---

[41] Bergson, *Productivity and the Social System,* p. 104.

[42] See Alec Nove, "The Politics of Economic Rationality," in Alec Nove, *Economic Rationality and Soviet Politics* (New York: Praeger, 1964), p. 53; and P. J. D. Wiles, *The Political Economy of Communism* (London: Blackwell, 1963), chap. 11.

[43] See Bergson, *Planning and Productivity,* pp. 16–19, and *The Economics of Soviet Planning,* chap. 14.

One further aspect of the relative efficiency of the Soviet economy that fails to show up in output or input measures is that such figures often indicate output per unit of *employed* labor and capital inputs.[44] Although the Soviets do not publish aggregate unemployment figures, one can probably safely assume that aggregate unemployment in the Soviet Union is less than in the United States, where unemployment occasionally rises to 8 or 9 percent of the entire labor force, with 5 percent considered as normal. Thus unemployment is a major source of inefficient resource utilization in the United States that the Soviets have largely avoided, although the Soviets do seem to suffer from "underemployment," as discussed in Chapter 6. In addition, capital capacity in the United States also tends to stand idle during downturns in the business cycle. On the other hand, it is difficult to predict the magnitude of the waste of capital resources in the Soviet Union that results from the stockpiling of fixed and working capital by the Soviet manager for the sake of building a safety factor and from poor choices of investment projects. In the American economy, such stockpiling adds to inventory costs and interest expenses, thereby reducing profits, and is therefore avoided as much as possible.

An even thornier issue in estimating factor productivity concerns the relative quality of output. Factor productivity measures relate the volume of output per unit of input, whereas the output measures (especially in the case of Soviet consumer goods) inadequately reflect the relative quality of output, which, according to numerous reports, is poor in the Soviet Union.[45] The production of a large quantity of defective goods using minimal inputs would show up well in factor productivity estimates, introducing a bias into such measures.

EQUITY OF INCOME DISTRIBUTION IN THE SOVIET UNION

A fourth performance criterion for evaluating economies is how "equitably" income is distributed among members of the population. Of all the suggested criteria, this is the most difficult to evaluate objectively because different individuals and different societies have different views on what constitutes an "equitable" or "inequitable" distribution of income. Some may argue that income is equitably distributed when divided equally; others may argue that equity requires large income differentials to reward risk, effort, and past frugality. Income derived from ownership of property is a very thorny question; in the United States, for example, large income differences among spending units result from differences in property income as opposed to wage and salary incomes. Whether it is equitable to allow such disparities in property income is a subjective judgment, yet it is crucial when contrasting equity in the Soviet Union and the United States.

[44] Hanson, "East-West Comparisons," 338.

[45] Bergson, *The Economics of Soviet Planning*, pp. 293–297, and Philip Hanson, *The Consumer in the Soviet Economy* (Evanston, Ill.: Northwestern University Press, 1968), p. 63.

In view of these issues, we suggest that the definition of "good" or "poor" income distribution must remain subjective over a fairly wide range.

The Soviets have not published much data on the distribution of income among families. This is more likely the result of the relatively low priority attached to the gathering of such information than to any official policy of secrecy. The available data on income distribution have been analyzed extensively by Alastair McCauley, Peter Wiles, Stefan Markowski, and Murray Yanowitch.[46] Although such data are far from complete and omit important income groups (the upper strata of the state and party bureaucracy, the state farmers), they do allow the researcher to draw certain conclusions. From the evidence that is available on industrial wage income, we note that Soviet wage differentials within industrial branches between high- and low-paid workers during the 1930s and early 1950s were probably greater than in the United States, but since the mid-1950s, Soviet differentials have been narrowed substantially until they are now probably smaller than American differentials. In general, the trend in recent years has been toward the concept of "equal pay for equal work," with wages to be determined by job content—working conditions, skill requirements, on-the-job incentives—rather than by some measure of productivity, which may be viewed as an attempt to introduce more equality into Soviet wage determination.[47] Such intercountry wage differential comparisons are quite crude and inexact, but the important point is that Soviet industrial wage differentials have at times been as large as in the United States. This result is in keeping with the Marxian theory of income distribution in the transitional stage of socialism, during which the workers' contribution to society should determine their share of society's output; inequality of income distribution would only be eliminated when society attained a higher stage of socialism—a state of absolute abundance—when distribution would proceed according to need.[48]

Beginning in the early 1930s, the Soviet leadership waged a consistent

---

[46] P. J. D. Wiles and Stefan Markowski, "Income Distribution Under Communism and Capitalism: Some Facts About Poland, the U.K., the USA and the USSR," *Soviet Studies*, vol. 22, nos. 3 and 4 (January and April 1971), 344–369 and 487–511; P. J. D. Wiles, *Economic Institutions Compared* (New York: Halsted Press, 1977), p. 443; Alastair McCauley, *Economic Welfare in the Soviet Union* (Madison: University of Wisconsin Press, 1979); Murray Yanowitch, *Social and Economic Inequality in the USSR* (White Plains, N.Y.: M. E. Sharpe, 1977).

[47] Leonard J. Kirsch, *Soviet Wages: Changes in Structure and Administration Since 1956* (Cambridge, Mass.: MIT Press, 1972), chaps. 1 and 8; Murray Yanowitch, "The Soviet Income Revolution," *Slavic Review*, vol. 22, no. 4 (December 1963), reprinted in Morris Bornstein and Daniel Fusfeld, eds., *The Soviet Economy*, 2nd ed. (Homewood, Ill.: Irwin, 1966), pp. 228–241; Bergson, *The Economics of Soviet Planning*, pp. 106–120; Wiles and Markowski, "Income Distribution," 501–507.

[48] Abram Bergson, "Principles of Socialist Wages," in *Essays in Normative Economics* (Cambridge, Mass.: Harvard University, Belknap Press, 1966).

battle against "equality mongering" (*uravnilovka*), a policy linked with utopian socialism and even Trotskyism. Indeed, during the 1930s, there was strong evidence of increasing inequality in the distribution of wage income, which persisted into the mid-1950s. Since the mid-1950s, there has been a remarkable decrease in such inequality. In 1956, the average wage earned by the top 10 percent of workers exceeded that of the bottom 10 percent by a factor of 4.4. By 1975, this ratio had been reduced to 2.9.[49] Although the move toward greater equality in the distribution of wage income has been justified ideologically by the "law of reimbursement,"[50] we suspect that economic considerations—namely, the greater supply of educated workers—served as the impetus for the leveling of wage incomes.

Comparisons of the *overall* distribution of income in the Soviet Union with that of other countries, both capitalist and socialist, is a risky business because of the omission of significant groups from the Soviet data and the questionable reliability of the data on included families.[51] With these reservations in mind, we cite some conclusions that we believe to be reasonably safe. The first is that the distribution of income probably became more equal between the late 1950s (1958) and the late 1960s (1967). This conclusion follows from evidence on state employees, a group accounting for 70 percent of all employment in 1967.[52] It would be surprising if such a leveling had not occurred in light of the marked reduction in industrial wage differentials during this period. The second conclusion (derived from a measure of income distribution that does cover all population groups) is that the overall distribution of money income after taxes (including income earned or retained by the farm population) in the USSR in 1967 was more unequal than in the other planned socialist economies of Eastern Europe, was about equal to the distribution of income in the "capitalist welfare states" (the United Kingdom and Sweden), and was more equal than in the capitalist nonwelfare states (United States, Canada, Italy).[53] Third, income distribution data for earlier periods are not available to make comparisons back over time. Fourth, contrary to the popular impression of the countryside, there is as much differentiation in the distribution of income among the farm population as among the city population.[54]

---

[49] Yanowitch, *Social and Economic Inequality*, p. 25.

[50] The "law of reimbursement" means that workers should receive wages sufficient to cover the normal costs of production of labor power; e.g., workers should receive sufficient income to cover their basic living requirements. *Ibid.*, pp. 27–28.

[51] McCauley, *Economic Welfare*, pp. 49–98, provides a survey of the available data on Soviet income distributions. The major omitted categories are the Soviet elite and state farm families.

[52] *Ibid.*, p. 57.

[53] This conclusion follows from McCauley, *Economic Welfare*, p. 66; and Wiles, *Economic Institution Compared*, p. 443. Also see P. J. D. Wiles, *Distribution of Income: East and West* (Amsterdam: North Holland, 1974), p. 48.

[54] McCauley, *Economic Welfare*, pp. 59–61.

The final conclusion is a striking one: namely the high incidence of "poverty" among the Soviet population, not only among the rural population and the pensioners but also among nonagricultural state employees. If one takes the Soviet's own "minimum material satisfaction budget" (the MMS budget), described as containing the "volume and structure of necessaries of life required for the reproduction of labor power among unskilled workers,"[55] then McCauley estimates that in 1967, 42 million nonagricultural employees and their dependents, 5 to 10 million state farm families, and 32 million *kolkhoznik* families had incomes at or below the MMS level. These figures add up to àn astonishing 79 million persons (or one-third of the Soviet population) living at or below the minimum material satisfaction budget. Given this large proportion, it is likely that the Soviet MMS budget is a liberal estimate of contemporary subsistence norms. However, if one adopts as the poverty norm one-half of the MMS budget, in 1967 approximately 25 million Soviet citizens were living at or below the poverty level (10 percent of the population).[56] From these figures, McCauley concludes that "there are significant lacunae in the network of support provided by Soviet social welfare programs."[57]

The cited income distribution data are based upon money incomes and fail to incorporate social services provided free of charge and perquisites (the use of official cars, dachas, foreign vacations, and other fringe benefits). Moreover, they do not include the income of top government and party officials, but the number of Soviet elite is so small (maybe 0.15 to 0.3 percent of the population[58]) that their inclusion would be unlikely to change any of the above results. Moreover, most of their income comes to them in the form of payments in kind and perquisites (Katsenelinboigen's law[59]) so that it would be difficult to incorporate them in the distribution. The distribution of noncash social consumption services (primarily education, child care, and medical services) received by Soviet workers cannot be specified with any degree of precision; such information must be culled from socioeconomic studies of workers at individual factories or municipalities. From this scattered information, it appears that noncash social services form a larger percentage of total family income among low paid workers (as would be expected) but that higher paid workers receive larger absolute benefits.

---

[55] *Ibid.*, p. 18.
[56] *Ibid.*, pp. 78–88.
[57] *Ibid.*, p. 74.
[58] M. Mathews, "Top Incomes in the USSR," in NATO Economics Directorate, *Economic Aspects of Life in the USSR* (Brussels: NATO, 1975), pp. 131–158.
[59] Aron Katsenelinboigen, p. 150. Katsenelinboigen contends that the proportion of total income received in the form of perquisites increases with the responsibility of the position. He believes this is a device used by the Soviet leadership to ensure the loyalty of high officials.

CONSUMER WELFARE IN THE SOVIET UNION

How well an economy meets the material wants and needs of its population with its *given productive capacity* is yet another way to evaluate economic performance. By "material wants and needs," we refer to those that can be satisfied through the consumption of material goods and services; items relating to mental and spiritual well-being are omitted, even though they are potentially important in determining overall welfare.

The level of consumer satisfaction in any given country must be evaluated in terms of existing productive capacity, for countries rich in terms of productive potential would naturally be expected to provide higher living standards than poor countries. This fact should be kept in mind throughout this section.

If one attempts to measure the level of consumer satisfaction in the Soviet Union relative to that of the United States or Western Europe, one encounters difficulties. First, the most frequently used measure of the relative level of consumer satisfaction is the per capita quantities of consumer goods and services made available to the consumer. According to this standard, either per capita quantities of selected consumer goods and services or aggregate per capita consumption may be compared. Both measures have their own deficiencies, aside from the almost impossible task of measuring quality differences. If one compares per capita consumption of selected commodities, one must realize that consumption patterns vary according to the level of development and cultural differences. For example, the per capita consumption of wheat products in the Soviet Union exceeds that of the United States, but the per capita consumption of most personal services and consumer durables in the United States exceeds that of the USSR. In this example, these differences are explained to a great extent by differences in per capita income, which means that single consumption indicators can provide misleading impressions of consumer welfare. The aggregative measure—total per capita consumption—must be computed in value terms; therefore, in comparisons between two countries, the prices of one country must be used to weigh the quantities of consumer goods and services available in both countries. Yet relative consumer prices vary among countries: commodities that are important consumption items in one country (where the price is relatively cheap) tend to be unimportant in another country (where the price is relatively expensive). Thus the relative per capita consumption level of one country will be *higher* when valued in the prices of a second country and vice versa—another example of index number relativity.

A further problem in the measurement of consumer satisfaction is that *average* consumption figures veil the underlying distribution of goods and services among the population, and the nature of this distribution has a great deal to do with the level of consumer satisfaction. Prominent Western economists have argued that relative, not absolute, consumption levels are most important in determining consumer satisfaction, for individuals tend to judge their own economic well-being relative to the level of living of their neighbors.[60] If income is distributed fairly evenly, the changes of feeling deprived relative to someone else are smaller than if income is unevenly distributed. For example, in 1957, the average personal income of the poorest fifth of American families was about the same as *average* income in the Soviet Union.[61] Is then the proper conclusion that the American poor are as "well off" as the average Soviet citizen? In terms of how well both are provisioned with physical quantities of goods and services (index number problems aside), the answer may be yes. Yet in terms of perceived welfare levels, the answer is probably no, because the American poor would feel relatively deprived because of much higher living standards around them.

The point of this discussion is that once a relatively comfortable standard of physical subsistence is reached, absolute measures of living standards may reflect the state of mental satisfaction less than relative measures do. In the foregoing section, we noted that a surprisingly large proportion of the Soviet population does not earn an income high enough to have a minimum material satisfaction budget. Does this mean that poverty is rampant in the Soviet Union? The answer is probably no, as perceived by the Soviet populace—a population that has experienced significant increases in its level of material well-being in recent years and that would be inclined to judge its contemporary well-being relative to its past experience. Insofar as the minimum material satisfaction budget has been recognized (tolerated?) by Soviet officialdom, this reflects the dissatisfaction of committees of specialists (health officials and sociologists) with existing consumption levels, which is itself a telling point.

Another problem in evaluating Soviet consumer welfare involves the relatively large share of communal consumption in the Soviet Union. Communal consumption—for example, communal services such as health care and education, provided free of charge—accounts for a substantial share of total consumption in the Soviet Union.[62] Such services are provided free of charge and are not subject to a market test as to the value of the satisfaction they provide. In fact, their value is determined by the costs of supplying them. Thus it is difficult to compare the consumption levels of countries having different shares of communal consumption.

---

[60] James Duesenberry, *Income, Saving and the Theory of Consumer Behavior* (Cambridge, Mass.: Harvard University Press, 1949).

[61] Janet G. Chapman, "Consumption," in Abram Bergson and Simon Kuznets, eds., *Economic Trends in the Soviet Union* (Cambridge, Mass.: Harvard University Press, 1963).

[62] Between 1937 and 1964, communal consumption accounted for between 8 and 9 percent of Soviet GNP. In the United States, it accounts for about 3 percent (1956). See Bergson, *The Real National Income of Soviet Russia*, p. 237; Becker, *Soviet National Income*, p. 220; Chapman, "Consumption," p. 263.

The foregoing discussion points to the loose relationship between the consumption of commodities and the level of satisfaction derived therefrom; yet it is perceived satisfaction that is of most interest. Thus it is possible to argue (as the Soviets have done) that the underprovisioning of the Soviet consumer relative to American or Western Europen standards does not imply lower levels of satisfaction because of the new social consciousness of the Soviet people, who will accept this as a necessary cost of building socialism and whose recognition of their patriotism enhances their perceived level of welfare. The validity of such arguments is well outside the scope of this work.

With the above reservations in mind, we present estimates of total per capita consumption in the Soviet Union (including communal services) as a percent of total per capita consumption in the United States and several other countries (Table 33). All figures are calculated in United States prices to present the Soviet figures in the most favorable light (in view of index number relativity).

The striking feature of Soviet per capita consumption is that it is quite low relative to the United States, the United Kingdom, France, and West Germany, both in 1955 and 1970. In 1955, it was roughly one-third of the American level and one-half of the British, French, and West German levels, and was more than three-quarters of the Italian level. Between 1955 and 1970, there was a catching up in relative terms. By 1970, Soviet

TABLE 33   Total Per Capita Consumption and Per Capita GNP of the Soviet Union as a Percent of the United States and Other Countries, 1955 and 1970 (valued in United States prices)

USSR as a Percent of:	1955		1970	
	Total Per Capita Consumption	GNP Per Capita	Total Per Capita Consumption	GNP Per Capita
United States	27	36	47	60
United Kingdom	41	53	67	88
France	47	59	61	73
West Germany	48	57	69	75
Italy	79	94	86	109
Japan	—	—	84	88

SOURCES: Joint Economic Committee, *Economic Performance and the Military Burden in the Soviet Union* (Washington, D.C.: U.S. Government Printing Office, 1970), pp. 14, 97; United Nations, *Yearbook of National Accounts Statistics* (1978); M. Gilbert and Associates, *Comparative National Products and Price levels* (Paris: Organization for European Economic Cooperation), p. 36; Irving Kravis et al., *A System of International Comparisons of Gross Product and Purchasing Power* (Baltimore and London: Johns Hopkins University Press, 1975), pp. 11, 189; Imogene Edwards, Margaret Hughes, and James Noren, "U.S. and USSR: Comparisons of GNP," in Joint Economic Committee, *Soviet Economy in a Time of Change* (Washington, D.C.: U.S. Government Printing Office, 1979), vol. 1, pp. 378–379. The USSR-U.S. 1976 relatives are backcast to 1970, using GNP and consumption indexes.

per capita consumption was one-half the United States, 60 to 70 percent of the British, French, and West German figures, and 86 percent of the Italian. Data are available for Japan for 1970, with the Soviet level 84 percent of the Japanese.

We suggested above that consumer welfare must be evaluated not in terms of absolute magnitudes but relative to productive capacity. Thus one should ask to what extent the relatively low Soviet per capita consumption is a consequence of relatively low per capita GNP. Table 33 indicates that the major portion of the low Soviet per capita consumption can be accounted for by low per capita GNP, which shows that even if the Soviets had devoted the same proportion of their resources to consumption as the other countries shown, there would still be a substantial "gap" in Soviet per capita consumption.[63] In all cases, Soviet per capita consumption compares much less favorably than per capita GNP, which shows that the Soviets directed a relatively larger share of total resources to nonconsumption items such as investment and defense, and this was of course an administrative decision. In the Japanese case, the difference is small because of the similar allocation of resources in Japan and the USSR. As Table 34 indicates, the Soviets devote a much larger share of GNP to investment than the major Western countries. The sole exception is Japan, which devotes only a negligible proportion of its resources to defense.

The reader should now well understand the importance of using multiple criteria to evaluate economies. The Soviet economy grew at such a rapid pace largely because it was decided to devote labor and capital resources to this pursuit. Per capita consumption remained below levels attainable from Soviet productive capacity as a consequence of these policies—thus a trade-off between growth and consumption. In a long-run sense, the two are not incompatible, for economic growth will raise productive capacity, which can eventually be used to raise consumption levels.

The structure of Soviet consumption reflects both the relatively low per capita income of the Soviet Union and the efforts of the state to educate and keep the population healthy. Relative to the United States, Soviet per capita consumption compares more favorably in necessities such as basic food products and health care than in nonnecessities such as durable goods. For example, in 1977, Soviet per capita consumption of food products was 54 percent of the United States (up from 39 percent in 1955); education was 75 percent and health expenditures were 37 percent of the United States (both down from 1955). On the other hand, expenditures for consumer durables were only 13 percent of the United States 1977 level.[64] A few individ-

[63] For further evidence on the Soviet consumption "gap," see Paul Gregory, *Socialist and Nonsocialist Industrialization Patterns* (New York: Praeger, 1971), p. 152.
[64] Edwards, Hughes, and Noren, "U.S. and USSR," p. 385.

TABLE 34   Gross Investment Expenditures as a Percent of GNP, USSR and Selected Countries, 1964 and 1978 (Soviet data in factor cost, other data in market prices)

	1964	1978
USSR	35	31
United States	17	16
France	23	21
West Germany	28	22
United Kingdom	19	18
Italy	22	19
Japan	39	33

SOURCES: Abraham Becker, *Soviet National Income, 1958–1964* (Berkeley: University of California Press, 1969), pp. 220, 271; National Foreign Assessment Center, *Handbook of Economic Statistics 1979*, p. 29.

ual comparisons bring this point home. In 1968, the average caloric intake of grain products and potatoes in the USSR exceeded that of the United States; yet the caloric intake of meat and fish was less than 50 percent of the United States figure, and this figure does not take quality differences into consideration—which may be substantial. In 1968, there were 412 automobiles per 1000 persons in the United States; the Soviet figure was 5 per 1000. On the other hand, in the Soviet Union, the number of doctors per person, hospital beds per person, and teachers per person exceeded that of the United States. The Soviet consumer remains relatively deprived as far as housing is concerned. The 1969 per capita availability of 77 square feet of housing space, although it represented a 20 percent improvement over 1960, was still well below the 97 square-foot minimum standard required for health and decency established by Soviet authorities.[65]

Let us now consider to what extent the Soviets have been able to reduce their per capita consumption gap between 1928 and the present. This is an important question because the current low Soviet consumption level would seem less significant if it was being steadily eliminated. We therefore compare the long-term growth rate of per capita consumption (including communal services) in the Soviet Union during the plan era with comparable United States rates (Table 35).

Table 35 indicates the very respectable performance of Soviet per capita consumption during the plan era as measured against long-term United States rates. The long-term Soviet rate of 2.8 percent (1928–1978) far ex-

[65] All of the above figures are from David W. Bronson and Barbara S. Severin, "Consumer Welfare," in Joint Economic Committee, *Economic Performance and the Military Burden in the Soviet Union* (Washington, D.C.: U.S. Government Printing Office, 1970), pp. 97–98. For more recent figures, see National Foreign Assessment Center, *Handbook of Economic Statistics 1979*, pp. 16–17.

TABLE 35   Annual Rates of Growth of Per Capita Consumption: USSR, 1928–1978—United States, 1869–1978 (including communal services)

USSR		United States	
1928–1978	2.8	1869–1873 to 1927–1929	2.4
1928–1937	1.1	1929–1978	1.7
1950–1969	4.5	1950–1969	2.3
1970–1978	2.5	1970–1978	2.7

SOURCES: Janet G. Chapman, "Consumption" in Abraham Bergson and Simon Kuznets, eds., *Economic Trends in the Soviet Union* (Cambridge, Mass.: Harvard University Press, 1963), pp. 238, 245–246; David W. Bronson and Barbara S. Severin, "Consumer Welfare" in Joint Economic Committee, *Economic Performance and the Military Burden in the Soviet Union* (Washington, D.C.: U.S. Government Printing Office, 1970), p. 97; M. Elizabeth Denton, "Soviet Consumer Policy: Trends and Prospects," in Joint Economic Committee, *Soviet Economy in a Time of Change* (Washington, D.C.: U.S. Government Printing Office, 1979), vol. 1, p. 768. The Soviet figures are in 1937 factor cost for the 1928 to 1958 period and in 1955 weights for 1958 to 1969. For the period 1970–1978, 1978 prices are used. The United States figures are from *Historical Statistics of the United States, Colonial Times to 1957*, pp. 7, 144; *Statistical Abstract of the U.S., 1970*, p. xiii; *The Economic Report of the President, 1979*, p. 184. The 1869–1873 to 1927–1929 figures are in 1929 dollars. The 1929–1978 figures are in 1958 dollars.

ceeds the comparable rate for the United States during the same period. It should be noted, however, that the United States rate from the Civil War to the Great Depression (1869–1873 to 1927–1929) compares more favorably with the Soviet plan era rate. The rate of growth of Soviet consumption during the first two Five Year Plans (1928–1937) was very slow compared with the postwar rate. Thus the fairly high long-term Soviet growth rate of per capita consumption is an average of the slow growth of per capita consumption during the 1930s and of the rapid growth of the postwar period.

To sum up trends in Soviet per capita consumption, we note that per capita consumption in the Soviet Union is low compared to consumption levels in the United States and Western Europe. The major portion of the Soviet consumption gap can be accounted for by low per capita income, but some of it is attributable to the administrative decision to devote a relatively larger proportion of total resources to investment. The pattern of Soviet consumption also reflects the decision of Soviet authorities to deemphasize nonnecessities and to concentrate on essential goods and health and education, all of which are required to maintain and increase the productivity of the Soviet labor force. Looking at trends in Soviet consumption over time, one must conclude that the rate of growth of per capita consumption in the Soviet Union during the plan era has been quite respectable, far exceeding comparable United States rates. If this trend continues, the consumption gap will be gradually reduced in the future, just as it has been since the end of World War II. In this sense, there may be some merit to the Soviet argument that living standards can be raised over the long-run by sacrificing current consumption.

ECONOMIC STABILITY (SECURITY) IN THE SOVIET UNION

The ability of an economic system to provide economic stability to its population is yet another indicator of economic performance. Economic stability is an amorphous concept, but it conveys the notion of "reasonable" stability of employment and real incomes. The economic stability (or security) of a nation's citizens can be threatened by declines in real output (or a declining rate of growth of real output), resulting in significant losses of jobs, and by inflation, which leads to substantial declines in the real incomes of population subgroups. The sources of economic instability can be either internal or external. In the latter category, one would have inflation transmitted into a country from abroad or by the interruption of petroleum deliveries. Economic stability, like consumer welfare, is a relative concept. In democratic countries, the electorate will determine "acceptable" and "unacceptable" levels of economic instability. In command systems, this function will be performed by political authorities, who may allow themselves to be influenced by public opinion. Different societies will have different attitudes, determined in part by past experience. American society is said to be more tolerant of inflation than German society because of Germany's experience with hyperinflation in the 1920s.

Three empirical measures are typically employed to quantify the degree of economic instability: the unemployment rate, the rate of inflation, and fluctuations in the rate of growth of real output. These three measures are not independent, as the well-known trade-off between employment and inflation attests. Which stability goals to pursue is therefore an important decision for a society to make. How well has the Soviet economy succeeded in providing economic stability, as measured by these three indicators? We begin with unemployment.

One has little notion of how much involuntary unemployment there is in the Soviet Union, as Soviet authorities claim to have "liquidated" unemployment in the early 1930s.[66] Such Soviet claims are exaggerated, for no society can completely eliminate unemployment. Frictional unemployment (the time spent unemployed while in the process of changing jobs) will be present at all times. In the Soviet Union in 1967–1968, the average period spent between jobs was 33 days for all workers and 47 days for female workers.[67] Because unemployment is said to no longer exist, there is no unem-

---

[66] The Soviets delight in contrasting the absence of unemployment in the USSR since October 1, 1930, with the high unemployment rates in the capitalist world. For an example, see *SSSR v tsifrakh v 1977 g.* [The USSR in figures 1977], (Moscow: Statistika, 1978), pp. 78–79.
[67] McCauley, *Economic Welfare*, p. 209.

ployment pay in the USSR. However, by any conceivable measure, the amount of involuntary unemployment in the Soviet Union is small relative to that of capitalist market economies.[68] Soviet law requires citizens of working age to be employed unless there are strong reasons against it, and in 1970, 92.4 percent of the working age population was either employed or engaged in full-time studies. The remaining 7.6 percent were either engaged in child care activities, incapacitated, or were working on private agricultural plots.[69]

One would thus have to conclude that Soviet citizens do have a greater degree of economic security with regard to job protection. This conclusion should come as no surprise to the reader, for we have already pointed out (Chapter 6) that Soviet planners have engaged throughout the plan era in deliberate full employment planning. Enterprises and local authorities are given quotas for hiring new entrants into the job market; national and regional planners must ensure the full utilization of labor resources. Unsuccessful enterprises are not allowed to fail, thereby eliminating a major source of job loss under capitalism. The guaranteeing of job security has not been without costs, however. Unproductive workers cannot be laid off except under extreme circumstances, even if the enterprise (which typically hoards labor anyway) desired to do so. That Soviet authorities have been willing to engage in the Shchekino experiment (Chapter 9) since 1967 indicates an understanding of the efficiency and incentive costs of total job security. However, the major incentive lever remains the differential wage, not the threat of dismissal.

The Soviet Union has to this point avoided episodes of negative real growth, unlike its capitalist competitors, who have experienced a depression in the 1930s and a series of recessions in the postwar era. The Soviet economy has, however, had "growth recessions," that is, episodes of reductions in the rate of growth, and as we demonstrated earlier in this chapter, the rate of Soviet growth has been declining steadily in recent years. In general, the command economies of the Soviet Union and Eastern Europe, although they do experience cycles in output and trade,[70] have been able to avoid the larger fluctuations suffered periodically by the capitalist world. This result is also not unexpected, given the manner in which the Soviet economy is planned and managed. Planners ensure that there is no deficiency in aggregate demand; output is credited to the enterprise (which is not permitted to fail), even if the output remains unsold. Workers continue to hold their jobs and receive their paychecks even if they are re-

---

[68] For an attempt to estimate the Soviet unemployment rate, see P. J. D. Wiles, "A Note on Soviet Unemployment in US Definitions," *Soviet Studies*, vol. 23, no. 2 (April 1972), 619–628.

[69] D. I. Valentei and M. Liatukh, eds., *Vosproizvodstvo naseleniia sotsialisticheskikh stran* [Reproduction of population of socialist countries], (Moscow: Statistika, 1977), p. 37.

[70] For references, consult footnote 3.

dundant. Under these circumstances, real output will continue to grow unless factor productivity declines to such an extent to offset increases in factor inputs. Thus negative real growth would require severe declines in productivity—a phenomenon that has not occurred to this point but may in the future.

The measurement of the rate of inflation in the Soviet Union is a matter of great complexity. The official retail price index claims that consumer prices were basically unchanged between 1955 and 1978. The official wholesale price index for industrial output shows an increase of less than 10 percent between 1955 and 1978.[71] If accurate, these indexes reveal a remarkable degree of price stability in a period (1970–1978) when retail prices were rising elsewhere at annual rates of from 5 percent (West Germany) to 13 percent (the United Kingdom).[72] Western analysts distrust official Soviet price statistics for a variety of reasons, the most important being the lack of representativeness of included products, the omission of commodities sold in relatively free markets, the common practice of claiming nonexistent quality improvements to raise prices, and so on.[73] Moreover, Western authorities (and Soviet émigrés) point to signs of repressed inflation—queues, waiting lists, and growing savings accounts "forced" by the inadequate supplies of consumer goods—as further indicators that Soviet inflation has been grossly understated by official statistics.[74]

The relevant question here is the Soviet Union's relative performance vis-à-vis the industrialized West, and there is fairly firm evidence that the Soviet inflation rate has been well below that of the West. Recalculations of official Soviet price indexes (which probably understate Soviet inflation) show retail and wholesale prices rising at some 1.5 percent annually after 1960,[75] and this rate (even if understated somewhat) is only a small fraction

---

[71] *Narodnoe khoziaistvo SSSR v 1978 g.* [The national economy of the USSR in 1978], (Moscow: Statistika, 1979), pp. 138, 448.

[72] National Foreign Assessment Center, *Handbook of Economic Statistics 1979*, pp. 46–47.

[73] Moris Bornstein, "Soviet Price Statistics," in Vladimir G. Treml and John P. Hardt, eds., *Soviet Economic Statistics* (Durham, N.C.: Duke University Press, 1972), pp. 355–376.

[74] There is a substantial literature on this subject. See for example, Bronson and Severin, "Consumer Welfare"; Keith Bush, "Soviet Inflation," in M. Yves Laulan, ed., *Banking, Money and Credit in Eastern Europe* (Brussels: NATO, 1973); Aron Katsenelinboigen, "Disguised Inflation in the Soviet Union," in NATO Economics Directorate, *Economic Aspects of Life in the USSR* (Brussels: NATO, 1975), pp. 101–109; Gertrude E. Schroeder, "Consumer Goods Availability and Repressed Inflation in the Soviet Union," in NATO Economics Directorate, *Economic Aspects of Life in the USSR* (Brussels: NATO, 1975).

[75] James E. Steiner, *Inflation in Soviet Industry and Machine-Building and Metalworking*, Office of Strategic Research, Washington, D.C., SRM78–10142, 1978, p. 44; Gertrude E. Schroeder and Barbara S. Severin, "Soviet Consumption and Income Policies in Perspective," in Joint Economic Committee, *Soviet Economy in a New Perspective* (Washington, D.C.: U.S. Government Printing Office, 1976), p. 631; M. Elizabeth Denton, "Soviet Consumer Policy: Trends and Prospects," in Joint Economic Committee, *Soviet Economy in a Time of Change* (Washington, D.C.: U.S. Government Printing Office, 1979), vol. 1, p. 766.

of the inflation rate in the industrialized capitalist nations. Such independent studies demonstrate that Soviet claims of total price stability are grossly exaggerated, but they fail to yield more than modest rates of price increase. Nor would one expect rapid inflation if the official wage series are to be believed. Between 1960 and 1977, wages rose at an annual rate of 3.9 percent.[76] It only takes an annual growth rate of labor productivity of 2.4 percent to yield an annual growth rate of unit labor costs of 1.5 percent, the inflation rate revealed by independent studies. Official Soviet wage policy over the years has been to permit wage increases equivalent to or below the rate of growth of labor productivity; thus wage inflation as a source of inflation has been held to moderate levels.

There is little doubt that repressed inflation was substantial during the period from 1929 to the mid-1950s, and individual products (automobiles, cooperative housing, imported consumer goods) remain in excess demand to the present day. Recent empirical studies of the savings behavior of Soviet households have revealed, however, that the accumulation of personal savings since the mid-1950s has followed normal patterns of rational consumer behavior and is not necessarily a sign of repressed inflation.[77] Soviet financial authorities are apparently less convinced than Western analysts on this point; these savings are regarded as postponed demand that could descend unexpectedly at any point on the consumer market or into the second economy.[78]

The fact that the Soviet economy was not caught up in the worldwide inflation of the 1970s may be regarded as justification of the long-standing pattern of trade aversion and economic independence. There are growing signs, however, that the domestic economy is coming to be influenced by capitalist inflation. The transmission mechanism is still not clearly defined, but Soviet pricing authorities now tend to pass on world market price increases of luxuries to the domestic consumer. Moreover, internal pricing decisions are influenced by world prices of machinery and oil. In general, there is an increased willingness to accept world market prices as the standard for domestic pricing decisions.[79] The point should be emphasized, however, that Soviet authorities are still in a position to insulate the domestic economy from external price disturbances if they choose to do so (for example, in the case of subsidized food prices).

[76] *Narodnoe khoziaistvo SSSR v 1978 g.*, p. 372.

[77] Joyce Pickersgill, "Soviet Household Saving Behavior," *Review of Economics and Statistics*, vol. 58, no. 2 (May 1976), 139–147.

[78] For a discussion of current Soviet attitudes toward accumulated savings, see Schroeder and Severin, "Soviet Consumption," pp. 637–639.

[79] Vladimir G. Treml, "Foreign Trade and the Soviet Economy: Changing Parameters and Interrelationships," in Egon Neuberger and Laura Tyson, eds., *Transmission and Response: The Impact of International Disturbances on the Soviet Union and Eastern Europe* (New York: Pergamon Press, 1980).

SOVIET ECONOMIC PERFORMANCE: AN ASSESSMENT

There is a unifying theme in this evaluation of Soviet economic performance: the crucial role of trade-offs. Over the years, the Soviet Union has consistently "traded off" consumption (and leisure) for rapid (by international standards) economic growth. Had the Soviets adopted the input growth patterns of the West, their output growth would have been lower *ceteris paribus*. The existence of this trade-off alone underscores the deficiencies of relying upon a single performance indicator to assess economic performance. The trade-offs are not limited to consumption and output growth, although these other trade-offs are more difficult to capture. The full employment and price stability policies of the Soviet government have likely reduced worker and management incentives and have made rational economic decision-making more difficult. Moreover, the impact of Soviet consumption policies upon incentives in general is an important unresolved issue.

The "high cost" nature of Soviet economic growth is evident from the productivity comparisons. Only one-third of Soviet output growth is accounted for by efficiency growth, whereas in the West the ratio is generally in the range of two-thirds. Moreover, the declining rate of productivity growth in the Soviet Union suggests that this situation is not improving. Although one cannot argue *a priori* that the Japanese experience is representative of capitalism under conditions of rapid input growth, the Japanese case does suggest that capitalism is capable of combining rapid growth of inputs with an "intensive" pattern of growth. Had the Soviets emulated this experience, they could have achieved the same rate of growth with considerably less sacrifice.

SELECTED BIBLIOGRAPHY

Overall Evaluation Problems

Bela Belassa, *The Hungarian Experience in Economic Planning* (New Haven, Conn.: Yale University Press, 1959), pp. 5–24.

Abram Bergson, "East–West Comparisons and Comparative Economic Systems: A Reply," *Soviet Studies*, vol. 23, no. 2 (October 1971), 282–295.

Abram Bergson, *The Economics of Soviet Planning* (New Haven, Conn.: Yale University Press, 1964), chap. 14.

Abram Bergson, "National Income," in Abram Bergson and Simon Kuznets, eds., *Economic Trends in the Soviet Union* (Cambridge, Mass.: Harvard University Press, 1963), pp. 1–37.

Robert Campbell et al., "Methodological Problems Comparing the US and USSR Economies," in Joint Economic Committee, *Soviet Economic Prospects for the Seventies* (Washington, D.C., U.S. Government Printing Office, 1973), pp. 122–146.

Alexander Eckstein, ed., *Comparison of Economic Systems* (Berkeley and Los Angeles: University of California Press, 1971).

Imogene Edwards, Margaret Hughes, and James Noren, "U.S. and USSR: Comparisons of GNP," in Joint Economic Committee, *Soviet Economy in a Time of Change* (Washington, D.C.: U.S. Government Printing Office, 1979), vol. 1, pp. 369–401.

Philip Hanson, "East–West Comparisons and Comparative Economic Systems," *Soviet Studies*, vol. 22, no. 3 (January 1971).

Vladimir G. Treml and Dimitri Gallik, *Soviet Studies on Ruble/Dollar Parity Ratios*, Foreign Economic Reports, no. 4, U.S. Department of Commerce, November 1973.

Vladimir G. Treml and John P. Hardt, eds., *Soviet Economic Statistics* (Durham, N.C.: Duke University Press, 1972).

Charles K. Wilber, "Economic Development, Central Planning, and Allocative Efficiency," *Yearbook of East-European Economics* (Munich: Günter Olzog Verlag, 1971), pp. 221–246.

Soviet Economic Growth

Abraham Becker, *Soviet National Income, 1958–1964* (Berkeley: University of California Press, 1969).

Abram Bergson, *Productivity and the Social System: The USSR and the West* (Cambridge, Mass.: Harvard University Press, 1978), part 3.

Abram Bergson, *The Real National Income of Soviet Russia Since 1928* (Cambridge, Mass.: Harvard University Press, 1961).

Herbert Block, "Soviet Economic Performance in a Global Context," in Joint Economic Committee, *Soviet Economy in a Time of Change* (Washington, D.C.: U.S. Government Printing Office, 1979), vol. 1, pp. 110–140.

M. Bornstein, "A Comparison of Soviet and United States National Product," in M. Bornstein and D. Fusfeld, eds., *The Soviet Economy* (Homewood, Ill.: Irwin, 1962).

Stanley Cohn, *Economic Development in the Soviet Union* (Lexington, Mass.: Heath, 1969), chap. 7.

Stanley H. Cohn, "General Growth Performance of the Soviet Economy," in Joint Economic Committee, *Economic Performance and the Military Burden in the Soviet Union* (Washington, D.C.: U.S. Government Printing Office, 1970).

Rush Greenslade, "The Real Gross National Product of the USSR, 1950–1975," in Joint Economic Committee, *Soviet Economy in a New Perspective* (Washington, D.C.: U.S. Government Printing Office, 1976), pp. 269–300.

Narodnoe khoziaistvo SSSR 3a 60 let [National economy of the USSR for 60 years] (Moscow: Statistika, 1977).

A. L. Vainshtein, *Narodnii dokhod Rossii i SSSR* [The national income of Russia and the USSR] (Moscow: Statistika, 1969).

Dynamic Efficiency and the Growth of Productivity

Abram Bergson, "Development Under Two Systems: Comparative Productivity Growth Since 1950," *World Politics*, vol. 23, no. 4 (July 1971), 579–617.

Abram Bergson, *Planning and Productivity Under Soviet Socialism* (New York: Columbia University Press, 1968).

Abram Bergson, *Productivity and the Social System: The USSR and the West* (Cambridge, Mass.: Harvard University Press, 1978), part 3.

Earl R. Brubaker, "Embodied Technology, the Asymptotic Behavior of Capital's Age, and Soviet Growth," *Review of Economics and Statistics*, vol. 50, no. 3 (August 1968), 304–311.

R. Moorsteen and R. Powell, *The Soviet Capital Stock, 1928–1962* (Homewood, Ill.: Irwin, 1966).

F. Douglas Whitehouse and Ray Converse, "Soviet Industry: Recent Performance and Future Prospects," in Joint Economic Committee, *Soviet Economy in a Time of Change* (Washington, D.C.: U.S. Government Printing Office, 1979), vol. 1, pp. 402–422.

Soviet Static Efficiency

Abram Bergson, "Comparative Productivity and Efficiency in the USA and USSR," in Alexander Eckstein, ed., *Comparison of Economic Systems* (Berkeley and Los Angeles: University of California Press, 1971), pp. 161–218.

Abram Bergson, *The Economics of Soviet Planning* (New Haven, Conn.: Yale University Press, 1964), chap. 14.

Abram Bergson, *Planning and Productivity Under Soviet Socialism* (New York: Columbia University Press, 1968).

Joseph S. Berliner, "The Static Efficiency of the Soviet Economy," *American Economic Review*, vol. 54, no. 2 (May 1964), 480–490.

Evsey Domar, "On the Measurement of Comparative Efficiency," in Alexander Eckstein, ed., *Comparison of Economic Systems* (Berkeley and Los Angeles: University of California Press, 1971), pp. 219–232.

Equity of Income Distribution in the Soviet Union

Abram Bergson, *The Structure of Soviet Wages* (Cambridge, Mass.: Harvard University Press, 1944).

Alastair McCauley, "The Distribution of Earnings and Income in the Soviet Union," *Soviet Studies*, vol. 29, no. 2 (April 1977), pp. 214–237.

Alastair McCauley, *Economic Welfare in the Soviet Union* (Madison: University of Wisconsin Press, 1979).

P. J. D. Wiles, *Distribution of Income: East and West* (Amsterdam: North Holland, 1974).

P. J. D. Wiles and Stefan Markowski, "Income Distribution Under Communism and Capitalism: Some Facts About Poland, the U.K., the USA and the USSR," *Soviet Studies*, vol. 22, nos. 3 and 4 (January and April 1971), 344–369, and 487–511.

Murray Yanowitch, *Social and Economic Inequality in the USSR* (White Plains, N.Y.: M. E. Sharpe, 1977).

Murray Yanowitch, "The Soviet Income Revolution," *Slavic Review*, vol. 22, no. 4 (December 1963).

Consumer Welfare in the Soviet Union

David W. Bronson and Barbara S. Severin, "Consumer Welfare," in Joint Economic Committee, *Economic Performance and the Military Burden in the Soviet Union* (Washington, D.C.: U.S. Government Printing Office, 1970), pp. 93–99.

David W. Bronson and Barbara S. Severin, "Soviet Consumer Welfare: The Brezhnev Era," in Joint Economic Committee, *Soviet Economic Prospects for the Seventies* (Washington, D.C.: U.S. Government Printing Office, 1973), pp. 376–403.

Janet G. Chapman, "Consumption," in Abram Bergson and Simon Kuznets, eds., *Economic Trends in the Soviet Union* (Cambridge, Mass.: Harvard University Press, 1963), pp. 235–282.

Janet G. Chapman, *Real Wages in the Soviet Union* (Cambridge, Mass.: Harvard University Press, 1963).

M. Elizabeth Denton, "Soviet Consumer Policy: Trends and Prospects," in Joint Economic Committee, *Soviet Economy in a Time of Change,* (Washington D.C. U.S. Government Printing Office, 1979) vol. 1, pp. 759–798.

Bernice Q. Madison, "Social Services: Families and Children in the Soviet Union Since 1967," *Slavic Review*, vol. 31, no. 4 (December 1972), 831–852.

Bernice Q. Madison, *Social Welfare in the Soviet Union* (Stanford, Calif.: Stanford University Press, 1968).

Robert J. Osborn, *Soviet Social Policies: Welfare, Equality, and Community* (Homewood, Ill.: The Dorsey Press, 1970).

Gertrude E. Schroeder and Barbara S. Severin, "Soviet Consumption and Income Policies in Perspective," in Joint Economic Committee, *Soviet Economy in a New Perspective* (Washington, D.C.: U.S. Government Printing Office, 1976), pp. 620–660.

Economic Stability (Security) in the Soviet Union

Morris Bornstein, "Unemployment in Capitalist Regulated Market Economies and Socialist Centrally Planned Economies," *American Economic Review, Papers and Proceedings,* vol. 68, no. 2 (May 1978), 38–43.

Keith Bush, "Soviet Inflation," in M. Yves Laulan, ed., *Banking, Money and Credit in Eastern Europe* (Brussels: NATO, 1973); 97–105.

NATO Economics Directorate, *Economic Aspects of Life in the USSR* (Brussels: NATO, 1976), contributions by Gertrude E. Schroeder and Aron Katsenelinboigen.

Joyce Pickersgill, "Soviet Household Saving Behavior," *Review of Economics and Statistics,* vol. 58, no. 2 (May 1976), 139–147.

P. J. D. Wiles, "A Note on Soviet Unemployment in US Definitions," *Soviet Studies,* vol. 23, no. 2 (April 1972), 619–628.

Chapter 11

Soviet Performance: Military Power. Technology. Economic Development. the Environment

FURTHER PERFORMANCE INDICATORS

In Chapter 10, we assessed the performance of the Soviet economy in terms of conventional economic performance criteria: economic growth, efficiency, living standards, income distribution, and economic stability. This list is a restrictive one in the Soviet context because other goals, pursued consistently by the Soviet leadership, are not included. The first of these is the objective, first sought by an "encircled" Bolshevik regime in 1917, of achieving a degree of military power sufficient to protect the Soviet experiment from its capitalist foes and, later, to expand the Soviet sphere of influence. One can debate current Soviet military objectives—are they designed to achieve parity or dominance?—but one thing is clear: the consistent priority assigned to military power. Soviet economic performance, especially in the postwar era, cannot be understood without an assessment of the resources devoted to the military and the military might these resources have produced, for these resources had to be diverted from consumption and investment. Trade-offs between military and civilian objectives would therefore be expected.

The second objective—the establishment of a high level of technology in the Soviet Union—is another that has been emphasized since the early days of the Soviet regime, when high technology heavy industry was proclaimed the instrument through which socialism would be built. To what extent has this objective been achieved? Has the Soviet economy succeeded in creating and utilizing advanced technology to its maximum potential, given the resource constraints in which it has had to operate? To a limited extent, this issue has been addressed in the previous chapter, for efficiency gains will depend upon the production and utilization of improved technology (including improved organizational arrangements). In this chapter, we will examine this issue directly by considering the Soviet record in the technology area. Unlike other performance indicators, global measures of technological performance (other than measures of productivity) are not available; therefore we must make do with partial indicators of technological achievement. The manner in which new technologies are created and utilized by the Soviet economic system will be considered as well, for in the absence of accurate global measures of technological performance, analyses of Soviet "rules of the game" for technological innovation may provide insights overlooked by empirical measures.

Rapid economic development is the third objective, pursued with full vigor in the 1930s. It also cannot be fully captured by conventional performance indicators. Since 1928, the Soviet leadership has been as concerned about the *pattern* of economic growth as with the pace of growth. Preobrazhensky and ultimately Stalin argued that the building of socialism required significant structural changes—the growth of heavy industry, the decline in private trade, the growth of communal forms of production in agriculture. It was realized that in some instances (the collectivization of agriculture, the destruction of private trade), the impact of the structural changes on overall growth might be negative initially, but it was believed that the long-term political and economic benefits of forcing rapid changes in the economic and social order would compensate for any losses. Official concern with the pattern of economic development is not purely ideological. The Soviet leadership has viewed the Soviet Union as an encircled country, forced to develop into a modern industrial economy rapidly on its own. Thus the luxury of allowing a slow and steady pace of economic development and structural change was not a viable option from the point of view of the Soviet leadership, as the supporters of the gradualist Bukharin program were taught. "Modernization" and all its concomitants—urbanization, the rising share of large scale industry, the transfer of labor out of agriculture and rural handicrafts, the lessening of dependence upon raw material exports and industrial imports—had to be speeded up in the Soviet case. How well the Soviet leadership succeeded in accelerating the pace of modernization will be discussed in this chapter under the heading "The Soviet Development Model of the 1930s."

The final performance criterion not encompassed in the conventional performance indicators is the degree to which the Soviet economy has been able to produce "environmental quality," or expressed in the negative form, has been able to prevent "environmental disruption." Widespread concern and analysis of environmental disruption is a postwar phenomenon. Many LDCs still view environmental protection as a luxury that only affluent countries can afford; and as the Soviet Union was engaged in a program of rapid industrialization, and thereafter a world war, one can understand that environmental concerns were of low priority during those early periods. Environmental disruption in the Soviet Union provides an interesting test case of the effect of the economic system on environmental quality, especially for those who have argued that environmental disruption is a product of capitalism.

SOVIET MILITARY POWER

We approach the topic of Soviet military power by posing two questions. The first is: how much military power have the Soviets been able to produce, given the limitations imposed by their economic base? This question is analogous to our earlier discussion of living standards, where we argued that per capita consumption levels must be judged relative to economic capacity. If one compares Soviet and American military power, it must be done with an appreciation of the different resource bases available to the two countries. To deal with this first question, we must above all have measures of military power, and as we shall point out, the measurement of military power raises severe conceptual and practical problems. The second question concerns the burden imposed on the Soviet domestic economy by the diversion of resources to military uses.

Problems of Measurement[1]

The military power of the Soviet Union can be quantified in two ways. The first is to list the physical quantities of the various inputs into the military power equation—armed service personnel, tanks, missiles, submarines, strategic supplies, and so on—and compare them with a similar list for the Soviet Union's major military competitors, the United States and its NATO allies and the People's Republic of China. In Table 36, such a compilation is supplied for the USSR and the United States.

Comparisons of physical quantities of military inputs are useful, and they confirm the general increase in Soviet military power vis-à-vis the United States. Yet such comparisons suffer from a series of deficiencies. Military hardware tends to be quite complex and heterogeneous, therefore the simple counting of physical units will not reveal their contribution to

[1] This discussion is based upon the following sources: Abraham Becker, "The Meaning and Measure of Soviet Military Expenditure," in Joint Economic Committee, *Soviet Economy in a Time of Change* (Washington, D.C.: U.S. Government Printing Office, 1979), vol. 1, pp. 352–368; Henry W. Shaeffer, "Soviet Power and Intentions: Military-Economic Choices," in Joint Economic Committee, *Soviet Economy in a Time of Change* (Washington, D.C.: U.S. Government Printing Office, 1979), vol. 1, pp. 341–351; William T. Lee, *The Estimation of Soviet Defense Expenditures, 1955–1975* (New York: Praeger, 1977); National Foreign Assessment Center, *Estimated Soviet Defense Spending: Trends and Prospects*, SR78–10121 (Washington, D.C., June 1978); National Foreign Assessment Center, *A Dollar Cost Comparison of Soviet and U.S. Defense Activities, 1968–78*, SR79–10004 (Washington, D.C., January 1979); Franklyn Holzman, "Are the Soviets Really Outspending the U.S. on Defense?," *International Security* (Spring 1980), pp. 86–104.

TABLE 36   Military Strength: USSR and USA, 1964 and 1978

	1964	1978
USSR		
Intercontinental ballistic missiles (ICBMs)	200	1400
Submarine launched ballistic missiles (SLBMs)	120	1015
Long range bombers	190	135
Armed services personnel (millions)	3.4	4.2
USA		
Intercontinental ballistic missiles (ICBMs)	834	1054
Submarine launched ballistic missiles (SLBMs)	416	656
Long range bombers	630	432
Armed services personnel (millions)	2.7	2.1

SOURCES: These data are based upon studies of the International Institute for Strategic Studies, London. They are cited in *The 1979 Hammond Almanac* (Maplewood, N.J.: Hammond Almanac, Inc., 1978), pp. 733–735; *The Official Associated Press Almanac 1973* (New York: Almanac Publishing Company, 1972), pp. 616–617. The Soviet armed services figures are from Murray Feshbach and Stephen Rapawy, "Soviet Population and Manpower Trends and Policies," in Joint Economic Committee, *Soviet Economy in a New Perspective* (Washington, D.C.: U.S. Government Printing Office, 1976), p. 132; Hearings Before the Subcommittee on Priorities and Economy in Government, *Allocation of Resources in the Soviet Union and China—1978; Part 4: Soviet Union* (Washington, D.C., June 26 and July 24, 1978), p. 68.

military power. To make such a judgment, one must have detailed information on the (perhaps thousands) characteristics of each type of military hardware. In the case of ICBMs, for example, one must know their payload, accuracy, speed of launch, degree of protection from nuclear attack, and so on. Even if this wealth of information were available, an *overall* measure of Soviet military power would still be lacking, for some means must be found of *aggregating* all the heterogeneous inputs (military personnel, tanks, bombs, ICBMs, strategic supplies, etc.).

The most straightforward means of converting physical indicators of military force into a common denominator is to multiply each by its price and then sum, that is, to compile a value aggregate of military power. Under ideal circumstances, relative prices will reflect both the opportunity cost of resources embodied in the commodity and the marginal rates at which defense planners are willing to substitute one item for another (holding the level of military power constant).[2] In our discussion of the Soviet price system (Chapter 5), we noted that Soviet ruble prices rarely mirror the opportunity costs of production (or the marginal rates of substitution of users); and in the case of pricing the defense commodities of the United States, it is difficult to know how rational such prices are (for example, until 1973 the wage rates of draftees were set

---

[2] Efficiency in the choice of military goods and services would require that the defense planners' marginal rates of substitution be equal to the marginal rates of transformation.

well below opportunity costs). Thus in making value comparisons of USSR and U.S. military power, one is unsure of the "rationality" of the prices used in aggregation.

In the case of compiling value aggregates of Soviet defense outlays, practical problems caused by data deficiencies are as serious as underlying theoretical issues. Official Soviet budgetary sources report defense spending as a single line item, and reported defense outlays are often manipulated to suit political needs. The announced state budget claims virtually no increase in defense spending (even prior to adjustment for inflation) between 1967 and 1978, a period when massive investments in military hardware systems were being made.[3] For these reasons, defense analysts in the United States have felt it necessary to make independent estimates of Soviet defense spending by employing U.S. defense budgetary practices. Two types of independent calculations have been made. The first, undertaken by the American intelligence community,[4] uses the "building block" approach, whereby the physical quantities of defense inputs (rockets, manpower, equipment, etc.) are multiplied by the presumed cost of producing the items in the United States (to obtain Soviet defense spending in U.S. prices for comparison with U.S. defense spending)[5] and by Soviet ruble prices.[6] The advantages of the building block approach are that the estimates are independent of official Soviet budgetary data and that they are in a form suitable for comparison with U.S. defense spending. The disadvantages are that one cannot assess the reliability of intelligence data on Soviet military hardware and that it is difficult to determine accurately costs in the United States and the Soviet Union. The second approach calls for the estimation of Soviet outlays on military hardware by subtracting civilian uses of industrial production from the ruble value of industrial production; the resulting residual is presumed to equal defense outlays.[7] The accuracy of both types of estimates is subject to serious question (although they have tended to agree with each other in recent years),[8] and scepticism concerning their reliabil-

---

[3] Hearings Before the Subcommittee on Priorities and Economy in Government, *Allocation of Resources in the Soviet Union and China—1978; Part 4: Soviet Union* (Washington, D.C., June 26 and July 24, 1978), pp. 11, 49.

[4] National Foreign Assessment Center's *Estimated Soviet Defense Spending* and *A Dollar Cost Comparison.*

[5] Information on Soviet military hardware is supplied to American defense contractors, who are asked to indicate what the system would have cost if produced in the United States.

[6] There is no direct information on the ruble costs of military hardware, so analysts convert dollar values into ruble values using conversion rates for similar products (relative U.S.–USSR machinery costs, for example). See Holzman, "Are the Soviets Really Outspending the U.S. on Defense? for a critique of these conversions.

[7] This is the procedure used by Lee, *Estimation of Soviet Defense Expenditures.*

[8] The various estimates for 1975 (cited in Becker, "Soviet Military Expenditure," p. 362) are:

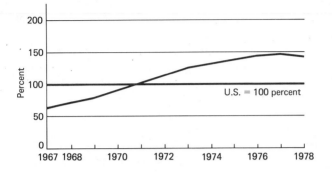

Figure 6 Dollar Cost of Soviet Activities as a Percent of U.S. Defense Outlays. (Source: National Foreign Assessment Center, *A Dollar Cost Comparison of Soviet and U.S. Defense Activities, 1968–78*, SR79–10004, Washington, D.C., January 1979, p. 10. The 1967 figure is from the previous
year's publication, which covers the years 1966–1977.)

ity was increased in 1976, when the Central Intelligence Agency raised its
estimate of Soviet defense spending by 100 percent.[9]

CIA Estimates

Using its building block approach, the CIA has derived estimates of the
dollar cost of Soviet defense activities for the period 1967–1978. These dollar cost figures can then be contrasted with the actual dollar costs of U.S.
defense outlays. The CIA findings are supplied in Figure 6. They show that
from 1967 (and earlier) U.S. defense spending outdistanced Soviet defense
outlays (by a factor of about one-third in 1967). Around 1971, Soviet defense
spending came to equal American spending, and thereafter exceeded
American defense outlays. In 1978, Soviet spending was estimated to exceed American outlays by 45 percent.

Expenditures on defense in any one year will not yield the total of military power, for military power is the product of cumulated past expenditures.[10] Therefore a more accurate measure of Soviet military power vis-à-
vis the United States would be the sum of military expenditures (in constant

Official Soviet: 17.4 (billion rubles)
CIA: 50–60
Lee: 72
French estimate: 42.3
Chinese estimate: 69.4

[9] Philip Hanson, "Review of Estimating Soviet Defense Expenditures," *Soviet Studies*, vol.
30, no. 3 (July 1978), 403.
[10] For a discussion of this point, see Becker, "Soviet Military Expenditure," pp. 352–366.

prices) over a substantial period of time. According to CIA calculations, cumulative Soviet defense outlays for the decade 1968–1978 exceeded American totals by 12 percent.[11] The implication of these findings is that the Soviet Union has overtaken the United States in its real defense spending, and that if current trends continue, it will outdistance the United States in military power in the future. This conclusion is not inconsistent with the evidence of the physical indicators presented in Table 36. Some reservations can be cited, however.

There is a range of considerable uncertainty surrounding these estimates, although the CIA believes its estimates are not more than 15 percent in error.[12] Given the problems of intelligence gathering and then of translating physical indicators into dollar or ruble values, one can understand why a substantial margin of error must be attached to these estimates. Second, the relationship between cumulated spending totals and military power is not clearly defined.[13] Military power depends not only upon sheer spending ability but also upon the wisdom of defense planners and the uses to which they put the expenditures. Third, there is the ambiguity introduced by the index number problem, which requires some comment.[14]

The dollar cost estimates of Soviet defense spending translate Soviet defense outlays into U.S. prices. Soviet ICBM systems are valued at U.S. prices, Soviet manpower is valued at U.S. military pay scales, fuels used by the military are computed in U.S. fuel prices. The United States is "rich" in advanced technology and "poor" in manpower relative to the Soviet Union, therefore the prices of high technology products will be low in the United States relative to Soviet ruble prices. The structure of Soviet defense outlays, however, is geared to domestic resource constraints, that is, Soviet defense planners will place relatively less emphasis on advanced technology (less use of advanced computer circuitry in ICBMs and greater use of large payloads) and more emphasis on labor intensive military expenditures (larger armed forces). When Soviet defense outlays are translated into U.S. prices, products that play a relatively small role (advanced technology computer products) are accorded a relatively low U.S. price, while those products that play a heavy role (manpower, rifles, etc.) are valued in relatively high U.S. prices. Thus dollar cost estimates of defense spending will yield a higher relative value for the USSR than comparisons conducted in ruble prices. To this point, the most reliable estimates are those in dollar values, but the available estimates in ruble prices do confirm the expected

[11] National Foreign Assessment Center, *A Dollar Cost Comparison*, p. 4.

[12] *Allocation of Resources in the Soviet Union and China*, p. 37.

[13] See Becker, "Soviet Military Expenditure," pp. 352–358, for a discussion of the tenuous relationship between outlays and military power; also see Holzman, "Are the Soviets Really Outspending the U.S. on Defense?" pp. 86–104.

[14] Holzman, "Are the Soviets Really Outspending the U.S. on Defense?" pp. 87–93.

relationship—namely, that if ruble prices are employed, the USSR spending advantage is reduced (to a 25 percent from a 45 percent advantage in 1978 according to the CIA).[15]

Despite these reservations, the conclusion to be drawn from figures on defense spending and physical indicators of military potential is that the Soviet Union has achieved an impressive degree of military might. Most analysts would agree that Soviet military might is at least equivalent to that of the United States, a nation that possesses considerably more economic power (as measured by the size of GNP). Soviet authorities have therefore achieved their objectives as far as the military power equation is concerned.

The Burden of Soviet Defense Expenditures

Obviously, these military power achievements have not taken place without sacrifice. The diversion of resources from the civilian economy has cost the Soviet economy production for consumption and investment. These costs can be illustrated in a number of ways: Soviet males reaching the age of 18 become subject to conscription, and in 1975, 87 percent of males turning 18 were drafted. It is projected that if current military manpower levels are to be maintained, over 100 percent of 18-year-olds must be conscripted in the 1980s, meaning that conscripts will have to be sought in other age groups.[16] Not only does Soviet defense require a drain of manpower from the civilian economy, it is also estimated that one-third of the product of the machine building industry (the primary source of investment goods) is devoted annually to the defense sector.[17] In general, defense takes a large share of the highest quality scientific, technical, and managerial talent, as well as having preferential access to scarce resources of all kinds.

The most frequently used measure of the total defense burden is the ratio of defense spending to GNP, as this denotes the share of total resources devoted to defense activities. From 1967 to 1978, the Soviets devoted approximately one-eighth of their output to defense, versus 5 percent for the United States.[18]

The exact costs of this military burden, as measured by the sacrifice of current consumption and the longer run effects on growth of reduced in-

[15] Holzman, "Are the Soviets Really Outspending the U.S. on Defense?" pp. 87–93, argues that the CIA grossly underestimates the effects of index number relativity. He maintains that it is quite possible that the U.S. outspends the Soviets if ruble prices would be correctly calculated. Holzman further argues that the higher quality of American manpower and military hardware are not captured by the CIA figures.

[16] Murray Feshbach and Stephen Rapawy, "Soviet Population and Manpower Trends and Policies," in Joint Economic Committee, *Soviet Economy in a New Perspective* (Washington, D.C.: U.S. Government Printing Office, 1976), p. 150.

[17] National Foreign Assessment Center, *Estimated Soviet Defense Spending*, p. i.

[18] See Holzman, "Are the Soviets Really Outspending the U.S. on Defense?" pp. 86–102, for a critique of estimates of defense expenditure shares.

vestment, are not known, but econometric estimates suggest that they are substantial.[19] Projections into the future are necessarily uncertain, primarily because it is difficult to predict productivity gains, but the ultimate cost of Soviet defense spending may prove to be a growth rate unacceptably low to Soviet authorities.

SOVIET TECHNOLOGY[20]

Measurement of Soviet technological performance is, like the assessment of Soviet military power, a complicated problem. Direct measures of Soviet technological achievement relative to that of capitalist countries can be made only on an industry case study basis, and the researcher will not know whether such results are representative for the economy as a whole. Moreover, case studies require the evaluation of the operating characteristics of the technology (reliability, power/weight ratios, energy efficiency, etc.) and of the quality of the end products produced, and the number of such technical-engineering characteristics is so large that the evaluation may depend upon the particular characteristics studied. Also the characteristics of the technology will depend upon the resource endowments of the country; so it may be optimal for one nation to adopt technology that is less "advanced" because factor proportions dictate such a choice.

Indirect measurement of technology represents the alternate to direct

[19] For a simulation of the effects of defense spending during the 1960s, see Donald Green and Christopher Higgins, *Sovmod I: A Macroeconometric Model of the Soviet Union* (New York: Academic Press, 1977), pp. 71–74. For a study of the 1970s and projections, see Hans Bergendorff and Per Strangert, "Projections of Soviet Economic Growth and Defense Spending," in Joint Economic Committee, *Soviet Economy in a New Perspective* (Washington, D.C.: U.S. Government Printing Office, 1976), pp. 394–430. Another important econometric study of the defense-consumption-GNP relationship is Lars Calmfors and Jan Rylander, "Economic Restrictions on Soviet Defense Expenditure," in Joint Economic Committee, *Soviet Economy in a New Perspective* (Washington, D.C.: U.S. Government Printing Office, 1976), pp. 377–392.

[20] This discussion is based largely on the following sources: Joseph S. Berliner, *The Innovation Decision in Soviet Industry* (Cambridge, Mass.: MIT Press, 1976); Joseph Berliner, "Prospects for Technological Progress," in Joint Economic Committee, *Soviet Economy in a New Perspective* (Washington, D.C.: U.S. Government Printing Office, 1976), pp. 431–446; Ronald Amman, Julian Cooper, and R. W. Davies, *The Technological Level of Soviet Industry* (New Haven, Conn.: Yale University Press, 1977); John R. Thomas and Ursula Kruse-Vaucienne, eds., *Soviet Science and Technology* (Washington, D.C.: George Washington University, 1977), parts 3 and 4; Eugene Zaleski et al., *Science Policy in the USSR* (Paris: OECD, 1969); John Martens and John P. Young, "Soviet Implementation of Domestic Inventions: First Results," in Joint Economic Committee, *Soviet Economy in a Time of Change* (Washington, D.C.: U.S. Government Printing Office, 1979), vol. 1, pp. 472–509; James Grant, "Soviet Machine Tools: Lagging Technology and Rising Imports," in Joint Economic Committee, *Soviet Economy in a Time of Change* (Washington, D.C.: U.S. Government Printing Office, 1979), vol. 1, pp. 524–553; Philip Hanson, "International Technology Transfer from the West to the USSR," in Joint Economic Committee, *Soviet Economy in a New Perspective* (Washington, D.C.: U.S. Government Printing Office, 1976), pp. 786–812.

case studies. The relative factor productivity of the USSR vis-à-vis other countries can be calculated (Chapter 10), but the relationship between factor productivity and Soviet technological achievement is not clearly defined. It is not directly apparent whether low Soviet factor productivity is a consequence of lagging technological performance or of "omitted factors" (qualitative differences in inputs, economies of scale, and so on). A low technological level is only one of several explanations of low Soviet factor productivity, as the factor productivity calculation represents "a measure of our ignorance."[21] Further measures of the technology level (lead time to the utilization of a new technology, number of patents, volume of scientific papers, scientific awards, citations in scientific papers) supplement our understanding of Soviet technology, but all suffer from serious deficiencies.

Granted that no single measure of technological performance will be adequate, we can nevertheless cite some of the basic results of research on Soviet technology. First, we should refer the reader back to the factor productivity results (Chapter 10), which show Soviet factor productivity to be low relative to the advanced industrialized countries. This finding is consistent with the conclusion that Soviet technological performance is below that of the industrialized West, but such evidence is not conclusive by itself. Case studies of the technological level of Soviet industry (even when chosen so as to select priority branches) suggest as well a relatively low level of Soviet technology, although this conclusion applies less strongly to the defense and iron and steel industries.[22] The most striking conclusion of case study research is that in most sectors, "there is no evidence of a substantial diminution of the technological gap between the USSR and the West in the past 15 to 20 years, either at the prototype/commercial application stages or in the diffusion of advanced technology."[23] This conclusion is generally consistent with the factor productivity studies, which show the rate of growth of factor productivity in the USSR to be only average relative to the industrialized West.

Another source of evidence concerning the relatively low technological level of the Soviet economy is its continued reliance on imports from the West to meet its advanced technology requirements. Case studies of computer and machine tool imports can be cited to confirm this continuing dependence.[24]

---

[21] A statement of Richard Nelson cited by Ronald Amman, "Soviet Technological Performance," in John R. Thomas and Ursula Kruse-Vaucienne, eds., *Soviet Science and Technology* (Washington, D.C.: George Washington University, 1977), p. 329.

[22] This is the basic conclusion of the Amman, Cooper, and Davies study, conducted at the University of Birmingham, England. See Amman, Cooper, and Davies, *The Technological Level of Soviet Industry.*

[23] Amman, "Soviet Technological Performance," p. 328.

[24] Grant, "Soviet Machine Tools," pp. 524–553; Kenneth Tasky, "Soviet Technology Gap and Dependence on the West: The Case of Computers," in Joint Economic Committee,

The technological level of a country will depend not only on the availability of new technology but also upon its diffusion throughout the economy. The limited evidence that is available suggests that the lead time between the granting of a patent for a new invention and its practical implementation are longer in the Soviet Union than in the United States and West Germany. In fact, the United States and West Germany tend to implement over one-half of their inventions in little more than a year, while the Soviets require three years to attain this ratio.[25] The slowness of diffusion of new technology applies to imported technology as well as domestic inventions.[26]

What conclusions are to be drawn from this mass of data? Our overall conclusion is that the information supplied by factor productivity studies, direct investigations of the technology of Soviet industry, reliance on high technology imports, lead times, and diffusion point to a relatively low level of technological achievement in the Soviet economy (with the exception of the military). Moreover, data over time suggest that the Soviet's technology gap has not been narrowed over the past two decades.

Causes of the Technology Gap

The probable causes of the Soviet technology gap have been identified by Joseph Berliner,[27] who argues that Soviet organizational structure, pricing system, and incentive rules discriminate against technological innovation. Although the Soviet economic system does have certain features favorable to innovation (patent restrictions do not limit the spread of an invention), other features inhibit technological innovation. The existing organizational structure gives maximal encouragement to decision makers to discriminate against innovations and to managers to shy away from doing new things. As noted in Chapter 6, Soviet managers have learned to minimize the risk of failure by developing secure channels of supply. Once a Soviet manager has established reliable supply relationships, the chance of failure is reduced. The installation of a new technology would change routine patterns and disrupt existing supply channels built up carefully over the years. New ways of doing things would also change established distribution arrangements and add another source of uncertainty to plan fulfillment. Moreover, most research and development work is done by research institutes and ministerial project-making organizations, whose responsibility for a project ends

---

Soviet Economy in a Time of Change (Washington, D.C.: U.S. Government Printing Office, 1979), vol. 1, pp. 510–523.

[25] Martens and Young, "Soviet Implementation," pp. 505–507.

[26] Philip Hanson, "The Diffusion of Imported Technology," in NATO Economics Directorate, *Economic Aspects of Life in the USSR* (Brussels: NATO, 1975).

[27] This discussion is based upon Berliner, *The Innovation Decision*, and Berliner, "Prospects for Technological Progress."

when a new design is approved by the ministry. The need for enterprises to rely on an outside supply of research and development services compounds the risk of failure.

As Berliner points out, innovation does increase managerial risks, but if the rewards to managers for innovation were large enough, managers could more readily be induced to innovate. One way to reward managers would be to grant them high prices relative to costs of production (and thus larger profits) for new products and then to pay them bonuses, either directly for innovative activity or through an increased share in enterprise profits. The existing pricing and incentive structures do neither. The principle of pricing according to the labor theory of value discriminates against product innovation, for savings in labor costs are passed on to the user in the form of lower prices rather than to the producer as higher profits. Efforts to exempt new products from branch average cost pricing have been largely unsuccessful, although some of the cruder disparities of earlier years have been eliminated.

The managerial bonus system also discourages innovation. Over the years, managers have been paid bonuses primarily for fulfillment of current year production targets. It was not until the mid-1950s that special bonuses for innovation were developed. But even after introducing a variety of rewards for innovation, it remains true that the managerial bonus still depends primarily upon fulfilling basic enterprise plan targets. Moreover, the bonus system is geared to rewarding short-term results. Innovative activity, by disrupting existing channels of supply and distribution, typically causes a short-term reduction in enterprise output, which is compensated for by a long-term increase as an innovation comes on-stream. Yet during this period, the manager will lose bonus funds and will thus be discouraged from innovation.

The economic reform begun in 1965 sought to reduce managerial resistance to change. Special bonuses for innovation were established, amended pricing rules for new products were introduced, and greater emphasis was placed upon long-term plan fulfillment. But as we noted in Chapter 9, economic reform has not altered the fundamentals of the Soviet economic system, and this conclusion applies to innovative activity as well. Berliner, after analyzing Soviet efforts to improve the incentive system, concluded that "the current incentive structure does not lend very strong support to the new growth strategy [based upon technological progress]."[28]

Berliner's work provides a vivid account of why Soviet enterprises are reluctant to engage in innovation and thus focuses on the micro context of innovation. The macro context is less clearly defined, for to do so requires knowledge of the workings of the Soviet scientific and technical community. This community includes the Soviet Academy of Sciences, the re-

[28] Berliner, "Prospects for Technological Progress," p. 445.

search and development establishment, and the project-making organizations, and is responsible for planning major investment projects (the Baikal-Amur mainline, for example) and enterprise investment projects. Although Western authorities have analyzed the financing of research and development, less is known about the internal operations of the Soviet scientific and technical community.[29] An assessment of its work must therefore await further research.

THE SOVIET DEVELOPMENT MODEL OF THE 1930s
Description

The small amount of attention devoted to the Soviet Development Model (SDM) by Western economists is surprising in view of its importance as a major alternative development pattern—although the gaps in our knowledge on this subject have been narrowed in recent years.[30] Using available research on the SDM, we delineate the following as its most essential components.[31]

1. Planners' preferences, dictated by the Communist Party through the planning hierarchy, replaced consumer preferences. This change-

[29] Eugene Zaleski, "Planning and Financing of Research and Development in the USSR," in John R. Thomas and Ursula Kruse-Vaucienne, eds., *Soviet Science and Technology* (Washington, D.C.: George Washington University, 1977), pp. 276–304; Louvan Nolting, *Sources of Financing the Stages of the Research Development and Innovation Cycle in the USSR*, Foreign Economic Reports, No. 3, U.S. Department of Commerce, September 1973.

[30] A comprehensive and controversial work is Charles K. Wilber, *The Soviet Model and Underdeveloped Countries* (Chapel Hill: University of North Carolina Press, 1969). Other authors making significant contributions are Oleg Hoeffding, "State Planning and Forced Industrialization," *Problems of Communism*, vol. 8, no. 6 (November–December 1959); Nicholas Spulber, *Soviet Strategy for Economic Growth* (Bloomington: Indiana University Press, 1964); Alec Nove, "The Soviet Model and Underdeveloped Countries," *International Affairs*, vol. 36, no. 1 (January 1961); Norton Dodge and Charles K. Wilber, "The Relevance of Soviet Industrial Experience for Less Developed Economies," *Soviet Studies*, vol. 21, no. 3 (January 1970), 330–349.

[31] Our elaboration of the components of the SDM is drawn from the following studies: Wilber, *The Soviet Model*, part I; Gur Ofer, *The Service Sector in Soviet Economic Growth* (Cambridge, Mass.: Harvard University Press, 1973); Gur Ofer, "Economizing on Urbanization in Socialist Countries," in Alan A. Brown and Egon Neuberger, eds., *Internal Migration: A Comparative Perspective* (New York: Academic Press, 1977), pp. 277–304; Gur Ofer, "Industrial Structure, Urbanization, and the Growth Strategy of Socialist Countries," *Quarterly Journal of Economics*, vol. 90, no. 2 (May 1976), 219–243; Paul R. Gregory, *Socialist and Nonsocialist Industrialization Patterns* (New York: Praeger, 1970); Frederic L. Pryor, *Public Expenditures in Communist and Capitalist Nations* (Homewood, Ill.: Irwin, 1968); Franklyn D. Holzman, *Soviet Taxation* (Cambridge, Mass.: Harvard University Press, 1955); Franklyn D. Holzman, "Foreign Trade," in Abram Bergson and Simon Kuznets, eds., *Economic Trends in the Soviet Union* (Cambridge, Mass.: Harvard University Press, 1963), pp. 283–332; Holland Hunter, *Soviet Transportation Policy* (Cambridge, Mass.: Harvard University Press, 1957); Ernest W. Williams, Jr, *Freight Transportation in the Soviet Union* (Princeton, N.J.: Princeton University Press, 1962); Simon Kuznets, "A Comparative Appraisal," in Abram Bergson and Simon Kuznets, eds., *Economic Trends in the Soviet Union*

over was made possible by the establishment of a political dictatorship that placed the means of production in the hands of the state. As a response to the imposition of planners' preferences, the structure demand was changed dramatically within a brief period of time in favor of selected (priority) heavy industry branches—in particular, metallurgy, machine building, and electricity. The allocation of resources to light industry and agriculture was severely restricted. These two trends reflected themselves in prominent structural shifts: the aggregate investment rate rose markedly and rapidly while the share of GNP devoted to personal consumption fell. The share of communal consumption (public health, education, etc.) rose at the expense of private consumption. The rise in public consumption, however, was not sufficient to counter the relative decline in total consumption (as a percentage of GNP).

The growth of the service sector was retarded despite the rise in health and education services, thereby limiting the flow of resources into "nonproductive" sectors.[32] Development of commerce was especially restricted because the limitations placed on consumer goods retarded the growth of retail trade; the absence of property ownership limited the need for banking, legal, and other commercial services; and the material balance system in large measure replaced the wholesale trade network.

2. Sectorial relationships changed. Agriculture was collectivized and private trade was virtually eliminated. In this way, the state could ensure deliveries of agricultural products to the cities by making the deliveries mandatory. The prices at which farms had to sell produce to the state were set at low levels for two purposes. The first was to force a transfer of savings from the countryside to industry to finance the industrial investment (via the turnover tax on food products). The second purpose was to reduce rural real incomes to facilitate the transfer of labor out of agriculture into higher priority industrial occupations, offering relatively higher real wages. The depression of rural living standards encouraged the more productive age groups to leave the collective farms for the city, and organized state recruitment campaigns in the countryside were used to promote this movement.

3. In industry, especially in high priority branches, highly capital intensive factor proportions were adopted. In this manner, the movement of population from the rural to urban areas, though quite rapid, was held down. The result was a below average ratio of urbanization, relative to the level of development, which enabled planners to restrict the flow of resources into nonproductive municipal services.[33] Urbanization was also held down by encouraging high labor participation rates among the existing

---

(Cambridge, Mass.: Harvard University Press, 1963). In this chapter, we do not footnote summary material drawn from earlier chapters.

[32] We use "nonproductive" sectors in the Marxian meaning of an economic sector that produces services not directly connected with the production of a physical commodity.

[33] Ofer, *The Service Sector*, chap. 1.

urban population, especially of women. The low absolute real income levels and (in later years) laws against parasitism and absenteeism were used to encourage such high labor participation rates.

The rapid expansion of priority industrial branches was made possible by generous allocations of scarce capital by planning authorities. In addition, in the priority areas, relatively high wages were set to attract skilled industrial workers. On the other hand, the most neglected light industrial sectors were those with high capital-output ratios, notably printing, paper, and food products.[34]

Not having developed sophisticated planning techniques, the Soviets used "campaigns" to eliminate bottlenecks that arose as a result of taut planning. In addition, industrial planning was simplified by limiting product differentiation. This product strategy was expected to encourage standardization, limit the spare parts problem, and facilitate maintenance and repair. Scarce industrial capital was stretched by multiple shift arrangements (often three per day) and by utilizing capital until it was totally worn out. Further capital saving techniques involved the combining of advanced capital intensive Western technology in primary processes with old-fashioned labor intensive methods in auxiliary processes and the limiting of social overhead investment in transportation, roads, apartment buildings, schools, and hospitals.[35] Instead, social overhead capital carried over from earlier periods was simply utilized more intensively.

Large-scale integrated plants were chosen. This gigantomania was sanctioned for reasons of international prestige (having the world's largest dam, for example) and because it was hoped that unit costs would eventually be lower owing to economies of scale.[36] Furthermore, a long planning time horizon was adopted and interest rate calculations were not used, both of which condoned the long gestation periods involved in such projects. Highly integrated plants were chosen because of the primitive state of the material supply system, a factor that made less integrated plants quite vulnerable to supply interruptions. Machinery plants, for example, produced their own steel and shipped their finished products.[37] The integrated nature of industrial plants enabled planners to limit the size of wholesale trade.

4. Inflation, monetary controls, and the "money illusion" played im-

---

[34] Gregory, *Socialist and Nonsocialist Industrialization Patterns*, p. 144.

[35] Dodge and Wilber, "The Relevance of Soviet Industrial Experience," part 2.

[36] An empirical study of the costs of gigantism is provided by Barbara Katz, " 'Gigantism' as an Unbalanced Growth Strategy: An Econometric Investigation of the Soviet Experience, 1928–1940," *Soviet Union*, vol. 4, part 2 (1977), pp. 205–222. For a statistical comparison of the scale of Soviet industrial establishments with American establishments, see Alexander Woroniak, "Industrial Concentration in Eastern Europe: The Search for Optimum Size and Efficiency," *Notwendigkeit und Gefahr der Wirtschaftlichen Konzentration* (Basel: Kyklos Verlag), pp. 265–284.

[37] David Granick, *Soviet Metal Fabricating and Economic Development* (Madison: University of Wisconsin Press, 1967).

portant roles. The shift of resources away from consumer goods meant that the growth of real income would be held below the overall growth rate, or in its extreme manifestation, would even decline.[38] However, it was necessary to preserve worker incentives. Wages were allowed to rise out of pace with consumer goods, thereby creating inflation. Prices of consumer goods were raised at a more rapid rate than wages, on the grounds that workers would be more concerned with what was happening to their *money* wages than to their *real* wages. To preserve equity during this period of rapid inflation, some rationing of necessities was implemented; sales at above-rationing prices were permitted—in fact, a complex multiple price system was used—to preserve the incentive effect of differential wages.

Personal income taxes were not used as a major source of state revenue because it was assumed that indirect taxes better preserve worker incentives. The form of indirect taxation adopted—the turnover tax—was a hidden tax, and consumers were unaware of the extent to which they were bearing the burden of industrialization.[39] In addition, the multiple price system was a rich source of tax revenue.

Tax revenues gathered in this fashion were then used to finance investment, the funds for which were allocated by an investment plan. Very little, if any, investment was determined at the plant level. The state bank monitored the cash in the hands of the public through its control of enterprise cash accounts and—via its control over credit and transactions—monitored plan fulfillment, thus providing a secondary source of information on enterprise operations for the planning apparatus.

5. A significant portion of government expenditure was used to finance industrial investment. The remainder served to finance defense, administration, and public consumption expenditures. Considerable public resources were channeled into public health and education, on the grounds that a healthy and well-trained labor force was required to man the economy. The focus of education was upon technical specialization. The state embarked on a mass campaign of vocational education that took place to a great extent on the job. In this manner, the state saved

---

[38] One can question whether the decline in real income is a fundamental aspect of the SDM rather than an unforeseen result of the world depression, collectivization problems, poor harvest of 1931, and so on. In fact (as indicated in Chapter 3), the First Five Year Plan projected a substantial increase in consumer goods as well as falling consumer prices. Also, industrial wages were not supposed to rise as fast as they did. Our view is that the SDM does call for a *relative* shift in resources away from consumption and for holding the rate of growth of real incomes below attainable levels. Whether this policy will result in absolute declines, as was true in the Soviet case, will depend on the situation. It will, however, result in a relative decline.

[39] Franklyn D. Holzman, "Financing Soviet Development," in M. Abramovitz, ed., *Capital Formation and Economic Growth* (Princeton, N.J.: Princeton University Press, 1955), pp. 229–287.

scarce capital by not having to build additional schools, universities, and technical institutes. A further device to stretch educational resources was the emphasis on night school training, correspondence courses, and self-instruction. Throughout, the worker was encouraged to acquire additional training by highly differentiated wages, which favored the skilled worker.

6. The expansion of transport capacity was limited in order to restrict investment in social overhead capital. Planners counted on substantial improvements in levels of *utilization*, coupled with a pattern of industrialization designed to minimize the need for transport services. To achieve this latter objective, strong emphasis was placed upon locating industrial establishments at the site of raw materials.[40] A further aspect was the emphasis on railways as opposed to other forms of surface transportation thereby enabling authorities to avoid highway construction.[41]

7. The economy's relationships with the outside world changed as well. The state established a foreign trade monopoly to ensure that dealings with the outside world were in accordance with the needs of industrialization. Initially, agricultural products were exchanged for the machinery—in particular, machine tools that could be used to make other machinery—vital to the early stages of industrialization, and heavy reliance was placed on imports of foreign technology. However, the long-term emphasis was placed upon lessening dependence on the rest of the world, for such reliance was viewed as incompatible with the planned nature of the economy. This autarky approach dictated that a complete range of industrial and agricultural products should be produced domestically. Domestic production was therefore substituted for imports and specialization according to comparative advantage was neglected.[42]

Comparison with Western Trends

The above summary outlines the major features of Soviet industrialization during the USSR economy's formative years. Upon closer examination, it could be argued that there is nothing patently new about Soviet develop-

---

[40] Soviet planners have long stressed the need for economic development in all regions of the country. The Ural-Kuznetsk Combine was designed to tap the mineral resources of the Ural mountains and the coal resources of the Kuznetsk area and to be appropriately combined to form a large industrial center. For a detailed discussion of the program, see, for example, Franklyn D. Holzman, "The Soviet Ural-Kuznets Combine: A Study of Investment Criteria and Industrialization Policies," *Quarterly Journal of Economics*, vol. 71, no. 3 (August 1957), 367–405.

[41] Hunter, *Soviet Transportation Policy*, chap. 3 and especially chart 4, p. 49; Williams, *Freight Transportation*, pp. 136–137.

[42] One could perhaps argue that the Soviet autarky model was not a true component of the SDM, rather a historical accident of the world depression and the hostility of capitalist

ment, for there are striking similarities with economic development in the West. For example, the share of heavy industry increases during the process of development.[43] The investment rate rises during the course of development. In most Western countries, import substitution has caused a lowering of foreign trade proportions, just as in the Soviet case.[44] A further common feature is the rapid expansion of universal education and specialized training during the development process.

Thus, many aspects of the SDM are not new. Others—for example, material balance planning, the substitution of planners' preferences, the collective farm, the deemphasis of services, and many others—are new features of the SDM. One important fact, however, should not be neglected—that is that the SDM involved considerable differences in magnitude and timing in the implementation of these common elements.

1. The relative increase in heavy industry, which generally occurs during development, was greater both in *magnitude* and in *speed* in the Soviet Union. The increase in the combined metallurgy and engineering product share of manufacturing in the USSR of 26 percentage points (from 19 to 45 percent) between 1928 and 1937 required from 50 to 75 years in other countries, and many industrialized Western countries have yet to attain a heavy industry share as larage as the USSR's in 1937.[45]

2. The rapidity of the increase in the investment rate in the Soviet Union is another distinctive feature of the SDM. In 1928, gross investment as a percent of GNP (measured in 1937 factor costs) was 12.5 percent; by 1937 this figure was 25.9 percent, after peaking at 32 percent in 1935.[46] Such high investment rates have been matched and even surpassed by several Western countries. However, in Western countries, the rise in the investment rate was gradual and began several decades after industrialization was under way, not during its initial stages.[47]

3. Another distinctive feature of the SDM was its combination of a high investment rate with a relatively low marginal capital-output ratio

---

trading partners. While these factors were of course important in forcing the USSR into a position of low reliance on trade, it is also true that there are noteworthy factors in the system itself (the inability of a planned economy to tie itself to outside economies) that have caused both the USSR and Eastern Europe to maintain low foreign trade proportions in spite of changing political climates.

[43] Walter Hoffman, *The Growth of Industrial Economies* (Manchester, England: Manchester University Press, 1958); Gregory, *Socialist and Nonsocialist Industrialization Patterns*, p. 168.

[44] Simon Kuznets, *Modern Economic Growth* (New Haven, Conn.: Yale University Press, 1967), pp. 300–303.

[45] Gregory, *Socialist and Nonsocialist Industrialization Patterns*, pp. 28–29, Appendix B.

[46] R. Moorsteen and R. Powell, *The Soviet Capital Stock, 1928–1962* (Homewood, Ill.: Irwin, 1966), pp. 358, 361. The 1935 figure is estimated by applying the Moorsteen and Powell investment rate index to the Bergson 1937 figure.

[47] Kuznets, "A Comparative Appraisal," pp. 353–354.

during the initial stages of industrialization.[48] In Western countries, either investment rates and marginal capital-output ratios were both low or high investment rates were combined with high marginal capital-output ratios. The Soviet marginal capital-output ratio did begin to rise substantially after 1958, but prior to that, it had remained stable. The Soviets were able to maintain the stability of the marginal capital-output ratio largely by limiting investment in residential construction and transportation (with high capital-output ratios) and by intensive multishift utilization of existing industrial capital stock.[49]

4. Extremely rapid shifts of resources out of agriculture into industry were also characteristic of the SDM. In the course of Western development, the labor force and product shares of agriculture generally declined, but in the Soviet Union, the decline between 1928 and 1940 (Table 8, Chapter 3) required from 30 to 50 years in other countries.[50]

5. As far as sectoral productivity relationships are concerned, the Soviet experience was distinctive for the relatively low output per worker in agriculture compared to industry. In fact, ratios of sectoral product per worker were quite similar to the LDCs, where traditional and backward agricultural sectors prevail. There is evidence that labor productivity (in full-time equivalents) in Soviet agriculture actually declined between 1928 and 1940, quite in contrast to the industrialization experiences of other countries, where agricultural labor productivity generally kept pace with the overall productivity growth of the economy.[51]

6. The SDM also differed from the Western experience with respect to private consumption. In the West, the GNP share of private consumption normally declined. The distinctive feature of the trend in private consumption in the Soviet Union was the magnitude and rapidity of its relative decline—not to mention the *absolute* decline. In 1928, private consumption accounted for 80 percent of Soviet GNP. By 1940, this figure had dropped to 50 percent (Table 8, Chapter 3). In other countries, the drop was from 80 percent to between 60 and 70 percent—a decline that required from 30 to 80 years to complete, versus 12 years in the Soviet case.[52]

7. A further distinctive feature of the SDM was the rapid rise in the labor participation rate. Between 1928 and 1940, the Soviet population grew at 1.2 percent annually, while the labor force grew at 3.7 percent. Thus there was a 2.5 percent annual rate of growth of the labor participation rate. As Simon Kuznets notes: "No such accelerated use of labor

---

[48] The marginal (or incremental) capital-output ratio is the ratio of the change in capital stock to the change in output ($\Delta K / \Delta Q$).

[49] Kuznets, "A Comparative Appraisal," pp. 354–357.

[50] *Ibid.*, pp. 345–347.

[51] *Ibid.*, pp. 350–352.

[52] *Ibid.*, pp. 358–361.

relative to population appears to have occurred in other countries."[53]

8. The relatively low Soviet foreign trade proportions during industri-alization were also a distinctive feature of the SDM. Commonly, a country's dependence on foreign trade is gradually reduced in the course of develop-ment.[54] In the Soviet case, the ratio of exports to national income dropped dramatically, from 3.5 percent in 1930 to 0.5 percent in 1937. Part of this drop can be explained by the collapse of world prices of primary products during the world depression, but Soviet trade ratios to and after the de-pression remained quite low by international standards. As Kuznets notes: "[The low Soviet foreign trade proportions] reflect a forced isolation of a large population from contact with the rest of the world, not paralleled in any non-Communist country within modern times."[55]

9. A final distinctive feature of the SDM was the extent to which the service sector, especially commercial services such as trade, banking, and insurance, was depressed below "normal" levels in the Soviet Union. When compared with the development experience of Western countries, a Soviet service gap is evident in the sense that the labor force share of ser-vice was much below that expected of a market economy at a similar level of development. Thus the Soviet economy developed without devoting as much resources to services as have "normally" been required in the West.[56]

Soviet Economic Development: An Assessment

The speed of the structural transformation of the Soviet economy in accord-ance with the proclaimed goals of heavy industry priority, massive capital accumulation, and the decline in private ownership indicates the success of the Soviet Development Model. The transformation that took place in the Soviet Union in the short span of 12 years (1928–1940) required a half cen-tury or more in the industrialized West. It would be difficult to argue in the face of such evidence that the Soviet leadership's goal of accelerating eco-nomic development was not met.

These are the benefits of the Soviet Development Model; its costs are more difficult to evaluate, primarily because a disentanglement of the basic features of the Soviet model from the unique features of the Stalin dictator-ship is required. Were the substantial losses of forced collectivization a characteristic of the model or a historical accident linked to Stalin's person-ality? This issue has long been debated in Western literature in the context of Alec Nove's question: "Was Stalin necessary?"[57] We cannot hope to re-

---

[53] *Ibid.*, p. 341.

[54] Kuznets, *Modern Economic Growth*, pp. 300–302.

[55] Kuznets, "A Comparative Appraisal," p. 367.

[56] Ofer, *The Service Sector*, chap. 3.

[57] Alec Nove, *Economic Rationality and Soviet Politics* (New York: Praeger, 1964), essay 1.

solve such weighty issues here; what we can do is to list some of the costs of rapid development. The forced transformation of Soviet agriculture from a private to a collective basis entailed significant costs that probably could not have been avoided with or without Stalin, and those costs have been discussed in Chapter 7. The relative decline of light industry undoubtedly affected industrial incentives and labor productivity. The general neglect of agriculture has required extraordinary injections of resources into agriculture in the postwar era. The one-sided priority of heavy industry has probably resulted in the maldistribution of capital resources by Western standards. We could add to this list, but choose instead to return to the basic point of trade-offs among economic objectives. Economic development was indeed accelerated in the Soviet case, but at the considerable expense of other areas. The reader should be reminded as well of the discussion in Chapter 7 concerning the existence of an "agricultural surplus" attributable to collectivization. It is not at all clear that collectivization did indeed cause a net transfer of resources (labor not included) into industry. If not, one of the main pillars of the Soviet model is removed.

SOVIET ENVIRONMENTAL QUALITY

Under capitalism, environmental disruption (ED) is thought to be caused by external effects. External effects arise whenever the private costs (or benefits) of a particular action diverge from its social costs (or benefits). If a profit-maximizing capitalist firm is able, for example, to pollute the air without being charged a price for this activity, the social cost of production will exceed the private cost and a greater than optimal level of environmental disruption will emerge. Only if private enterprises can be charged for the social costs (via a tax, for example) of their pollution or if such activities are internalized will the level of environmental disruption be optimal.[58] The optimality criterion is such that pollution should be allowed up to that level at which its marginal social cost equals the marginal cost of pollution abatement.[59] This is the standard adopted by most economists to the chagrin of many environmental groups, who deny the existence of "optimal" levels of pollution.

Advocates of socialism have long argued on theoretical grounds that ED will not arise in a socialist society. Although specifics have varied, the essential thread is the *level* of decision-making. Where decisions are centralized and the objective function—the outcome that planners are trying

---

[58] Internalization occurs when costs that were previously external to the polluting enterprise become internal costs. For example, if all enterprises located along a river are merged, then the water pollution abatement costs of these enterprises become private costs.

[59] Robert McIntyre and James Thornton, "On the Environmental Efficiency of Economic Systems," *Soviet Studies*, vol. 30, no. 2 (April 1978), 173–192.

to achieve—includes environmental quality, there need never be externalities, since there is literally nothing external to the decision makers. A similar argument is made for local decision-making if the planners develop an incentive structure that ensures the harmony of local decisions with central goals (assuming the necessary concomitant of perfect information). It is necessary that appropriate resource valuations, which reflect central goals, be available to the central decision makers.[60]

Oskar Lange, a classic advocate of the socialist cause, argued in his famous article, *On the Economic Theory of Socialism*,[61] that under socialism, the price system will be more comprehensive, and in effect, a high value will be placed by the Central Planning Board upon a clean environment. Maurice Dobb makes a similar argument when he suggests that although information availability and digestion may be a problem in the real world, socialist planners will tend to make decisions with maximum global vision and an eye to their environmental impact.[62] Jan Tinbergen, the noted Dutch economist, has also endorsed the notion that in general, decisions made at the highest possible levels will minimize the problem of externalities.[63]

Such theoretical arguments to the contrary, there is a well-documented literature that environmental disruption is, in fact, a problem in the Soviet Union.[64] The Soviet press and literature abound with cases of soil erosion, poisoning of rivers and lakes with industrial effluents and chemical fertilizers, industrial air pollution, and so on—problems that have become common in the industrialized West. Growing concern in the Soviet Union is reflected in the formation of conservationist groups, increasing press atten-

---

[60] Arthur Wright, "Environmental Disruption and Economic Systems: An Attempt at an Analytical Framework," *The ASTE Bulletin*, vol. 13, no. 1 (Spring 1971), 11–12.

[61] Lange's paper appears in Benjamin E. Lippincott, ed., *On the Economic Theory of Socialism* (Minneapolis: University of Minnesota Press, 1938), pp. 103 ff., reprinted by McGraw-Hill, 1964.

[62] Maurice Dobb, *Welfare Economics and the Economics of Socialism* (Cambridge: Cambridge University Press, 1969), p. 133.

[63] For a discussion of this point, see Dobb, *Welfare Economics*, pp. 133–134. For a survey of theorizing on environmental quality, see Marshall I. Goldman, *The Spoils of Progress: Environmental Pollution in the Soviet Union* (Cambridge, Mass.: MIT Press, 1972), pp. 12–22.

[64] Marshall I. Goldman, "Externalities and the Race for Economic Growth in the Soviet Union: Will the Environment Ever Win?" *Journal of Political Economy*, vol. 80, no. 2 (March/April, 1972); Keith Bush, "Environmental Disruption: The Soviet Response," *L'Est*, no. 2 (June 1972); Donald Kelley, Kenneth Stunkel, and Richard Wescott, *The Economic Superpowers and the Environment: The United States, the Soviet Union, and Japan* (San Francisco, Calif.: Freeman, 1976); W. A. Jackson, ed., *Soviet Resource Management and the Environment* (Columbus, Ohio: Anchor Press, 1978); Victor Mote, "Environmental Protection and the Soviet Tenth Five Year Plan," *Geographical Survey*, vol. 7, no. 2 (April 1978); Philip R. Pryde, *Conservation in the Soviet Union* (Cambridge, Mass.: Harvard University Press, 1972); Fred Singleton, *Environmental Misuse in the USSR* (New York: Praeger, 1976).

tion, and the passage of a number of (generally ineffective) laws concerned with environmental quality.[65]

Measurement of Environmental Pollution

To assess the Soviet record of environmental protection, one must begin with some notion of the stock of pollution in the USSR relative to the stock in the industrialized capitalist countries. Of all the performance criteria, we are on the most treacherous footing with regard to the measurement of pollution levels.[66] Although it may be possible to establish the physical quantities of harmful air pollutants, water pollutants, noise pollution, and radiation, there is no established system of weights that allows the researcher to aggregate environmental disruption into a single global measure. In place of a global measure, one must rely on various partial measures, the firmest of which are for air pollution. According to calculations by Victor Mote (for 1968–1969), the gross weights of air pollutants produced in the USSR were as follows: dust, 61 percent of U.S.; sulfur dioxide, 49 percent of U.S.; carbon monoxide, 19 percent of U.S.; and hydrocarbons, 22 percent of U.S.[67] Although a number of studies of Soviet water, noise, and radiation pollution have been undertaken, the USSR production of these forms of environmental disruption relative to other countries cannot yet be estimated.

The air pollution data, however, suggest (by all conceivable weighting schemes) that the USSR produces less air pollution than does the United States. Does this demonstrate superior Soviet performance? A number of conditioning factors must be considered, some of which would contribute to higher levels of expected pollution (the greater frequency of air inversions, the lesser emphasis on "clean" industry and services) and others to lower expected levels. The USSR's lower level of economic output and lower per capita income are factors that would be expected to lower Soviet levels of environmental disruption. Soviet GNP in 1976 was roughly three-quarters that of the United States, while expenditures on consumption were 54 percent of those of the United States.[68] Given lower levels of output and consumption, one would expect lower levels of pollution, independent of environmental performance.

---

[65] Although the power of the state and the Soviet view of the superiority of the public sector should be positive forces in the control of environmental disruption, the specific techniques used in the Soviet case, notably administrative penalties and criminal prosecution, seem to have been most ineffective. On this see Goldman, *The Spoils of Progress*, pp. 28–37.
[66] For a discussion of measurement problems, see McIntyre and Thornton, "Environmental Efficiency," pp. 182–183.
[67] *Ibid.*, p. 181.
[68] Imogene Edwards, Margaret Hughes, and James Noren, "US and USSR: Comparisons of GNP," in Joint Economic Committee, *Soviet Economy in a Time of Change* (Washington, D.C.: U.S. Government Printing Office, 1979), vol. 1, pp. 378 and 385.

The lower level of consumption, especially the decision to not produce automobiles, is a significant explanatory factor behind the lower observed levels of Soviet pollution. The Soviets have yet to reach the age of mass motoring, with the stock of passenger automobiles roughly equivalent to American 1913 levels.[69] The flush toilet, with its tremendous demand on fresh water, is still not universal in Soviet urban housing. The density of population is still relatively low. Packaging in light industries and food industries is still a rarity, thus reducing the solid waste disposal problem that has plagued industrialized Western countries.

Because environmental disruption does seem to be a concomitant of the industrialization process, it is difficult to evaluate the performance of the Soviet system without some quantifiable notion of what constitutes a "normal" level of pollution for a given level of economic development. Only in this way can one judge whether the Soviet economy has performed "better" or "worse" in providing a suitable environment. In some areas, the Soviet system may have natural advantages over market economies—for example, the unwillingness of Soviet planners to meet the pent-up demand for private automobiles and their stress upon cheap mass urban transit, the ability of urban and regional planners to develop master plans for areas independently of private developers, the stress on multifamily dwellings that make use of centrally supplied warm water for washing and heating, and so on. However, it is not possible to draw an overall balance.

Even if we were able to determine whether Soviet environmental performance is better or worse than that of capitalist countries at the same stage of economic development, a measure of the *efficiency* of Soviet environmental policy is still lacking.[70] An efficient environmental program is one that equates the marginal costs and benefits of pollution abatement, and as different societies have varying preferences concerning the costs and benefits of environmental protection, it is theoretically possible to combine efficiency with relatively high (or low) environmental disruption.

Causes of Pollution in the Soviet Union

Why is there pollution in the Soviet economy? Three possible reasons might be considered. First, it may be that planners were not concerned with environmental quality until the level of development became such that, in combination with the international demonstration effect, its presence became pervasive. More important however is the possibility that environmental quality had been consciously discarded as one of the costs of rapid economic growth. In effect, the Soviets raised growth in the short-run by simply not placing a high price on pollution costs—in

[69] Keith Bush, "Environmental Disruption: The Soviet Response," *L'EST*, No. 2 (June, 1972).

[70] This point is stressed by McIntyre and Thornton, "Environmental Efficiency," 174.

effect, postponing some of the costs by letting them accumulate in the form of a stock of pollution. Thus disinvestment in the environment would be considered as a rather typical aspect of Soviet economic development, just as it has characterized economic growth generally in market economies.

A second factor leading to environmental disruption in the Soviet Union is the breakdown of *valuation*—a problem not unique to the Soviet Union. Planners are simply unaware of appropriate resource valuations, including the costs of environmental disruption, and hence may be unable to allocate them in a "rational" manner even if they so desired. This in effect is a breakdown of the information mechanism common to both market and planned economies. We suggest that this is a likely partial explanation in view of the Soviets' inability to compute scarcity prices in general either with or without social costs.[71] In the Soviet context, the valuation problem is further complicated by Marxian theory, which is prejudiced against charging for natural resources (the labor theory of value). Like the right to pollute the environment, natural resources have in effect been given to enterprises free of charge, thereby encouraging them to overuse depletable natural resources.[72]

Third, perfectly centralized decision-making as visualized in the idealized versions of the socialist economic model has not proved to be practical in the real world. In fact, most crucial economic decisions are made not by a small group of planners at the apex of the planning hierarchy who take the broad overview of the economy, but by ministerial and regional authorities and by plant managers, none of whom can see (or cares to see) the total impact of his actions. In effect, there has been no pressure group concerned with the environment. Instead, administrators and managers are concerned with performing well, in line with directives given them by their superiors; and as we noted above, success in the Soviet economy has been determined primarily on the basis of fulfilling short-term output goals. Less easily quantifiable goals (especially in view of the price system) such as cost reductions, innovations, and environmental quality have not played a role in influencing decision-making. Thus, where environmental groups exist in the Soviet Union, they find themselves in the awkward position of having to lobby against regional *Gosplan* organizations, national ministries, or even the party itself on projects that create environmental disruption, in other words, against the very organizations that in theory are to prevent environ-

---

[71] Some Soviet economists have argued that each factory should be accountable for both direct *and* social costs. However, such has not been the case, primarily due to the absence of appropriate cost measurement and the potential conflict with Marxian ideology. On this see Goldman, *The Spoils of Progress*, pp. 46 ff.

[72] Judith Thornton, "Resources and Property Rights in the Soviet Union," in W. A. Jackson, ed., *Soviet Resource Management and the Environment* (Columbus, Ohio: Anchor Press, 1978), pp. 1–12.

mental disruption from taking place.[73] In fact, there is no all-union agency for protecting the environment. Rather, environmental protection has tended to be placed in the hands of various agencies, all with limited powers.

The final source of environmental disruption in the Soviet Union is the lack of a clear assignment of "property rights" (the assignment of rights to use, benefit from, and bear the costs of scarce resources).[74] Under capitalism, property rights belong to private owners, who bear the costs and reap the benefits from the use of the resource. In the case of resources with a long-life span (renewable and nonrenewable natural resources, capital equipment), the capitalist owner will weigh current and future benefits and will forgo current use if the prospect of future reward is sufficiently high. Thus there is a natural incentive to conserve. Under socialism, property rights are assigned to society as a whole, not to individual workers or to plant managers. These persons are rewarded according to short-term performance criteria and will not personally benefit from refraining from current use for the sake of future use. The incentive to conserve is therefore lacking, unless imposed from above via a change in the existing incentive system.

SELECTED BIBLIOGRAPHY

Soviet Military Power

Abraham Becker, "The Meaning and Measure of Soviet Military Expenditure," in Joint Economic Committee, *Soviet Economy in a Time of Change* (Washington, D.C.: U.S. Government Printing Office, 1979), vol. 1, pp. 352–368.

Hans Bergendorff and Per Strangert, "Projections of Soviet Economic Growth and Defense Spending," in Joint Economic Committee, *Soviet Economy in a New Perspective* (Washington, D.C.: U.S. Government Printing Office, 1976), pp. 394–430.

Lars Calmfors and Jan Rylander, "Economic Restrictions on Soviet Defense Expenditure," in Joint Economic Committee, *Soviet Economy in a New Perspective* (Washington, D.C.: U.S. Government Printing Office, 1976), pp. 377–392.

William T. Lee, *The Estimation of Soviet Defense Expenditures, 1955–1975* (New York: Praeger, 1977).

[73] The Ministry of Power's handling of Lake Baikal is a case in point. Despite protests from residents concerning the environmental damage that such a project would cause, dam construction was pushed through, although other sources of electricity were already available at cheaper cost. See Goldman, "Externalities." Another case in point is the Central Committee's irrigation program that calls for the diversion of Siberian rivers to irrigate dry regions in Kazakhstan and Central Asia, which will have an important impact on the climate of the Far North. On this see Bush, "Environmental Disruption."

[74] This discussion is based upon Thornton, "Resources and Property Rights," pp. 1–12.

National Foreign Assessment Center, *A Dollar Cost Comparison of Soviet and U.S. Defense Activities, 1968–78,* SR79–10004, Washington, D.C., January 1979.

National Foreign Assessment Center, *Estimated Soviet Defense Spending: Trends and Prospects,* SR78–10121, Washington, D.C., June 1978.

Henry W. Shaeffer, "Soviet Power and Intentions: Military-Economic Choices," in Joint Economic Committee, *Soviet Economy in a Time of Change* (Washington, D.C.: U.S. Government Printing Office, 1979), vol. 1, pp. 341–351.

Soviet Technology

Ronald Amman, Julian Cooper, and R. W. Davies, *The Technological Level of Soviet Industry* (New Haven, Conn.: Yale University Press, 1977).

Joseph Berliner, *The Innovation Decision in Soviet Industry* (Cambridge, Mass.: MIT Press, 1976).

James Grant, "Soviet Machine Tools: Lagging Technology and Rising Imports" in Joint Economic Committee, *Soviet Economy in a Time of Change* (Washington, D.C.: U.S. Government Printing Office, 1979), vol. 1, pp. 524–553.

Philip Hanson, "The Diffusion of Imported Technology," in NATO Economics Directorate, *Economic Aspects of Life in the USSR* (Brussels: NATO, 1976).

Philip Hanson, "International Technology Transfer from the West to the USSR," in Joint Economic Committee, *Soviet Economy in a New Perspective* (Washington, D.C.: U.S. Government Printing Office, 1976), pp. 786–812.

John Martens and John P. Young, "Soviet Implementation of Domestic Inventions: First Results," in Joint Economic Committee, *Soviet Economy in a Time of Change* (Washington, D.C.: U.S. Government Printing Office, 1979), vol. 1, pp. 472–509.

John R. Thomas and Ursula Kruse-Vaucenne, eds., *Soviet Science and Technology* (Washington, D.C.: George Washington University, 1977), parts 3 and 4.

Eugene Zaleski et al., *Science Policy in the USSR* (Paris: OECD, 1969).

The Soviet Development Model of the 1930s

Paul Gregory, *Socialist and Nonsocialist Industrialization Patterns* (New York: Praeger, 1970).

Franklyn D. Holzman, "Foreign Trade," in Abram Bergson and Simon Kuznets, eds., *Economic Trends in the Soviet Union* (Cambridge, Mass.: Harvard University Press, 1963), pp. 283–332.

Franklyn D. Holzman, *Soviet Taxation* (Cambridge, Mass.: Harvard University Press, 1955).

Holland Hunter, *Soviet Transportation Policy* (Cambridge, Mass.: Harvard University Press, 1957).

Barbara Katz, " 'Gigantism' as an Unbalanced Growth Strategy: An Econometric Investigation of the Soviet Experience, 1928–1940," *Soviet Union,* vol. 4, part 2 (1977), pp. 205–222.

Simon Kuznets, "A Comparative Appraisal," in Abram Bergson and Simon Kuznets, eds., *Economic Trends in the Soviet Union* (Cambridge, Mass.: Harvard University Press, 1963), pp. 333–382.

Gur Ofer, "Economizing on Urbanization in Socialist Countries," in Alan Brown and Egon Neuberger, eds., *Internal Migration: A Comparative Perspective* (New York: Academic Press, 1977), pp. 277–304.

Gur Ofer, "Industrial Structure, Urbanization, and the Growth Strategy of Socialist Countries," *Quarterly Journal of Economics*, vol. 90, no. 2 (May 1976), pp. 219–243.

Gur Ofer, *The Service Sector in Soviet Economic Growth* (Cambridge, Mass.: Harvard University Press, 1973).

Frederic Pryor, *Public Expenditures in Communist and Capitalist Nations* (Homewood, Ill.: Irwin, 1968).

Charles K. Wilber, *The Soviet Model and Underdeveloped Countries* (Chapel Hill: University of North Carolina Press, 1969).

Ernest W. Williams, Jr., *Freight Transportation in the Soviet Union* (Princeton, N.J.: Princeton University Press, 1962).

Environmental Quality

Keith Bush, "Environmental Disruption: The Soviet Response," *L'Est*, no. 2 (June 1972).

Marshall I. Goldman, "Externalities and the Race for Economic Growth in the Soviet Union: Will the Environment Ever Win?" *Journal of Political Economy*, vol. 80, no. 2 (March/April, 1972).

W. A. Jackson, ed., *Soviet Resource Management and the Environment* (Columbus, Ohio: Anchor Press, 1978).

Donald Kelley, Kenneth Stunkel, and Richard Wescott, *The Economic Superpowers and the Environment: The United States, the Soviet Union, and Japan* (San Francisco, Calif.: Freeman, 1976).

Robert McIntyre and James Thornton, "On the Environmental Efficiency of Economic Systems," *Soviet Studies*, vol. 30, no. 2 (April 1978), 173–192.

Victor Mote, "Environmental Protection and the Soviet Tenth Five Year Plan," *Geographical Survey*, vol. 7, no. 2 (April 1978), 25–34.

Philip R. Pryde, *Conservation in the Soviet Union* (Cambridge, Mass.: Harvard University Press, 1972).

Fred Singleton, *Environmental Misuse in the USSR* (New York: Praeger, 1976).

Judith Thornton, "Resources and Property Rights in the Soviet Union," in W. A. Jackson, ed., *Soviet Resource Management and the Environment* (Columbus, Ohio: Anchor Press, 1978), pp. 1–12.

Chapter 12

Conclusions and Prospects

ACHIEVEMENTS

The Soviet Union enters the 1980s, more than a half century after the First Five Year Plan, with some impressive achievements. The Soviet economy's position vis-à-vis the industrialized West has improved substantially. In 1928, Soviet GNP was roughly one-quarter that of the United States; by 1980, the ratio had risen to three-quarters (both ratios measured in U.S. prices).[1] This improvement in relative position was the result of a more rapid growth than in the industrialized West, where only Japan has rivaled the Soviet long-run growth record. For example, an annual growth rate differential of 1.5 percentage points compounded over 50 years will cause an improvement in relative GNP by a factor of more than two. Soviet achievements in the military area need not be repeated beyond noting that Soviet military power is now rivaled only by the United States, a country whose GNP well surpasses that of the USSR. The advent of centralized planning appears to have accelerated both the growth rates of output and of military power, as dictated by a succession of leaders. The historical rate of growth of the tsarist economy during its industrialization era (1885–1913) was slightly in excess of 3 percent per annum. From the First Five Year Plan to 1980, the Soviet growth rate has averaged 5 percent, if the war years are ignored. We cannot rule out the possibility that a capitalist Russia would also have experienced a rapid increase in its relative economic position after 1917, as did the United States in the nineteenth century and Japan in the twentieth century, but such cases are rare in world economic history.

We believe it fair to conclude, therefore, that the introduction of the Soviet system of central planning and management did indeed cause an ac-

---

[1] This section is drawn from Paul R. Gregory, "Economic Growth and Structural Change in Tsarist Russia and the Soviet Union: A Long-Term Comparison," in Steven Rosefielde, ed., *Economic Welfare and the Economics of Soviet Socialism* (Cambridge: Cambridge University Press, 1981).

celeration of the growth rate and that without the change in the economic system, the relative position of the Soviet Union would not have improved as dramatically as it did. The structural changes desired by the Soviet leadership (the rise in heavy industry, the destruction of private economic activity, the reduced dependence on foreign trade) were implemented at an unprecedented pace by the Soviet economic system. The structural changes that occurred in the USSR between 1928 and 1940 typically required 50 years or more in the industrialized West.

What features of the Soviet economic system were responsible for Soviet growth achievements? Simply stated, Soviet planners were able to accelerate growth by allocating resources in such a manner as to maximize the growth of labor and capital inputs. If factor inputs had continued to grow at the rates of the late tsarist era, it is unlikely that any acceleration would have taken place.[2] The mechanisms for maximizing the growth of factor inputs have been described in earlier chapters: administrative allocation to favor producer goods at the expense of consumer goods, the use of administrative and market mechanisms to raise labor force participation rates and to encourage the flow of labor out of agriculture and handicrafts into priority branches, the reliance on turnover taxes to create funds for investment, the use of the collective farm to ensure deliveries and to depress rural living standards, and so on.

The rapid expansion of Soviet economic and military power was purchased at considerable expense to the Soviet Union. The growth of living standards was virtually halted during the 1930s and remained depressed after the death of Stalin. It can be safely said that the Soviet consumer, both in the city and the countryside, bore the burden of rapid industrialization. The relation between the Soviet economic system and Soviet productivity performance remains poorly understood, but a couple of points need to be repeated. The Soviet Union began the era of central planning with a large technology gap relative to the industrialized West. Yet since 1928, the growth rate of factor productivity has been at best average relative to these countries; there is no evidence that the USSR has succeeded in closing the technology gap it inherited from its tsarist predecessors. The sole exception to this judgment is military technology, an area where the technology gap has indeed been narrowed (or even eliminated). Expert studies of Soviet technology cited in this book conclude that the past two decades have not witnessed a noticeable reduction in the USSR's technological backwardness.

The most serious disappointment of the Soviet economy has been its inability to create intensive economic growth, that is, growth based upon increases in efficiency rather than upon the growth of factor inputs. In the industrialized West, at least two-thirds of economic growth is typically ac-

[2] *Ibid.*

counted for by the growth of efficiency. In the Soviet case, the ratio is one-third. This means that Soviet economic growth has been of a high cost variety, for growth that depends upon the expansion of factor inputs calls for sacrifices of consumption and leisure. The relationship between the supply of consumer goods and productivity is a cloudy one, but it is likely that the deprivation experienced by Soviet consumers has impacted negatively over the years upon their performance as workers.

The probable causes of the Soviet technology gap have been duly noted. The existing system appears to discourage innovation and new ways of doing things because the reward structure fails to compensate Soviet managers for the risks of innovative activity. The pervasive emphasis on short-term performance, particularly output goals, has created an environment that does not encourage the efficient combination of resources to produce output. A side effect of the emphasis on the short run has been the failure to discourage environmental disruption, much like such activities are not penalized in the West.

Is the Soviet economic system of 1980 the same as that which evolved in the 1930s or has the Soviet system "converged" toward that of capitalism? Convergence could be noted either as a convergence of Soviet resource allocation patterns toward patterns prevailing in the West, as a change in Soviet economic institutions to resemble more closely those of capitalist countries, or as a growing homogeneity of all industrial societies.[3] The postwar era has indeed witnessed some change in the pattern of Soviet resource allocation, namely, the increasing share of resources devoted to agriculture and rising foreign trade proportions, but the central features of the Soviet allocational model—the priority of heavy industry, a high investment rate for the level of economic development, the relative neglect of services, a consumption gap—have persisted to the 1980s.

The degree of institutional convergence depends upon the impact of

[3] For discussions of the convergence hypothesis, see Jan Tinbergen, "Do Communist and Free Economies Show a Converging Pattern?" *Soviet Studies*, vol. 12, no. 4 (April 1961), 331–341; P. J. D. Wiles, "Will Capitalism and Communism Spontaneously Converge?" *Encounter*, vol. 20, no. 6 (June 1963), 84–90. For a summary of general arguments, see H. Linnemann, J. P. Pronk, and J. Tinbergen, "Convergence of Economic Systems in East and West," in Emile Benoit, ed., *Disarmament and World Economic Interdependence* (New York: Columbia University Press, 1967), pp. 246–260. For more critical views, see L. Leontiev, "Myth About Rapprochement of the Two Systems," in Jan S. Prybyla, ed., *Comparative Economic Systems* (New York: Appleton-Century-Crofts, 1969), pp. 477–483; James R. Millar, "On the Merits of the Convergence Hypothesis," *Journal of Economic Issues*, vol. 2, no. 1 (March 1969), 60–68; Jan S. Prybyla, "The Convergence of Market-Oriented and Command-Oriented Systems: A Critical Estimate," in Jan S. Prybyla, *Comparative Economic Systems* (New York: Appleton-Century-Crofts, 1969), pp. 467–476; Robert C. Stuart and Paul R. Gregory, "The Convergence of Economic Systems: An Analysis of Structural and Institutional Characteristics," *Jahrbuch der Wirtschaft Osteuropas* [Yearbook of East-European Economies], Band 2 (Munich: Gunter Olzog Verlag, 1971), pp. 425–442.

economic reform on Soviet resource allocation arrangements. The initial discussion of economic reform suggested that important injections of "economic levers" might be introduced into the Soviet system, and reform experiments have indeed tested the use of some capitalist techniques. The official reform of 1965 sought to strengthen the existing system by allowing enterprise managers only a limited degree of extra flexibility, which was then withdrawn in the early 1970s. Most observers believe that "reform is dead" and that Soviet authorities have again turned to organizational shuffling to resolve economic problems. The basic restraint on economic reform is that it requires a diminution of centralized authority, something the party and state hierarchies have been unwilling to accept.

PROBLEMS OF THE SEVENTIES

The Soviet economy enters the 1980s after a troubled decade. The industrialized West had its share of economic troubles as well—the energy crisis, rising inflation rates, the need to establish a new world monetary system— but this fact provides small consolation to the troubled Soviet economic system. This system saw its growth rate fall from 6 percent per annum in the 1950s to less than 4 percent in the 1970s. At the end of the decade, the growth rate had declined to 3 percent, the same growth rate as the tsarist economy.[4] The falling productivity of the Soviet economy was especially alarming. After 1973, the growth rate of factor productivity was negative in most years, and capital productivity (after growing at negative rates after 1960) declined to even lower rates. Even in industry, the priority interest of Soviet planners, factor productivity became negative after 1975.[5] The declining rates of growth of output and productivity emphasized that unless the Soviet leadership were to impose enormous additional burdens on a population that had become accustomed to a rising living standard, a new Soviet model of intensive growth would be required to restore the rate of growth to an acceptable level.

In the 1970s, the Soviet economy turned increasingly outward to meet its needs for grain and advanced technology. The proportion of imports to GNP rose substantially, and these imports were financed in large part by Western credits. Soviet indebtedness to Western countries increased but remained within manageable proportions. Hard currency earnings were based principally on exports of petroleum products and raw materials, the

[4] Herbert Block, "Soviet Economic Performance in a Global Context," in Joint Economic Committee, *Soviet Economy in a Time of Change* (Washington, D.C.: U.S. Government Printing Office, 1979), vol. 1, pp. 110–141. These figures have been updated from press accounts of Soviet economic growth in 1979 and 1980; Gregory, "Economic Growth and Structural Change."

[5] National Foreign Assessment Center, *Handbook of Economic Statistics 1979*, ER79-10274, Washington, D.C., August 1979, pp. 64–65. These figures have been updated from press accounts for 1979 and 1980.

supplies of which grew increasingly tight in the Soviet domestic economy. Although the declining ability to rely on petroleum exports could be countered initially by tightening up exports to COMECON nations, Soviet authorities began to realize that their imports from the West must remain limited. Moreover, the failure to gain trade and credit concessions from the United States during the 1970s worsened the Soviets' prospects of competing effectively in Western markets.

The 1970s also brought home the fact that economic reform, in the modest form tolerated by Soviet officialdom, would not release large volumes of "hidden reserves" as had been hoped. When faced with the choice of significant decentralization of economic authority or a return to the problems of the traditional planning system, the leadership chose the latter.

OPTIONS FOR THE 1980s

Projections for the 1980s offer little prospect of quick solution to the problems of the 1970s. For two decades, Soviet birthrates have been declining (more so in the Slavic republics than in the Asian republics), and this means that the working age population will necessarily grow at very slow rates in the 1980s. The prime working age population is scheduled to grow only 5 percent (0.5 percent annually) in the 1980s.[6] The slow growth of the working age population will be particularly apparent in the younger age groups, which will actually decline in absolute terms in the 1980s. Any growth that does occur will be in the non-Slavic republics, where the bulk of industry is not located. Moreover, the willingness of the non-Slavic nationalities to migrate to labor deficit areas is in doubt.[7] Thus, the Soviet leadership must increasingly channel resources into republics that have traditionally had lower productivity, possibly complicating the productivity problem.[8] One option to counter the quantitative decline in the growth rate of labor is to increase its quality. This option has not been exhausted, and the median years of schooling of the working age population is forecast to increase at an annual rate of one percent in the 1980s. This projection may be overly optimistic, insofar as students will be under increasing pressure to enter the

[6] Godfrey Baldwin, *Population Projections by Age and Sex: For the Republics and Major Economic Regions of the USSR, 1970 to 2000,* International Population Reports, Series P–91, No. 26, September 1979, Table 3.
[7] Murray Feshbach, "Prospects for Outmigration from Central Asia and Kazakstan in the Next Decade," in Joint Economic Committee, *Soviet Economy in a Time of Change* (Washington, D.C.: U.S. Government Printing Office, 1979), vol. 1, pp. 656–709.
[8] Martin Spechler, "Regional Developments in the USSR, 1958–1978," in Joint Economic Committee, *Soviet Economy in a Time of Change* (Washington, D.C.: U.S. Government Printing Office, 1979), vol. 1, pp. 141–164; NATO Economics Directorate, *Regional Development in the USSR: Trends and Prospects* (Newtonville, Mass.: Oriental Research Partners, 1979).

labor force and as an increasing portion of the labor force will be drawn from the Asian republics, where mean education is lower. Under most scenarios, the impact of rising education will have only a small compensating effect on the growing scarcity of labor.[9]

The Soviet Union ended the 1970s with a gross investment share of over 30 percent and a ratio of defense expenditures to GNP of 13 percent. Thus less than 57 percent of GNP is left to meet consumption, public services, and administration requirements.[10] These figures fairly well rule out the possibility of a significant expansion in the share of resources devoted to investment without a drastic reallocation of priorities away from either defense or the consumer. If output grows at a slow pace, rates of growth of investment well above the output rate will be difficult to maintain. In the late 1970s, Soviet capital stock was growing at an annual rate in excess of 7 percent.[11] If the growth rate of output continues to slow, it will be difficult to maintain this growth rate without imposing hardships on the consumer. Even if the Soviets are able to maintain a rapid rate of growth of capital stock, there are serious questions about the continuing effectiveness of this strategy. In the 1960s and 1970s, increasing difficulties in substituting capital for labor were encountered, and with the expected decline in the growth rate of labor, one would expect such substitution difficulties to multiply.

According to Keith Bush, the Soviet leadership is faced with five options.[12] They are: (1) to continue the Stalinist model, with high rates of growth of capital stock; (2) to reduce the burden of military expenditures; (3) to increase the import of Western technology; (4) to engage in a radical reform of the economic system; and (5) to do very little. If the last option is pursued (and this appears most likely), American analysts project that Soviet economic growth will decline to an annual rate of 3 to 3.5 percent and perhaps lower. Such low rates would not spell the end of the Soviet system, but they would make the competition for scarce resources intense.[13] They would also mean the acceptance of a growth rate roughly equivalent to that of the industrialized West and thus an acceptance of the economic status quo (an abandoning of the leadership's effort to overtake the West). Long-range forecasts must contain margins of error. In the Soviet case, the major

[9] National Foreign Assessment Center, *USSR: Trends and Prospects in Educational Attainment, 1959–85*, ER79–10344, Washington, D.C., June 1979.

[10] National Foreign Assessment Center, *Handbook of Economic Statistics 1979* p. 29.

[11] *Ibid.,* p. 65.

[12] Keith Bush, "The Tenth Five-Year Plan and the USSR's Economic Prospects," in John R. Thomas and Ursula Kruse-Vaucienne, eds., *Soviet Science and Technology* (Washington, D.C.: George Washington University, 1977), pp. 256–276.

[13] Hearings Before the Subcommittee on Priorities and Economy in Government, *Allocation of Resources in the Soviet Union and China—1978; Part 4:* (Washington, D.C., June 26 and July 14, 1978), pp. 38, 78.

unknowns are labor productivity and agricultural production.[14] The first option is not a viable one, for reasons spelled out above. If the rate of GNP growth is low, high rates of capital accumulation require that living standards be sacrificed. One would doubt that the current leadership (and the one to come) will be secure enough in its position to risk a major alienation of the Soviet consumer.

The third option (to import Western technology) will be of limited value unless the imported technology is put to effective use in the Soviet economy, which means that it will have to be effectively selected and then diffused throughout the economy. Insofar as imported technology will continue to represent a minor portion of Soviet capital stock, its indirect effects (felt through the diffusion of new technology) will have to be great in order to have a noticeable effect on Soviet GNP.[15] The available Western studies of the Soviet experience with imported technology disagree on its impact: some argue that it has been negligible; others, that it has been important.[16] Even if it is proved that imported technology can be utilized to raise the Soviet growth rate, there is the further question of the Soviets' ability over the long haul to afford the importation of large quantities of imported capital. Much would depend upon the rate of growth of Soviet oil output, grain harvests, gold prices, and the West's willingness to grant credits.[17]

The second option (to reduce the defense burden) would, according to American analysts, have a surprisingly small effect on the Soviet growth rate unless the USSR leadership were to drop out of the international arms race. Under conceivable scenarios, the defense burden could be reduced only to the extent of raising the growth rate by about a quarter of one percent.[18]

[14] For an analysis of climatic change and its effect on agriculture, see Central Intelligence Agency, *USSR: The Impact of Recent Climate Changes on Grain Production*, ER76–10577J, Washington, D.C., October 1976.

[15] Philip Hanson, "International Technology Transfer from the West to the USSR," in John Thomas and Ursula Kruse-Vaucienne, eds., *Soviet Science and Technology* (Washington, D.C.: George Washington University, 1977), pp. 353–385.

[16] For papers presenting different viewpoints on the impact of Western technology, see Donald Green and Herbert Levine, "Implications of Technology for the USSR," in NATO Economics Directorate, *East-West Technological Cooperation* (Brussels: NATO, 1976); Martin Weitzman, "Technology Transfer to the USSR: An Econometric Analysis," *Journal of Comparative Economics*, vol. 3, no. 2 (June 1979), 167–177; Yasushi Toda, "Technology Transfer to the USSR: The Marginal Productivity Differential and the Elasticity of Intra-Capital Substitution in Soviet Industry," *Journal of Comparative Economics*, vol. 3, no. 2 (June 1979), 181–194.

[17] National Foreign Assessment Center, *USSR: Long-Term Outlook for Grain Imports*, ER79–10057, Washington, D.C., January 1979; Select Committee on Intelligence, *The Soviet Oil Situation: An Evaluation of CIA Analyses of Soviet Oil Production* (Washington, D.C.: U.S. Government Printing Office, 1978).

[18] Testimony of Douglas Diamond, in *Allocation of Resources in the Soviet Union and China*, p. 35.

The fourth option (a radical reform of the Soviet economy) appears at this moment unlikely. The Soviet leadership has rejected for the time being the notion of decentralization reform, and those advocating significant reform have gone underground. The experience with the moderate 1965 reform was that if decentralization were offered it would require a loss of political authority, and the party and state leadership were unwilling to part with their political power. Whether they will be willing to do so in the 1980s is an open question, for they now understand the personal costs of such reform. The most likely scenario for such a reform would be an unforeseen change in the political leadership in favor of some liberal leader or a drastic economic failure.

PROSPECTS TO THE YEAR 2000: A POSTSCRIPT[19]

Looking ahead to the year 2000, what are the trends and prospects for the Soviet economy and for Soviet society in general? Long range projections are difficult to make. Some trends can be projected well into the future (such as trends in the able-bodied population); other phenomena are much less certain (such as changes in the political leadership).

What things are known? What things are unknown concerning the next two decades? On the side of the "knowns" is the fact that labor will become an increasingly scarce factor of production. The growth rate of the able-bodied population (from which the working population is drawn) will average around ½ percent per year over the next two decades; so the Soviet economy must learn how to adjust to a labor force that is scarcely expanding. Other economies have successfully bridged the transition from a fast to a slow growing labor force; whether the Soviet economy can do so will be a crucial determinant of future economic performance. Basic demographic trends also show that the regional allocation of Soviet population will be unfavorable, for population will continue to expand most rapidly in those republics where labor is in most abundant supply. The success of Soviet planners in adjusting the regional labor imbalance will be as critical as their response to the slowdown in labor force growth.

The prospect for a return to rapid rates of growth of investment and capital stock to compensate for the declining growth of labor appears to be dim. First, the Soviet consumer can no longer be treated as a residual claim-

[19] This discussion is based upon papers presented at the Conference on the Soviet Economy Toward the Year 2000 at Airlie House, Airlie, Virginia, October 23–25, 1980, organized by Abram Bergson and Herbert Levine. Papers were presented by Daniel Bond and Herbert Levine (econometric projections), Abram Bergson (factor productivity), Murray Feshbach (population and labor force), D. Gale Johnson (agricultural organization), Douglas Diamond, Lee Bettis, and Robert Ramsson (agricultural production), Robert Campbell (energy), Edward Hewett (trade), Martin Weitzman (industrial production), Gertrude Schroeder (consumption), Joseph Berliner (planning and management), Seweryn Bialer (politics), and Leslie Dienes (regional development).

ant to resources (as the 1980 overthrow of a communist government in Poland once again demonstrated); the claims of the Soviet defense establishment also will remain strong. As a consequence, there is little "give" in the system for large reallocations to investment. Second, there is the question of the wisdom of allowing investment to grow at a rate disproportionately higher than that of GNP. With high rates of growth of capital and low rates of growth of labor, it has become increasingly difficult to effectively substitute capital for labor. The payoff of accelerated investment growth may therefore be meager and its costs high. Moreover, the Soviet leadership must be concerned about an incentive "threshold" if investment is favored at the expense of consumption. The loss of output due to declining incentives may offset the gains of greater investment.

The great unknown in projecting Soviet economic performance to the year 2000 is productivity performance. Will the Soviet economy learn how to grow rapidly with slowly growing inputs? It would appear that the potential for efficiency gains is great. The Soviet Union has yet to undertake the substitutions for petroleum forced upon Western countries by the rising relative price of energy. Therefore, the extent to which the Soviet economy will be able to economize on scarce energy inputs remains a real question mark. This is a vital question of wide ranging economic and political significance, for it will affect Soviet relations with Eastern Europe, Soviet hard currency earnings, and East-West competition for imported oil.

The available evidence also suggests that substantial efficiency gains in the use of labor are also possible. Over-full employment planning still prevails in the Soviet Union; much labor is redundant and could be used more effectively if transferred to other jobs. Yet better utilization of manpower resources would require significant changes in the Soviet system—the reduction of job security, greater pay differentiation among workers, greater freedom for managers to hire and fire workers, and the revision of managerial incentives to encourage the better use of labor.

There is little evidence that the Soviets are moving in these directions. The late 1970s witnessed the movement towards more (not less) equality among industrial wage earners; the abandonment of partial reforms to improve managerial incentives and grant more managerial flexibility; and the failure to expand the one experiment that reduced job security.

One means of achieving efficiency gains over the next two decades is greater integration of the Soviet economy into the world economy. In this way, the Soviets could acquire advanced technology, become more intimately acquainted with Western business practices, and subject their own industries to outside competition. The 1970s did indeed witness a dramatic increase in Soviet participation in international trade. Much of this, however, may have been a matter of luck such as the rise in gold, oil and raw material prices that improved the Soviet terms of trade with the West. It is questionable whether such good fortune will continue into the 1980s and

1990s. If it does not, then the Soviet's ability to import from the West will depend more and more on the vitality of the domestic USSR economy. Can the planning system be restructured to improve the product quality of Soviet exports? Can the Soviets compete effectively in Western markets for manufactures? Can the Soviets make do with less oil and free this oil for exports? Moreover, can the Soviet economy assimilate imported Western technology effectively? Increased reliance on foreign markets does not represent a "quick fix" for accumulated problems. The effective utilization of foreign trade may ultimately depend upon the improved performance of the domestic Soviet economy rather than vice versa.

Will the Soviet leadership take bold steps to improve the prevailing system of planning and management? The options are broad and range from a "muddling along" approach (making do with the existing system); to a policy of removing the more obvious inefficiencies in the existing system (removing agricultural price supports, charging the world market price for oil, loosening restrictions on private plots, and so on); to a veritable liberalizing reform such as that currently underway in Hungary. It is unlikely that bold steps will be undertaken during the long transition period as a new leadership of the communist party replaces the old. Instead, the "muddling along" option is likely to be selected. Consequently, growth projections are best predicated on the continuation of the existing system of planning and management with only minor cosmetic changes.

Informed observers agree that the Soviet leadership must accept a rate of GNP growth that is low by Soviet historical standards. The growth rate of GNP to the year 2000 will likely be in the 2–3 percent per annum range, and the rate of growth of per capita consumption will be even lower than this rate. The ongoing decline in the rate of growth of factor productivity may be halted, but there is little prospect of raising this rate to above 1 percent per annum. In fact, rates of factor productivity growth below 1 percent would not be surprising because of the disincentive effects caused by slow consumption growth.

Soviet agriculture will continue to be a troubled sector. In the last decade, productivity growth has virtually disappeared and the annual growth rate of agricultural output has fallen below 2 percent per annum despite massive infusions of investment and subsidies into agriculture. The USSR will therefore continue to depend upon foreign suppliers of grain, and a continuation of growth rates of the last decade means that the average Soviet family's diet will not equal that of the average 1978 Polish family until the year 2000.

Are there any bright spots for the Soviet leadership in these otherwise gloomy projections? The most important is the fact that the Western world enters the 1980s with significant troubles of its own. Productivity growth is declining, high rates of inflation coexist with high rates of unemployment, and real wages are actually declining in some countries. The Soviet Union has no monopoly on economic problems. Moreover, the Soviet population may have adjusted its expectations downward, so that slower rates of growth of consumption may be tolerated without open political strife. Finally, the Soviet economy continues to supply the Soviet leadership with military power that is at least equal to that of its major competitor, the United States.

SELECTED BIBLIOGRAPHY

Godfrey Baldwin, *Population Projections by Age and Sex: For the Republics and Major Economic Regions of the USSR, 1970 to 2000*, International Population Reports, Series P–91, No. 26, September 1979, Table 3.

Herbert Block, "Soviet Economic Performance in a Global Context," in Joint Economic Committee, *Soviet Economy in a Time of Change* (Washington, D.C.: U.S. Government Printing Office, 1979), vol. 1, pp. 110–141.

Keith Bush, "The Tenth Five-Year Plan and the USSR's Economic Prospects," in John Thomas and Ursula Kruse-Vaucienne, eds., *Soviet Science and Technology* (Washington, D.C.: George Washington University, 1977), pp. 256–276.

Central Intelligence Agency, *USSR: The Impact of Recent Climate Changes on Grain Production*, ER76–10577J, Washington, D.C., October 1976.

Murray Feshbach, "Prospects for Outmigration from Central Asia and Kazakhstan in the Next Decade," in Joint Economic Committee, *Soviet Economy in a Time of Change* (Washington, D.C.: U.S. Government Printing Office, 1979), vol. 1, pp. 656–709.

Donald Green and Herbert Levine, "Implications of Technology for the USSR," in NATO Economic Directorate, *East–West Technological Cooperation* (Brussels: NATO, 1976).

Holland Hunter, ed., *The Future of the Soviet Economy: 1978–1985* (Boulder, Colo.: Westview Press, 1978).

Philip Hanson, "International Technology Transfer from the West to the USSR," in John Thomas and Ursula Kruse-Vaucienne, eds., *Soviet Science and Technology* (Washington, D.C.: George Washington University, 1977), pp. 353–385.

Hearings Before the Subcommittee on Priorities and Economy in Government, *Allocation of Resources in the Soviet Union and China–1978, Part 4: Soviet Union* (Washington, D.C., June 26 and July 14, 1978), pp. 38, 78.

Joint Economic Committee, *Soviet Economy in a Time of Change* (Washington, D.C.: U.S. Government Printing Office, 1979), vols 1–3.

T. Khachaturov, *The Economy of the Soviet Union Today*, translated from the Russian (Moscow: Progress Publishers, 1977).

H. Linnemann, J. P. Pronk, and J. Tinbergen, "Convergence of Economic Systems in East and West," in Emile Benoit, ed., *Disarmament and World Economic Interdependence* (New York: Columbia University Press, 1967), pp. 246–260.

James R. Millar, "On the Merits of the Convergence Hypothesis," *Journal of Economic Issues*, vol. 2, no. 1 (March 1969), 60–68.

National Foreign Assessment Center, *USSR: Long-Term Outlook for Grain Imports*, ER79–10057, Washington, D.C., January 1979.

National Foreign Assessment Center, *USSR: Trends and Prospects in Educational Attainment, 1959–1985,* ER79–10344, Washington, D.C., June 1979.

NATO Economics Directorate, *Regional Developments in the USSR: Trends and Prospects* (Newtonville, Mass.: Oriental Research Partners, 1979).

Martin Spechler, "Regional Developments in the USSR, 1958–1978," in Joint Economic Committee, *Soviet Economy in a Time of Change* (Washington, D.C.: U.S. Government Printing Office, 1979), vol. 1, pp. 141–164.

Yasushi Toda, "Technology Transfer to the USSR: The Marginal Productivity Differential and the Elasticity of Intra-Capital Substitution in Soviet Industry," *Journal of Comparative Economics,* vol. 3, no. 2 (June 1979), 181–194.

Martin Weitzman, "Technology Transfer to the USSR: An Econometric Analysis," *Journal of Comparative Economics,* vol. 3, no. 2 (June 1979), 167–177.

Index

Price system (*Continued*)
  reform of, 165–168. *See also* Price reform
    (1966–1967)
  two-tiered, 160, 161
Primitive capitalist accumulation, 67, 69
Primitive socialist accumulation, 74–75,
  246
Priority system, managers and, 180, 181
Private industry, 39, 48
Private plots of peasants, 224, 229–231
Private trade, 41, 43, 48, 55–56, 59
Production associations, 309, 310, 314–315
Productivity. *See also* Efficiency
  of agriculture, 250–253
  dynamic efficiency and, 338–346
  factor. *See* Factor productivity
  labor. *See* Labor productivity
  Soviet Industrialization Debate and, 387
Profits, 156, 164, 178
  Liberman reform proposals and, 303–304
  1965 reform and, 308–309
  price reforms of 1966–1967 and, 317–318

Railroads in Russia, 16, 17, 25
Ratchet effect, 179, 181
Regional planning, 58, 120, 300
  Sovnarkhozy and, 117, 120, 139, 301
Repressed inflation, 148–149, 363–364
  in the postwar period, 149–152
Requisitioning policy, 40–43, 54
Research and development, 208–209
Resource allocation, 55, 57, 113, 219–220.
  See also Capital allocation; Labor allo-
    cation, Planning
  pragmatic approach to, 293
  prices and, 162–163
Retail price index, 149–151
Retail prices
  setting of, 158–160
  turnover tax and, 147, 158–160
Ruble, 264, 269
Ruble control, system of, 142, 154, 185
Russia (Russian Empire)
  agriculture in, 18–19, 22–25, 34
  demographic trends in, 30
  dependence on foreign capital, 31–32
  economic and social indicators for 1861
    and 1913 (*table*), 20–21
  economic development of, 15–16
  economic growth in, 24–33, 331
  economic history to 1917, 15–34
  foreign trade of, 284–285
  growth of per capita NNP in, 26–27

industrial growth in, 16–18
investment in human capital in, 28–29
in 1917, 1, 3, 70
relative backwardness of, 16–18, 25,
  32–33
structural change in, 27–28
as underdeveloped, 31–34

Safety factor phenomenon, 180–181
Savings, 147, 151, 152
  rural-urban transfer of, 246–248
Schroeder, Gertrude F., 121n., 122n., 139n.,
  140n., 150, 170n., 180n., 201n., 239n.,
  240n., 266n., 302n., 310n., 311n.,
  315n., 320n., 321n., 349n., 363n., 364n.
Scissors Crisis (1923), 53–56, 60
Second economy, 170–172
Self-sufficiency, 284, 385
Serf labor, 16, 19
Severin, Barbara, 150, 161n., 239n., 240n.,
  298n., 359n., 363n., 364n.
Sex discrimination, 206–207
Shanin, Lev, 64, 75–78, 82n., 88, 90
Shock system, 44–45, 58
Smychka, 46–47, 65, 79, 100
Socialism
  environmental disruption and, 389–390
  expansion of, 1–2
  market, 168n.
  Marx on, 67–69
  "in one country," 70–71, 82
Socialist economy. *See also* Soviet economy
  goal of, 8–9
Socialist revolution
  Lenin on, 69–71
  Marx on, 67
Soviet Development Model of the 1930s
  (SDM), 370, 381–389
  assessment of, 388–389
  definition of, 33
  description of, 381–385
  Western trends compared to, 385–388
Soviet economy. *See also specific topics*
  achievements of, 397–400
  as centrally managed rather than cen-
    trally planned, 121
  as command economy, 2–3
  naturalization of, 40, 42
  1970s problems of, 400–401
  1980s options of, 401–404
  organization chart of administrative
    structure of, 118–119

Valuation, environmental disruption and, 393

Value. *See also* Labor theory of value price formation and, 165–166

Value judgments, comparison of economic systems and, 8–11

Vinogradov, V. A., 37–39n., 41n., 43n., 47n., 148n.

Vinokur, Aaron, 171, 207

Virgin lands campaign, 232–233, 251–252

Volin, Lazar, 23, 99n., 103n., 104n., 231n.

VSNKh (Supreme Council of the National Economy), 43–44, 49, 55, 116, 117
role of, 96, 97

Vyas, Arvind, 99n., 247–248

Wage differentials, 5, 158, 384. *See also* Incentive wages
allocative efficiency of labor policy and, 205
for dangerous or arduous work, 192–193
distribution of labor in the 1930s and, 200–201
labor allocation and, 190–194
male-female, 207
modernization of manpower and, 202
regional, 192, 201
setting of, 190–192
supply and demand for labor and, 193–194
United States–USSR comparison, 352

War Communism and, 45

Wages. *See also* Industrial wages
inflation of the 1930s and, 146–148
1972–1976 reform of, 190–191
War Communism and, 42, 45

War Communism (1918–1921), 37–46
agriculture and, 38–39, 43
evaluation of, 42–46
industry and, 40, 41, 43–45
money supply during, 39–40
peasants and, 38–40, 43
policies of, 40–42
precedents established by, 57–60
roots of, 38
shock system under, 44–45, 58

West Germany, 334, 335, 342, 348, 349, 357, 358, 379

Wholesale prices, industrial, 155–158

Wiles, Peter J. D., 350, 352n., 353n., 362n., 399n.

Women in labor force, 206–207

Workers. *See also* Industrial workers; Labor
free occupational choice by, 59
placement of, 203–204

World War I, 54

World War II, 11, 107–109

Zaleski, Eugene, 37n., 43n., 95n., 97n., 98, 107, 108n., 121, 129n., 305, 307n., 377n., 381n.,

Zauberman, Alfred, 208n., 210, 212n., 213n., 297n., 303n.

81 82 83 9 8 7 6 5 4 3 2 1